RMAN Recipes for Oracle Database 12c

A Problem-Solution Approach
Second Edition

Darl Kuhn

Sam Alapati

Arup Nanda

⟨**IOUG**⟩
independent oracle users group

Apress·

RMAN Recipes for Oracle Database 12c: A Problem-Solution Approach, 2nd Ed.

ISBN-13 (pbk): 978-1-4302-4836-1

ISBN-13 (electronic): 978-1-4302-4837-8

President and Publisher: Paul Manning
Lead Editor: Jonathan Gennick
Technical Reviewer: Bernard Lopuz; Jay Nielson
Editorial Board: Steve Anglin, Mark Beckner, Ewan Buckingham, Gary Cornell, Louise Corrigan, Morgan Ertel, Jonathan Gennick, Jonathan Hassell, Robert Hutchinson, Michelle Lowman, James Markham, Matthew Moodie, Jeff Olson, Jeffrey Pepper, Douglas Pundick, Ben Renow-Clarke, Dominic Shakeshaft, Gwenan Spearing, Matt Wade, Tom Welsh
Coordinating Editor: Katie Sullivan
Copy Editors: Antoinette Smith
Compositor: SPi Global
Indexer: SPi Global
Artist: SPi Global
Cover Designer: Anna Ishchenko

Distributed to the book trade worldwide by Springer Science+Business Media New York, 233 Spring Street, 6th Floor, New York, NY 10013. Phone 1-800-SPRINGER, fax (201) 348-4505, e-mail orders-ny@springer-sbm.com, or visit www.springeronline.com. Apress Media, LLC is a California LLC and the sole member (owner) is Springer Science + Business Media Finance Inc (SSBM Finance Inc). SSBM Finance Inc is a Delaware corporation.

For information on translations, please e-mail rights@apress.com, or visit www.apress.com.

Apress and friends of ED books may be purchased in bulk for academic, corporate, or promotional use. eBook versions and licenses are also available for most titles. For more information, reference our Special Bulk Sales–eBook Licensing web page at www.apress.com/bulk-sales.

Any source code or other supplementary materials referenced by the author in this text is available to readers at www.apress.com. For detailed information about how to locate your book's source code, go to www.apress.com/source-code/.

About IOUG Press

*IOUG Press is a joint effort by the **Independent Oracle Users Group (the IOUG)** and **Apress** to deliver some of the highest-quality content possible on Oracle Database and related topics. The IOUG is the world's leading, independent organization for professional users of Oracle products. Apress is a leading, independent technical publisher known for developing high-quality, no-fluff content for serious technology professionals. The IOUG and Apress have joined forces in IOUG Press to provide the best content and publishing opportunities to working professionals who use Oracle products.*

Our shared goals include:

- Developing content with excellence
- Helping working professionals to succeed
- Providing authoring and reviewing opportunities
- Networking and raising the profiles of authors and readers

To learn more about Apress, visit our website at **www.apress.com**. Follow the link for IOUG Press to see the great content that is now available on a wide range of topics that matter to those in Oracle's technology sphere.

Visit **www.ioug.org** to learn more about the Independent Oracle Users Group and its mission. Consider joining if you haven't already. Review the many benefits at www.ioug.org/join. Become a member. Get involved with peers. Boost your career.

www.ioug.org/join

Apress®

Contents at a Glance

Contents

Foreword

What skills set the database administrator (DBA) apart from other technologists? Of the many responsibilities laid upon a DBA, which cannot be performed by someone else? Adding database accounts? Creating tables and indexes? Installing and configuring databases? Optimizing the database and the applications that access and manipulate it?

All of these things are regularly performed by people who do not consider themselves database administrators. They consider themselves to be programmer/analysts, to be application developers, to be managers and directors, and they do all these things just to be able to move forward with their own job. Most application developers know how to run the Oracle Universal Installer—it's just another graphical application, and these days accepting all the default choices is a perfectly valid way to get the job done. Adding database accounts? That's easy! Granting database privileges? Just give 'em "DBA" or "SYSDBA" and no more problems! Creating tables and indexes? C'mon, that's more of a developer's job than the DBA's job, isn't it? Tuning Oracle databases is mostly about crafting efficient SQL statements, and while this job often falls to DBAs, it is best handled by the developers and programmers who write the SQL in the first place.

While many of these duties are correctly assigned to a DBA, they are not hallmarks of the job.

Think about the people flying airliners. With the degree of automation in aircraft cockpits now, it can be argued (with a lot of merit) that the planes can fly themselves, from takeoff, through navigated flight, to touchdown. So, what are the pilots for?

If something goes wrong with the plane, you want the best pilots at the controls. Because when things go wrong, they go wrong in a hurry, and it takes somebody who knows exactly what all that PlayStation gadgetry is really controlling in that cockpit, and it takes somebody who can intelligently take control and land the thing safely when dozens of lights are flashing and dozens of alarms are buzzing. It's not too hard to justify the presence of pilots on airplanes, in the end.

Likewise, fifty years ago, at the dawn of the American space program, a debate was under way then, as it is now: Should space flights be manned or unmanned? There were good arguments in favor of the latter. The first astronauts weren't human—they were dogs and chimps. When humans were finally included, the spacecraft engineers assured them that they were redundant, just along for the ride, superfluous—that they were just "Spam in a can," went the gallows humor.

But it didn't take long to prove those people wrong. The presence of a well-trained and comprehensively knowledgeable pilot in the spacecraft has proven its worth time and time again. A classic example is the final two minutes of the historic Apollo 11 moon landing, when Neil Armstrong looked out the window of the Eagle lunar module and realized that their automated descent, controlled from Houston via computer, was dropping them into a boulder field. Only a few hundred meters from the lunar surface, Armstrong flipped the controls to manual and pushed the lunar module higher, seeking a more viable landing site. While Houston nervously and repeatedly queried for status, Armstrong calmly replied, "Hold, Houston," until, with only 30 seconds of fuel remaining, he set the lunar module down and declared that the Eagle had landed.

That's why we have human astronauts. This is what sets "Spam in a can" apart from a pilot. This is why airliners, while heavily automated, have highly trained pilots at the controls.

Which brings us back to database administrators . . . I hope!

What sets a DBA apart from an ambitious programmer or a developer doing what needs to be done to move forward?

It is the ability to prepare for trouble and recover from it. Database recovery in the event of failure or mishap is the most vital skill in a DBA's toolkit.

The Oracle RDBMS has been around now for about 30 years. The internal mechanisms for backup and recovery have changed very little in the past 20 years. Of course there have been enhancements, but the basic mechanism for basic "hot" or online backups has changed very little.

However, it is the mechanism for restore and recovery that took a great leap forward 10 years ago, when Oracle Recovery Manager (RMAN) was introduced with Oracle8. In a world where misnomers abound, Recovery Manager is quite aptly named. The focus of the product is not on automating backups, but rather on automating the steps of restore and recovery as much as possible. Much of the early reluctance to adopt RMAN came about not from any failings in the product, but rather from disappointment that the product did not make the job of performing backups any easier. Since backups are the operations DBAs see most often, what RMAN does for recovery operations was not fully appreciated.

As I teach people how to use RMAN, I attempt to stress the mind-set that RMAN is not just about performing backups. Rather, it is about "feeding" the RMAN "recovery catalog." Backups are not ends in themselves, but simply entries in the recovery catalog used by RMAN during restore and recovery operations. If a DBA considers it his duty to feed the recovery catalog with backup operations and other maintenance, such as crosschecks, then we have someone who is truly preparing for the eventuality, not just the remote possibility, of restore and recovery—someone who understands the tool, and is not just applying a different tool to bang in nails the same old way.

The knowledge and capability to recover a database from catastrophic failure is what separates a real DBA apart from someone who found the installer or who knows how to do the clickety-clickety thing in Oracle Enterprise Manager. And not just once, by luck, but knowing how to use RMAN to its full advantage, to work around those confusing and misleading error messages, to verify backups and maintain and protect the recovery catalog(s) so as to virtually guarantee recoverability, each and every time.

It is this protective mind-set, liberally seasoned with caution and pessimism, that separates DBAs from other technologists. Systems administrators and network administrators have much the same tendencies, but only database administrators are made responsible for never losing data. Systems and networks can be made redundant, and if they fail it is only a matter of bringing them back to service, but data loss is forever and is never forgiven.

Years ago I worked with a no-nonsense vice president. She didn't want to know the details of my job, and rightly so. She simply stated, very clearly, "Failures happen, but don't EVER tell me that you could not recover my data." Message received.

This book is written by seasoned professionals who have been using RMAN since its inception. They recognize that RMAN can be confusing and feel that no one should have to go through the same learning curve to arrive at the same conclusions. So, they have gathered together their best practices and tried-and-true procedures and compiled them into this wonderful book.

If you are an Oracle database administrator, this could very well be the most important book you read. Technology books are famous for becoming "shelf-ware," pristine and unopened books adorning shelves everywhere. This book will be the exception—the book that is dog-eared and worn, the cover falling off and pages smudged, found more often opened facedown on a desk than perched serenely on a shelf. The information within this book is the very essence of the job of the Oracle DBA, the most important facet of the job, and I am grateful to Sam, Arup, and Darl for sharing.

Tim Gorman
Evergreen, Colorado
February 2013

About the Authors

Darl Kuhn is currently a DBA working for Oracle. He has written books on a variety of IT topics including SQL, performance tuning, Linux, backup and recovery, RMAN, and database administration. Darl also teaches Oracle classes for Regis University and does volunteer DBA work for the Rocky Mountain Oracle Users Group.

Sam Alapati works as a manager and senior database architect at Cash America, in Fort Worth, Texas. Earlier, Sam worked for many years at Boy Scouts of America, as well as a senior principal consultant for Oracle Corporation. Sam has written twelve books relating to Oracle Database and Oracle Middleware. Sam lives in Flower Mound, near Dallas, Texas, with his wife, Valerie; daughter, Nina; and sons, Shannon and Nicholas.

Arup Nanda has been an Oracle DBA since 1993, when the world was slowly turning its attention to a big force to reckon with—Oracle 7. But he was not so lucky; he was entrusted with a production Oracle database running Oracle 6. Since then he has never been out of the Oracle DBA career path, weaving several interesting situations from modeling to performance tuning to backup/recovery and beyond, with lots of gray hairs to document each ORA-600. He has written more than 500 articles for publications such as Oracle Magazine and OTN, has presented about 300 sessions at conferences such as Oracle World and IOUG Collaborate, and has coauthored three other books. He is an Oracle ACE director, a member of Oak Table Network, and an editor of SELECT Journal, the IOUG publication. As recognition of his expertise and user group contributions, Oracle chose him as DBA of the Year 2003 and as Enterprise Architect of the Year in 2012. He lives in Danbury, Connecticut, with his wife, Anu, and their son, Anish. When he is not working, he loves to read mysteries, paint watercolors, and photograph nature.

About the Technical Reviewers

Bernard Lopuz has been a senior principal technical support analyst at Oracle Corporation since 2001, and he is an Oracle Certified Professional (OCP). Before he became an Oracle DBA, he was a programmer developing Unisys Linc and Oracle applications, as well as interactive voice response (IVR) applications such as telephone banking voice-processing applications. Bernard was coauthor of the Linux Recipes for Oracle DBAs (Apress, 2008) and technical reviewer of three other books, namely, Oracle RMAN Recipes (Apress, 2007), Pro Oracle Database 11g Administration (Apress, 2010), and Pro Oracle SQL (Apress, 2010). He has a bachelor's degree in computer engineering from the Mapúa Institute of Technology in Manila, Philippines. Bernard was born in Iligan, Philippines, and now resides in Ottawa, Canada, with his wife, Leizle, and daughters, Juliet and Carol. Aside from tinkering with computers, Bernard is a soccer and basketball fanatic.

Jay Nielsen is an OCP developer (6i) and OCP DBA (10g) and has worked in an Oracle environment since January 1989. He started with Oracle version 5.1 while in the U.S. Air Force. He retired from the USAF in 1995 and has continued as a contractor for the Department of Defense in the DC metro area. He has been married since 1975 and has thirteen children.

He is almost finished with a master's degree in database technology from Regis University. Darl Kuhn is his favorite instructor from Regis University Online.

Acknowledgments

Special thanks go to the lead editor, Jonathan Gennick. His vision and keen organizational and technical skills have made this book a much greater sum than its pieces.

We owe a huge thanks to Bernard Lopuz, the technical reviewer for this book. Bernard made countless suggestions and modifications that greatly contributed to the quality of the final product.

We also appreciate the efforts of Jay Nielsen, who jumped in to help review several chapters. Thanks also to our coordinating editor, Kathleen Sullivan, who guided us through this project and kept us on schedule. Thanks also to our copy editor, Antoinette Smith; we appreciate her contributions toward improving the quality of this book.

—Darl Kuhn, Sam Alapati, and Arup Nanda

It's been a pleasure working again with coauthors Sam Alapati and Arup Nanda. These guys are expert real-world DBAs and excellent communicators. Also thanks to the numerous DBAs, SAs, and developers I've learned database administration techniques from over the years: Dave Jennings, Bob Suehrstedt, Scott Schulze, Pete Mullineaux, Shawn Heisdorffer, Roger Murphy, Tim Gorman, Gary Dodge, Sujit Pattanaik, Ken Toney, Janet Bacon, Sue Wagner, Doug Davis, Ken Roberts, Mehran Sowdaey, Dan Fink, Guido Handley, Nehru Kaja, Tim Colbert, Glenn Balanoff, Bill Padfield, Bob Mason, Ravi Narayanaswamy, Kevin Bayer, Abdul Ebadi, Kevin Hoyt, Trent Sherman, Sandra Montijo, Sean Best, Ennio Murroni, Roy Backstrom, Mohan Koneru, John Lilly, Todd Wichers, Will Thornburg, Ashley Jackson, Mike Tanaka, Andy Hewitt, Kevin Cook, Doug Cushing, Jeff Sherard, and Jim Stark.

—Darl Kuhn

As was the case with the first edition, it was a great pleasure to work with my two coauthors, who are very accomplished Oracle DBAs. As usual, Jonathan Gennick reviewed the chapters during the first pass and made valuable suggestions that helped us improve the style and content and the chapters. Thank you, Jonathan, for putting up with all the stuff I wrote during the initial draft and patiently showing me ways to improve my work! Bernard Lopuz helped significantly by closely reading the chapters and not only catching critical errors, but also pointing out the relevant documentation for clarifying key areas.

My colleagues at Cash America play a huge role in my professional life, and my happiness in my job has helped me devote my spare time to this book. I owe a great amount of thanks to the great leadership exhibited by Reddy Kankanala, my manager. I also would like to express my appreciation for all the help and support from John Ninan, my senior colleague. I owe a huge round of thanks to Anil Daniyala, Henry Patrick, and Francisco Banda for being great friends and for helping out so many times at my job.

I'd like to express my immense gratitude for the great love and affection of my parents, Appa Rao and Swarna Kumari, and brothers, Hari Hara Prasad and Siva Sankara Prasad. I don't want to forget Aruna, Vanaja, Teja, Ashwin, Aparna, and Soumya. My wife, Valerie, has as usual provided the peaceful environment for working on the book. My children, Shannon, Nina, and Nicholas, have done their bit to help by letting me focus on the book when I needed to—I thank Valerie and the kids for their great support and help!

—Sam Alapati

First and foremost, I thank my wife, Anindita, and son, Anish, for letting me pound away on the keyboard—especially Anish, who must have missed his daddy playing with him, although he was very considerate for his ripe old age of eight! Thank you, my parents, Ajay and Asha Nanda, for guiding my life and making me what I am today.

Beyond my immediate family, I sincerely thank my extended family of friends, colleagues, customers, and associates for enriching me and my professional life. Thank you to the team that started me off in Oracle Database management: the ISBS crew. Thank you, Lance Tucker, Vijaya Kommineni, Mike Clasby, William Chen, Ken Noel, and others at Boston College; Suresh Karunakaran at Stroz Friedberg; Serge Nikulin and the team at IntraLinks; Daniel Lyakovetsky, Robert Vittori, and others at IntelliClaim (now McKesson); Jim Roland, Ramesh Venkatakrishnan, Nick Yelashev, Celine Hatch, and the others at Cigna HealthCare; Jonas Rosenthal, Matt Augustine, Scott Uhrick, Mladen Gogala, and the awesome team at Oxford Health (now United Healthcare); Rajesh Chauhan, Alan Patierno, Bob Kess, Bonnie Majeski, and others at Lucent and IBM; Barry Sergeant and the rest of the Financials team at Priceline; and Tom Urban, Chris Overbey, Dave Hallman, and others at Blue Cross Blue Shield of VA for believing in me and supporting me whenever and wherever they could. Last but not least, Chris Clanton, Tim Hickey, Bill Camp, Christos Kotsakis, Steve Golinski, and my own special DBA team of Harish Patel, Pradeep Nair, and others at Starwood Hotels, thank you for believing in me and pushing and challenging me to explore new frontiers.

Many thanks to Tom Kyte, Jonathan Lewis, and other luminaries of the Oracle user world for shining on the path less traveled and gently pushing me back on track whenever I veered off; Tony Jedlinski, George Trujillo, Alex Gorbachev, April Sims, John Kanagaraj, and others at Independent Oracle Users Group; Paul Dorsey, Mike LaMagna, Rob Edwards, Mike Olin, Caryl Lee Fisher, and others at New York Oracle User Group; David Teplow, Lyson Ludvic, Jameson White, Jean Mutha, and the wonderfully appreciative crowd at Boston DBA SIG; Donna Cooksey, Tim Chien, Mughees Minhas, Prabhaker "GP" Gongloor, Hermann Baer, and many others at Oracle whose help and support I have counted on and received. I can't express my thanks enough to Tom Haunert and Justin Kestelyn for bringing the best out of my writing and reiterating their faith in me every day; Steven Feuerstein for making an author out of me; Darl and Sam for welcoming me into the team; Jonathan for making me look good while being completely in the background; and the rest of the crew at Apress for making this book a reality.

But above all, thank you, dear reader, for that ultimate support you have shown that makes every keystroke worthwhile.

—Arup Nanda

Introduction

Every company relies on data to operate efficiently. Protecting corporate data is a critical task. One major responsibility of a DBA is to ensure that information stored in corporate databases is safe and available. This is what makes a database administrator valuable.

Oracle is a leading vendor of database technology. Many companies use Oracle databases to store mission-critical data. Recovery Manager (RMAN) is Oracle's flagship database backup and recovery solution. A DBA's job security depends on being able to back up and safely recover databases. Therefore, RMAN is a tool that every Oracle DBA must be proficient with.

RMAN can be used out of the box for simple backup and recovery needs or can be configured to meet the most sophisticated requirements. When you are implementing RMAN backups, sometimes it can be difficult to find clear examples of how to accomplish a specific task. Or worse, you find yourself in an uber-stressful recovery situation and you can't quickly find a solution to get your mission-critical database restored and available.

In those hectic circumstances, you don't want to wade through pages of architectural discussions or complex syntax diagrams. Rather, you require a solution right then and there. You want a quick step-by-step cookbook example that is easy to read and to the point.

This book provides you with task-oriented, ready-made solutions to both common and not-so-common backup and recovery scenarios. You do not need to read this book cover to cover. You can pick and choose whatever topic requires your attention. Whether you just need to brush up on an old backup and recovery subject or you want to implement an RMAN feature that is new in Oracle Database 12c, this book allows you to focus on a topic and its corresponding solution.

Audience

This book is for any DBA who wants to quickly find accurate solutions to his RMAN backup and recovery operations. Any database administrator from rookie to expert can leverage the recipes in this book to implement RMAN's features and resolve troublesome issues.

This book is also for system administrators, who are responsible for keeping the overall system backed up and available. The delineation between system administration and database administration tasks is often nebulous. This is especially true when troubleshooting and tuning disk, tape, hardware, and network issues. System administrators and database administrators must work together to ensure that the database servers are backed up, scalable, and highly available.

Using This Book
Problem

You often find yourself thinking, "Dang it, I just want to see a good example and an explanation of how to implement this RMAN feature. . . ."

Solution

Use this book to locate a recipe that matches your scenario, and then use the corresponding example solution to solve your problem.

How It Works

RMAN Recipes for Oracle Database 12c is a cookbook of solutions for a wide variety of backup and recovery scenarios. The recipe titles act as an index to the task you need help with. You should be able to search for the recipe that fits your scenario and then find a concise answer you can use to solve the issue you face. Each recipe starts with a description of the problem, followed by a to-the-point solution, and then a thorough explanation of how it works.

What This Book Covers

This book covers the gamut of RMAN backup and recovery subject matter—from simple to advanced, to disk or tape, running command line or GUI, any type of backup, or any type of recovery. Major topics included within are:

- Backing up your database
- Performing complete and incomplete recovery
- Using flashback database technology
- Implementing a media management layer
- Troubleshooting and tuning RMAN
- Differences between Unix and Windows environments
- Using Enterprise Manager with RMAN
- Utilizing new RMAN features in Oracle Database 12c
- Working with container and pluggable databases

Where appropriate, we highlight the differences between RMAN in Oracle Database 12c and older versions. There have been significant improvements to RMAN with each new release of Oracle. Where relevant, we point out what version the particular RMAN feature was introduced.

Comments and Questions

We've tried to make this book as error free as possible. However, mistakes happen. If you find any type of error in this book, whether it be a typo or an erroneous command, please let us know about it. You can submit any issues by going to the main Apress web page at www.apress.com. Search for this book and then use the errata page to submit corrections.

Contacting the Authors

You can contact the authors directly at the following e-mail addresses:

Darl Kuhn: darl.kuhn@gmail.com

Sam Alapati: samalapati@yahoo.com

Arup Nanda: arup@proligence.com

CHAPTER 1

■ ■ ■

Backup and Recovery 101

Oracle *backup and recovery* refers to the theory and practice of protecting a real-life Oracle database against data loss and recovering data after a loss. You can lose data either because of a technical problem, such as media failure, or because of errors made by the users, such as a wrong update or an overeager sysadmin or DBA deleting the wrong file. Oracle backup is the set of concepts, strategies, and steps to make copies of a database so you can use them to recover from a failure/error situation. Backups in this sense refer to physical backups of database files, control files, and archived redo log files. Oracle recovery is the set of concepts, strategies, and steps to actually recover from a system/ user error or a potential data loss due to media-related problems, such as the loss of a disk drive.

In an ideal world, no one would ever have any data loss or downtime because of a database failure. However, the constraints of both humans and machinery, such as disk drive technology, mean that there's bound to be some type of failure over the course of your life as a practicing DBA, since you're the one in charge of maintaining and tuning databases that support the business. So, here is your more realistic set of goals:

- Protect the database from as many types of failure as possible.

- Increase the mean time between failures.

- Decrease the mean time to recover.

- Minimize the loss of data when there is a database failure.

Recovery Manager (RMAN) is Oracle's main backup and recovery tool and is a built-in component of the Oracle server. You don't have to pay additional licensing fees to use RMAN, as is the case when you use other Oracle products, such as the Enterprise Manager Grid Control. Since its introduction as part of the Oracle 8 release, RMAN has improved considerably to the point that it has become the most powerful tool to back up and recover Oracle databases, with its wide array of sophisticated and powerful capabilities. You can still use traditional user-managed backup and recovery techniques, but the powerful backup and recovery features offered by RMAN mean you won't be taking full advantage of your Oracle server software if you don't use RMAN. This book provides comprehensive coverage of RMAN's backup and recovery capabilities. Before we start our discussion of how to perform backup and recovery tasks with RMAN, it's important to get an overview of key backup- and recovery-related concepts. We discuss the following topics in this chapter before turning to a detailed discussion of RMAN backup and recovery techniques starting in Chapter 2:

- Types of database failures

- Oracle backup and recovery concepts

- Backup types

- Recovery types

- An introduction to RMAN

- Backup and recovery best practices

We use the Oracle Database 12c release throughout this book, thus providing you with cutting-edge RMAN backup and recovery solutions. Most of what we say, however, applies equally to Oracle Database 11g. We specifically mention whenever we're discussing a feature not available in Oracle Database 12c.

Types of Database Failures

Since database backups are made to protect against a database failure, let's quickly review the types of database failures that can occur. A database can fail, either entirely or partially, for various reasons. You can recover from some types of database failure with scarcely any effort on your part, because the Oracle database can recover automatically from some types of failures. The more critical types of failures require you to go in and "recover" the database by using your backups. You can divide database failures into the categories covered in the following sections.

Statement Failure

A typical example of a statement failure is when a program attempts to enter invalid data into an Oracle table. The statement will fail because of the checks built into the data insertion process. The solution here is to clean up the data by validating or correcting it. Sometimes a program may fail to complete because of programmatic logical errors. You must then refer the problem to the development group for corrections.

It is fairly common for a long data insertion job or a data import job to fail midway because there is no more room to put in the data. If you haven't already invoked the *resumable space allocation* feature, you must add space to the relevant tablespace. Another common cause of a statement failure is not having the proper privileges to perform a task. Your task as a DBA is to simply grant the appropriate privileges for the user who invoked the failed SQL statement.

User Process Failure

Sometimes a user process may be terminated abruptly because of, say, the user performing an abnormal disconnect or performing a terminal program error and losing the session connection. As a DBA, there is not much you need to do here: the Oracle background processes will roll back any uncommitted changes to the data and release the locks that were held by the abnormally disconnected user session. The user will have to reconnect after the abrupt termination.

Network Failure

A network failure can also cause a database failure. Network failures can occur because the Oracle Net listener, the network interface card (NIC), or the network connection has failed. The DBA must configure multiple network cards and a backup network connection and backup listener to protect against these errors. In addition, you can use the connect-time failover feature to protect against a network failure.

Instance Failure

You experience an Oracle instance failure when your database instance comes down because of an event such as a hardware failure, a power failure, or an emergency shutdown procedure. You may also experience an instance shutdown when the key Oracle background process, such as PMON, shuts down because of an error condition.

Following an instance failure, first you check the alert log and trace files for any potential hints about the cause of the instance failure. Following this, you can just restart the database instance by using the Oracle command startup from the SQL*Plus command line.

Since the database wasn't cleanly shut down and the database files aren't synchronized, Oracle will perform an automatic instance or crash recovery at this point. Oracle will automatically perform a rollback of the uncommitted transactions by using data from the undo segments and will roll forward the committed changes it finds in the online redo log files. You don't need to use any sort of backup when restarting the database instance following an instance failure. Once the uncommitted changes are backed out and the committed changes are rolled forward, the data files are in sync again and will contain only committed data.

User Error

Inadvertently dropping a table is every DBA's nightmare. In addition to accidentally dropping a table, users can also wrongly modify or delete data from a table. You can use techniques such as the flashback table or the new Oracle 12c RMAN command recover table to restore a table to a previous point in time. You can use the flashback drop feature to recover an accidentally dropped table. Of course, if the transaction isn't committed yet, you can simply roll back the unwanted changes. Oracle's LogMiner tool also comes in handy in such situations.

Media Failure

Media failure occurs when you lose a disk or a disk controller fails, hindering access to your database. A head crash, a file corruption, and the overwriting or deletion of a data file are all examples of a media failure. In general, any failure to read from or write to a disk constitutes a media failure. Although the first four types of failures don't require you to resort to a backup (except the new RMAN command recover table, which does need an RMAN backup), media failure in most cases would require performing a media recovery with the help of backups of the data files and archived redo logs.

Each type of media failure may have a different solution as far as recovery is concerned. For example, if a control file copy is accidentally deleted, you won't have to go to your backups. On the other hand, deleting a data file most likely requires you to restore the data file from a backup as well as use the archived redo logs to bring the database up-to-date. If only a few blocks in a data file are corrupt, you may use RMAN's block media recovery feature instead of restoring data files and performing media recovery.

In this book, we are mostly concerned with problems caused by media failures and how to recover from them. For this reason, let's analyze how database failures can occur because of media problems. Once your Oracle database instance is running in open mode, it could crash because of the loss of several types of files. For example, the database will crash if any of the following are true:

- Any of the multiplexed control files are deleted or lost because of a disk failure. You must restore the missing control file by copying from an existing control file and restarting the instance.

- Any data file belonging to the system or the undo tablespace is deleted or lost because of a disk failure. If you lose one of these files, the instance may or may not shut down immediately. If the instance is still running, shut it down with the shutdown abort statement. You then start up the database in mount state, restore the lost data file, and recover it before opening the database for public access.

- An entire redo log group is lost. If you have at least one member of the redo log group, your database instance can continue to operate normally. Restore the missing log file by copying one of the other members of the same group.

The database won't crash if any of the following are true:

- Any nonsystem or undo tablespace data file is lost. If you lose a nonsystem or undo tablespace file, also known as a noncritical data file from the point of view of the Oracle server, you must first restore and then recover that data file. The database instance can continue operating in the meantime.

- At least a single member of each redo log group is available, although you might have lost other members of one or more groups.

Oracle Backup and Recovery Concepts

Before you jump into Oracle backup and recovery concepts, it's a good idea to review the basic Oracle backup and recovery architecture. Oracle uses several background processes that are part of the Oracle instance, and some of these background processes play a vital role in backup and recovery tasks. For a quick understanding of the Oracle background processes involved in backup and recovery, please see Figure 11-1 (in Chapter 11). Oracle also has several physical structures that are crucial components of backup and recovery, which we discuss in the following sections.

Backup and Recovery Instance Architecture

The Oracle instance consists of the system global area (SGA), which is the memory allocated to the Oracle instance, and a set of Oracle processes called the *background processes*. The Oracle processes start when you start the instance and keep running as long as the instance is alive. Each of the Oracle background processes is in charge of a specific activity, such as writing changed data to the data files, cleaning up after disconnected user sessions, and so on. We'll briefly review the key Oracle background processes that perform critical backup- and recovery–related tasks, which are the checkpoint process, the log writer process, and the archiver process.

The Checkpoint Process

The checkpoint process does three things:

- It signals the database writer process (DBWn) at each checkpoint.

- It updates the data file headers with the checkpoint information.

- It updates the control files with the checkpoint information.

The Log Writer Process

Oracle's online redo log files record all changes made to the database. Oracle uses a write-ahead protocol, meaning the logs are written to before the data files. Therefore, it is critical to always protect the online logs against loss by ensuring they are multiplexed. Any changes made to the database are first recorded in the redo log buffer, which is part of the SGA.

Redo log files come into play when a database instance fails or crashes. Upon restart, the instance will read the redo log files looking for any committed changes that need to be applied to the data files. Remember, when you commit, Oracle ensures that what you are committing has first been written to the redo log files before these changes are recorded in the actual data files. The redo log is the ultimate source of truth for all changes to the data in an Oracle database, since an instance failure before the changes are written to the data files means that the changes are only in the redo log files but not in the data files.

The log writer (LGWR) process is responsible for transferring the contents of the redo log buffer to the online redo log files. The log writer writes to the online redo files under the following circumstances:

- At each commit

- Every three seconds

- When the redo log buffer is one-third full

The important thing to remember here is that the log writer process writes before the database writer does, because of the write-ahead protocol. Data changes aren't necessarily written to data files when you commit a transaction, but they are always written to the redo log.

■ **Note** In fact, some esoteric features in the Oracle database allow you to make changes without generating redo log entries. Such features are helpful, for example, when loading large amounts of data. However, their benefits do not come without additional risk. The important point to take away from this section is that unless you are specifically using a feature that disables logging, any changes you commit are first written to the redo log files, and it is the log writer process that does the writing.

The Archiver Process

The archiver (ARCn) is an optional background process and is in charge of archiving the filled online redo log files, before they can be overwritten by new data. The archiver background process is used only if you're running your database in archivelog mode.

Physical Database Structures Used in Recovering Data

You need to deal with four major physical database structures during a database recovery:

- Data files
- Redo logs (archived and online)
- Control files
- Undo records

In a basic database recovery situation, you would need to first restore data files by using backups (from a past period, of course). Once the restoration of the data files is completed, you issue the recover command, which results in the database rolling forward all committed data and thus bringing the database up-to-date. The database also rolls back any uncommitted data that's recorded in the undo segments that are part of the undo tablespace. The database server automatically performs the rollback of uncommitted data by using undo records in the undo tablespace to undo all uncommitted changes that were applied to the data files from the redo logs during the recovery process. This rolling-back of uncommitted data takes place by using the information about all the changes made since the last database startup. Oracle records all changes made to the database in files called the *online redo log files*. Since Oracle uses a round-robin method of writing the online redo log members, it is critical that you save the filled online redo logs before they are written. The process of saving the filled redo log files is called *archiving*, and the saved redo log files are termed *archived redo log files*. A media recovery process uses both the archived redo log files and the online redo log files.

The control file is essential for the Oracle instance to function, because it contains critical information concerning tablespace and data file records, checkpoints, redo log threads in the current online redo log, log sequence numbers, and so on.

RMAN lets you back up all the files you need for a database recovery, including data files, control files, the spfile, and archived redo logs. RMAN also lets you make image copies of both data files, the spfile and control files, in addition to the standard RMAN-formatted backup pieces. You should never back up online redo log files; instead, always duplex these files to protect against the loss of an online redo log.

Archivelog and Noarchivelog Mode of Operation

You can operate your Oracle database in either *archivelog* mode or *noarchivelog* mode. In noarchivelog mode, Oracle will overwrite the filled online redo logs, instead of archiving (saving) the online redo logs. In this mode, you're protected only from instance failures, such as those caused by a power failure, for example, but not from a media failure. Thus, if there is a media failure, such as a damaged disk drive, the changes that were overwritten are gone forever, and the database won't be able to access those data modifications to recover the database up to the current point in time. The transactions made since the last backup are lost forever, and you can restore the database only to the point of the last backup you made.

If you are running your database in noarchivelog mode and you happen to lose a data file, for example, you follow these steps to get back to work again:

1. If the instance isn't already shut down, first shut it down.

2. Restore the entire database (data files and control files) from the backups.

3. Restart the database by using the `startup` (open mode) command.

4. Users lose any data that was changed or newly entered in the database since you took the backup that was just restored. You can enter the data if you have a source, or you're going to have a data loss situation.

If you are running a production database—or if you want to make sure that all the data changes made to any database, for that matter, are always protected—you must operate your database in archivelog mode. Only a database running in archivelog mode can recover from both instance and media failures. You can't perform a media recovery on a database running in noarchivelog mode.

If you're running the database in noarchivelog mode, remember that you can make a whole-database backup only after first shutting down the database. You can't make any online tablespace backups in such a database. A database in noarchivelog mode also can't use the tablespace point-in-time recovery technique. Make sure you take frequent whole-database backups if an important database is running in noarchivelog mode for some reason.

Flashback Technology

Traditionally, restoring backed-up data files and recovering the database with the help of archived redo logs was the only way you could rewind the database to a previous point in time or view older data. Oracle's *flashback* technology offers new techniques that let you recover from several types of errors without ever having to restore backup files. The key idea behind the flashback technology is to improve database availability while you're fixing logical data errors. While you're correcting the logical data errors in one or more errors, all the other database objects continue to be available to the users unhindered. Flashback technology actually consists of a half dozen specific features, most but not all of which rely on the use of undo data to undo the effect of logical errors:

Oracle flashback query (uses undo data): This feature lets you view results from a past period in time. You can choose to use this query to retrieve lost or wrongly deleted data.

Oracle flashback version query (uses undo data): This feature lets you view all versions of a table's rows during a specific interval. You can use this feature for retrieving old data as well as for auditing purposes.

Oracle flashback transaction query (uses undo data): This feature enables you to view all the changes made by one or more transactions during a specified period of time.

Oracle flashback transaction (uses undo data): This feature that was added in the Oracle Database 11g release lets you back out unwanted transactions by using compensating transactions.

Oracle flashback table (uses undo data): This feature lets you recover a table (online) to a previous point in time. You can recover a table or a set of tables to a past point in time by using the contents of the undo tablespace. The database can remain online during this time, thus enhancing its availability. All of a table's constraints, triggers, and indexes are restored during the recovery, while the database remains online. You don't have to restore from a backup when you perform a flashback table operation. Since you're using undo data to restore the table instead of media recovery, you'll get done faster, and with less effort to boot.

Oracle flashback drop (uses the recycle bin): This relies on the concept of a recycle bin and lets you restore a dropped table. When you accidentally drop a table with the drop table statement, information about the purged table is saved in the recycle bin (which is actually a data dictionary table) under a system-assigned name. Actually, the table's contents remain intact and in place, but the data dictionary marks the table as having been dropped. You can then "undrop" the table at a later time by using the flashback table ... to before drop statement, which recovers the dropped object from the recycle bin. The flashback table feature relies entirely on the recycle bin concept.

The *flashback data archive* capability lets you use the previously described flashback features to access data from a period of time that's as old as you want. By using a flashback data archive, you overcome the limitation of a short undo retention time in the undo tablespace.

Oracle's *flashback database* feature serves as an alternative to traditional database point-in-time recovery. You use this feature to undo changes made by logical data corruption or by user errors. The essential point to understand here is that the opposite of flashback is to *recover*. In normal database recovery, you update the backups by applying logs forward. In flashback, you rewind the database by applying flashback logs backward. Thus, in most cases, a flashback database operation will take much less time than it takes to restore and recover during the traditional alternative, which is a database point-in-time recovery. The flashback database feature takes the database back in time, essentially rewinding it to a past point in time by undoing all changes made to the database since that time. Unlike traditional point-in-time recovery, you don't have to perform a media recovery by restoring backups. You simply use the flashback logs (stored in the fast recovery area) to access older versions of the changed data blocks. In addition, the database makes use of the archived redo logs as well.

■ **Note** The flashback database feature is useless in dealing with cases of lost data files or damaged media. You can use this feature to undo the changes made to an Oracle database's data files only by reverting the contents of the data files to a previous point in time.

When you enable flashback logging so that you can use the flashback database feature, you may not always be able to return to a specific point in time, if the flashback logs for that period aren't available. Oracle's *guaranteed restore points* feature lets you specify a system change number (SCN) to which you can always restore the database. That is, the database will ensure that the flashback logs from the specific SCN on are saved, no matter what. Thus, guaranteed restore points, which are an adjunct to the flashback database feature, let you ensure that you'll at least be able to recover until the specified SCN, even if you aren't necessarily able to recover up to the current SCN.

Backup Types

When we talk about a database backup, your first thought might be that it is simply a copy of all the database physical files. However, an Oracle database offers several types of backups. We summarize the main types in the following sections.

Physical and Logical Backups

When you make a copy of a database file using an operating system utility, such as cp, you are making an actual physical copy of the database file. You can use this file to restore the database contents if you happen to lose the disk containing that file. Physical backups are simply physical copies of the files used by the database, such as data files, redo logs, and control files. However, making exact physical copies of the database file isn't the only way to copy the contents of an Oracle database. You can also make a logical backup by using Oracle's Data Pump Export tool, wherein you copy the definitions and contents of all of the database's logical components, such as tables and so on. You can use Oracle's Data Pump Import utility to later import the logical data into the same or another Oracle database. Logical backups are, however, not a complete backup and recovery solution; they serve as a secondary means of backing up key tablespaces or tables in some situations.

Whole and Partial Backups

A *whole-backup* of a database is the backup of the *entire* database; this is the most commonly made type of Oracle database backup. A whole-database backup includes all the data files plus the control files. A *partial backup* refers to backups of a tablespace or data file in a database. A data file backup will include only a single operating system file. A tablespace backup includes all the data files that are part of that tablespace. You can also back up just the control file by making either a text or a binary copy of it. The control file is a crucial part of the recovery process, since it contains key information about various recovery-related structures.

Online and Offline Backups

RMAN supports both *offline* and *online* backups. An offline backup, also called a *cold backup*, is one made after shutting down the database using the shutdown command or the shutdown command with the immediate or transactional clause. An offline backup, provided you make one after the database is shut down gracefully, is always consistent, whether you're operating in archivelog or noarchivelog mode. When making an offline backup with RMAN, however, you must start the database you want to back up in the mount mode.

An online backup, also called a *hot* or *warm* backup, is one made while the database instance is still open. By definition, an online backup is always inconsistent. During a recovery, the application of the necessary archived redo logs will make the backup consistent. Thus, you can make online backups of any database you're operating, and the resulting inconsistent backups can be made consistent with the application of archived redo logs. However, for databases running in noarchivelog mode, open inconsistent backups aren't recommended.

Full and Incremental Backups

A full backup of a database will contain complete backups of all the data files. Incremental backups contain only the changed data blocks in the data files. Obviously, then, incremental backups can potentially take a much shorter time than full backups. You can make incremental backups only with the help of RMAN—you can't make incremental backups using user-managed backup techniques.

Consistent and Inconsistent Backups

To understand the crucial difference between consistent and inconsistent backups, you must first understand the concept of the system change number (SCN). The SCN is an Oracle server–assigned number that indicates a committed version of the database. It's quite possible that different data files in the database might have a different SCN at any given point in time. If the SCNs across all the data files are synchronized, it means that the data across the data files comes from a single point in time and, thus, is consistent.

During each checkpoint, the server makes all database file SCNs consistent with respect to an identical SCN. In addition, it updates the control file with that SCN information. This synchronization of the SCNs gives you a consistent backup of your database. Not only does each of the data files in the database have the same SCN, it must also not contain any database changes beyond that common SCN.

If you back up your database while it's running, you may end up with backups of the various data files at various time points and different SCNs. This means your backups are inconsistent, since the SCNs aren't identical across all the data files.

If you're operating the database in noarchivelog mode, you can use only consistent backups to restore your database. If you're operating in archivelog mode, however, you can use consistent or inconsistent backups to restore the database. If you're using a consistent backup, you can open a whole-database backup without recovery and without using the open resetlogs command. If you're using inconsistent backups, however, you must use archived redo logs to make the data current and synchronize the SCNs across the data files.

The key fact here is that the recovery process will make your inconsistent backups consistent again by using the data from the archived redo logs and the online redo log files to apply all the necessary changes across the data files to make them all consistent with reference to a single SCN.

If you're running the database in noarchivelog mode, the recommended approach to backing up the database is to shut down the database cleanly first and then to back up all the data files. If you're using RMAN to perform an offline backup, the database must be mounted before you can actually perform the RMAN backup. This is because RMAN needs to update the target database control file.

When you follow the approach suggested in the previous paragraph, you'll be backing up a consistent database. It's not recommended that you back up an inconsistent database resulting from an abrupt shutdown using the shutdown abort command, for example.

If you're running the database in archivelog mode, you can back up a whole database in any of the following ways:

- Closed and consistent

- Closed and inconsistent

- Open and inconsistent

The ability to back up a database while it is open and in use is a key benefit of running a database in archivelog mode.

Recovery Types

There are several methods of recovering data, and to a large extent the particular recovery strategy you adopt will depend on your backup strategy. For example, if you are operating in noarchivelog mode, then in most cases you can't go perform a complete recovery. You can restore only the latest backup and will lose all the data that was entered since the time of the backup. In the following sections, we'll briefly describe the major recovery techniques you can use. Similarly, the flashback database technique offers a much faster means of restoring a database to a previous point in time than traditional media recovery, but of course, you can't avail yourself of this wonderful feature if you haven't configured and used a fast recovery area (to store the flashback logs).

Database Recovery and Consistent vs. Inconsistent Backups

If you shut down your database using either shutdown normal (same as the shutdown command), shutdown immediate, or shutdown transactional, you'll have a *consistent* database. A shutdown following each of the previously mentioned variations of the shutdown command will result in the following actions:

- All uncommitted changes are rolled back first.

- The contents of the database buffer cache are written to the data files on disk.

- All resources, such as locks and latches, are released.

Since the database was cleanly shut down, when you restart the database, there is no need for an instance recovery, which is the main implication of performing and using a consistent backup.

If you shut down your database using either the shutdown abort or shutdown force command or if there is an instance failure, you'll end up with an *inconsistent* database, wherein the database is said to be in a "dirty" state. Once the shutdown command is issued or the instance is terminated abruptly for some reason, the following things will be true:

- Any committed changes are *not* rolled back automatically.

- Changes made to the database buffers aren't written to the data files on disk.

- All resources, such as locks and latches, are still held and aren't released.

In other words, there is simply no time to perform a graceful and tidy closure of the database. Your database instance is simply terminated, even though it may be in the middle of processing user transactions and hasn't properly recorded all the modified data to the data files. Upon restarting your database, the Oracle database instance will do the following things first:

- Use the information in the online redo logs to reapply changes.

- Use the undo tablespace contents to roll back the uncommitted changes to data.

- Release the held resources.

The work that the Oracle database performs upon a restart following an inconsistent shutdown is known as *instance recovery*. Instance recovery is thus mandatory and entirely automatic, with the database itself performing all the work without any intervention by the DBA.

Crash Recovery and Media Recovery

As noted in the previous section about instance or crash recovery, if your Oracle instance crashes, because of a power failure, for example, you don't have to perform a media recovery of the database, which requires that you restore backups of the database and bring them up-to-date with the help of the archived redo logs. The Oracle server will perform an automatic crash recovery when you restart the instance. However, if you lose a disk drive, for example, or you can't access the disk's contents because of some kind of media failure, you may have to restore your backups and bring them up-to-date using the archived redo logs.

Crash Recovery

Crash recovery or instance recovery is the automatic recovery of the database by the Oracle server, without any intervention by the DBA. For example, if a power outage brings down your database instance, when the power supply resumes, you only need to restart the database instance. You don't have to perform any restore or recovery tasks, because the server will use the information in the undo tablespace to perform automatic instance recovery by rolling back uncommitted transactions in the database. The server uses the online redo logs to record in the data files the changes that were committed before the outage but couldn't be written to the database files before the occurrence of the failure.

The Oracle server automatically performs crash recovery whenever you open a database whose files were not cleanly synchronized before shutting down. Since an abrupt shutdown doesn't provide a chance to synchronize the data files, it is a given that, in most cases, an instance recovery will be performed by the Oracle server when you restart the Oracle instance. The Oracle server will use the information saved in the online redo log files to synchronize the data files. Instance recovery involves the following two key operations:

> *Rolling forward:* During this operation, the Oracle server will update all data files with the information from the redo log files. The online redo log files are always written to before the data is recorded in the data files. Thus, an instance recovery usually leaves the online log files "ahead" of the data files.

> *Rolling back:* During this operation, uncommitted changes that were added to the data files during the rollforward operation are rolled back. Oracle does this by using the undo tablespace contents to return uncommitted changes to their original states. At the end of the rollback stage, only committed data at the time of the instance failure is retained in the data files.

During instance recovery, in the first rollforward operation, the database server must apply all transactions between the last checkpoint and the end of the redo log to the data files. Thus, in order to tune instance recovery, you control the gap between the checkpoint position and the end of the redo log. You use the Oracle initialization parameter `fast_start_mttr_target` to specify the number of seconds you want the crash recovery to take. Oracle will try to recover the instance as close as possible to the time that you specify for the `fast_start_mttr_target` parameter. The maximum value of this parameter is 3,600 seconds (one hour).

Media Recovery

When a disk drive fails and you can't access the contents of an Oracle data file, you're looking at a potentially much more serious situation than a crash recovery, since the server won't be able to automatically recover from such a catastrophe. You must provide the lost data files from backup. Since it's likely that data has changed in the meantime, you must provide the changes stored both in the archived redo log files and in the online redo log files. When the Oracle database issues an error indicating media problems, you must first find which files to recover by querying the V$RECOVER_FILE view, which lists all files that need media recovery.

RMAN completely automates the process of media recovery. You use two basic commands—`restore` and `recover`—to perform media recovery. The `restore` command restores the necessary data files from RMAN's backup sets or image copies to the same or an alternate location on disk. The `recover` command performs the recovery process by applying necessary archived redo logs or incremental backups to the restored data files. You must do the following as part of a media recovery operation:

- Restore the necessary data files from backup, either to the old or to an alternate location.

- Rename the data files, if necessary, so the database will know about their new location.

- Recover the data files (bring them up-to-date), if necessary, by applying redo information to them.

To open the database after a successful restore and recovery, the following must be true:

- You must have synchronized copies of all the control files.

- You must have synchronized online data files.

- You must have at least one member of each redo log group.

If all these are true, you can open the recovered database.

Complete and Point-in-Time Recovery

You perform a complete recovery when you bring a database, a tablespace, or a data file up-to-date with the most current point in time possible. It's important to emphasize that complete recovery isn't synonymous with recovering the complete database. Rather, completeness here alludes to the completeness of the entire database or part of it (tablespace or data file) with reference to the time element. If you update the database tablespace or data file completely by applying all changes from the archived redo logs to the backup files, you're performing a complete backup. In other words, complete recovery will ensure that you haven't lost any transactions. Note that when using RMAN, you may also use incremental backups as well, in addition to archived redo logs, during the recovery process.

When you perform media recovery, it isn't always the case that you can or should bring the database up-to-date to the latest possible point in time. Sometimes you may not want to recover the database to the current point in time. Following a loss of a disk or some other problem, the complete recovery of a database will make the database current by bringing all of its contents up to the present. A *point-in-time recovery*, also known as *incomplete recovery*, brings the database to a specified time in the past. A point-in-time recovery implies that changes made to the database after the specified point may be missing. On the face of it, a point-in-time recovery may seem strange. After all, why would you recover your database only to a past period in time and not bring it up-to-date? Well, there may be situations where a point-in-time recovery is your best bet, as in the following examples:

- You lose some of the archived redo logs or incremental backups necessary for a complete recovery following a media failure.

- The DBA or the users delete data by mistake or make wrong updates to a table.

- A batch job that's making updates fails to complete.

In all of these situations, you can use either point-in-time recovery or Oracle's flashback technology to get the database back to a previous point in time. Prior to the introduction of the flashback technology, a database point-in-time recovery (DBPITR) and a tablespace point-in-time recovery (TSPITR) were the automatic solutions when confronted by situations such as an erroneous data entry or wrong updates. Flashback technology offers you the capability to perform point-in-time recovery much quicker than the traditional point-in-time recovery techniques that rely on media recovery. The flashback database feature is the alternative to traditional database point-in-time recovery, while the flashback table feature lets you avoid having to perform a media recovery in most cases.

Deciding on the Appropriate Recovery Technique

Fortunately for Oracle database administrators, several recovery techniques are available, such as media recovery, Oracle flashback, and so on, each geared toward recovering from a certain type of problem. Here's a summary of when to use the various types of recovery techniques:

- Use media recovery if you're confronted with damaged, missing, or inaccessible data files.

- If a user drops a table or commits a major data entry error, you can perform a point-in-time media recovery, but the best option is to use the flashback drop feature. You can also import the affected table using the Data Pump Import utility or have users reenter data in some situations. You can also use the RMAN command recover table, which is a brand-new Oracle Database 12c feature.

- If you run into logical errors, perform a TSPITR or consider using an appropriate flashback technique to make a point-in-time recovery.

- If you have data corruption in a few blocks in a data file or a set of data files, use block media recovery. Again, there's no need to perform a media recovery and make the rest of the database inaccessible.

- If a user error affects a large set of tables or the entire database, use the flashback database feature to revert the database to a previous "good" time by undoing all the changes since that point in time.

- Use the flashback table feature to revert to a previous state of a table in order to undo unwanted changes. Starting with Oracle Database 12c, you can also use the RMAN recover table command to recover a table to a specified point in time.

RMAN Architecture

You can start performing backups with RMAN without installing or configuring a thing. Simply invoke the RMAN client by using the RMAN executable (named rman) from the $ORACLE_HOME/bin directory, and you're ready to go. Just specify the target database you want to work with at the command line, and that's it. You can perform backup and recovery actions with RMAN through the RMAN client or through the Enterprise Manager GUI.

In addition to the RMAN client, you may use additional optional components to make your backup and recovery strategy robust and easy:

> *The recovery catalog*: The target database control file will always store the RMAN repository, which is the set of RMAN-related backup and recovery information. This data is also referred to as RMAN's *metadata*. However, it's smarter to use a dedicated database to store the RMAN repository. You can then create a special schema called the *recovery catalog* in this dedicated database and have RMAN store its repository in it, thus avoiding the risk of the critical metadata being overwritten when the control file runs out of space. As you'll see in Chapter 6, using a recovery catalog, which is optional, has several other advantages.

The fast recovery area: This is a location on disk where the database will store the backup- and recovery-related files. This is also optional but highly recommended. See Chapter 3 for a detailed discussion of the fast recovery area.

Media management layer: As mentioned earlier, RMAN can directly interact only with disk drives. If you want to use tape drives to store your backups, you'll need a media management layer in addition to RMAN, since RMAN can't directly interact with the tape drives. You can use any of several Oracle-certified third-party media management layers. Oracle also provides Oracle Secure Backup, which it claims is the "most well-integrated media management layer for RMAN backups." Together, RMAN and Oracle Secure Backup provide a complete end-to-end backup solution for all Oracle environments. Chapter 18 deals with the media management layer.

An RMAN session in Unix/Linux systems consists of the following processes:

- The RMAN client process.

- A default channel, which is the connection to the target database.

- Additional channels you allocate and the corresponding target connection to each of the target databases.

- If you're using the recovery catalog, there will be a catalog connection to the recovery catalog database.

- During database duplication or TSPITR operations, there will be an auxiliary connection to the auxiliary instance.

- By default, RMAN makes one polling connection to each of the target databases to help monitor the execution of RMAN commands on the different allocated channels.

Figure 1-1 shows the RMAN architecture in detail and illustrates the linkages among the various components.

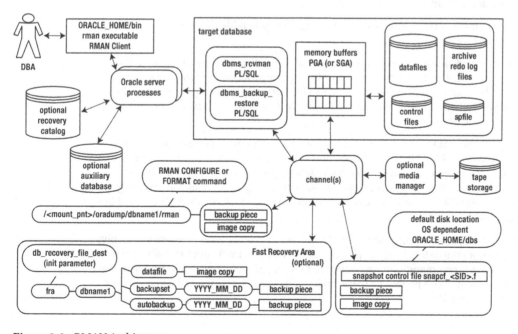

Figure 1-1. *RMAN Architecture*

The following list describes the RMAN architectural components:

DBA: Appears somewhat short and bald in the diagram, which isn't far from the truth (in our case, with the exception of Arup Nanda).

Target database: The database being backed up by RMAN. You connect to the target database with the RMAN command-line TARGET parameter (more on this in the next section of this chapter).

RMAN client: The rman utility from which you issue BACKUP, RESTORE, and RECOVER commands. On most database servers, the rman utility is located in the ORACLE_HOME/bin directory (along with all the other Oracle utilities, such as sqlplus, expdp, and so on).

Oracle server processes (channels): When you execute the rman client and connect to the target database, two Oracle server background processes are started. One process interacts with the PL/SQL packages to coordinate the backup activities. The secondary process occasionally updates Oracle data-dictionary structures. You can query the RMAN metadata information via views such as V$SESSION_LONGOPS.

PL/SQL packages: RMAN uses two internal PL/SQL packages (owned by SYS) to perform B&R tasks: DBMS_RCVMAN and DBMS_BACKUP_RESTORE. DBMS_RCVMAN accesses information in the control file and passes that to the RMAN server processes. The DBMS_BACKUP_RESTORE package performs most of RMAN's work. For example, this package creates the system calls that direct the channel processes to perform B&R operations.

Memory buffers (PGA or SGA): RMAN uses a memory area in the program global area (and sometimes in the system global area) as a buffer when reading from data files and copying subsequent blocks to back up files.

Auxiliary database: A database to which RMAN restores target database data files for the purpose of duplicating a database, creating a Data Guard standby database, or performing a database point-in-time recovery.

Channel(s): Oracle server processes for handling I/O between files being backed up and the backup device (disk or tape).

Backups and backup sets: When you run an RMAN BACKUP command, it creates one or more backup sets. A *backup set* is an internal RMAN construct that logically groups backup piece files. You can think of the relationship of a backup set to a backup piece as similar to the relationship between a tablespace and a data file. One is a logical construct, and the other is a physical file.

Backup piece file: RMAN binary backup files. Each logical backup set consists of one or more backup piece files. These are the physical files that RMAN creates on disk or tape. They're binary, proprietary format files that only RMAN can read or write to. A backup piece can contain blocks from many different data files. Backup piece files are typically smaller than data files because backup pieces contain only blocks that have been used in the data files.

Image copy: A type of backup in which RMAN creates identical copies of a data file, archive redo log file, or control file. Image copies can be operated on by OS utilities, such as the Linux cp and mv commands. Image copies are used as part of incrementally updated image backups. Sometimes it's preferable to use image copies over backup sets if you need to be able to restore quickly.

Recovery catalog: An optional database schema that contains tables used to store metadata information regarding RMAN backup operations. Oracle strongly recommends using a recovery catalog, because it provides more options for B&R.

Media manager: Third-party software that allows RMAN to back up files directly to tape. Backing up to tape is desirable when you don't have enough room to back up directly to disk or when disaster-recovery requirements necessitate a backup to storage that can be easily moved off-site.

Fast-recovery area: An optional disk area that RMAN can use for backups (formerly known as the flash recovery area). You can also use the FRA to multiplex control files and online redo logs. You instantiate a fast recovery area with the database initialization parameters DB_RECOVERY_FILE_DEST_SIZE and DB_RECOVERY_FILE _DEST.

Snapshot control file: RMAN requires a read-consistent view of the control file when either backing up the control file or synchronizing with the recovery catalog (if it's being used). In these situations, RMAN first creates a temporary copy (snapshot) of the control file. This allows RMAN to use a version of the control file that is guaranteed not to change while backing up the control file or synchronizing with the recovery catalog.

Benefits of Using RMAN

You can perform basic backup and recovery tasks using operating system utilities and standard SQL commands. However, there are several drawbacks to using these so-called user-managed backup and recovery techniques. For example, you can't perform incremental backups using user-managed techniques. In general, user-managed backup and recovery techniques require you to manually keep track of your backup files, their status, and their availability. You must write your own SQL and operating system scripts to manage the backup and recovery operations. In addition, you must provide the necessary data files and archived log files during a database recovery operation. If the database is operating during your backups (online or hot backups), you must place the database files in the backup mode before performing the actual file backups.

Oracle explicitly states that you can use user-managed techniques to perform backup/recovery activities. Oracle actually states that both user-managed techniques and RMAN are alternative ways of performing backup and recovery tasks. However, Oracle strongly recommends using RMAN to make your backups and perform database recovery, because of the tool's strengths and powerful features. Although you can perform a basic backup and recovery task with user-managed techniques without ever having to even start the RMAN interface, you should make RMAN your main backup and recovery tool for several reasons. Several important backup and recovery features are available to you only through RMAN.

Here's a brief description of the important benefits of using RMAN instead of user-managed backup and recovery techniques:

- You can take advantage of the powerful Data Recovery Advisor feature, which enables you to easily diagnose and repair data failures and corruption (Chapter 20 discusses the Data Recovery Advisor).

- There are simpler backup and recovery commands.

- It automatically manages the backup files without DBA intervention.

- It automatically deletes unnecessary backup data files and archived redo log files from both disk and tape.

- It provides you with detailed reporting of backup actions.

- It provides considerable help in duplicating a database or creating a standby database.

- It lets you test whether you can recover your database, without actually restoring data.

- It lets you verify that available backups are usable for recovery.

- It lets you make incremental backups, which isn't possible by any other means of backup.

- It lets you perform database duplication without backups by using the network-enabled database duplication feature, also known as *active duplication*.

- It automatically detects corrupt data blocks during backups, with the corruption-relevant information recorded in the V$DATABASE_BLOCK_CORRUPTION view.

- When only a few data blocks are corrupted, you can recover at the data block level, instead of recovering an entire data file.

- You can take advantage of the unused block compression feature, wherein RMAN skips unused data blocks during a backup.

- Only RMAN provides the ability to perform encrypted backups.

- You can use RMAN with a variety of third-party storage systems.

- You can use a powerful yet easy-to-use scripting language, which lets you write custom backup and recovery scripts quickly.

Backup and Recovery Best Practices

To successfully recover from unforeseen database mishaps, you must of course be fully conversant with the Oracle recovery techniques and concepts. In addition, you must ensure you are following certain basic steps to make sure you can successfully carry out the database recovery when you're pressed for time.

In addition, you must always document your backup and recovery procedures. You must have a detailed recovery plan for each type of failure you anticipate. If possible, you must write scripts to automate the execution of the recovery plan during a crisis. You must also update the written backup and recovery procedures on a regular basis and communicate these changes to all the personnel involved in the backup and recovery process in your organization. The following is a summary of basic Oracle backup and recovery best practices that will ensure that your database recovery efforts are successful.

Configure a Fast Recovery Area

It's common for backed-up data files and archived redo logs to be archived to tape storage. However, the problem is that when you're recovering a database, tape drives are rather slow media to copy to disk. Oracle strongly supports *automatic disk-based backup and recovery*, wherein all the necessary backup files are stored on the disk itself. You make the initial copy of the necessary data files and archived redo log files to the fast recovery area and, from here, copy them to tape so you can store them off-site in a secure location.

Oracle recommends using the *fast recovery area* to store the entire set of backup- and recovery-related files. The fast recovery area is simply a location on a server where you decide to store backup- and recovery-related files, such as RMAN's backup pieces, copies of control files, and the online redo log files, and so on. At the minimum, Oracle recommends that you size the fast recovery area large enough to hold all archived redo logs that have not yet been copied to tape. It's easy to maintain the fast recovery area—all you have to do is specify the size of the area and the retention policy, which dictates when RMAN will discard unnecessary files from the fast recovery area. It's RMAN's job to keep the maximum number of backups possible in the fast recovery area, while discarding both obsolete backups and the backup files already copied to tape.

Oracle recommends that you size the fast recovery area large enough that it equals the sum of the size of the database plus the size of the archived redo logs not yet copied to tape and the size of any incremental backups.

Although the fast recovery area is by no means mandatory, Oracle recommends that you use one. You must have activated a fast recovery area in order to avail of the flashback database or the guaranteed restore point feature. In addition, using a fast recovery area means you're reducing your recovery time, since necessary backups and archived redo logs can be kept on disk instead of having to recover from tape backups. Since obsolete backups are automatically deleted when space is needed for fresh files, you won't be running the risk of accidentally deleting necessary files.

Make and Protect a Database Redundancy Set

You may have to perform a database recovery when you lose or can't access (because of a media problem) any of these three types of Oracle database files: data files, online redo log files, and control files. Oracle recommends that you maintain a *database redundancy set*, which is a set of files that'll help you recover any of the three key types of Oracle files when they become unavailable to the database. This essential set of recovery-related files, called the *redundancy set*, will enable you to recover your database from any contingency. Here are the components of the redundancy set:

- Most recent backups of all data files plus the control file

- All archived redo logs made after the last backup

- Current control files and online redo file copies

- Oracle database-related configuration file copies (spfile, password file, tnsnames.ora, and listener.ora files, for example)

To maintain the database redundancy set described here, you must duplex the control file as well as the online redo log files *at the database level*. That is, although a mirrored disk setup means that a copy of the redo log files and the control file will be automatically made at the operating-system level, that doesn't provide you with complete safety.

Although you can mirror the online redo files at the operating-system level, Oracle advises against this. Follow these Oracle best practices for protecting your database files:

- Multiplex the online redo log file at the database level. If you're using the fast recovery area, make this the destination for the duplexed copies of the online redo log file.

- Ensure that you use hardware or software (OS) mirroring to duplex the control file. This way the database will always continue to operate following the loss of one control file.

- Mirror the data files in the database so you don't have to perform media recovery for simple disk failures.

- Keep more than one set of backups so you can withstand a database corruption issue.

- Consider making more than one copy of the redundancy set on tape if you aren't going to be using a disk-based recovery plan.

Oracle recommends that you use at least two disk drives on all production systems (one for the redundancy set and the other for the data files) and completely separate them by using different volumes, file systems, disk controllers, and RAID devices to hold the two sets of files: database files and the files in the redundancy set. One way to do this is to simply use the Oracle recommended fast recovery area. In fact, Oracle recommends the fast recovery area as a logical candidate to keep a copy of all the files belonging to the redundancy set (which includes the most recent database backup) on disk.

Create Powerful Backup Strategies

The strength of your backup strategy determines the strength of your recovery strategy. No backups, no recovery! Your backup strategies are derived entirely from your recovery strategies. Ideally, you must plan your recovery strategy based on the potential types of database failures you might encounter. The more types of database failures you want to guard against, the more complex your backup strategy will be.

Schedule Regular Backups

Schedule your backups on a regular basis, thus reducing your exposure to media failures. You, of course, can recover any database from a backup made at any remote time in the past, provided you have all the archived redo logs from that point forward. But can you imagine applying all those archived redo logs to the backups and suffering a horrendous downtime?

Create Regular Backups of the Control File

Back up a database's control file after any structural change to your database, such as creating a new tablespace or adding or renaming a data file or an online redo log member. The best way to do this is to issue the RMAN command `configure controlfile autobackup on`. By default, the automatic backup of the control file is turned off. By turning control file autobackups on, you make sure that at the end of every RMAN backup command, RMAN automatically backs up the control file. When you make some changes via SQL*Plus, even though you're outside the purview of RMAN, the control file is automatically backed up, if you set the control file autobackup feature on. Using the control file autobackup, you can restore RMAN's backup and recovery information (called RMAN's *repository*) when you lose all your control files and aren't using the optional recovery catalog.

Run the Database in Archivelog Mode

To be able to restore a database completely (that is, bring it up-to-date with all the changes ever made to that database), you must run the database in archivelog mode. Only development and test databases where data loss isn't an issue should be run in noarchivelog mode.

Multiplex the Control File

Since the control file is absolutely necessary during a recovery, use the following guidelines to safeguard the control file:

- Keep the Oracle-recommended three copies of the control file.
- Put each copy of the control file on a separate disk.
- Place at least one of the three copies on a separate disk controller.

Multiplex the Redo Log Groups

If you lose your online redo logs, you may not be able to recover all committed changes to your database following a media failure and subsequent recovery. You must always duplex the online redo logs, using the following guidelines:

- Have a minimum of two members in each redo log group.
- Place each member on a separate disk drive.
- Place each redo log member on a separate disk controller.

Adopt the Right Backup Storage Strategy

Where you store your backups is quite critical to your recovery strategy, since different storage strategies have different implications for recovery time. If you use a fast recovery area, of course, the backups are all on disk, and consequently, you can recover with the least amount of elapsed time. If you store your backups only on tape or you store them off-site, you have to endure a longer interval to restore and recover your database.

Plan Your Backup-Retention Duration

One of the key questions every backup strategy must address is how long you want to keep a backup. Although you can specify that a backup be kept forever without becoming obsolete, it's not common to follow such a strategy, unless you're doing it for a special reason. Instead, backups become obsolete according to the retention policy you adopt. You can select the retention duration of backups when using RMAN in two ways. In the first method, you can specify backup retention based on a *recovery window*. That is, all backups necessary to perform a point-in-time recovery to a specified past point of time will be retained by RMAN. If a backup is older than the point of time you chose, that backup will become obsolete according to the backup retention rules. The second way to specify the retention duration is to use a *redundancy-based* retention policy, under which you specify the number of backups of a file that must be kept on disk. Any backups of a data file greater than that number will be considered obsolete.

You can set a default retention policy for all files that RMAN backs up. Once you do this, you can choose to delete any files that are obsolete under that retention policy using simple RMAN commands. The files you delete may be on disk or on tape storage. When you delete the obsolete files using RMAN commands, RMAN will remove the relevant information from its metadata. If, however, you're using the fast recovery area to store your backups, RMAN will automatically delete all obsolete files as and when it needs space for accommodating newer data file backups or archived redo logs in the fast recovery area.

Plan Your Backup Schedules

Determining a backup schedule means how often you use RMAN to back up your database files, as well as what files you back up. Do you perform nightly or weekly backups, or do you back up different files at different intervals? How frequently you create a backup will, of course, depend on how fast the data in your database is changing. If your database performs a very large number of DML operations on a daily basis, for example, you must back it up daily rather than weekly. If, on the other hand, a database is being used mostly for lookup purposes, with minimal DML changes, you can back up at a less frequent interval, say, on a weekly basis. An incremental backup strategy may be especially apt in such a case, because of the small amount of changes.

Validate Your Recovery Strategy

A key part of a backup and recovery strategy is the validation of your backups. Merely backing up the database regularly doesn't guarantee that you can recover your database successfully with those backups. You must choose a method to regularly validate the backups you take with RMAN. Since the only goal in creating database backups is to use them in a recovery situation, you must make sure you regularly validate your backups and test your data recovery strategy. RMAN provides commands that let you validate the database files you're planning to back up by reading those files without actually backing them up.

Conduct Regular Trial Recoveries

Another key part of a solid backup and recovery strategy is to schedule regular trial recoveries using your current recovery plan and the latest backups for various simulated scenarios. In addition to verifying that your backups are being made correctly, you'll also get plenty of practice with the recovery techniques and commands. Aside from that, it is only during the test restore/recovery that you'll know the duration of a restore/recovery and, therefore, how fast you can perform the actual restore/recovery.

It's much better to get acquainted with the recovery techniques this way than to try them for the first time after a production database runs into problems and you're under the gun to recover it fast.

■ **Note**   You can configure the `nls_date_format` environment variable to include the date and time format, such as DD-MON-RRRR HH24:MI:SS (in the Korn shell, use the command `export nls_date_format = YYYY-MM-DD:HH24:MI:SS`) because by default only the date is displayed in the RMAN log. This is helpful when troubleshooting, because most often you want to know the exact date and time a specific problem or error occurred. Furthermore, this will also display the date/time of the RMAN backup completion and data file checkpoints.

Record Accurate Software and Hardware Configuration

Always keep handy vital information that you might have to send to the Oracle Support personnel, such as the following:

- Server model and make

- Operating system version and patch number

- Oracle database version number and patch release

- Database identifier (DBID)

- Names and location of all your data files

- Version of the recovery catalog database and the recovery catalog schema, if you're using one

- Version of the media management software you are using

Of course, it's always a good idea to keep the complete RMAN log file generated during the RMAN backup (even though this is already captured in the V$RMAN_OUTPUT), which is useful when you lose the control file or recovery catalog that has information about the RMAN backups you want to restore from.

In this introductory chapter, we have provided a quick review of the essentials of Oracle backup and recovery concepts and have defined key terms. We also introduced the Recovery Manager tool and explained its basic architecture and an overview of its important features. Later chapters, of course, delve into the intricacies of using RMAN to perform backup and recovery.

CHAPTER 2

■ ■ ■

Jump-Starting RMAN

This chapter is for those who are fairly new to Oracle and RMAN. The purpose of this material is to show you how simple it can be—even for a novice—to back up, restore, and recover a database using RMAN. You'll see that it's possible to use RMAN with little or no training. This chapter will walk you through critical tasks, such as how to connect to your database, start it, enable archiving, and then perform basic backup and recovery tasks.

If you're a seasoned Oracle DBA and are already somewhat familiar with RMAN, this chapter is not for you. As an experienced DBA, the recipes that come after this chapter contain the information you need.

This chapter starts with simple examples of how to connect to your database, how to start/stop it, and how to enable archiving. Once your database is in archivelog mode, then you can use RMAN to take online backups, restore, and recover your database.

■ **Note**   This chapter is not intended to demonstrate how to implement RMAN backup and recovery for a production environment. Rather, this chapter is meant only to help get you started with RMAN. If you're new to RMAN, we feel it is very instructional to see how RMAN operates with out-of-the-box default settings. This will provide a foundation for understanding material in subsequent chapters.

2-1. Connecting to Your Database
Problem

You're new to Oracle and wonder how to connect to your database via SQL*Plus so that you can perform basic commands, such as starting and stopping your database and enabling archivelog mode.

Solution

Before you connect to an Oracle database, you must establish operating system variables before connecting to the database, and you also need access to either a privileged OS account or a database user granted the appropriate privileges (via a password file). These topics are discussed in the following subsections.

Establishing OS Variables

The OS environment variables are usually set when you log on to your database server. DBAs typically set these variables automatically in a startup file (such as .bashrc on Linux/Unix). Minimally, you need to set:

- ORACLE_SID to the name of your target database

- ORACLE_HOME to the parent directory where you installed the Oracle RDBMS software (binaries)

- PATH to include ORACLE_HOME/bin

In a Linux/Unix environment, Oracle provides an oraenv script for the Korn/Bash/Bourne shells and coraenv for the C shell to set the required OS variables. For example, you can run the oraenv script from the operating system prompt as follows:

```
$ . oraenv
```

You'll be prompted for the name of your database. You can verify the settings of these variables as follows:

```
$ echo $ORACLE_SID
$ echo $ORACLE_HOME
$ echo $PATH
```

If the need arises, you can override these settings by establishing OS environment variables from the command line. Here's an example of manually establishing these variables in a Linux/Unix environment:

```
$ export ORACLE_SID=o12c
$ export ORACLE_HOME=/u01/app/oracle/product/12.1.0.1/db_1
$ export PATH=$ORACLE_HOME/bin:$PATH
```

Keep in mind the prior code is just an example. You will need to modify the prior commands to match the target ORACLE_SID and ORACLE_HOME in your environment.

■ **Note** In Windows the operating system variables are set in the registry.

After you've established your operating system variables, you need to connect to the database with the proper privileges. You can do this in one of two ways: using OS authentication or using a password file.

Using OS Authentication

If your Linux/Unix account is a member of the dba group (your shop might use a different group name, but dba is the most common), you can connect to your database with the required privileges via SQL*Plus by virtue of being logged in to your Linux/Unix account. On Windows, the OS user must be part of either the ora_dba group or the ora_oper group.

On Linux/Unix you can quickly verify the operating system groups that your account belongs to using the id command without any parameters:

```
$ id
uid=500(oracle) gid=500(oinstall) groups=500(oinstall),501(dba),502(oper),503(asmdba),
504(asmoper),505(asmadmin),506(backupdba)
```

The prior output indicates that the oracle user is included in several groups, one of which is dba. Any user who belongs to the dba group can connect to the database with sysdba privileges. A user with sysdba privileges can start and stop the database. This example uses OS authentication to connect to your database as the user sys:

```
$ sqlplus / as sysdba
```

No username or password is required when using OS authentication (hence just the slash without a user/password) because Oracle first checks to see if the OS user is a member of a privileged OS group, and if so, connects without checking the username/password. You can verify that you have connected as sys by issuing the following:

```
SQL> show user
USER is "SYS"
```

Using a Password File

You can also connect to your database by providing the username and password of a database user who has been granted proper privileges. When you provide a username/password and attempt to connect to the database with sys* level (sysdba, sysoper, sysbackup, and so on) privileges, Oracle will check to see if the username and password provided are within the password file associated with your database. The password file must be manually created with the orapwd utility and is populated via the SQL grant command (see the How It Works section of this recipe for details on creating a password file).

This example shows the syntax for using a password file to connect to a database:

```
$ sqlplus <username>/<password>[@<db conn string>] as sys[dba|oper|backup]
```

For example, if you wanted to connect to a local database with a user named chaya with a password of heera with sysdba privileges, you would do as follows:

```
$ sqlplus chaya/heera as sysdba
```

Because you are providing a username/password and attempting to connect with a sys* level privilege, Oracle will verify that a password file is in place (for the local database) and that the username/password is in the password file.

One key aspect about using a password file is that this is the mechanism that allows you to use SQL*Plus or RMAN to connect to a remote database over the network with sys* privileges. For example, if you want to connect to a user named chaya with a password of heera to a remote database named HATHI with sysdba privileges, you would do as follows:

```
$ sqlplus chaya/heera@HATHI as sysdba
```

Oracle will verify that the username/password combination exists in a password file on the remote server that is associated with the database defined by the HATHI net service name. In this example, Oracle uses the information in a local tnsnames.ora file to determine the location of the database on the network (host, port, and database).

■ **Tip** Using a local tnsnames.ora file is known as the *local naming* connection method. There are other remote database name resolution methods, such as easy connect, directory naming, and external naming. See the *Oracle Database Net Services Administrator's Guide* for details on how to implement these.

How It Works

Before you can connect to the Oracle database, you need to have the proper OS variables set. Additionally, if you want to connect to Oracle as a privileged user, then you must also have access to either a privileged OS account or a privileged database user. Connecting as a privileged user allows you to perform administrative tasks, such as starting and stopping a database. You can use either OS authentication or a password file to connect to your database as a privileged user.

The concept of a privileged user is also important to RMAN backup and recovery. RMAN uses OS authentication and password files to allow privileged users to establish a privileged database session (via the rman utility). Only a privileged account is allowed to back up, restore, and recover a database.

Explaining OS Authentication

OS authentication means that if you can log on to an authorized OS account, then you are allowed to connect to your database as a privileged user without the requirement of an additional password. OS authentication is administered by assigning special groups to OS accounts.

When preparing to install the Oracle binaries, you are required to first create the OS groups and then when installing the Oracle software, associate the names of the OS groups with various levels of database privileges. Typically the three OS groups that pertain to backup and recovery are:

- dba

- oper

- backupdba (new in Oracle Database 12c)

Each OS group corresponds to certain database privileges. Table 2-1 shows the mapping of OS groups to database system privileges and operations.

Table 2-1. *Mapping of OS groups to privileges related to backup and recovery*

Operating System Group	Database System Privilege	Authorized Operations
dba	sysdba	Start up, shut down, alter database, create and drop database, toggle archivelog mode, back up and recover database.
oper	sysoper	Start up, shut down, alter database, toggle archivelog mode, back up and recover database.
backupdba	sysbackup	New in Oracle Database 12c, this privilege allows you to start up, shut down, and perform all backup and recovery operations.

Any OS account assigned to the authorized OS groups can connect to the database without a password and perform administrative operations. In Linux/Unix, it's common to create an oracle OS account and assign its primary group to be dba, which in turn authorizes it to perform sysdba operations. If you need more granular control over privileges, you can create other operating system accounts and assign them to groups as appropriate (such as oper and backupdba).

In Windows environments, you can verify which OS users belong to the ora_dba group as follows: select Control Panel, Administrative Tools, Computer Management, Local Users and Groups, Groups. You should see a group named something like ora_dba. You can click that group and view which OS users are assigned to it.

Additionally, for OS authentication to work in Windows environments, you must have the following entry in your sqlnet.ora file:

```
SQLNET.AUTHENTICATION_SERVICES=(NTS)
```

Explaining Password File Authentication

You can also use a password file to authenticate users connecting to the database with sys* (sysdba, sysoper, sysbackup, and so on) privileges. A password file allows you to do the following from SQL*Plus or RMAN:

- Connect to your database with sys* privileges as a non-sys database user

- Connect to remote database (over the network) with sys* privileges

To implement a password file, perform the following steps:

1. Create the password file with the orapwd utility.

2. Set the initialization parameter remote_login_passwordfile to exclusive.

In a Linux/Unix environment, use the orapwd utility to create a password file as follows:

```
$ cd $ORACLE_HOME/dbs
$ orapwd file=orapw<ORACLE_SID> password=<sys password>
```

In a Linux/Unix environment, the password file is usually stored in the ORACLE_HOME/dbs directory, and in Windows, it's typically placed in the ORACLE_HOME\database directory. The format of the filename that you specify in the previous command may vary by OS. For example, on Windows the format is PWD<ORACLE_SID>.ora. The following shows the syntax in a Windows environment:

```
c:\> cd %ORACLE_HOME%\database
c:\> orapwd file=PWD<ORACLE_SID>.ora password=<sys password>
```

To enable the use of the password file, set the initialization parameter remote_login_passwordfile to exclusive (this is the default value). You can verify its value as shown next:

```
SQL> show parameter remote_login_password
```

NAME	TYPE	VALUE
remote_login_passwordfile	string	EXCLUSIVE

If need be, you can manually set the remote_login_passwordfile parameter as shown:

```
$ sqlplus / as sysdba
SQL> alter system set remote_login_passwordfile=exclusive scope=spfile;
```

You will then need to stop and start your database for this parameter to take effect. The prior example assumes you are using a server parameter file (spfile). If you are not using a spfile, you will have to manually edit the init.ora file by adding this entry with a text editor:

```
remote_login_passwordfile=exclusive
```

■ **Note**   The default location on Linux/Unix for the spfile or init.ora file is the ORACLE_HOME/dbs directory. The default location on Windows is usually the ORACLE_HOME/database directory.

Then stop and start your database to instantiate the parameter. Once the password file is enabled, you can then create database users and assign them the sys* privileges as required. For example, suppose you had a database user named dba_maint that you wanted to grant sysbackup privileges:

```
$ sqlplus / as sysdba
SQL> grant sysbackup to dba_maint;
```

Now the dba_maint database user can connect to the database with sysbackup privileges:

```
$ sqlplus dba_maint/foo as sysbackup
```

You can verify which users have sys* privileges by querying the V$PWFILE_USERS view:

```
SQL> select * from v$pwfile_users;
```

Here is some sample output:

USERNAME	SYSDB	SYSOP	SYSAS	SYSBA	SYSDG	SYSKM	CON_ID
SYS	TRUE	TRUE	FALSE	FALSE	FALSE	FALSE	0
DBA_MAINT	FALSE	FALSE	FALSE	TRUE	FALSE	FALSE	0

OS AUTHENTICATION VS. PASSWORD FILE

For local connections, operating system authentication takes precedence over password file authentication. In other words, if you're logged on to an OS account that is a member of an authenticated group, such as dba, it doesn't matter what you type in for the username and password when connecting to a local database with sys* privileges. For example, you can connect as sysdba with a nonexistent username/password:

```
$ sqlplus bogus/wrong as sysdba
SQL> show user;
USER is "SYS"
```

The prior connection works because Oracle ignores the username/password provided, as the user was first verified via OS authentication. However, a password file is used when you're not using OS authentication to establish a privileged local connection or when you're trying to make a privileged connection to a remote database via the network.

2-2. Starting and Stopping Your Database
Problem

You want to start or stop your Oracle database.

Solution

Connect to the database with a `sys*` privileged user (`sysdba`, `sysoper`, or `sysbackup`), and issue the `startup` and `shutdown` statements. If you're not sure which account you should use, refer to Recipe 2-1 for details on connecting to your database. The following example uses OS authentication to connect to the database:

```
$ sqlplus / as sysdba
```

After you are connected as a privileged account, you can start up your database as follows:

```
SQL> startup;
```

You should then see messages from Oracle indicating that the system global area (SGA) has been allocated and the database is mounted and then opened. For example:

```
ORACLE instance started.
Total System Global Area  300630016 bytes
Fixed Size                  2259768 bytes
Variable Size             222299336 bytes
Database Buffers           71303168 bytes
Redo Buffers                4767744 bytes
Database mounted.
Database opened.
```

Use the `shutdown immediate` statement to stop a database. The `immediate` parameter instructs Oracle to halt database activity and roll back any open transactions:

```
SQL> shutdown immediate;
Database closed.
Database dismounted.
ORACLE instance shut down.
```

In most cases, `shutdown immediate` is an acceptable method of shutting down your database.

■ **Note** Stopping and restarting your database in quick succession is known colloquially in DBA land as bouncing the database.

How It Works

Starting and stopping your database is a fairly simple process. If the environment is set up correctly, you should be able to connect to your database as a privileged user and issue the appropriate startup and shutdown statements.

When shutting down your database, usually `shutdown immediate` is sufficient. If `shutdown immediate` appears to be hanging, then don't be afraid to try `shutdown abort`; it's not as bad as it sounds. The `shutdown abort` command immediately terminates the database instance and transactions are killed and are not rolled back. Oracle will ensure uncommitted transactions are rolled back when you subsequently restart the database (after `shutdown abort`).

2-3. Toggling Archivelog Mode

Problem

You attempted to use RMAN to back up your database and received this error message:

```
ORA-19602: cannot backup or copy active file in NOARCHIVELOG mode
```

This message indicates that before you can create an RMAN online backup, you need to place your database into archivelog mode.

Solution

To place your database in archivelog mode, perform the following steps:

1. Connect as a sys* privileged user (sysdba, sysoper, or sysbackup). You can use either RMAN or SQL*Plus.

2. Shut down your database.

3. Start up the database in mount mode.

4. Alter the database into archivelog mode.

5. Alter the database open.

If you want to disable archivelog mode, then you would execute all the previous steps, with one change; in step 4, you will need to use the noarchivelog parameter (instead of archivelog).

Enabling Archivelog Mode

First connect to your database with a user who has sys* privileges. You can enable archivelog mode from within SQL*Plus or RMAN; the commands are identical regardless of the tool used. This example shows how to enable archivelog mode via SQL*Plus:

```
$ sqlplus / as sysdba
SQL> shutdown immediate;
SQL> startup mount;
SQL> alter database archivelog;
SQL> alter database open;
```

■ **Caution**   If you don't specify a location (via a fast recovery area or the log_archive_dest_n parameter) for the archive redo logs, then a default location is used. For this simple example, the default location is fine. The default location varies by operating system; on Linux/Unix systems the default location is usually ORACLE_HOME/dbs. For production databases, you will need to give careful consideration to where your archive redo logs are written on disk (Chapter 3) and how you back them up (Chapter 7).

Disabling Archivelog Mode

If you need to disable archiving, connect to your database with a sys* privileged user. You can disable archivelog mode from within SQL*Plus or RMAN. This example shows how to disable archivelog mode from SQL*Plus:

```
$ sqlplus / as sysdba
SQL> shutdown immediate;
SQL> startup mount;
SQL> alter database noarchivelog;
SQL> alter database open;
```

How It Works

Your database is required to be in archivelog mode for online backups. RMAN will return an error if you attempt to take an online backup when your database isn't in archivelog mode.

After you have changed the archivelog mode of your database, you can verify that the mode has been set properly. To display the status of archiving, you can query V$DATABASE as follows:

```
SQL> select log_mode from v$database;
```

Here is some sample output:

```
LOG_MODE
--------------------
ARCHIVELOG
```

You can also query the name and destination to show where the archive redo logs are being written via this query:

```
SELECT
 dest_name
,destination
FROM v$archive_dest
WHERE destination is not null;
```

The SQL*Plus archive log list command displays a useful summary of the archiving configuration of your database:

```
SQL> archive log list;
```

As shown in the following output, it includes information such as the archivelog mode, automatic archiving, archive destination, and log sequence numbers:

```
Database log mode              Archive Mode
Automatic archival             Enabled
Archive destination            /u01/app/oracle/product/12.1.0.1/db_1/dbs/arch
Oldest online log sequence     20
Next log sequence to archive   21
Current log sequence           21
```

Archivelog mode is the mechanism that allows you to recover all committed transactions. This mode protects your database from media failure because your transaction information can be restored and recovered (applied to the data files) from the archived redo log files. Archivelog mode ensures that after every online redo log switch, the contents of the logs are successfully copied to archived redo log files.

When in archivelog mode, Oracle will not allow an online redo log file to be overwritten until it is copied to an archived redo log file. If Oracle cannot copy an online redo log file to an archived redo log file, then your database will stop processing and hang. Therefore, it's critical that you have a strategy to manage the available free space where the archived redo log files are being stored.

We must point out that when working with a production database, you need an intelligent strategy for implementing archiving, mainly for two reasons. First, the archive redo logs are crucial for recovering transactions in the event of a failure. Therefore, you need a strategy for backing up these files. Second, the archive redo logs consume disk space; if left unattended, these files will eventually consume all the space allocated for them. If this happens, the archiver background process can't write a new archive redo log file to disk, and your database will stop processing transactions. At this point you have a hung database. You need to manually intervene by creating space for the archiver to resume work.

For these reasons, there are several architectural decisions you must carefully consider before implementing archiving in a production environment:

- Where to place the archive redo logs, and whether to use the fast-recovery area (FRA) to store the archive redo logs
- How to name the archive redo logs
- How much space should be allocated to the archive redo log location
- How often to back up the archive redo logs
- When it's okay to permanently remove archive redo logs from disk
- Whether multiple archive redo log locations should be enabled
- When to schedule the small amount of downtime that's required to enable archiving

Minimally, you should have enough space in your primary archive redo location to hold at least a day's worth of archive redo logs. This lets you back them up on a daily basis and then remove them from disk after they've been backed up.

If you decide to use a FRA for your archive redo log location, you must ensure that it contains sufficient space to hold the number of archive redo logs generated between backups (see Chapter 3 for complete details on how to use a FRA).

You need a strategy to automate the backup and removal of archive redo log files. As you see in later chapters in this book, RMAN automates the backup and removal of archive redo log files.

If your business requirements are such that you must have a high degree of availability and redundancy, then you should consider writing your archive redo logs to more than one location. Some shops set up jobs to copy the archive redo logs periodically to a different location on disk or tape, or even copy them to a different server.

2-4. Connecting to RMAN
Problem
You want to connect to RMAN and prepare to perform backup and recovery tasks.

Solution
To connect to RMAN, you need to establish the following:

- OS environment variables
- Access to a privileged operating system (OS) account or schema with sys* privileges (sysdba, sysoper, or sysbackup)

These are the same conditions that need to be in place before connecting to your database and that are described in Recipe 2-1. If you haven't already done so, review Recipe 2-1 and ensure that you have the proper OS variables set and that you have access to a privileged database user.

You can connect to RMAN either through the operating system command-line interface or through Enterprise Manager (EM). Using EM for backup and recovery is covered in Chapter 19 of this book. This chapter uses the command-line interface for its examples.

■ **Tip**   Even if you use the screen based Enterprise Manager tool, it's useful to understand the RMAN commands used for backup and recovery operations. This knowledge can be particularly useful when debugging and troubleshooting problems.

The following example assumes you have logged on to a Linux/Unix server using the oracle operating system account assigned to a privileged group, such as dba. You can then invoke RMAN and connect to the target database as follows:

```
$ rman target /
```

Here is a snippet of the output:

```
connected to target database: O12C (DBID=3412777350)
```

If you're using a password file, then you need to specify the username and password that have been granted proper system privileges:

```
$ rman target <user>/<password>
```

If you're accessing your target database remotely via Oracle Net, you will need a password file on the target server and will also need to specify a connection string as follows:

```
$ rman target <user with sys* priv>/<password>@<database connection string>
```

You can also invoke RMAN and then connect to your target database as a second step, from the RMAN prompt:

```
$ rman
RMAN> connect target /
```

To exit RMAN, enter the exit command as follows:

```
RMAN> exit
```

■ **Tip**   On Linux systems, when typing in the rman command from the OS prompt, if you get an error, such as "rman: can't open target," make sure your PATH variable includes ORACLE_HOME/bin directory before the /usr/X11R6/bin directory.

How It Works

Before you can connect to RMAN, you need to ensure that you have the proper OS variables set and that you have access to an account with sys* privileges. Once those are in place, you can start RMAN and connect to your target database via the rman command-line utility.

When connecting to RMAN, you do not have to specify the sys* clause. This is because RMAN always requires that you connect as a user with sys* privileges. Therefore, you must connect to RMAN with either a user who is OS authenticated or a username/password with sys* privileges granted to it (and therefore exists in the password file). This is unlike SQL*Plus, where you have the option of connecting as a non-privileged user. In SQL*Plus, if you want to connect as a user with sys* privileges, you are required to specify a sys* clause when connecting.

If you attempt to connect to RMAN without the proper privileges, you'll receive this error:

```
ORA-01031: insufficient privileges
```

A useful way to troubleshoot the root cause of an ORA-01031 error is to attempt to log in to SQL*Plus with the same authentication information as when trying to connect through RMAN. This will help verify either that you are using an OS-authenticated account or that the username and password are correct. If OS authentication is working, you should be able to log in to SQL*Plus as follows:

```
$ sqlplus / as sysdba
```

If you're using a password file, you can verify that the username and password are correct (and that the user has sysdba privileges) by logging in as shown here:

```
$ sqlplus <username>/<password> as sysdba
```

If you receive an ORA-01031 error from attempting to log in to SQL*Plus, then either you aren't using an OS-authenticated account or your username and password combination does not match what is stored in the password file (for users attempting to connect with sys* privileges).

Once connected to RMAN, you can issue administrative commands, such as startup, shutdown, backup, restore, and recover. For example, if you want to start and stop your database, you can do so from within RMAN as follows:

```
$ rman target /
RMAN> startup;
RMAN> shutdown immediate;
```

This saves you the inconvenience of having to jump back and forth between SQL*Plus and RMAN (when issuing administrative commands). You'll see in other recipes throughout the book that many SQL*Plus commands can be run directly from within RMAN.

RUNNING SQL COMMANDS FROM WITHIN RMAN

New in Oracle Database 12c, you can run many SQL commands directly from the RMAN command line. In prior versions of Oracle, when running certain SQL commands from within RMAN, you had to specify the sql clause. For example, say you wanted to run the alter system switch logfile command. Prior to Oracle Database 12c, you would have to specify that command as shown:

```
RMAN> sql 'alter system switch logfile';
```

In Oracle Database 12c, you can now run the SQL directly:

```
RMAN> alter system switch logfile;
```

This is a nice ease-of-use enhancement because it eliminates the need for additional clauses and quotes around the command.

2-5. Backing Up Your Database

Problem

You're new to RMAN, and you want to back up your database. You just need to get a backup created, and you want to take the simplest possible approach.

Solution

Connect to your target database via the rman utility, and use the backup database command to back up your entire database:

```
$ rman target /
RMAN> backup database;
```

You should now see a list of RMAN messages displaying information about which files are being backed up and to which file and location. Here's an abbreviated portion of that output:

```
allocated channel: ORA_DISK_1
channel ORA_DISK_1: SID=45 device type=DISK
channel ORA_DISK_1: starting full datafile backup set
channel ORA_DISK_1: specifying datafile(s) in backup set
input datafile file number=00003 name=/u01/dbfile/o12c/undotbs01.dbf
input datafile file number=00001 name=/u01/dbfile/o12c/system01.dbf
input datafile file number=00002 name=/u01/dbfile/o12c/sysaux01.dbf
input datafile file number=00004 name=/u01/dbfile/o12c/users01.dbf
piece handle=/u01/app/oracle/product/12.1.0.1/db_1/dbs/01nfuc0b_1_1
```

To display information about your backup, use the list backup command as follows:

```
RMAN> list backup;
```

Here's a partial snippet of the output that you can expect to see:

```
List of Backup Sets
===================
BS Key  Type LV Size       Device Type Elapsed Time Completion Time
------- ---- -- ---------- ----------- ------------ ---------------
1       Full    633.41M    DISK        00:00:55     12-JUL-12
        BP Key: 1   Status: AVAILABLE  Compressed: NO  Tag: TAG20120712T210515
        Piece Name: /u01/app/oracle/product/12.1.0.1/db_1/dbs/01nfuc0b_1_1
  List of Datafiles in backup set 1
  File LV Type Ckp SCN    Ckp Time  Name
  ---- -- ---- ---------- --------- ----
  1       Full 368430     12-JUL-12 /u01/dbfile/o12c/system01.dbf
  2       Full 368430     12-JUL-12 /u01/dbfile/o12c/sysaux01.dbf
  3       Full 368430     12-JUL-12 /u01/dbfile/o12c/undotbs01.dbf
  4       Full 368430     12-JUL-12 /u01/dbfile/o12c/users01.dbf
```

```
┌─────────────────────────────────────────────────────────────────────────┐
│              SETTING THE NLS_DATE_FORMAT OS VARIABLE                      │
└─────────────────────────────────────────────────────────────────────────┘
```

By default RMAN displays the date information only (in its output). To include the time component in the RMAN output, we recommend that you set NLS_DATE_FORMAT="DD-MON-RRRR HH24:MI:SS" at the OS level prior to running RMAN, for example:

```
$ export NLS_DATE_FORMAT="DD-MON-RRRR HH24:MI:SS"
```

This is useful especially when checking the exact time an RMAN command ran as viewed in the RMAN output.

How It Works

Backing up a database with RMAN was designed to be simple. All the required configuration settings are automatically set to sensible defaults. Therefore, you can perform basic backup and recovery tasks without any configuration of your RMAN environment.

By default RMAN will allocate a channel and back up to a location on disk. The default location is operating system dependent. The `list backup` command will show you where the backup piece files are located.

If you want to specify a location for your backup pieces, you can stipulate this either by enabling a fast recovery area as described in Chapter 3 or by specifically setting the backup location through the format command described in Chapter 5.

2-6. Simulating a Failure

Problem

You want to simulate a failure as a prelude to testing RMAN's restore and recovery capabilities.

Solution

To simulate a failure, perform the following steps:

1. Ensure you have a backup.

2. Determine the location and name of a data file to rename. You will simulate media failure by renaming a data file so that it appears to have been lost.

3. Stop the database.

4. Rename a data file at the OS level (simulates media failure).

5. Attempt to start the database.

Before simulating a media failure, ensure that you're in a noncritical test database environment and that you have a good RMAN backup of your database. Run the following command in your target database, and ensure that you have a good backup:

```
$ rman target /
RMAN> list backup;
```

■ **Caution**   If no backup information is listed, then stop here. You need to ensure that you have a good backup of your database before you simulate media failure.

Determine the location of a target database data file so that you can rename it to simulate media failure:

```
RMAN> report schema;
```

Shown next is an abbreviated portion of the output of the previous command:

```
List of Permanent Datafiles
===========================
File Size(MB) Tablespace          RB segs Datafile Name
---- -------- ------------------- ------- ------------------------
1    500      SYSTEM              ***     /u01/dbfile/o12c/system01.dbf
2    500      SYSAUX              ***     /u01/dbfile/o12c/sysaux01.dbf
3    800      UNDOTBS1            ***     /u01/dbfile/o12c/undotbs01.dbf
4    50       USERS               ***     /u01/dbfile/o12c/users01.dbf
```

Note the location and name of the data file associated with the users tablespace in your target database. In this example, the file name is /u01/dbfile/o12c/users01.dbf. This is the file that will be moved to simulate media failure. Keep in mind what we're showing here is just an example, and the data file names and locations may be different in your environment.

Next, shut down your target database, and rename the data file.

```
RMAN> shutdown immediate;
RMAN> exit
```

If you are in a Linux/Unix environment, use the mv command to rename the data file as follows:

```
$ mv /u01/dbfile/o12c/users01.dbf  /u01/dbfile/o12c/users01.old
```

Once the data file has been renamed, connect to RMAN and attempt to start your database as follows:

```
$ rman target /
RMAN> startup
```

You should see a message similar to the following:

```
ORA-01157: cannot identify/lock data file 4 - see DBWR trace file
ORA-01110: data file 4: '/u01/dbfile/o12c/users01.dbf'
```

How It Works

To simulate media failure, you can rename a data file at the OS level on your target database server. After the data file has been renamed, when Oracle starts up, it reads the control file and compares the information to all the data file headers. If Oracle can't find a data file, it will display a message indicating that it can't find the file. You won't be able to open your target database until you restore and recover your database.

2-7. Restoring and Recovering Your Database

Problem

You've experienced a failure and want to use RMAN to restore and recover your database. You have a current backup in the default location, and all needed control files, archived redo log files, and online redo log files are available.

Solution

Connect to RMAN, and use the following commands to restore and recover your database. In this recipe you'll perform the following steps:

1. Connect to the target database.

2. Mount the database.

3. Restore the database.

4. Recover the database.

5. Open the database.

To keep this example as simple as possible, we'll show how to restore and recover the entire database.

```
$ rman target /
RMAN> startup mount;
RMAN> restore database;
```

You'll see several lines of output as RMAN tells you what it is restoring. Here is a snippet of the output for this example:

```
using target database control file instead of recovery catalog
allocated channel: ORA_DISK_1
channel ORA_DISK_1: SID=21 device type=DISK
channel ORA_DISK_1: starting datafile backup set restore
channel ORA_DISK_1: specifying datafile(s) to restore from backup set
channel ORA_DISK_1: restoring datafile 00001 to /u01/dbfile/o12c/system01.dbf
channel ORA_DISK_1: restoring datafile 00002 to /u01/dbfile/o12c/sysaux01.dbf
channel ORA_DISK_1: restoring datafile 00003 to /u01/dbfile/o12c/undotbs01.dbf
channel ORA_DISK_1: restoring datafile 00004 to /u01/dbfile/o12c/users01.dbf
```

After RMAN restores your database, next recover the database as follows:

```
RMAN> recover database;
```

You should see a message similar to this:

```
starting media recovery
media recovery complete, elapsed time: 00:00:02
```

You can now open your database for use:

```
RMAN> alter database open;
```

How It Works

If you have a good backup of your database, it's fairly simple to use RMAN to restore and recover your database. By default, RMAN uses information stored in the control file to determine where to retrieve backups and which files to restore and recover.

Restore and recovery are two separate steps. Restore is the process of copying back data files from the backup files. Recovery is the process of applying transaction information (contained in either the online redo logs or archive redo logs) to the data files to recover them to the state they were in just before the failure occurred.

■ **Tip**   Restore and recovery are analogous to the healing process when you break a bone. Restoring is similar to the process of setting the broken bone back to its original position. This is like restoring the data files from a backup and placing them in their original locations. Recovering a data file is similar to the healing process that recovers the bone back to its state before it was broken. When you recover your data files, you apply transactions (stored in the redo files) to get the data files back to the state they were in before the media failure took place.

RMAN ships with practical default values that allow you to use it immediately to back up, restore, and recover your database. Although these default settings are reasonable, you'll want to read the subsequent chapters in this book for best practices on how to configure RMAN for an industrial-strength backup and recovery strategy.

CHAPTER 3

Using the Fast Recovery Area

In Chapter 2 you learned how to take an RMAN backup to a storage location on the disk. Disk-based backup offers significant benefits over backing up to tape, such as a considerably faster backup (and an even faster recovery), the ability to merge backups to make the recovery quicker, the constant validation of incremental backups, and so on. In subsequent chapters, you will learn more about those operations.

One of the important considerations in the process of setting up a disk-based backup is the location of the backup. You can choose any location, such as a file system, a directory on a file system or an ASM disk group, or a directory under a disk group. The only requirement is that the location must be visible to and writable by the instance performing the backup.

Another important consideration is the management of the space inside the disk-based backup location. You, as the DBA, must ensure that the location has enough free space to hold all the backups required—backups of data files, archive logs, and so on. When new backups require more space, it's your responsibility to make sure the space is available, which you can achieve by either adding space or deleting redundant backups. If you choose the latter, you must decide which files are redundant.

What if Oracle Database did all the work for you? It can, if you let it know the location to use. Starting with Oracle Database 10g Release 1, you can define a special area on disk called the Flash Recovery Area (FRA) that the database uses as a backup location. In Oracle Database 11g Release 2, this was renamed to Fast Recovery Area (so keeping the acronym—FRA—unchanged). By default, RMAN creates backups of all types—regular backup sets, image copies, and archived logs—in that area. Since RMAN knows about the existence of this area, it automatically deletes unneeded backups (based on redundancy and retention periods) to make room for new backups.

In addition to backups, the fast recovery area can also store flashback logs, online redo log files, archived redo log files, and control files. Again, these are optional; you can always define the location of those files to be anywhere, not necessarily inside the fast recovery area. Since the fast recovery area is generally used for backup files, you should consider creating it on disks different from your main database disks. Doing so helps protect you from losing both your main database and your backup files from a single failure. You can further take advantage of this probability by putting one member of the redo log group or one control file on the fast recovery area. This reduces the possibility of all members of a redo log group or all control files getting damaged at the same time.

3-1. Creating the Fast Recovery Area
Problem

You want to create the fast recovery area for your database.

Solution

Before creating the fast recovery area, you should decide the following:

- Where you want the FRA to be created

- How much space should be allocated to the FRA

Having the answers to these questions in mind, you can then use the following process to create the fast recovery area:

1. Disable the parameters `log_archive_dest` and `log_archive_duplex_dest`, if they are set in the database. You can do that by issuing the following commands:

    ```
    alter system set log_archive_duplex_dest = '';
    alter system set log_archive_dest = '';
    ```

2. Log on as a user with the sysdba role (such as the user sys) in preparation for creating the fast recovery area:

    ```
    sqlplus / as sysdba (if logged in as the Oracle software owner)
    sqlplus sys/<PasswordOfUserSys> as sysdba
    ```

3. Issue the following commands to size and create the fast recovery area:

    ```
    SQL> alter system set db_recovery_file_dest = '+FRA';

    System altered.

    SQL> alter system set db_recovery_file_dest_size = 10G;

    System altered
    ```

The sequence of these commands is important; you have to issue them in that order, not the reverse. However, do replace the size and path name with the values you have chosen for your system.

That's it; the fast recovery area is ready for operation.

How It Works

The issues of location and size are keys to creating a fast recovery area. The location issue is straightforward if you use a single-instance database. Any location, as long as it's a directory (or a file system), should be acceptable as the FRA. If you use ASM, you can use a disk group as the FRA as well. You can also use the same disk group you use for the database files. However, you cannot use a raw device.

To decide the size of the FRA, use the detailed analysis shown in Recipe 3-16.

As a best practice, you should avoid putting the fast recovery area and the database files on the same mount point (if a file system) or disk group (if on ASM). This way a failure in the underlying physical disks will not affect both the database files and the FRA files at the same time. You thus ensure your ability to quickly recover from a failure by again pointing the damaged data file to the copy in the fast recovery area.

Remember, you can always define a different location for archived redo logs. If you use a different location, then you can't just erase the values of the parameters `log_archive_dest` and `log_archive_duplex_dest`, as suggested in the earlier solution:

```
alter system set log_archive_duplex_dest = '';
alter system set log_archive_dest = '';
```

To place your log files elsewhere than the fast recovery area, you should use a different parameter to specify the archived redo log location; use `log_archive_dest_1` instead of `log_archive_dest`. Suppose `log_archive_dest` used to be /dbarch. You can use `log_archive_dest_1` to specify the same location for archived redo logs.

First, check the value of the parameter log_archive_dest:

```
SQL>show parameter log_archive_dest
NAME                                    TYPE           VALUE
---------------------------------------- -------------- -----------
log_archive_dest                        string         /dbarch
```

The current setting of the archived redo log destination is /dbarch. Next, set the log_archive_dest_1 parameter to that location:

```
SQL> alter system set log_archive_dest_1 = 'location=/dbarch';
```

Note the different syntax for this parameter; it has a location clause. Now, set log_archive_dest to NULL:

```
SQL> alter system set log_archive_dest = '';
```

If you have set the two parameters—log_archive_dest and log_archive_duplex_dest—in the initialization parameter file, you should edit the file to remove these two parameters completely. Remember to recycle the database after editing the file for the changes to take effect. If you don't set these parameters before adding FRA, you will get the error: *ORA-16018: cannot use LOG_ARCHIVE_DEST with LOG_ARCHIVE_DEST_n or DB_RECOVERY_FILE_DEST.*

3-2. Writing Regular RMAN Backups to the FRA

Problem

Now that you have configured a fast recovery area, you want RMAN to use it when creating disk-based backups.

Solution

You can easily make RMAN store backups in the fast recovery area. Here are the steps to follow:

1. Start RMAN:

2. Connect to the target database:

    ```
    RMAN> connect target /

    connected to target database: CDB1 (DBID=762264187)
    ```

3. Now, initiate a backup without specifying a format option:

    ```
    RMAN> backup database;
    Starting backup at 21-JUL-12
    using target database control file instead of recovery catalog
    allocated channel: ORA_DISK_1
    channel ORA_DISK_1: SID=29 device type=DISK
    channel ORA_DISK_1: starting full datafile backup set
    channel ORA_DISK_1: specifying datafile(s) in backup set
    input datafile file number=00003 name=+DATA/cdb1/datafile/sysaux.257.788546597
    input datafile file number=00001 name=+DATA/cdb1/datafile/system.258.788546653
    ```

```
input datafile file number=00009
name=+DATA/cdb1/c4bd35d102b92f07e04380a8840a6a44/datafile/sysaux.275.788546943
input datafile file number=00007
name=+DATA/cdb1/c4bd2d3ad8c42bf9e04380a8840a451e/datafile/sysaux.270.788546799
input datafile file number=00005
name=+DATA/cdb1/c4bd2d3ad8c42bf9e04380a8840a451e/datafile/system.271.788546799
input datafile file number=00008
name=+DATA/cdb1/c4bd35d102b92f07e04380a8840a6a44/datafile/system.274.788546943
input datafile file number=00004 name=+DATA/cdb1/datafile/undotbs1.260.788546719
input datafile file number=00006 name=+DATA/cdb1/datafile/users.259.788546719
input datafile file number=00010
name=+DATA/cdb1/c4bd35d102b92f07e04380a8840a6a44/datafile/users.277.788546967
channel ORA_DISK_1: starting piece 1 at 21-JUL-12
channel ORA_DISK_1: finished piece 1 at 21-JUL-12
piece handle=+FRA/cdb1/backupset/2012_07_21/nnndf0_tag20120721t173019_0.256.789240621
tag=TAG20120721T173019 comment=NONE
channel ORA_DISK_1: backup set complete, elapsed time: 00:00:55
channel ORA_DISK_1: starting full datafile backup set
channel ORA_DISK_1: specifying datafile(s) in backup set
including current control file in backup set
including current SPFILE in backup set
channel ORA_DISK_1: starting piece 1 at 21-JUL-12
channel ORA_DISK_1: finished piece 1 at 21-JUL-12
piece handle=+FRA/cdb1/backupset/2012_07_21/ncsnf0_tag20120721t173019_0.257.789240677
tag=TAG20120721T173019 comment=NONE
channel ORA_DISK_1: backup set complete, elapsed time: 00:00:01
Finished backup at 21-JUL-12
RMAN>
```

Note the command in step 3 carefully; you issued just the backup database command. You specified nothing else—no channel creation, no format, nothing. Since you have defined a fast recovery area, the backups go in there by default. Of course, you can issue a format command and use channels to redirect the backup to a different location, but as you will see later in this chapter, the fast recovery area provides greater control if you choose to place the backups there.

How It Works

The solution in this recipe creates backup sets under the directory specified as the fast recovery area. Note the output carefully and, more specifically, the following line:

```
piece
handle=+FRA/cdb1/backupset/2012_07_21/nnndf0_tag20120721t173019_0.256.789240621
tag=TAG20120721T173019 comment=NONE
```

This line of output shows the file created by the RMAN backup process. The file is named nnndf0_tag20120721t173019_0.256.789240621, which is a pretty strange name in any language. This is what is known as an Oracle managed file. Ordinarily you don't need to worry about the name since Oracle manages the file on your behalf—it creates the file with a unique name, deletes the file when not needed, and so on. Since you don't deal with it, the daunting name does not sound so daunting after all.

Also note the directory in which the backup file was stored. Remember, you set the fast recovery area in Recipe 3-1 to +FRA. The RMAN backup process created a subdirectory called CDB1, the same name as the database you are backing up. This way, you can use the same fast recovery area for as many databases as you want. Under the directory corresponding to a database name, Oracle creates several other directories:

> backupset: This subdirectory is for RMAN regular backups.

> datafile: This subdirectory is for RMAN image copies.

> autobackup: This subdirectory is for control file autobackups.

> flashback: If your database runs in flashback mode, you will see flashback logs in this subdirectory.

> archivelog: Archived redo logs can optionally be stored in the FRA (Recipe 3-6). If so, they go in this subdirectory.

> controlfile: The control file, if configured to go to the fast recovery area (Recipe 3-8), goes in this subdirectory.

> onlinelog: Online redo logs can also be made to go to the fast recovery area (Recipe 3-9). In that case, they go in this subdirectory.

Under each of the directory's backupset, autobackup, and archivelog, Oracle also creates a subdirectory named per the date of the backup in the format YYYY_MM_DD (2012_07_21 in this case, indicating July 21, 2012). So on another day, the backup goes into a different directory. Oracle creates all these directories and subdirectories automatically.

■ **Note**   Even if you see that the fast recovery area is filled up close to the size you specified in the initialization parameter db_recovery_file_dest_size (4GB in this case), never delete files manually to make room. Oracle automatically removes any files unnecessary for a subsequent recovery operation. Later in this chapter you will learn how to see the contents of the fast recovery area.

3-3. Freeing FRA Space in an Emergency
Problem

The fast recovery area has run out of space. You see a message in the alert log similar to the following:

```
Can not open flashback thread because there is no more space in fast recovery area
```

If the database has aborted earlier because of any flashback errors and you attempt to start it, you get the following error:

```
SQL> alter database open;
alter database open
*
ERROR at line 1:
ORA-38760: This database instance failed to turn on flashback database
```

You want to correct the problem, or at least shut down the flashback so that the normal database operations can continue.

There are three solutions. Which to choose depends upon the nature of the emergency and the resources you have at your disposal.

Solution 1: Delete Unneeded Files

When the FRA does not have enough space for the newer files, Oracle deletes the unneeded files to make room; but not everything at the same time. Therefore, there may be a time when Oracle does actually delete some redundant files but not enough to free up sufficient space. You can manually clean up a lot of files yourself by using this command in RMAN:

```
RMAN> delete obsolete;
```

This causes RMAN to clean up unneeded files immediately. Files needed for recovery are not touched.

Solution 2: Increase Space

You can increase the size of the flashback area dynamically. To increase it to, say, 10GB, you would issue the following:

```
SQL> alter system set db_recovery_file_dest_size = 10G;
```

By the way, the converse is also possible; you can reduce the FRA size using this command, although that will not solve the problem addressed in this recipe.

Solution 3: Remove Restore Points

The alternative to increasing the size of the flashback area is to remove some of the older restore points that you no longer need. The following is a query to list the restore points you currently have:

```
SQL> col name format a15
SQL> select name, storage_size
  2  from v$restore_point;

NAME            STORAGE_SIZE
--------------- ------------
GRP1                       0
GRP2                52428800
GRP3                52428800
RP1                        0
RP2                        0

4 rows selected.
```

These results show that restore points GRP2 and RP2 have storage associated with them. This is because they are guaranteed restore points (see "How It Works" for an explanation of what that means). You should remove them to make some room in the fast recovery area. To remove a restore point, issue a drop restore point command:

```
SQL> drop restore point grp2;

Restore point dropped.

SQL> drop restore point grp2;

Restore point dropped.
```

Dropping restore point should clear up space inside FRA, and you may be able to start the database.

Solution 4: Disable Flashback

If solutions 1, 2, and 3 fail or are not applicable, you may want to take the drastic step of disabling flashback in the database temporarily.

```
SQL> alter database flashback off;

Database altered.
```

This will stop the flashback operations and will stop generating flashback logs. This should reduce the space requirement on the fast recovery area.

■ **Note**   In some earlier versions of the Oracle Database, you may have to shut down the database and restart to mount mode to turn off flashback.

To free up some space, you may want to delete some more files, such as archived redo logs, unneeded backups, and so on. In RMAN delete these:

```
RMAN> delete noprompt archivelog all;

using target database control file instead of recovery catalog
allocated channel: ORA_DISK_1
channel ORA_DISK_1: SID=264 device type=DISK
RMAN-08139: WARNING: archived redo log not deleted, needed for guaranteed restore point
archived log file
name=+FRA/cdb1/archivelog/2012_07_21/thread_1_seq_47.260.789243259 thread=1 sequence=47
List of Archived Log Copies for database with db_unique_name CDB1
=====================================================================

Key     Thrd Seq     S Low Time
------- ---- ------- - ---------
2       1    48       A 21-JUL-12
        Name: +FRA/cdb1/archivelog/2012_07_21/thread_1_seq_48.261.789243361

3       1    49       A 21-JUL-12
        Name: +FRA/cdb1/archivelog/2012_07_21/thread_1_seq_49.262.789243365

... output truncated ...
deleted archived log
archived log file
name=+FRA/cdb1/archivelog/2012_07_21/thread_1_seq_54.267.789243373 RECID=8
STAMP=789243372
Deleted 7 objects
```

Similarly, you may want to delete copies of the database and backup sets:

```
RMAN> delete noprompt backup of database;
RMAN> delete noprompt copy of database;
```

Now open the database, if needed. The database is now fully functional, but without the flashback ability. If you want to reenable flashback later, you can do so. Because you've cleared unneeded files, the fast recovery area is fully usable whenever you choose to again enable flashback. Until then, you can always back up the database using RMAN without a fast recovery area.

How It Works

The first solution is intuitive—you removed some files to make room for new files.

The second solution is probably the easiest to understand. It merely increased the fast recovery area's size to accommodate the new contents.

In the third solution, you removed restore points. Restore points are created by executing SQL statements such as the following:

```
SQL> create restore point rp1;
```

This statement creates a named point in time to which you can flash back the database, through the SQL statement (provided, of course, that you have turned on the flashback for the database). Once you have a restore point, you can rewind or flash back to that point in time using a statement such as this:

```
SQL> flashback database to rp1;
```

There are two types of restore points: normal and guaranteed. The preceding example of creating a restore point creates a normal one. You may be able to flash back to that point, provided enough flashback logs are available. If the flashback logs are not available (perhaps because the space in the flashback recovery area ran out and Oracle had to delete some flashback logs to make room for the newer occupants), then your flashback operation will fail. The solution: a guaranteed restore point. To create a guaranteed restore point, you will have to specifically ask for the guarantee:

```
SQL> create restore point grp1 guarantee flashback database;
```

A guaranteed restore point stores information needed to flash back in a special way. When space pressures in the fast recovery area force the database to remove the unneeded files, flashback logs are the first to go, unless these are for a guaranteed restore point. The flashback logs of the guaranteed restore points are stored even when the fast recovery area runs out of space. The only way to reclaim the space is to drop the guaranteed restore point. Dropping the guaranteed restore points frees up that space.

■ **Note** Disabling flashback on the database does not remove the space occupied by the guaranteed restore points. Once the damaging situation has been cleared, you may want to start the flashback option again.

3-4. Checking Space Usage in the FRA
Problem

After setting up the fast recovery area, you want to check on the types of files that are present inside, and you want to report on the space occupied by each type of file.

Solution

The data dictionary view V$RECOVERY_FILE_DEST shows the sum of various types of files in the fast recovery area in terms of percentages of the total space. It has only one row. Here is an example of how you can use the view:

```
SQL> select * from v$recovery_file_dest;

NAME           SPACE_LIMIT SPACE_USED SPACE_RECLAIMABLE NUMBER_OF_FILES CON_ID
-------------- ----------- ---------- ----------------- --------------- ------
+FRA           1.0737E+10 2962227200          18874368               9      0
```

To see space used by different types of files in the fast recovery area, you should check the view V$FLASH_RECOVERY_AREA_USAGE. Here is an example of how you can see the contents of the fast recovery area:

```
SQL> select * from v$flash_recovery_area_usage;
```

FILE_TYPE	PERCENT_SPACE_USED	PERCENT_SPACE_RECLAIMABLE	NUMBER_OF_FILES	CON_ID
CONTROL FILE	.18	0	1	0
REDO LOG	1.49	0	3	0
ARCHIVED LOG	0	0	0	0
BACKUP PIECE	24.91	.18	3	0
IMAGE COPY	0	0	0	0
FLASHBACK LOG	1	0	2	0
FOREIGN ARCHIVED LOG	0	0	0	0
AUXILIARY DATAFILE COPY	0	0	0	0

Note the number of files of each category. The sum of the total number of files (1+3+3+2) equals 9, as shown in the previous example querying V$RECOVERY_FILE_DEST.

V$FLASH_RECOVERY_AREA_USAGE shows the percentages of the total space consumed, not the space itself. You may want to join it to V$RECOVERY_FILE_DEST to see the total space occupied by each type of file, as shown here:

```
select
  file_type,
  space_used*percent_space_used/100/1024/1024 used,
  space_reclaimable*percent_space_reclaimable/100/1024/1024 reclaimable,
  frau.number_of_files
from v$recovery_file_dest rfd, v$flash_recovery_area_usage frau;
```

FILE_TYPE	USED	RECLAIMABLE	NUMBER_OF_FILES
CONTROL FILE	13.5054	0	1
REDO LOG	111.7947	0	3
ARCHIVED LOG	1410.564	.1464	79
BACKUP PIECE	3698.979	.2135	6
IMAGE COPY	0	0	0
FLASHBACK LOG	261.8547	0	7
FOREIGN ARCHIVED LOG	0	0	0
AUXILIARY DATAFILE COPY	0	0	0

The report generated by this example may prove to be a more useful display of the space occupancy inside the fast recovery area compared to information in the view V$FLASH_RECOVERY_AREA_USAGE. The key is to understand how much space is left as reclaimable. By observing this view for a while, you should be able to figure out how much space is necessary for a day's backup. If that much space is not available as reclaimable, then you may run out of space later. If you detect an impending shortage of space, you can mark some of the old backups as expired, or you can extend the space in the fast recovery area.

■ **Note** The view V$FLASH_RECOVERY_AREA_USAGE has been deprecated since Oracle Database 11g Release 2 and beyond. The new view is V$RECOVERY_AREA_USAGE. However, the former view is still available and is used in this book for the sake of version independence.

How It Works

Table 3-1 and Table 3-2 describe the columns in the two V$ views used in the solution. Both the views display useful information, but they are not useful individually. For instance, the view V$FLASH_RECOVERY_AREA_USAGE displays information on the percentage of space used, but not the value whose percentage is referred. That total value is found in V$RECOVERY_FILE_DEST, in the column PERCENT_SPACE_USED. Joining the two views yields more useful information than either does separately.

Table 3-1. *Columns of the View V$RECOVERY_FILE_DEST*

Column Name	Contents
NAME	This is the directory used as the fast recovery area. In case an ASM disk group is used, then this is the name of the disk group.
SPACE_LIMIT	This is the total space allocated to the fast recovery area.
SPACE_USED	This is the total space used right now.
SPACE_RECLAIMABLE	When all the space is consumed in the fast recovery area, Oracle must remove the redundant files to make room for the newer backups. The total space contained in these redundant files is shown here.
NUMBER_OF_FILES	This is the total number of files present in the fast recovery area.
CON_ID	This is the container ID of the database (only for Oracle Database 12c).

Table 3-2. *Columns of the View V$FLASH_RECOVERY_AREA_USAGE*

Column Name	Contents
FILE_TYPE	This is the type of the files, such as a control file.
PERCENT_SPACE_USED	This is the total space occupied by that type of file as a percentage of the total space allocated to the fast recovery area.
PERCENT_SPACE_RECLAIMABLE	Of the total space, this is how much (a percentage) is reclaimable because of the redundant backups.
NUMBER_OF_FILES	This is the total number of files of that type.
CON_ID	This is the container ID of the database (only for Oracle Database 12c).

3-5. Expanding or Shrinking the FRA

Problem

From time to time you may need to expand your fast recovery area. Expansion may be required because of a variety of reasons—the size of the database keeps increasing, or you may want to increase the retention period, leaving more backups in the fast recovery area and reducing the reclaimable space.

Solution

To increase space in the fast recovery area, just use the command shown in the following example:

```
SQL> alter system set db_recovery_file_dest_size = 2G;

System altered.
```

This example sets the maximum size of fast recovery area to 2GB. You can use the same command to reduce space as well. For example:

```
alter system set db_recovery_file_dest_size = 1G;
```

The fast recovery area size has now been reduced from 2GB to 1GB.

How It Works

The alter system set db_recovery_file_dest_size command expands or shrinks the allocated space in the fast recovery area. There is something important you have to know, though: if you are shrinking the fast recovery area and if the total space occupied in the fast recovery area is more than your new, lower target value, then the command to shrink succeeds; however, the files in the fast recovery area are not deleted, keeping the total space occupied at more than the new target.

Returning to the example shown in this recipe's solution, the following query illustrates the shrinkage issue we've just described. Remember, the fast recovery area space has just been reduced to 1GB:

```
SQL> select * from v$recovery_file_dest;
```

NAME	SPACE_LIMIT	SPACE_USED	SPACE_RECLAIMABLE	NUMBER_OF_FILES	CON_ID
+FRA	1073741824	7867465728	0	96	0

Note the column SPACE_USED is about 7.8 GB, whereas the column SPACE_LIMIT is 1GB, which is less than the space actually used. Also note that the column SPACE_RECLAIMABLE, which shows the space that can be freed up should the new backups need space, is zero, indicating that there is no room for any additional backup. At this time, if you decide to take any backup, however small, you will receive an error, as shown in the following attempt to get a backup of the tablespace users:

```
RMAN> backup as copy tablespace users;

RMAN-00571: ===========================================================
RMAN-00569: =============== ERROR MESSAGE STACK FOLLOWS ===============
RMAN-00571: ===========================================================
RMAN-03009: failure of backup command on ORA_DISK_1 channel at 07/31/12
ORA-19809: limit exceeded for recovery files
ORA-19804: cannot reclaim 5242880 bytes disk space from 1073741824 limit
```

Note the error ORA-19804: cannot reclaim 5242880 bytes disk space from 1073741824 limit. To reclaim space from the fast recovery area at this time, you have to delete the redundant backups yourself. For example:

```
RMAN> report obsolete;

using target database control file instead of recovery catalog
RMAN retention policy will be applied to the command
RMAN retention policy is set to redundancy 1
Report of obsolete backups and copies
Type                 Key    Completion Time    Filename/Handle
-------------------- ------ ------------------ --------------------
Backup Set           1      21-JUL-12
  Backup Piece       1      21-JUL-12          +DATA/cdb1/backupset/2012_07_21/ncsnf0_tag20120721t16
5826_0.278.789238709
Archive Log          10     21-JUL-12          +FRA/cdb1/archivelog/2012_07_21/thread_1_
seq_56.266.789243567
Backup Set           3      21-JUL-12
  Backup Piece       3      21-JUL-12          +FRA/cdb1/backupset/2012_07_21/ncsnf0_tag20120721t17
3019_0.257.789240677
Archive Log          11     21-JUL-12          +FRA/cdb1/archivelog/2012_07_21/thread_1_
seq_58.264.789243569
Archive Log          12     21-JUL-12          +FRA/cdb1/archivelog/2012_07_21/thread_1_
seq_57.265.789243569
Backup Set           6      21-JUL-12
  Backup Piece       6      21-JUL-12          +FRA/cdb1/backupset/2012_07_21/nnndn1_tag20120721t18
3841_0.268.789244779
```

To create even more space in the fast recovery area, you may want to remove the old backups. The RMAN command delete obsolete does the trick:

```
RMAN> delete obsolete;

RMAN retention policy will be applied to the command
RMAN retention policy is set to redundancy 1
allocated channel: ORA_DISK_1
channel ORA_DISK_1: SID=32 device type=DISK
Deleting the following obsolete backups and copies:
Type                 Key    Completion Time    Filename/Handle
-------------------- ------ ------------------ --------------------
Backup Set           1      21-JUL-12
  Backup Piece       1      21-JUL-12          +DATA/cdb1/backupset/2012_07_21/ncsnf0_tag20120721t16
```

```
5826_0.278.789238709
Archive Log            10      21-JUL-12          +FRA/cdb1/archivelog/2012_07_21/thread_1_
seq_56.266.789243567
Backup Set              3      21-JUL-12
   Backup Piece         3      21-JUL-12          +FRA/cdb1/backupset/2012_07_21/ncsnf0_tag20120721t17
3019_0.257.789240677
Archive Log            11      21-JUL-12          +FRA/cdb1/archivelog/2012_07_21/thread_1_
seq_58.264.789243569
Archive Log            12      21-JUL-12          +FRA/cdb1/archivelog/2012_07_21/thread_1_
seq_57.265.789243569
Backup Set              6      21-JUL-12
   Backup Piece         6      21-JUL-12          +FRA/cdb1/backupset/2012_07_21/nnndn1_tag20120721t18
3841_0.268.789244779
```

At this time, RMAN will display the following message:

```
Do you really want to delete the above objects (enter YES or NO)?
```

Answer YES at the prompt. RMAN will delete the files:

```
deleted backup piece
backup piece
handle=+DATA/cdb1/backupset/2012_07_21/ncsnf0_tag20120721t165826_0.278.789238709
RECID=1 STAMP=789238708
deleted archived log
archived log file
name=+FRA/cdb1/archivelog/2012_07_21/thread_1_seq_56.266.789243567 RECID=10 STAMP=789243566
deleted backup piece
backup piece
handle=+FRA/cdb1/backupset/2012_07_21/ncsnf0_tag20120721t173019_0.257.789240677
RECID=3 STAMP=789240676
deleted archived log
archived log file
name=+FRA/cdb1/archivelog/2012_07_21/thread_1_seq_58.264.789243569 RECID=11 STAMP=789243568
deleted archived log
archived log file
name=+FRA/cdb1/archivelog/2012_07_21/thread_1_seq_57.265.789243569 RECID=12 STAMP=789243568
deleted backup piece
backup piece
handle=+FRA/cdb1/backupset/2012_07_21/nnndn1_tag20120721t183841_0.268.789244779
RECID=6 STAMP=789244779
Deleted 6 objects
```

If you want to delete the files without being prompted, you can issue the following command:

```
delete noprompt obsolete;
```

When you include the noprompt option, RMAN will delete the files without prompting you. This might open up enough space inside the fast recovery area for future backups. If it does not, then you have to add some more space to the fast recovery area (as shown at the beginning of this recipe's solution).

■ **Caution**   As this recipe illustrates, reducing the size of the fast recovery area may not result in a reduction of the actual space consumed. When you reduce the size, Oracle tries to remove the nonessential backups to reduce the space consumed; however, if the backups are considered essential, then they are not removed, and the fast recovery area may consume more than what you had requested it to be shrunk to. As a best practice, check the actual space consumed after a resize operation.

3-6. Configuring Archived Redo Logs to Go to FRA
Problem
You want to configure your database so that archived redo log files are written to the fast recovery area.

Solution
When you run the database in archivelog mode, you have to configure a location to which the archived redo logs are written when they are generated. The default location for archived redo logs is $ORACLE_HOME/dbs in Unix-based system and %ORACLE_HOME%\database for Windows-based systems. Of course, you can always configure a specific location by executing the command `alter system set log_archive_dest_1`. In this recipe, you will see how to use the fast recovery area as the destination of the archived redo logs.

Here are the steps to follow to send archived redo logs to the fast recovery area:

1. Configure the fast recovery area with adequate space (Recipe 3-1).

2. If the fast recovery area is already defined, then make sure you have enough space to hold at least one archived log (Recipe 3-4).

3. Log on to the database as a user with the `sysdba` privilege (such as `sys`), and issue the following command:

    ```
    alter system set log_archive_dest_1 = 'LOCATION=USE_DB_RECOVERY_FILE_DEST';
    ```

    This command instructs the database to use the fast recovery area as the destination for archived redo logs.

4. Make sure the archived redo log destination 1 is enabled. By default it's enabled, but someone may have disabled it. Issue the following SQL:

    ```
    SQL>show parameter log_archive_dest_state_1
    NAME                                 TYPE             VALUE
    ------------------------------------ ---------------- ---------------- ----------
    log_archive_dest_state_1             string           ENABLE
    ```

5. The presence of ENABLE confirms that the destination is enabled.

6. If the destination is not enabled, enable it now by issuing this:

    ```
    alter system set log_archive_dest_state_1 = enable;
    ```

7.   Check the correct setting by issuing an `archive log list` command at the SQL prompt:

```
SQL>archive log list
Database log mode              Archive Mode
Automatic archival             Enabled
Archive destination            USE_DB_RECOVERY_FILE_DEST
Oldest online log sequence     47
Next log sequence to archive   49
Current log sequence           49
```

Note the line `Archive destination USE_DB_RECOVERY_FILE_DEST`, which confirms that the archived redo log destination is set to the fast recovery area.

8.   Check the operation by issuing a log switch that forces the generation of an archived redo log:

```
alter system switch logfile;
```

9.   Execution of this command should come back with the message "System altered." If you see any other message, then you will get a clue for your next action from the message itself. For instance, a common message is as follows:

```
ORA-00257: archiver error. Connect internal only, until freed.
```

10. This message indicates that the location specified for archived redo logs is possibly full, so you need to address that, as shown in Recipe 3-5.

11. Confirm that an archived redo log was created in the fast recovery area. Oracle will automatically create a directory called archivelog in the FRA and also a subdirectory under that named as the day's date specified in the format YYYY-MM-DD. You can go to that directory and check for the existence of a new, archived redo log file.

12. Alternatively, or in addition to checking for the physical presence of the file, you can check the database for the existence of the archivelog:

```
SQL>select name from v$archived_log
  2  order by completion_time;

NAME
--------------------------------------------------------------------------------
... output truncated ...
+FRA/cdb1/archivelog/2012_08_01/thread_1_seq_128.342.790207235
+FRA/cdb1/archivelog/2012_08_01/thread_1_seq_129.343.790207281
+FRA/cdb1/archivelog/2012_08_01/thread_1_seq_130.344.790208967
+FRA/cdb1/archivelog/2012_08_02/thread_1_seq_131.345.790239647
+FRA/cdb1/archivelog/2012_08_02/thread_1_seq_132.346.790279237
```

13. This shows the last archived redo log was created in the fast recovery area as an Oracle managed file (note the long name).

14. Now the archived redo log destination is set to the fast recovery area.

How It Works

Before you start on this recipe, ask yourself whether you really want to direct the archived redo logs to the fast recovery area. Let's see the pros and cons of doing so.

The following are the benefits of directing archived redo logs to the fast recovery area:

- Doing so allows Oracle to back up the archived redo logs and to delete them when a space shortage occurs.

- Using the single command backup recovery area (Recipe 3-15), you can back up everything, including archived redo logs, to tape at once.

- You have one location where the database recovery-related files are kept. You can make this location very reliable through the use of RAID structures.

- You can monitor the space easily.

And the disadvantage is only one:

- Since all the recovery-related files are in one place, a disaster in that file system or ASM disk group will make everything unavailable for recovery. This is a practical consideration and can't be ignored.

■ **Caution**   As a best practice, we do not advise that you put the archived redo logs in the fast recovery area. When a disaster makes the disks inoperable and you need to recover the data files, archived redo logs are very important. If you miss an archived redo log, you can't recover beyond that point. Sometimes you can't even perform an incomplete recovery when an archived redo log is missing, since that archived redo log may contain some changes to the system tablespace. Even in the case when a data file has no backup, you can re-create it if you have all the archived redo logs generated since the creation of the data file. Therefore, archived redo logs are far more important than data file backups. Also, they sometimes compensate for each other's absence. Because of this, you should place the archived redo logs and data file backups in two different locations so that at least one of them is available. We recommend keeping the data file backups, but not the archived redo logs, in the fast recovery area. Use the parameter log_archive_dest_1 to set an explicit location for the archived redo logs. You should, however, place backups of archived redo logs in the fast recovery area.

3-7. Using the Same FRA for Two Databases with the Same Name

Problem

In the preceding recipes, you learned that the different files are placed inside the fast recovery area in the following directory structure:

```
<Fast recovery area>/<Database Name>/<Type of File>/<Date>
```

For instance, the archived redo logs for database PRODB2 for August 2, 2012, are stored here:

```
+FRA/prodb2/archivelog/2012_08_02/thread_1_seq_132.346.790279237
```

The structure allows several databases to share the same fast recovery area. However, you may wonder, what happens when two databases with the same name want to share the same fast recovery area? They can't have two directories with the same name.

Solution

The solution is rather simple. The directory for <Database Name> does not refer to the database name; rather, it refers to the unique name of the database. To check the unique name, use the following query:

```
SQL> select db_unique_name
  2  from v$database;

DB_UNIQUE_NAME
-------------------------------
PRODB2
```

By default, the unique name of a database is the same as the database name. If you want to use the same fast recovery area for two databases, you must use different unique names. Unfortunately, you can't change this dynamically. You have to put the following parameter in the initialization file and restart the database:

```
db_unique_name = <Unique Name of the Database>
```

Once done, the RMAN backups are automatically created in the appropriate directory.

How It Works

This solution has some caveats. It works fine in most cases but not all. For instance, suppose you had a database called PRODB2 and the unique name was also PRODB2. The backups go in the directory +FRA/prodb2/backuppiece/2012_08_02. Later you configure another database also called PRODB2 to share the same fast recovery area. Of course you have to use a different unique name, but for which database? You have two choices:

- Change the unique name of the new database to PROD2, and let the old one keep the unique name PRODB2.

- Change the unique name of the old database to PROD2, and let the new one have the unique name PRODB2.

If you choose the former, then a new subdirectory, PROD2, will be created in the directory specified as the fast recovery area, and all the backups of the new database will go there. This is the easiest and the least intrusive option. We recommend this, if you have a choice. In most cases, this will be possible.

However, sometimes it may not be possible to give a new unique name to the new database. You may have to change the unique name of the old database. This will also create a new subdirectory—PROD2—in the fast recovery area. But here is the problem: prior to renaming the unique name, the backups of the old database were going to the following directory:

```
+FRA/prodb2/backuppiece/2012_08_02
```

After renaming, however, the backup pieces go in this directory instead:

```
+FRA/prod2/backuppiece/2012_08_02
```

However, the backup pieces taken earlier will still be in +FRA/prodb2/backuppiece/2012_08_02, along with the backup pieces of the new database PRODB2. This may cause some confusion. Therefore, instead of leaving the backup pieces there, you may want to move them to the newly created directory +FRA/prod2/backuppiece/2012_08_02. You can do this by using the unix mv command (for Unix-based filesystems). For ASM files, you can either use dbms_file_transfer package or use asmcmd (only on Oracle Database 10g Release 2 or later). Chapter 24 shows the recipes for managing ASM files.

The RMAN repository will not be aware of the move, so it will continue to report the existence of the backup pieces in the old directory. So, you have to make the repository know that the location of the backup piece has changed. You can accomplish that by simply uncataloging and recataloging the backup pieces in their appropriate directories. Here are the steps:

1. First, check the backup pieces in the old location:

```
RMAN> list backup of database;
List of Backup Sets
===================
BS Key  Type LV Size       Device Type Elapsed Time Completion Time
------- ---- -- ---------- ----------- ------------ ---------------
159     Full   796.63M     DISK        00:01:57     02-AUG-12
        BP Key: 153   Status: AVAILABLE  Compressed: NO  Tag: TAG20061110T175734
        Piece Name: +FRA/prodb2/backupset/2012_08_02/o1_mf_nnndf_TAG20061110T175734_2ob0yzgp_.bkp
  List of Datafiles in backup set 159
  File LV Type Ckp SCN    Ckp Time  Name
  ---- -- ---- ---        ----------------  --------------------------
  1       Full 3350546    02-AUG-12 /home/oracle/oradata/PRODB2/SYSTEM.dbf
  2       Full 3350546    02-AUG-12 /home/oracle/oradata/PRODB2/UNDOTBS1.dbf
  3       Full 3350546    02-AUG-12 /home/oracle/oradata/PRODB2/SYSAUX.dbf
  4       Full 3350546    02-AUG-12 /home/oracle/oradata/PRODB2/USERS.dbf
  5       Full 3350546    02-AUG-12 /home/oracle/oradata/PRODB2/EXAMPLE.dbf
  6       Full 3350546    02-AUG-12 +DG2/accdata_01.dbf

BS Key  Type LV Size       Device Type Elapsed Time Completion Time
------- ---- -- ---------- ----------- ------------ ---------------
161     Full   796.65M     DISK        00:01:45     02-AUG-12
        BP Key: 155   Status: AVAILABLE  Compressed: NO  Tag:TAG20061110T180848
        Piece Name: +FRA/prodb2/backupset/2012_08_02/o1_mf_nnndf_TAG20061110T180848_2ob1n1ol_.bkp
  List of Datafiles in backup set 161
  File LV Type Ckp SCN    Ckp Time  Name
  ---- -- ---- ---------- --------- ----
  1       Full 3353618    02-AUG-12 /home/oracle/oradata/PRODB2/SYSTEM.dbf
  2       Full 3353618    02-AUG-12 /home/oracle/oradata/PRODB2/UNDOTBS1.dbf
  3       Full 3353618    02-AUG-12 /home/oracle/oradata/PRODB2/SYSAUX.dbf
  4       Full 3353618    02-AUG-12 /home/oracle/oradata/PRODB2/USERS.dbf
  5       Full 3353618    02-AUG-12 /home/oracle/oradata/PRODB2/EXAMPLE.dbf
  6       Full 3353618    02-AUG-12 +DG2/accdata_01.dbf
```

2. From the previous output, you can see that the backup piece with the name +FRA/prodb2/backupset/2012_08_02/o1_mf_nnndf_ TAG20061110T175734_2ob0yzgp_.bkp is in the old place. Move it to the right directory using the appropriate tool. Here is an example in ASMCMD:

```
ASMCMD> cp
+fra/prodb2/backupset/2012_07_21/nnndn0_TAG20120721T183841_0.262.789244721 +fra/prod2/bs1.rmb
copying
+fra/prodb2/backupset/2012_07_21/nnndn0_TAG20120721T183841_0.262.789244721 -> +fra/prod2/bs1.rmb
```

3. Now that the backup piece is in the right directory, you must tell that fact to RMAN. First you need to remove the identity of the backup piece from the RMAN repository using a process generally known as uncataloging:

```
RMAN> change backuppiece
'+FRA/prodb2/backupset/2012_08_02/o1_mf_nnndf_TAG20061110T175734_2ob0yzgp_.bkp' uncatalog;
uncataloged backuppiece
backup piece handle=+FRA/cdb1/backupset/2012_08_02/o1_mf_nnndf_TA G20061110T175734_2ob0yzgp_.bkp
recid=153 stamp=606160655
Uncataloged 1 objects
```

4. Then catalog the piece again with the correct file:

```
RMAN> catalog backuppiece '+FRA/prod2/backupset/2012_08_02/o1_mf_nnndf_TA
G20061110T175734_2ob0yzgp_.bkp';
cataloged backuppiece
backup piece handle+FRA/PROD2/backupset/2012_08_02/o1_mf_nnndf_TAG20061110T175734_2ob0yzgp_.bkp
recid=157 stamp=606163369
```

Note there is no need to tell what type of file you are cataloging. RMAN queries the file header and gets that information. If you have a lot of files in this directory, instead of issuing the command once per file, you can use the following command:

```
RMAN> catalog start with '+FRA/prod2/backupset/2012_08_02';
```

It will automatically scan the headers of each file in that directory and catalog them with proper types.

5. Test whether RMAN knows this file is a backup piece of the database:

```
RMAN> list backup of database;

List of Backup Sets
===================
BS Key  Type LV Size        Device Type Elapsed Time Completion Time
------- ---- -- ---------- ----------- ------------ ---------------
159     Full   796.63M    DISK        00:01:57     02-AUG-12
        BP Key: 157    Status: AVAILABLE  Compressed: NO  Tag:TAG20061110T175734
        Piece Name: +FRA/PROD2/backupset/2012_08_02/o1_mf_nnndf_TAG20061110T175734_2ob0yzgp_.bkp
  List of Datafiles in backup set 159
```

```
File LV Type Ckp SCN    Ckp Time    Name
---- -- ---- --------   ----------  ---------  ---------  ----
1         Full 3350546     02-AUG-12 /home/oracle/oradata/PRODB2/SYSTEM.dbf
2         Full 3350546     02-AUG-12 /home/oracle/oradata/PRODB2/UNDOTBS1.dbf
... output truncated ...
```

As you can see, the backup piece is correctly displayed as +FRA/PROD2/backupset/2012_08_02/o1_mf_nnndf_
TAG20061110T175734_2ob0yzgp_.bkp, just the way you intended. Now all backup pieces are located properly and
also recorded accurately in the repository.

You can use this technique in cases where two databases share the same fast recovery area and have the same name.

3-8. Placing a Control File in the FRA

Problem

You want to create a database and have one of the control file mirrors placed into the fast recovery area, or you have
an existing database and want to create a control file mirror in the fast recovery area.

Solution

The control files are created only once—during the database creation. Later the control files can be re-created from
either a backup or a script possibly produced by a control file trace. So, there are only three occasions when the
control files could be placed in the fast recovery area:

- When the database is created for the first time

- When the control file is re-created through a SQL script to recover from a failure, just prior to
  restoring the backup

- When the control file is restored from a backup

During any one of these cases, you make the database create one of the control files in the fast recovery area by
making the required changes to the initialization parameter file. You have two options:

- Place the control files parameter explicitly in the initialization parameter file, taking care to
  place at least one control file in a location different from the fast recovery area. For instance,
  if the fast recovery area is /home/oracle/fastarea, you put the following entry in the
  initialization parameter file:

```
control_files = ('+FRA/cdb1/controlfile/control01.ctl', '/home/oracle/oradata/control02.ctl')
```

- The second option is to let the database guess the control file location in the fast recovery area:

  a. Specify the fast recovery area location and size (Recipe 3-1)

  b. Put the following parameters in the initialization parameter file:

  ```
  DB_CREATE_FILE_DEST = '/home/oracle/oradata'
  ```

  c. Check that these two parameters are not in the initialization parameter file:

  ```
  db_create_online_log_dest_1
  db_create_online_log_dest_2
  ```

If they exist, remove them. In either option, one control file is created in the fast recovery area.

How It Works

While deciding where to place the control file, the database uses a decision plan, as shown here. Essentially, the decision is based on which initialization parameters are set. Table 3-3 shows the location of the control files based on the settings of the various initialization parameters. The headings are the abbreviations of the initialization parameters.

Table 3-3. *Decision for Location of the Control File*

DCOLD1	DCOLD2	DCFD	DRFD	Location of Control File(s)
Set	Set	Not Set	Not set	Two members created, one each in db_create_online_log_dest_1 and db_create_online_log_dest_2.
Not set	Not set	Set	Set	Two members created, one each in db_create_file_dest and the fast recovery area.
Not set	Not set	Set	Not set	Only one member is created in db_create_file_dest.
Not set	Not set	Not set	Set	Only one member is created in the fast recovery area.

DCOL1: db_create_online_log_dest_1

DCOL2: db_create_online_log_dest_2

DCFD: db_create_file_dest

DRFD: db_recovery_file_dest

As you can see, the only cases where control files are created in the fast recovery area is the case where parameter db_recovery_file_dest is set and db_create_online_log_dest_1 and _2 are not set. So, to make sure the control file is created there, you should specify the fast recovery area (assumed true since we are talking about that in this whole chapter). To make sure these parameters are not set, issue the following SQL statement:

```
SQL> show parameter db_create_online_log_dest
NAME                                  TYPE         VALUE
------------------------------------  -----------  ------------------------------
db_create_online_log_dest_1           string
db_create_online_log_dest_2           string
```

The output shows nothing as values of these parameters, which is what we expect. When the conditions of these two parameters being NULL and the fast recovery area being set are met, at least one control file will be created in the fast recovery area when the database is created or the control file is re-created.

Before implementing this recipe, it's wise to consider the pros and cons of placing a control file in the fast recovery area.

Advantages

The easiest advantage to understand is the visibility across all instances of a real application cluster (RAC) database. Since the fast recovery area must be visible to all the nodes of the RAC database (Recipe 3-1), it makes a perfect location for a control file, which must be visible to all the nodes as well. Only one control file should be placed there. The rest should be placed in other locations.

It's the other advantage that is more significant, one that relates to availability. If their primary database fails and you need to recover (or restore, whatever is appropriate), the fast recovery area is used, which has the backups of the database. So, technically, you have positioned the fast recovery area on such areas of the storage that the placement reduces the probability of failure at the same time as the failure of the primary database. For instance, you may have put your database disks on a SAN different from where the fast recovery area disks are. So, the chances of both disks (the database and the fast recovery area) going down at the same time are substantially reduced. If the primary database files are down and you have access to the most current online redo log files, you may avoid the possibility of an incomplete recovery, since you have a control file and will not need to start a recovery using a backup control file. If you don't have a control file on the fast recovery area, then there is a fair chance you will have to resort to a backup control file during recovery, which means an incomplete recovery, even if you have access to the current redo log files. So, there is a strong argument for placing one control file in the fast recovery area.

Disadvantages

It's not a slam-dunk argument; there is a significant disadvantage that you should consider. In a more practical situation, you probably have limited resources (read: money to buy disks) and want to maximize your investment for performance and reliability. So, you probably made the storage location of the main database files on RAID level 0+1, have a more reliable SAN, and so on. And you may have placed the fast recovery area on a less reliable (and less expensive) storage area network (SAN), even on network attached storage (NAS), and perhaps with RAID 5 or even no RAID at all. The latter is not advisable but is not unusual. So, the chance of failure in the fast recovery area is greater compared to that of the main database disks. If the fast recovery area fails, then you lose one of the control files. This by itself is not the end of the world. Let's hope you have been prudent in putting the other control files in other locations. So, when the database comes down after the control file in the fast recovery area suddenly becomes inaccessible, all you have to do is to remove that control file from the control file parameter in the initialization parameter file and restart the database. There is no data loss; you will have an interruption of service, since the database is unavailable from the time the fast recovery area is unavailable and the database is back up after removing the control file from the initialization parameter.

Choice

Here comes the tough question: should you put a control file in the fast recovery area? If your fast recovery area is in a storage location as reliable as the main database storage, then we strongly urge you to put one control file there.

If that is not true (and most likely the case), decide how important complete recovery is to you. If you must have a complete recovery after a failure regardless of other consequences including a possible interruption in service, then put one control file in the fast recovery area. If the potential service interruptions in case of the fast recovery area failure are not acceptable, do not use it as a location for even one control file.

Without knowing your exact circumstances, it's not easy for us to recommend one solution over the other. In general, however, we find it safer not to put even one control file in the fast recovery area. Under no circumstances should you put all your control files in the fast recovery area.

3-9. Placing Online Redo Log Files in FRA

Problem

You want to create online redo logs in the fast recovery area.

Solution

Online log files are not created by default in the fast recovery area. It's possible to place them there, however, and you can do so when creating the database or when adding a new log file group. Furthermore, when adding a new log file group, you have two choices regarding the placement of online redo logs in the fast recovery area:

- Creating both members of the group in the fast recovery area

- Creating only one member in the fast recovery area and creating the other member in the regular data file location

The following sections cover the two scenarios just described.

During Database Creation

During database creation, Oracle creates the online redo log files in the locations specified in the initialization parameter file. The parameters that affect the placement are db_create_online_log_dest_1 and db_create_online_log_dest_2.

1. Put the following lines in the initialization parameter file:

   ```
   db_create_online_log_dest_1 = '+FRA'
   db_create_online_log_dest_2 = '+FRA'
   ```

   When the database is created, Oracle will create two members of each online redo log group and both members in the fast recovery area.

2. If the parameter db_create_file_dest is set in the initialization parameter file, either remove it or set it to '' (null string), as shown here:

   ```
   db_create_file_dest = ''
   ```

3. After the database is created, confirm the creation of online redo log files by selecting the member names from the data dictionary view V$LOGFILE:

   ```
   SQL> select member
     2  from v$logfile
     3  where group# = 1;

   MEMBER
   --------------------------------------------------------------------------
   +FRA/cdb1/onlinelog/o1_mf_1_2psd26ox_.log
   +FRA/cdb1/onlinelog/o1_mf_1_2lpsd285q_.log
   ```

Note how the online redo log files were created in the fast recovery area.

Adding a New Log File Group: Both Members in the FRA

Follow these steps to place both members of an online redo log group in the fast recovery area. We're assuming you have already defined the fast recovery area (Recipe 3-1).

1. Make sure the fast recovery area is set:

```
SQL> show parameter db_recovery_file_dest
NAME                                 TYPE          VALUE
------------------------------------ ------------- ------------------ -----------
db_recovery_file_dest                string        +FRA
```

2. Also make sure that the parameters db_create_file_dest and db_create_online_log_dest_* are all set to NULL. For example:

```
SQL> show parameter db_create_online_log_dest
NAME                                 TYPE          VALUE
------------------------------------ ------------- -----------------------------
db_create_online_log_dest_1          string
db_create_online_log_dest_2          string
db_create_online_log_dest_3          string
db_create_online_log_dest_4          string
db_create_online_log_dest_5          string

SQL> show parameter db_create_file_dest
NAME                                 TYPE          VALUE
------------------------------------ ------------- -----------------------------
db_create_file_dest                  string
```

3. Now, add the log file group with the appropriate number. For example, to add a log file group 4, do this:

```
SQL> alter database add log file group 4;

Database altered.
```

The log file group is created in the fast recovery area in the subdirectory onlinelog, in a naming convention for Oracle managed files. The log file created this way is 100MB.

4. Confirm placement of the new member in the fast recovery area by selecting the member names from the data dictionary view V$LOGFILE:

```
SQL> Select Member
  2    from v$logfile
  3    where group# = 4;
MEMBER
-----------------------------------------------------------------------------
+FRA/cdb1/onlinelog/group_4.268.790292145
```

5. Optionally check for the member's existence in the onlinelog directory at the fast recovery area destination:

```
$ asmcmd
ASMCMD> cd +FRA/cdb1/onlinelog
ASMCMD> ls -ls
Type        Redund  Striped  Time             Sys  Block_Size  Blocks     Bytes      Space      Name
ONLINELOG   UNPROT  COARSE   AUG 02 21:00:00  Y           512  204801  104858112  106954752
group_4.268.790292145
```

This has a small problem, however. As you can see, there is only one log file member for that group. Best practices suggest that there should be at least two members per group to eliminate any single point of failure. You can accomplish this by specifying two additional parameters for the online redo log creation, shown in the following steps:

1. Set the parameters db_create_online_log_dest_1 and db_create_online_log_dest_2 to the fast recovery area location:

    ```
    SQL> alter system set db_create_online_log_dest_1 = '+FRA';
    System altered.

    SQL> alter system set db_create_online_log_dest_2 = '+FRA';
    System altered.
    ```

2. Now add the log file group without mentioning any specific file or directory names:

    ```
    SQL> alter database add logfile group 5;
    Database altered.
    ```

3. Confirm the creation of online redo log files by selecting the member names from the data dictionary view V$LOGFILE:

    ```
    SQL> select member
      2    from v$logfile
      3    where group# = 5;

    MEMBER
    ---------------------------------------------------------------------------
    +FRA/cdb1/onlinelog/group_5.268.790292145
    +FRA/cdb1/onlinelog/group_5.265.790292147
    ```

    This confirms that two members were created for the log file group, not one.

4. Optionally, you can also verify that these files were created in the fast recovery area destination:

    ```
    $ cd +FRA/cdb1/onlinelog
    $ ls -l
    total 205016
    -rw-r-----   1 oracle    oinstall 104858112 Oct 10 23:43 o1_mf_4_2lrt26ox_.log
    -rw-r-----   1 oracle    oinstall 104858112 Oct 10 23:43 o1_mf_4_2lrt285q_.log
    ```

■ **Caution**   If you add online log files in this manner, they will be created in the fast recovery area, but the FRA will not know of their existence. So, they will not be counted toward the total number of files or the space consumed in the FRA. This may cause you to miscalculate the FRA space, causing space starvation in FRA.

Using the following command, you can add a logfile group quickly without specifying anything else, such as the group number:

```
alter database add logfile;
```

This will create a new log file group at a sequence of one more than the last log file group sequence. So, if currently the group number of the last added log file group is 6, the previous command will add a group 7 with just one file in the Oracle managed file format. You can check that through the following query:

```
SQL> select member
  2  from v$logfile
  3  where group# = 7;
MEMBER
-------------------------------------------------------------
+FRA/cdb1/onlinelog/o1_mf_6_2lrvlth1_.log
```

Adding a New Log File Group: Only One Member in the FRA

If you want only one member of the group in the fast recovery area and the other one in the regular database file location, you should define two parameters: the fast recovery area and db_create_file_dest. This parameter determines where a data file should be created if no location is given.

1. Set the parameter where you want to create the first member of the online redo log groups. To specify the location, such as the ASM disk group DATA, issue the following SQL statement:

    ```
    SQL> alter system set db_create_file_dest = '+DATA';

    System altered.
    ```

2. Ensure that the parameter db_create_file_dest is set:

    ```
    SQL> show parameter db_create_file_dest
    NAME                                 TYPE        VALUE
    ------------------------------------ ----------- ------------------------------
    db_create_file_dest                  string      +DATA
    ```

Like the fast recovery area, the directory you specify as a location of the previously mentioned parameter must already exist. Oracle will not create it for you.

3. Make sure the fast recovery area is set:

```
SQL> show parameter db_recovery_file_dest

NAME                     TYPE    VALUE
------------------------ ------  --------- ------------
db_recovery_file_dest      string +FRA
```

4. Unset log destinations:

```
SQL> alter system set db_create_online_log_dest_1 = '';

System altered.

SQL>alter system set db_create_online_log_dest_2 = '';

System altered.
```

Note these are two consecutive single quotes.

With this configuration, if you decide to add a log file group, the group will be created with two members, and they will be in the fast recovery area and the directory specified by db_create_file_dest. Let's see how that is done:

1. First add a log file group:

```
SQL> alter database add logfile group 7;
```

2. Check how many members are created and where:

```
SQL> select member
  2  from v$logfile
  3  where group# = 7;

MEMBER
MEMBER
-----------------------------------------------------------------------------
+DATA/cdb1/onlinelog/group_7.278.790292907
+FRA/cdb1/onlinelog/group_7.264.790292907
```

3. In the physical fast recovery area location and in the view V$LOGFILE, verify the existence of the new redo log files.

How It Works

One of the lesser known features of Oracle database administration is the ability to create data files, online redo log files, and so on, without specifying file names and locations. You do this by specifying some locations in the initialization parameter file as the location for these files. These locations could be ASM disk groups or file systems or directories under file systems. The location must be available to all instances in case of a Real Application Cluster (RAC) database. Please note that the directory you specify as a location must already exist. Oracle will not create it for you. If you have defined the fast recovery area, the redo logs will be created there.

You must carefully decide whether you really want to create redo logs in the fast recovery area. The arguments pro and con are the same as for the question of putting the control file in the FRA (see Recipe 3-8). Read up on those arguments, and arrive at your own conclusion.

Advantages of Putting Redo Log Members in the FRA

In summary, the argument for putting at least one member of a redo log group in the fast recovery area hinges on the assumption that the fast recovery area and the main database disks are located in such a way that the probability of both going down at the same time is very slim, almost to the point of being negligible. You attain that probability by putting the fast recovery area disks on a SAN or NAS other than where the main database is located. Even if the fast recovery area and main database are both on the same SAN (or NAS), if they do not share the same physical disks, then it further reduces the probability of simultaneous failure. The idea is to make sure that whatever causes the main database disks to go down will not affect the fast recovery area disks. This way, should the main database disks get corrupted, you can still access the backup of the database files in the fast recovery area.

With the assumption we've just described, the idea of putting one member of an online redo log group on the fast recovery area ensures that at least one member of the group will still be available in case the main database disks experience a failure. For instance, suppose your database has three log groups, each with two members, and one member of each group is on the fast recovery area, as shown in Figure 3-1.

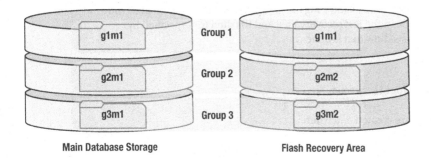

Figure 3-1. *Ideal placement of redo log members if FRA is used as a location*

The members in Figure 3-1 are named in the following form: g<group#>m<member#>. Since the database is in archivelog mode, each log file group can be in one of three states:

Current: The online redo log group is the current group. If the group fails, the database immediately aborts with an error. If all the members of the group are damaged, then you need to perform an incomplete recovery from previous backups.

Active: The group is not the current one, but it was earlier. Now it's being archived, and that operation is not completed yet. If the group fails, the database is not halted, but the log file will not have been archived, and any subsequent recovery operation will stop at this group. When an active group fails, you should take a fresh backup of the database so that you do not need to roll forward from a previous backup with archived redo logs. You don't want the rollforward operation to be dependent upon a failed group.

Inactive: The group is not current now, and it has already been archived. The loss of this group does not affect database operations, and it doesn't affect any recovery that you might perform in the future.

Having these explanations in mind, now assume that the status of the online redo log groups in Figure 3-1 is as follows:

> Group 1: Current
>
> Group 2: Active
>
> Group 3: Inactive

With this information, suppose one member (or even both) of the online redo log group is damaged. Let's see the consequences. You can find a more detailed description of the redo log failure in Chapter 14; we will look at only one scenario here. Member g3m1 of Group 3 gets damaged. Since this member is INACTIVE, it has no impact on the database operation. But when the current log group gets filled, Group 3 must be available, so we need to fix the damaged member now. The solution is really simple. Since the other member of the group—g3m2—is in a different part of our storage, in the fast recovery area, that is most likely intact. We can copy it over the damaged file and be on our way:

```
$ cp g3m2 g3m1
```

No other action is required. Had g3m2 been on the same storage area as g3m1, then the probability of g3m2 being intact would have been much less because it would have been prone to the same failure that affected g3m1. So, there is a strong reason to place redo log group members on different storage areas, even if one of them is not the fast recovery area. Since we are assuming in case of database failure that the fast recovery area might survive, keeping one member of the redo log groups will reduce the chances of failure of both members of the online redo log group.

Disadvantages of Placing One Member of the Online Redo Log Group in FRA

Putting members of the redo log groups in the fast recovery area is not a slam-dunk decision either. Let's revisit the scenario in Figure 3-1. Suppose that one member—g1m1—of Group 1 fails. Since the group is now current, the failure of the member will cause a failure in the database, and the database instance will abort.

You can correct the situation by copying the intact member of the online redo log group to the damaged member and starting the database. Since we describe the process of recovery in case of redo log failure in detail in Chapter 14, we will skip the details here. The important point to understand is that the sole reason of success in re-creating the redo log member was because we had an intact copy. Keeping one member of the log file group in the fast recovery area improves the odds of that, as shown in the previous section. However, on the flip side, the failure of a current redo log member temporarily shuts the database down, even if you can repair it and bring the database up quickly. This creates a denial-of-service situation and should be avoided at all costs. Prevention of the loss is the key, not the repair afterward. The fast recovery area is usually built on cheaper, less reliable disks and is more prone to failure than the more reliable database disks. Therefore, putting even one member of the redo log group there increases your chances of failure.

So, in summary, you should decide with care to place a member of the redo log group on the fast recovery area. You can use the decision grid shown in Table 3-4 to support your decision.

Table 3-4. Decision Grid to Decide Placement of One Redo Log Member on the FRA

Reliability of the Disk Under	Risk of Temporary Database	Failure the Fast Recovery Area
	Acceptable	Not Acceptable
Low	Yes	No
High	Maybe	Yes

■ **Caution** We do not recommend creating all members of online redo logs in the fast recovery area. As a best practice, we recommend keeping the redo logs out of the fast recovery area in general, unless the reliability of the area is pretty close to the main database disks.

3-10. Sending Image Copies to the FRA
Problem

You have configured the fast recovery area, and you want to make sure image copies of the data files go there.

Solution

There is no special command to specify the fast recovery area as the target of the image copies. All you have to do is make sure of the following:

- The fast recovery area is configured.

- The RMAN script does not have any format command in the channel configuration.

Once these two conditions are met, you can issue a simple backup as copy database command, and the image copies will go there. Here is a sample command and output:

```
RMAN> backup as copy database;

Starting backup at 02-AUG-12
using target database control file instead of recovery catalog
allocated channel: ORA_DISK_1
channel ORA_DISK_1: SID=259 device type=DISK
channel ORA_DISK_1: starting datafile copy
input datafile file number=00003 name=+DATA/cdb1/datafile/sysaux.257.788546597
output file name=+FRA/cdb1/datafile/sysaux.257.790293315 tag=TAG20120802T215514
RECID=1 STAMP=790293329
channel ORA_DISK_1: datafile copy complete, elapsed time: 00:00:15
... output truncated ...
channel ORA_DISK_1: specifying datafile(s) in backup set
including current SPFILE in backup set
channel ORA_DISK_1: starting piece 1 at 02-AUG-12
channel ORA_DISK_1: finished piece 1 at 02-AUG-12
piece
handle=+FRA/cdb1/backupset/2012_08_02/nnsnf0_tag20120802t215514_0.267.790293387
tag=TAG20120802T215514 comment=NONE
channel ORA_DISK_1: backup set complete, elapsed time: 00:00:01
Finished backup at 02-AUG-12

RMAN>
```

As you can see in the resultant output, the image copies are now in the fast recovery area.

How It Works

The solution should be self-explanatory. When the RMAN image copy command is given, the database makes the copies and places them in the fast recovery area. The image copies are placed in the directory +FRA/cdb1/datafile, that is, <fast recovery area>/<DB Unique Name>/datafile. As we explained earlier, Oracle will now manage these files—deleting redundant ones to make room for new ones, and so on.

3-11. Deleting Backup Sets from the FRA

Problem

Recall from the earlier discussion that one of the biggest appeals of using the fast recovery area is that Oracle automatically deletes the unnecessary files from this location whenever additional space is needed. So, you may not need to delete files manually. However, in some rare occasions you may want to delete backup sets, such as cleaning up under space constraints, where you are forced to remove some nonredundant backup set.

Solution

Like archived redo logs, there is no special command to delete backup sets from the fast recovery area. You delete a backup set in the same way as you would have deleted one while not using a fast recovery area. Here's the process to follow:

1. First check the backup sets existing in the RMAN repository. Look for the value under the column "BS Key:"

```
RMAN> list backupset;

List of Backup Sets
===================

BS Key  Type LV Size        Device Type Elapsed Time Completion Time
------- ---- -- ---------- ----------- ------------ ---------------
4       Incr 0  2.42G       DISK        00:00:50     21-JUL-12
        BP Key: 4   Status: AVAILABLE  Compressed: NO  Tag: TAG20120721T183841
        Piece Name: +FRA/cdb1/backupset/2012_07_21/nnndn0_tag20120721t183841_0.262.789244721
  List of Datafiles in backup set 4
  File LV Type Ckp SCN    Ckp Time  Name
  ---- -- ---- ---------- --------- ----
  1    0  Incr 2196533    21-JUL-12 +DATA/cdb1/datafile/system.258.788546653
  3    0  Incr 2196533    21-JUL-12 +DATA/cdb1/datafile/sysaux.257.788546597
  4    0  Incr 2196533    21-JUL-12 +DATA/cdb1/datafile/undotbs1.260.788546719
  5    0  Incr 1619431    13-JUL-12 +DATA/cdb1/c4bd2d3ad8c42bf9e04380a8840a451e/datafile/
system.271.788546799
  6    0  Incr 2196533    21-JUL-12 +DATA/cdb1/datafile/users.259.788546719
  7    0  Incr 1619431    13-JUL-12 +DATA/cdb1/c4bd2d3ad8c42bf9e04380a8840a451e/datafile/
sysaux.270.788546799
  8    0  Incr 2192687    21-JUL-12 +DATA/cdb1/c4bd35d102b92f07e04380a8840a6a44/datafile/
system.274.788546943
  9    0  Incr 2192687    21-JUL-12 +DATA/cdb1/c4bd35d102b92f07e04380a8840a6a44/datafile/
sysaux.275.788546943
```

```
BS Key  Type LV Size        Device Type Elapsed Time Completion Time
------- ---- -- ---------- ----------- ------------ ---------------
5       Incr 1  17.11M      DISK        00:00:02     21-JUL-12
        BP Key: 5   Status: AVAILABLE  Compressed: NO  Tag: TAG20120721T183841
        Piece Name: +FRA/cdb1/backupset/2012_07_21/ncsnn1_tag20120721t183841_0.261.789244779
    SPFILE Included: Modification time: 21-JUL-12
    SPFILE db_unique_name: CDB1
    Control File Included: Ckp SCN: 2196567      Ckp time: 21-JUL-12

BS Key  Type LV Size        Device Type Elapsed Time Completion Time
------- ---- -- ---------- ----------- ------------ ---------------
7       Full    80.00K      DISK        00:00:01     02-AUG-12
        BP Key: 7   Status: AVAILABLE  Compressed: NO  Tag: TAG20120802T215514
        Piece Name: +FRA/cdb1/backupset/2012_08_02/nnsnf0_tag20120802t215514_0.267.790293387
    SPFILE Included: Modification time: 02-AUG-12
    SPFILE db_unique_name: CDB1
```

    2.   Now, to delete a backup set, let's say number 7, issue a delete backupset command:

```
RMAN> delete backupset 7;

using channel ORA_DISK_1

List of Backup Pieces
BP Key  BS Key  Pc# Cp# Status      Device Type Piece Name
------- ------- --- --- ----------- ----------- ----------
7       7       1   1   AVAILABLE   DISK        +FRA/cdb1/backupset/2012_08_02/nnsnf0_tag20120802t21
5514_0.267.790293387

Do you really want to delete the above objects (enter YES or NO)? yes
deleted backup piece
backup piece handle=+FRA/cdb1/backupset/2012_08_02/nnsnf0_tag20120802t215514_0.267.790293387
RECID=7 STAMP=790293386
Deleted 1 objects
```

The backup set is now removed.

    3.   If you want to delete a backup set without being prompted for confirmation issue a delete noprompt backupset command.

How It Works

This process is no different than deleting the backup sets from any other location. When you give a delete backupset command, RMAN knows about all the available backup sets and deletes the one specified by the user. However, please note that RMAN must know about the existence of the backup set. If the backup set is removed from the RMAN metadata, then RMAN does not know about it, and the delete operation will not work.

3-12. Deleting Archived Redo Logs from the FRA

Problem

You want to delete archived redo logs from the fast recovery area, possibly to free up space quickly to avoid running out of room.

Solution

One strong motivation for using the fast recovery area as the archivelog destination is the automated way redundant archivelogs are deleted by Oracle, so you do not need to worry about the redundant archivelogs. Therefore, you may not ever need to delete them manually, and this recipe may not be required on a regular basis. In some rare circumstances, however, you may want to delete the archived redo logs in the fast recovery area. One case could be that you have taken the backup of the archived redo logs to a different location, which is not yet cataloged in the RMAN repository, and you are running out of space in the fast recovery area. To quickly make room, you may want to delete some archived redo logs, such as those you've backed up somewhere else, from the fast recovery area. Here are the steps to follow:

1. First, find out the archived redo logs to delete. List all archived redo logs like so:

   ```
   RMAN> list archivelog all;
   ```

   Here is the partial output. Look for the values under the column "Seq." That is the sequence# of the archived log.

```
List of Archived Log Copies for database with db_unique_name CDB1
=====================================================================

Key     Thrd Seq     S Low Time
------- ---- ------- - ---------
14      1    60        A 21-JUL-12
        Name: +FRA/cdb1/archivelog/2012_07_21/thread_1_seq_60.269.789244815

15      1    61        A 21-JUL-12
        Name: +FRA/cdb1/archivelog/2012_07_21/thread_1_seq_61.270.789244817
```

2. To delete the archived log sequences 60 through 61, you can use the following commands:

   ```
   RMAN> delete archivelog from logseq=60 until logseq=61;
   ```

   The output comes back as follows:

```
released channel: ORA_DISK_1
allocated channel: ORA_DISK_1
channel ORA_DISK_1: SID=259 device type=DISK
RMAN-08139: WARNING: archived redo log not deleted, needed for guaranteed restore point
archived log file
name=+FRA/cdb1/archivelog/2012_07_21/thread_1_seq_60.269.789244815 thread=1 sequence=60
List of Archived Log Copies for database with db_unique_name CDB1
=====================================================================
```

```
Key      Thrd Seq      S Low Time
-------  ---- -------  - ---------
15       1    61       A 21-JUL-12
              Name: +FRA/cdb1/archivelog/2012_07_21/thread_1_seq_61.270.789244817

Do you really want to delete the above objects (enter YES or NO)? yes
deleted archived log
archived log file
name=+FRA/cdb1/archivelog/2012_07_21/thread_1_seq_61.270.789244817 RECID=15 STAMP=789244816
Deleted 1 objects
```

3. Verify in the directory that the archived redo logs got deleted. For instance, in Unix, you can do this using the standard ls command. In case of ASM, you can use asmcmd ls command.

How It Works

Just like any other backups, the Oracle database knows where the archived redo logs are stored. The delete archivelog command deletes the archived redo logs pretty much the same way it would have done if the archived redo logs were stored in any other directory.

One very important point to note above is that the archived log sequence #60 was not deleted. Notice the presence of the following line in the output:

```
RMAN-08139: WARNING: archived redo log not deleted, needed for guaranteed restore point
```

This line is self-explanatory. The archived log file is needed for the guaranteed restore point created earlier. This is one of the reasons why a fast recovery area gets filled and the database can't allocate any space by removing old archived log files.

3-13. Reinstating a Damaged Data File from an Image Copy

Problem

One of the database files has been damaged, and you have to repair the file quickly to bring the associated tablespace back online. Instead of restoring the data file from backup, you want to use the image copy in the fast recovery area.

Solution

When a database file fails and you need to repair the file, you can just reinstate the image copy of the file from the fast recovery area instead of actually repairing it. This reduces the time for the operation significantly.

1. First check the files of the database:

```
RMAN> report schema;
Report of database schema for database with db_unique_name CDB1
```

```
List of Permanent Datafiles
===========================
File Size(MB) Tablespace           RB segs Datafile Name
---- -------- -------------------- ------- ----------------------
1    790      SYSTEM               ***     +DATA/cdb1/datafile/system.258.788546653
3    970      SYSAUX               ***     +DATA/cdb1/datafile/sysaux.257.788546597
4    50       UNDOTBS1             ***     +DATA/cdb1/datafile/undotbs1.260.788546719
5    250      PDB$SEED:SYSTEM      ***     +DATA/cdb1/c4bd2d3ad8c42bf9e04380a8840a451e/datafile/
system.271.788546799
6    5        USERS                ***     +DATA/cdb1/datafile/users.259.788546719
7    490      PDB$SEED:SYSAUX      ***     +DATA/cdb1/c4bd2d3ad8c42bf9e04380a8840a451e/datafile/
sysaux.270.788546799
8    250      PDB1:SYSTEM          ***     +DATA/cdb1/c4bd35d102b92f07e04380a8840a6a44/datafile/
system.274.788546943
9    530      PDB1:SYSAUX          ***     +DATA/cdb1/c4bd35d102b92f07e04380a8840a6a44/datafile/
sysaux.275.788546943
10   5        PDB1:USERS           ***     +DATA/cdb1/c4bd35d102b92f07e04380a8840a6a44/datafile/
users.277.788546967

List of Temporary Files
=======================
File Size(MB) Tablespace           Maxsize(MB) Tempfile Name
---- -------- -------------------- ----------- --------------------
1    532      TEMP                 32767       +DATA/cdb1/tempfile/temp.269.788546767
2    20       PDB$SEED:TEMP        32767       +DATA/cdb1/c40f9b49fc9c19e0e0430baae80aff01/tempfile/
temp.272.788546809
3    20       PDB1:TEMP            32767       +DATA/cdb1/c4bd35d102b92f07e04380a8840a6a44/tempfile/
temp.276.788546957
```

Suppose file 6, +DATA/cdb1/datafile/users.259.788546719, has been damaged.

2. Check for the existence of image copies of the damaged data file:

```
RMAN> list copy of datafile 6;

List of Datafile Copies
=======================

Key     File S Completion Time Ckp SCN    Ckp Time
------- ---- - --------------- ---------- ---------------
9       6    A 02-AUG-12       2913735    02-AUG-12
        Name: +FRA/cdb1/datafile/users.352.790293385
        Tag: TAG20120802T215514
```

As you can see from the output, there is an image copy of the damaged file in the fast
recovery area (users.352.790293385).

3. Take the damaged data file offline, if not offline already:

```
RMAN> sql 'alter database datafile 6 offline';
sql statement: alter database datafile 6 offline
```

In Oracle Database 12.1 and above you do not need to have the "sql" prefix. You can give the "alter database" command directly from the RMAN prompt.

Now, instruct the database to make the copy of the file in the fast recovery area, the production data file:

```
RMAN> switch datafile 6 to copy;

datafile 6 switched to datafile copy "+FRA/cdb1/datafile/users.352.790293385"
```

4. Recover the copy to make it consistent with the current state of the database:

```
RMAN> recover datafile 6;

Starting recover at 02-AUG-12
using channel ORA_DISK_1

starting media recovery
media recovery complete, elapsed time: 00:00:01

Finished recover at 02-AUG-12
```

5. Bring the recovered data file online:

```
RMAN> sql 'alter database datafile 6 online';
sql statement: alter database datafile 6 online
```

Again, in Oracle Database 12.1 and above you don't need to pass the "sql" prefix to the alter database command. When you bring the data file back online, the tablespace will be brought online as well. The tablespace is now operational. Don't leave the database using a file in the fast recovery area, though, especially not for the long term. When you have some time, follow the steps in Recipe 3-14 to switch to the original data file.

■ **Note**   If data files belonging to SYSTEM are damaged, the database can be only in the mounted state; not open. So, step 3 above is not needed. The database must be in mounted state at that step (only for data files of SYSTEM tablespace).

How It Works

It is important to contrast this recipe's approach to recovery with the traditional Oracle database recovery technique. If one of your database data files fails, the traditional solution is to restore the data file from your RMAN backup and then recover it. In summary, the steps are roughly as follows:

1. Take the tablespace offline (if not already).

2. Restore the data file from RMAN backup.

3. Apply the incremental backups.

4. Recover the data file by applying archived redo logs.

5. Bring the tablespace online.

These steps will recover the data file, but note the steps carefully. Steps 2 and 3 involve actual data transfer from the RMAN backup to the original data file location, and those transfers will take a considerable amount of time, depending on the type of RMAN storage, the speed of the connection, the other load on the SAN at the time, and so on. During these steps, the tablespace remains offline, and data in the tablespace remains inaccessible.

Now consider the approach shown in this recipe. If you took data file image copies in RMAN, you can switch to using the copy of the damaged data file instead of restoring from that copy. The advantage here is that pointing to a different file is for all practical purposes an instant operation—you save all the time you would normally spend copying from a backup. Figure 3-2 should make the concept easier to understand. For simplicity, assume the database has only three data files: File1, File2, and File3. The RMAN backups are done as image copies, which are made in the fast recovery area.

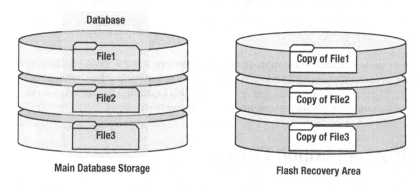

Figure 3-2. *Presence of image copies in the fast recovery area*

Suppose now File1 gets damaged. Ordinarily you would resort to restoring the file from the image copy and recovering it. However, the image copy is actually a copy of the data file File1, and it can be used as a substitute. Of course, the copy was taken at some point in the past, so it's not up-to-date, and it must be updated before being used. You do this update by applying the archived redo logs to the image copy. Finally, after the image copy is current, you use the switch command to make the data file copy part of the database.

Now you are running the database with one file in the fast recovery area. Figure 3-3 depicts the data files being used now.

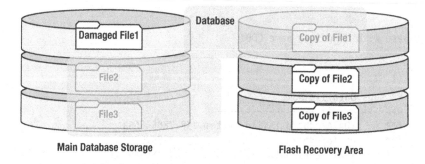

Figure 3-3. *Use of image copy of data file File1*

As an illustration, Table 3-5 compares the elapsed times under both approaches. The time estimates are highly approximate and depend on your specific conditions such as hardware, disk speed, and so on. It is shown as an illustration for the relative analysis, not for empirical establishment of elapsed times.

Table 3-5. *Comparison of Elapsed Times During Traditional and Image Copy Switch Approaches*

Step	Original Approach	Switch Approach	Time
1	Make data file offline	Make data file offline	1 minute
2	Restore copy of data file from the backup location to the main data file location	N/A	2 hours
3	Apply incremental backup	N/A	30 minutes
4	N/A	Switch to copy	1 minute
5	Recover data file	Recover data file	30 minutes
6	Make data file online	Make data file online	1 minute

As you can see from the comparison in Table 3-5, the switch approach eliminates steps 2 and 3, saving 2.5 hours (your time savings will vary). The switch approach takes about 33 minutes to get a tablespace back online, while the original approach takes more than 3 hours. (Again, your time savings may vary from this example.) If time to return to service is a priority, then you should seriously consider this recipe's approach as a recovery strategy.

3-14. Switching Back from an Image Copy

Problem

You've followed Recipe 3-13 to quickly get back online after a data file failure. You did that by having your database switch to the image copy of the failed file in the fast recovery area. Now you have some time, and you want to undo that switch.

Solution

Begin by creating a copy of the data file at the main location. Then switch to using that copy. Here are the steps to follow:

1. Check the data files once again:

```
RMAN> report schema;
Report of database schema for database with db_unique_name CDB1

List of Permanent Datafiles
===========================
File Size(MB) Tablespace          RB segs Datafile Name
---- -------- ------------------- ------- ------------------------
1    790      SYSTEM              ***     +DATA/cdb1/datafile/system.258.788546653
3    970      SYSAUX              ***     +DATA/cdb1/datafile/sysaux.257.788546597
4    50       UNDOTBS1            ***     +DATA/cdb1/datafile/undotbs1.260.788546719
5    250      PDB$SEED:SYSTEM     ***     +DATA/cdb1/c4bd2d3ad8c42bf9e04380a8840a451e/datafile/
system.271.788546799
6    5        USERS               ***     +FRA/cdb1/datafile/users.352.790293385
7    490      PDB$SEED:SYSAUX     ***     +DATA/cdb1/c4bd2d3ad8c42bf9e04380a8840a451e/datafile/
sysaux.270.788546799
```

8	250	PDB1:SYSTEM	***	+DATA/cdb1/c4bd35d102b92f07e04380a8840a6a44/datafile/	

system.274.788546943

9	530	PDB1:SYSAUX	***	+DATA/cdb1/c4bd35d102b92f07e04380a8840a6a44/datafile/	

sysaux.275.788546943

10	5	PDB1:USERS	***	+DATA/cdb1/c4bd35d102b92f07e04380a8840a6a44/datafile/	

users.277.788546967

```
List of Temporary Files
=======================
File Size(MB) Tablespace        Maxsize(MB) Tempfile Name
---- -------- -----------------  ----------- --------------------
1    532      TEMP               32767       +DATA/cdb1/tempfile/temp.269.788546767
2    20       PDB$SEED:TEMP      32767       +DATA/cdb1/c40f9b49fc9c19e0e0430baae80aff01/tempfile/
temp.272.788546809
3    20       PDB1:TEMP          32767       +DATA/cdb1/c4bd35d102b92f07e04380a8840a6a44/tempfile/
temp.276.788546957
```

Note how data file 6 is in the fast recovery area. You want to move it to its original location.

2. Remove the file at the OS level from the original location, if present. The file is unused, so it can be removed without any effect on the database. Since this is in ASM, we can use the ASMCMD command:

```
ASMCMD> cd +DATA/cdb1/datafile
ASMCMD> rm USERS.259.788546719
```

3. Connect to RMAN:

```
$ rman target=/
```

4. Create an image copy of the file, in this case file 6. Place that image copy in the file's original location:

```
RMAN> backup as copy datafile 6 format='+DATA';

Starting backup at 02-AUG-12
using channel ORA_DISK_1
channel ORA_DISK_1: starting datafile copy
input datafile file number=00006 name=+FRA/cdb1/datafile/users.352.790293385
output file name=+DATA/cdb1/datafile/users.259.790295525 tag=TAG20120802T223203
RECID=12 STAMP=790295524
channel ORA_DISK_1: datafile copy complete, elapsed time: 00:00:01
Finished backup at 02-AUG-12
```

5. Take the data file offline:

```
RMAN> sql 'alter database datafile 6 offline';
sql statement: alter database datafile 6 offline
```

In Oracle 12.1 and above you don't need to use the "sql" prefix. You can give the alter database command directly from the RMAN prompt.

6. Switch the data file to the copy you just placed in the original location:

```
RMAN> switch datafile 6 to copy;

datafile 6 switched to datafile copy "+DATA/cdb1/datafile/users.259.790295525"
```

7. Recover the data file to bring it up-to-date with changes that occurred between step 4 and step 5:

```
RMAN> recover datafile 6;

Starting recover at 02-AUG-12
using channel ORA_DISK_1

starting media recovery
media recovery complete, elapsed time: 00:00:00

Finished recover at 02-AUG-12
```

8. Bring the data file online:

```
RMAN> sql 'alter database datafile 6 online';
sql statement: alter database datafile 6 online
```

Again, as mentioned earlier, you can issue the alter database command directly from RMAN prompt; there is no need to have the "sql" prefix.

9. Check the location of the file once again:

```
RMAN> report schema;

Report of database schema for database with db_unique_name CDB1

List of Permanent Datafiles
===========================
```

File	Size(MB)	Tablespace	RB segs	Datafile Name
1	790	SYSTEM	***	+DATA/cdb1/datafile/system.258.788546653
3	970	SYSAUX	***	+DATA/cdb1/datafile/sysaux.257.788546597
4	50	UNDOTBS1	***	+DATA/cdb1/datafile/undotbs1.260.788546719
5	250	PDB$SEED:SYSTEM	***	+DATA/cdb1/c4bd2d3ad8c42bf9e04380a8840a451e/datafile/ system.271.788546799
6	5	USERS	***	+DATA/cdb1/datafile/users.259.790295525
7	490	PDB$SEED:SYSAUX	***	+DATA/cdb1/c4bd2d3ad8c42bf9e04380a8840a451e/datafile/ sysaux.270.788546799
8	250	PDB1:SYSTEM	***	+DATA/cdb1/c4bd35d102b92f07e04380a8840a6a44/datafile/ system.274.788546943
9	530	PDB1:SYSAUX	***	+DATA/cdb1/c4bd35d102b92f07e04380a8840a6a44/datafile/ sysaux.275.788546943
10	5	PDB1:USERS	***	+DATA/cdb1/c4bd35d102b92f07e04380a8840a6a44/datafile/ users.277.788546967

```
List of Temporary Files
=======================
File Size(MB) Tablespace          Maxsize(MB) Tempfile Name
---- -------- ------------------- ----------- --------------------
1    532      TEMP                32767       +DATA/cdb1/tempfile/temp.269.788546767
2    20       PDB$SEED:TEMP       32767       +DATA/cdb1/c40f9b49fc9c19e0e0430baae80aff01/tempfile/
temp.272.788546809
3    20       PDB1:TEMP           32767       +DATA/cdb1/c4bd35d102b92f07e04380a8840a6a44/tempfile/
temp.276.788546957
```

The file is in the proper location now.

10. As a best practice, you should now create a fresh image copy of the file and place it in the fast recovery area:

```
RMAN> backup as copy datafile 6;
```

This step creates a new image copy of the file in the fast recovery area. Now you are well prepared for any future failure involving that same file.

How It Works

Although a quick switch to an image copy in the fast recovery area can get you back up and running with a minimal loss of time after a data file failure, running with a data file in the fast recovery area offers its own problems. The fast recovery area, by definition, is for backups. Many sites choose to put their fast recovery area on disks that are not as reliable as those used for the main database files. Perhaps those disks are not mirrored or are slower. You may not want to keep your now main data files there for long.

Even if your fast recovery area is on reliable disks, consider the implications of another failure. By design, you have strived to separate the storage of the main database and the fast recovery area to reduce the possibility of failure in both locations simultaneously. Keeping one data file in the fast recovery area violates that principle. You should move the data file back to the original location as soon as possible.

3-15. Backing Up the FRA to Tape

Problem

You want to back up the contents of the fast recovery area to tape to be shipped off-site and reuse the storage in the fast recovery area.

Solution

The fast recovery area is, after all, a disk location. This location is prone to the same failures as any other disk-based location. Again, because the Oracle Database starting with version 10g knows about the special purpose of the fast recovery location, it knows how to back it up to tape using just one command. Just define a channel to tape, and issue the special RMAN command backup recovery area:

```
RMAN> run {
2>   allocate channel c1 type sbt_tape;
3>   backup recovery area;
4> }
```

This run block backs up the entire fast recovery area to tape.

How It Works

This recipe first creates a channel based on tape. A lot of details have been omitted here on the channel allocation for tape drive. These details rely heavily on the type of media management library used. We discuss media management libraries used in tape backups in Chapter 18.

After the channel creation, the next command in the script backs up the fast recovery area to tape using a single command. RMAN knows the existence of the various types of files in the fast recovery area. After the backup to tape, RMAN marks the backed-up files as redundant and as candidates for deletion in the event that space needs to be freed. For instance, suppose your retention policy is that only one version of a backup is to be retained, and the backup of the files in the fast recovery area are themselves backed up to tape. Those backup files will be made obsolete. If there is no room on the fast recovery area and new backups need space, Oracle deletes those obsolete backup files since they are already available on the tape.

3-16. Sizing the Fast Recovery Area

Problem

While setting up the fast recovery area, you have to specify its size. If you specify a very low setting, backups will fail, and a high setting will waste space without adding a real value. How can you determine the correct size?

Solution

Sizing the fast recovery area is a rather complex topic, and getting to a reasonable size will require some analysis on your part. In this recipe, you will see how to use a worksheet to arrive at the optimal size of the fast recovery area for your database.

Here are the different files you are concerned with:

- Copy of all data files

- Incremental backups, as used by your chosen backup strategy

- Flashback logs (if enabled)

- Online redo logs

- Archived redo logs not yet backed up to tape

- Control files

- Control file auto backups (which include copies of the control file and spfile)

- Foreign archived logs (which are used in case of a logical standby database)

Since flashback logs are created only when the database runs in flashback mode, we will not include the space for those in this calculation. Decide how many versions to keep for each type, and determine how big each version of each file will be. You can get the size of each version by watching it for a few days. For instance, if the control file is 10MB, then you can assume that the control file auto backup will also be 10MB per backup set. For image copies, the size of the backups will be the same as the size of data files. For regular RMAN backups, you should observe the backup sets for a few days to get an idea about their sizes.

Once you determine the size of each type of file and have decided how many versions you should keep, you are ready for the next step. In this step, you decide what type of backup you will use. Your choices are as follows:

Regular RMAN backups: You back up incrementally (Level 1) every day and create a full backup (Level 0) at a longer frequency, say once a week. In this case, you will need to keep at least the prior Level 0 backup and all the Level 1 backups until the next Level 0 backup. However, you must keep the first Level 0 backup intact until the second Level 0 backup successfully completes. If the second Level 0 backup fails, you will need the first one to recover. For archived redo logs, you can back up and delete them after you create an incremental Level 1 backup. So, here is the minimum number of files you should plan for:

- Two copies of Level 0 backup

- Six days of incremental Level 1 backups

- Two days of archived redo logs

Of course, these are suggested minimums. If you plan to have redundancy in the backups or you plan to retain longer for the purpose of doing a point-in-time recovery, you will need more space for more files, and you'll need to increase the numbers given here to values appropriate for your plans.

RMAN image copies: The frequency is similar to the regular backup option. You'll take a Level 0 backup every week and a Level 1 backup every day. Again, here are some suggestions regarding minimum file counts:

- Two copies of Level 0 backup

- Six days of incremental Level 1 backups

- Two days of archived redo logs

RMAN image copies with the merge backup option: Here you can take an incremental backup every day but merge that with the Level 0 backup already present. This option does not need the incremental backups to be kept, since they are merged with the Level 0 backup. You need space for only one incremental backup and only one Level 0 backup. Here are the minimum quantities of files that you need to keep:

- One image copy

- One incremental Level 1 backup

- Two days of archived redo logs

Once you decide the exact alternative to choose from the preceding list, figure out the size of the following components:

RMAN regular backup set Level 0 backup: You can get the size of this component by watching the space it takes from one RMAN run. Since RMAN regular backups skip the unused blocks, the size will be less than the total database size, and you can determine that by watching a Level 0 backup set. Assume it is 2,500GB.

RMAN image copies: Getting the size of these files is simple. Just add up the size of all the data files. The following query shows it:

```
SQL> select sum(bytes)/1024/1024
  2  from dba_data_files;
```

```
SUM(BYTES)/1024/1024
--------------------
          3188263.55
```

Now you know that each Level 0 image copy of the database takes about 3,188,263.55MB, or 3TB.

RMAN incremental level 1 backup: this is something you have to determine by watching how big each incremental level 1 takes. Assume it's 200gb.

Archived redo logs for a day: You can get the total size of the archived redo logs generated and the count by issuing the following query:

```
select count(1), avg(blocks*block_size)/1024 MB
from v$archived_log
where completion_time between sysdate-1 and sysdate
```

Suppose the output comes back as follows:

```
   COUNT(1)                    MB
---------- ---------------------
        10             103657472
```

From the output, you know every day the database generates about ten archived redo logs of the total size 103,657,472KB, or about 100GB.

Size of the control file: Assume it to be 200MB for this example's purposes.

Taking the numbers you've come up, you can use the worksheet shown in Table 3-6 to arrive at the size of the fast recovery area.

Table 3-6. *Worksheet to Calculate the Size of the FRA*

Type	Size per File or Set	Total per Cycle (Week)	Total	Description
Full backup set				Put how many of the Level 0 backup sets are required and the size of each.
Image copies				If you use image copies instead of backup sets, use this instead.
Archived redo logs				Calculate how many archived redo logs are needed. If you take a daily incremental Level 1 or Level 0 backup, you need about two days of archived about two days of archived redo logs. Remember, this is themselves.not the archived redo logs the archived redo log backups, themselves.
Incremental copy of the data files				Size of incremental Level 1 RMAN backup.
Control file auto backup				Put the size of the control file auto backup.
Total space required				Count the sum of the space needed.

How It Works

Sizing a fast recovery area is simple in concept. Decide on a backup strategy. Work through each file type to determine how much fast recovery area space each file type needs. Add everything up. Allocate that amount of space. The key to success is to carefully think through the details.

By the way, in this recipe we have assumed that the fast recovery area to be sized will be used for only one database. If you have more than database to back up to the same area, calculate the space for each database, and sum the resulting values to arrive at a size that will suffice for a combined fast recovery area serving all the databases.

Tables 3-7 through 3-9 show several working examples of our sizing worksheet. There's one example for each of the three backup strategies that we listed earlier in the solution section. Our file sizes and counts won't match yours, of course, but you can see how the different values in the worksheets ultimately lead to a size recommendation for the fast recovery area.

Table 3-7. *Sizing the FRA for Regular RMAN Backup*

Type	Size per File or Set	Total per Cycle (Week)	Total	Description
Full backup set	2,500	2	5,000	We need 2 Level 0 backups per cycle, that is, a week.
Image copies	0	0	0	We take RMAN backup sets in this option, so this is not required.
Archived redo logs	100	2	200	Two days' worth of archived redo logs backup.
Incremental copy of the data files	200	6	600	
Control file auto backup	0.2	7	1.4	
Total space required			5,801.40	

Table 3-8. *Sizing the FRA for RMAN Image Backup*

Type	Size per File or Set	Total per Cycle (Week)	Total	Description
Full backup set	0	0	0	We use image copies, so this is zero.
Image copies	3,000	2	6,000	We need 2 Level 0 backups per cycle, that is, a week.
Archived redo logs	100	2	200	Two days' worth of archived redo logs backup.
Incremental copy of the data files	200	6	600	
Control file auto backup	0.2	7	1.4	
Total space required			6,801.40	

Table 3-9. *Sizing the FRA for RMAN Image Backup with Merge*

Type	Size per File or Set	Total per Cycle (Week)	Total	Description
Full backup set	0	0	0	We use image copies, so this is zero.
Image copies	3,000	1	3,000	We need only one Level 0 backup per cycle, that is, a week, which is updated every day by merging the incremental.
Archived redo logs	100	2	200	Two days' worth of archived redo logs backup.
Incremental copy	200	1	200	Since we merge the Level 1 incremental backups with the Level 0 one, we will not need six of them; only one will be present at any point.
Control file auto backup	0.2	2	0.4	There is no need to control file backups since each day the incremental is merged with the Level 0.
Total space required			3,400.40	

CHAPTER 4

■ ■ ■

Using RMAN

You can start using RMAN to back up and recover your databases with very little fanfare. When you install the Oracle server software, you'll automatically install RMAN as well. You only absolutely need two things to start using RMAN: the database you want to back up (referred to as the *target database*) and the RMAN client, which is the interface you use to interact with the RMAN server processes that perform the actual backup and recovery tasks.

When you use RMAN to back up and recover your database files and objects, you use the RMAN client to interact with the database. The RMAN client interprets the RMAN commands you issue and starts up the necessary server sessions to process those commands. The term *RMAN repository* refers to the record of RMAN metadata about all backup and recovery actions on the target database. RMAN relies on this metadata when it performs backup and recovery operations.

By default, RMAN always stores a copy of the RMAN repository in the target database's control file. Optionally, you can also use a *recovery catalog* for long-term storage of the RMAN repository. Whenever there is a change in the database structure, archived redo logs, or backups, RMAN updates the recovery catalog with the new information from the target database control file. This way, you have an alternate source for the all-important RMAN repository data if you lose or can't access the control file of the target database. In addition, the recovery catalog provides a long-term storage capacity for all RMAN backup and recovery information, whereas such older data is liable to be overwritten in the control file. The recovery catalog exists as a separate database schema, located ideally in a database separate from the target database(s). You can simplify your RMAN administration by using a single recovery catalog for all your Oracle databases.

You start up the RMAN client using the RMAN executable rman, which you'll find in the $ORACLE_HOME/bin directory. In addition to the rman executable, RMAN also comes with two other internal components: one a set of PL/SQL procedures in the target database and the other a file named recover.bsq. RMAN turns the backup and recovery commands you issue into PL/SQL procedure calls using the recover.bsq file to construct the calls. After you start the RMAN client, you must log in using either operating system credentials or database authentication. After logging in, you can issue backup and recovery instructions either by entering RMAN commands at the command line or by executing a script file that contains RMAN commands. You can also issue several types of SQL commands from the RMAN command line. After you finish your backup and recovery session, you exit the RMAN client.

In addition to the target database and the RMAN client, the RMAN environment can have other optional elements. If you follow the Oracle's backup and recovery recommendations (see Chapter 1), you may also have a fast recovery area. In addition, you must have a media management layer (MML) to interact with tape drives, since RMAN can't work directly with the tape drives. RMAN can use either a third-party MML or Oracle's own backup and recovery offering, called Oracle Secure Backup. The MML accesses and controls the tape libraries and manages the loading and unloading of tapes.

Finally, if you plan on working with several databases, it may be a smart idea to use an RMAN catalog database, which is a separate Oracle database dedicated to storing the recovery catalog. Although the recovery catalog isn't mandatory, it provides two important advantages over using the database control file to store the RMAN metadata relating to backup and recovery activity: you can store vastly greater amounts of data in the recovery catalog as compared to a control file, and you can store RMAN scripts inside the recovery catalog. By default, all RMAN-related records in the target database's control file are overwritten after seven days, but you can control the length of retention by setting a higher value for the initialization parameter control_file_record_keep_time.

One may argue that since the control file can record all of RMAN's metadata, there is no need to create and manage a separate recovery catalog database to store RMAN metadata. However, consider a situation where you lose all your control file copies at once. You can, of course, rebuild the control file quickly using the output of a recent `alter database backup controlfile to trace` command. However, when you re-create the control file using the output of that command, the one thing you do not get back is all the RMAN metadata that used to be stored in the control file! This and the fact that Oracle may always overwrite even useful RMAN metadata in the control file means you should seriously consider using the recovery catalog. Oracle recommends using a recovery catalog in order to provide redundancy for your RMAN metadata. Chapter 6 discusses the recovery catalog in detail.

4-1. Starting the RMAN Client

Problem

You want to start working with the RMAN tool and need to use the RMAN client.

Solution

Invoke the RMAN executable, which is named rman, to start the RMAN client. The RMAN executable file is always in the $ORACLE_HOME/bin directory. If you've set your ORACLE_HOME environment variable, you'll be able to invoke RMAN from any directory by simply entering the command rman at the command prompt:

```
[oracle@virtual1 ~]$ rman

Recovery Manager: Release 12.1.0.0.2 - Beta on Tue Jul 24 10:41:54 2012

Copyright (c) 1982, 2012, Oracle and/or its affiliates. All rights reserved.

RMAN>
```

When the RMAN prompt is displayed, you aren't connected to a target database or the recovery catalog. You must, of course, connect to the target database, the recovery catalog, or the auxiliary database (or sometimes all of them) to perform backup and recovery tasks. Once you finish working with RMAN, you shut down the Recovery Manager by using the command exit at the RMAN prompt:

```
RMAN> exit

Recovery Manager complete.
[oracle@virtual1 ~]$
```

You can also use the QUIT command to terminate your rman session, as shown here:

```
RMAN> quit
```

How It Works

The command rman starts the RMAN client. Once the RMAN prompt is displayed, you can choose to connect to the target database, the recovery catalog, or an auxiliary database. If you issue any RMAN command at this stage, RMAN will use the RMAN repository in the default nocatalog mode. You can't use the connect catalog command to connect to the recovery catalog after having issued RMAN commands in the nocatalog mode—you must first exit RMAN before you can restart and make a connection to the recovery catalog.

■ **Note** Your connection to a database through RMAN is authenticated just as a regular connection to a database through a tool such as SQL*Plus. If you're using an Oracle 12c release database, you must just make sure to grant the user the SYSBACKUP privilege to enable the user to make an RMAN connection to a database.

Even if you've set the Oracle-specific operating system environment variables correctly, you may find that absolutely nothing happens when you execute the rman command, as shown in the previous example. If you have a problem starting the client, simply specify the complete path to the RMAN executable when you invoke RMAN:

```
$ $ORACLE_HOME/bin/rman
```

The reason you may need to specify the full path names is that in some operating systems, the command rman may be pointing not to the Recovery Manager executable but to another executable on Linux with an identical name (rman). You can verify whether that's the case by issuing the which command in Linux (and Unix), which tells you which particular version of an executable is being executed. For example, the following command will reveal the exact RMAN executable that's executed:

```
[oracle@virtual1 ~]$ which rman
/u01/app/oracle/product/12.1.0/db_1/bin/rman
[oracle@virtual1 ~]$
```

If you've placed the $ORACLE_HOME/bin location at the beginning of the PATH environmental variable, you should have no problems accessing the rman executable just as you would any other Oracle executable such as SQL*Plus, for example.

4-2. Issuing RMAN Commands

Problem

You'd like to start working with RMAN and issue the various RMAN commands to back up your database and to manage those backups.

Solution

RMAN uses a free-form command language. Each RMAN command statement starts with a keyword, is followed by specific arguments, and ends with a semicolon. A command can be one line or multiple lines. For example, the following single-line command initiates a backup of the target database:

```
RMAN> backup database;
```

If you enter a partial command and hit Enter, RMAN will prompt you to continue the input and will provide a line number as well. In the following example, the command requests RMAN to back up the database along with its control file:

```
RMAN> backup database
   2> include current
   3> controlfile
   4> ;
```

You can add comments to your RMAN commands, which makes it easy to follow the logic of your RMAN commands when you use several of them inside a command file (we discuss RMAN command files later in this chapter). Each comment must be preceded by the # sign. Here's an example of an RMAN command file that performs an incremental backup of the database:

```
# this command will be run daily
backup incremental level 1
for recover of copy # uses incrementally updated backups
database;
```

This RMAN code includes two comments, each preceded by the hash (#) sign. Notice how you can make an entire line into a comment, or merely append a comment to the end of a line containing a command. The example shows both approaches.

How It Works

When you begin entering a command, RMAN buffers every line that you enter until you end a line with a semicolon. Any text on a line following a # sign is considered commentary and is ignored. When you enter the terminating semicolon, RMAN executes the command that you've entered. Although you aren't supposed to use reserved keywords as part of the arguments you supply to RMAN commands, you can, if you want, use reserved keywords (such as file name, tablespace name, or tag name) by simply enclosing them within single or double quotes, as shown in the following example, which specifies a tag named "full" (which is an RMAN reserved word):

```
RMAN> backup database tag 'full';
```

In general, it's probably best to avoid using RMAN keywords for things such as channel names.

4-3. Saving RMAN Output to a Text File
Problem

You want to save the output of an RMAN session to a text file.

Solution

You can save RMAN output to a text file by issuing the spool command and specifying the name of the log file. You don't have to create the log file beforehand. Here's an example showing how to use the spool command:

```
RMAN> spool log to '/tmp/rman/backuplog.f';
RMAN> backup datafile 1;
RMAN> spool log off;

Spooling for log turned off

Recovery Manager12.1.0.0.2

RMAN>
```

RMAN will create the log file if it doesn't already exist. If a file with the same name exists, RMAN will overwrite the older file.

How It Works

The `spool` command works the same way as it does in SQL*Plus. If the file with the same name you specify already exists, RMAN will overwrite the file, unless you specify the append option. For example:

```
spool log to '/tmp/rman/backuplog.f' append
```

The `spool` command will add the new contents to the end of the log file named backuplog.f.

4-4. Logging Command-Line RMAN Output
Problem

You want to log the output of RMAN commands you issue in command-line mode.

Solution

If you want RMAN to log all its output when you use RMAN from the operating system command line, just add the keyword `log` to the command line, and supply the name of the log file to use. For example:

```
[oracle@virtual1 ~]$ rman target / cmdfile commandfile1.rcv  log /u01/app/oracle/outfile.txt
[oracle@virtual1 ~]$
```

In this case, RMAN will write the output of the RMAN commands in the command file named commandfile1.rcv to the log file outfile.txt. If you later want to run another set of RMAN commands and want to append the log messages to the same log file, you can do this by using the append option along with the log option. Here's an example:

```
[oracle@virtual1 ~]$ rman target / cmdfile commandfile2.rcv log /u01/app/oracle/outfile.txt append
[oracle@virtual1 ~]$
```

The previous command will append the output from executing the command file commandfile2.rcv to the text file outfile.txt.

How It Works

The command-line argument `log` causes RMAN to send all its output to the log file you specify. Failure to add the keyword append when referring to an existing log file will result in the overwriting of that older log file.

If you are running RMAN interactively and you want to see output on your terminal screen as well as have it written to a log file, you can take advantage of the Unix/Linux `tee` command. The `tee` command sends output both to a text file and to the terminal. Here's how you use the `tee` command:

```
[oracle@virtual1 ~]$ rman | tee rman.log

Recovery Manager: Release 12.1.0.0.2 - Beta on Tue Jul 24 10:46:25 2012

Copyright (c) 1982, 2012, Oracle and/or its affiliates. All rights reserved.

RMAN>
```

All is not lost if you don't specify a log file to capture the RMAN output. The view V$RMAN_OUTPUT returns detailed information about RMAN jobs in progress. For example, if your media manager runs into a problem with a tape drive, RMAN records the associated error messages in V$RMAN_OUTPUT and also outputs the message to the terminal or to a log file. As with all dynamic performance views, the contents of the V$RMAN_OUTPUT view are refreshed when you restart the database. The V$RMAN_STATUS view contains information about completed RMAN jobs as well as all RMAN jobs in progress.

4-5. Connecting to a Target Database from the RMAN Prompt
Problem

You want to connect to your target database from the RMAN prompt.

Solution

After you invoke the RMAN client, you can connect to a target database from the RMAN prompt to perform backup and recovery tasks. A target database is the database where you want to perform RMAN backup or recovery actions. You can connect only to a single target database at a time. You can connect with operating system authentication, or by validating your password against a password file. You must have the SYSDBA (or another administrative privilege, such as SYSBACKUP) to connect to the target database. However, you do not use the as sysdba clause that you have to use in SQL*Plus when connecting to a database with sysdba privileges. RMAN automatically expects that you have the sysdba privilege and attempts the database connection with that privilege.

You can connect to a target database either by using an operating system authentication method or by supplying the database credentials (provided you use a password file). Here's an example showing how to make a connection using operating system authentication (first make sure you have set the correct ORACLE_SID variable):

```
RMAN> connect target /

connected to target database: ORCL (DBID=1316762630)

RMAN>
```

And here's an example showing how to log in using a database username and password that are authenticated against the password file:

```
[oracle@virtual1 ~]$ rman

Recovery Manager: Release 12.1.0.0.2 - Beta on Tue Jul 24 10:51:39 2012

Copyright (c) 1982, 2012, Oracle and/or its affiliates. All rights reserved.

RMAN> connect target sys/Ninamma11@orcl

connected to target database: ORCL (DBID=1316762630)

RMAN>
```

This method of connection is also called the *Oracle Net password file* authentication method.

How It Works

To use operating system authentication rather than database authorization to connect to a target database, you must first set your environment correctly so that the ORACLE_SID points to the correct database. Having done that, you can specify target / to connect to the target database. As long as you belong to the dba group in Unix/Linux or to the ora_dba group on Windows, you can connect to the database without specifying a username and password.

When you're using password file authentication, the keyword target must specify a database connection string, such as target sys/sammyy1@mydb. If you want to make a privileged database connection from RMAN, you must have already created an Oracle password file. The username and password that you give to RMAN must match those recorded in the password file.

> **Note** See the sidebar Creating an Oracle Password File for help creating such a file.

CREATING AN ORACLE PASSWORD FILE

You can easily create an Oracle password file with the help of the orapwd utility. Just type orapwd at the operating system command line to view the syntax of the command:

```
[oracle@virtual1 ~]$ orapwd
Usage: orapwd file=<fname> entries=<users> force=<y/n> ignorecase=<y/n>
       asm=<y/n> dbuniquename=<dbname> format=<legacy/12> sysbackup=<y/n>
       sysdg=<y/n> delete=<y/n> input_file=<input-fname>
  where
    file - name of password file (required),
    password - password for SYS will be prompted
               if not specified at command line.
               Ignored, if input_file is specified,
    entries - maximum number of distinct DBA (optional),
    force - whether to overwrite existing file (optional),
    ignorecase - passwords are case-insensitive (optional),
    asm - indicates that the password to be stored in
          Automatic Storage Management (ASM) disk group
          is an ASM password. (optional).
    dbuniquename - unique database name used to identify database
                   password files residing in ASM diskgroup only.
                   Ignored when asm option is specified (optional),
    format - use format=12 for new 12c features like SYSBACKUP, SYSDG and
             SYSKM support, longer identifiers, etc.
             If not specified, format=12 is default (optional),
    delete - drops a password file. Must specify 'asm',
             'dbuniquename' or 'file'. If 'file' is specified,
             the file must be located on an ASM diskgroup (optional),
    sysbackup - create SYSBACKUP entry (optional and requires the
                12 format). Ignored, if input_file is specified,
    sysdg - create SYSDG entry (optional and requires the 12 format).
            Ignored, if input_file is specified,
```

```
    input_file - name of input password file, from where old user
                entries will be migrated (optional).

   There must be no spaces around the equal-to (=) character.
 [oracle@virtual1 ~]$
```

There are a lot more options you can specify for the orapwd utility in the Oracle Database 12g release. Of the twelve options for the orapwd utility, only the file option is mandatory. You can create a simple Oracle password file using the following syntax:

```
[oracle@virtual1 ~]$ orapwd file=mydb_pwd

Enter password for SYS:
[oracle@virtual1 ~]$
```

The orapwd command shown here creates the password file named *mydb_pwd*. Once you restart your database after this, you'll be able to log in as the sys user.

4-6. Connecting to a Target Database from the Operating System Command Line

Problem

You want to invoke the RMAN client and connect to the target database from the operating system command line.

Solution

You can make a connection to the target database from the operating system by using the same two methods of connection you use to connect to a target database from within RMAN. That is, you can use either operating system authentication or Oracle Net authentication.

Here's an example showing how to connect to a target database from the command line using operating system authentication:

```
[oracle@virtual1 ~]$ rman target /

Recovery Manager: Release 12.1.0.0.2 - Beta on Mon Aug 6 09:59:44 2012

Copyright (c) 1982, 2012, Oracle and/or its affiliates. All rights reserved.

connected to target database: ORCL (DBID=1316762630)

RMAN>
```

You can also connect to the target database from the command line using Oracle Net password file authentication, as shown here:

```
% rman target sys/<sys password>@trgt
```

How It Works

Once you see the RMAN prompt, you're ready to issue the RMAN commands. RMAN always attempts a database connection assuming you are connecting with the SYSDBA (or other administrative privileges such as SYSOPER, SYSASSM, SYSDG or SYSKM, with some of these being new privileges introduced in the Oracle Datbase 12c release) sysdba privilege. If you're having problems connecting to a target database, first check that you can connect to the database from SQL*Plus using the sysdba privilege, as shown in this example:

```
SQL> connect sys/Ninamma11@orcl as sysdba
Connected.
SQL>
```

4-7. Executing Operating System Commands from Within RMAN
Problem

You've invoked the RMAN client, and now you need to issue some operating system commands.

Solution

Use the RMAN command host to invoke an operating system subshell. You can execute this command in two ways: you can issue it from the RMAN prompt, or you can execute it from inside a run block, which is a group of RMAN commands executed as a single unit. If you issue the host command stand-alone, without any parameters, RMAN will take you to the operating system command line. Thus, the host command works the same in RMAN as it does from within SQL*Plus. If you issue the command host followed by a valid operating system command as a parameter, then RMAN will execute that operating system command and continue to process the rest of the commands in the run block, if there are any.

In the following example, we use the HOST command to list all files ending with *DBF*, after backing up a data file from the RMAN prompt:

```
RMAN> shutdown immediate;
RMAN> startup mount;
RMAN> backup datafile '/u01/app/oracle/oradata/targ/system01.dbf'
      format  '/tmp/system01.dbf';
RMAN> host  'ls -l /tmp/*dbf';
RMAN> alter database open;
```

Note that when you execute the host command from within RMAN, you must enclose the command with single quotes or double quotes, and also terminate the command with a semicolon, as shown in the host command example here. The following example uses the host command with no parameters, which enables you to temporarily escape to the operating system level during an interactive RMAN session:

```
RMAN> backup datafile 3 format '/u01/app/oracle/oradata/targ_db/dbs01.cpy';
RMAN> host;
   $ ls $ORACLE_HOME/oradata/dbs01.cpy
     /net/oracle/oradata/dbs01.cpy
   $ exit
RMAN>
```

How It Works

As you can see in the two examples, you can use the host command with or without an operating system command as a parameter. If you run the host command as part of a series of RMAN commands, RMAN executes the host command and continues with the rest of the commands. When you execute the host command by itself, RMAN displays the operating system command prompt and resumes after you exit the command-line subshell.

4-8. Scripting RMAN

Problem

You want to automate an RMAN process by executing a set of commands that you've placed into a script file. You don't want to type each command one at a time. You want to start the entire sequence of commands and walk away while they execute. You may even want to execute your script periodically via a job scheduler, such as cron.

Solution

It's common practice to include RMAN backup scripts within an operating system shell script. Doing so allows you to schedule your backup jobs via cron to run automatically. The following is an example of an operating system shell script to back up a database. The script executes various RMAN backup commands to perform an incremental backup of a database as well as delete all expired archive logs.

Notice the <<- EOF notation in lines 2 and 5 and the corresponding EOF markers in lines 4 and 18. Use <<- EOF to tell the shell interpreter that input to the command in question is to be read from the shell script file until an EOF marker is encountered. You can replace the letters EOF with any sequence that you like, but you really should stick with the universally recognized convention of EOF.

```
#!/bin/ksh
export ORACLE_SID=$1
export LEVEL=$2
export TIMESTAMP='date +'%Y%m%d''
export BACKUP_DIR=/u01/app/oracle/backup
export LOGFILE=${BACKUP_DIR}/rman-level$(LEVEL)_$(TIMESTAMP).log
rman target / catalog rman/rman@rcat > ${LOGFILE} <<- EOF
sql 'alter system archive log current';
change archivelog all crosscheck;
allocate channel for maintenance type disk;
delete noprompt expired archivelog all;
run {
allocate channel ch1 type disk format
'${BACKUP_DIR}/%d_level${LEVEL}_${TIMESTAMP}_%s_U%U.bak';
set limit channel ch1 kbytes=2000000;
backup incremental level ${LEVEL} (database);
release channel ch1;
resync catalog;
}
EOF
```

Once you create the script and make it executable, you run it as follows, by specifying the database name and the backup level (1 in this example):

```
[oracle@virtual1 rman]$ ./backup.sh orcl 1.
```

When this script executes, whether it is run from the command line or fired off as a cron job, the script will start up RMAN, connect to the target database, and execute the commands to back up that database.

Alternatively, you can write RMAN files that are sequences of RMAN commands. Then you can invoke RMAN from the command line to execute those files. For example, suppose you have a file called *full_backup.rman* consisting of the following run block:

```
run {
   allocate channel d1 type disk;
   backup full database format '/export/rman/rman_%n_%T_%s_%p.bus';
   }
```

You can then invoke RMAN from the operating system command line to execute this file as follows:

```
$ rman target / @full_backup.rman
```

The use of @ followed immediately by the file name causes RMAN to read and execute commands from the specified file.

How It Works

The full benefits of RMAN come when you use it to automate your backup and recovery tasks. Key to doing that is the ability to define sequences of commands that you can execute on demand or on a regular schedule. The solution section shows two general approaches you can take:

- You can embed your RMAN scripts within shell scripts. The advantage here is that you have all commands—both shell and RMAN commands—in one place.

- You can place your RMAN scripts into their own files. This approach works on non-Unix systems, such as Windows. It also enables you to execute those files interactively from the RMAN client.

The solution shows @ as a command-line parameter to rman. You can also use @ from within RMAN to interactively execute a file. For example, you can run the following three scripts to first shut down the database, then perform a full backup of the database, and finally open the database after the backup is completed:

```
RMAN> @close_database
RMAN> @full_backup.rman
RMAN> @open_database
```

The @ parameter works from within a run block as well as directly from the RMAN prompt. You can substitute the command cmdfile for @, but most DBAs use @ because it's easier to type and because @ has a long history of being used to invoke scripts in Oracle.

4-9. Executing RMAN Command Files
Problem
You want to automate an RMAN process by executing a set of commands you've placed into a script file. You don't want to type each command one at a time. You want to start the entire sequence of commands and walk away while they execute.

■ **Note** This recipe shows you how to execute a file containing just RMAN commands. This differs from the solution in Recipe 4-7, which shows you how to embed RMAN commands in operating system shell scripts.

Solution
Instead of entering each command piecemeal, you can create a *command file* with a number of commands and execute the command file. Use the keyword `cmdfile` to let RMAN know that it must execute the commands inside the script file command. The individual commands in the command file will execute as if they were entered from the command line. Here's an example showing how to execute a command file named commandfile.rcv:

```
$ rman target / cmdfile commandfile.rcv
```

In this example, the commandfile.rcv file is in the same directory from which you're executing the `cmdfile` command. If the command file is elsewhere, you must provide the complete path name to access that file. For example:

```
$ rman target / cmdfile /oracle/dbs/cmd/commandfile.rcv
```

You can also execute a command file by placing the @ sign in front of the command file, as shown in the following example:

```
$ rman target / @commandfile.rcv
```

You aren't limited to invoking command files from the command line, though that is very useful when using `cron` to automate your work. You also have the option of running command files interactively from the RMAN prompt:

```
$ rman target /
RMAN> @commandfile.rcv
RMAN>
```

This approach is useful when you want to execute a script of RMAN commands and then do more work from the RMAN command line. After executing the command file, you'll be back at the RMAN prompt.

Once RMAN finishes executing the contents of the command file you specify, control returns to RMAN once again, and you'll see the following comment on the screen:

```
RMAN> **end-of-file**
```

You'll still be at the RMAN command line after the command file finishes executing.

How It Works

The RMAN session will terminate immediately after the command file finishes executing. There's an important difference to be aware of regarding how RMAN reacts to syntax errors in command files. The difference depends upon whether you invoke RMAN to execute a command file from the operating system prompt or whether you invoke a command file interactively from the RMAN prompt. Here's what you need to know:

- When you run an RMAN file from the operating system line, RMAN will first try to parse all the RMAN commands in the file. Then RMAN will start executing each in a sequential fashion. If RMAN encounters any errors at the parse stage or during the execution phase, it'll immediately exit.

- On the other hand, when you run an RMAN file from the RMAN prompt, RMAN executes each command separately and will exit only after it attempts the execution of the last command in the file.

In addition to executing a command file from the RMAN prompt, you can also call a command file from within another command file. Use the double at (@@) command for that purpose. When you issue the @@ command inside a command file, RMAN will look for the file specified after the @@ command in the same directory as that of the command file from which it was called. For example:

```
$ rman @$ORACLE_HOME/rdbms/admin/dba/scripts/cmd1.rman
```

In this example, the command @@cmd2.rman is specified within the cmd1.rman command file. Once you execute the main or parent command file (cmd1.rman), the @@ command within the cmd1.rman file makes RMAN l look for and execute the cmd2.rman command file in the directory $ORACLE_HOME/rdbms/admin/dba/scripts/, the same directory that holds the parent command file. The @@ command is useful when you have a set of related command files, because you can place all those files into one directory and they can all find each other automatically after that point.

4-10. Creating Dynamic Command Files

Problem

You want to create dynamic command files that can be used for multiple jobs by passing substitution variables.

Solution

You can create dynamic shell scripts by using substitution variables in the RMAN command files inside the shell scripts. You can specify values for use in substitution variables through the new using clause when calling an RMAN command file. You use the *&integer* syntax (&1, &2, and so on) to indicate to which variable your substitution values should be assigned, just as in SQL*Plus.

Let's review an example that shows how to create a dynamic backup shell script.

1. Create the RMAN command file that uses two substitution variables:

```
#backup.cmd
connect target sys/<sys_password>@prod1
run {
backup database
tag &1
format '&2 ';
}
exit;
```

2. The command file shown here will back up the database using two substitution variables (&1 and &2), one for the backup tag and the other for the string value in the `format` specification.

3. Create the shell script to run the backup command file you created in step 1:

```
#!/bin/ksh
# script name: nightly_backup.sh
set tag=$argv[1]
set format=$argv[2]
rman  @backup.cmd using  $tag $format
```

4. Now that you have created a dynamic shell script, you can specify the arguments for the `tag` and `format` variables on the command line, thus being able to modify them for different jobs. Here's an example:

```
$ nightly_backup.sh longterm_backup back0420
```

The example shows how to execute the shell script `nightly_backup.sh` with two dynamic parameters, `longterm_backup` (tag) and `back0420` (format string).

How It Works

The ability to use substitution variables in RMAN scripts is new in Oracle Database 11g. The use of substitution variables in RMAN scripts is similar to the way you specify substitution variables in operating system and SQL*Plus scripts. Specifying substitution variables lets you use the same command file by modifying it appropriately for different backup tasks, thus making the command file dynamic.

4-11. Connecting to an Auxiliary Database
Problem

You need to connect to an auxiliary database to duplicate a database or to perform a tablespace point-in-time recovery.

Solution

You can connect to an auxiliary instance either from the operating system command line or from the RMAN prompt. To connect to an auxiliary database instance from the operating system command line, simply replace the usual keyword `target` with the keyword `auxiliary`, as shown here:

```
$ rman auxiliary sys/<sys_password>@aux
```

You can also start the RMAN client first and then connect to the auxiliary instance from the RMAN prompt, as shown in this example:

```
$ rman
RMAN> connect auxiliary sys/<sys_password>@aux
```

How It Works

You mostly connect to an auxiliary database to perform a duplicate command or to perform a tablespace point-in-time recovery (TSPITR) operation. The syntax is the same as for connecting to a target database, except that you specify the keyword auxiliary rather than target.

Note that you can't connect to the three types of databases—auxiliary, target, and catalog database—with one connection string once you're working from the RMAN command prompt, whereas you can connect to all three types from the operating system prompt. Once you're operating from an RMAN prompt, you have to connect using separate connect commands for each of the three databases, one after the other, as shown in the following examples:

```
RMAN> connect target sys/<sys_password>@trgt
RMAN> connect catalog rman/<rman_password>@catalog
RMAN> connect auxiliary sys/<sys_password>@aux
```

The following example shows how you can connect to all three types of database in one go from the operating system command line:

```
% rman target sys/oracle@trgt catalog rman/cat@catalog auxiliary sys/aux@aux
```

As you'll see in Chapter 15, when creating a duplicate database, you may not be able to connect to all three instances at once in this fashion, since the auxiliary database may not be open and hence may not permit the use of a connection string to connect to it.

4-12. Executing Multiple RMAN Commands as a Single Unit

Problem

When you are setting up the environment for some RMAN backup and recovery commands from the command line, you'll sometimes need to execute multiple RMAN commands as one atomic operation. That is, you want all commands to be run sequentially if they are syntactically correct but want the entire operation to fail if any of the commands in the group aren't valid.

Solution

You use the RMAN special syntax known as the run block when you want to group a set of RMAN commands into a block and execute the commands serially. RMAN will treat the entire set of commands as one single block, which it'll execute sequentially. The series of commands is enclosed within a beginning and an ending set of curly braces, and the entire set of commands is called a run block.

A common use to which you can put the run block is to override one or more default configuration settings for the duration of a backup job. For instance, you can use a run block to allocate channels using the allocate command to override the automatic channels that you configured using the configure command. In the following example, the run block first manually allocates two channels for the disk devices and then backs up the database:

```
RMAN> run
2> {
3> allocate channel t1 device type disk format '/u01/app/oracle/backup/%U';
4> allocate channel t2 device type disk format '/u01/app/oracle/backup/%U';
5> backup database;
6> }
```

Here's one more example, this time showing how you use the `set` command to temporarily change the value of a parameter within a `run` block. Let's say you configured data file copies to three using the following command:

```
RMAN> configure datafile backup copies for device type sbt to 3;
```

You can override the default of three copies by using the following `run` block, where the `set` command sets the number of backup copies to only two. You'll thus get two copies of each data file and archive log that's part of the backup.

```
run
{
  allocate channel  dev1 device type sbt;
  set backup copies = 2;
  backup datafile 1,2,3,4,5;
  backup archivelog all;
}
```

Once the `run` block finishes executing, the data file copies for tape devices will be set to three again, per your configured settings.

How It Works

You can execute a `run` block from the RMAN command line by entering each line sequentially, but it's more common to employ the `run` block from inside a command file. You can then execute the command file from the RMAN prompt or use it inside a `cron` job. The `run` block is useful when you want to schedule RMAN jobs, say, through the `cron` facility. Once RMAN completes checking the syntax of the input lines in the `run` block, it'll execute each statement sequentially.

When RMAN encounters the closing brace of a `run` block, it groups the commands into one or more job steps and starts executing the job step(s) immediately. Frequently you use a `run` block to override the default configured channels or other parameters for a certain task and then reset the channels or parameters to their original values before finishing the `run` block. RMAN uses the `allocate channel` and `release channel` commands to override the default configured channels for a task. You use the `set` command to change other parameters. You can specify the allocate channel and set commands within a `run` block to override the default values of key RMAN backup and recovery settings for a particular job.

You can use some RMAN commands only within a `run` block. These commands, such as `allocate channel` and `set newname for datafile`, are typically used to set the execution environment for the other RMAN commands within the `run` block. Conversely, you can't use some of the RMAN commands dealing with configuration and environmental settings within a `run` block. For example, you can't use the following commands from within a `run` block:

```
connect, configure
create catalog, drop catalog, upgrade catalog
create script, delete script, replace script
list
report
```

Note that you can use any of the commands listed previously inside a command file, as long as you don't enclose them inside a `run` block. In Chapter 9 you'll learn about storing RMAN scripts, known as *stored scripts*, within the recovery catalog. Since all commands inside a stored script must be enclosed in a `run` block, it means you can't use any of the commands listed here in a stored script as well.

When you invoke an RMAN script, you must do so only within a run block, as shown in the following example, where the script backup_db is executed using a run block:

```
run {execute script backup_db; }
```

We discuss RMAN scripting in detail in Chapter 9.

4-13. Issuing SQL Statements from the RMAN Client

Problem

You're using RMAN to issue backup and recovery commands, and you find that you need to issue some SQL statements as well.

Solution

It's easy to execute an SQL statement from RMAN. All you need to do is type the keyword SQL followed by the actual SQL statement. Make sure you enclose the actual SQL statement inside single or double quotes, if you're dealing with a pre–Oracle Database 12c release database. For example:

```
RMAN> SQL 'alter system archive log all';
```

You can execute SQL statements from within a run block, too. The following run block restores and then recovers the tablespace tools:

```
run
{
  SQL "alter tablespace tools offline immediate";
  restore tablespace tools;
  recover tablespace tools;
  SQL "alter tablespace tools online";
}
```

The example shown here illustrates how you can interleave SQL statements and RMAN commands within a single run block. The first SQL statement takes the tools tablespace offline. Following this, the two RMAN commands first restore and then recover the tools tablespace. The final SQL statement at the end of the run block brings the tools tablespace online.

In Oracle Database 12c (12.1), it's easier to execute SQL commands and PL/SQL procedures because you don't have to enclose the SQL commands in quotes—nor do you need to prefix them with the keyword SQL as we did in our examples here. So, if you want to switch a log file in an Oracle Datbase 12c database from RMAN, all you need to do is issue the following statement:

```
RMAN> alter system switch logfile;

Statement processed

RMAN>
```

Here's an example that shows how to execute a SELECT statement from RMAN:

```
RMAN> select tablespace_name from dba_data_files;

TABLESPACE_NAME
------------------------------
SYSTEM
SYSAUX
USERS
EXAMPLE
UNDOTBS1

RMAN>
```

The ability to issue a SELECT statement is an Oracle Database 12c new feature and isn't available in older releases.

In addition to SELECT statements, you can issue other SQL statements, such as ALTER TABLESPACE, CREATE DIRECTORY, etc. from RMAN in Oracle Database 12c.

How It Works

Usually you use the RMAN command line or an RMAN script to issue RMAN backup and recovery commands. However, from time to time, you may need to issue some SQL commands from within the RMAN interface.

The SQL command that you can execute from RMAN in Oracle Database 12c affords you a lot of the same functionality of the normal SQL command. As mentioned earlier, you had to specify the keyword SQL and also enclose the commands in quotations in a pre-Oracle Database 12c release database—this functionality, now called SQL(Quoted), is available in Oracle Database 12c only for backward compatibility purposes.

The following sets of commands must be preceded by the keyword SQL in Oracle Database 12c, to distinguish RMAN commands from SQL commands.

- DELETE: Executes the SQL DELETE command

- DROP DATABASE: Executes the SQL DROP DATABASE command

- FLASHBACK: Executes the SQL FLASHBACK command

In releases older than Oracle Database 12c, if you're passing file names with the SQL string you use from the RMAN prompt, you must remember to do the following:

- Enclose the entire SQL string in double quotes.

- Enclose the file name in duplicate single quotes.

Here's an example that shows how to specify a file name in an SQL command issued from the RMAN prompt. Note the use of *two* single quotes inside the SQL statement:

```
SQL "create tablespace test1
    datafile ''/u01/app/oracle/oradata/mydb/test01.dbf''
    size 100m temporary";
```

You can execute PL/SQL blocks in the same manner as SQL statements. Remember that a block includes the **begin** and **end** keywords, as shown here:

```
SQL 'begin rman.rman_purge; end;';
```

Similarly, you can execute a PL/SQL block from within a run block.

4-14. Starting and Shutting Down a Database with RMAN

Problem

You need to start and shut down the Oracle database from the RMAN client during a backup- and recovery–related task.

Solution

You can both shut down and start up a database using the equivalent of the usual SQL*Plus startup and shutdown commands from the RMAN client. The following sections show how to issue the startup and shutdown commands from RMAN.

Starting a Database

You can use the startup command with several options. Here's an example that shows how the database is opened using the startup command:

```
RMAN> startup
```

RMAN enables you to do more with the nomount option, however. In the following example, you can see how you can go through all the steps of opening a database: starting the instance, restoring the control file, mounting the control files, recovering the database, and finally, opening the database. The example shows how to restore the control file while connected to the recovery catalog. After restoring the control file, the database is mounted with the alter database mount command. Next you see the recover command, which is mandatory after restoring a control file. Finally, the database is opened with the open resetlogs option:

```
RMAN> connect target /
RMAN> connect catalog rman/rman@catdb
RMAN> startup nomount;
RMAN> restore controlfile;
RMAN> alter database mount;
RMAN> recover database;
RMAN> alter database open resetlogs;
```

The nomount option also comes in handy when you lose your spfile or are forced to start the instance without a spfile (and any init.ora file). You can then use the nomount option to start up the database with a dummy parameter file. For example:

```
set DBID 1296234570;
startup force nomount; # RMAN will start the instance with a dummy parameter file
```

If you aren't connected to the recovery catalog, you just need to set the following minimum parameters in the init{SID}.ora file under the $ORACLE_HOME/dbs directory, as shown here.

- DB_NAME

- DB_RECOVERY_FILE_DEST

- DB_RECOVERY_FILE_DEST_SIZE

Once rman starts the database with the dummy parameter file, you can restore the actual spfile from the autobackup:

```
restore spfile from autobackup; # restore a server parameter file
startup force; # restart instance with the new server parameter file
```

After restoring the spfile, you can start the database using that spfile.

You can also use the dba option with the shutdown command to restrict access to those users who've been granted the restricted session privilege. Here's how:

```
RMAN> startup dba pfile=/tmp/initprod1.ora;
```

The database is now open, but only users with the restricted session privilege will be able to connect. Typically DBAs give the restricted session privilege only to each other. It gives you a way to do work in the database while ensuring that no business users are connected.

Shutting Down a Database

Issue the shutdown command to close down the database and stop the instance. All the standard SQL*Plus options you can use with the shutdown command—normal, immediate, abort, and transactional—have the same effect and meaning when used from within RMAN. Here's an example:

```
RMAN> shutdown immediate;

RMAN> startup mount;

RMAN> backup  database;

RMAN> alter database open;
```

This example shuts down the database, kicking off any current users as soon as their currently executing SQL statements finish. The database is then backed up and reopened for use.

How It Works

All the shutdown and startup commands shown here pertain only to the target database. You can't start and stop the recovery catalog instance from RMAN. The only way to start up and shut down the recovery catalog instance is by connecting to the recovery catalog database as the target database and by issuing the relevant commands to start or stop the instance.

4-15. Checking the Syntax of RMAN Commands

Problem

You want to check the syntax of your RMAN commands without actually executing the commands.

Solution

To check the syntax of RMAN commands, you must start the RMAN client with the operating system command-line argument checksyntax. You can easily check the syntax of commands prior to their execution either by entering them at the command prompt or by reading in the commands through a command file. Here's how you check the syntax of a single RMAN command (run {backup database;}) by first starting the RMAN client with the checksyntax argument:

```
[oracle@virtual1 ~]$ rman checksyntax

Recovery Manager: Release 12.1.0.0.2 - Beta on Tue Jul 24 11:00:46 2012

Copyright (c) 1982, 2012, Oracle and/or its affiliates. All rights reserved.

RMAN> run {backup database;}

The command has no syntax errors

RMAN>
```

In this example, there were no errors in the syntax of the simple run block, and RMAN confirms that. You can also use the checksyntax argument to check the syntax of RMAN commands that are part of a command file. Simply specify the checksyntax argument before invoking the command file that consists of the RMAN commands. In the following example, the file goodcmdfile contains a couple of restore and recovery commands:

```
$ rman checksyntax @/tmp/goodcmdfile
RMAN> #  file with legal syntax
   2> restore database;
   3> recover database;
   4>
The cmdfile has no syntax errors
 Recovery Manager complete.
$
```

You can also open an RMAN session solely for the purpose of checking the syntax of commands that you type interactively:

```
$ rman checksyntax
```

An important point about the checksyntax argument is that you can't use it after starting RMAN. That is, you can't include the checksyntax argument from the RMAN command line. You must pass checksyntax as an argument to the rman command when you start the RMAN client and without connecting to any target or recovery catalog.

How It Works

When you either execute an RMAN command file by preceding it with the checksyntax argument or enter any RMAN commands after starting RMAN with the checksyntax argument, RMAN won't actually execute any RMAN commands. RMAN will check and report only on the syntax of those commands. If the RMAN commands that you type at the command line or that you include as part of a command file have no errors, you get the "The command has no syntax errors" message from RMAN (if you use a command file instead of an RMAN command, you'll instead get the message: "The cmdfile has no syntax errors"). Otherwise, RMAN will issue an error message, as shown in the following example:

```
[oracle@virtual1 rman]$ rman checksyntax @badcmdfile

RMAN> # file with illegal syntax
2> run (
RMAN-00571: ===========================================================
RMAN-00569: =============== ERROR MESSAGE STACK FOLLOWS ===============
RMAN-00571: ===========================================================
RMAN-00558: error encountered while parsing input commands
RMAN-01009: syntax error: found "(": expecting one of: "{"
RMAN-01007: at line 2 column 5 file: badcmdfile
[oracle@virtual1 rman]$
```

The output of the checksyntax command in this example reveals there is a syntax error in your run block. The checksyntax command is handy for checking scripts for syntax errors. With RMAN, there's no need for a script to fail unexpectedly because you mangled the syntax of a command. If you're surprised by an error, it's because you didn't test with checksyntax first.

4-16. Hiding Passwords When Connecting to RMAN
Problem
You want to hide the database passwords when connecting to the RMAN client.

Solution
One of the easiest ways to prevent others from gleaning sensitive database passwords by looking over your shoulder is simply to never type a password directly at the operating-system level when starting the RMAN client. One approach is to pass only your username on the command line, letting RMAN prompt for your password:

```
[oracle@virtual1 ~]$ rman target sys@orcl

Recovery Manager: Release 12.1.0.0.2 - Beta on Tue Jul 24 11:02:18 2012

Copyright (c) 1982, 2012, Oracle and/or its affiliates. All rights reserved.

target database Password:
connected to target database: ORCL (DBID=1316762630)

RMAN>
```

When RMAN prompts you for the target database password, it won't echo the characters you type to the terminal, and thus your password is safe from prying eyes.

If you're using a command file that employs database credentials (username and password), you must ensure that the connection string doesn't get written to any log files that capture the RMAN output. One good way to prevent the Oracle user password from being captured by an RMAN log file is to run command files using the @ command-line option. In the following example, the command file backup.rman contains the following lines:

```
connect target sys/syspassword@trgt
backup database;
```

Execute the backup.rman command file by using the @ option at the command line:

```
$ rman @backup.rman
```

When the command file executes, the connect command will make the connection to the target database using the database credentials you supplied, but it won't reveal the database password. RMAN replaces the connection credentials (username and password) with an asterisk, as shown here:

```
[oracle@virtual1 rman]$ rman @backup.rman

Recovery Manager: Release 12.1.0.0.2 - Beta on Mon Aug 6 11:55:03 2012

Copyright (c) 1982, 2012, Oracle and/or its affiliates. All rights reserved.

RMAN> connect target *
2> backup database;

connected to target database: ORCL (DBID=1316762630)

Starting backup at 06-AUG-12
...
```

In this case, the command file issued a connect target command. That command included a password. RMAN displays the command, but with an asterisk in place of the password.

How It Works

An important fact to remember is that you'll be exposing the database credentials when you connect to RMAN from the operating system command line. For example, a scan of the Unix processes using ps -ef will reveal any RMAN command lines, including passwords. You can avoid this problem by always using the connect string from the RMAN prompt to connect to the recovery catalog, the target database, and the auxiliary database.

■ **Note**   Anyone with read permissions on the command file containing the connect string with the password will be able to read that file and obtain the password. For this reason, you should look to secure that file, limiting read access to only DBAs.

4-17. Identifying RMAN Server Sessions
Problem

RMAN performs all its backup and recovery tasks using server sessions. You want to know more about these server sessions, such as how many server sessions are created and how to identify them.

Solution

You can find out the number of RMAN server sessions using this formula:

```
Number of sessions = C+N+2
```

where the following is true:

- C is the number of channels allocated.

- N is the number of "connect" options used in the allocate channel commands (if no connect options are used, N has the value of 1).

If you're using a recovery catalog, there are always at least two sessions: one for connecting to the recovery catalog and the other for the default connection to the target database. The default connection is needed to perform tasks such as applying archived redo logs during a recovery task.

You can find out exactly who is currently running the RMAN client by issuing a command such as ps -ef on a Unix system:

```
RMAN> host 'ps -ef|grep rman';

oracle   15960  7412  2 11:57 pts/2    00:00:00 rman target /
oracle   15986 15960  0 11:57 pts/2    00:00:00 /bin/bash -c ps -ef|grep rman
oracle   15988 15986  0 11:57 pts/2    00:00:00 grep rman
host command complete

RMAN>
```

Having a list of RMAN client sessions like this, you can pick one in which you're interested. Say, for example, that you're interested in the session for process ID 9255. You can then issue the following command, which will find all the child processes associated with that instance of the client:

```
RMAN> host 'ps -ef|grep 15960';

oracle   15960  7412  0 11:57 pts/2    00:00:00 rman target /
oracle   15965 15960  0 11:57 ?        00:00:00 oracleorcl (DESCRIPTION=(LOCAL=YES)
(ADDRESS=(PROTOCOL=beq)))
oracle   15966 15960  0 11:57 ?        00:00:00 oracleorcl (DESCRIPTION=(LOCAL=YES)
(ADDRESS=(PROTOCOL=beq)))
oracle   16041 15960  0 11:58 pts/2    00:00:00 /bin/bash -c ps -ef|grep 15960
oracle   16043 16041  0 11:58 pts/2    00:00:00 grep 15960
host command complete

RMAN>
```

To identify the Oracle session ID of the RMAN session, look for the following types of messages in the RMAN log:

```
channel ch2: sid=12 devtype=SBT_TAPE
```

On a Windows server, you can use the Task Manager to identify the RMAN client sessions. Then you can drill down into associated server processes by clicking the Process tab and clicking the relevant server process under the process list.

How It Works

Identifying RMAN server sessions is crucial for tasks such as terminating an unwanted RMAN session. The best way to terminate an RMAN session that's executing commands is to simply use the Ctrl+C combination. You can kill a server session corresponding to an RMAN channel by executing the SQL statement `alter system kill session`.

4-18. Dropping a Database Using the RMAN Client
Problem

You are planning to drop a database and want to make sure you drop all the data files, online logs, and control files pertaining to the database. Of course, you can drop a database from SQL*Plus using the `drop database` command. However, if you can't access SQL*Plus, you can drop a database from RMAN instead.

Solution

Use the `drop database` command to drop a database from the RMAN prompt. Here are the steps to follow:

1. Start up the database in :mount exclusive mode:

    ```
    SQL> startup mount exclusive;
    ORACLE instance started.

    Total System Global Area  626327552 bytes
    Fixed Size                  2263520 bytes
    Variable Size             457180704 bytes
    Database Buffers          163577856 bytes
    Redo Buffers                3305472 bytes
    Database mounted.
    SQL> exit
    ```

2. From the RMAN interface, use the following command to drop the database:

    ```
    RMAN> connect target /

    connected to target database: ORCL (DBID=1316762630, not open)

    RMAN> drop database;
    ```

3. RMAN will require a confirmation from you that you really do want to drop the database. Respond with yes, if that's what you intend to do:

    ```
    Do you really want to drop the database (enter YES or NO)? yes
    Database dropped.
    RMAN>
    ```

Note how RMAN prompts you if you really want to drop the target database. By using the optional keyword `noprompt`, you can prevent such a message. However, considering how critical the dropping of a database is, you may simply ignore the `noprompt` keyword.

The drop database command drops only the data files, the online redo log files, and the control files. You can get rid of all the backups and copies in one fell swoop by adding the including backups option to the drop database command:

```
RMAN> drop database including backups;
```

Needless to say, you should use this command with the utmost care.

How It Works

RMAN will ensure that all data files, online redo logs, and control files belonging to the database are removed from the operating system file system. Optionally, you can also specify that all the archive logs, backups, and copies that belong to the database be dropped as well.

CHAPTER 5

■ ■ ■

Configuring the Rman Environment

To work with RMAN, you must configure several things, such as the default backup type (disk or tape), the number of channels, and the degree of parallelism. For simple backup tasks, you probably can get by with RMAN's default configuration settings. However, for complex jobs involving sophisticated backup strategies, you need to customize one or more of RMAN's configuration settings.

Broadly speaking, you can configure the RMAN environment in two ways:

- Make the configuration settings persistent across different RMAN sessions.

- Manually modify configuration settings for only a particular backup or recovery job.

You can also set different persistent configuration settings for each of the target databases registered in your recovery catalog if you are using a recovery catalog. Thus, you can configure different backup retention policies, for example, for different databases. In this chapter, we'll look at several important recipes that show you how to configure the RMAN backup and recovery environment, including configuring the backup device type, configuring the backup type, generating the backup file names, and creating backup retention polices.

■ **Note** Chapter 3 discusses configuring the fast recovery area. Configuring RMAN to make backups to a media manager is an important part of RMAN configuration. We discuss how to configure a media manager in Chapter 18.

5-1. Showing RMAN Configuration Settings
Problem

You want to see your current RMAN configuration settings. For example, you may be seeing unexpected RMAN behavior, or you may be encountering performance issues because of how you've configured RMAN in your environment.

Solution

Use the RMAN command show to view the current value of one or all of RMAN's configuration settings. The show command will let you view the value of a specified RMAN setting. For example, the following show command displays whether the auto backup of the control file has been enabled:

```
RMAN> show controlfile autobackup;

using target database control file instead of recovery catalog
RMAN configuration parameters for database with db_unique_name ORCL are:
CONFIGURE CONTROLFILE AUTOBACKUP OFF; # default

RMAN>
```

The show all command displays both settings that you have configured and any default settings. Any default settings will be displayed with a # default at the end of the line. For example, the following is the output from executing the show all command:

```
RMAN> connect target /

RMAN> show all;

RMAN configuration parameters for database with db_unique_name ORCL are:
CONFIGURE RETENTION POLICY TO REDUNDANCY 1; # default
CONFIGURE BACKUP OPTIMIZATION OFF; # default
CONFIGURE DEFAULT DEVICE TYPE TO DISK; # default
CONFIGURE CONTROLFILE AUTOBACKUP OFF; # default
CONFIGURE CONTROLFILE AUTOBACKUP FORMAT FOR DEVICE TYPE DISK TO '%F'; # default
CONFIGURE DEVICE TYPE DISK PARALLELISM 1 BACKUP TYPE TO BACKUPSET; # default
CONFIGURE DATAFILE BACKUP COPIES FOR DEVICE TYPE DISK TO 1; # default
CONFIGURE ARCHIVELOG BACKUP COPIES FOR DEVICE TYPE DISK TO 1; # default
CONFIGURE MAXSETSIZE TO UNLIMITED; # default
CONFIGURE ENCRYPTION FOR DATABASE OFF; # default
CONFIGURE ENCRYPTION ALGORITHM 'AES128'; # default
CONFIGURE COMPRESSION ALGORITHM 'BASIC' AS OF RELEASE 'DEFAULT' OPTIMIZE FOR LOAD TRUE ; # default
CONFIGURE ARCHIVELOG DELETION POLICY TO NONE; # default
CONFIGURE SNAPSHOT CONTROLFILE NAME TO '/u01/app/oracle/product/12.1.0/db_1/dbs/snapcf_orcl.f'; # default

RMAN>
```

Table 5-1 lists all the parameters you can use with the show command and describes each parameter.

Table 5-1. *Parameters for RMAN's show Command*

Parameter	Description
all	Shows all parameters
archivelog deletion policy	Shows the archivelog deletion policy
archivelog backup copies	Shows the number of archivelog backup copies
auxname	Shows the auxiliary database information

(continued)

Table 5-1. (*continued*)

Parameter	Description
`backup optimization`	Shows whether optimization is on or off
`[auxiliary] channel`	Shows how the normal channel and auxiliary channel are configured
`channel for device type [disk |` `<media device>;`	Shows the characteristics of the channel
`controlfile autobackup`	Shows whether auto backup is on or off
`controlfile autobackup format`	Shows the format of the auto backup control file
`datafile backup copies`	Shows the number of data file backup copies being kept
`default device type`	Shows the default type (disk or tape)
`encryption algorithm`	Shows the encryption algorithm currently in use
`encryption for [database | tablespace]`	Shows the encryption for the database and every tablespace
`Exclude`	Shows the tablespaces excluded from the backup
`Maxsetsize`	Shows the maximum size for backup sets. The default is unlimited
`retention policy`	Shows the policy for data file and control file backups and copies that RMAN marks as obsolete
`snapshot controlfile name`	Shows the snapshot control filename
`compression algorithm`	Shows the compression algorithm in force. The default is the ZLIB algorithm

■ **Note** You can also display nondefault RMAN configuration settings by querying the V$RMAN_CONFIGURATION view.

To simplify ongoing use of RMAN, you can set several persistent configuration settings for each target database. These settings control many aspects of RMAN behavior. For example, you can configure the backup retention policy, default destinations for backups, default backup device type, and so on.

How It Works

The `show` command queries the target database control file to retrieve RMAN configuration settings. You can use the `configure` command to view and change RMAN configurations.

Configuration settings are stored in the target database control file regardless of whether you are using a recovery catalog. Once configured, settings persist until you change them again.

Because RMAN settings are stored in the control file, your target database must be mounted or open when issuing the `show` command.

The `show all` command reveals the present configuration regarding several important RMAN backup and recovery settings. The following list summarizes the meaning of the most important of these settings, shown by issuing the `show all` command:

- `configure retention policy to redundancy 1` means that RMAN retains only one set of backup copies.

- `configure backup optimization off` means that by default RMAN won't skip the backing up of unchanged data blocks in the data files.

- configure default device type to disk means that by default RMAN sends backup output to a disk drive.

- configure controlfile autobackup off means that by default RMAN doesn't automatically back up the control files when it performs a backup task.

- configure device type disk parallelism 1 backup type to backupset means that the default RMAN backup type is a backup set (and not an image copy) and the degree of parallelism is 1.

- configure datafile backup copies for device type disk to 1 means that by default RMAN doesn't make multiple copies of a backup file.

- configure maxsetsize to unlimited means that there's no limit on the size of a backup set by default.

- configure encryption for database off means that by default RMAN backups aren't encrypted.

Notice that the output of the show all command shows the existing RMAN configuration in the form of RMAN commands to re-create that configuration. Therefore, if you are planning to use the same type of configuration on a different database, just save the output from the show all command to a text file that you can then execute from the RMAN command line after connecting to the target database to which you're planning to migrate those settings.

You can view information about RMAN's persistent configuration settings by querying the V$RMAN_CONFIGURATION view, as shown here:

```
SQL> select * from v$rman_configuration;
     CONF# NAME                                       VALUE
---------- ----------------------------------         --------------------------
         1 RETENTION POLICY                           TO REDUNDANCY 3
         2 BACKUP OPTIMIZATION                        ON
         3 DEFAULT DEVICE TYPE TO                     sbt_tape
         4 CONTROLFILE AUTOBACKUP                     ON
         5 DEVICE TYPE                                DISK PARALLELISM 2
5 rows selected.
```

The NAME column in the V$RMAN_CONFIGURATION view shows the type of RMAN configuration, and the VALUE column shows the present configure command setting for that type, for example, configure retention policy to redundancy 3, in our example here.

■ **Note** The V$RMAN_CONFIGURATION view shows only those parameters for which you've set a nondefault value.

5-2. Configuring RMAN
Problem

You want to configure RMAN to suit the requirements of the particular backup and recovery strategy you choose to implement in your organization.

Solution

You can create or modify any of RMAN's persistent configuration settings affecting backup and recovery through the configure command. The general format of the configure command is as follows:

```
RMAN> configure [<parameter> <syntax>];
```

If you want, you can script an entire set of configuration changes and run it from within a run block. Alternatively, you may execute the configure command from the RMAN command prompt in order to change a single parameter at a time. The following example changes many settings all at once from within a run block:

```
run
{
configure retention policy to redundancy 2;
configure backup optimization off;
configure default device type to disk;
configure controlfile autobackup on;
configure controlfile autobackup format for device type disk to
'/proj/11/backup/%F';
configure device type disk parallelism 2;
configure datafile backup copies for device type disk to 1;
configure archivelog backup copies for device type disk to 1;
configure maxsetsize to unlimited;
configure snapshot controlfile name to '/proj/11/backup/snapf_prod11.f';
 }
```

It's quite common to specify the configure command within backup and recovery scripts to change the default settings for one or more RMAN persistent configuration settings.

How It Works

Use the configure command to configure persistent settings for backup, restore, duplication, and maintenance jobs. Once set, the settings will apply to all future RMAN sessions until you clear or modify those settings by using the configure command again. RMAN stores the configuration for each of the target databases in that database's control file. The recovery catalog, if you're using one, contains the configuration for all the databases that are registered in the catalog.

You must connect to the target database, which must be in mount or open state, since RMAN configuration settings are stored in the control file. In Chapter 15, you'll learn about the configure auxname command, which lets you rename files when you're duplicating databases using RMAN.

5-3. Restoring Default Parameter Settings
Problem

You want to restore RMAN's default settings after performing a special task that required you to modify some parameters.

Solution

If you don't explicitly use the `configure` command to specify the value of any RMAN parameters, RMAN will use default values for those parameters. By using the `configure ... clear` command, you can return an individual configuration setting to its default value, as shown in the following example:

```
RMAN> configure backup optimization clear;

using target database control file instead of recovery catalog
old RMAN configuration parameters:
CONFIGURE BACKUP OPTIMIZATION ON;
RMAN configuration parameters are successfully reset to default value

RMAN>

RMAN> configure retention policy clear;

RMAN configuration parameters are successfully reset to default value

RMAN>
```

The first example shows how to turn off backup optimization, since by default the backup optimization is set to off. The second example sets the retention policy to the default value of `redundancy 1`.

How It Works

You can't clear individual parameters affecting a particular RMAN component by using the `configure ... clear` command. For example, you may have configured several options using the `configure channel ...` command. However, you can't erase the individual options by using the `configure ... clear` command. That is, you can't run a command such as the following, which attempts to clear only the individual option `maxpiecesize`:

```
RMAN> configure channel device type sbt maxpiecesize 100m clear;
```

However, you can use the following command successfully:

```
RMAN> configure channel device type sbt clear;
```

The previous command will clear the permanent setting for the device type and set it back to the default setting, which of course is disk.

5-4. Enabling and Disabling Automatic Control File Backups
Problem

You want to configure RMAN so it automatically backs up the control file and the server parameter file whenever RMAN repository data in the control file changes, since those changes critically affect the ability of RMAN to restore the database.

Solution

To enable automatic control file backups, use the autobackup clause with the configure command as follows:

```
RMAN> configure controlfile autobackup on;
```

If for any reason you want to disable automatic control file backups, run the following command:

```
RMAN> configure controlfile autobackup off;
```

An alternative way to disable automatic control file backups is to clear (see Recipe 5-3 for instructions on clearing configured RMAN settings) the auto backup setting. For example:

```
RMAN> configure controlfile autobackup clear;
```

This command will set the control file auto backup to off, which is the default setting.

How It Works

By default, automatic control file backups are disabled. Even when the auto backup feature is disabled, RMAN will back up the current control file and the server parameter file whenever any backup command includes data file 1 from the data files that belong to the target database. In an Oracle database, data file 1 is always part of the system tablespace, which contains the data dictionary. You can configure RMAN to automatically back up the control file following *every* backup and any database structural change by using the configure command. We highly recommend you configure automatic control file backups for two reasons:

- To ensure that the critical control file is backed up regularly following a backup or structural change to the database

- To simplify the scripts used to back up your database

■ **Note** Oracle recommends you enable the control file auto backup feature if you aren't using a recovery catalog.

Once you configure automatic control file backup, RMAN will automatically back up your target database control file, as well as the current server parameter file, when any of the following events occurs:

- Successful completion of either a backup or the copy command

- After a create catalog command from the RMAN prompt is successfully completed

- Any structural changes to the database modify the contents of the control file

After a backup or copy command completes and the recovery catalog—if you are using one—is successfully updated, RMAN will then back up the control file to its own backup piece. In addition, any changes to the physical structure of your database, even if they are made through SQL*Plus, will trigger a control file auto backup. (For example, the following actions will trigger an auto backup of the control file: adding a tablespace or data file, dropping a data file, placing a tablespace offline or online, adding an online redo log, and renaming a data file.) When automatic backup is triggered by a structural change, an Oracle server process (not an RMAN process) will automatically create the auto backup of your control file.

■ **Note**   If you are using a binary server parameter file (spfile), it will also be automatically included in the control file backup piece.

Why back up the control file after database structure changes? Having a backup of the control file that reflects the current physical structure of the database simplifies your recovery process. Without such a control file, you'll have to re-create your control file using the create controlfile statement with the updated physical structure of the database.

The auto backup of the control file is independent of any backup of the current control file that you may make as part of a backup command. The automatic control file backup that follows a database structural change is always a backup to a disk location. See Recipe 5-5 to learn how to specify that location. Automatic control file backups that occur after a data file backup can be created on disk or on tape, however.

Once you configure auto backup of the control file, RMAN can recover a database even if the current control file, the recovery catalog, and the server parameter file all turn out to be inaccessible. The following are the steps RMAN takes in recovering the database:

1. RMAN will first restore the server parameter file from the location where RMAN automatically backed up the file.

2. RMAN will start the instance with the help of the server parameter file it restored in step 1.

3. RMAN will restore the control file from the same auto backup.

4. Once the control file is mounted, RMAN will connect to the target database in the nocatalog mode and use the RMAN repository available in the control file to restore the data files and then recover the database.

5. At this point, you may re-create a new recovery catalog and register your target databases in it.

6. Finally, RMAN will copy all the RMAN repository records from the target database control files to the new recovery catalog.

This recovery sequence shows the importance of configuring the auto backup of the control file.

5-5. Specifying the Auto Backup Control File Directory and File Name
Problem

You've just enabled the auto backup of the control file feature, but you don't know where the files are physically being written. You want to ensure that these critical backups are being written to a location you know about so that you can maintain and monitor that location.

Solution

You can override where RMAN will write the auto backup control file and its name using the configure command. For example, the following configure command changes both the directory where RMAN stores the auto backup of the control file and the file name of the auto backup:

```
RMAN> configure controlfile autobackup format
2> for device type disk to '/u01/app/oracle/backup/autobackup/controlfile_%F';
```

To set the directory and file format back to the default value, run this command:

```
RMAN> configure controlfile autobackup format for device type disk clear;
```

You can use the command `set control file autobackup format`, either within a `run` block or at the RMAN prompt (the `run` block has precedence over the RMAN prompt), to override the configured auto backup format for the duration of an RMAN session.

How It Works

If you have enabled a fast area as well as the auto backup of the control file, then RMAN will write the backup to the directory defined for the fast area. By default, RMAN creates these files as Oracle managed files.

When specifying a file name as well as a target directory, you must include the format variable %F in the filename. The format variable %F yields a unique combination of the database ID, day, month, year, and sequence.

When you clear the control file auto backup format for disk as shown in the Solution section of this recipe, the control file will be backed up to the fast recovery area, provided you have enabled it first. If you haven't enabled a fast recovery area, RMAN will create the auto backups in an operating system–specific location ($ORACLE_HOME/dbs on Unix and %ORACLE_HOME%\database on Windows).

You can also configure the auto backup to back up the control file to an automatic storage management (ASM) disk group, as shown in the following example:

```
RMAN> configure controlfile autobackup format
        for device type disk to '+dgroup1/%F';
```

The control file autobackup will be stored in the disk group +*dgroup1* when you execute this `configure` command.

5-6. Specifying the Snapshot Control File's Name and Location
Problem

RMAN occasionally creates a special control file called the *snapshot control file*. You want to specify your own name for this file as well as the location for storing it.

Solution

Use the `configure snapshot controlfile to ...` command to change the snapshot control file's name and the directory in which it is stored:

```
RMAN> configure snapshot controlfile name to '/u01/app/oracle/rman/snapct.ctl';

new RMAN configuration parameters:
CONFIGURE SNAPSHOT CONTROLFILE NAME TO '/u01/app/oracle/rman/snapct.ctl';
new RMAN configuration parameters are successfully stored

RMAN>
```

Use the show command to display the current location of the snapshot control file:

```
RMAN> show snapshot controlfile name;

RMAN configuration parameters for database with db_unique_name ORCL are:
CONFIGURE SNAPSHOT CONTROLFILE NAME TO '/u01/app/oracle/rman/snapct.ctl';
```

RMAN> To reset the snapshot control file's name and location to the default values, use the configure command as follows:

```
RMAN> configure snapshot controlfile name clear;

old RMAN configuration parameters:
CONFIGURE SNAPSHOT CONTROLFILE NAME TO '/u01/app/oracle/rman/snapct.ctl';
RMAN configuration parameters are successfully reset to default value

RMAN>
```

The output of the show snapshot controlfile name command at this point reveals that the current location, which is actually $ORACLE_HOME/dbs (on a Linux/Unix system) is the default location.

How It Works

RMAN requires a consistent view of the control file under two circumstances:

- When resynchronizing with the recovery catalog
- When making a backup of the control file

■ **Note** Oracle allows only one RMAN session to access the snapshot control file at a time. This ensures that multiple RMAN sessions do not concurrently write and read from the snapshot control file.

To achieve these two goals, RMAN creates a temporary backup copy of the control file called the *snapshot control file*, which enables RMAN to resynchronize with the recovery catalog or back up the control file, using a read-consistent version of the control file. The default location and name of the snapshot control file is operating system dependent. On Windows servers, the default location is ORACLE_HOME/database, and the default name of the snapshot control file is of the form SNCF<database name>.ORA. On Unix the default directory is $ORACLE_HOME/dbs, and the default name is snapcf_<database name>.f.

■ **Note** RMAN uses the default snapshot directory and name regardless of whether you have configured a fast recovery area.

5-7. Specifying the Retention Period for RMAN History
Problem

You're using only a control file, and not the recovery catalog, to record RMAN's backup and recovery activity. You want to change the length of time for which the Oracle server will retain history data in the control file before overwriting it.

Solution

Use the control_file_record_keep_time initialization parameter to specify the minimum length of time that RMAN history is saved in the control file before being overwritten.

Here's an example showing how to set the retention period to 15 days:

```
RMAN> alter system set control_file_record_keep_time=15;

Statement processed

RMAN>
```

As explained in Recipe 4-12, it is only in Oracle Database 12c that you can excute an SQL command in RMAN without any quotations around the SQL statement. In earlier releases, you'll need to specify the keyword SQL, and you must also enclose the statement in quotes, as shown in the following example:

```
RMAN> SQL "alter system set control_file_record_keep_time=15";

sql statement: alter system set control_file_record_keep_time=15

RMAN>
```

The alter system statement in this example specifies that all reusable records in the control file be kept for at least 15 days before they are eligible for overwriting.

How It Works

The control file contains two types of sections: reusable and nonreusable. The control_file_record_keep_time parameter applies only to the reusable section of the control file. If RMAN needs to add new backup and recovery–related records to the control file, any records that expired as per the control_file_record_keep_time parameter are overwritten. If there are no eligible records to be overwritten, the reusable section of the control file (and therefore the control file itself) expands.

The default value of the control_file_record_keep_time parameter is seven days. You can dynamically change the value of the parameter through the alter system statement as shown in the previous example. The range of values you may use can be anywhere from 0 to 365 days. If you set the retention time to zero, it means the reusable sections of the control file will not expand when there aren't any more empty reusable records and the database starts overwriting the existing records as and when it needs them.

The Oracle database records all RMAN backup information in the control file, whether you use a recovery catalog or not. If there is no limit to the number of days that information can be kept, the control file will keep growing without a limit. To avoid letting the control file grow without limit, the Oracle database overwrites backup records that are older than a threshold you specify.

If you choose the default value of seven days for the parameter, for example, any reusable records older than seven days can be overwritten by the Oracle server when it needs space to write new history. If no reusable record is old enough to be overwritten and yet more space is needed for new history, then Oracle will expand the control file's size. If space limitations preclude the expansion of the control file, Oracle will be forced to overwrite the oldest reusable record in the control file anyway, even if that record's age is less than the value of the control_file_record_keep_time parameter.

The control_file_record_time initialization parameter controls the overwriting of only the circularly reusable records, such as the archive log records and the backup records. The value for the parameter has no bearing on the control file records pertaining to data files, tablespaces, and redo thread records, which are reused only after the relevant object is dropped from the database. The V$CONTROLFILE_RECORD_SECTION view provides information about the control file record sections.

5-8. Configuring the Default Device Type
Problem

You want to change the default backup device from disk to tape or from tape to disk.

Solution

By default, *disk* is the default device type for all automatic channels. However, you can use the configure command with the default device type option to make a tape device the default device type instead. The following example shows how to do this:

```
RMAN> configure default device type to sbt;

new RMAN configuration parameters:
CONFIGURE DEFAULT DEVICE TYPE TO 'SBT_TAPE';
new RMAN configuration parameters are successfully stored

RMAN>
```

You can use the clear option to return the default device type to disk again:

```
RMAN> configure default device type clear;

old RMAN configuration parameters:
CONFIGURE DEFAULT DEVICE TYPE TO 'SBT_TAPE';
RMAN configuration parameters are successfully reset to default value

RMAN>
```

Alternatively, you can also explicitly reset the default device type to disk, as shown here:

```
RMAN> configure default device type to disk;

new RMAN configuration parameters:
CONFIGURE DEFAULT DEVICE TYPE TO DISK;
new RMAN configuration parameters are successfully stored

RMAN>
```

Once you configure the default device type to disk, all backups will be made to disk.

How It Works

You can override RMAN's default device type settings by specifying the backup device type as a part of the backup command itself, as shown in the following two commands, the first backing up to a tape device and the second to a disk device:

```
RMAN> backup device type sbt database;
RMAN> backup device type disk database;
```

When you issue a backup command, RMAN will allocate channels of the default device type only. For example, let's say you configure automatic channels for both disk and tape (sbt), but you set the default device type to disk. When you subsequently issue a backup database command, RMAN will allocate only a disk channel, and not an sbt channel, for the backup job.

The following example illustrates this point. The first command configures a channel for a tape device (sbt). The second command sets the default device type to tape (sbt). The third command backs up the archived logs through the default sbt channel that you set through the second command. Finally, the last command backs up the database to disk, rather than to the default tape device (set by the second command). Thus, the backup device type disk ... command overrides the default device type setting of sbt.

```
RMAN> configure channel device type
sbt parms='sbt_library=/mediavendor/lib/libobk.so
env=(nsr_server=tape_svr,nsr_client=oracleclnt,
nsr_group=ora_tapes)';
RMAN> configure default device type to sbt;
RMAN> backup archivelog all;
RMAN> backup device type disk database;
```

You can also override RMAN's behavior regarding the default device type, which is to manually allocate a specific channel within the RUN command, as shown here:

```
RMAN> run
      {
      allocate channel c1 device type disk maxpiecesize 1G;
      backup database plus archivelog;
      }
```

The previous command will make a backup to disk, even if the default device type is a tape device.

Here's an example showing how you can first make a backup to a default disk device and then back up the resulting backup sets to tape for safekeeping off the premises:

```
RMAN> run
      {
      backup database plus archivelog;
      backup device type sbt backupset all;
      }
```

You only ever need to worry about overriding the default device type when issuing a backup command. The default device type is not an issue with the restore command. That's because the restore command will allocate channels of both configured device types, no matter what the default device type is. RMAN works this way because you may be restoring files from both disk-based and tape-based backups.

5-9. Configuring the Default Backup Type

Problem

You want to change the default backup type to image copies from the default backup type, which is a backup set.

Solution

The default backup type in RMAN, whether you're backing up to disk or to tape, is a backup set. You can change the default backup type to an image copy by using the following command:

```
RMAN> configure device type disk backup type to copy;
```

You can revert to the original setting of backup set backup type by using either of the following two commands:

```
RMAN> configure device type disk clear;
RMAN> configure device type disk backup type to backupset;
```

How It Works

You have the option to set image copies as your backup type only when making backups to disk. If you're using a tape device, you don't have an image copy option—you can make backups only in the form of a backup set when using a tape device.

5-10. Making Compressed Backup Sets the Default

Problem

You want to make compressed backups using RMAN in order to save storage space and reduce the network traffic.

Solution

By default, all RMAN backups are made in a noncompressed format. You can, however, configure RMAN to make compressed backup sets, both for disk-based as well as for tape-based backups. Here's the command for specifying the compression of a disk-based backup:

```
RMAN> configure device type disk backup type to compressed backupset;

new RMAN configuration parameters:
CONFIGURE DEVICE TYPE DISK BACKUP TYPE TO COMPRESSED BACKUPSET PARALLELISM 1;
new RMAN configuration parameters are successfully stored
released channel: ORA_DISK_1
```

RMAN> And here's how you specify compression when making backups to a tape device:

```
RMAN> configure device type sbt backup type to compressed backupset;

old RMAN configuration parameters:
CONFIGURE DEVICE TYPE 'SBT_TAPE' PARALLELISM 3 BACKUP TYPE TO BACKUPSET;
new RMAN configuration parameters:
```

```
CONFIGURE DEVICE TYPE 'SBT_TAPE' BACKUP TYPE TO COMPRESSED BACKUPSET PARALLELISM 3;
new RMAN configuration parameters are successfully stored

RMAN>
```

Both in the case of disk and tape backups, you can revert to the default noncompressed backup format by omitting the keyword compressed in the two commands shown in this solution.

```
Starting backup at 07-AUG-12
using channel ORA_DISK_1
channel ORA_DISK_1: starting compressed full datafile backup set...
```

How It Works

RMAN uses binary compression to produce compressed backup sets. Since a compressed backup means fewer bytes are transmitted across the network, it makes it a lot easier for you to safely schedule a daily backup of the database without adversely affecting other users of your network. Of course, even compression may not permit you to back up a very large database during the backup window.

When you restore a compressed backup set, RMAN can read the backup set directly, without having to first uncompress it, thus saving you a considerable amount of time. If you compress backup sets through some other means, such as the Unix/Linux tar command, then you'll incur significant overhead in time and in disk space when uncompressing them.

When using the RMAN compression feature, you can choose among different compression algorithms. You can query the view V$RMAN_COMPRESSION_ALGORITHM to view the compression algorithms available to you, as shown here:

```
RMAN> select algorithm_name,algorithm_description, is_default
  2* from v$rman_compression_algorithm;
ALGORITHM_NAME       ALGORITHM_DESCRIPTION                              IS_

BZIP2                good compression ratio                             NO
BASIC                good compression ratio                             YES
LOW                  maximum possible compression speed                 NO
ZLIB                 balance between speed and compression ratio        NO
MEDIUM               balance between speed and compression ratio        NO
HIGH                 maximum possible compression ratio                 NO

RMAN>
```

The ZLIB compression algorithm offers speed but not the best compression ratio. The alternate compression algorithm, BZIP2, is slower but provides a better compression ratio. In Oracle Database 12c, both the ZLIB and the BZIP2 compression algorthims are deprecated. A new compression algorithm named BASIC is the default starting with Oracle Database 12c. The BASIC algorithm replaces the BZIP2 algorithm.

These three compression algorithms—BZIP2, ZLIB, and BASIC—are available to you out of the box and with no additional cost. Starting with the Oracle Database 11g Release 2, you can choose from among three additional compression levels, by enabling the Advanced Compression option. As with the free compression options, the Advanced Compression option offers three different compression levels: HIGH, MEDIUM, and LOW.

If your network speed is the limting factor, you may want to look at the HIGH compression level. For most environments, Oracle recommends the MEDIUM level, because it offers an ideal compromise between speed and compression ratios. The LOW compression level has the least effect on backup throughput. Note that the MEDIUM compression algorithm is a replacement for the ZLIB, which is deprecated starting with the Oracle Database 12.1.2 release.

You can use the show command to check the current compression algorithm in use, as shown here:

```
RMAN> show compression algorithm;

using target database control file instead of recovery catalog
RMAN configuration parameters for database with db_unique_name ORCL are:
CONFIGURE COMPRESSION ALGORITHM 'BASIC' AS OF RELEASE 'DEFAULT' OPTIMIZE FOR LOAD TRUE ; # default

RMAN>
```

In addition to offering multiple options to compress your backup sets, starting with the Oracle Database 12.1 release, RMAN also lets you specify options for *precompression processing* (precompression block processing) by consolidating free space in data blocks. Precompressing data is especially beneficial in cases where the data blocks were subjected to multiple inserts and deletes. By default, precompression processing of backups is enabled (OPTIMIZE FOR LOAD TRUE). This means that RMAN will precompress block processing, ignoring the increase in CPU usage. Preprocessing in this manner will help you attain superior compression ratios, but of course, you need to be ready to pay the price in terms of higher CPU usage during the preprocessing phase.

By doing the following you can ensure that RMAN won't preprocess blocks that it's going to compress:

```
RMAN> CONFIGURE COMPRESSION ALGORITHM 'BASIC' AS OF RELEASE 'DEFAULT' OPTIMIZE FOR LOAD FALSE;

old RMAN configuration parameters:
CONFIGURE COMPRESSION ALGORITHM 'BASIC' AS OF RELEASE 'DEFAULT' OPTIMIZE FOR LOAD TRUE;
new RMAN configuration parameters:
CONFIGURE COMPRESSION ALGORITHM 'BASIC' AS OF RELEASE 'DEFAULT' OPTIMIZE FOR LOAD FALSE;
new RMAN configuration parameters are successfully stored

RMAN>
```

5-11. Configuring Multiple Backup Copies
Problem

You want to initiate a backup (as a backup set) and have RMAN automatically make multiple copies of the resulting backup sets. You do not want to make any persistent configuration changes to your RMAN environment.

Solution

RMAN provides a backup *duplexing* feature under which you can direct RMAN to make multiple copies of the backup pieces inside a backup set. Using a single backup command, you can make up to four copies of each backup piece in a *backup set* on four separate devices. *Copy* in this context means an exact copy of each of the backup pieces in a backup set.

You can use the copies parameter with the configure command to specify the duplexing of backup sets. Here's an example showing how to use the configure ... backup copies command:

```
RMAN> configure datafile backup copies for device type disk to 2;
```

The configure ... backup copies command shown here specifies that RMAN must make two copies of each backup piece for all types of backups (archived redo logs, data files, control files) made to a disk device.

You can configure the number of backup set copies for each type of device—disk and tape—separately. The following example shows how to configure multiple copies when backing up to a tape device:

```
RMAN> configure datafile backup copies for device type sbt to 2;
```

Use the format option of the backup command to specify the multiple destinations for the multiple backups you're making when duplexing backups. With the format option when using a disk channel, you can specify that multiple copies be sent to different physical disks. For example, if you want to place one copy of a backup set in three different locations on disk, you would configure RMAN as follows:

```
RMAN> configure channel device type disk format '/save1/%U','/save2/%U','save3/%U';
```

■ **Note** You can't make duplex backups to the fast recovery area.

When you next execute a backup command, RMAN will place one copy each of the resulting backup piece in the /save1, /save2, and /save3 directories. For tape backups, if your media manager supports version 2 of the SBT API, RMAN will automatically place each copy on a separate tape.

How It Works

You can use the configure ... backup copies command to specify how many copies of each backup piece should be made on a specified type of device. Not only can you specify the number of copies, but you also can specify the type of backup file, such as data file, archived redo, log, or control file. Using the configure command this way specifies a new default level of duplexing. The original default level of duplexing is set to 1, meaning that RMAN will make only a single copy of each backup piece.

You must understand that when duplexing backups, RMAN produces multiple identical copies of each backup piece in a backup set, rather than producing multiple backup sets. There's only one backup set with a unique backup set key with multiple copies of its member backup pieces.

You can check the current configuration for multiple backup copies by using the SHOW ... BACKUP COPIES command. For example, the following command shows the default configuration of the DATAFILE BACKUP COPIES setting:

```
RMAN> show datafile backup copies;

RMAN configuration parameters for database with db_unique_name ORCL are:
CONFIGURE DATAFILE BACKUP COPIES FOR DEVICE TYPE DISK TO 1; # default

RMAN>
```

Once you configure the number of backup copies to a nondefault value with the help of the configure command, the show command shows the settings that you've configured:

```
RMAN> CONFIGURE DATAFILE BACKUP COPIES FOR DEVICE TYPE DISK TO 2;

old RMAN configuration parameters:
CONFIGURE DATAFILE BACKUP COPIES FOR DEVICE TYPE DISK TO 1;
new RMAN configuration parameters:
CONFIGURE DATAFILE BACKUP COPIES FOR DEVICE TYPE DISK TO 2;
new RMAN configuration parameters are successfully stored
```

```
RMAN> show datafile backup copies;

RMAN configuration parameters for database with db_unique_name ORCL are:
CONFIGURE DATAFILE BACKUP COPIES FOR DEVICE TYPE DISK TO 2;
```

RMAN> By replacing the keyword *datafile* with *archivelog*, you can view the current configuration for multiple backups of archived logs, as shown here:

```
RMAN> show archivelog backup copies;

RMAN configuration parameters for database with db_unique_name ORCL are:
CONFIGURE ARCHIVELOG BACKUP COPIES FOR DEVICE TYPE DISK TO 1; # default
```

```
RMAN>
```

Note that the backup duplexing feature is limited to backups made as backup sets—you can't direct RMAN to make multiple simultaneous copies of image copies—you first have to make a single image copy before you can make multiple copies of it. Also note that you can't use the fast recovery area as one of the destinations for a duplexed copy.

Ideally, you should keep the multiple backup copies on multiple media. For example, say you want to keep one copy on disk and another on tape. Instead of making persistent configuration changes to make multiple backup copies as shown in this recipe, you can specify the number of copies only for a specific backup job using the backup copies and set backup copies commands. Please refer to Chapter 7 to learn how to use the copies parameter in the set and backup commands to specify multiple copies when using the backup command.

5-12. Skipping Previously Backed-Up Files
Problem

You want to use the *backup optimization* feature of RMAN to save on backup time by making RMAN skip those files that it has already backed up.

Solution

By default, backup optimization is set to off, meaning RMAN will back up every file, whether an identical copy was backed up previously or not. You can configure backup optimization by using the following command:

```
RMAN> configure backup optimization on;
```

From here on out, RMAN will attempt to avoid backing up files that have already been backed up the specified number of times to each device type—disk and sbt. If you've set a recovery window-based retention policy, then configuring backup optimization won't result in RMAN skipping a backup unless the backups get older than the recovery window you've configured. For example, if you've set the following retention policy, RMAN will continue to back up a data file even if an identical backup of that data file exists that falls within the recovery window of the past seven days:

```
RMAN> show retention policy;

RMAN configuration parameters for database with db_unique_name ORCL are:
CONFIGURE RETENTION POLICY TO RECOVERY WINDOW OF 7 DAYS;
```

```
RMAN>
```

How It Works

By enabling backup optimization, you can make RMAN skip those files that it has already backed up. The backup optimization feature applies to three types of files: data files, archived redo logs, and backup sets. Optimizing backups can lead to a considerable reduction in the time it takes to back up a database. For the backup optimization to work, you must satisfy the following conditions after first turning on backup optimization using the `configure` command, as described in the Solution section of this recipe:

- You must run a `backup database`, or a `backup archivelog` command with the `all` or `like` options, or run the `backup backupset all` command. You can also execute a `backup recovery area`, `backup recovery files`, or `backup datafilecopy` command.

- You must not mix both disk and sbt channels in the same backup command—all channels must be of the same type.

You can turn off backup optimization during a particular RMAN session and force RMAN to back up a file regardless of whether it's identical to a previously backed-up file by specifying the `force` option with your backup command, as shown here:

```
RMAN> backup database force;
```

Similarly, you can force the backing up of archivelogs by issuing the following command:

```
RMAN> backup archivelog all force;
```

By using the `force` option, you make RMAN back up all the specified files, even if the backup optimization feature is turned on. To turn off backup configuration on a more permanent basis, use the `configure` command, as shown here:

```
RMAN> configure backup optimization off;
```

■ **Note** RMAN also provides *restore optimization*, which lets it avoid restoring data files wherever possible. If, after checking a data file's file headers, RMAN concludes that the header contains the correct information and that the data file is in the correct location, it will skip the restoration of that data file from backup.

Once you configure backup optimization, RMAN will skip backing up previously backed-up files if they are exactly identical to their previously backed-up versions (that is, if they haven't changed at all since the last backup). The following example shows the result of trying to back up the database immediately after a backup of that database was made, assuming you've turned on backup optimization:

```
RMAN> backup database;
Starting backup
...
using channel ORA_DISK_2
using channel ORA_DISK_1
using channel ORA_DISK_3
skipping datafile 1; already backed up 2 time(s)
skipping datafile 1; already backed up 2 time(s)
skipping datafile 1; already backed up 2 time(s)
skipping datafile 1; already backed up 2 time(s)
```

```
skipping datafile 1; already backed up 2 time(s)
finished backup
...
RMAN>
```

RMAN uses specific rules for each type of file it backs up to determine whether the file is identical to a previously backed-up version. For example, a data file must have the same DBID and checkpoint SCN as a previously backed-up file to be deemed identical to it. Similarly, an archived redo log must have the same DBID, thread, and sequence number as a previously backed-up version, and a backup set must have the same backup set record ID and stamp.

The fact that a data file, archived redo log, or backup set is identical to a previously backed-up file doesn't mean that RMAN will automatically skip backing up that file. When RMAN detects an identical file, that file initially is deemed only a *candidate* for optimization. Once RMAN determines that an identical file (data file, archived redo log file, or backup set) has already been backed up, that file becomes a candidate for backup optimization. RMAN must consider the retention policy in force at the time and the backup duplexing feature before determining whether it has sufficient backups on the specified device to let it skip the particular file.

RMAN uses a backup optimization algorithm to determine whether it should skip backing up a previously backed-up file. The optimization algorithm takes into account two factors: the retention policy currently in use and RMAN's backup duplexing feature. The rules specified by the optimization algorithm vary, depending on the type of file or whether you're dealing with the backing up of a backup set. We summarize the rules of the optimization algorithm for data files, archived redo logs, and backup sets in the following sections.

Data Files

The key determinant of how RMAN decides to treat the backup optimization issue for a data file depends on whether you have a retention policy in use and, if so, the type of retention policy in effect. Here's a brief summary of how RMAN approaches backup optimization under different circumstances.

- If you're using a recovery window–based retention policy, then the backup media type determines whether RMAN will skip a data file. If you are making tape backups, RMAN will make another backup of a data file even if it has a backup of an identical file, if the latest backup is older than the configured recovery window. That is, RMAN ignores the backup optimization policy you've configured. For example, let's say today's date is April 1, and we're dealing with the backup of a read-only tablespace whose contents don't change by definition. If the last backup of this read-only tablespace was made on March 15 and you have configured a recovery window of seven days, it means that the backup is older than the recovery window. RMAN will make another backup of that tablespace, even though its contents haven't changed a bit. If you're backing up to disk instead, RMAN will not back up a datafile if the backup of an identical file is already on disk. It doesn't matter whether the latest disk backup is older than the beginning of RMAN's recovery window.

- If you're using a redundancy-based retention policy (and, say, the redundancy is set to r), RMAN will skip backing up a file if n (defined as r+1) copies of an identical file exist on the specified device, whether it's disk or tape.

- If you don't have a retention policy in effect, RMAN skips a backup if n number of copies of that file exist on the specified backup device. RMAN determines the value of n in the following order of precedence, with higher values on the list overriding the lower values:

  1. The number of backup copies when using the backup ... copies n command

  2. The number of backup copies when using the set backup copies n command

3. The number of backup copies configured by using the `configure datafile backup copies for device type ... to n` command

4. n=1

Accordingly, if the number of backup copies is set to the default number of 1, after you make two identical copies of a data file, RMAN will skip that data file in future backups.

Archived Redo Logs

In the case of archived redo logs, RMAN will determine the value of n according to the following order of precedence and will skip backing up a file if at least n backups already exist on the specified device:

1. The number of backup copies when using the `backup ... copies n` command

2. The number of backup copies when using the `set backup copies n` command

3. The number of backup copies configured by using the `configure data file backup copies for device type ... to n` command

4. n=1

Suppose the value of n in your `backup ... copies` command is 2 and you issue the following command first:

```
RMAN> backup device type sbt copies 3 archivelog all;
```

Let's say you turn on backup optimization sometime later with the following command:

```
RMAN> configure backup optimization on;
```

Issue the following command to back up the archived redo logs:

```
RMAN> backup device type sbt copies 2 archivelog all;
```

RMAN will set the value of n to 2 in this case, and RMAN will back up only those archive logs that haven't been backed up more than twice. That is, all archived redo logs that were backed up by the very first backup command will be skipped during the second backup command. However, RMAN will make two copies of any archived redo logs produced subsequent to the first backup when you issue the second backup command.

Backup Sets

RMAN uses the following order of precedence to determine n, which is the number of copies of a backup set that must already exist if RMAN is to skip backing up that backup set:

1. The number of backup copies when using the `backup ... copies n` command

2. The number of backup copies when using the `set backup copies n` command

By default, n = 1. To be considered eligible for backup optimization, a backup set must have an identical record ID and stamp as another existing backup set.

■ **Caution**   Media managers may have their own expiration policies. Therefore, RMAN may sometimes skip a backup according to its optimization algorithm, but the media manager may have already discarded the older backup stored to tape that formed the basis for RMAN's decision to skip the backup. To avoid a discrepancy between RMAN's metadata and that of a media manager, you must issue the `crosscheck` command frequently to synchronize the RMAN repository with the media manager's metadata.

5-13. Specifying Backup Piece File Names
Problem

You want to specify your own names for RMAN backup pieces.

Solution

You can specify your own meaningful names for backup pieces using the `format` option in the backup command. You can provide substitution variables for use in the generation of unique file names for image copies and backup pieces.

Here's how you incorporate the `format` parameter within a backup command when using backup pieces:

```
RMAN> backup tablespace users format='/u01/app/oracle/backup_%u%p%c';
```

RMAN uses the substitution variables you provide to create meaningful names for the backup pieces. The example here is meant only to show you how to specify the `format` parameter during a backup—you'll learn all about the backing up of tablespaces in Chapter 8.

How It Works

If you don't use the `format` option within your backup command to generate names for the backup pieces, RMAN will automatically generate a unique name for each of those backups in the default backup location. If you're using a media manager, check your vendor documentation for specific restrictions on using the `format` parameter—for example, the length of the name.

■ **Note**   In addition to the `format` option, you can also use the `db_file_name_convert` parameter to generate unique file names for RMAN image copies. The `db_file_name_convert` parameter is a database initialization parameter that you set either in the database parameter file or by issuing an `alter database` command. You use the same syntax to set the `db_file_name_convert` parameter as when you specify the `format` option.

5-14. Generating File Names for Image Copies
Problem

You want to set meaningful names for image copies instead of letting RMAN generate its own default names.

Solution

You can use the format parameter to generate unique names for RMAN image copies. The default format %U is defined differently for image copies of data files, control files, and archived redo logs, as shown in Table 5-2.

Table 5-2. *Default Formats for Various Types of Files*

Type of File	Meaning of %U
Data file	data-D-%d_id-%I_TS-%N_FNO-%f_%u
Archived log	arch-D_%d-id-%I_S-%e_T-%h_A-%a_%u
Control file	cf-D_%d-id-%I_%u

You can specify up to four values for the format parameter, but the second through fourth values are used only if you're making multiple copies. That is, the second, third, and fourth format values are used when you execute the backup copies, set backup copies, or configure ... backup copies command.

For image copies, you can also use the db_file_name_convert option of the backup command to generate your own file names for RMAN image copies. When you use this option, you must provide a pair of file name prefixes to change the names of the output files. The first file name prefix refers to the file names of the files that are being copied by RMAN. The second file name prefix refers to the file names for the backup copies. In the following example, we use the db_file_name_convert option to specify that the backup copies of a file that starts with /u01/oradata/users are prefixed with /backups/users_ts:

```
RMAN> backup as copy
db_file_name_convert=('/u01/app/oracle/oradata/orcl/users',
'/u01/app/oracle/backup/users_ts')
tablespace users;
```

The db_file_name_convert option to set the image copy file names is useful in situations where you may want to direct the backups of tablespaces to different locations, as shown in the following example:

```
RMAN> backup as copy device type disk
    db_file_name_convert = ('/u01/app/oracle/table',
    '/u05/app/oracle/copy_table',
    '/u01/app/oracle/index','/u05/app/oracle/copy_index')
    tablespace data, index;
```

This example shows how you can easily direct the image copies of the data and index tablespaces to different locations on disk.

How It Works

When you use the db_file_name_convert option within a backup command when creating image copies, RMAN will first try to use the pair of names (for the original file and backup copy) you provide to convert file names. If it fails to do this, RMAN will try to name the image copy according to any format parameter values you may have specified. If you didn't use the format parameter within the backup command, RMAN will use the default format %U.

5-15. Tagging RMAN Backups

Problem

You want to name your RMAN backup pieces and image copies with symbolic names so that it's easy to refer to them.

Solution

You can assign a character string called a *tag* to either a backup set or an image file. A tag is simply a symbolic name such as nightly_backup, for example, that helps you identify the contents of a backup file. Once you associate a tag with a backup, you can refer to just the tag later in RMAN commands. For example, when executing a restore command, you can specify the tag nightly_backup instead of having to specify the actual backup file name.

The following example shows how to associate a tag with a backup set:

```
RMAN> backup copies 1 datafile 5 tag test_bkp;
```

The following example shows how to associate a tag with an image copy:

```
RMAN> backup as copy tag users_bkp tablespace users;
```

To copy an image copy with a specific tag, you can use the following command format:

```
RMAN> backup as copy
        copy of database
        from tag=full_cold_cpy
        tag=new_full_cold_cpy;
```

In the following example, we show how you can create backup sets of image copies of the tablespace users, which has the tag weekend_users, and the tablespace system, which has the tag weekend_system. Note that both of the new backup sets you're creating are given the same tag, new_backup.

```
RMAN> backup as backupset tag new_backup
        copy of tablespace users from tag weekend_users
        copy of tablespace system from tag weekend_system;
```

Tags are case-insensitive. Even if you specify a tag in lowercase, RMAN will store and display the tag in uppercase.

How It Works

The main benefit in using tags for backups is that a tag can clearly tell you what a given backup's purpose is. For example, you can have two copies of a backup, one with the tag switch_only and the other with the tag for_restore_only. During a restore/recovery situation, you can use the first tag if you're using the switch command and the second if you are restoring the actual file.

You can use tags to identify backups taken for a specific purpose or at a specific time. Examples of such tags are weekly_incremental and 2006_year_end. It's common to use tags to distinguish among a set of backups that are part of a backup strategy, such as an incremental backup strategy. If you back up a backup set, you can provide a different tag for the new copy of the backup set.

Even if you don't expressly specify a tag using the keyword tag, Oracle assigns a default tag to every backup except for control file backups. The default tag is of the format TAGYYYYMMDDTHHMMSS, where YYYY refers to the year, MM to the month, DD to the day, HH to the hour, MM to the minutes, and SS to the seconds. For example, a backup of data file 1 made on July 31, 2012, will receive the tag TAG20120731T062822.

5-16. Configuring Automatic Channels

Problem

You want to configure channels for use with either a disk device or a tape on a persistent basis for all RMAN sessions.

Solution

Use the `configure` command to cause RMAN to automatically allocate channels. Automatic channel allocation lets you configure persistent channels for use in all RMAN sessions.

■ **Note** Remember that any specification of automatic channels using the `configure` command can be overridden by manually setting different channels within a `run` block.

You can configure the degree of parallelism, the default device type, and the default device type settings for your RMAN channels by using the options `configure device type ... parallelism`, `configure default device type`, and `configure channel [n] device type`, respectively. Let's look at the three-channel `configure` command options in more detail.

Specifying a Default Device Type

You can specify a default device type for automatic channels by using the `configure default device type` command, as shown here:

```
RMAN> configure default device type to sbt;
```

The result of configuring the device type to sbt (tape drives) in this example is that RMAN will use only the sbt type channels for backups, because sbt (tape) was selected as the default device. As you learned earlier, the default device type for automatic channels is disk.

Specifying the Degree of Parallelism for Channels

The degree of parallelism for a specific device type controls the number of server sessions that will be used for I/O for a specific device type. You use the `configure device type ... parallelism` command to specify the number of automatic channels to be assigned for both types of device types: disk and tape. The default degree of parallelism is 1. It's best to allocate only one channel for each physical device on the server. That is, if you have only a single disk drive, don't set the degree of parallelism (default is 1).

You can use the `show device type` command to see the current parallelism settings:

```
RMAN> show device type;

RMAN configuration parameters for database with db_unique_name ORCL are:
CONFIGURE DEVICE TYPE SBT_TAPE PARALLELISM 1 BACKUP TYPE TO BACKUPSET; # default
CONFIGURE DEVICE TYPE DISK PARALLELISM 1 BACKUP TYPE TO BACKUPSET; # default

RMAN>
```

You can use the following set of commands to back up to a media manager by using three tape drives in parallel:

```
RMAN> configure device type sbt parallelism 3;
RMAN> backup device type sbt database plus archivelog;
```

Each of the three tape channels that you configured will back up roughly a third of the database files and archive logs.

You can configure a maximum of 255 channels, with each channel capable of reading 64 files in parallel. The number of channels you specify for use with a particular device determines whether RMAN writes to (or reads from, if it's a recovery) this device in parallel when performing a backup. If you configure three tape channels, for example, each channel may back up more than one file, but a single file won't be backed up simultaneously by the three channels. For RMAN to use multiple channels to back up a data file, you must use the RMAN backup feature called *multisection backups*, which is explained in detail in Chapter 7.

Specifying the Maximum Backup Piece Size

You can specify the maximum size of a backup piece by using the maxpiecesize option, as shown here (1g stands for 1 gigabyte):

```
RMAN> configure channel device type disk
    maxpiecesize 1g;
```

The previous command will limit the size of an individual backup piece to 1 gigabyte.

■ **Note**   RMAN allocates only a single type of channel—disk or sbt—when you execute a backup command. However, when you issue a restore command (or a maintenance command, such as delete), RMAN allocates all necessary channels, including both disk and sbt.

Generic Settings for Automatic Channels

If you don't specify a number (up to *nn*) while allocating a channel, RMAN configures a *generic channel*. You use the configure channel device type command to configure a template of generic parameter settings for all automatic channels that belong to either the disk or the sbt type. Here's an example that shows how you can specify the disk rate and format settings for backup pieces, assuming that the default device type is set to disk:

```
RMAN> configure channel device type disk
2> maxpiecesize 1g;

old RMAN configuration parameters:
CONFIGURE CHANNEL DEVICE TYPE DISK MAXPIECESIZE 1 G;
new RMAN configuration parameters:
CONFIGURE CHANNEL DEVICE TYPE DISK MAXPIECESIZE 1 G;
new RMAN configuration parameters are successfully stored
```

RMAN> As another example, look at the following command, where all backups using a tape device will use the channel settings specified:

```
RMAN> configure channel device type sbt parms='ENV=(NSR_SERVER=bksvr1)';
```

If you don't explicitly configure settings for a specific named channel, the generic settings will come into play. Thus, generic channel settings are applied to all channels you don't explicitly configure. Whenever you reconfigure a generic channel of either disk or tape, any previous settings for that device type are erased. In the following example, the format setting in the second command erases the maxpiecesize value set by the first configure command:

```
configure channel device type sbt maxpiecesize 1G;
configure channel device type sbt format 'bkup_%U';
```

Configuring Specific Channels for a Device Type

Sometimes you want to control each channel's parameters separately instead of using generic channel settings for all your channels. By assigning a number to a channel, you can configure a specific channel for each device type. Note that if you want to use a specific channel for a device, you must specify at least one channel option such as maxpiecesize or format for that channel. In the following example, we use three specific channels to send disk backups to three separate disks:

```
RMAN> configure channel 1 device type disk format '/disk1/%U';
RMAN> configure channel 2 device type disk format '/disk2/%U';
RMAN> configure channel 3 device type disk format '/disk3/%U';
```

How It Works

When you send a command to the target database through the RMAN interface, the command is sent through an RMAN *channel*. An RMAN channel is simply a connection that RMAN makes from itself to the server session on the target database for performing a backup or recovery task. Each connection will initiate a database server session on the target or auxiliary database. This server session is the one that actually performs the backup and recovery tasks for RMAN. Each server session that performs a backup, restore, or recovery job relies on an RMAN channel representing a stream of data *to a particular device type* such as a disk or a tape drive. Thus, an RMAN channel is simply an input or output channel for RMAN backup and recovery jobs. Since each RMAN channel works on a single backup set or image copy at a given time, by allocating multiple channels you can have RMAN execute some commands in parallel. That is, different server sessions can be instructed to concurrently execute the same remote procedural call (RPC). RMAN will read or write multiple backup sets or copies in parallel when you allocate multiple channels for a job. Each of the allocated channels will work on a separate backup set or disk copy.

You can have two different types of RMAN channels: disk and sbt. Using a disk channel, a server process can read and write to a disk. Similarly, the sbt channel will let the server process read or write from a tape device. Note that regardless of the channel type (disk or tape), RMAN can always read from or write to a disk by default, and RMAN always allocates a single disk channel for all backup and recovery operations.

You must either manually allocate a channel (explained in the next recipe) or preconfigure channels for automatic allocation before you can execute any of the following RMAN commands:

- backup

- recover

- restore

- duplicate

- create catalog

- validate

For each RMAN channel, a connection is made to the target database. That is, each channel will spawn a separate process. It is important to understand that a single RMAN session corresponds to multiple server sessions, each for a different channel. If you're using disk devices only, you don't have to configure automatic channels, since RMAN preconfigures a disk channel for you by default. If you're using tape drives, you'll have to configure the channels, whether explicitly in the RMAN run blocks or by using automatic channel configuration. Automatic channel configuration is the way to go in most cases; it makes life easy for you because you don't have to manually allocate the channels each time you perform a backup, restore, or recovery task.

You can configure persistent channel settings to simplify your usage of RMAN by using the configure channel commands shown earlier in this recipe. These persistent channel settings are stored in the RMAN repository, thus making it unnecessary for you to use the allocate channel command with each RMAN backup, recovery, restore, or maintenance command. RMAN first looks for any generic settings you might have set for any channel you don't explicitly configure. If you haven't manually set any channel configurations, RMAN will use the automatic channel configuration.

You use the clear option with the configure command to clear any automatic channel settings. You must use a separate configure ... clear command to set the configuration back to its default value. Here are some examples:

```
RMAN> configure default device type clear;        # reverts to the default
device type (DISK)
RMAN> configure channel device type sbt clear;     # erases all
options that were set for the sbt channel
RMAN> configure channel 1 device type disk clear;   # erases
configuration values set specifically for channel 1.
```

There is a difference between how RMAN treats a backup or copy command and a restore command when it comes to the allocation of channels. Even if you configure automatic channels for sbt, if your default disk type is disk, RMAN will allocate only disk channels when you run a backup or copy command. If you want RMAN to use the sbt channel, you have to use one of the following two methods:

- Use the allocate channel command in a run block to allocate the sbt channel.

- Specify the device type as disk directly within the backup command.

By default, RMAN sends all backups to the fast recovery area if you've already configured one. That is, you don't have to expressly specify the location by using the format option of the configure channel command. However, sometimes you may want to bypass the fast recovery area and send the RMAN backups elsewhere to disk. You can do so by explicitly configuring a backup device type with a specific format option. In the following example, we show how you can use the configure channel device type disk format command to specify that all RMAN disk backups be made to the /backup directory:

```
RMAN> configure channel device type disk format '/backup/ora_df%t_s%s_s%p';
```

In the format specification:

- %t stands for four-byte timestamp.

- %s stands for the backup set number.

- %p stands for the backup piece number.

If you use the configure command as shown in the previous example, all RMAN backups will be made in the /backup directory, even if you've configured a fast recovery area and there is plenty of free space in it. Thus, you must be prepared to lose the benefits of having the fast recovery area when you use the configure channel device type disk format command shown previously.

You can also send the backups to an automatic storage management (ASM) disk group, as shown in the following example:

```
RMAN> configure channel device type disk format '+dgroup1';
```

All backups will now be stored in the ASM disk group +dgroup1.

5-17. Manually Allocating RMAN Channels

Problem

You want to manually allocate RMAN channels for a specific backup or recovery command within a run block.

Solution

You can manually specify channels inside a run block by using the allocate channel command as shown here, where we allocate a single channel that we named c1, for the backup:

```
run
{
  allocate channel c1 device type sbt;
  backup database plus archivelog;
}
```

The use of the channel ID, which is c1 in the previous example, is optional. Oracle will use the channel ID when reporting input and output errors during the execution of an RMAN job.

The following example shows how to use multiple RMAN channels to spread a backup over multiple disk drives:

```
run
{
  allocate channel disk1 device type disk format '/disk1/backups/%U';
  allocate channel disk2 device type disk format '/disk2/backups/%U';
  allocate channel disk3 device type disk format '/disk3/backups/%U';
  backup database plus archivelog;
}
```

Each of the three allocate channel commands allocates a separate disk channel for each of three disk drives and also employs the format option to specify file names that point to the different disk drives.

How It Works

You can use all options of the configure channel command when you use the allocate channel command to manually allocate RMAN channels. You can use the allocate channel command only within a run block. A manually allocated channel applies only to the run block in which it's issued. If you don't manually allocate channels during any RMAN job, automatic channels will apply to that job. Manual channels override automatic channels. You can manually allocate channels for a backup, copy, or restore task.

■ **Note**   Once you specify manual channels, you can't specify either the backup device type or restore device type command to use automatic channels.

Since a manually allocated channel works only within a run block, as soon as the run block finishes executing, RMAN automatically releases the manually allocated channels. However, you can release a channel manually by using the same identifier as when you allocated a channel.

In the following example, we show how to use the ability of manually releasing channels to configure different options (format and maxpiecesize) for tape backups:

```
run {
    allocate channel c1 device type sbt format 'bkup_%U';
    allocate channel c2 device type sbt maxpiecesize = 5M;
    backup channel c1 datafile 1,2,3;
    release channel c1;
    backup datafile 4,5,6;
}
```

The first backup command backs up the data files numbered 1, 2, and 3 to a tape drive using channel c1. Once these three data files are backed up, the release channel command releases channel c1. The second backup data file command will then use the only remaining open channel, channel c2, to back up data files 4, 5, and 6.

5-18. Allocating an RMAN Maintenance Channel

Problem

You want to allocate a channel in order to perform maintenance tasks, such as deleting obsolete RMAN backups.

Solution

Use the allocate channel for maintenance command to allocate a maintenance channel before running a change, delete, or crosscheck command. Suppose you've already backed up to a tape device and sent off-site all RMAN backups you made to a tape device first. You now want to delete permanently the original backups on tape so you can reuse those tapes for future backup space. Assume you've configured only a disk device by default. You can then allocate a maintenance channel as a preparatory step to deleting those backups you don't need on tape any longer:

```
RMAN> allocate channel for maintenance device type sbt;
RMAN> delete backup of database completed before 'sysdate-30';
```

The allocate channel command allocates the previously unallocated tape channel to perform the deletion of the backups. The delete command will then delete all backups of the database that were completed before 'sysdate-30.' RMAN will ask you for confirmation before it deletes all the backup objects:

```
List of Backup Pieces
BP Key  BS Key  Pc# Cp# Status       Device Type Piece Name
-------  -------  --- --- ----------- ----------- ----------
6       6       1   1   AVAILABLE    DISK        /u01/app/oracle/backup/ORCL_level__16_U0gnhv6hg_1_1.bak
7       6       1   2   AVAILABLE    DISK        /u01/app/oracle/backup/ORCL_level__16_U0gnhv6hg_1_2.bak
...
36      25      1   1   AVAILABLE    DISK        /u01/app/oracle/backup_1bnhvpig11

Do you really want to delete the above objects (enter YES or NO)?
```

If there are no backups older than 30 days, RMAN will present the following:

```
RMAN> delete backup of database completed before 'sysdate-30';

using channel ORA_DISK_1
specification does not match any backup in the repository

RMAN>
```

How It Works

The `allocate channel for maintenance` command is meant to be used for maintenance tasks such as a change, delete, or crosscheck operation. You can use maintenance channels only at the RMAN prompt. That is, you can't use maintenance channels within a run block. You can also allocate a maintenance channel automatically. Whether you allocate a maintenance channel manually or automatically, you can't use it for a backup or restore operation. You won't have to allocate a maintenance channel when executing a `maintenance` command, such as crosscheck, change, or delete, against a disk-based file (such as an archived redo log, for example), because RMAN preconfigures an automatic disk channel for those operations.

■ **Note** As long as you configure at least one channel for each device type you're using, you don't need to use maintenance channels. RMAN recommends preconfiguring the channels of tape and disk instead of using the maintenance channel command. Since RMAN always comes configured with a disk channel, this means you must configure the tape channel as well to avoid using the `allocate channel` command in each run block in preference to configuring persistent settings for the channels.

Suppose your current backup strategy uses only disk, but you have several old tape backups you want to get rid of. You can allocate a maintenance channel for performing the deletion of the tape backups by using the dummy sbt API (because the media manager isn't available any longer). You can then use the `delete obsolete` command to remove the tape backups. Here's an example showing how to do those things:

```
RMAN> allocate channel for maintenance device type sbt
      parms 'SBT_LIBRARY=oracle.disksbt,
      ENV=(BACKUP_DIR=/tmp)';

RMAN> delete obsolete;
```

Although the media manager isn't available any longer, RMAN simulates a callout to the media management layer (MML) and successfully initiates the `maintenance` command to delete the old tape backups you want to get rid of.

5-19. Creating a Backup Retention Policy
Problem

You're in charge of coming up with a backup retention policy for your enterprise. You want to create a retention policy to optimize storage space and other expenses involved in retaining backups.

Solution

You can specify a backup retention policy in two ways:

- Use a recovery window (based on the length of time to retain backups).

- Use the concept of redundancy (number of backup copies to retain).

In both cases, you use the `configure` command to set the backup retention policy.

Backup Retention Policy Based on a Recovery Window

You can decide that you want your backups to be retained in the fast recovery area for a specific number of days. After the specified number of days, RMAN will mark the backups as obsolete, making them eligible for deletion. By using a recovery window, you're ensuring that you can recover your database to any point within the recovery window. For example, if your recovery window is configured to be seven days, you can recover the database to any day and time within the past week.

Here's how you use the `configure retention policy ...` command to set a recovery window–based backup retention policy:

```
RMAN> configure retention policy to recovery window of 7 days;

old RMAN configuration parameters:
CONFIGURE RETENTION POLICY TO REDUNDANCY 2;
new RMAN configuration parameters:
CONFIGURE RETENTION POLICY TO RECOVERY WINDOW OF 7 DAYS;
new RMAN configuration parameters are successfully stored

RMAN>
```

This command specifies that RMAN must retain all backups for the duration of seven days before marking them obsolete. Any backup file that's older than seven days is marked obsolete by RMAN. If you're using RMAN incremental backups, the retention period will be greater than seven days, since RMAN has to consider not only the incremental level 0 backup but also all the incremental level 1 backups in this case. In such a situation, the actual retention period for the backups will exceed the configured retention period of seven days.

Backup Retention Policy Based on Redundancy

By default, RMAN keeps a single copy of each backed-up data file and control file. However, you can specify that RMAN retain more than a single copy of a backed-up data file or control file by using the `redundancy` parameter of the `configure retention policy` command. RMAN will mark any additional copies of a data file backup or a control file that exceed the value of the redundancy parameter as obsolete.

In the following example, we set the backup redundancy value at 2:

```
RMAN> configure retention policy to redundancy 2;

old RMAN configuration parameters:
CONFIGURE RETENTION POLICY TO RECOVERY WINDOW OF 7 DAYS;
new RMAN configuration parameters:
CONFIGURE RETENTION POLICY TO REDUNDANCY 2;
new RMAN configuration parameters are successfully stored

RMAN>
```

Let's say you make five backups of a specific data file, one on each day of the workweek, starting on a Monday. Thus, on Friday, you end up with five different backups of that data file. However, the first three days' backups of the data file are deemed obsolete by RMAN, since you've set your backup redundancy value at 2. That is, only the Thursday and Friday backups are considered nonobsolete backups.

How It Works

Storing backups indefinitely isn't impossible, but it's impractical—you clearly don't need to save very old backups. However, you must guard against the opposite problem of not retaining enough backups. For one reason or another, all your most recent backups may become unusable. You then have no recourse but to use older backups to perform a database recovery.

By using RMAN's backup retention policies, you can direct RMAN to retain specific backups of the database and archived redo logs in the fast recovery area. Any backup files or archived redo logs that aren't covered by the backup retention policy guidelines are automatically declared obsolete, making them candidates for deletion if space requirements demand it.

To view the current backup retention policy in effect, use the `show retention policy` command, as shown in this example:

```
RMAN> show retention policy;

RMAN configuration parameters for database with db_unique_name ORCL are:
CONFIGURE RETENTION POLICY TO REDUNDANCY 2;

RMAN>
```

The output of this `show retention policy` command shows that RMAN is currently using a redundancy-based retention policy and that the redundancy is set to two copies.

RMAN marks any backups that fail to meet the backup retention policy constraints as *obsolete* backups. This, of course, means that the other backups that meet the retention policy criterion are considered not obsolete. The distinction between obsolete and nonobsolete backups is quite crucial, since RMAN will always retain all archived redo logs and incremental backups necessary to recover just the nonobsolete backups. It's important to understand that RMAN won't automatically delete obsolete backup files—that job falls to the DBA, who must delete the obsolete files explicitly with the `delete obsolete` command. Use the `report obsolete` command first to see which files are marked obsolete by RMAN. You can also query the V$BACKUP_FILES view to check on obsolete backups.

■ **Note** Explicitly setting the retention policy to neither a window nor a redundancy-based policy (`configure retention policy to none`) completely disables a backup retention policy. This isn't the same as using the command `configure retention policy clear`, which resets the retention policy to its default value, which is redundancy 1.

RMAN uses a redundancy-based backup retention policy by default, with a default redundancy of 1. By using the command configure retention policy to nonw, you can specify that RMAN follows no retention policy whatsoever. This means RMAN will never consider any backup as obsolete. If you're using a fast recovery area, this means RMAN can't delete a file from the fast recovery area until you first back up the file to either disk or tape. You therefore run the risk of running out of room in the fast recovery area because of the unavailability of any reclaimable space, and eventually you'll receive an ORA-19809 error (limit exceeded for recovery files). In most cases, an ORA-19809 error results in a hung database.

5-20. Configuring an Archived Redo Log Deletion Policy

Problem

You want to configure an archived redo log deletion policy so that you can make unnecessary archived redo logs eligible for deletion.

Solution

By default, RMAN doesn't use an archived redo log policy—that is, the configure archivelog deletion policy is set to the value of none by default. However, you can specify your own archived redo log deletion policy using the `configure` command. After connecting to the target database, issue the `configure archivelog deletion policy ...` command, as shown in the following example:

```
RMAN> configure archivelog deletion policy to
2> backed up 2 times to sbt;

new RMAN configuration parameters:
CONFIGURE ARCHIVELOG DELETION POLICY TO BACKED UP 2 TIMES TO 'SBT_TAPE';
new RMAN configuration parameters are successfully stored

RMAN>
```

The preceding `configure` command specifies that once an archived redo log has been backed up twice to tape, it's eligible for deletion from all archived redo log locations, including the fast recovery area. The configuration of an archived redo log deletion policy is a new feature introduced in the Oracle Database 11g release.

How It Works

The `configure archived redo log deletion policy` command specifies only which archived redo logs are *eligible* for deletion—it doesn't automatically delete all those archived redo logs. RMAN automatically deletes only those archived redo logs in the fast recovery area that become eligible as per this deletion policy. Any archived redo logs that exist in other locations will remain there, even after becoming eligible for deletion, until you manually delete them.

In Chapter 8, where you learn about manually deleting archived redo logs using the `delete input` and `delete all input` commands, you'll see that those commands can't violate any configured archived redo log policies you may have set, unless you specify the `force` option when using those commands. By using the `force` option with either of the archived redo log deletion commands (`delete input` and `delete all input`), you can override any configured archived redo log deletion policy.

Note that the archived redo log deletion policy you set through the `configure` command doesn't affect the archived redo logs in backup sets. The deletion policy applies only to local archived redo logs. Foreign archived redo logs, meaning those received by a logical standby database for a LogMiner session, aren't affected by the deletion policy.

5-21. Limiting the Size of Individual Backup Pieces

Problem

You want to restrict the size of each individual backup piece produced by RMAN. For example, you want to limit backup piece size to something that will fit on a single backup tape.

Solution

To limit the size of a backup piece, you must specify the `maxpiecesize` option of the `configure` channel or `allocate` channel commands. The following example illustrates how you can limit the maximum size of a backup piece to 1 gigabyte:

```
RMAN> configure channel device type disk maxpiecesize = 1g;
RMAN> backup as backupset tablespace users;
```

The first command configures an automatic disk channel and limits the maximum size of a backup piece to 1 gigabyte. The second command backs up the tablespace named users.

How It Works

One reason to limit the size of backup pieces is to accommodate physical limitations inherent in your storage devices. For example, if it looks like backup pieces are going to be greater in size than the capacity of a single tape drive, assuming you are backing up to tape, you can use the `maxpiecesize` parameter to ensure that a single backup piece isn't larger than the tape drive's capacity. Then, if the backup of a data file or tablespace is larger than the configured maximum size of a backup piece, RMAN will create as many backup pieces as necessary to conform to the `maxpiecesize` value you set.

5-22. Configuring the Maximum Size of Backup Sets
Problem

You want to limit the size of an individual backup set because your operating system won't support files larger than a certain size.

Solution

Use the `maxsetsize` parameter in either the `configure` or `backup` command to set the maximum size of backup sets created on disk or tape devices. A maximum backup set size you set using the `configure` command will serve as the default for all backups performed using whatever channel you are configuring. You can set the `maxsetsize` parameter in units of bytes, kilobytes (K), megabytes (M), and gigabytes (G). By default, `maxsetsize` is set in bytes. Here's an example that shows how to set the maximum backup set size to 1 gigabyte:

```
RMAN> configure maxsetsize to 1g;
```

The second way to configure the maximum size of backup sets is to specify the `maxsetsize` parameter directly within a backup command, as shown here:

```
RMAN> backup database maxsetsize=1g;

Starting backup at 06-AUG-12
...
RMAN>
```

The backup command first sets the `maxsetsize` parameter to 1 gigabyte before backing up the database.

How It Works

The size of a backup set made using RMAN equals the sum of the bytes in each of the backup pieces that are part of that backup set. By default, the maximum size of a backup set is unlimited, as you can see by issuing the following command:

```
RMAN> show maxsetsize;

RMAN configuration parameters for database with db_unique_name ORCL are:
CONFIGURE MAXSETSIZE TO 1 G;

RMAN>
```

The `configure maxsetsize` command applies to both disk and tape backups.

■ **Note** You can't specify the number of backup pieces in a backup set.

Since your backup will fail if a large file in the database being backed up is larger than the value of the `maxsetsize` parameter, make sure the value of this parameter is at least as large as the largest data file being backed up by RMAN. If you're backing up to tape, you run the risk of losing all your data even if just one of the tapes fails. Using the `maxsetsize` parameter, you can force RMAN to back up each backup set to a separate tape, thus limiting the damage to the contents of only the single failed tape.

Finally, know that the `maxsetsize` parameter doesn't give you absolute control over the size of the backup set that RMAN will create. The `maxsetsize` parameter is only one of the factors determining the size of backup sets. In addition to the setting of the `maxsetsize` parameter, RMAN takes into account the following factors when determining the sizing of RMAN backup sets:

- Number of input files specified in each backup command.
- Number of channels you allocate. Each allocated channel that's not idle will produce at least one backup set. RMAN also aims to divide work so all allocated channels have roughly an equal amount of work to do.
- Default number of files in each backup set.
- Default number of files that a single channel reads simultaneously (eight).

■ **Note** You can't limit the size of image copies. By definition, an image copy must be identical to the original data file, so you really don't have a choice here regarding the size of a copy—it'll simply be the same size as the original data file.

In Chapter 8, you'll learn about RMAN's restartable backups feature. Following a backup failure, RMAN will back up only the data that wasn't backed up before. That is, once it's backed up, the same data won't be backed up again if a backup fails midway. Using the `maxsetsize` parameter of your backup command, you can make smart use of this restartable backup feature. For example, if you set `maxsetsize` to 10MB for a backup, RMAN produces a new backup set after every 10MB worth of backup output. Let's say your backup failed after backing up 12 backup sets. Following a restart of the backup after a backup failure, RMAN won't have to back up the data already backed up to the 12 backup sets before the backup failure.

CHAPTER 6

◼ ◼ ◼

Using the Recovery Catalog

A *recovery catalog* is an optional database schema consisting of tables and views, and RMAN uses it to store its repository data. The control file of each target database always serves as the primary store for the repository, but you may want to create a recovery catalog as secondary storage for the repository, thus providing redundancy for the repository. For most small databases, you can get away with using just the control file to store the RMAN metadata. However, the recovery catalog provides a larger storage capacity, thus enabling access to a longer history of backups, and it is an ideal solution when dealing with a large number of databases. In addition, you can create and store RMAN scripts in the recovery catalog. Any client that can connect to the recovery catalog and a target database can use these stored scripts. We discuss how to create and use RMAN-stored scripts in Chapter 9.

◼ **Note** Even when you choose to use a recovery catalog, backup information will continue to be stored in the control file as well by default.

The recovery catalog contains information about both RMAN backups and the target database. More specifically, the recovery catalog contains the following:

- RMAN configuration settings
- RMAN-stored scripts that you create
- Target database tablespace and data file information
- Information pertaining to data file backup sets and backup pieces
- Information pertaining to archived redo log backup sets and backup pieces
- Information pertaining to data files and archived redo log copies

---

◼ **Tip** A recovery catalog is mandatory in an Oracle Data Guard environment.

The recovery catalog isn't a default entity—you must create it manually. Since the recovery catalog instance is a regular Oracle database like any other, you must also regularly back up this critical database. Sometimes you may have to export and import or restore and recover the recovery catalog. The recipes in this chapter show you how to create, use, merge, move, upgrade, and drop the recovery catalog. In addition, you'll also learn how to restrict access to the central or base recovery catalog by creating *virtual private recovery catalogs*.

Using a recovery catalog requires you to create and maintain a recovery catalog schema in an Oracle database. You may create the recovery catalog in an existing Oracle database or create it in a new Oracle database created specifically for the recovery catalog. We recommend creating a dedicated recovery catalog database if you already have a decent number of databases to manage. If you're creating a new database for housing the recovery catalog, you must create that database with a set of tablespaces such as these:

- System tablespace
- Sysaux tablespace
- Temporary tablespace
- Undo tablespace
- Recovery catalog tablespace

■ **Caution**   You can create the recovery catalog in a target database that you want to back up using the recovery catalog, but that's an unwise choice! In such a case, losing the target database means you've lost the recovery catalog as well, thus making recovery much harder or even impossible.

Back up your recovery catalog database just as you would any other production database by making it part of your regular backup and recovery strategy. It's a good policy to back up the recovery catalog right after you back up the target databases. This way, you can secure the most recent backup information records of all your production databases. Always run the recovery catalog instance in the archivelog mode, and try to make at least one backup on disk and on tape each time you back up the catalog database.

■ **Note**   In this book, when we use the words *recovery catalog*, we are referring to the *base* recovery catalog.

The owner of a recovery catalog, called the *recovery catalog owner*, can grant restricted access of the recovery catalog to other users. The restricted access is called a *virtual private catalog*. The main or central recovery catalog that acts as the repository for all databases is called the *base recovery catalog*. The owner of the base recovery catalog determines which databases the virtual catalog owner can access. There can be multiple virtual catalogs but there should be only one base recovery catalog.

■ **Note**   Oracle recommends creating one central recovery catalog to act as the repository for all your databases.

6-1. Creating the Recovery Catalog

Problem

You are planning to use a recovery catalog, have already created a recovery catalog database, and want to create a recovery catalog in that database.

Solution

Creating the recovery catalog consists of two major steps. First, you must create the recovery catalog owner or schema in the database where you want to house the recovery catalog. Second, once you successfully create the recovery catalog schema, you must create the recovery catalog itself.

Creating the Recovery Catalog Owner

Follow these steps to create the recovery catalog owner:

1. Using SQL*Plus, connect as the user sys to the database where you want to create the recovery catalog. For example:

```
SQL> connect sys/oracle@catdb as sysdba
```

2. Create a default tablespace for the RMAN recovery catalog owner you're about to create. Otherwise, the system tablespace may be used by default to hold the recovery catalog structures, and it's not a smart idea to let that happen. This example creates a tablespace named cattbs:

```
SQL> create tablespace cattbs
  2  datafile '/u01/app/oracle/oradata/catdb/cattbs_01.dbf' size 500M;

Tablespace created.

SQL>
```

3. Create the recovery catalog owner. This example creates a user named rman to own the catalog:

```
SQL> create user rman identified by rman
        temporary tablespace temp
        default tablespace cattbs
        quota unlimited on cattbs;

User created.
SQL>
```

The default tablespace of the recovery catalog owner in this example is the cattbs tablespace, which was created in the previous step.

4. Once you create the recovery catalog owner, you must grant that user the recovery_catalog_owner privilege in order for that user to have the authority to work with the recovery catalog you'll create in the next step. This recovery catalog owner is named rman, so grant the recovery_catalog_owner privilege to that user:

```
SQL> grant recovery_catalog_owner to rman;
SQL> exit;
```

Creating the Recovery Catalog

Once you've created the recovery catalog schema, your next step is to create the recovery catalog. You must connect to the recovery catalog, but not to a target database, when you do this. Here are the steps you must follow to create the recovery catalog:

1. Connect to the RMAN catalog database. You must connect as the recovery catalog owner you created in the previous section.

2. Using the `create catalog` command, create the recovery catalog. RMAN will create the recovery catalog in the default tablespace of the recovery catalog owner (cattbs in our example here). For example:

```
RMAN> create catalog;

recovery catalog created

RMAN>
```

You're now ready to use RMAN with the recovery catalog, which will store RMAN's backup and recovery metadata.

How It Works

Whether you decide to create a new recovery catalog using the database or merely create a recovery catalog schema in an existing database, you must configure the size of the default tablespace for the recovery catalog owner (schema). Several factors determine the sizing of the recovery catalog owner's default tablespace. The most important factors are as follows:

- The size of the databases you need to back up and recover with RMAN

- The frequency of the RMAN backups

- The number of databases you are planning to back up

- The number and size of the archived redo logs produced from each database

- The number and size of the scripts you plan to save in the recovery catalog

Each backup piece you create with RMAN will require an entry in the backup piece table, stored in the recovery catalog. So, the amount of space you need to allocate to the recovery catalog schema will depend on the size of a database. This means the number of data files in a database is a key determinant of the size of the recovery catalog.

The most important factor when determining the size of the recovery catalog is the frequency of backups. Even if you have a large database with a huge number of data files, if you are backing it up only infrequently, say, once a month, the amount of space taken up in the recovery catalog over time won't be significant. However, if you're making daily backups of even a medium-sized database with hundreds of data files, you'll end up needing a lot more space in the recovery catalog.

Another key determinant of the size of the recovery catalog is the number of archived redo logs produced by each database. If a database is churning out archived redo logs every few seconds, the recovery catalog will require more space to record metadata about these archived redo logs. On the other hand, a database with few DML operations won't put out too many archived redo logs and, consequently, would take up very little space in the recovery catalog.

In practical terms, Oracle suggests that if you perform a daily RMAN backup of a target database with about 100 data files, it takes roughly 60MB of storage space. Assuming the same amount of space for storing metadata for the archived redo log backups, you'll need about 120MB for the recovery catalog tablespace for the year. If you aren't making a daily backup, your storage requirements would, of course, be considerably lower. You can allocate minimal space for the temp and undo tablespaces in the recovery catalog database, since those tablespaces are sparingly used.

6-2. Granting Restricted Access
Problem

You want to grant restricted recovery catalog access to some users, granting them access to only some of the databases registered in the base recovery catalog.

Solution

You can grant a user restricted access to the base recovery catalog by granting that user read/write access only to that user's RMAN metadata, also known as a *virtual private catalog*. Creating a virtual private catalog actually encompasses two tasks: First you must create the virtual private catalog owner and grant that user the recovery_catalog_owner role and the catalog for database privilege. Then the virtual private catalog owner must connect to the base recovery catalog and create the virtual catalog.

In our example, we've registered two databases—orcl and catdb (shown below). Registering a database simply means enrolling a database in the recovery catalog, so the catalog can start recording pertinent information for a database. See Recipe 6-5 for examples of registering a database. We want to grant a restricted view of the base recovery catalog by granting a user access to the metadata for only one database, orcl.

The following are the basic steps for creating a virtual private catalog:

1. If the user who will own the new virtual private catalog doesn't exist yet in the database, then create the user (in our example, the username is virtual1):

    ```
    SQL> create user virtual1 identified by virtual1
      2  temporary tablespace temp
      3  default tablespace cattbs
      4* quota unlimited on cattbs
    SQL> /

    User created.

    SQL>
    ```

Once you create the new user, you must grant the recovery_catalog_owner role to that user.

2. Grant the new user the recovery_catalog_owner role, just as you do when you create a base recovery catalog:

    ```
    SQL> grant recovery_catalog_owner to virtual1;

    Grant succeeded.
    SQL>
    ```

User virtual1 now has the privileges to work with a recovery catalog.

3. Connect to the recovery catalog database as the base recovery catalog owner, and grant the new user virtual1 restricted access (virtual private catalog access) to just one database, orcl, from the base recovery catalog. You grant the catalog for database privilege to the new user in order to do this:

    ```
    $  [oracle@virtual1 ~]$ rman

    RMAN> connect catalog rman/rman@catdb
    ```

```
connected to recovery catalog database

RMAN> grant catalog for database orcl to virtual1;

Grant succeeded.

RMAN>
```

Note that you must first register the database with the register database command (example shown above), which enrolls the database in the recovery catalog. The grant catalog command shown in the example grants the user virtual1 access to the metadata for just a single database named orcl.

4. Now that the virtual private catalog owner has access to the metadata for the database orcl, that user can log in to the base recovery catalog and create the virtual private catalog:

```
oracle@virtual1 ~]$ rman

RMAN> connect catalog virtual1/virtual1@catdb

connected to recovery catalog database

RMAN> create virtual catalog;

found eligible base catalog owned by RMAN
created virtual catalog against base catalog owned by RMAN

RMAN>
```

The previous command creates the virtual private catalog for the user VIRTUAL1.You can confirm that the user VIRTUAL1 can access only the orcl database (and not any of the other databases registered in the base recovery catalog) by issuing the following command, after logging in as the user VIRTUAL1

```
RMAN> list incarnation;

List of Database Incarnations
DB Key  Inc Key DB Name  DB ID            STATUS  Reset SCN  Reset Time
------- ------- -------- ---------------- --- ---------- ----------
1       20      ORCL     1316762630       PARENT  1          04-JUL-12
1       2       ORCL     1316762630       CURRENT 1609405    18-JUL-12

RMAN>
```

If you log in as the owner of the base recovery catalog owner and issue the list incarnation command, you'll see the other two databases in the base recovery catalog as well, as shown in the following output:

```
RMAN> connect catalog rman/rman@catdb

connected to recovery catalog database

RMAN> list incarnation;
```

```
List of Database Incarnations
DB Key  Inc Key DB Name  DB ID              STATUS   Reset SCN  Reset Time
-------  ------- --------  ----------------   ---  ----------  ----------
501      520     ORCL     1316762630         PARENT   1          04-JUL-12
501      502     ORCL     1316762630         CURRENT  1609405    18-JUL-12
2601     2602    CATDB    2337498815         CURRENT  1          20-AUG-12

RMAN>
```

You can see that only the owner of the base recovery catalog can view the metadata for all the databases registered in that catalog, unlike the owner of the virtual private catalog, who is restricted to a specific database or databases.

How It Works

The virtual private catalog is really a set of views and synonyms based on the central or base recovery catalog. These views and synonyms are copied to the schema of the virtual catalog owner.

The virtual private catalog is a subset of the base recovery catalog to which you can grant access to users in the recovery catalog database. You can create multiple recovery catalog users, but by default, only the creator of the base recovery catalog has access to all its metadata. A virtual recovery catalog owner has no access to the metadata of the entire base recovery catalog.

■ **Note** By default, the virtual recovery catalog owner can't access the base recovery catalog.

You must be familiar with the RMAN command grant, which lets you assign privileges to database users for a virtual private catalog. You must first create a virtual private catalog before you can use the grant command to assign privileges on that private catalog to users. The grant command lets you grant two important virtual recovery catalog-related privileges, register database and catalog for database, which we explain next.

The catalog for database privilege shown here grants the virtual catalog user access to a database already registered in the base recovery catalog:

```
RMAN> connect catalog rman/rman@catdb
RMAN> grant catalog for database prod1 to virtual1;
```

By granting the register database privilege as shown in the following example, you grant a user the ability to register new databases in the virtual private catalog and, implicitly, in the base recovery catalog as well:

```
RMAN> connect catalog rman/rman@catdb
RMAN> grant register database to virtual1;
```

The register database privilege automatically grants the user the catalog for database privilege as well. Once you grant a user the register database privilege, that user has the ability to register *new databases* in the recovery catalog. The virtual private catalog owner can register new databases—that is, databases that aren't part of the base recovery catalog—by issuing the register database command. Any databases that the virtual private catalog owner registers in this way are also registered automatically in the base recovery catalog.

Even if the virtual private catalog owner has registered a particular database, the base recovery catalog owner can always unregister that database from the central recovery catalog and thus from the virtual recovery catalog, which is a subset of the main catalog.

Just as the grant command lets you grant various privileges to the recovery catalog users, the revoke command lets you take those rights away. Here's a summary of the revoke command's usage:

- By using the catalog for database clause, you can revoke recovery catalog access to a database from a user, as shown in the following example:

```
RMAN> revoke catalog for database prod1 from virtual1;
```

- The register database clause lets you revoke the ability of a recovery catalog user to register new databases.

```
RMAN> revoke register database from virtual1;
```

- The all privileges from clause, as shown in the following example, helps revoke both the catalog and the register privileges from a user:

```
RMAN> revoke all privileges from virtual1;
```

If you're using an Oracle 10.2 or older release of RMAN, you must perform the following steps to use a virtual private catalog. Connect to the base recovery catalog as the virtual catalog owner, and execute the create_virtual_catalog procedure as shown here:

```
SQL> execute base_catalog_owner.dbms_rcvcat.create_virtual_catalog;
```

If all your target databases are from an Oracle Database 11.1g or newer release, you can omit the previous step. The step is necessary only if you're planning to use a virtual private catalog with an Oracle Database 10.2g or older release. The step doesn't create a virtual private catalog—you've created the private catalog already. You need to execute this step before you can use a database belonging to an older release.

6-3. Connecting to the Catalog from the Command Line
Problem
You want to connect to the recovery catalog and the target database directly from the operating system command line.

Solution
You always use Oracle Net authentication information to connect to the recovery catalog database, but you can connect to the target database using either operating system authentication or Oracle Net authentication. The following example shows how to connect from the operating system command line using operating system authentication for the target database connection and Oracle Net authentication for the recovery catalog:

```
[oracle@virtual1 ~]$ rman target / catalog rman/rman@orcl

Recovery Manager: Release 12.1.0.0.2 - Beta on Mon Aug 20 11:29:36 2012

Copyright (c) 1982, 2012, Oracle and/or its affiliates.  All rights reserved.

connected to target database: ORCL (DBID=1316762630)
connected to recovery catalog database

RMAN>
```

In the example, we're assuming that you've already created the rman schema in the catalog database, as we described in Recipe 6-1. Since you must always connect to the recovery catalog as the owner of the catalog schema, you must, in this case, connect as the recovery catalog database user rman; whatever username you connect with in your environment should be the owner of your recovery catalog.

Instead of using operating system authentication with your target database, you can use Oracle Net credentials to connect to *both* the target database and the recovery catalog, as shown here:

```
$ rman target sys/sammyy1@target_db catalog rman/rman@catalog_db
```

Just make sure that your tnsnames.ora file, if you're using one, lists both the catalog database and the target database to which you're connecting.

How It Works

The catalog connection connects you to the recovery catalog database, and the target connection connects you to the target database you want to back up or recover. You must make some changes in the tnsnames.ora file on the server from which you're connecting to the recovery catalog, before trying the operating system–level commands shown in this solution. For example, if your recovery catalog database(catdb) is running on the server prod1, you must add the following entry in your tnsnames.ora file in the $ORACLE_HOME/network/admin directory:

```
catdb =
(DESCRIPTION =
    (ADDRESS_LIST =
        (ADDRESS =  (PROTOCOL = TCP) (HOST = prod1) (PORT=1521))
        )
    (CONNECT_DATA =
        (SERVICE_NAME = catdb)
    )
  )
```

You must also add the following entry to the listener.ora file on the server where the recovery catalog instance is running. The listener.ora file is also located in the $ORACLE_HOME/network/admin directory on Unix/Linux systems and the ORACLE_HOME\network\admin directory on Windows servers.

```
(SID_DESC =
    (ORACLE_HOME = /u01/app/oracle/db/prod1)
    (sid_name=catdb)
)
```

The portion of the listener.ora file shown here includes the protocol address, which is the network address of any object on the network, in this case the Oracle database cat_db. The Oracle listener service will accept connection requests for all databases listed in the listener.ora file.

Don't forget to specify your catalog database when invoking RMAN. Otherwise, RMAN will use the control file by default, since the recovery catalog is only an optional construct. If you don't specify catalog or nocatalog when you make a connection to the target database, you'll be using the control file as the source of all repository information. Make one mistake, and you will have broken the link between target and catalog. The following example demonstrates this:

```
$ rman

RMAN> connect target sys/Ninamma11@orcl
```

```
connected to target database: ORCL (DBID=1316762630)

RMAN> backup datafile 1;

Starting backup at 10-SEP-12
using target database control file instead of recovery catalog
allocated channel: ORA_DISK_1
channel ORA_DISK_1: SID=48 device type=DISK
channel ORA_DISK_1: starting full datafile backup set
channel ORA_DISK_1: specifying datafile(s) in backup set
input datafile file number=00001 name=/u01/app/oracle/oradata/orcl/system01.dbf
channel ORA_DISK_1: starting piece 1 at 10-SEP-12
channel ORA_DISK_1: finished piece 1 at 10-SEP-12
piece handle=/u01/app/oracle/fast_recovery_area/ORCL/backupset/2012_09_10/o1_mf_nnndf_
TAG20120910T125910_84wbmhhm_.bkp tag=TAG20120910T125910 comment=NONE
channel ORA_DISK_1: backup set complete, elapsed time: 00:01:25
Finished backup at 10-SEP-12

Starting Control File Autobackup at 10-SEP-12
piece handle=/u01/app/oracle/fast_recovery_area/ORCL/autobackup/2012_09_10/o1_
mf_n_793630838_84wbp94b_.bkp comment=NONE
Finished Control File Autobackup at 10-SEP-12

RMAN> connect catalog rman/rman@catdb

RMAN-00571: ===========================================================
RMAN-00569: =============== ERROR MESSAGE STACK FOLLOWS ===============
RMAN-00571: ===========================================================
RMAN-06445: cannot connect to recovery catalog after NOCATALOG has been used

RMAN>
```

This example connects only to the target database. Notice the message given by RMAN in response to the backup command (using target database ...). That message alerts you that you've just broken the link to your catalog database. Notice the error given next when a connection to the catalog is subsequently attempted. Just making that one backup without connecting to the catalog first has severed the link between catalog and target.

In the example shown previously, your failure to first connect to the recovery catalog before performing the backup of the target database means the recovery catalog won't have a record of this backup. The entire metadata for this backup will be absent from the recovery catalog, which will cost you dearly if you have to restore the database using RMAN. Not to worry, because you can always update or synchronize the recovery catalog from the contents of the control file. Recipe 6-8 shows how to perform a resynchronization of the recovery catalog.

6-4. Connecting to the Catalog from the RMAN Prompt
Problem

You have invoked RMAN without connecting to anything, you are sitting at the RMAN prompt, and now you want to connect to your target and catalog databases.

Solution

An easy solution is to connect to each database as a separate step. You can use operating system authentication to connect to the target database in the following way:

```
RMAN> connect target /

connected to target database: CATDB (DBID=2337498815)

RMAN>
```

You can then use Oracle Net authentication to connect to the recovery catalog:

```
RMAN> connect catalog rman/rman@catdb

connected to recovery catalog database

RMAN>
```

And, of course, you can issue the connect auxiliary command to connect to an auxiliary database, should you need to do so.

How It Works

Connecting to the target database and the recovery catalog (and to the auxiliary database) from the RMAN interface is a good way to keep key passwords from being revealed to other users in the system. If you connect directly from the operating system prompt, you'll be exposing your passwords to everyone, because they are (often) visible in the results from a ps command. However, the ps command does not "see" what you type after you invoke RMAN.

6-5. Registering Target Databases
Problem

You want to use a recovery catalog to manage the RMAN repository data for a new database.

Solution

To use a recovery catalog to store RMAN repository data concerning any target database, you must first *register* the target database with that catalog. The following steps show how to register a database in a recovery catalog:

1. Make a connection to the recovery catalog, as well as to the target database you want to register:

    ```
    % rman target / catalog rman/rman@catdb
    ```

2. If the target database isn't mounted yet, start it in the mount state:

    ```
    RMAN> startup mount;
    ```

3. Issue the register database command to register the target database to which you are currently connected:

```
RMAN> register database;
database registered in recovery catalog
starting full resync of recovery catalog
full resync complete
RMAN>
```

You can ensure that you have successfully registered the target database by issuing the list incarnation command. Here's an example:

```
RMAN> list incarnation;

List of Database Incarnations
DB Key  Inc Key  DB Name  DB ID             STATUS   Reset SCN  Reset Time
-------  -------  --------  ----------------  ---  -----------  ----------
1       20       ORCL      1316762630        PARENT   1          04-JUL-12
1       2        ORCL      1316762630        CURRENT  1609405    18-JUL-12

RMAN>
```

The list incarnation command is actually meant to show the various incarnations of a database, but we're using it here to confirm database registration in the recovery catalog by using the DB_NAME and DB_ID columns. Another way to confirm that you have successfully registered a database is to run the report schema command after registering a database, as shown here:

```
RMAN> connect target /

connected to target database: CATDB (DBID=2337498815)

RMAN> report schema;

starting full resync of recovery catalog
full resync complete
Report of database schema for database with db_unique_name CATDB

List of Permanent Datafiles
===========================
File Size(MB) Tablespace          RB segs Datafile Name
---- -------- -------------------- ------- ------------------------
1    368      SYSTEM              YES     /u01/app/oracle/product/12.1.0/db_1/dbs/dbs1catdb.dbf
2    240      SYSAUX              NO      /u01/app/oracle/product/12.1.0/db_1/dbs/dbx1catdb.dbf
3    259      SYS_UNDOTS          YES     /u01/app/oracle/product/12.1.0/db_1/dbs/dbu1catdb.dbf
4    500      CATTBS              NO      /u01/app/oracle/oradata/catdb/cattbs_01.dbf
5    100      VIRT_CATALOG        NO      /u01/app/oracle/oradata/catdb/virt_catalog1.dbf
```

```
List of Temporary Files
========================
File Size(MB) Tablespace          Maxsize(MB) Tempfile Name
---- -------- ------------------- ----------- -------------------
1    100      TEMP                100         /u01/app/oracle/oradata/catdb/temp01.dbf
```

RMAN>

As you can tell, the output of the `report schema` command clearly indicates that the catdb database was successfully registered in the recovery catalog.

How It Works

When you register a new target database in your recovery catalog, RMAN reads the control file of the target database and copies the RMAN metadata into tables in the recovery catalog. After registration, the control file and the recovery catalog will contain identical information regarding RMAN backups.

■ **Note**   Should your target database control file ever become out of sync with your recovery catalog, as it will when there are structural changes in the database, see Recipe 6-7 for instructions on how to resynchronize the two.

You can register multiple target databases in the same recovery catalog. Conversely, you can register the same target database in multiple recovery catalogs. If you have several target databases that you plan to register in a given recovery catalog, you must connect to each of them separately and register them one at a time. Make sure that each of the target databases has a unique database ID (DBID). Usually that is the case; however, if you copy a database, you might end up with multiple databases with the same DBID. Because RMAN relies on the DBID to distinguish between databases, you won't be able to register the source database and the copied database in the same recovery catalog unless you change the DBID of the copied database.

■ **Tip**   In the event you do find yourself with two databases having the same DBID, first change the DBID of one of the databases using the `dbnewid` utility. Then you can register that database in the recovery catalog.

6-6. Unregistering a Database
Problem

You want to remove a target database from the recovery catalog because you have decided to rely instead on the control file to hold backup and recovery metadata.

Solution

You can remove a target database's information from a recovery catalog and stop RMAN from tracking a target database's activity in that catalog by using the unregister database command. Here are the steps for unregistering a database from the recovery catalog:

1. Connect both to the recovery catalog and to the target database:

    ```
    [oracle@virtual1 ~]$ rman target / catalog rman/rman@catdb

    Recovery Manager: Release 12.1.0.0.2 - Beta on Mon Sep 10 13:05:43 2012

    Copyright (c) 1982, 2012, Oracle and/or its affiliates.  All rights reserved.

    connected to target database: ORCL (DBID=1316762630)
    connected to recovery catalog database

    RMAN>
    ```

2. Issue the unregister database command to unregister the target database to which you're currently connected:

    ```
    RMAN> unregister database;

    database name is "ORCL" and DBID is 1316762630

    Do you really want to unregister the database (enter YES or NO)? yes
    database unregistered from the recovery catalog

    RMAN>

    RMAN>
    ```

You may also explicitly specify the name of the database you want to unregister from the recovery catalog, along with the unregister command, as in unregister database tenner, for example.

How It Works

When you unregister a target database from the recovery catalog, the backups pertaining to that database aren't affected—you now rely on the control file, instead of the recovery catalog, to store the history of those backups. Just a reminder—prior to the Oracle Database 10g release, you were required to execute the dbms_rcvcat.unregisterdatabase(db_key, db_id) procedure from SQL*Plus to unregister a database from the recovery catalog.

Prior to unregistering a database, it's a smart idea to record the complete set of backups known to the recovery catalog by issuing the commands list backup summary and list copy summary. Then, if you later decide to reregister the database, you'll know exactly which backups are not recorded in that database's control file. You'll need to recatalog those backups. Recipe 6-6 shows you how.

You may someday find yourself in the situation of needing to unregister a database that no longer exists. In such a case, you can't, of course, connect to the nonexistent database in order to unregister it. The solution is to connect to your catalog database independently and issue an unregister command specifying exactly which database you want to unregister. For example:

```
RMAN> unregister database orcl;
```

It is further possible that you might have another database of the same name, perhaps because it is running on a different server. In such a case, use the set dbid command to specify the particular database that you want to unregister. The following example shows how to remove a specific database named orcl when multiple databases named testdb are registered:

```
RMAN> run
        {
         set dbid 1316762630;
         unregister database orcl;
        }
```

In the event that you need to issue a set dbid command, you can easily determine the DBID to use. Whenever you connect to a target database, RMAN displays the DBID for that database. In addition, you can query the recovery catalog or check the file names of the control file auto backup to find the DBID for a database. To find out how to determine the database identifier (DBID), please refer to Recipe 10-3.

6-7. Cataloging Older Files
Problem

You have some image copies, some RMAN backup pieces, and some archived redo log files that were backed up before your recovery catalog was created. You want to make all these part of the recovery catalog so that information about them is available to RMAN.

Solution

You can catalog any existing data file copies, backup pieces, or archived redo logs by using the catalog command, as shown in the following example, which catalogs an operating system–based copy of a data file:

```
RMAN> catalog datafilecopy '/u01/app/oracle/users01.dbf';
cataloged datafile copy
datafile copy filename=/u01/app/oracle/users01.dbf recid=2 stamp=604202000
RMAN>
```

Similarly, you can use the following two commands to catalog an RMAN-made backup piece and an archivelog, respectively:

```
RMAN> catalog backuppiece '/disk1/backups/backup_820.bkp';
RMAN> catalog archivelog '/disk1/arch_logs/archive1_731.dbf',
                 '/disk1/arch_logs/archive1_732.dbf';
```

The files you want to catalog can exist only on disk and not on tape, and they must belong to one of the following types:

- Data file copy
- Control file copy
- Archived redo log
- Backup piece

Cataloging a Data File Copy as an Incremental Backup

You can use the `catalog` command to catalog a data file copy that you want to use as a level 0 incremental backup. Simply add `level 0` to the `catalog datafilecopy` command, as shown here:

```
RMAN> catalog datafilecopy '?/oradata/users01.bak' level 0;
```

Once you catalog a data file copy as a level 0 backup, you can then perform an incremental backup by using that copy as your base.

Cataloging Sets of Files

If you have a whole bunch of files you need to record in the recovery catalog, you can save time and effort by using the `catalog start with` command. After the keywords `catalog start with`, you specify a string pattern. The command catalogs all valid backup sets, data file copies, archived redo logs, and control file copies whose names start with the string pattern you specify. The string pattern can refer to an OMF directory, an ASM disk group, or part of a file name.

RMAN will automatically catalog all the backups found in the locations that match the string pattern that follows the `catalog start with` command. For example, to catalog all files in the `/disk1/arch_logs` directory, use this:

```
RMAN> catalog start with '/disk1/arch_logs/';
```

In this case, the `catalog start with` command will catalog an entire directory of archived redo logs. By default, RMAN will prompt you after each match to verify that you want the item to be cataloged. You can skip this prompting by using the additional keyword `noprompt`, as shown here:

```
RMAN> catalog start with '/disk1/arch_logs/' noprompt;
```

Remember that while the "catalog" commands shown here are useful if you know the backup files that you are missing, a full resyncing of the catalog will also achieve the same purpose.

■ **Tip** You can't use the `catalog` command to add backup pieces and images that are on a tape (SBT) device.

Cataloging the Fast Recovery Area

You can also use the `catalog recovery area` command to catalog the contents of the fast recovery area. All the backup sets, archived redo logs, and datafile copies that are part of the fast recovery area will be cataloged. Here's how to do that:

```
RMAN> catalog recovery area;
```

The clause `recovery area` in this command is an exact synonym for `db_recovery_file_dest.`

How It Works

The `catalog` command comes in handy when you want to record information pertaining to backup-related files that were created outside the context of the recovery catalog. It's important to understand that this `catalog` command is completely different from the `connect catalog` command used when connecting to the recovery catalog. The `catalog` command helps you add to the RMAN repository any backup pieces and image copies you may have on disk. In addition, you can also employ the `catalog` command to record a data file copy as a level 0 incremental backup within the RMAN repository, making that backup eligible for use in an incremental backup strategy.

When you create a recovery catalog, an initial automatic synchronization occurs. During this synchronization process, RMAN gets all backup-related data from the current control file and stores the data in its own internal tables. However, as you probably are aware by now, the control file doesn't necessarily save *all* the older backup-related data. It's quite likely that some of the older backup data has aged out of the control file because of space limitations. You can make all the aged-out, older backup data available to RMAN by explicitly using the `catalog` command to register the older backups, recording them in your recovery catalog.

6-8. Updating the Recovery Catalog
Problem

The recovery catalog is sometimes not available when issuing certain RMAN commands. In addition, RMAN updates of the recovery catalog may be made infrequently under some conditions. You want to make sure the recovery catalog is updated with all the current backup information.

Solution

You use the `resync catalog` command to update or resynchronize a recovery catalog. You must connect to the recovery catalog as well as to the target database to perform the resynchronization. First, start the target database in mount mode:

```
RMAN> startup mount;
```

Next, once you connect to the target database, issue the `resync catalog` command:

```
RMAN> resync catalog;
  starting full resync of recovery catalog
  full resync complete
RMAN>
```

■ **Note** You must connect as `target` to a mounted or open database. To the recovery catalog database, you must connect as `catalog`.

■ **Note** Full resynchronization uses a snapshot of the target database control file as the source to resynchronize the recovery catalog.

How It Works

To update the recovery catalog using the current control file information, RMAN will first create a snapshot control file. It'll then compare the contents of the recovery catalog to the contents of the snapshot control file and update the recovery catalog by adding the missing information and modifying the changed backup- and schema-related records.

How often you must use the `resync catalog` command will depend on your backup frequency as well as the number of archived redo logs and online log switches produced by the target database. At the least, you must ensure that you resynchronize the recovery catalog often enough that the data in the control file gets transferred to the recovery catalog before that data is overwritten because the control file is full. This means you must keep the value of the initialization parameter `control_file_record_keep_time` longer than your backup interval. This is also a good reason you must never set the value of this parameter to 0.

Two basic types of records get updated in the recovery catalog during the resynchronization process. The first type of records consists of mostly archive log and backup–related data, such as the following:

- Online log switch information

- Archived redo log information

- Backup history, such as backup sets, backup pieces, and proxy copies

- Database incarnation history

The other major type of recovery catalog data that's updated is data relating to the *physical schema*, such as data relating to data files and tablespaces, for example. When you issue certain RMAN commands such as the `backup` command, RMAN automatically performs a resynchronization. A resynchronization involves the comparison of the recovery catalog to the current control file and the updating of the recovery catalog with the information that is either missing or changed. A resynchronization is said to be *partial* when RMAN updates only information about archived redo logs and new backups. During a *full* synchronization, in addition to the backup-related information, RMAN also updates metadata about the physical schema, such as tablespaces, data files, online redo logs, and undo segments. Thus, RMAN performs a full resynchronization whenever the schema metadata is changed; otherwise, it does only a partial synchronization.

Although RMAN automatically resynchronizes the recovery catalog pursuant to most RMAN commands, such as `backup` and `delete`, it is easy to think of situations when you may not be able to avail of this feature. For example, you may decide to perform the backups of a database without connecting to the catalog database, or you may be prevented from connecting to the recovery catalog database before the backup of a target database. Clearly, in such cases, the control file will contain the backup information but not the recovery catalog, since you weren't even connected to the recovery catalog during the backup of the target database. In cases such as these, you must connect to the recovery catalog when you get a chance and perform a resynchronization using the `resync catalog` command.

Another scenario requiring you to resort to the manual resynchronization of the recovery catalog is when you don't perform frequent backups, such as a nightly backup, but instead perform, say, a weekly or monthly backup. If you were to perform a daily backup, RMAN would've automatically synchronized the recovery catalog as part of the backup command. However, since you aren't performing a nightly backup, the recovery catalog gets updated only once a week or once a month, depending on the frequency of your backups. If you're running your database in archivelog mode and the database churns out a million of these between backups, the recovery catalog won't contain the information relating to these archived redo logs, although the control file will. The same will also be true of all online redo log switches—data regarding what is stored only in the control file but not propagated automatically to the recovery catalog. In situations such as these, manually resynchronizing the recovery catalog with the help of the resync catalog command is the only way to update the catalog.

If you've never backed up the recovery catalog or if you've backed it up but are missing some necessary archived redo logs, you can use the resync catalog command to bail yourself out. If you don't have a backup of the recovery catalog or you can't recover the recovery catalog for some reason from the backups, you must re-create the recovery catalog. You can use the resync catalog command to update the newly re-created recovery catalog with the information from the control file of the target database. However, you'll be missing the metadata for those records that have aged out of the control file. You can then use the catalog start with ... command to enter any available older backup information in the freshly re-created recovery catalog.

6-9. Dropping the Recovery Catalog

Problem

You decide to do away with your base recovery catalog, because you've decided that the control file is adequate to maintain your RMAN backup and recovery needs. Or you want to remove just a particular virtual private catalog but keep the base recovery catalog intact.

Solution

To drop the base recovery catalog, you must drop the recovery catalog schema from the recovery catalog database by using the drop catalog command. Here are the steps to follow:

1. Connect to the base recovery catalog. You don't need to be connected to a target database to drop the recovery catalog. Here's how to connect:

    ```
    RMAN> connect catalog rman/rman@catdb
    Connected to recovery catalog database
    ```

2. Issue the DROP CATALOG command. For example:

    ```
    RMAN> drop catalog;

    recovery catalog owner is RMAN
    enter DROP CATALOG command again to confirm catalog removal

    RMAN>
    ```

RMAN will force you to enter the drop catalog command a second time to ensure that you really do want to drop the recovery catalog. You want to drop the catalog for sure, so issue the drop catalog command again:

```
RMAN> drop catalog;
recovery catalog dropped
RMAN>
```

■ **Caution** When you drop the base recovery catalog, you lose the backup information for all databases registered in the base recovery catalog.

The steps for dropping a *virtual* private catalog are identical to those for the base recovery catalog. You must first connect to the recover catalog database as the virtual private catalog owner before issuing the drop catalog command. Here's an example that shows how to drop a virtual catalog:

```
$ rman
RMAN> connect catalog virtual1@catdb;
RMAN> drop catalog;
```

Here, user virtual1 is the virtual private catalog owner and not the owner of the base recovery catalog.

How It Works

The drop catalog command will remove all RMAN backup metadata from the base recovery catalog or the virtual private catalog database. You thus lose the ability to use any of the backups formerly registered in the catalog if the backups were recorded in the dropped recovery catalog but not in the control file. If you've backed up your recovery catalog prior to dropping it, you can restore it and access the backup metadata. The only other way to make those backups available to RMAN again is to create a new recovery catalog and then manually use the catalog command to record those backups in the new recovery catalog.

You can drop a virtual private catalog by logging in as the virtual catalog owner. Dropping a virtual catalog has no impact on the base recovery catalog.

6-10. Merging Recovery Catalogs
Problem

You have multiple recovery catalogs, each for a different version of your Oracle databases. You want to merge all of these recovery catalogs into one.

Solution

Use the import catalog command to merge recovery catalog schemas. Let's say you have a destination recovery catalog that has two databases registered in it. You can check the number of registered databases by issuing the list incarnation command.

Let's say you also have a different recovery catlog schema with a 10.2 version

Your goal is to merge a release 11 recovery catalog into the 12.1 release recovery catalog, thus creating a consolidated recovery catalog schema with all three databases registered in that catalog. To do this, connect to the destination catalog (12.1 release), and issue the import catalog command, as shown in the following example:

```
$ rman

RMAN> connect catalog rman/rman@twelve
RMAN> import catalog rman/rman@eleven;
```

In the previous command, you must specify the connection string for the source catalog whose metadata you want to import into the destination catalog. Issue the `list incarnation` command again to ensure that all three databases are now part of the single consolidated recovery catalog:

RMAN> list incarnation;

You'll also find that there are no databases registered in the source database any longer, when you issue the `list incarnation` command in the source recovery catalog.

You don't see any databases registered in the source database, since RMAN automatically unregisters all databases from the source recovery catalog after importing the contents of that catalog into the destination recovery catalog. If you don't want RMAN to unregister the databases from the source catalog after importing the metadata for the databases registered in that catalog, issue the following `import catalog` command, with the `no unregister` option:

```
RMAN> import catalog rman11/rman11@eleven no unregister;
```

In cases where you want to re-create a recovery catalog from a source catalog, you will not want to unregister all databases from the source catalog.

How It Works

Importing a catalog into another and merging it with the destination catalog all takes place without connecting to a target database. You simply need to connect to the source and destination recovery catalogs with the RMAN client.

The `import catalog` command will import the metadata for all the databases that are currently registered in the source catalog schema into the destination catalog schema. If you'd rather import a specific database(s), you can do so using the following variation on the `import catalog` command wherein you specify the DBID or database name of the database you want to import:

```
RMAN> import catalog rman11/rman11@eleven dbid = 123456, 123457;
RMAN> import catalog rman11/rman11@eleven db_name = testdb, mydb;
```

If a database is registered in both the source and destination target recovery catalogs, first unregister that database from one of the catalogs before proceeding. You can't perform an import when a database is simultaneously registered in both the source and destination catalogs.

You can issue the `import catalog` command only if the source database's version is identical to the version of the RMAN client you're using. If the source recovery catalog schema belongs to an older version, upgrade that catalog schema first using the `upgrade catalog` command.

6-11. Moving the Recovery Catalog to Another Database
Problem

You want to move a recovery catalog from one database to another.

Solution

You can move a recovery catalog to a different database from the present recovery catalog database by using the import catalog command. Here are the steps to move a recovery catalog:

1. Create a new recovery catalog in the target database, but don't register any databases in it.

2. Use the import catalog command in RMAN after connecting to the target database:

```
$ rman
RMAN> connect catalog rman/rman@target_db
RMAN> import catalog rman11/rman11@source_db;
```

The import catalog command will import the source recovery catalog contents into the target recovery catalog.

How It Works

Moving a recovery catalog to another database is similar to merging recovery catalogs discussed in the previous recipe, since both operations make use of the import catalog command to import a recovery catalog from one database to another.

6-12. Creating a High-Availability Recovery Catalog

Problem

You have registered a large number of databases in a single recovery catalog and want to ensure that the recovery catalog is always available to perform backup and recovery tasks. That is, you want a high-availability solution for the RMAN recovery catalog.

Solution

The solution is to maintain multiple, redundant recovery catalogs. If you're using the recovery catalog to manage the backup and recovery tasks for a large number of production databases, maintaining high availability becomes critical. You can ensure high availability of the recovery catalog just as you would any other Oracle database—by using a *standby* recovery catalog instance. In the case of recovery catalogs, however, you really don't use a special standby database for the alternate recovery catalog instance—you simply maintain a *secondary recovery catalog* that can take over from the primary recovery catalog in the event disaster strikes.

Here's a simple outline of the strategy for using a standby recovery catalog:

1. Create a secondary recovery catalog in a separate Oracle database.

2. Register all databases—all that you have registered in your primary catalog—in the secondary recovery catalog.

3. The primary recovery catalog is synchronized automatically during the normal backups of the target databases.

4. Synchronize the secondary recovery catalog manually with the resync catalog command after connecting to each of the target databases registered in the catalog.

5. Switch to the secondary catalog as the primary recovery catalog when necessary after resynchronizing it first. Switching to the secondary catalog is as easy as can be. Simply connect to that catalog instead of to the primary one. The secondary catalog will now be your primary catalog.

How It Works

It's important to synchronize the secondary recovery catalog manually on a frequent basis so the catalog remains current. This way, when you are forced to fall back on the secondary catalog, it'll have all the backup metadata you need.

You must back up the secondary recovery catalog database just as you would the primary catalog database to provide high availability.

6-13. Viewing Backup Information
Problem

You want to access information stored in the recovery catalog. You know you can use the database views in the individual target databases to find out information about their backups, but you'd like to get data about all your target databases from the recovery catalog itself.

Solution

The recovery catalog comes with its own special set of dynamic views that are analogous to the database performance views (V$ views). These recovery catalog views have the prefix RC_. Each such recovery catalog view contains information for all the target databases registered in the recovery catalog.

Most of the RC_ views use the DB_KEY column to uniquely identify a target database registered in the recovery catalog. That is, the DB_KEY column is the primary key in each of the recovery catalog views or RC_ views. To obtain the DB_KEY for a database, first identify the DBID for that database. Each DBID is mapped to a unique database and is connected to a single DB_KEY value. You can find out the DBID of a database with the following query:

```
RMAN> connect target orcl

target database Password:
connected to target database: ORCL (DBID=1316762630)

RMAN> select DBID from v$database;

      DBID
----------
1316762630

RMAN>
```

Once you have the DBID for a database, you can get the DB_KEY from the RC_DATABASE view after first connecting to the recovery catalog database:

```
SQL> connect rman/rman@catdb
SQL> select db_key from rc_database where dbid = 1316762630;

    DB_KEY
----------
       501

SQL>
```

The following are brief descriptions of the most important recovery catalog views:

RC_STORED_SCRIPT: *This view lists information about RMAN scripts stored in the recovery catalog.*

RC_UNUSABLE_BACKUPFILE_DETAILS: *This view shows the unusable backup files recorded in the recovery catalog.*

RC_RMAN_STATUS: *This view is similar to the V$RMAN_STATUS view and shows the status of all RMAN operations. This view doesn't contain information about any operations that are currently executing.*

RC_RMAN_CONFIGURATION: *This view provides information about persistent configuration settings.*

RC_DATAFILE: *This view shows all data files registered in the recovery catalog.*

RC_DATABASE: *This view shows the databases registered in the recovery catalog.*

RC_ARCHIVED_LOG: *This view provides historical information on both archived as well as unarchived redo logs.*

How It Works

Remember that you can also use RMAN commands such as list to view the information stored in the recovery catalog tables. It's often far easier to use commands than to query the views. For example, we find it generally easier to issue a list script names command than to write a select statement against the RC_STORED_SCRIPT view. Unlike normal V$ views, the recovery catalog views described in this recipe aren't normalized, since they exist mainly for the use of RMAN and Enterprise Manager. Owing to the joining of multiple tables to build each of the recovery catalog views, you see a lot of redundant information when you query these views.

6-14. Uncataloging RMAN Records
Problem

You want to remove information from the recovery catalog, perhaps pertaining to a deleted backup or to a file that you have deleted with an operating system utility.

Solution

Use the change ... uncatalog command to alter or remove specific RMAN repository records. The following are two examples of the usage of this command. The first one deletes the record of a control file copy, and the second deletes the record of a data file copy:

```
RMAN> change controlfilecopy '/u01/app/oracle/rman/backup/control01.ctl' uncatalog;
RMAN> change datafilecopy '/u01/app/oracle/rman/backup/users01.dbf' uncatalog;
```

If you want, you can query the RC_DATAFILE_COPY and RC_CONTROLFILE_COPY views to confirm deletions such as these.

How It Works

Use the change ... uncatalog command for two specific purposes:

- To update a deleted backup record's status to *deleted* in the control file repository.

- To delete a backup record from the recovery catalog. For example, if you delete an archived redo log through an operating system command instead of deleting it through RMAN, you can use the change archivelog ... uncatalog command to remove the record of that now-deleted archived redo log from the recovery catalog.

When you execute the change ... uncatalog command, RMAN doesn't remove any physical files—it merely removes references to the specified file from the recovery catalog. Only the records pertaining to the uncataloged files are removed from the recovery catalog.

6-15. Using a Release 12.*x* Client with Older Catalogs
Problem

You've installed the new Oracle 12.*x* release RMAN software. When you try to connect to an RMAN recovery catalog you created with the Oracle 10.X or 11.X release, you get an error.

Solution

If you try to connect to older versions of the recovery catalog schema using the new Oracle 12 release RMAN client, you'll receive an error saying the recovery catalog is too old. The solution is to upgrade the recovery catalog to the newer version required by the RMAN client using the upgrade catalog command. The following is a set of examples that shows how you get an error and what to do about it.

First check the version of your recovery catalog by issuing the following command from SQL*Plus after logging in as the recovery catalog owner:

```
SQL> select * from rcver;
VERSION
------------
10.02.00.00
SQL>
```

The preceding query shows that your recovery catalog is release 10.2. Now, try connecting to this recovery catalog by invoking your Oracle 12.1 release RMAN client, as shown in the following example:

```
$ rman

Recovery Manager: Release 12.1.0.0.2 - Beta on Fri Sep 21 12:37:09 2012

Copyright (c) 1982, 2012, Oracle and/or its affiliates.  All rights reserved.

RMAN>
```

You'll receive an error stating that the recovery catalog version in the recovery catalog database is too old. To be able to connect to the older recovery catalog, you must upgrade the recovery catalog in the following manner (you'll have to issue this command twice, as shown in the example, by using the upgrade catalog command):

```
RMAN> upgrade catalog;

recovery catalog owner is RMAN
enter UPGRADE CATALOG command again to confirm catalog upgrade

RMAN> upgrade catalog;

recovery catalog upgraded to version 12.01.00.00
DBMS_RCVMAN package upgraded to version 12.01.00.00
DBMS_RCVCAT package upgraded to version 12.01.00.00

RMAN>
```

After the catalog is successfully upgraded, confirm the version of the recovery catalog in SQL*Plus, again logging in as the recovery catalog owner, as shown in this example.

```
SQL> conn rman/rman
Connected.
SQL> select * from rcver;

VERSION
------------
12.01.00.00

SQL>
```

You've successfully upgraded your 10.2 version of your recovery catalog schema to the 12.1 release version.

How It Works

Not all catalog schema versions are usable with all target database releases. Please check the compatibility matrix provided by Oracle to learn about which recovery catalog schema versions are compatible with a particular version of RMAN. You can also refer to Recipe 6-12, which deals with the resolution of RMAN compatibility issues.

The RMAN client you're using can't be a more recent version than the target or auxiliary database to which you're connecting. The recovery catalog schema version must be at least the same as the RMAN client version or greater.

You can't upgrade a virtual private catalog with the upgrade catalog command—you must upgrade the base recovery catalog. When RMAN connects to the virtual private catalog the next time, it automatically performs any necessary changes in the virtual private catalog.

CHAPTER 7

■ ■ ■

Making Backups with RMAN

You can use the backup command to back up data files, archived redo logs, or control files. You can also use the backup command to make copies of data files and backups of backup sets. Because RMAN provides (since the Oracle9i Database release) the default configuration for all backup-related parameters, such as devices, formats, and tags, if you want you can back up your entire database by simply typing the command backup database at the RMAN prompt. You must, of course, first connect to the target database before backing it up, and the database must be in mount or open state if it's running in archivelog mode and must be in the mount state if it's operating in noarchivelog mode.

Key Concepts

Before we discuss various RMAN backup-related recipes in this chapter, we'll quickly review key RMAN backup-related concepts before jumping into the mechanics of performing the backups.

Backup Sets and Image Copies

The backup command lets you make two types of RMAN backups: *backup sets* and *image copies*. By default, all RMAN backups are in the form of backup sets. Each backup set contains one or more backup pieces, which are files in an RMAN-specific format. Backup sets are the default backup type for both disk- and tape-based backups.

A backup set is a logical structure that consists of a minimum of one *backup piece*, which is a physical, RMAN-specific format file that actually contains the backed-up data. A backup set can contain data from one or more data files, archived log files, or control files A backup set can't contain a combination of data files and archived log files. By default, a backup set contains just one backup piece. However, you can limit the size of a backup piece by using the maxpiecesize parameter. If you do this and the backup set size is larger than the backup piece size specified by the maxpiecesize parameter, there'll be multiple backup pieces within that backup set.

Each of the objects you back up with the backup command—database, tablespace, archived redo logs, and so on—will result in at least one backup set if you specify backup set as the backup type. RMAN determines the number of backup sets for a backup according to an internal algorithm. However, you can limit the size of a backup set by specifying the maxsetsize parameter. You can also indirectly control the number of backup sets made by RMAN for each backup by specifying the filesperset parameter, which limits the number of input files (data files, archived redo log files, and so on) that can be backed up into a single backup set.

The key difference between an image copy and a backup set is that RMAN can write blocks from many files into the same backup set (known as *multiplexing*) but can't do so in the case of an image copy—an image copy is identical, byte by byte, to the original data file, control file, or archived redo log file. An RMAN image copy and a copy you make with an operating system copy command, such as dd (which makes image copies), are identical.

■ **Note** RMAN treats all user-made backups as image copies.

Since RMAN image copies are identical to copies made with operating system copy commands, you may use user-made image copies for an RMAN restore and recovery operation after first making the copies "known" to RMAN by using the catalog command, as shown in Recipe 6-7. After this point, there's no difference between those image copies made by you and those made by RMAN. During a restore operation, if you have both image copies and backup sets from the same time period, RMAN prefers to use an image copy over a backup set. This is because there is more overhead involved in sorting through a backup set to get the files to restore. In addition, image copies offer yet another benefit during a restore and recovery operation. If you need to restore a current data file and happen to have an image copy of that data file available, you can use the switch command to simply point the database to the replacement file instead of the original data file. This eliminates the need to restore the data file, thus speeding up database recovery considerably.

RMAN Backup Modes

A control file or an archived redo log file is always backed up completely and in a consistent fashion. A data file, however, may be backed up partly or completely. You can also make consistent or inconsistent backups with data files. The various backup types are as follows:

> *Full vs. incremental backups:* A full backup is a backup of a data file that includes every allocated block in that file. Note that an image copy backup of a data file will always include every block in that file. A backup of a data file as a backup set, however, may skip data blocks that aren't in use. An incremental backup can be one of two levels: a level 0 backup including all blocks in the data file except those blocks compressed because they have never been used, or a level 1 backup including only those blocks that have changed since the parent backup.

> *Consistent vs. inconsistent backups:* A backup taken after a database was shut down gracefully (as opposed to using the shutdown abort command or a shutdown following an abrupt database crash) and restarted in mount state is said to be consistent. A consistent backup doesn't require recovery after you restore the database. A backup taken while the database is online or after it was brought into mount state after being shut down abruptly is called an inconsistent backup. An inconsistent backup always needs recovery to make the backup consistent.

If you're running in archivelog mode, the target database must be mounted or be open before you can issue an RMAN backup command. If you're running the database in noarchivelog mode, the database must first be shut down cleanly and started up in mount state before you can use RMAN for backups. If the database was abruptly shut down and restarted, RMAN can't make the backups. You mustn't back up a database running in noarchivelog mode while the database is open.

■ **Note** Starting with the Oracle Database 11*g* release, RMAN excludes the backup of undo in the undo tablespace, which is not necessary for recovering an RMAN backup. Unlike the backup optimization feature, you have no control over whether to use this feature—it works by default. You can, if necessary, disable the UNDO BACKUP OPTIMIZATION feature by setting the hidden parameter _undo_block_compression to FALSE.

By default, all RMAN backups—whole database, tablespace level, and so on—are full backups. That is, all data blocks in the data files that were ever used, even if they are currently empty, are included in the backup. You can specify the command backup full database, for example, to start a whole-database backup, but it's not necessary to do so. Just use the command backup database to do the same thing. However, when you are performing an incremental RMAN backup, you must specify the keyword incremental in your backup commands since it isn't the default backup type.

Types of Files RMAN Can Back Up

RMAN lets you back up all the files you would need for a database recovery, such as:

- Data files

- Control files

- Archived redo logs

- Image copies of data files and control files, including those made by RMAN

- Backup pieces that contain RMAN backups

The Oracle database uses three types of "live" files during its operation: data files, online redo log files, and control files. Of these three types, RMAN backs up only the data files and the control files. You can't use RMAN to back up the online redo log files. If you're operating in noarchivelog mode, you won't need the online redo logs, since the database files are always consistent when you back up the database using the only permitted modes of backing up a database in noarchivelog mode, which are closed whole backups. You won't need the online redo log backups if you're operating in archivelog mode either, since RMAN is continually backing up all your archived redo logs. However, you must make sure you always multiplex the online redo log so you won't lose all members of a group and thus all the committed changes as yet unrecorded in the data files.

In addition to the previously mentioned types of files, RMAN also can back up the server parameter file, or *spfile*, which contains the initialization parameter for starting up your database. You *can't*, however, back up the following types of files using RMAN:

- External files

- Network configuration files

- Password files

- Any Oracle home-related files

Use normal operating system copy utilities to back up any of these four types of files.

RMAN Backup Destinations

RMAN can back up to the following destinations:

- Any disk directory, including an automatic storage management (ASM) disk group.

- A media management library (tape device).

- A fast recovery area, which is the heart of Oracle's disk-based backup and recovery strategy. The fast recovery area is a disk area reserved entirely for backup and recovery purposes as well as for storing flashback logs used to support the flashback database feature.

■ **Note**   RMAN places all backups of the data files, archived redo logs, and control files in the fast recovery area by default.

7-1. Specifying Backup Options

Problem

You want to back up your database using the backup command but want to override some of the default options for the backup command as well as some of the preconfigured persistent settings made with the `configure` command.

Solution

To back up anything using RMAN, you use the backup command, as shown in the following example, which backs up the entire database:

```
RMAN> backup database;
```

Although the simple command backup `database` would suffice to perform a whole-database backup, it's smart to understand the most common options that you can specify with the backup command.

Specifying Channels

By default, RMAN comes with a single disk channel preconfigured, starting with the Oracle9*i* release of the database. So, if you're backing up to a disk, you don't have to manually allocate a channel. However, if you're backing up to tape, you must either configure an automatic channel for the tape device or manually allocate a tape (sbt) channel as part of the backup commands you issue. The following example shows how to set a channel for a tape device before making a backup of the database:

```
RMAN> connect target orcl

target database Password:
connected to target database: CATDB (DBID=2337498815)
using target database control file instead of recovery catalog

run {
    allocate channel c1 device type sbt;
    backup database;
}
```

You can use the allocate channel option to specify the channel to use when creating backups. RMAN also uses the channel id you provide to report i/o errors. You can use a meaningful name such as *CH1* or *DEV1* as the channel name. If you don't use the channel parameter, RMAN dynamically assigns the backup set to one of the available channels.

Specifying the Output Device Type

As you saw in Chapter 5, you can configure the backup device (disk or tape drive) by using the `configure` command. However, you can use the device type clause with the backup command to specify whether you want a disk device or tape device for a specific backup. The device type you specify with the device type clause will override the persistent configuration setting you created for the device type. The following example shows how to specify a tape device for a backup instead of the default disk device:

```
RMAN> backup
        device type sbt
        database;
```

Note that you must first run the `configure device type` command for a tape device before you can choose tape as the backup device type in the previous backup command.

Specifying Image Copy or Backup Set Output

When you're backing up to a disk, you have the choice of creating backups as *backup sets* or *image copies*. If you don't specify whether RMAN should make an image copy or a backup set, RMAN will make a backup set, which is the default backup type. You can use the `as copy` and `as backupset` clauses with a backup command to override the configured default device type.

You can explicitly specify that a backup be made as a backup set by using the `as backupset` clause within the backup command:

```
RMAN> backup as backupset
      database;
```

The following command shows how to specify a tape device as the backup destination and specify that the backup be made as a backup set:

```
RMAN> backup as backupset
      device type sbt
      database;
```

To make image copies of the database, use the `as copy` clause instead, as shown here:

```
RMAN> backup as copy
      database;
```

You can make image copies only on disk, not on a tape device. Therefore, you can use the `backup as copy` option only for disk backups, and the `backup as backupset` option is the only option for making tape backups.

Specifying a Backup Format

Backup format refers to the naming of the RMAN backup files. There are several ways in which you can specify the backup file name. Here are the set of rules governing the file names, in order of precedence:

- Specify the `format` clause in the `backup` command to generate the backup file name.

- Configure a `format` setting for the specific channel that you use in the backup.

- Configure a `format` setting for the device type used in the backup.

- If you enabled a fast recovery area, RMAN will generate a name for the backups in the fast recovery area if you don't specify the `format` clause.

If none of the four formatting rules applies, RMAN will name the backups and store them in locations based on operating system–specific rules. Since the `format` clause is at the top of the formatting rules in order of precedence, let's look at that clause in detail in this section.

You can specify the format option with the backup command to direct the RMAN backup output to a specific location. In the following example, RMAN's backup output is directed to the /u01/backup/ directory, and the backup files are stored with unique names generated by the random string generator %U:

```
RMAN> backup
         database
         format= '/u01/backup/%U ';
```

If your default backup device is a disk, by default all RMAN backups are sent to the fast recovery area (if you've configured it) and stored there with automatically generated file names. If you don't specify the format option and you haven't configured a fast recovery area, the backups are stored in an operating system–specific default location.

You may also use an ASM disk group as the destination for the RMAN backups, as shown in the following example:

```
RMAN> backup
         database
         format '+dgroup1';
```

The database backups will be stored in the diskgroup +dgroup1.

Specifying Tags for Backup Output

You can use the tag option to make RMAN assign a unique name to each of the backups that you make. In the following example, the tag parameter of the backup command specifies that the backup must be tagged with the identifier weekly_backup:

```
RMAN> backup
         database
         tag  'weekly_backup';
```

If you don't use the tag parameter to assign your own customized tag, RMAN will attach a default tag to every backup it creates. Chapter 4 discusses RMAN tags.

How It Works

If you're operating the target database in archivelog mode, the database must be mounted or open before you can issue an RMAN backup command. If you are running the database in noarchivelog mode, the database must first be shut down cleanly and started up in mount state before you can use RMAN for backups. If the database was abruptly shut down and restarted, RMAN can't make the backups. You mustn't back up a database running in noarchivelog mode while the database is open.

You can use RMAN's backup command to back up the following entities:

- Tablespaces
- Data files (current or copy)
- Control file (current or copy)
- Spfiles
- Archived logs
- Backup sets

In this recipe, we showed you how to use the most common options that control the types, naming, and formatting of RMAN's backup output files. However, you don't need to use all those options. Since RMAN uses default values for all those options, your backups will still be made successfully without you specifying values for each possible option. You need to specify an option only when the default value is not something you like.

The following are the key points you must remember about the basic RMAN options described in this recipe:

- The backup set is the default backup type.

- The default device is disk.

- RMAN assigns default tags if you omit the tag clause in your backup commands.

- You can't set the number of backup pieces in a given backup set—that's something RMAN will determine based on an internal algorithm.

- If you don't use the device type clause in your backup command, RMAN will back up to the currently configured default device type.

- You can't back up a backup set from tape to another tape or from tape to disk, although you can go from disk to tape.

7-2. Backing Up the Control File

Problem

You want to back up the control file often so that your backup copy always reflects the current structure of the database.

Solution

In Recipe 5-3, you learned how to use the configure command to enable automatic backups of the control file:

```
RMAN> configure controlfile autobackup on;

old RMAN configuration parameters:
CONFIGURE CONTROLFILE AUTOBACKUP ON;
new RMAN configuration parameters:
CONFIGURE CONTROLFILE AUTOBACKUP ON;
new RMAN configuration parameters are successfully stored

RMAN>
```

From here on out, RMAN will create a backup of the control file (as well as the server parameter file) whenever you perform any backup with RMAN or make structural database changes.

If you prefer not to configure automatic control file backups, you can use the backup command's current controlfile clause to perform a manual backup of the current control file, as shown here:

```
RMAN> backup current controlfile;
```

You also have the option to manually include the control file with any other backup that you make. You do that by adding the include current controlfile option to any backup command. For example, you can back up the control file as part of a tablespace backup operation:

```
RMAN> backup tablespace users include current controlfile;
```

If you make any backup that includes data file 1, RMAN automatically backs up both the control file and the server parameter file. You can use the `include current controlfile` clause with a `backup database` command as well.

You can also execute the `alter database backup controlfile` command from within RMAN as of Oracle 12c, in the following manner:

```
RMAN> alter database backup controlfile to '/u01/app/cf_back.ctl';

Statement processed

RMAN>
```

In earlier database versions, you'd have to employ the RMAN `sql` command to issue the SQL `alter database backup controlfile` command. For example:

```
RMAN> sql "alter database backup controlfile to ''/orabac/prod1/cf_back.ctl''";
```

Issuing an `alter database backup controlfile` command is probably the least desirable method for backing up the control file. Unlike a control file auto backup, this backup doesn't have the metadata for the previous backup, which is essential for database recovery. Therefore, you have to manually keep track of when and where such a backup took place.

■ **Note**   See Recipe 5-4 for a complete description of enabling/disabling the `controlfile` autobackup feature.

How It Works

You can have RMAN automatically back up the control file as part of regular database backups, or you can explicitly issue commands whenever you want to back up your control file. We strongly recommend using the auto backup feature for control file backups, as explained in Chapter 5.

When you issue the `backup current controlfile` command, RMAN will create a backup set that contains a copy of the control file. If you are using a server parameter file (spfile), RMAN includes it in the same backup set. If you are using a fast recovery area, RMAN will place the backup piece in the location specified by the initialization parameter `db_recovery_file_dest`. If you aren't using a fast recovery area, the control file is backed up to an OS-dependent directory under ORACLE_HOME. For example, with Windows the default directory is ORACLE_HOME/database. From then on, RMAN will back up the control file anew whenever you initiate a backup operation from RMAN that includes data file 1.

RMAN actually backs up the control file whenever you back up data file 1, regardless of the auto backup setting. If you haven't set the control file auto backup to on, RMAN will include the control file as well as the server parameter file (if you have started the instance with a server parameter file) as part of the backup of data file 1. If, on the other hand, you've configured the control file auto backup to on, RMAN won't include the control file as part of the data file 1 backup, but it generates a separate control file auto backup piece for it.

The control file auto backups contain metadata about the previous backup. RMAN makes a control file auto backup after every backup command you issue from the command line and after every backup command in a run block that's not followed by another backup command. Control file auto backups are significant because RMAN can restore the control file even if you lose both the control file and the recovery catalog.

7-3. Backing Up the Server Parameter File

Problem

You want to make a copy of the database's server parameter (spfile) file using RMAN so that you have a record of the most recent database configuration.

Solution

Use the `backup spfile` command to back up the server parameter file, as shown here:

```
RMAN> backup spfile;
```

The previous command backs up the server parameter file currently in use by the database instance. Note that you'll be able to backup the SPFILE only if you've started the instance with the SPFILE.

How It Works

To successfully back up a given server parameter file through RMAN, you must first make sure you start the database with that server parameter file. You don't want to have used the text-based, init.ora style of parameter file. If you start the database using an init.ora file instead of an spfile, RMAN won't back up the spfile, since it really isn't currently in use by the instance.

■ **Note** RMAN can't make backups of the multiple server parameter files you may have on the server. It backs up only the *current* server parameter file.

7-4. Backing Up Data Files

Problem

You have a large database with thousands of data files, and you don't have the resources to take a daily backup of your database. You therefore need to implement a strategy that can back up a subset of the database by copying a set number of data files each day.

Solution

RMAN gives you the option of backing up individual data files. You can back up a data file either by using the data file number or by using the data file name. The following example shows how to back up data files by specifying their numbers. The `format` option specifies the format of each backup piece file name:

```
RMAN> backup datafile 1,2,3,4
    format '/u01/app/oracle/rman/%d_%U.bus';
```

Instead of specifying a data file number, you can specify the names of the data files you want to back up. In the following example, the first command configures a channel with a specific file name format, and the second command backs up two data files:

```
RMAN> configure channel device type disk format '/oraback/prod1/%d_%U.bus';
RMAN> backup datafile '/u01/app/oracle/oradata/system01.dbf',
       '/u01/app/oracle/oradata/users01.dbf';
```

■ **Note**   Once you configure a channel, there is no need to specify it in other backup commands unless you need to change it. These configuration settings are persistent.

You can also take *incremental backups* of data files. The following example takes an incremental level 1 backup of data file 5:

```
RMAN> backup incremental level 1 datafile 5;
```

As you'll learn later in this book, you must already have made a level 0 incremental backup of the database (with the command backup incremental level 0 datafile 5) before you can take an incremental level 1 backup.

You can use RMAN to make a physical copy, also called an *image copy*, of a data file. The next example makes an image copy of the data file users01.dbf and uses the format parameter to specify the backup file name. The actual file users01.dbf is located in the directory /u01/app/oracle/oradata/orcl, and its image backup, also named users01.dbf, is stored in the directory /u01/app/oracle/backup.

```
RMAN> backup as copy datafile '/u01/app/oracle/oradata/orcl/users01.dbf'
2> format '/u01/app/oracle/backup/users01.dbf';

Starting backup at 11-SEP-12
using channel ORA_DISK_1
channel ORA_DISK_1: starting datafile copy
input datafile file number=00006 name=/u01/app/oracle/oradata/orcl/users01.dbf
output file name=/u01/app/oracle/backup/users01.dbf tag=TAG20120911T111006 RECID=6 STAMP=793710608
channel ORA_DISK_1: datafile copy complete, elapsed time: 00:00:03
Finished backup at 11-SEP-12

Starting Control File Autobackup at 11-SEP-12
piece handle=/u01/app/oracle/fast_recovery_area/ORCL/autobackup/2012_09_11/o1_mf_n_793710610_
84yrm3wj_.bkp comment=NONE
Finished Control File Autobackup at 11-SEP-12

RMAN>
```

The as copy clause directs RMAN to make an image copy instead of the default backup sets.

How It Works

The backup datafile command is fairly straightforward. RMAN will back up the specified data files and put them into backup pieces. If auto backup of the control file is disabled and data file 1 (SYSTEM) is backed up, RMAN will include a backup of the current control file. If the auto backup of the control file is disabled and the system tablespace isn't included in the tablespace list, then no backup of the control file is created.

When you perform a full data file backup (as against an incremental data file backup), RMAN reads every block that has ever been used in a data file into the input buffer and eventually backs it up to the specified device. RMAN skips all data blocks in a data file that have never been used. That saves space and is unlike an image file backup, which makes a byte-per-byte copy of the source file.

Only never-used data blocks are skipped to save on space. Even if a previously used data block is currently empty because the data was deleted at some point, RMAN still backs up the data block. The reason for this seemingly odd behavior is that RMAN was designed to back up data even when the database isn't open when you can't access the data dictionary to check whether a specific data block is on the free list (blocks get on the free list once all data has been deleted from them).

If you haven't configured a format for the location and name of the backup pieces, RMAN will write files to the fast recovery area. If the fast recovery area is not configured, then it is operating system dependent on where the backup pieces are written.

If you're using the backup as copy command and don't specify a destination for the image copies, RMAN chooses the storage locations according to the following criteria:

- If the output channel has a default configure...format setting, that setting will be the basis for the output file names.

- If you configure a fast recovery area, the backups will be sent there.

- If you haven't configured a fast recovery area, an operating system–specific default format is used (that is, the format parameter, which includes a %U for the generation of unique filenames, is used).

You can view data file numbers and data file names in the V$DATAFILE, V$DATAFILE_COPY, or V$DATAFILE_HEADER view. For example, to view data file numbers and data file names in your database, issue this SQL command:

```
RMAN> select file#, name from v$datafile;
```

You can also issue the RMAN report schema command to display data file names and numbers. Once you know the name or number for each file you want to back up, you can use the backup datafile command to perform the actual backup operation.

7-5. Backing Up Tablespaces

Problem

You want to back up one or more tablespaces, either as a part of a regular backup schedule or for some special purpose.

Solution

Use the backup tablespace command to back up one or more tablespaces. The following example shows how to back up two tablespaces, users and tools:

```
RMAN> backup tablespace users,example;
```

Since we didn't specify an image copy, RMAN will create a backup set containing the two specified tablespaces. The following example shows how to specify the format parameter in a backup tablespace command:

```
RMAN> backup tablespace system format '/u01/app/oracle/backup/%d_%U.bus';
```

The next example shows how to make an image copy of a tablespace:

```
RMAN> backup as copy tablespace users;
```

If you want to take an incremental backup of a tablespace, include the incremental clause in the backup command:

```
RMAN> backup incremental level 1 tablespace example;
```

The incremental backup command shown here performs a level 1 incremental backup of the tablespace named example.

To back up a tablespace of the seed (pluggable) database PDB$SEED, you need to enclose the seed database name in double or single quotes, as shown here:

```
RMAN> backup tablespace "PDB$SEED":SYSTEM;
```

OR

RMAN> backup tablespace 'PDB$SEED':SYSTEM;

The examples shown here will back up the tablespace SYSTEM.

How It Works

In Oracle a tablespace is a logical grouping of data files. Sometimes you'll need the flexibility to back up these logical subsets of your database. Using the backup tablespace command provides you with an easy way to back up parts of your database. You can use the backup tablespace command to back up both read/write and read-only tablespaces.

■ **Tip**   If you're using an Oracle Database 11.1*g* or newer release, transportable tablespaces don't have to be in read/write mode. You can't, however, perform a backup of read-only transportable tablespaces if you're dealing with older databases.

When backing up tablespaces, RMAN will back up all data files that belong to those tablespace(s). RMAN takes each tablespace name and translates it into the corresponding data file names. RMAN then copies the data file blocks to the backup pieces. If auto backup of the control file is disabled (the default) and the system tablespace is backed up, RMAN automatically includes a backup of the control file.

If you don't specify the location and name of the backup pieces by using the format option or by using the configure command, RMAN will write files to the fast recovery area. If you haven't configured the fast recovery area, the backup pieces are written to an operating system–dependent location.

7-6. Making a Whole-Database Backup

Problem

You want to back up the entire database.

Solution

You can perform a whole-database backup with the database started in mount state or the database open. Issue the simple backup database command, as shown here:

```
RMAN> backup database;
```

The backup database command will back up all data files. And, assuming you've set configure controlfile autobackup to on, it'll back up the current control file and the current server parameter file as well at the end of the backup.

To make sure you have a complete set of archived redo logs through the time of the backup, it is common practice to archive the current online redo log, as shown in the following example:

```
RMAN> backup database;

RMAN> alter system archive log current;

Statement processed

RMAN>
```

In pre–Oracle Database 12c release databases, you need to use the following statement instead:

```
RMAN> SQL "alter system archive log current";
```

The first of these commands backs up the database. The second (and its alternate version for earlier versions of the database) archives the current redo log right after the backup completes.

How It Works

The backup database command backs up all data files and the control file but not the archived redo logs. If you take a consistent backup of the database, you can later use this backup to restore and recover without performing media recovery. That is, you won't have to apply any changes from the archived redo logs before opening the database.

To take a consistent backup, you must satisfy the following two conditions:

- You must first shut down the database normally, that is, use one of the following statements: shutdown, shutdown normal, shutdown immediate, or shutdown transactional.

- You must start up the database in mount state before taking the backup.

If you're recovering a database using inconsistent backups, you must first make the database consistent through applying the archived redo logs before you can open it. Backups taken under the following conditions are inconsistent:

- If you create a backup of a database after restarting a database that was shut down abruptly (say, because of a power failure) or with the shutdown abort command

- If you create a backup of the database while the database is open

There's nothing wrong with inconsistent backups—by definition, all open database backups are inconsistent. You can safely use inconsistent backups as the foundation of your backup and recovery strategy. Since database uptime is critical, most production databases depend on inconsistent backups. All you have to do is to make sure you're running your database in archive log mode and that you're backing up your archived redo logs along with your data files.

7-7. Backing Up Archived Redo Logs

Problem

You want to back up the archived redo logs by themselves.

Solution

Use the backup archivelog command to back up archived redo logs. To back up one copy of each log sequence number for all the archived redo logs, for example, you can issue the following command:

```
RMAN> backup archivelog all;
```

The backup archivelog command shown in this example will back up only a single copy of each of the archived redo logs, even if there are multiple copies of those logs. That is, the command will back up a single copy of each distinct log sequence number per thread.

The following example shows how to use the archivelog like clause with the backup command to back up one archived redo log for each unique log sequence number:

```
RMAN> backup device type sbt
        archivelog like '/disk%arc%'
        delete all input;
```

Let's say you have two archiving destinations, one called /disk1/arch/ and the other called /disk2/arch/. If a certain archived redo log, say, log 9999, is in both directories, RMAN will back up only one of the copies, not both. The delete all input clause deletes all archived redo logs from all (in this case, two) destinations after the backup.

You can limit the backup of the archived redo logs based on a specific time, SCN, or log sequence number. In the following example, the clauses from time and until time limit the range of the archived redo log backups:

```
RMAN> backup archivelog
        from time "sysdate-15" until time "sysdate-7";
```

The previous command uses a specified time period to direct the backing up of all archive logs generated between two weeks ago and last week. To back up archived redo logs based on specific log sequence numbers, use the keyword sequence and provide either a specific log sequence number or a range for the sequence numbers. Here are some examples:

```
RMAN> backup archivelog sequence 99
        delete input;        # specifies a particular log sequence number
RMAN> backup archivelog sequence between 99 and 199 thread 1
        delete input;        # specifies range of records by log sequence numbers
```

In both examples, the delete input clause directs RMAN to delete the backed-up archived redo log files after they're successfully backed up.

How It Works

You can make a backup of the archived redo logs using any of the following clauses with the backup command:

- `archivelog all`
- `plus archivelog`
- `archivelog from...`

When you issue the backup command with the `archivelog all` or `plus archivelog` clause, either of these commands will back up the archived redo logs, and RMAN first directs the database to switch the current online redo log group. After this, all unarchived redo logs, including the one the database just switched out of, are archived. This process guarantees that the backup contains all the redo information generated until the backup started.

When you use the `backup database plus archivelog` command to back up archive logs as part of another backup, RMAN will perform the following operations in the sequence listed here:

1. Run the `alter system archive log current` command.
2. Run the `backup archivelog all` command.
3. Back up the rest of the data files specified by the `backup database` command.
4. Run the `alter system archive log current` command.
5. Back up the new archive logs generated during the backup operation.

The sequence of operations listed here means that RMAN will have all the necessary archived redo log information it'll need down the road if it has to perform a complete recovery of the database.

■ **Note**   The `backup database plus archivelog` command will back up the entire database and all the archived redo logs as well as the current control file in a single command. See the next recipe for details.

Instead of backing up archive logs specifically by using the `backup archivelog` command, you can back up the archive logs as part of a database backup or some other data file backup. The following recipe shows how you can back up the database, along with all the archive logs, using a single command, `backup database plus archivelog`.

7-8. Backing Up Everything
Problem

You want to create a backup of the entire database, meaning all the data files, the archived redo logs, and the control file.

Solution

To make sure the control file is backed up automatically as part of the database backup, first make sure you have configured automatic control file backups by using the following command:

```
RMAN> configure controlfile autobackup on;

old RMAN configuration parameters:
CONFIGURE CONTROLFILE AUTOBACKUP ON;
```

```
new RMAN configuration parameters:
CONFIGURE CONTROLFILE AUTOBACKUP ON;
new RMAN configuration parameters are successfully stored

RMAN>
```

Then you can issue the backup database plus archivelog command to back up the database along with the archived redo logs:

```
RMAN> backup database plus archivelog;

Starting backup at 12-SEP-12
current log archived
using channel ORA_DISK_1
skipping archived logs of thread 1 from sequence 33 to 38; already backed up
channel ORA_DISK_1: starting archived log backup set
...
channel ORA_DISK_1: backup set complete, elapsed time: 00:00:26
Finished backup at 12-SEP-12

Starting backup at 12-SEP-12
using channel ORA_DISK_1
channel ORA_DISK_1: starting full datafile backup set
channel ORA_DISK_1: specifying datafile(s) in backup set
input datafile file number=00005 name=/u01/app/oracle/oradata/orcl/cattbs_01.dbf
...
channel ORA_DISK_1: backup set complete, elapsed time: 00:00:45
input datafile file number=00001 name=/u01/app/oracle/oradata/orcl/system01.dbf
...
channel ORA_DISK_1: backup set complete, elapsed time: 00:01:25
Finished backup at 12-SEP-12

Starting backup at 12-SEP-12
current log archived
using channel ORA_DISK_1
channel ORA_DISK_1: starting archived log backup set
...
channel ORA_DISK_1: backup set complete, elapsed time: 00:00:01
Finished backup at 12-SEP-12

Starting Control File Autobackup at 12-SEP-12
...
Finished Control File Autobackup at 12-SEP-12

RMAN>
```

The BACKUP command shown in this example backs up the data files, the archived redo log files, and the control file (because control file autobackup is on), as well as the current spfile. If you issue the LIST BACKUP BY FILE command now, you can see that RMAN has a record of all the backed-up files, sorted by the backup file type (data files, archive logs, control files, and the spfile). For example:

```
RMAN> list backup by file;

List of Datafile Backups
========================
```

File	Key	TY	LV	S	Ckp SCN	Ckp Time	#Pieces	#Copies	Compressed	Tag
1	143	B	F	A	2150919	12-SEP-12	1	1	NO	TAG20120912T103431
	131	B	F	A	2078370	10-SEP-12	1	1	NO	TAG20120910T125910
2	141	B	F	A	2150875	12-SEP-12	1	1	NO	TAG20120912T103431
	138	B	F	A	2113798	11-SEP-12	1	1	NO	TAG20120911T111156

```
...
List of Archived Log Backups
============================
```

Thrd	Seq	Low SCN	Low Time	BS Key	S	#Pieces	#Copies	Compressed	Tag
1	29	1925370	07-AUG-12	140	A	1	1	NO	TAG20120912T103405
1	30	1925437	07-AUG-12	140	A	1	1	NO	TAG20120912T103405

```
...
List of Control File Backups
============================
```

CF Ckp SCN	Ckp Time	BS Key	S	#Pieces	#Copies	Compressed	Tag
2150970	12-SEP-12	145	A	1	1	NO	TAG20120912T103740
2113818	11-SEP-12	139	A	1	1	NO	TAG20120911T111232

```
...
List of SPFILE Backups
======================
```

Modification Time	BS Key	S	#Pieces	#Copies	Compressed	Tag
20-AUG-12	130	A	1	1	NO	TAG20120820T113325
20-AUG-12	129	A	1	1	NO	TAG20120820T112324
07-AUG-12	128	A	1	1	NO	TAG20120807T145320

RMAN>The list backup by file command shows you the data files, the archived redo logs, the control file, and the spfile that was backed up with the backup database plus archivelog command.

How It Works

You can use the backup database command to make a backup of all the data files in a database. The backup database command by itself can back up only data files and control files but not the archived redo log files. You must add the plus archivelog clause to back up the archived redo logs.

If the control file autobackup feature is turned off, RMAN *won't* automatically include the control file in the database backup. To force RMAN to include a backup of the current control file in the backup in such a situation, you must add the `include current controlfile` clause to your backup command, as shown here:

```
RMAN> backup database
   2> include current controlfile;
```

The previous command will back up all the data files, the control file, and the spfile. You can't add the `include current controlfile` clause to a backup that includes the archived redo logs. You can use the clause only in a data file backup.

7-9. Backing Up Recovery Files in the FRA

Problem

You want to back up all the recovery files located in the fast recovery area of a database so that you can store them offline on tape.

Solution

Use either the `recovery area` clause or the `db_recovery_file_dest` clause with your backup command to back up all the recovery files for a database (*recovery area* and `db_recovery_file_dest` are synonymous). To back up the recovery files in the fast recovery area, use the following command (you must first configure sbt as the backup channel):

```
RMAN> backup recovery area;
```

If the default device type is disk, you may issue the following command instead to back up the fast recovery area:

```
RMAN> backup device type sbt recovery area;
```

By adding the subclause `destination` to the `backup recovery area` command, you can specify a disk channel as the location for the backing up of the recovery area files.

```
RMAN> backup recovery area to destination '/u01/app/oracle/backup';
```

Both of the previous commands will back up recovery files that were created not only in the current fast recovery area but also in all previous fast recovery area locations.

If you want to back up the recovery files located in all locations, not merely the fast recovery area, use the following command instead after configuring a tape backup channel:

```
RMAN> backup recovery files;
```

If the default device type is disk, then you may issue the following RMAN command instead:

```
RMAN> backup device type sbt recovery files;
```

By adding the subclause `destination` to the `backup recovery files` command, you can specify a disk channel as the location for the backing up of the recovery area files:

```
RMAN> backup recovery files to destination '/u01/app/oracle/backup';
```

All three of the previous three commands will back up *all* recovery files on disk, whether they're part of the fast recovery area or are stored elsewhere on disk.

How It Works

Recovery files include full and incremental backup sets, control file auto backups, archived redo logs, and data file copies. Recovery files do not include files such as flashback logs, the current control file, and the online redo log files. If the fast recovery area isn't currently enabled, RMAN will back up eligible recovery files from previously configured and enabled fast recovery area destinations.

When RMAN is backing up the fast recovery area, it has the capability to fail over to alternate archiving destinations if necessary. For example, if an archived redo log in the fast recovery area is missing or corrupted, RMAN will instead back up a good archived redo log from the alternative location.

It's important to remember that you must specify a tape device when backing up any fast recovery area files. By default, RMAN turns backup optimization on during a fast recovery area backup, even if that feature is currently turned off. You may, however, override this behavior by adding the force option when configuring backup optimization.

7-10. Performing Incremental Backups
Problem

Instead of making a complete backup of your database every night, you want to be able to back up only the changed data in order to complete backups within the time interval provided by your backup window and also to save storage space.

Solution

An *incremental backup* includes only changed data blocks instead of entire data files, as normal full backups do. You can make two types of incremental backups with RMAN—*differential incremental backups* and *cumulative incremental backups*—and both of these types are explained in the following sections.

■ **Note** If you don't specify either the full or the incremental option during a backup, RMAN will perform a full backup by default.

Differential Incremental Backups

A *differential incremental backup* is an incremental backup of all data blocks that changed subsequently to a level 0 or a level 1 backup. RMAN first looks for a level 1 backup and, in its absence, looks for a level 0 backup and backs up all changes since that level 0 backup. Here's an example of a differential incremental level 0 backup:

```
RMAN> backup incremental level 0 database;
```

Incremental level 0 backups can be made as image copies or backup sets.

Here's how you would perform a level 1 differential incremental backup that backs up the data blocks changed since the most recent level 0 or, if there's no level 0 backup, a level 1 backup:

```
RMAN> backup incremental level 1 database;
```

> ▨ **Note**   Backup sets are the only choice you have for creating level 1 incremental backups to either a tape device or a disk device.

Since a level 1 incremental backup backs up only the changed blocks, it tends to be faster than a level 0 backup in most cases. You can make backups of the backup set type only when making a level 1 incremental backup.

> ▨ **Note**   RMAN makes differential incremental backups by default if you don't specify the incremental backup type.

Cumulative Incremental Backups

A *cumulative incremental backup* is an incremental backup of *all* data blocks that changed subsequently to the most recent level 0 incremental backup. The following command shows how to make a cumulative incremental backup of a database:

```
RMAN> backup incremental level 1 cumulative database;
```

The previous command backs up all data blocks that have changed since the last *level 0* backup.

How It Works

An incremental backup is designed to make shorter and faster backups of your data files by backing up only changed data blocks instead of all the data blocks in a data file. RMAN uses the SCNs present in each of Oracle's data blocks in every data file as the basis of its incremental backup policy. If the SCN of a data block in the data file that's a backup candidate is the same or greater than the SCN of the parent incremental backup, RMAN will back up that data block. Otherwise, RMAN will exclude that data block from the incremental backup.

The basis for all incremental backups is the parent backup, also called a *level 0* backup. A level 0 backup includes all the data blocks in all the datafiles and serves as the base or foundation for future incremental backups. Note that even though a full backup also includes all data blocks, it can't serve as the basis for future incremental backups—you can use a level 0 backup only as the parent for incremental backups.

Often the choice between a cumulative differential and incremental differential backup comes down to a trade-off between space and recovery time. If you use cumulative backups, you'll use more storage space, but you can recover faster, since you'll need to apply fewer incremental backups. Differential incremental backups, on the other hand, take less space to store, but you'll take more time to recover with them, because in most cases you'll need to apply a lot more of these than the cumulative differential backups.

When you issue the following command to perform a differential incremental backup, if neither a level 1 nor a level 0 incremental backup is available, RMAN will back up all blocks changed since the creation of that data file and save the backup as a level 1 backup (for database compatibility greater than or equal to 10.0.0).

```
RMAN> backup incremental level 1 database;
```

Here's an example of how the default differential incremental backup works in an Oracle database:

1. Let's say you take an incremental level 0 backup on a Sunday night. This backup will include all the blocks in the database that were used and will serve as the foundation for future incremental backups.

2. On Monday, you take a differential incremental level 1 backup that backs up all changed blocks since the level 0 backup on Sunday.

3. From Tuesday through Saturday, you take a level 1 differential backup that copies all changed blocks since the level 1 backup the day before.

4. If you have to recover the database on a Saturday morning, you'll need the previous Sunday's level 0 backups plus all the differential incremental level 1 backups from Monday through Friday.

A cumulative level 1 backup always takes longer than a differential backup, since it backs up all changed blocks since the last level 0 incremental backup. Thus, cumulative backups need more time as well as space, since they "repeat" or "duplicate" the copying of changed blocks. Differential backups, on the other hand, don't duplicate the work performed by previous backups at the same level—a differential incremental level 1 backup done on a given day is always distinct from the same-level backup done the day before.

You can perform incremental backups of any of the following:

- Data file
- Data file copy
- Tablespace
- Database

You *can't* perform an incremental copy of a control file, archived redo log, or backup set.

While incremental backups do, in general, take significantly less time to complete than a full backup of the same files, you can't be absolutely sure that this is always true. This is because of how RMAN checks data blocks for changes. Even during an incremental backup (at a greater than level 0 incremental backup), RMAN still reads all data blocks in a data file into the memory to check the block's SCN number. Any block with an SCN more recent than the SCN of the level 0 incremental backup is moved from the input buffer to the output buffer, and from there it's written to the backup piece.

■ **Note** If you want fast incremental backup performance, use the block change tracking feature, where RMAN doesn't scan all the data blocks to see whether they've changed, to determine whether they are candidates for the incremental backup.

You can't use an incremental backup directly during a database restore operation since it's only a complement to a full backup and can't be "restored." It's only to provide a faster recovery time (faster mean time to recovery, or MTTR). The following example serves to demonstrate this point:

```
RMAN> run
    {
      restore datafile 7;
      recover datafile 7;
    }
```

Once RMAN restores data file 7 from the latest level 0 incremental backup, it has two choices. It can use incremental level backups since the most recent level 0 backup and add any necessary archive logs to recover the database to the present point in time. Alternatively, RMAN can choose to use archived logs only from the level 0 backup time to recover. RMAN always prefers using incremental backups to archive logs.

7-11. Reducing Incremental Backup Time

Problem

You want to reduce the time it takes to perform incremental backups.

Solution

Implement RMAN's *block change tracking* feature to reduce the time it takes to make an RMAN incremental backup. By default, the block change tracking feature is disabled. Use the following command to create a change tracking file in the specified location (if you leave out the location, RMAN creates the block change tracking file in the location specified by the db_create_file_dest initialization parameter).

1. First, make sure the db_create_file_dest parameter is set. If it isn't, set it using the alter system command, as shown in this example:

    ```
    SQL> alter system set
            db_create_file_dest='/u01/app/oracle/dfiles'
            scope= both;
    ```

2. Enable block change tracking by using the following alter database statement:

    ```
    RMAN> alter database enable block change tracking using file
    '/u01/app/oracle/backup/change_track.f';

    Statement processed

    RMAN>
    ```

    The name of the change tracking file is *change_track.txt* in our example.
    You can *disable* block change tracking by using the following command:

```
RMAN> alter database disable block change tracking;

Statement processed

RMAN>
```

The change tracking file is automatically deleted when you execute the previous command.

How It Works

RMAN uses a binary file referred to as the *block change tracking file* to record the changed blocks in each data file in a database. When you perform an incremental backup, RMAN refers to this change tracking file instead of scanning all the data blocks in all the data files in the database, thus making the incremental backups finish faster. You can use the alter database statement to change the name of the change tracking file.

The V$BLOCK_CHANGE_TRACKING view shows whether change tracking is enabled as well as other things such as the change tracking file name.

If you need to move the change tracking file, use the following procedure:

1. Determine the current location of the change tracking file with the following command:

```
RMAN> select filename from v$block_change_tracking;

FILENAME
---------------------------------------------------------------------------

/u01/app/oracle/backup/change_track.f

RMAN>
```

2. Shut down the database.

3. Move the change tracking file to the new location using the following command:

```
$ mv /u01/app/oracle/backup/change_track.f  /u01/app/oracle/rman/change_track.f
```

4. Start up the database in mount mode:

```
SQL> startup mount
```

5. Use the `alter database rename file` command to rename the change tracking file in the Oracle database:

```
SQL> alter database rename file
    '/u01/app/oracle/backup/change_track.f' to
    '/u01/app/oracle/rman/change_track.f';
```

6. Open the database:

```
SQL> alter database open;
```

If you can't shut down the database for some reason, you have to first disable change tracking and then reenable it after you rename the change tracking file, as shown here:

```
SQL> alter database disable block change tracking;
SQL> alter database enable block change tracking using file
    '/u01/app/oracle/rman/change_track.f';
```

■ **Note**   You can turn on block change tracking in a physical standby database, thus making the incremental backups of the standby database run faster.

As a result of directing output to the new change tracking file without shutting down the database, you'll lose the contents of the original change tracking file. RMAN will scan the entire file as a result until the next time you perform a level 0 incremental backup.

The size of the change tracking file is not proportional to the number of updates in the database. Instead, the size of the file depends on how large the database is, the number of data files, and how many threads of redo are enabled. Initially, the change tracking file starts at 10MB and grows in 10MB increments. Since RMAN allocates 320KB of space in the change tracking file for each data file in the database, a database with a very large number of data files would require a larger allocation of space for the change tracking file than a database with a small number of data files.

7-12. Creating Multiple Backup Sets
Problem

You want to initiate a backup and have RMAN automatically make multiple copies of the resulting backup set. You don't want to make any persistent configuration changes to your RMAN environment.

Solution

You can specify the making of multiple copies (duplexing) of backup sets by using the backup command's copies option or by issuing the set backup copies clause in a backup command. The following example shows how to use the copies option to make multiple backup copies. Of course, you need to tell RMAN where the multiple destinations for the duplexed backups are by using the format option. Here's our example:

```
RMAN> backup
      copies 2
      database
      format  '/u01/app/oracle/backup/db_%U',
              '/u02/app/oracle/backupdb_%U';
```

In the example shown here, the copies parameter produces two backups of the database, each on a different disk, with disk locations being specified by the format parameter.

The next example shows how to use the set backup copies command to make two backup copies of the database:

```
run
{
  allocate channel c1 device type sbt
  parms 'ENV=(OB_DEVICE_1=testtape1,OB_DEVICE_2=testtape2)';
  set backup copies = 2;
  backup database  plus archivelog;
}
```

The OS environment variables specific to Oracle Secure Backup (OSB), such as OB_DEVICE_1, must be in uppercase. Otherwise, the corresponding OSB job will not be restricted to a specific drive. Instead, the corresponding OSB job will use whatever tape drive is available, which is the default behavior.

■ **Note**　If you want to duplex your backups when using a tape device, you must enable the backup_tape_io_slaves initialization parameter on the target database you are backing up.

Assuming you are using a media manager that supports version 2 of the SBT API, the media manager will automatically write the two identical backup copies resulting from the previous `run` block to different tape drives. If you're using a disk channel instead, you must specify the `format` parameter to direct the copies to their destination physical disk locations.

When you use the `set` command from the RMAN command line by using a command such as `set backup copies=2`, the configuration specified by the `set` command will remain in force until the end of the session. If you use the same `set` command in a `run` block, the configuration will be in force until the `run` block completes executing.

How It Works

Whenever RMAN creates a backup set (but not an image copy), you can take advantage of RMAN's built-in *duplexed backup set* feature to make multiple copies of that backup set. You can specify a maximum of four copies of each backup piece in a backup set. This applies to backups of data files, archived redo log files, and control files. You can use the `configure ... backup copies` command to persistently configure backup duplexing, as explained in Recipe 5-11. If you'd rather not persistently configure multiple backup copies, you can use either of the two commands shown in the Solution section of this recipe—`set backup copies` or `backup copies`—to configure duplexed backup sets. By default, the `configure ... backup copies` is set to 1 for both disk and tape backups. You can use the `configure` command to change the default duplexing level of 1 for all future backups. You can also use either the `backup copies` command or the `set backup copies` command to override the configured setting for multiple copies.

Here's the order of precedence for the three ways in which you can configure RMAN backup duplexing, with settings higher in the list overriding the others:

```
backup copies
set backup copies
configure ... backup copies
```

You can't use the `as copy` option when duplexing, since you can duplex only backup sets and not image copies. You also can't use duplexing when creating backup files in the fast recovery area. However, this is true only when making image copies (using the `backup as copy` command). You can duplex backups as a backup set when the fast recovery area is the destination. The following example shows this:

```
RMAN> run {
        allocate channel d1 type disk;
        set backup copies = 2;
        backup
        as backupset
        datafile 2
        format '+BACKUP',
        '+BACKUP';
        release channel d1;
        }
allocated channel: d1
channel d1: SID=124 device type=DISK
executing command: SET BACKUP COPIES
Starting backup
...
released channel: d1
RMAN>
```

If you don't specify the format parameter and you haven't configured a fast recovery area, RMAN will still make the multiple copies and send them to operating system–specific locations. For example, on a Windows-based system, the backups are sent to the $ORACLE_HOME/database directory.

Note that when you specify the duplexing of a backup set, RMAN doesn't produce multiple *backup sets*—it produces multiple copies of the *backup pieces* in that backup set. That is, if you set duplexing to the maximum of four, for example, RMAN will produce only one backup set and then generate four copies of each backup piece in that backup set.

You can't back up from a tape device to another tape device. You also can't back up from a tape device to disk. You can, however, use the backup . . . backupset command with the device type sbt clause to back up disk-based backups to a tape device.

7-13. Making Copies of Backup Sets
Problem

You have previously made backups in the form of backup sets and want to make copies of these backups for off-site storage and other purposes.

Solution

Use the backup . . . backupset command to back up a previously made backup set. Here's an example showing how to use the backup . . . backupset command to back up the backups you've made to disk:

```
RMAN> backup device type sbt
2> backupset
3> completed before 'sysdate -2';

Starting backup at 12-SEP-12
allocated channel: ORA_DISK_1
channel ORA_DISK_1: SID=48 device type=DISK
skipping backup set key 130; already backed up 1 time(s)
skipping backup set key 132; already backed up 1 time(s)
Finished backup at 12-SEP-12

RMAN>
```

The backup . . . backupset command shown here backs up to tape all backup sets more than a month old.

How It Works

The backup . . . backupset command is useful in moving backup sets from disk to a tape storage device. The command comes in handy when you want to save storage space by removing older backup sets from disk after first copying them to tape for long-term storage. It's especially important to free up space in the fast recovery area for new backups by moving the older backups from disk to tape.

It's important to understand that the backup ... backupset command produces additional copies of the backup pieces in the backup set but doesn't create a new backup set itself with a different backup set key.

7-14. Making Copies of Image Copy Backups
Problem
You want to make copies of image copy backups you've already made using RMAN.

Solution
Use the backup as copy or backup as backupset command to make copies of image copies made by RMAN. Here are some examples:

```
RMAN> backup as copy copy of database;
RMAN> backup as backupset copy of tablespace users;
RMAN> backup as backupset copy of datafile 4;
```

The first backup as copy command makes an image copy of an image copy of the database. Make sure you make an image copy of the database first! The second command, backup as backupset, creates a backup set from an image copy of a tablespace. The third command, backup as backupset, creates a backup set from an image copy of a data file.

The following example shows how to copy two data files using the tag weekly_copy. The example creates the data file copies in a new location and names them using substitution variables:

```
RMAN> backup as copy
        copy of datafile 2,3
        from tag 'weekly_copy'
        format '/backup/datafile%f_Database%d';
```

In the previous example, the format parameter uses the percent sign (%) as a wildcard that means zero or more characters. Use an underscore (_) instead of the percent sign to refer to exactly one character. The syntax element f refers to the absolute file number, and the syntax element d specifies the name of the database.

The following example shows how to make an image copy of a database copy to the default destination:

```
RMAN> backup as copy
        copy of database
        from tag "test";
```

The previous command will create new copies of the original image copy of the database with the tag test.

How It Works
You can use either the copy of database, copy of tablespace, or copy of datafile clause to make a backup of an image copy of a database, tablespace, or data file, respectively. Note that the output of any of these commands can be either an image copy or a backup set.

> ■ **Note** If you happen to have multiple image copies of a data file and you issue an RMAN backup command with the copy of database clause, RMAN uses the most recent image copy of that data file to make the backup.

As shown in the examples, you can refer to a file by its name or by its number. You may also specify copies by their tag names and let RMAN find the specified files from those tags.

7-15. Making Tape Copies of Disk-Based Image Copies

Problem

You've already made an image copy of a data file on disk and want to move it to a tape drive for off-site storage.

Solution

You can use either the backup datafilecopy or backup ... copy of command to back up image copies from disk to tape (you can use either command to back up an image copy from disk to disk as well). Here's how you use the backup datafilecopy command:

```
RMAN> backup device type sbt datafilecopy '/u05/app/oracle/system01.dbf';
```

The previous command backs up the image copy of the /u05/app/oracle/system01.dbf data file to a tape drive. Instead of the actual data file name as shown in this example, you can alternatively specify a backup *tag* to identify the input image copies. This makes it easy for you to specify the input data file copy when you happen to have multiple backups of that data file. The following command backs up all data file copies that have the tag whole_db:

```
RMAN> backup datafilecopy from tag whole_tag;
```

The new image copy made from the original image copy will inherit the tag of the source image copy.

Here's an example showing how to use the backup ... copy of database command to back up image copies from disk to tape:

```
RMAN> backup as backupset
      device type sbt_tape
      tag "monthly_backup"
      copy of database;
```

The previous backup command will make a backup of the image copies of all data files and the control file of the target database. Since we specified a backup set as the backup type, RMAN will generate backup sets, even though you're making the copy of the database from an image copy of the database.

How It Works

Often, you may first copy a data file to disk and then want to transfer the backup to a tape device for storing it off-site. The backup datafilecopy and backup ... copy of commands come in handy at times like this.

You can use the noduplicates option when backing up datafile copies to ensure that only a single copy of each data file copy is backed up by RMAN. The following example comprising a series of backup commands illustrates this point:

```
RMAN> run {
backup as copy
datafile 1
format '/u01/app/oracle/backups/df1.copy';
backup as copy
datafilecopy '/u01/app/oracle/backups/df1.copy'
format '/u02/app/oracle/backups/df1.copy';
backup as copy
datafilecopy '/u01/app/oracle/backups/df1.copy'
format '/u03/app/oracle/backups/df1.copy';
backup
device type sbt
datafilecopy all noduplicates;
}
```

The first backup command creates an image copy of data file 1. The second and third backup commands use the datafilecopy clause to back up the image copy of data file 1 to two other locations on disk. The last backup command backs up only one of the two copies on disk to a tape drive (sbt).

7-16. Excluding a Tablespace from a Backup
Problem

You have a tablespace whose contents don't change over time or a tablespace that contains temporary data, such as test data, that you don't need to back up. You want to exclude such tablespaces from a whole backup of the database.

Solution

Use the configure exclude for tablespace command to exclude a tablespace from a whole-database backup. First use the show exclude command to see whether any tablespaces are already configured to be excluded from backups:

```
RMAN> show exclude;

RMAN configuration parameters for database with db_unique_name ORCL are:
RMAN configuration has no stored or default parameters
RMAN>
```

By default, RMAN includes all the tablespaces in the database for a whole backup. To exclude a particular tablespace from future backups, you would use the following command (users is the tablespace you want to exclude):

```
RMAN> configure exclude for tablespace users;

tablespace USERS will be excluded from future whole database backups
new RMAN configuration parameters are successfully stored
RMAN>;
```

Any tablespace exclusion you specify in a RMAN session through the configure command will last through that RMAN session.

How It Works

You may exclude any tablespace from a whole backup, except the system tablespace. You can disable tablespace exclusion and include a previously excluded tablespace in future backups by using the following command:

```
RMAN> configure exclude for tablespace users clear;

Tablespace USERS will be included in future whole database backups
old RMAN configuration parameters are successfully deleted
RMAN>
```

Even after excluding a specific tablespace as shown in the previous section, you can back up that tablespace either by using the noexclude option in a backup database or backup copy of database command or by issuing a backup tablespace command. If you use the noexclude option as part of a backup database or backup copy of database command, RMAN will back up all tablespaces, including those tablespaces that you expressly excluded from the backup earlier with a configure exclude command. Here's how you use the noexclude option as part of a backup database command:

```
RMAN> backup database noexclude;
```

Since the exclusion from the RMAN backup is stored as a property of the tablespace and not of the individual data files in the tablespace, the exclusion will apply to any new data files you may add to an excluded tablespace.

7-17. Skipping Read-Only, Offline, or Inaccessible Files

Problem

You want RMAN to skip the backing up of read-only, offline, or inaccessible data files and archived redo log files.

Solution

You can skip the backup of offline, read-only, or inaccessible data files and archived redo log files by using the skip option, as shown in the following example:

```
RMAN> backup database
      skip inaccessible
      skip readonly
      skip offline;
```

The explicit skipping of inaccessible, read-only, and offline data files means that RMAN won't issue an error when it confronts a data file that falls into one of these three categories.

How It Works

Since read-only tablespaces don't change over time, you need to back up these tablespaces only once, after you first make a tablespace read-only. Note that you can persistently skip read-only, offline, and inaccessible tablespaces by using the configure exclude command, as explained in Recipe 7-16.

You can use the skip inaccessible clause with your backups to specify the exclusion of any data files or archived redo logs that couldn't be read by RMAN because of I/O errors. For example, some archived redo logs may have been deleted or moved and thus can't be read by RMAN. In such cases, the skip inaccessible clause will avoid errors during a backup.

7-18. Encrypting RMAN Backups

Problem

You want to encrypt the backups made with RMAN to meet your organization's security guidelines.

Solution

By default, all RMAN backups are unencrypted (encryption is turned off), but you can encrypt any RMAN backup in the form of a backup set. You can encrypt the backup sets in two ways: transparent encryption and password encryption.

Transparent Encryption

The default encryption mode in RMAN is transparent encryption. Transparent encryption uses the Oracle encryption key management infrastructure to create and restore encrypted backups. Transparent encryption is the way to go if you want to persistently configure encrypted backups. Here are the steps to encrypt backups using this method:

1. Configure the Oracle Encryption Wallet (Oracle Wallet) if it hasn't already been configured before. You can do this in several ways, including using the Oracle Wallet Manager. However, using the SQL command we show you here is probably the easiest way to create the wallet. Before you create the Oracle Wallet, first create a directory named *wallet* in the directory $ORACLE_BASE/admin/$ORACLE_SID. After that, issue the following statement from SQL*Plus:

   ```
   SQL> alter system set encryption key identified by "sammyy11";
   System altered.
   SQL>
   ```

   The `alter system` statement will do the following for you:

   - If you already have an Oracle Wallet, it opens that wallet and creates (or re-creates) the master encryption key.

   - If you don't have an Oracle Wallet already, it creates a new wallet, opens the wallet, and creates a new master encryption key.

2. If you're using the encrypted wallet, open the wallet. If you're using the auto login form of the Oracle Wallet, you don't have to do this, since the Oracle Wallet is always open under this method. The SQL statement in the previous step automatically opens a new wallet after creating it.

3. Configure encrypted backups using the `configure` command, as shown in the following example:

   ```
   RMAN> configure encryption for database on;
   new RMAN configuration parameters:
   CONFIGURE ENCRYPTION FOR DATABASE ON;
   new RMAN configuration parameters are successfully stored
   RMAN>
   ```

The previous command will configure automatic backup encryption for all database files using the default 128-bit key (AES128) algorithm. You can use an alternative encryption algorithm by specifying the `algorithm` parameter with the value for the alternative encryption algorithm (AES256, for example). You don't have to specify any encryption-related options or clauses with your backup commands when you configure encryption using the `configure` command, as shown in the example.

4. Make encrypted backups by using the usual backup or backup . . . backupset command, as shown here:

```
RMAN> backup database;
```

Make sure that the Oracle Wallet is open before you issue the previous backup command because you've configured database encryption in the previous step, which requires the use of the Oracle wallet as explained earlier.

Password Encryption

If you don't want to configure an Oracle Wallet, you can still perform encrypted backups by using the `set encryption` command. This method is called *password encryption* of backups since the DBA must provide a password both for creating an encrypted backup and for restoring an encrypted backup.

Use the `set encryption` command to use password encryption, as shown here:

```
RMAN> set encryption on identified by <password> only;
```

The `set encryption on` command lets you make password-protected backups. If you've also configured *transparent encryption*, then the backups you make after this will be dual protected—with the password you set here as well as by transparent encryption.

How It Works

You use normal RMAN backup commands to perform backup encryption once you set up configuration using the Oracle Wallet (and the `configure` command) or the password encryption (and the `set encryption` command). Oracle uses a backup encryption key encrypted with either the password or the database master key, depending on whether you choose password-based encryption or the Oracle Wallet–based encryption.

In addition to the transparent encryption and password encryption modes, you also have the option of using a dual mode of encryption, wherein you may create the encrypted backups using a password (using the `set encryption on identified by <password>` command) but can decrypt the backups using either a password or Oracle Wallet credentials. This method is appropriate in cases where you may have to perform off-site restoration of encrypted backups without access to the Oracle Wallet.

It's a good idea to configure multiple channels when performing backup encryption using RMAN because of the additional demands on resources for encrypting backup data.

You can select the level (database, tablespace) of backup encryption as well as the algorithm to use for the encrypted backups through the `configure` command. By default, RMAN uses the 128-bit AES encryption algorithm. If you configured persistent encryption settings through the `configure` command, you can turn encryption off when necessary by using the following command:

```
RMAN> configure encryption for database off;
```

The following command shows a variation of the configure command, where we use the tablespace option with the configure command to specify encryption for a specific tablespace named example:

```
RMAN> configure encryption for tablespace example on;

tablespace EXAMPLE will be encrypted in future backup sets
new RMAN configuration parameters are successfully stored

RMAN>
```

When you back up the database, only the example tablespace backup will be in an encrypted form. You can disable encryption for the tablespace example by using the following command:

```
RMAN> configure encryption for tablespace example off;

Tablespace EXAMPLE will not be encrypted in future backup sets
new RMAN configuration parameters are successfully stored

RMAN>
```

If you back up an already encrypted backup set using the backup ... backupset command, no further encryption takes place. Oracle simply backs up the previously encrypted backup set. However, if you use transparent data encryption in some tables to encrypt selected columns, the encrypted RMAN backups will encrypt the already encrypted columns again when backing up the data.

You can look up the available algorithms for encryption in the V$RMAN_ENCRYPTION_ALGORITHMS view. You can configure the compression alogorithm to something other than the default by executing the configure encryption algorithm command, as shown here:

```
RMAN> configure encryption algorithm 'AES256';

new RMAN configuration parameters:
CONFIGURE ENCRYPTION ALGORITHM 'AES256';
new RMAN configuration parameters are successfully stored
RMAN>
```

The previous command configures the compression algorithm to AES 256-bit encryption.

It's important to note the following about RMAN backup encryption:

- RMAN backups created as a backup set can be encrypted. RMAN image copies cannot be encrypted.

- RMAN encrypted backups can be taken to disk. ASO licensing is required.

- RMAN encrypted backups to tape are possible only with Oracle Secure Backup as the media manager. ASO licensing is not required.

7-19. Making a Compressed Backup

Problem

You want to compress RMAN backups to save storage space.

Solution

Specify the as compressed backupset option with your backup command to direct RMAN to produce a binary compressed backup set, as shown in the following example:

```
RMAN> backup
  2> as compressed backupset
  3> database plus archivelog;
2> 3>

Starting backup at 21-SEP-12
current log archived
allocated channel: ORA_DISK_1
channel ORA_DISK_1: SID=52 device type=DISK
skipping archived logs of thread 1 from sequence 29 to 59; already backed up
channel ORA_DISK_1: starting compressed archived log backup set
...
Starting backup at 21-SEP-12
using channel ORA_DISK_1
channel ORA_DISK_1: starting compressed full datafile backup set
channel ORA_DISK_1: specifying datafile(s) in backup set
```

The previous command will back up all data files and the archived redo log files as a compressed backup set. The backup may be made to disk or tape, depending on which one you configured as the default backup destination.

How It Works

RMAN's compression capabilities are especially useful when you're backing up to disk and confront a tight disk space situation. Just make sure you schedule the compressed backups during a low database usage period, because of the higher CPU overhead for compression.

You don't need to explicitly uncompress a compressed backup during recovery. RMAN recommends that you not use RMAN's backup set compression feature if you're backing up to a tape device and the media manager is using its own compression capability.

You don't have to worry about any extra work during the recovery of a compressed backup—you restore a compressed backup the same way as an uncompressed backup set.

By using what's called *unused block compression*, Oracle reads only the currently allocated blocks to a database table and doesn't write the unused blocks to the backup. If the database satisfies the following five conditions, RMAN automatically applies the *unused block compression* feature.

- The compatible initialization parameter must be set to 10.2 or higher.

- There are no guaranteed restore points in the database.

- The data files are locally managed.

- You must either back up to disk, or use Oracle Secure Backup as the media manager.

- You're backing up the data file to a backup set, either as part of a full backup or a level 0 incremental backup.

7-20. Parallelizing Backups

Problem

You want to make the backups complete faster by parallelizing them.

Solution

You can parallelize a backup by configuring channel parallelism using the channel parameter. Each allocate channel command you specify will dictate the files each channel should back up, along with the locations where RMAN should place those backups. Here's an example that shows how to use a parallelism of degree 2 by specifying two separate tape channels for a single backup job:

```
run
{
allocate channel ch1 device type sbt
      parms 'ENV=(OB_DEVICE=testtape1)';
allocate channel ch2 device type sbt
      parms 'ENV=(OB_DEVICE=testtape2)';
backup
database channel ch1
archivelog all channel ch2;
}
```

If you're backing up to multiple disk drives, you can allocate a disk channel for each disk drive. You can use the format clause of the allocate channel command to spread the backups across multiple disks to enhance backup performance. Here's an example that shows how to spread the backup of a database across four disks:

```
run
{
  allocate channel d1 device type disk  format '/u01/%d_backups/%U';
  allocate channel d2 device type disk  format '/u02/%d_backups/%U';
  allocate channel d3 device type disk  format '/u03/%d_backups/%U';
  allocate channel d4 device type disk  format '/u04/%d_backups/%U';
  backup database;
}
```

If you want to configure persistent backup parallelism, first specify the degree of parallelism for the device type you want, as shown here:

```
RMAN> configure device type disk parallelism 4;

new RMAN configuration parameters:
CONFIGURE DEVICE TYPE DISK PARALLELISM 4 BACKUP TYPE TO BACKUPSET;
new RMAN configuration parameters are successfully stored

RMAN>
```

In the previous example, we specify a degree of parallelism of 4 for the device type disk. Once you configure the degree of parallelism, configure channels as follows (assuming you want parallelism of degree 4) using the parallelism clause to specify the degree of parallelism:

```
configure device type disk parallelism 4;
configure default device type to disk;
configure channel 1 device type disk format '/u01/%d_backups/%U';
configure channel 2 device type disk format '/u02/%d_backups/%U';
configure channel 3 device type disk format '/u03/%d_backups/%U';
configure channel 4 device type disk format '/u04/%d_backups/%U';
```

RMAN will henceforward distribute all your backups over the four disks by default. You can undo the configuration of parallelism for the disk device in the following manner:

```
RMAN> configure device type disk clear;

old RMAN configuration parameters:
CONFIGURE DEVICE TYPE DISK PARALLELISM 4 BACKUP TYPE TO BACKUPSET;
RMAN configuration parameters are successfully reset to default value
RMAN>
```

You can also specify the degree of parallelism for tape backups by using the following command:

```
RMAN> configure device type sbt parallelism 3;
```

The previous command uses a degree of parallelism of 3 for all subsequent tape backups. Once again you can use the clear option to revert to the default parallelism setting, as shown here:

```
RMAN> configure device type sbt clear;
```

This command will set the degree of parallelism to the default value of 1, which means future tape backups will not be parallelized.

How It Works

You can parallelize an RMAN backup by using either the configure command (as explained in Chapter 5) or the allocate channel command to manually specify multiple channels for a backup job.

The parallelism clause configures the number of automatic channels of a specific type, disk, or tape that RMAN allocates to a job. The default degree of parallelism is 1, and you can set the degree of parallelism for both disk and tape drives, as shown in the "Solution" section of this recipe. RMAN determines the degree of parallelism for a job based on which device type you specify as the device type for the backup.

7-21. Making Faster Backups of Large Files

Problem

You want to make faster backups of a large data file.

Solution

You can back up a large data file faster by dividing the backup work among multiple channels so they can back up the large data file in parallel. To do this, you can make a *multisection backup*, wherein each channel backs up a section of a data file, thus enhancing performance.

You perform a multisection backup by specifying the section size parameter in the backup command. Here are the steps you must follow to make a multisection backup:

1. Connect to the target database.

   ```
   $ rman target sys/<sys_password>@target_db
   ```

2. Configure channel parallelism. In this example, we use a parallel setting 3 for the sbt device, as shown here:

   ```
   run{
   allocate channel c1 device type sbt
        parms 'ENV=(OB_DEVICE=testtape1)';
   allocate channel c2 device type sbt
        parms 'ENV=(OB_DEVICE=testtape2)';
   allocate channel c3 device type sbt
        parms 'ENV=(OB_DEVICE=testtape3)';
   ```

3. Execute the backup, specifying the section size parameter:

   ```
   RMAN> backup
   2> section size 150m
   3> tablespace system;

   Starting backup at 28-SEP-12
   using target database control file instead of recovery catalog
   allocated channel: ORA_DISK_1
   ...
   channel ORA_DISK_1: starting full datafile backup set
   channel ORA_DISK_1: specifying datafile(s) in backup set
   including current control file in backup set
   channel ORA_DISK_1: starting piece 1 at 28-SEP-12
   channel ORA_DISK_1: finished piece 1 at 28-SEP-12
   piece handle=/u01/app/oracle/fast_recovery_area/CATDB/backupset/2012_09_28/o1_mf_ncnnf_
   TAG20120928T102135_86cj5x8x_.bkp tag=TAG20120928T102135 comment=NONE
   channel ORA_DISK_1: backup set complete, elapsed time: 00:00:01
   Finished backup at 28-SEP-12

   RMAN>
   ```

In this example, the tablespace system has one data file, size 600m. The `section size` parameter (set to 150m) breaks up the data file backup into four chunks of about 150m each.

How It Works

In a multisection backup, multiple channels back up a single data file. Each of the channels you specify will back up a single file section, which is a contiguous set of blocks in a data file. Each of the data file sections is backed up to a different backup piece.

■ **Note** You can't specify the `section size` parameter along with the `maxpiecesize` parameter.

By default, RMAN won't let you make multisection backups for any data file smaller than 1GB, but you can override this by simply specifying a smaller size than 1GB in the **section size** parameter of the RMAN **backup** command. You can have up to 256 sections per data file. RMAN makes uniform-size sections, except the very last one, which may or may not be the same size as all the other sections.

Use the backup command clause `section size` to perform multisection backups. If you don't specify a value for the sections with the `section size` parameter, RMAN computes an internal default section size for that backup job. Multisection backups offer performance benefits, since you can back up a single data file simultaneously in multiple sections, thus parallelizing the backup. You also don't have to back up a large file all over again, if the backup fails midway—you need to back up only those sections that weren't backed up the first time around.

You must set the initialization parameter `compatibility` to at least 11.0 when performing multisection backups, since it's not possible to restore multisection backups with a release earlier than 11.0.

You can also use the `section size` clause with the `validate datafile` command.

The `section_size` column in both the V$BACKUP_DATAFILE and RC_BACKUP_DATAFILE views shows the number of blocks in each section of a multisection backup. If you haven't performed any multisection backups, the section_size column would have a zero value. The V$BACKUP_SET and RC_BACKUP_SET views tell you which backups or multisection backups. The following example shows a query on the V$BACKUP_DATAFILE view:

```
SQL> select pieces, multi_section from V$BACKUP_SET;
```

```
PIECES      MUL
------      --------
     1      NO
     2      YES
     7      YES
     4      NO
SQL>
```

The V$BACKUP_DATAFILE shows information about control files and data files in backup sets. The previous command shows that data file 7's backup is a multisection backup.

7-22. Specifying Backup Windows
Problem

The DBA has a limited window for running the RMAN backups. The backups must complete within this specified backup window every day.

Solution

By using the `duration` parameter as part of your `backup` command, you can specify a window for an RMAN backup. The backup either will complete during the time interval you specify with the `duration` parameter or will stop midway through the backup if it doesn't finish within the specified time. RMAN may or may not issue an error when an ongoing backup runs past the backup window, based on your selection of certain options.

Here's an example that shows how to limit an RMAN backup to six hours:

```
RMAN> backup duration 6:00
      database;
```

You can use the `duration` clause along with other clauses to control what happens when a backup fails to complete within the specified time interval. By default, RMAN reports an error when the backup is interrupted because of the end of the backup interval. If your `backup` command is part of a `run` block, that `run` block will also terminate immediately. By using the optional clause `partial`, you can suppress the RMAN error reports and instead have RMAN merely report which data files it couldn't back up because of a lack of time. Here's an example:

```
RMAN> backup duration 6:00 partial
      database
      filesperset 1 ;
```

In addition to not issuing any error messages, the `partial` clause also lets the other commands within a `run` block continue to execute after the termination of a backup when the window of time for backups expires. You can also use the `duration` clause along with one of two other options to control the *speed* of the backup. To perform the backup in the shortest time possible, specify the `minimize time` option, as shown here:

```
RMAN> backup
      duration 6:00 partial
      minimize time
      database
      filesperset 1;
```

On the other hand, if you think that the backup may not go over the backup window, you can reduce the overhead imposed by the backup with the `minimize load` option with the `duration` clause, as shown here:

```
RMAN> backup
      duration 6:00 partial
      minimize load
      database
      filesperset 1;
```

When you specify the `minimize load` clause, RMAN extends the backup (slows it down) to take advantage of all the time that's available to it.

How It Works

Each of the `backup` commands shown in the Solution section specifies the `filesperset` parameter. When you specify `filesperset=1`, each file gets its own backup set. Thus, when the backup is terminated when you bump up against the backup window, only the backup of a particular data file is lost, and all the other backup sets already made will be good. When you resume the backup afterward, you don't have to back up these data files again (this may not be true if the SCNS of the data file headers have changed since the most recent backup).

When you specify the minimize load clause, RMAN periodically estimates the completion time for a currently running backup. If RMAN estimates that a backup will complete within the backup window, it slows down the backup to fit the entire backup window so as to reduce the overhead on the database.

If you're using a tape device to make the backup, you must understand the implications of using the minimize load clause during backups. When you use the minimize load clause, tape streaming may be below the optimal level because of the slowing down of the rate of backups by RMAN. Since RMAN has the exclusive use of the tape device for the entire duration of the backup, you can't use that tape device for any other purpose during the backup. For the reasons listed here, Oracle recommends that you not use the minimize load option when using a tape drive to make your backups.

7-23. Reusing RMAN Backup Files

Problem

You want to reuse some existing RMAN backup files by overwriting existing backups with new backups.

Solution

You can use the reuse option with your backup commands to enable RMAN to overwrite existing backups, as shown in the following example:

```
RMAN> backup reuse database FORMAT '/u01/app/oracle/backup/backup01.rman';
```

How It Works

When you include the reuse option with a backup command, RMAN will overwrite the existing backups with the newer backups. The existing backup files, both backup sets and image copies, will be overwritten by a file with an identical name. You must provide the FORMAT clause, as we showed in the example in the Solution section. Otherwise, the backup command we showed will create a new backup piece, instead of reusing the existing backup.

7-24. Retaining Backups for a Long Time

Problem

You want to retain certain backups beyond what the retention policy for the database will allow for archival purposes.

Solution

Use the keep option with the backup command to retain backups beyond what's mandated by the retention polices that you've configured. In the following example, the keep until time clause tells RMAN to retain the backup for a period of six months:

```
run
{
backup database
tag quarterly
keep until time 'sysdate+180'
restore point '2012Q1';
}
```

The BACKUP command with the KEEP UNTIL TIME clause ensures that RMAN exempts this backup from any configured retention polices and retains it for six months after the backup. The BACKUP command also creates the *restore point* 2012Q1 to mark the SCN at which the backup will be consistent.

■ **Note** Backups that use the backup . . . keep command are also known as *archival backups*.

Note that you need to specify a location other than the fast recovery area for any backup files you want to make with the keep attributes. If you try to store these files in the fast recovery area, you may encounter the following error:

```
RMAN> backup database keep forever tag 'semi_annual_bkp';

Starting backup at 12-SEP-12
starting full resync of recovery catalog
full resync complete
current log archived

channel ORA_DISK_1: starting piece 1 at 12-SEP-12

RMAN-00571: ===========================================================
RMAN-00569: =============== ERROR MESSAGE STACK FOLLOWS ===============
RMAN-00571: ===========================================================
RMAN-03002: failure of backup command at 09/12/2012 14:22:59
ORA-19811: cannot have files in DB_RECOVERY_FILE_DEST with keep attributes

RMAN>
```

You may sometimes need to retain a given backup *forever*. As long as you're using a recovery catalog, you can simply use the keep forever option during a backup command to exempt a backup copy from any retention policies:

```
run
{
backup database
tag quarterly
keep forever
restore point Y2012Q1;
}
```

One of the common uses of archival backups is to use them for creating a test database on a different server. Since you won't need the backups after you create the test database from the backups, you can set the keep parameter to sysdate+1, meaning that the backup will become obsolete a day after the backup is made, regardless of your backup retention policy. Here's an example:

```
Run
{
backup database
tag quarterly
keep until time 'sysdate+1'
restore point Y2012Q1;
}
```

You can then use the RMAN duplicate command to create your test database from this archival backup, as shown in Chapter 15. If you don't delete the backup after a day, it'll become obsolete anyway and thus eligible for automatic deletion by RMAN.

Once you exempt a backup from the retention policy using the keep option, you can also mark the backups as unavailable so RMAN knows that this backup can't be used for a normal restore/recovery operation. Here's an example that shows how to do this using the keyword unavailable to mark a backup as unavailable in the RMAN repository:

```
RMAN> backup database keep forever tag 'semi_annual_bkp';

RMAN> change backup tag 'semi_annual_bkp' unavailable;
```

The unavailable option of the change command changes the status of the backup to unavailable in the RMAN repository. You can use this option when a file is missing or you have moved it off-site. When you find the file or move it back to your site, you can specify the available option of the change command to make it once again available to RMAN.

How It Works

You want to exempt backups from your retention polices at times when you want to retain a backup long term for archival purposes. For example, you may want to store a historical record of the database by taking a cold backup of the database every six months. Your main purpose in creating this backup, then, isn't to use it in a future recovery/ restore effort but rather to serve as a permanent record of the database as of the time when you made the backup.

When you issue a backup . . . keep command, RMAN does the following:

- It automatically backs up all data files, the control file, and the server parameter file.

- To ensure that it can restore the database to a consistent state, RMAN creates an archived redo log backup automatically as well.

- You can use the optional restore point clause, which is a label or name for the particular SCN to which RMAN must recover the database to make it consistent.

■ **Note**   You must use a recovery catalog to specify the KEEP FOREVER option.

In all three examples shown in the previous section, the backup . . . keep command will back up both the data files and the archived redo log files. RMAN backs up only those archived redo logs that are necessary to restore the backups to a consistent state. Before the RMAN backup starts, the database performs an online redo log switch, thus archiving all redo that's currently in the online redo logs and that will be necessary later to make the database consistent.

The control file auto backup that RMAN automatically makes when you use the backup . . . keep command has a copy of the restore point. During a restore operation, the control file is restored first. After the control file is restored, the restore point that's recorded in the control file is looked up to see what SCN the database must be restored to in order to make it consistent.

Archival backups are usually made to tape so they can be stored off-site.

7-25. Backing Up Only Those Files Previously Not Backed Up

Problem

You want to create a backup of only new files that have been recently added or those files that failed to get backed up during the normal backup schedule.

Solution

You can limit RMAN to backing up only specific files using the not backed up or since time clause within a backup command. Using the not backed up clause, you can instruct RMAN to back up only those data files or archived log files that were never backed up previously. Here's the backup command that shows how to back up only previously backed-up files:

```
RMAN> backup database not backed up;

Starting backup at 12-SEP-12
using channel ORA_DISK_1
skipping datafile 1; already backed up on 12-SEP-12
skipping datafile 2; already backed up on 12-SEP-12
skipping datafile 3; already backed up on 12-SEP-12
skipping datafile 4; already backed up on 12-SEP-12
skipping datafile 5; already backed up on 12-SEP-12
skipping datafile 6; already backed up on 12-SEP-12
skipping datafile 7; already backed up on 12-SEP-12
Finished backup at 12-SEP-12

Starting Control File Autobackup at 12-SEP-12
piece handle=/u01/app/oracle/fast_recovery_area/ORCL/autobackup/2012_09_12/o1_mf_n_793808685_
851rcxnt_.bkp comment=NONE
Finished Control File Autobackup at 12-SEP-12

RMAN>
```

You can also use the not backed up command with additional specifications such as the number of backups. The following example shows how to back up only those archived redo logs that were backed up less than twice on tape:

```
RMAN> backup device type sbt archivelog all not backed up 2 times;
```

RMAN considers only backups created on identical device type as the current backup when counting the number of backups it has already made. Thus, the not backed up clause is ideal for specifying the number of archived redo logs to be stored on a specific type of media. The previous example specifies RMAN to keep at least two copies of archived redo logs on *tape*.

How It Works

The backup ... not backed up command comes in handy when you add one or more new files and want to ensure that the new file's contents are backed up soon rather than waiting for the regular scheduled time for backup.

If you're making backup sets (instead of image copies), RMAN considers the completion time for any file in the backup set as the completion time for the entire backupset. That is, all files in a backup set must have the same finishing time. Let's say you're making a backup that involves multiple backup sets. If the target database crashes midway through a database backup, you don't have to start the backup from the beginning. You can use the `not backed up since time` command to back up only those data files that haven't been backed up since the specified time, as shown in the following example:

```
RMAN> backup database not backed up since time 'sysdate-31';
```

If you use the `not backed up since time` clause when you restart the RMAN backup, RMAN will skip backing up the files it already backed up prior to the instance failure. Recipe 7-26 explains this in more detail. If you're using the `since time` clause, you can specify either a date in the `nls_date_format` or an SQL data expression such as sysdate-7. Note that RMAN considers only backups made on the same device type as the current backup when figuring out whether a new backup ought to be made.

7-26. Restarting Backups After a Crash
Problem

The RMAN backup process fails midway through a database backup, say, because of a database instance crash or because of the unavailability of some data files. You want to resume the backup but save time by backing up only those parts of the database that failed to be backed up the first time.

Solution

Use the *restartable backup* feature to back up only those files that failed to be backed up the first time around. Use the `not backed up since time` clause of the backup command to restart a backup after it partially completes. If the time you specify for the `since time` clause is a more recent time than the backup completion time, RMAN backs up the database file.

Here's an example that shows how to restart an RMAN backup that failed midway through a nightly backup. You discover the backup failure in the morning and decide to back up only those parts of the database that weren't backed up by RMAN before the backup failed. Simply run the following backup command to achieve your goal.

▪ **Note** If you use the `backup database not backed up` command without the `since time` clause, RMAN backs up only those files that were never backed up before by RMAN.

```
RMAN> backup not backed up since time 'sysdate-1'
2> database plus archivelog;

Starting backup at 12-SEP-12
current log archived
using channel ORA_DISK_1
skipping archived logs of thread 1 from sequence 29 to 53; already backed up
channel ORA_DISK_1: starting archived log backup set
channel ORA_DISK_1: specifying archived log(s) in backup set
input archived log thread=1 sequence=54 RECID=48 STAMP=793808242
...
channel ORA_DISK_1: backup set complete, elapsed time: 00:00:03
Finished backup at 12-SEP-12
```

```
Starting backup at 12-SEP-12
using channel ORA_DISK_1
skipping datafile 1; already backed up on 12-SEP-12
skipping datafile 2; already backed up on 12-SEP-12
skipping datafile 3; already backed up on 12-SEP-12
skipping datafile 4; already backed up on 12-SEP-12
skipping datafile 5; already backed up on 12-SEP-12
skipping datafile 6; already backed up on 12-SEP-12
skipping datafile 7; already backed up on 12-SEP-12
Finished backup at 12-SEP-12

Starting backup at 12-SEP-12
current log archived
using channel ORA_DISK_1
...
Finished backup at 12-SEP-12

Starting Control File Autobackup at 12-SEP-12
piece
Finished Control File Autobackup at 12-SEP-12

RMAN>
```

The previous backup command will back up all the database files and archive logs that weren't backed up during the past 24 hours. Any database file or archive logs that were backed up during the past 24 hours won't be backed up again. You thus avoid backing up files you already backed up. When RMAN encounters database files that it had already backed up before the backup failed, it issues messages such as these:

```
RMAN-06501: skipping datafile 1; already backed up on SEP 12 2012  20:12:00
RMAN-06501: skipping datafile 2; already backed up on SEP 12 2012  20:13:35
RMAN-06501: skipping datafile 3; already backed up on SEP 12 2012  20:14:50
```

The backup command that produced this output used a SQL expression of type date (sysdate-1). You may also specify a date string as a literal string that matches the nls_date_format environment variable setting.

How It Works

The restartable backup feature backs up only those files that weren't backed up since a specified date and uses the last completed backup set or image copy as the restart point for the new backup. By using the restartable backup feature after a backup failure, you back up the parts of the database that the failed backup didn't back up. If your backup consists of multiple backup sets and the backup fails midway, you don't have to back up the backup sets that were already backed up. However, if your backup consists only of a single backup set, a backup failure means that the entire backup must be rerun.

All the database files are affected when you place the not backed up since clause right after the backup command, as shown in our example. By placing the not backed up since clause after a specific backup set, you can limit the backup to only the objects that are part of the backup set.

It's important to understand that when considering the number of backups, RMAN takes into account only those backups made on a device identical to the device in the current backup command.

7-27. Updating Image Copies

Problem

You want to update image copies to keep them current without having to perform lengthy image copy backups of entire data files.

Solution

By using *incrementally updated image copies*, you can avoid making time-consuming full image copy backups of data files. To use the incrementally updated backups feature, you first make a full image copy backup of a data file and, at regular intervals, update the initial image copy of the data file with level 1 incremental backups of that data file.

You use the backup ... for recover of copy form of the backup command to incrementally update an image copy, as shown here:

```
run {
 recover copy of database
 with tag 'incr_update';
 backup
 incremental level 1 for recover of copy with tag 'incr_update'
 database;
}
```

By running the previous script daily, you'll never have to apply more than a day's worth of redo to recover the database, thus dramatically reducing the time needed to perform a media recovery of the database.

How It Works

You can use Oracle's incrementally updated backups feature to update image copy backups. For example, you can start by making an image copy backup of the database on day one. You can then take a daily, level 1 incremental backup of that data file and apply it to the image copy, thus updating or rolling forward the image copy on a regular basis, in this case daily. The advantage is that during a recovery situation you can simply restore the incrementally updated image copy and recover with the help of archived redo logs, just as if you were using a recent (taken at the same time as the latest incremental level 1 backup) full backup of the database. The great benefit of using incrementally updated backups is that at any given time you won't have more than a single day's worth of redo to apply. This is of course assuming that you update your image copies daily.

It's a little hard to see how our solution script implements the incrementally updated backups strategy, so we'll explain the sequence of events in more detail. We're reproducing the script here so you can follow the logic clearly:

```
RMAN> run
2> {
3> recover copy of database
4> with tag 'incr_update';
5> backup
6> incremental level 1
7> for recover of copy with tag 'incr_update'
8> database;
9> }
```

Assuming that on a daily basis you run the backup script shown previously, the following is what happens from here on:

1. The first day the backup script runs, the `recover copy of database with tag` `'incr_update'` clause doesn't find anything to recover. The backup command that follows it will create an image copy of the disk with the tag `incr_update`. The first part of the backup command's output shows this:

    ```
    Starting recover at 21-SEP-12
    using channel ORA_DISK_1
    no copy of datafile 1 found to recover
    no copy of datafile 2 found to recover
    no copy of datafile 3 found to recover
    no copy of datafile 4 found to recover
    Finished recover at 21-SEP-12
    Starting backup at 21-SEP-12
    using channel ORA_DISK_1
    no parent backup or copy of datafile 1 found
    no parent backup or copy of datafile 3 found
    no parent backup or copy of datafile 2 found
    no parent backup or copy of datafile 4 found
    channel ORA_DISK_1: starting datafile copy
    ```

The output also shows that the `recover` command couldn't find any copies of data files to recover.

2. On the second day of the script's execution, the script will create a level 1 incremental backup of the database, as shown in the following chunk from the backup command's output:

    ```
    Starting recover at 21-SEP-12
    using channel ORA_DISK_1
    no copy of datafile 1 found to recover
    no copy of datafile 2 found to recover
    no copy of datafile 3 found to recover
    no copy of datafile 4 found to recover
    Finished recover at 21-SEP-12
    Starting backup at 21-SEP-12
    channel ORA_DISK_1: starting incremental level 1 datafile backupset
    channel ORA_DISK_1: backup set complete, elapsed time: 00:00:03
    Finished backup at 21-SEP-12
    RMAN>
    ```

3. On the third day and all subsequent days, the backup script will perform both the recovery and backup steps. The script first applies the level 1 incremental backup to the data file copy and then creates a new level 1 backup. The following output shows the two parts of the script execution:

    ```
    Starting recover at 21-SEP-12
    using channel ORA_DISK_1
    channel ORA_DISK_1: starting incremental datafile backupset restore
    channel ORA_DISK_1: specifying datafile copies to recover
    recovering datafile copy fno=00001

    ...
    channel ORA_DISK_1: restored backup piece 1
    ```

```
channel ORA_DISK_1: restore complete, elapsed time: 00:00:03
Finished recover at 21-SEP-12

Starting backup at 21-SEP-12
channel ORA_DISK_1: starting incremental level 1 datafile backupset
channel ORA_DISK_1: specifying datafile(s) in backupset

...
channel ORA_DISK_1: backup set complete, elapsed time: 00:00:03
Finished backup at 21-SEP-12

RMAN>
```

The incrementally updated backups feature is a truly powerful feature that lets you cut back on both the daily backup duration and the time for media recovery, should you need one.

RMAN also provides the incremental Roll Forward of Database Copy feature to let you synchronize a standby database with the source database by using incremental backups of the source database. RMAN applies the incremental backups of the source database to the standby database using the recover command to bring the standby database up-to-date with the source database.

7-28. Backing Up a Container Database

Problem

You want to back up a whole container database (CDB).

Solution

Before you can back up an entire CDB, you must connect as target to the *root*. You can connect in one of the following ways:

1. Connect locally with RMAN to the root:

    ```
    $ rman target sys
    target database Password:
    connected to target database: CDB (DBID=659628168)
    ```

2. Connect with RMAN to the root with OS authentication:

    ```
    $ rman target /
    connected to target database: CDB (DBID=659628168)
    ```

3. Connect with RMAN to the root with a Net Service Name:

    ```
    $ rman target c##bkuser@sales
    target database Password:
    connected to target database: CDB (DBID=659628168)
    ```

You may optionally connect to a recovery catalog as well. Use the syntax described in Chapter 6 for that purpose. Issue the following RMAN command to back up the database:

```
RMAN> backup database;
```

If you want to back up the archived logs as well, issue the following variation on the command:

```
RMAN> backup database plus archivelog;
```

How It Works

As the Solution section shows, you back up a container database the same way you would a normal database. You can also implement an incremental backup strategy for a container database, the same as you do for your other databases. When you back up a whole CDB, you're backing up the root of the CDB and all the PDBs that are part of the CDB. You can use this whole backup of the CDB to recover the whole CDB, or to recover one or more PDBs.

Although the backup of the root and all the PDBs in a container database amounts to backing up the entire CDB, the approach you choose makes a difference when you need to recover the CDB. Using the method in this recepe allows you to recover the container database using fewer commands than if you had backed up all the various parts separately.

Backing up the entire container database isn't your only alternative. As the following recipes show you, you can also back up individual pluggable databases (PDBs), or even individual tablespaces and data files that are part of a pluggable database.

7-29. Backing Up the Root in a Container Database
Problem

You want to back up only the root of a container database.

Solution

Follow these steps to back up the root of a container database.

1. Connect to the root as a user with the SYSBACKUP or SYSDBA privilege:

   ```
   $ rman target sys
   target database Password:
   connected to target database: CDB (DBID=659628168)
   ```

2. Issue the following command to start the backup of the root:

   ```
   RMAN> backup database root;
   ```

How It Works

RMAN gives you the option to back up the entire CDB or just the root, or the PDBs that are part of a CDB. The root of a container database contains critical metadata for the whole CDB. Therefore, Oracle recommends that you frequently back up the root, if you can't back up the whole CDB.

7-30. Backing Up a Pluggable Database

Problem

You want to back up a pluggable database (PDB).

Solution

Follow these steps to back up a pluggable database after first directly connecting to the pluggable database.

1. Connect as target to the PDB you want to back up:

```
$ rman target hrbkup@hrpdb
target database Password:
connected to target database: CDB (DBID=659628168)
```

In this example, the local user hrbkup is a user created in the PDB named hrpdb.

2. Issue the RMAN backup command to back up the pluggable database hrpdb.

```
RMAN> backup pluggable database hrpdb;
```

You can back up multiple pluggable databases by first connecting to the root. Here are the steps:

1. Start up RMAN and connect to the root.

2. Issue the following backup command to back up multiple pluggable databases:

```
RMAN> backup pluggable database sales, hr;
```

How It Works

If you need to back up multiple pluggable databases with a single backup command, you can do so by connecting as root. You can then issue the backup pluggable database command to perform the backups of multiple pluggable databases with just one command. Coonecting directly to a pluggable database is an alternative, but you can back up only the specific pluggable database you connect to.

■ **Note** When you connect as target to a pluggable database, you must specify an Oracle net service name that resolves into the database service for the pluggable database. If you use operating system authentication instead to connect to a pluggable database, you'll be connected to the root and not to the pluggable database.

7-31. Backing Up Tablespaces and Data Files in a PDB

Problem

You want to back up specific tablespaces or data files in a PDB.

Solution

Follow these steps to back up a tablespace in a pluggable database.

1. Start RMAN and connect to the pluggable database as a local user.

2. Issue the following command to back up tablespaces. In our example, we want to back up the tablespaces *users* and *example*.

```
RMAN> backup tablespace users, example;
```

To back up data files belonging to a pluggable database, follow these steps.

1. Start RMAN and connect to the pluggable database as a local user.

2. Isssue the following command to back up tablespaces. In our example, we want to back up the data files 9 and 10.

```
RMAN> backup datafile 9, 10;
```

How It Works

If you have multiple pluggable databases, it's possible that you may have tablespaces with identical names in different PDBs. This is why you must first connect to a specific PDB before backing up its tablespaces. Doing this ensures you are backing up the correct tablespace.

Data files, however, are different in this regard—each data file is uniquely identified by the data file number as well as the file's path. Therefore, it's safe to back up data files of a specific PDB after connecting to either the root or a PDB. By connecting to a specific PDB, you can back up up data files belonging only to that PDB. You can back up data files belonging to multiple PDBs by connecting to the root.

CHAPTER 8

■ ■ ■

Maintaining RMAN Backups and the Repository

To get the most out of RMAN as your main backup and recovery tool, you must master the various RMAN backup and repository maintenance tasks. Managing RMAN backups involves managing the backups themselves as well as performing the record-keeping chores for those backups in the RMAN repository. The RMAN stores its metadata in the control file of the target database, whether you use a recovery catalog or not. If you use a recovery catalog, RMAN will store its metadata in the recovery catalog as well. You don't have to have a recovery catalog to perform any of the backup maintenance tasks.

Oracle recommends that you implement the following policies as the foundation of your RMAN backup and repository maintenance strategy:

- A fast recovery area

- An archived redo log deletion policy

- A backup retention policy

If you adhere to all the recommended backup and repository maintenance tasks, RMAN will take care of creating and managing maintenance tasks, such as deleting unneeded backup files and archived redo logs. Even if you have configured the recommended policies listed here, sometimes you may need to manually delete backups, say, from a tape device, or perform related tasks such as validating data files and backup sets. Some of the backup and repository maintenance tasks are relatively trivial, such as using the `list` and `report` commands, which help find out which backups exist and the status of those backups. Other tasks are more significant, such as the actions you must take when you manually delete a backup with an operating system utility. To avoid a discrepancy between what RMAN records in the control file and the actual backup files caused by accidental or intentional deletions of backup files, disk failures, and tape failures, you must use RMAN maintenance commands to update the repository so it accurately reflects the true state of affairs regarding your backups. Validating data files, backup sets, and backup copies are important tasks that ensure your RMAN backups are usable during a recovery.

From time to time, you'll have to perform some maintenance tasks to keep the flash recovery area working well. You may, for example, add more space to the flash recovery area when it's getting full or move the flash recovery area to a different location. Chapter 3 covers the flash recovery area maintenance tasks.

8-1. Adding User-Made Backups to the Repository
Problem

You've made some data file copies on disk, which you want to add to the RMAN repository.

Solution

You can add any user-managed copies, such as a data file copy (that you made with an operating system utility), to the RMAN repository using the catalog command. Here's a basic example:

```
RMAN> catalog datafilecopy '/u01/app/oracl/example1.bkp';
```

The preceding catalog command catalogs the data file copy you made of the example01.dbf data file as an RMAN-recognized backup. You can, if you want, catalog the data file copy as an incremental level 0 backup by issuing the following command:

```
RMAN> catalog datafilecopy '/u01/app/oracle/example01.bkp' level 0;
```

There's absolutely no difference between a data file copy you first copy and then record in the recovery catalog using the catalog command and an RMAN incremental level 0 backup of that data file. You can use this cataloged file as part of your RMAN incremental backup strategy.

How It Works

To catalog a copy made by you in the RMAN repository, the copy must be available on disk, and it must be a complete image copy of a single data file, control file, archived redo log file, or backup piece. Use the catalog command in the following situations:

- You use an operating system command to make copies of data files, archived redo log files, or control files and want to record them in the RMAN repository.

- If you change the archiving destination during a recovery, you must use the catalog command to catalog those archived redo logs in the RMAN repository.

- You want to use a data file copy as a level 0 backup, in which case you can perform incremental backups with that level 0 backup as the basis, provided you catalog it in the RMAN repository. You can also use a cataloged data file copy for block media recovery (BMR) even if you didn't back up the data file using RMAN.

If you copy or move an RMAN backup piece manually, you can use the catalog command to make that backup piece usable by RMAN. The following is an example of cataloging an RMAN backup piece on tape. The list command shows that a certain backup piece is uncataloged.

```
RMAN> list backuppiece 'ilif2lo4_1_1';
RMAN-00571: ===========================================================
RMAN-00569: =============== ERROR MESSAGE STACK FOLLOWS ===============
RMAN-00571: ===========================================================
RMAN-03002: failure of list command at 09/28/2012 13:39:53
RMAN-06004: ORACLE error from recovery catalog database:

RMAN-20260: backup piece not found in the recovery catalog
RMAN-06092: error while looking up backup piece
RMAN>
```

Use the catalog command to make the uncataloged backup piece available to RMAN, as shown here:

```
RMAN> catalog device type sbt backuppiece 'ilif2lo4_1_1';
released channel: ORA_SBT_TAPE_1
allocated channel: ORA_SBT_TAPE_1
channel ORA_SBT_TAPE_1: sid=38 devtype=SBT_TAPE
channel ORA_SBT_TAPE_1: WARNING: Oracle Test Disk API
cataloged backuppiece
backup piece handle=ilif2lo4_1_1 recid=3878 stamp=619796430
RMAN>
```

You can check that the backup piece has been cataloged successfully by issuing the list command again, as shown here:

```
RMAN> list backuppiece 'ilif2lo4_1_1';
List of Backup Pieces
BP Key  BS Key  Pc# Cp# Status       Device Type Piece Name
------- ------- --- --- ----------- ----------- ----------------
3473331 3473326 1   1   AVAILABLE    SBT_TAPE     ilif2lo4_1_1
RMAN>
```

If you have to catalog multiple files that you had backed up to a directory, use the catalog start with command, as shown in the following example:

```
RMAN> catalog start with '/u01/app/oracle/backup' noprompt;
```

The start with clause specifies that RMAN catalog all valid backup sets, data file copies, and archived redo logs starting with the string pattern you pass. This string pattern can be part of a file name, an Oracle managed file (OMF) directory, or an automatic storage management (ASM) disk group. By default, RMAN prompts you after every name match for a file. In this example, we used the optional noprompt clause to suppress these automatic prompts.

You can catalog all files in the flash recovery area by using the following command:

```
RMAN> catalog recovery area;
```

When you issue the catalog recovery area command, RMAN searches for all files in the recovery area and issues a message if it doesn't find any files known to the database, as shown here:

```
RMAN> catalog recovery area;

searching for all files in the recovery area
no files found to be unknown to the database

RMAN>
```

8-2. Finding Data Files and Archive Logs that Need a Backup
Problem

You want to find out which of the data files and archived redo logs in a database need a backup.

Solution

Use the report need backup form of the report command to find out which backups you need to make to conform to the retention policy you put in place. Here's how you execute the report need backup command to see which database files are in need of backup:

```
RMAN> report need backup;

RMAN retention policy will be applied to the command
RMAN retention policy is set to redundancy 1
Report of files with less than 1 redundant backups
File #bkps Name
---- ----- -------------------------------------------------------
2    0     /u01/app/oracle/product/12.1.0/db_1/dbs/dbx1catdb.dbf
3    0     /u01/app/oracle/product/12.1.0/db_1/dbs/dbu1catdb.dbf
4    0     /u01/app/oracle/oradata/catdb/cattbs_01.dbf
5    0     /u01/app/oracle/oradata/catdb/virt_catalog1.dbf

RMAN>
```

The output of the report need backup command tells you that you must back up several database files to comply with your retention policy.

How It Works

The report need backup command reports which data files and archived redo logs need to be backed up to conform to the backup retention policy you have put in place. You must have configured your own retention policy, or at least have enabled the default retention policy, for the report need backup command to work. If you disable the default retention policy, RMAN won't be able to figure out which of your data files or archived redo logs need a backup. Here's an example that shows the result of running the report need backup command after disabling the default retention policy, which is set to 1.

The following command shows the current retention policy:

```
RMAN> show retention policy;

RMAN configuration parameters for database with db_unique_name ORCL are:
CONFIGURE RETENTION POLICY TO REDUNDANCY 1;

RMAN>
```

The command shows that the retention policy is configured to a redundancy of 1. Let's change the configured retention policy from one backup to none, as shown here:

```
RMAN> configure retention policy to none;

old RMAN configuration parameters:
CONFIGURE RETENTION POLICY TO REDUNDANCY 1;
```

```
new RMAN configuration parameters:
CONFIGURE RETENTION POLICY TO NONE;
new RMAN configuration parameters are successfully stored

RMAN>
```

If you now issue the report need backup command, you'll see the following error:

```
RMAN> report need backup;

RMAN-00571: ===========================================================
RMAN-00569: =============== ERROR MESSAGE STACK FOLLOWS ===============
RMAN-00571: ===========================================================
RMAN-03002: failure of report command at 09/21/2012 14:09:13
RMAN-06525: RMAN retention policy is set to none

RMAN>
```

The error occurs because the RMAN retention policy was set to none, thus making it impossible for RMAN to figure out whether you need to make any backups.

You can specify different options with the report need backup command. Here are the most useful options you can use with this command:

This command shows objects that require a backup to conform to a redundancy-based retention policy:

```
RMAN> report need backup redundancy n;
```

This command shows objects that require a backup to conform to a window-based retention policy:

```
RMAN> report need backup recovery window of n days
```

This command shows data files that require more than n days' worth of archived redo logs for a recovery:

```
RMAN> report need backup days=n;
```

This command shows only the required backups on disk:

```
RMAN> report need backup device type disk;
```

This command shows only required backups on tape:

```
RMAN> report need backup device type sbt;
```

8-3. Finding Data Files Affected by Unrecoverable Operations
Problem

You want to identify which data files have been affected by unrecoverable operations, since RMAN needs to back up those files as soon as possible after you perform an unrecoverable operation.

Solution

Use the `report unrecoverable` command to find out which data files in the database have been marked unrecoverable because they're part of an unrecoverable operation. Here's an example showing how to use the `report unrecoverable` command:

```
RMAN> report unrecoverable;

Report of files that need backup due to unrecoverable operations
File    Type of Backup   Required Name
-----   --------------   ----------------------------------------
1       full             /u01/app/oracle/data/prod1/example01.dbf

RMAN>
```

The `report unrecoverable` command reveals that the example01.dbf file is currently marked unrecoverable and that it needs a full backup to make it recoverable if necessary.

How It Works

If you perform a nonrecoverable operation, such as a direct load insert, the changes made won't be logged in the redo log files. You must, therefore, immediately perform either a full backup or an incremental backup of the data files involved in the nonrecoverable operation.

The `report unrecoverable` command tells you both the names of the data files that were part of a nonlogged operation (and therefore nonrecoverable by normal media recovery) and the type of backup (full or incremental) required to recover the data file from an RMAN backup.

8-4. Identifying Obsolete Backups
Problem

You want to find out whether any backups are obsolete according to the retention policy you configured.

Solution

The `report obsolete` command reports on any obsolete backups. Always run the `crosscheck` command first to update the status of the backups in the RMAN repository to that on disk and tape. In the following example, the `report obsolete` command shows no obsolete backups:

```
RMAN> crosscheck backup;
RMAN> report obsolete;
RMAN retention policy will be applied to the command
RMAN retention policy is set to redundancy 1
no obsolete backups found
```

The following execution of the report obsolete command shows that there are both obsolete backup sets and obsolete backup copies. Again, run the crosscheck command before issuing the report obsolete command.

```
RMAN> crosscheck backup;
RMAN> report obsolete;
RMAN> report obsolete;

RMAN retention policy will be applied to the command
RMAN retention policy is set to redundancy 2
Report of obsolete backups and copies
Type                 Key    Completion Time    Filename/Handle
-------------------- ------ ------------------ --------------------
Datafile Copy        1      06-AUG-12          /u01/app/oracle/backup/users_ts01.dbf
Control File Copy    5      11-SEP-12          /u01/app/cf_back.ctl
Datafile Copy        6      11-SEP-12          /u01/app/oracle/backup/users01.dbf
Backup Set           152    12-SEP-12
  Backup Piece       163    12-SEP-12          /u01/app/oracle/fast_recovery_area/ORCL/
backupset/2012_09_12/o1_mf_nnnd1_TAG20120912T105000_851csrct_.bkp
Backup Set           156    12-SEP-12
  Backup Piece       167    12-SEP-12          /u01/app/oracle/fast_recovery_area/ORCL/
backupset/2012_09_12/o1_mf_nnnd1_TAG20120912T105238_851cypr7_.bkp
Backup Set           161    12-SEP-12
  Backup Piece       172    12-SEP-12          /u01/app/oracle/fast_recovery_area/ORCL/
backupset/2012_09_12/o1_mf_nnndf_TAG20120912T141028_851qkokn_.bkp
Backup Set           162    12-SEP-12
  Backup Piece       173    12-SEP-12          /u01/app/oracle/fast_recovery_area/ORCL/
backupset/2012_09_12/o1_mf_nnndf_TAG20120912T141028_851qkpw2_.bkp
Backup Set           163    12-SEP-12
  Backup Piece       174    12-SEP-12          /u01/app/oracle/fast_recovery_area/ORCL/
backupset/2012_09_12/o1_mf_nnndf_TAG20120912T141152_851qms4y_.bkp
Backup Set           168    12-SEP-12
  Backup Piece       179    12-SEP-12          /u01/app/oracle/fast_recovery_area/ORCL/
autobackup/2012_09_12/o1_mf_n_793808776_851rgrk4_.bkp
Datafile Copy        9      12-SEP-12          /u01/app/oracle/fast_recovery_area/ORCL/
datafile/o1_mf_cattbs_851rqj92_.dbf
Datafile Copy        10     12-SEP-12          /u01/app/oracle/fast_recovery_area/ORCL/
datafile/o1_mf_example_851rrmdv_.dbf

RMAN>
```

The report obsolete command shows all backups sets, backup pieces, and data file copies that RMAN considers obsolete since it doesn't need them to meet the specified backup retention policy.

How It Works

As in the case of the report need backup command, you must configure a retention policy, or at least not disable the default retention policy that's preconfigured for you already, for the report obsolete command to run without an error.

When using the `report obsolete` command, it's always a good idea to run the `crosscheck database` command beforehand to ensure that RMAN has the latest information about the status of different types of backups.

When using the `report obsolete` command, you can also specify the redundancy and recover window options, as shown here:

```
RMAN> report obsolete recovery window of 5 days;
RMAN> report obsolete redundancy 2;
RMAN> report obsolete recovery window of 5 days device type disk;
```

Note that the last command in the preceding code examples specifies that only disk backups be considered in determining whether there are any obsolete backups. If you don't specify the device type, RMAN takes into account both disk and sbt backups in determining whether a backup is obsolete according to the configured policy.

8-5. Displaying Information About Database Files
Problem
You want to display information about all the data files in the target database.

Solution
You can get a report about all the data files in a database by using the `report schema` command, as shown in the following example. The `report schema` command in the following example reports on all data files:

```
RMAN> report schema;

Report of database schema for database with db_unique_name ORCL

List of Permanent Datafiles
===========================
File Size(MB) Tablespace          RB segs Datafile Name
---- -------- ------------------- ------- ------------------------
1    800      SYSTEM              ***     /u01/app/oracle/oradata/orcl/system01.dbf
2    341      EXAMPLE             ***     /u01/app/oracle/oradata/orcl/example01.dbf
3    680      SYSAUX              ***     /u01/app/oracle/oradata/orcl/sysaux01.dbf
4    50       UNDOTBS1            ***     /u01/app/oracle/oradata/orcl/undotbs01.dbf
5    500      CATTBS              ***     /u01/app/oracle/oradata/orcl/cattbs_01.dbf
6    6        USERS               ***     /u01/app/oracle/oradata/orcl/users01.dbf
7    100      VIRT_CATALOG        ***     /u01/app/oracle/oradata/orcl/virt_catalog_01.dbf

List of Temporary Files
=======================
File Size(MB) Tablespace          Maxsize(MB) Tempfile Name
---- -------- ------------------- ----------- --------------------
1    105      TEMP                32767       /u01/app/oracle/oradata/orcl/temp01.dbf

RMAN>
```

The `report schema` command is helpful in finding out the names of all the data files of the target database.

How It Works

You can use the `report schema` command to get more than the routine listing of all data files at the current time. You can, for example, get a listing of all database files from a past point in time by using the `at time` clause, as shown in the following example:

```
RMAN> report schema at time 'sysdate-1';
```

The previous command requires that you use a recovery catalog. You can also specify the `at scn` or `at sequence` clause instead of the `at time` clause to get a report specific to a certain SCN or log sequence number.

8-6. Listing RMAN Backups

Problem

You want to see the backups that are recorded in the RMAN repository for a target database.

Solution

Use the `list` command to review RMAN backups of data files, archived redo logs, and control files. The `list` command uses the RMAN repository data to provide the list of backups and copies. Here's an example of the basic `list` command:

```
RMAN> list backup;

List of Backup Sets
===================

BS Key  Type LV Size        Device Type Elapsed Time Completion Time
------- ---- -- ---------- ----------- ------------ ---------------
130     Full    9.73M       DISK        00:00:02     20-AUG-12
        BP Key: 141   Status: AVAILABLE  Compressed: NO  Tag: TAG20120820T113325
        Piece Name: /u01/app/oracle/fast_recovery_area/ORCL/autobackup/2012_08_20/
o1_mf_s_791811205_834sppgs_.bkp
  SPFILE Included: Modification time: 20-AUG-12
  SPFILE db_unique_name: ORCL
  Control File Included: Ckp SCN: 1957559      Ckp time: 20-AUG-12

  List of Archived Logs in backup set 146
  Thrd Seq     Low SCN    Low Time  Next SCN   Next Time
  ---- ------- ---------- --------- ---------- ---------
  1    29      1925370    07-AUG-12 1925437    07-AUG-12
  1    30      1925437    07-AUG-12 1925468    07-AUG-12
  ...
  1    53      2150846    12-SEP-12 2150961    12-SEP-12
```

```
List of Datafiles in backup set 152
File LV Type Ckp SCN    Ckp Time  Name
---- -- ---- ---------- --------- ----
  3   1  Incr 2152892   12-SEP-12 /u01/app/oracle/oradata/orcl/sysaux01.dbf
  4   1  Incr 2152892   12-SEP-12 /u01/app/oracle/oradata/orcl/undotbs01.dbf
  7   1  Incr 2152892   12-SEP-12 /u01/app/oracle/oradata/orcl/virt_catalog_01.dbf
...
---- -- ---- ---------- --------- ----
  2      Full 2209483   21-SEP-12 /u01/app/oracle/oradata/orcl/example01.dbf
  5      Full 2209483   21-SEP-12 /u01/app/oracle/oradata/orcl/cattbs_01.dbf

RMAN>
```

The basic list command shown in the previous example lists all backups in the RMAN repository for the target database by serially listing each backup set (including the backup pieces information) and proxy copy. It also identifies all the files that are part of the backup. If you would rather list the backups by just the backup files, you can do so by using the list backup by file command, as shown in the following example:

```
RMAN> list backup by file;

List of Datafile Backups
========================

File Key     TY LV S Ckp SCN    Ckp Time  #Pieces #Copies Compressed Tag
---- ------- -  -- - ---------- --------- ------- ------- ---------- ---
1    157     B  1  A 2153006    12-SEP-12 1       1       NO         TAG20120912T105238
     153     B  1  A 2152904    12-SEP-12 1       1       NO         TAG20120912T105000
2    174     B  F  A 2209483    21-SEP-12 1       1       NO         TAG20120921T140136
...
List of Archived Log Backups
============================

Thrd Seq     Low SCN    Low Time  BS Key  S #Pieces #Copies Compressed Tag
---- ------- ---------- --------- ------- - ------- ------- ---------- ---
1    29      1925370    07-AUG-12 146     A 1       1       NO         TAG20120912T104426
1    30      1925437    07-AUG-12 146     A 1       1       NO         TAG20120912T104426
...
List of Control File Backups
============================

CF Ckp SCN Ckp Time  BS Key  S #Pieces #Copies Compressed Tag
---------- --------- ------- - ------- ------- ---------- ---
2196190    21-SEP-12 170     A 1       1       NO         TAG20120921T095227
...
```

```
List of SPFILE Backups
=======================

Modification Time BS Key  S #Pieces #Copies Compressed Tag
----------------- ------- - ------- ------- ---------- ---
20-AUG-12             130 A 1       1       NO         TAG20120820T113325

RMAN>
```

The list backup by file command groups all backups by file and lists all data files, their backup sets, and any proxy copies.

How It Works

You can use the list command to list the following:

- Backup pieces, image copies, and proxy copies of databases, tablespaces, data files, archived redo logs, and the control file
- Expired backups
- Backups classified by time period, recoverability, path name, device type, or tag

Using the list command isn't the only way to view the status of RMAN backups. You can also check backup status by querying the recovery catalog views RC_DATAFILE_COPY, RC_ARCHIVED_LOG, and V$BACKUP_FILES.

You can also get the output of the list command in a summarized form by specifying the keyword summary when using the list command, as shown here:

```
RMAN> list backup summary;         # lists backup sets, proxy copies, and image copies
RMAN> list expired backup summary; # lists expired backups in summary form
```

You can use optional clauses with the list command to narrow down your search of backup information or to list only a specific type of backup. Here are some of the important optional clauses you can employ with the list command, with examples showing how to use those clauses.

This command lists only backup sets and proxy copies but not image copies:

```
RMAN> list backupset;
```

This command lists only data file, archived redo log, and control file copies:

```
RMAN> list copy;
```

This command lists a particular data file copy:

```
RMAN> list datafilecopy '/a01/app/oracle/users01.dbf';
```

This command lists backups by tag:

```
RMAN> list backupset tag 'weekly_full_db_backup';
```

This command lists backups according to when the backup was made:

```
RMAN> list copy of datafile 1 completed between '01-JAN-2012' AND '15-JAN-2012';
```

This command lists backups by the number of times they were backed up to tape:

```
RMAN> list archivelog all backed up 2 times to device type sbt;
```

This command lists the backups of all data files and archivelogs of the target database:

```
RMAN> list backup of database;
```

The list command is really not limited to merely listing the metadata about backups and copies, although that is its primary function. You can also use the list command to mine all kinds of information from the RMAN repository. For example, you can use the following versions of the list command to gather information other than that pertaining to just RMAN backups:

> list incarnation: Lists all incarnations of a database (shown in Recipe 8-10)

> list restore point: Lists all restore points in the target database (shown in Recipe 8-9)

> list script names: Lists the names of all recovery catalog scripts (shown in Chapter 9)

> list failure: Lists failures recorded by the Data Recovery Advisor (shown in Chapter 20)

You can run the crosscheck and delete commands against the backups and copies displayed by the list command.

8-7. Listing Expired Backups

Problem

You want to find out which of your backups are marked in the RMAN repository as expired, meaning they were not found during the execution of an RMAN crosscheck command.

Solution

The list expired backup command shows which of the backups of the target database have an expired status in the repository. Here's an example:

```
RMAN> list expired backup;
```

Of course, if there aren't any expired backups, the previous command won't return any output. You can also find out which of the archived redo log backups have the expired status by using the following command:

```
RMAN> list expired archivelog all;

specification does not match any archived log in the recovery catalog

RMAN>
```

The output of the list command shows that there are no archived redo logs with the expired status.

How It Works

The list expired backup command shows all backups not found during an RMAN cross-check. You can use the list expired copy command to list all copies not found during a cross-check. Of course, if you haven't run the crosscheck command for quite some time, the output of the list expired command isn't going to be very useful to you. To guarantee the best results from this command, you must make a habit of executing the crosscheck command frequently, especially if you've been manually deleting any kind of RMAN-related backup files at the OS level. This is yet another reason for you to adhere to Oracle's recommendation of configuring both a backup retention policy and an archived redo log deletion policy, in addition to using the flash recovery area. When you follow the recommended maintenance strategy, RMAN backup and repository maintenance becomes more or less automatic, obviating the need for you to constantly execute commands such as crosscheck to verify your backups.

8-8. Listing Only Recoverable Backups and Copies
Problem

You want to review all data file backups and copies that you can actually use for a restore and recovery.

Solution

Use the list backup command with the recoverable clause to restrict the list of backups to only those backups and copies whose status is listed as available. Here's an example:

```
RMAN> list recoverable backup;

List of Backup Sets
===================

/u01/app/oracle/fast_recovery_area/ORCL/autobackup/2012_08_20/o1_mf_s_791811205_834sppgs_.bkp
  ...
  List of Archived Logs in backup set 146
  Thrd Seq     Low SCN    Low Time   Next SCN   Next Time
  ---- ------- ---------- ---------- ---------- ---------
  1    29      1925370    07-AUG-12  1925437    07-AUG-12
  ...
  List of Archived Logs in backup set 166
  Thrd Seq     Low SCN    Low Time   Next SCN   Next Time
  ---- ------- ---------- ---------- ---------- ---------
  1    54      2150961    12-SEP-12  2163833    12-SEP-12
  ...
  Control File Included: Ckp SCN: 2164280     Ckp time: 12-SEP-12
...
  List of Datafiles in backup set 174
    5        Full 2209483    21-SEP-12 /u01/app/oracle/oradata/orcl/cattbs_01.dbf

RMAN>
```

The recoverable clause restricts the list of backups and copies to only those that are listed as available in the repository and, as such, can actually be used for a restore and recovery operation.

How It Works

The list backup command shows all backups and copies from the repository, irrespective of their status. Since you can use the backups and copies only with the available status, it's a good idea to run the list recoverable backup command instead when you want to know what usable backups you really do have.

8-9. Listing Restore Points
Problem

You want to list all restore points or a specified restore point in the target database.

Solution

Use the list restore point command to view a specific restore point in a database. You can use the all option to view all the restore points in the database, as shown in the following example:

```
RMAN> list restore point all;

SCN                RSP Time   Type       Time      Name
---------------    ---------  ---------- --------- ---------
2210949                                  21-SEP-12 RESTORE_1

RMAN>
```

The list restore point all command reports that you have a single restore point named restore_1 that covers SCN 2210949.

How It Works

You can use the list restore point command to effectively manage any restore points you created in a database. Any guaranteed restore points will never age out of the control file. You must manually delete a guaranteed restore point by using the drop restore point command. Oracle retains the 2,048 most recent restore points, no matter how old they are. In addition, Oracle saves all restore points more recent than the value of the control_file_record_keep_time initialization parameter. All other normal restore points automatically age out of the control file eventually.

8-10. Listing Database Incarnations
Problem

You want to find out what incarnations of a database are currently recorded in the RMAN repository so you can use this information during potential restore and recovery operations.

Solution

When you perform an open resetlogs operation, it results in the creation of a new incarnation of the database. When performing recovery operations on such a database, you might want to check the database incarnation. The list incarnation command is handy for this purpose, as shown in the following example:

```
RMAN> list incarnation;

List of Database Incarnations
DB Key  Inc Key DB Name DB ID            STATUS  Reset SCN  Reset Time
------- ------- ------- ---------------- ------  ---------- ----------
1       1       ORCL    1316762630       PARENT  1          04-JUL-12
2       2       ORCL    1316762630       CURRENT 1609405    18-JUL-12

RMAN>
```

The list incarnation command output lists all incarnations of the target database.

How It Works

If the list incarnation command shows three incarnations of a database, for example, it means you've reset the online redo logs of this database twice. Each time you reset the online redo logs, you create a new incarnation of that database.

RMAN can use backups both from the current incarnation of a database and from a previous incarnation as the basis for subsequent incremental backups if incremental backups are part of your backup strategy. As long as all the necessary archived redo logs are available, RMAN can also use backups from a previous incarnation for performing restore and recovery operations.

8-11. Updating the RMAN Repository After Manually Deleting Backups

Problem

You have deleted some unneeded archived redo logs from disk using an operating system command instead of using the RMAN delete command. The RMAN repository, however, continues to indicate that the deleted archived redo logs are available on disk. You want to update this outdated RMAN repository information about the deleted backups.

Solution

Execute the change ... uncatalog command to update the RMAN repository after you manually delete a backup. Let's say you delete the data file copy /u01/app/oracle/users01.dbf using the rm command from the Linux operating system. Here's an example of how you would then use the change ... uncatalog command to change the RMAN repository information pertaining to the removed data file copy:

```
RMAN> change datafilecopy '/u01/app/oracle/users01.dbf' uncatalog;
```

Here's another example showing how to uncatalog a specific backup piece:

```
RMAN> change backuppiece 'ilif2lo4_1_1' uncatalog;

uncataloged backuppiece
backup piece handle=ilif2lo4_1_1 recid=3876 stamp=619796229
Uncataloged 1 objects
RMAN>
```

If you're using a recovery catalog, the change ... uncatalog command will also delete the backup record you are specifying in the change ... uncatalog command from the recovery catalog.

How It Works

The change ... uncatalog command changes only the RMAN repository information pertaining to the manually deleted backups, but it doesn't actually delete the physical backups and copies of backups. The command removes all references to data file copies, backup pieces, and archived redo logs from the recovery catalog. It also updates the status of those records in the control file to be deleted.

Run the change ... uncatalog command anytime you delete a backup or an archived redo log with an operating system command. The command removes all RMAN repository references for the file you manually deleted. Otherwise, RMAN won't know about the files you deleted unless you run the crosscheck command.

8-12. Synchronizing the Repository with the Actual Backups
Problem

You've manually removed some old archived redo logs from disk and want to make sure you update the RMAN repository (in the control file and in the recovery catalog) to match the actual backup situation both on disk and in the media management catalog.

Solution

Use the crosscheck command to update the RMAN repository with the correct information about available backups. If you physically remove an RMAN backup file, the crosscheck command will update the RMAN repository so its records match the physical status of the backups. The crosscheck command synchronizes the backup data in the RMAN repository (in the control file and the recovery catalog) with the actual backups both on disk and in the media management catalog.

■ **Note** If you use all three of Oracle's recommended backup maintenance polices—a backup retention policy, an archived redo log deletion policy, and the flash recovery area—you don't need to resort to the crosscheck command often. If you happen to be manually deleting backup files, run the crosscheck command often to make sure the RMAN repository is current.

In the following example, we issue a delete backup command, which results in a warning that an object couldn't be deleted because of "mismatched status." That is one of the typical errors that results from manually deleting archived redo logs as described in the Problem section. Here's an example:

```
RMAN> delete backup;

using channel ORA_DISK_1

List of Backup Pieces
BP Key  BS Key  Pc#  Cp#  Status       Device Type  Piece Name
-------  ------  ---  ---  -----------  -----------  ----------
141     130      1    1    AVAILABLE    DISK         /u01/app/oracle/fast_recovery_area/ORCL/
autobackup/2012_08_20/o1_mf_s_791811205_834sppgs_.bkp
...

Do you really want to delete the above objects (enter YES or NO)? YES
deleted backup piece
backup piece handle=/u01/app/oracle/fast_recovery_area/ORCL/autobackup/2012_08_20/
o1_mf_s_791811205_834sppgs_.bkp RECID=141 STAMP=791811206
...
Deleted 18 objects

RMAN>
```

You attempt to delete a backup with a mismatched status, which leads to a recommendation from RMAN to run the crosscheck command to fix the status of the backup in the repository. The crosscheck command will update the RMAN repository records with the correct status of the backups. If you manually delete a backup file, for example, a subsequent crosscheck command will result in RMAN marking that file status as expired in the RMAN repository. In the following example, once you issue the crosscheck command, RMAN marks the missing file as expired. Once a file is marked as expired, it's eligible for deletion from the RMAN repository (with the delete expired command), although the physical file itself may have been deleted long ago.

Here's how you run the basic crosscheck command:

```
RMAN> crosscheck backup;

using channel ORA_DISK_1
crosschecked backup piece: found to be 'AVAILABLE'
backup piece handle=/u01/app/oracle/fast_recovery_area/CATDB/backupset/2012_09_28/o1_mf_nnndf_
TAG20120928T102135_86cj409w_.bkp RECID=1 STAMP=795176496
crosschecked backup piece: found to be 'AVAILABLE'
backup piece handle=/u01/app/oracle/fast_recovery_area/CATDB/backupset/2012_09_28/o1_mf_nnndf_
TAG20120928T102135_86cj53od_.bkp RECID=2 STAMP=795176531
crosschecked backup piece: found to be 'AVAILABLE'
backup piece handle=/u01/app/oracle/fast_recovery_area/CATDB/backupset/2012_09_28/o1_mf_nnndf_
TAG20120928T102135_86cj5lwd_.bkp RECID=3 STAMP=795176546
crosschecked backup piece: found to be 'AVAILABLE'
backup piece handle=/u01/app/oracle/fast_recovery_area/CATDB/backupset/2012_09_28/o1_mf_ncnnf_
TAG20120928T102135_86cj5x8x_.bkp RECID=4 STAMP=795176557
Crosschecked 4 objects

RMAN>
```

The previous `crosscheck` command will search for all backups on all channels with the same device type as the channel that was used to make the RMAN backups.

How It Works

The `crosscheck` command helps you update backup information about corrupted backups on disk and tape, as well as any manually deleted archived redo logs or other backup files. For disk backups, the `crosscheck` command validates the file headers, and for tape backups, it checks whether the backups are in the media management layer (MML) catalog.

It's a good strategy to always first use the `list` command to see what backups you have and follow it up with the `crosscheck` command to make sure you really do have those backups. You can use the `delete expired` command to remove RMAN repository data for all those backups that fail the checking performed by the `crosscheck` command.

The `crosscheck backup` command checks all backups on both disk and tape, provided you've already configured an automatic channel for your tape backups. As you know, RMAN already comes with a single preconfigured disk channel.

If you haven't configured an automatic sbt channel, you must allocate a maintenance channel within a `run` block before you execute the `crosscheck` command, as shown here:

```
RMAN> allocate channel for maintenance device type sbt;
    crosscheck backup;
```

Once you've configured an sbt channel through the `configure` command or manually allocated it through the `allocate channel` command shown previously, you can then check backups on both disk and tape with a single `crosscheck` command, as shown here:

```
RMAN> crosscheck backup;
```

There are three possible values for the status of a file following the execution of the `crosscheck` command—available, unavailable, and expired.

When the `crosscheck` command fails to locate the backups and copies you're looking for on disk or tape (files are absent or RMAN can't access them), it'll update the RMAN repository to show the backup record status for those backups and copies as expired. You can then consequently use the `delete expired` command to delete the expired backup records (metadata) from the RMAN repository. Thus, you use the following sequence of commands to delete expired backups:

```
RMAN> crosscheck backup;
RMAN> delete expired backup;
```

The `crosscheck` command checks whether the backups still exist. The command checks backup sets, proxy copies, and image copies. The `delete expired backup` command will delete the expired backups. Here's another example:

```
RMAN> crosscheck backupset of tablespace users
    device type sbt completed before 'sysdate-14';
RMAN> delete expired backupset of tablespace users
    device type sbt completed before 'sysdate-14';
```

The `crosscheck` command checks the media manager for expired backups of the tablespace users, and the delete command removes their repository records.

If you want to search for and check only image copies and not backup sets, you can do so by using the copy option with the crosscheck command, as shown in the following example:

```
RMAN> crosscheck copy;
```

You may want to run the crosscheck copy command when verifying the current status and the availability of image copies that you made yourself or through RMAN.

You can use various options of the crosscheck command to perform the cross-checking of a specific tablespace, data file, archived redo log, control file, and so on. Here are some examples that show how to restrict the cross-checking to specify types of backups:

```
# cross-checking just backup sets.
RMAN> crosscheck backupset;
# cross-checking a copy of a database
RMAN> crosscheck copy of database;
# cross-checking specific backupsets;
RMAN> crosscheck backupset 1001, 1002;
# cross-checking using a backup tag
RMAN> crosscheck backuppiece tag = 'weekly_backup';
# cross-checking a control file copy;
RMAN> crosscheck controlfilecopy '/tmp/control01.ctl';
# cross-checking backups completed after a specific time
RMAN> crosscheck backup of datafile   "/u01/app/oracle/prod1/system01.dbf" completed
after 'sysdate-14';
# cross-checking of all archivelogs and the spfile;
RMAN> crosscheck backup of archivelog all spfile;
# cross-checking a proxy copy
RMAN> crosscheck proxy 999;
```

Use the completed after clause to restrict the crosscheck command to check only those backups that were created after a specific point in time. The following command will check only for backups of a data file made in the last week:

```
RMAN> crosscheck backup of datafile 2
      completed after 'sysdate -7';
```

It's important to understand that the crosscheck command doesn't *delete* the RMAN repository records of backup files that were manually removed. It simply *updates* those records in the repository to reflect that the backup isn't available any longer by marking the file status as expired. You must use the delete command to actually remove the records of these expired backups from the RMAN repository. On the other hand, if a file was expired at one time and is now made available again on disk or on media management layer, RMAN will mark the file's status as available.

8-13. Deleting Backups
Problem

You want to delete unwanted backups.

Solution

Use the delete or backup ... delete command to remove both archived redo logs and RMAN backups. You can remove backup sets, image copies, proxy copies, and archive log backups through the delete command. The most general form of the delete command is delete backup. This command deletes all backup pieces for the target database that are recorded in the RMAN repository. Here's an example:

```
RMAN> delete backup;

using channel ORA_DISK_1

List of Backup Pieces
BP Key  BS Key  Pc# Cp# Status       Device Type Piece Name
------- ------- --- --- ------------ ----------- ----------
1       1       1   1   AVAILABLE    DISK        /u01/app/oracle/fast_recovery_area/CATDB/
backupset/2012_09_28/o1_mf_nnndf_TAG20120928T102135_86cj409w_.bkp
2       1       2   1   AVAILABLE    DISK        /u01/app/oracle/fast_recovery_area/CATDB/
backupset/2012_09_28/o1_mf_nnndf_TAG20120928T102135_86cj53od_.bkp
3       1       3   1   AVAILABLE    DISK        /u01/app/oracle/fast_recovery_area/CATDB/
backupset/2012_09_28/o1_mf_nnndf_TAG20120928T102135_86cj5lwd_.bkp
4       2       1   1   AVAILABLE    DISK        /u01/app/oracle/fast_recovery_area/CATDB/
backupset/2012_09_28/o1_mf_ncnnf_TAG20120928T102135_86cj5x8x_.bkp

Do you really want to delete the above objects (enter YES or NO)? YES
deleted backup piece
backup piece handle=/u01/app/oracle/fast_recovery_area/CATDB/backupset/2012_09_28/o1_mf_nnndf_
TAG20120928T102135_86cj409w_.bkp RECID=1 STAMP=795176496

...
Deleted 4 objects

RMAN>
```

RMAN always prompts you for confirmation before going ahead and deleting the backup files. You can issue the delete noprompt command to suppress the RMAN confirmation prompt. You can use the delete command with various options, as shown in the following examples:

```
RMAN> delete backuppiece 999;
RMAN> delete copy of controlfile like '/u01/%';
RMAN> delete backup tag='old_production';
RMAN> delete backup of tablespace sysaux device type sbt;
```

In some special situations, you may want to delete all backups—including backup sets, proxy copies, and image copies—belonging to a database. This can happen when you decide to drop a database and get rid of all of its backups as well. Use a pair of crosscheck commands first, one for backups and the other for the image copies, to make sure the repository and the physical media are synchronized. Then issue two delete commands, one for the backups and the other for the copies. Here are the commands:

```
RMAN> crosscheck backup;
RMAN> crosscheck copy;
RMAN> delete backup;
RMAN> delete copy;
```

If you configure a tape channel, RMAN will use both the (preconfigured) disk and the tape channels to delete the backups and copies.

How It Works

When you issue the `delete backup` command, RMAN does the following:

1. Removes the physical file from the backup media

2. Marks the status of the deleted backup in the control file as deleted

3. Deletes the rows pertaining to the deleted backup from the recovery catalog repository, which is actually stored in database tables, if you are using a recovery catalog and are actually connected to it while deleting the backup

If you issue the `delete backup` command, you may sometimes get the RMAN prompt back right away without any messages about deleted backups. However, that doesn't mean RMAN has deleted all backups. This actually means RMAN didn't find any backups to delete. Here's an example:

```
RMAN> delete backup;

using channel ORA_DISK_1

RMAN>
```

If you issue the simple `delete` command, without specifying the `force` option, the deletion mechanism works in the following manner under different circumstances:

- If the status of the object is listed as available in the repository but the physical copy isn't found on the media, RMAN doesn't delete the object or alter the repository status.

- If the status is listed as unavailable in the repository, RMAN deletes the object if it exists and removes the repository record for the object.

- If the object has the expired status and RMAN can't find the object on the media, RMAN doesn't delete the object or update its repository status.

Here are some options you can use with the `delete` command when deleting backups:

`delete force`: Deletes the specified files whether they actually exist on media or not and removes their records from the RMAN repository as well

`delete expired`: Deletes only those files marked *expired* pursuant to the issuance of the `crosscheck` command.

`delete obsolete`: Deletes data file backups and copies and the archived redo logs and log backups that are recorded as *obsolete* in the RMAN repository

Instead of using the basic `delete backup` command, you can also use the alternative deletion command, `backup ... delete [all] input`, to first make a backup of and then delete the input files (source files) of backup sets, data file copies, and archived redo logs. Typically you use the `backup ... delete` command to back up the source files to tape and then delete them after a successful backup. We show you how to use the `backup ... delete` command in the next recipe, where we focus on deleting archived redo logs.

8-14. Deleting Archived Redo Logs

Problem

You want to manually delete some unneeded archived redo logs.

Solution

You can delete any eligible archived redo log by using the `delete archivelog` or `backup ... delete input` command. Here's an example showing how to delete all archived redo logs with the `delete archivelog all` command:

```
RMAN> delete archivelog all;
```

The `delete archivelog all` command deletes all archived redo logs on disk that aren't necessary to meet the configured archived redo log deletion policy. It's more likely that you would want to use the following `delete` command, which deletes archived redo logs from disk based on whether they have been first backed up to tape a certain number of times:

```
RMAN> delete archivelog all
        backed up 3 times to sbt;
```

You can delete specific archived redo logs by using the `delete` command, as shown in the following example:

```
RMAN> delete archivelog until sequence = 999;
```

The `backup ... delete` command lets you first back up an archived redo log and then delete the source archived redo log file. To delete the source file, you use the additional clause `delete input`, as shown in the following example:

```
RMAN> backup device type sbt
        archivelog all
        delete all input;
```

The previous `backup ... delete` command backs up all the archived redo logs and then deletes all those archived redo logs (input files). The `delete all input` clause results in the deletion of all backed-up archived redo logs from all archived redo log destinations. If you want to delete only the specified archived redo log that you've just backed up to a backup set, use the `delete input` clause instead, as shown in the following example:

```
RMAN> backup archivelog like '/arch%'
        delete input;
```

Note that it's common to use the `backup ... delete` command to back up archived redo logs to tape and then delete the source files.

How It Works

RMAN uses the configured archived redo log deletion policy to determine which of the archived redo logs are eligible for deletion, including those archived redo logs that are stored in the flash recovery area. RMAN automatically deletes the eligible archived redo logs from the flash recovery area. An archived redo log is considered eligible for deletion when the flash recovery area becomes full.

Suppose you have configured the following archived redo log deletion policy:

```
RMAN> configure archivelog deletion policy
        to backed up 2 times to device type sbt;
```

The previous command specifies that all archived redo log files will be eligible for deletion from all locations when those files have been backed up twice or more to tape. Once you set the archived redo log deletion policy shown here, a `delete archivelog all` or `backup ... delete input` command will delete all archived redo logs that satisfy the requirements of your configured deletion policy, which requires that RMAN back up all archived redo logs to tape twice.

If you *haven't* configured an archived redo log deletion policy (by default there is no policy set), RMAN will deem any archived redo log file in the flash recovery area eligible for deletion, if both of the following are true:

- The archived redo logs have been successfully sent to all the destinations specified by the `log_archive_dest_n` parameter.

- You have copied the archived redo logs to disk or to tape at least once, or the archived redo logs are obsolete per your configured backup retention policy.

Use the `configure archivelog deletion policy` command to specify your own archive redo log deletion criteria instead of leaving the deletion timing to RMAN. Once you configure an archived redo log deletion policy this way, it applies to all archived redo log locations, including the flash recovery area, if you've configured one.

RMAN stores the archived redo logs as long as possible in the flash recovery area. When the flash recovery area is under space pressure, RMAN tries to ensure that any flashback retention time you've set is being satisfied before automatically deleting the archived redo logs. RMAN deletes eligible archived redo logs stored in all areas other than the flash recovery area when you execute one of the two deletion commands shown in the Solution section of this recipe, `backup ... delete input` or `delete archivelog`.

If you execute the `delete` command with the `force` option, RMAN will ignore any configured archived redo log retention polices and delete all the specified archived redo logs.

8-15. Deleting Obsolete RMAN Backups

Problem

You want to delete just those RMAN backups that are obsolete according to the defined retention policy.

Solution

Use the `obsolete` option of the `delete` command to remove just the obsolete backups. The following command shows how to remove all backups that are obsolete according to the retention policy that's currently configured:

```
RMAN> delete obsolete;

RMAN retention policy will be applied to the command
RMAN retention policy is set to redundancy 1
using channel ORA_DISK_1
Deleting the following obsolete backups and copies:
...
Do you really want to delete the above objects (enter YES or NO)? YES
RMAN>
```

The `delete obsolete` command shown here will delete all backups deemed obsolete per your configured backup retention policy.

■ **Note** The `delete obsolete` command relies only on the backup retention policy in force. It doesn't consider the configured archived redo log deletion policy in effect to determine which archived redo logs are obsolete. The `delete archivelog all` command, on the other hand, relies entirely on the configured archived redo log deletion policy.

The following examples show how to use either the `redundancy` or `recovery window` clause to delete backups that are deemed obsolete according to a retention policy you have configured:

```
RMAN> delete obsolete redundancy = 2;
```

The command shown here deletes backups that exceed the redundancy requirement of 2:

```
RMAN> delete obsolete recovery window of 14 days;
```

The previous command deletes backups and the archived redo logs that aren't necessary to recover the database to an arbitrary SCN within the past two weeks.

How It Works

Obsolete backups are any backups that you don't need to satisfy a configured retention policy. You may also delete obsolete backups according to any retention policy you may specify as an option to the `delete obsolete` command. The `delete obsolete` command will remove the deleted files from the backup media and mark those backups as deleted in both the control file and the recovery catalog.

When deleting obsolete backups, it's important to understand how the `keep until` clause impacts how RMAN deems a backup obsolete. No matter what `keep until` time you specify, RMAN will never consider a backup obsolete if that backup is needed to satisfy any retention policy you might have configured. This applies to both a recovery window–based and a redundancy-based retention policy. If you set the `keep until` time for some backups longer than a configured retention policy interval, however, RMAN will retain those backups. Regardless of any configured backup retention policy, a backup will be considered obsolete as soon as its `keep until` period expires, and the `delete obsolete` command will delete all such obsolete backups.

8-16. Changing the Status of an RMAN Backup Record
Problem

You have migrated some backups off-site and want to let RMAN know that those files aren't available to it.

Solution

Use the `change ... unavailable` command when you move backups off-site or can't find a backup for some reason. Here's an example showing how you can change the status of a backup set to unavailable because you've temporarily moved the backup set to a different location because of a lack of space on a disk:

```
RMAN> change backupset 10 unavailable;
```

```
changed backup piece unavailable
...
Changed 1 objects to UNAVAILABLE status

RMAN>
```

Use the change ... unavailable option when you know you don't want a particular backup or copy to be restored yet but don't want to delete that backup or copy either. If you uncatalog the backup set, it'll have a status of deleted in the repository. However, if you just use the change command to make the backup set unavailable, you can always make that available again when you have more space on this disk and are able to move the backup set to its original location.

How It Works

Once you mark a backup file unavailable, RMAN won't use that file in a restore or recover operation. Note that you can't mark files in the flash recovery area as unavailable. Once you find copies of the unavailable, misplaced, or lost backups and restore them, you can mark all the backups you had marked unavailable previously as available again by using the keyword available as part of the change command, as shown here:

```
RMAN> change backupset 10 available;
using channel ORA_DISK_1
changed backup piece available
...
Changed 1 objects to AVAILABLE status
RMAN>
```

When you change the status of a file to available, RMAN searches for that file and makes sure it actually exists. You can use the change option to modify the status of backups and copies from previous incarnations of a database.

You can use the change command in a Data Guard environment to update the status of backups. The command itself doesn't check whether a file is accessible on the backup media but simply changes the status of that backup in the repository to whatever you specify. For example, if you performed a backup using an NFS-mounted disk and that disk subsequently becomes inaccessible, you can connect to either the primary database or the standby database and issue the change command to set the status of the backup as unavailable. Later, once the disk becomes accessible again, you can change its status back to available.

8-17. Changing the Status of Archival Backups
Problem

You have made an archival backup for long-term storage to comply with some business requirements. These requirements have changed over time, and you now want to change the status of the archival backup.

Solution

Use the change command when you want to change the status of an archival backup pertaining to the long-term retention of that backup. You can use the change command in two ways to alter the retention requirements of your archival backups.

If you have previously specified the keep forever option to create an archival backup and have now decided to alter the status of this backup to that of a regular backup, use the change ... nokeep command to alter the status of the archival backup. Here's an example:

1. Use the change command to modify a regular consistent database backup into an archival backup:

```
RMAN> change backup tag 'consistent_db_bkup'
        keep forever;
```

Since this is a consistent backup, it won't need any recovery, and as such, you won't need any archived redo log backups.

2. Use the CHANGE command to change the archival backup to a normal database backup subject to the backup obsoletion policies you have in place:

```
RMAN> change backup tag 'consistent_db_backup' nokeep;
```

When you make an archival backup with the keep ... forever option, RMAN disregards the backup retention time for these backups. Once you run the change ... nokeep command, the backup set with the tag consistent_db_backup, which was previously designated as a long-term archival backup, will once again come under the purview of your configured retention policy. The backup will become obsolete per the configured retention policy and can be removed by the delete obsolete command.

How It Works

Remember that you can create archival backups (with the keep forever option) only if you're using a recovery catalog. You can't also set, and therefore alter, the keep attribute for any backup files that are stored in the flash recovery area.

If you want to modify the time period for which you want to retain the archival backups, you can do so by using the change ... keep command. Here's an example:

```
RMAN> change backupset 111 keep until time 'sysdate+180';
```

When you execute the change ... keep command as shown in the example, the previously (permanently) archived backup (backup set 111) will now be retained only for a period of 180 days starting from today. After the 180 days are up, the backup will become obsolete and is eligible for deletion by the delete obsolete command.

8-18. Testing the Integrity of an RMAN Backup
Problem

You want to test your backup operation without actually performing a backup to a disk or tape device to make sure that RMAN can indeed make good backups of your data files. Your goal is to ensure that all the data files exist in the correct locations and that they aren't physically or logically corrupt.

Solution

Use the backup validate command to perform an integrity testing of RMAN backups without actually performing the backup. Here's an example that shows how to check all the data files and the archived redo logs for physical corruption:

```
RMAN> backup validate database archivelog all;

Starting backup at 21-SEP-12
using channel ORA_DISK_1
channel ORA_DISK_1: starting archived log backup set
channel ORA_DISK_1: specifying archived log(s) in backup set
input archived log thread=1 sequence=29 RECID=23 STAMP=790698859
input archived log thread=1 sequence=30 RECID=24 STAMP=790698872
...
channel ORA_DISK_1: backup set complete, elapsed time: 00:00:15
List of Archived Logs
=====================
Thrd Seq     Status Blocks Failing Blocks Examined Name
---- ------- ------ -------------- --------------- ---------------
1    29      OK     0              7               /u01/app/oracle/fast_recovery_area/ORCL/
archivelog/2012_08_07/o1_mf_1_29_822vfvs7_.arc
...
channel ORA_DISK_1: starting full datafile backup set
channel ORA_DISK_1: specifying datafile(s) in backup set
input datafile file number=00005 name=/u01/app/oracle/oradata/orcl/cattbs_01.dbf
input datafile file number=00002 name=/u01/app/oracle/oradata/orcl/example01.dbf
...
File Name: /u01/app/oracle/oradata/orcl/users01.dbf
  Block Type Blocks Failing Blocks Processed
  ---------- -------------- ----------------
  Data       0              106
  Index      0              42
  Other      0              487

channel ORA_DISK_1: starting full datafile backup set
channel ORA_DISK_1: specifying datafile(s) in backup set
including current control file in backup set
channel ORA_DISK_1: backup set complete, elapsed time: 00:00:01
List of Control File and SPFILE
===============================
File Type     Status Blocks Failing Blocks Examined
-----------   ------ -------------- ---------------
Control File OK     0              618
Finished backup at 21-SEP-12

RMAN>
```

The backup validate command shows that all the necessary data files and archived redo logs can be backed up successfully by RMAN. The output of this command is identical to that of an actual RMAN backup command, but as with the other validation command shown in this recipe, no actual backup takes place.

To check for logical corruption, use the following variation of the backup validate command:

```
RMAN> backup validate
      check logical
      database archivelog all;
```

The check logical clause means that RMAN will check for logical corruption only.

How It Works

The backup ... validate command confirms that all the data files are indeed where they are supposed to be. The command also checks for both physical and logical corruption. Look up the V$DATABASE_BLOCK_CORRUPTION view for any corruption identified by RMAN after the backup ... validate command finishes executing.

RMAN reads all the database files that are covered by the backup command without creating any backup files themselves. Since all the data blocks are examined for corruption, the backup ... validate command provides a good way to check your backup strategy without being surprised during an actual backup to find that either the necessary data files are missing or they are corrupt.

8-19. Validating Data Files, Backup Sets, and Data Blocks

Problem

You aren't sure whether a particular data file is missing and you want to run a check to validate the file(s). In addition, you may also want to check whether a particular backup set or a data block is corrupt.

Solution

You can validate data files, backup sets, or even individual data blocks by using the validate command. The following example shows how to validate a single backup set with the validate command:

```
RMAN> validate backupset 3;

Starting validate at 28-SEP-12
using channel ORA_DISK_1
channel ORA_DISK_1: starting validation of archived log backup set
channel ORA_DISK_1: reading from backup piece /u01/app/oracle/fast_recovery_area/CATDB/
backupset/2012_09_28/o1_mf_annnn_TAG20120928T112559_86cmwr8j_.bkp
channel ORA_DISK_1: piece handle=/u01/app/oracle/fast_recovery_area/CATDB/backupset/2012_09_28/
o1_mf_annnn_TAG20120928T112559_86cmwr8j_.bkp tag=TAG20120928T112559
channel ORA_DISK_1: restored backup piece 1
channel ORA_DISK_1: validation complete, elapsed time: 00:00:01
Finished validate at 28-SEP-12

RMAN>
```

You can also use the validate command to check all data files at once, as shown here:

```
RMAN> validate database;

Starting validate at 28-SEP-12
using channel ORA_DISK_1
channel ORA_DISK_1: starting validation of datafile
channel ORA_DISK_1: specifying datafile(s) for validation
input datafile file number=00004 name=/u01/app/oracle/oradata/catdb/cattbs_01.dbf
...
File Status Marked Corrupt Empty Blocks Blocks Examined High SCN
---- ------ -------------- ------------ --------------- ----------
5    OK     0              12673        12800           498714
   File Name: /u01/app/oracle/oradata/catdb/virt_catalog1.dbf
   Block Type Blocks Failing Blocks Processed
   ---------- -------------- ----------------
   Data       0              0
   Index      0              0
   Other      0              127
...
Control File OK     0                494
Finished validate at 28-SEP-12

RMAN>
```

Note that when you issue the backup ... validate command, the command begins with the message "Starting validate" and not "Starting backup," as is the case with the backup ... validate command.

How It Works

The semantics of the validate command are similar to those of the backup ... validate command, with the big advantage that the validate command can check at a much more granular level than the backup ... validate command. You can use the validate command with individual data files, backup sets, and even data blocks.

■ **Note** The validate command checks only for intrablock corruption, which may be either physical or logical in nature.

You can speed up the validation of a large data file by using the section size clause with the validate command after first configuring multiple channels. The allocation of multiple channels with the section size clause parallelizes the data file validation, making it considerably faster. Here's an example using two disk channels, with the section size clause dividing up the validation work between the two channels:

```
RMAN> run {
2> allocate channel ch1 device type disk;
3> allocate channel ch2 device type disk;
4> validate datafile 1 section size = 250m;
5> }
```

```
released channel: ORA_DISK_1
allocated channel: ch1
channel ch1: SID=40 device type=DISK

Starting validate at 28-SEP-12
channel ch1: starting validation of datafile
channel ch1: specifying datafile(s) for validation
input datafile file number=00001 name=/u01/app/oracle/product/12.1.0/db_1/dbs/dbs1catdb.dbf
validating blocks 1 through 32000
channel ch1: validation complete, elapsed time: 00:00:27
List of Datafiles
=================
File Status Marked Corrupt Empty Blocks Blocks Examined High SCN
---- ------ -------------- ------------ --------------- ----------
1    OK     0                 6466          47294          680442
   File Name: /u01/app/oracle/product/12.1.0/db_1/dbs/dbs1catdb.dbf
   Block Type Blocks Failing Blocks Processed
   ---------- -------------- ----------------
   Data       0                19767
   Index      0                6281
   Other      0                14780

Finished validate at 28-SEP-12
released channel: ch1
released channel: ch2

RMAN>
```

The validate command always skips all the data blocks that were never used, in each of the data files it validates. The larger the value of the section size clause you set, the faster the validation process completes. You can use the validate command with the following options, among others:

- validate recovery area

- validate recovery files

- validate spfile

- validate tablespace <tablespace_name>

- validate controlfilecopy <filename>

- validate backupset <primary_key>

Scripting RMAN

Although RMAN allows interactive commands to be entered from the command line, there is little use for some of them in real life, especially for the commands that back up the database. In almost all cases, you'll want to automate your processes to back up your databases, delete archived redo logs, and so on. You should set up these tasks in such a way that they can run without any human intervention. This means you need to script RMAN commands, and the scripts need to be run by some sort of automated scheduler, such as cron. In this chapter, you will learn different ways to script and schedule RMAN commands, both in Unix and in Windows.

Approaches to Scripting

RMAN provides for several approaches to scripting. We discuss each approach in the following sections.

With so many options comes the natural question, what is the best approach in your case? While deciding on the exact option to use, you should consider the usage of your scripts. If yours is a Unix server and you are fairly good at shell scripting, the command file option with shell scripts might be attractive. Even if you are not that proficient at shell scripting, you can use the shell script we provide in Recipe 9-1, which might be the only one you ever need. If your server is Windows, you can use the Windows batch file example in Recipe 9-3.

Stored scripts, meaning scripts stored in an RMAN repository, are attractive since they store the code in the catalog database. So, you can connect from any target and run these scripts as long as you are connected to the catalog. This reduces your coding effort significantly. However, in Oracle Database 10g and older, stored scripts are not good at parameter passing and replacing parameters at runtime, whereas shell scripts are good at those tasks. So, stored scripts are attractive for repetitive tasks that you generally use interactively but not against a specific database, such as delete archivelog all, crosscheck backup, list copy of datafiles, and so on. Such scripts are the same regardless of the database and therefore can be executed against any target, saving you a lot of typing effort. On the other hand, shell scripts (or batch files) are better for tasks such as backing up a database, where you can write a generic script and merely substitute parameter values depending on the database target.

The Script Delimiter Approach

You can embed RMAN commands within a shell script by using input redirection along with a delimiter. For instance, here are some RMAN commands embedded within a Unix shell script:

```
... snipped ...
rman target / << EOF
... RMAN commands come here ...
... more RMAN commands
EOF
... and the rest of the script ...
```

The RMAN commands until the EOF marker are all executed.

Command File

You can create regular text files containing RMAN commands. These are regular text files just as you would create using an operating-system utility such as vi. In RMAN, you can call them in a variety of ways, one of which is putting an at (@) sign in front of them, similarly to how you execute an SQL*Plus script file. For example:

```
RMAN>@cmd.rman
```

Unlike the behavior of SQL*Plus, which expects the script file to have an extension of .sql, RMAN does not expect any extension. If your script file name includes an extension, you'll need to specify that extension when you invoke the script.

The cmdfile Option

You can use the cmdfile command-line option to call a command file while calling RMAN from the Unix shell prompt, as shown here:

```
$ rman target=/ catalog=u/p@catalog cmdfile cmd.rman
```

You can also use the cmdfile option with an equal sign:

```
$ rman target=/ catalog=u/p@catalog cmdfile=cmd.rman
```

You can use the SQL*Plus–like notation to call a script by placing an @ before the name. For example:

```
$ rman target=/ catalog=u/p@catalog @cmd.rman
```

At the RMAN command line, the @ is synonymous with cmdfile.

Stored Scripts

You can store scripts in a catalog and call them from the RMAN command prompt, as shown here:

```
RMAN> run { execute script stored_script; }
```

The stored script is in an RMAN catalog database, not on any file system.
You can also call a stored script using the script parameter on the command line, as shown here:

```
$ rman target=/ catalog=u/p@catalog script stored_script
```

9-1. Developing a Unix Shell Script for RMAN

Problem

You want to develop a shell script to be run by an automated process to back up the database via RMAN.

Solution

The most common platforms for Oracle databases are Unix and its variants, such as Linux, Solaris, HPUX, and so on. The presence of a shell programming language is extremely handy when using these variants. In this recipe, you will learn how to develop a complete shell script to call any RMAN script. Here are some expectations for the script:

- It should be able to be run from some automated utility, such as cron.

- It should send an e-mail to a set of addresses after successful completion.

- It should send an e-mail to another set of addresses after a failure.

- It should back up to multiple mount points. In this example, we have assumed nine mount points.

- It should produce a log file whose name follows this format:

  <ORACLE_SID>_<BACKUP_TYPE>_<BACKUP_MEDIA>_<TIMESTAMP>.log

- The log file should show the time stamp in mm/dd/yy hh24:mi:ss format, not the default dd-MON-yy format.

- This log file should be copied over to a central server where all the DBA-related logs are kept. In addition, the log file should be copied to one of the backup mount points as well.

- The script should be generic enough to be called for any database. In other words, the script should not hard-code components that will be different from database to database, such as Oracle Home, SID, and so on.

- The script should have a built-in locking mechanism; in other words, if the script is running and is being called again, it shouldn't start.

With these requirements in mind, you can develop a script similar to the one that follows, which enables you to back up any database automatically and on a recurring basis by using cron or some other job-scheduling utility. (Our listing has line numbers to aid explanation; the actual script does not have those line numbers.) The script has a configurable section in which you can replace the variable values to suit your environment.

```
1. # Beginning of Script
2. # Start of Configurable Section
3. export ORACLE_HOME=/opt/oracle/12.1/db_1
4. export ORACLE_SID=PRODB1
5. export TOOLHOME=/opt/oracle/tools
6. export BACKUP_MEDIA=DISK
7. export BACKUP_TYPE=FULL_DB_BKUP
8. export MAXPIECESIZE=16G
9. # End of Configurable Section
10. # Start of site specific parameters
11. export BACKUP_MOUNTPOINT=/oraback
12. export DBAEMAIL="dbas@proligence.com"
13. export DBAPAGER="dba.ops@proligence.com"
14. export LOG_SERVER=prolin2
15. export LOG_USER=oracle
16. export LOG_DIR=/dbalogs
17. export CATALOG_CONN=${ORACLE_SID}/${ORACLE_SID}@catalog
18. # End of site specific parameters
```

```
19. export LOC_PREFIX=$BACKUP_MOUNTPOINT/loc
20. export TMPDIR=/tmp
21. export NLS_DATE_FORMAT="MM/DD/YY HH24:MI:SS"
22. export TIMESTAMP='date +%T-%m-%d-%Y'
23. export LD_LIBRARY_PATH=$ORACLE_HOME/lib:/usr/lib:/lib
24. export LIBPATH=$ORACLE_HOME/lib:/usr/lib:/lib
25. export SHLIB_PATH=$ORACLE_HOME/lib:/usr/lib:/lib
26. export LOG=${TOOLHOME}/log
27. LOG=${LOG}/log/${ORACLE_SID}_${BACKUP_TYPE}_${BACKUP_MEDIA}_${TIMESTAMP}.log
28. export TMPLOG=$TOOLHOME/log/tmplog.$$
29. echo 'date' "Starting $BACKUP_TYPE Backup of $ORACLE_SID \
30. to $BACKUP_MEDIA" > $LOG
31. export LOCKFILE=$TOOLHOME/${ORACLE_SID}_${BACKUP_TYPE}_${BACKUP_MEDIA}.lock
32. if [ -f $LOCKFILE ]; then
33. echo 'date' "Script running. Exiting ..." >> $LOG
34. else
35. echo "Do NOT delete this file. Used for RMAN locking" > $LOCKFILE
36. $ORACLE_HOME/bin/rman log=$TMPLOG <<EOF
37. connect target /
38. connect catalog $CATALOG_CONN
39. CONFIGURE SNAPSHOT CONTROLFILE NAME TO
40.  '${ORACLE_HOME}/dbs/SNAPSHOT_${ORACLE_SID}_${TIMESTAMP}_CTL';
41. run
42. {
43. allocate channel c1 type disk
44. format '${LOC_PREFIX}1/${ORACLE_SID}_${BACKUP_TYPE}_${TIMESTAMP}_%p_%s.rman'
45. maxpiecesize ${MAXPIECESIZE};
46. allocate channel c2 type disk
47. format '${LOC_PREFIX}2/${ORACLE_SID}_${BACKUP_TYPE}_${TIMESTAMP}_%p_%s.rman'
48. maxpiecesize ${MAXPIECESIZE};
49. allocate channel c3 type disk
50. format '${LOC_PREFIX}3/${ORACLE_SID}_${BACKUP_TYPE}_${TIMESTAMP}_%p_%s.rman'
51. maxpiecesize ${MAXPIECESIZE};
52. allocate channel c4 type disk
53. format '${LOC_PREFIX}4/${ORACLE_SID}_${BACKUP_TYPE}_${TIMESTAMP}_%p_%s.rman'
54. maxpiecesize ${MAXPIECESIZE};
55. allocate channel c5 type disk
56. format '${LOC_PREFIX}5/${ORACLE_SID}_${BACKUP_TYPE}_${TIMESTAMP}_%p_%s.rman'
57. maxpiecesize ${MAXPIECESIZE};
58. allocate channel c6 type disk
59. format '${LOC_PREFIX}6/${ORACLE_SID}_${BACKUP_TYPE}_${TIMESTAMP}_%p_%s.rman'
60. maxpiecesize ${MAXPIECESIZE};
61. allocate channel c7 type disk
62. format '${LOC_PREFIX}7/${ORACLE_SID}_${BACKUP_TYPE}_${TIMESTAMP}_%p_%s.rman'
63. maxpiecesize ${MAXPIECESIZE};
64. allocate channel c8 type disk
65. format '${LOC_PREFIX}8/${ORACLE_SID}_${BACKUP_TYPE}_${TIMESTAMP}_%p_%s.rman'
66. maxpiecesize ${MAXPIECESIZE};
67. backup
68. incremental level 0
69. tag = 'LVL0_DB_BKP'
```

```
70. database
71. include current controlfile;
72. release channel c1;
73. release channel c2;
74. release channel c3;
75. release channel c4;
76. release channel c5;
77. release channel c6;
78. release channel c7;
79. release channel c8;
80. allocate channel d2 type disk format
81. '${LOC_PREFIX}8/CTLBKP_${ORACLE_SID}_${TIMESTAMP}.CTL';
82. backup current controlfile;
83. release channel d2;
84. }
85. exit
86. EOF
87. RC=$?
88. cat $TMPLOG >> $LOG
89. rm $LOCKFILE
90. echo 'date' "Script lock file removed" >> $LOG
91. if [ $RC -ne "0" ]; then
92. mailx -s "RMAN $BACKUP_TYPE $ORACLE_SID $BACKUP_MEDIA Failed" \
93. $DBAEMAIL,$DBAPAGER < $LOG
94. else
95. cp $LOG ${LOC_PREFIX}1
96. mailx -s "RMAN $BACKUP_TYPE $ORACLE_SID $BACKUP_MEDIA Successful" \
97. $DBAEMAIL < $LOG
98. fi
99. scp $LOG \
100. ${LOG_USER}@${LOG_SERVER}:${LOG_DIR}/${ORACLE_SID}/.
101. rm $TMPLOG
102. fi
```

The "How It Works" section describes the mechanics of the script.

■ **Note**   You don't need to type this solution script. If you want to use it or adapt it to your own use, you'll find the script in the zip file of script examples that you can download for this book from the Apress website.

How It Works

We made this script as generic as possible. All the parameters are configurable. Keeping in that spirit, pretty much everything in the script is parameter-driven. You can use the same script on any database on any Unix server. You merely need to modify the parameters appropriately.

One issue we must clarify before you start the database backup to tape based on this script is the location of the backup files. You can store the backup pieces on one mount point, such as /oraback. All the backup files go there. However, sometimes it may not be advisable to store everything on a single mount point. Some tape backup systems work more efficiently if the files are spread over multiple file systems (or mount points), since they allow for parallel backup from all those mount points. If the files are on the same file system, the files are backed up to tape serially.

In this case, it makes sense for RMAN to create the backup pieces on multiple file systems. Usually you define as many channels as there are mount points. So, you can have mount points such as /oraback/loc1, /oraback/loc2, and so on. In our example script, we're assuming there are eight mount points: /oraback/loc1 through /oraback/loc8. Accordingly, we have configured eight channels.

We use three types of parameters in the script:

Fixed: The parameters that are fixed for a site. Examples of such parameters are the e-mail addresses of DBAs, the name of the central log server, and so on. These parameters do not change from database to database.

DB specific: The parameters that change between databases. Examples are the Oracle SID, the Oracle Home, the type of the backup (full, incremental, and so on), and the media, such as tape and disk.

Derived: The parameters that are derived from the previous two types of parameters. Examples are the location of the rman executable in the bin directory of Oracle Home, and so on. You don't need to change these parameters.

Table 9-1 shows a line-by-line explanation of the script.

Table 9-1. *Line-by-Line Explanation of the Unix Shell Script to Back Up via RMAN*

Line Number	Explanation
3	The Oracle Home for that database. Change for another database.
4	The SID of the database being backed up.
5	The location on the server where this script is executed.
6	The media where the backup is stored, such as tape or disk. This parameter is only for naming the log file, not for directing the target of the backup.
7	The type of backup, such as full or incremental. This is only for naming the log file. This parameter does not actually cause the backup to be full or otherwise.
8	The MAXPIECESIZE parameter for RMAN. This parameter in RMAN creates the backup pieces to be limited to a certain size, which is a limitation on some operating systems. The limit should be based on the database size as well. If your database is fairly small and you want to remove any limit, just specify a very high number. In this example, we have assumed a 16GB limit.
11	The backups will be made to /oraback/loc1 through /oraback/loc8.
12	The e-mail that says where the successful notification should be sent.
13	The e-mail that says where the failure e-mail should be sent, usually a pager.
14	The server where the log files of each run are stored.
15	The user ID of the log server.
16	The directory where the logs are kept on the central log server.
17	The connection string for the catalog connection. Here we assume that your catalog database connect string is catalog and you have defined a separate catalog owner for each database, where the owner's name is the same as the SID of the database being backed up and the password is the same as the owner name. This is not absolutely necessary; you can have a common owner for catalogs of all databases. Whatever your decision is, update this parameter to reflect that.

(continued)

Table 9-1. (*continued*)

Line Number	Explanation
19	The mount points where the backups will be taken have a common format, such as /oraback/ loc<n>, where <n> varies from 1 to 8. The format is mentioned here.
20	The directory where the temporary file log file of the script is generated. Later this temp file and the RMAN log file are merged and sent out as the log file.
21	The date format that the time stamps in the RMAN log files are shown as.
22	The time stamp; the log files are generated in this name.
23–25	Various path variables that need to be there. Remember, this script is called from a cron job, so the user's profile is not executed, and no variables are set.
26	The log file name is constructed.
27	The temporary log file is created in this name. The parameter $$ indicates the PID in the shell script. Since the PID of each process is different, a different log file will be created each time.
31	Since we want to prevent the script from starting if it is running currently, we're using a lock file. At the beginning of each run, the script checks the lock file. If it is present, it indicates the script is running now, and the current run is aborted. At the end of the run, the script deletes the lock file.
32	We check whether the lock file exists. If it does, then the script is running, so we abort this run.
35	If the lock file does not exist, we create one. The contents of the file do not matter, but we put the lines "Do NOT delete this file. Used for RMAN locking" in the file, just in case someone gets curious and opens this file. The message should be crystal clear.
36	We start the RMAN command. The << EOF clause at the end of the line indicates that the RMAN executable should accept all the lines until the string EOF is encountered.
37	We connect to the target database.
38	We connect to the catalog.
39	When RMAN starts backing up the database, it must get an exclusive lock on the control file. Since that creates the disruption of the database, RMAN takes a snapshot of the control file and uses that. Here, in this line, we decide the snapshot control file location.
43–45	We allocate the first channel, specifying the format string so that the backups go there. We also specify MAXPIECESIZE, which determines how big each piece should be. Note the format string: ${LOC_PREFIX}1/${ORACLE_SID}_${BACKUP_TYPE}_${TIMESTAMP}_%p_%s.rman The location of the file will be constructed as /oraback/loc1, a mount point.
46–66	We do the same for channels 2 through 8. They go to the mount points /oraback/loc2 through /oraback/loc8.
67–71	The actual backup command comes here. You can specify any RMAN command you want here.
72–79	The channels are explicitly released, a best practice.
80–83	We take an explicit backup of the current control file. Note that in line 69 we have included the control file as part of the backup, but the control file gets embedded in the backup pieces. If you have the catalog, it is simple to get the control file from the backup pieces. But imagine the worst-case scenario where the catalog is lost and so is the control file. It will be hard to locate the control file from the many backup piece files. Therefore, as a good practice, we take an explicit backup of the control file, which has a clearly identified name.

(*continued*)

Table 9-1. (*continued*)

Line Number	Explanation
87	After we exit the RMAN command line, we capture the return code, $?.
88	We merge the RMAN log with the script log file.
89	We remove the lock file created earlier to indicate that the script has completed its run and a new script run may be started.
87	We check the status of the RMAN execution. 0 indicates successful execution.
91	If the script fails for any reason, the return code will not be 0. The exact return code is immaterial; the cause of the error will be captured in the RMAN log file. The error is notified to the DBA's pager. The log file is sent to the pager and the DBA's e-mail.
95	If the RMAN execution was successful, we copy the log file to one of the locations where the backups are generated. The tape backup software will pick it up from that location.
99–100	The log file is also copied to the central log server.
101	The temporary log file is removed.

The beauty of the solution script is that it's useful for any type of RMAN run—full, incremental, merge, archivelog, and so on; it also can be applied to any database on any server. All you have to do is change the values of the parameters in the script to reflect the correct target.

9-2. Scheduling a Unix Shell File

Problem

You want to run a backup shell script using a Unix scheduler, such as cron.

Solution

The cron utility in Unix is a built-in scheduler that can kick off any shell script at a certain time. You can decide a specific day to run a script, or you can repeatedly run a script based on weekday and time, such as every Monday at 8 a.m. You enable a shell script to be run from cron by placing a reference to it in the crontab file. The crontab file is a text file with one line per execution. The lines have several fields indicating the execution times, with each field separated by a space. Here is an example of a crontab file:

```
00 11 * * 0 /opt/oracle/tools/rman_full.disk.sh > /opt/oracle/tools/rman_full.disk.log 2>&1
00 11 * * 0 /opt/oracle/tools/rman_arc.disk.sh > /opt/oracle/tools/rman_arc.disk.log 2>&1
```

These two lines show the execution properties of two programs under the cron scheduler: rman_full.disk.sh and rman_arc.disk.sh. The lines have several fields separated by spaces. These fields denote the execution times. Table 9-2 later in the chapter describes the fields. In general, the fields are shown as follows:

```
<minute> <hour> <date> <month> <weekday> <program>
```

The cron tool then runs the <program> at <hour>:<minute> on the <date> of the <month>. If <weekday> is specified, the program is run on the weekday at that time. If any of these entries have an asterisk (*) in them, the asterisk is ignored.

Direct Editing of Crontab

To schedule a program via `cron`, you have two options. One is to directly edit the crontab entries. Here is the process to follow:

1. Issue the following Unix command:

   ```
   $ crontab -e
   ```

   This opens your crontab file in the vi editor. If you don't have any entry yet in crontab, you will see an empty file. Place whatever line you want in the file. Be sure to adhere to the format described in Table 9-2 later in this chapter.

2. Save the file and exit. The line is now scheduled in crontab.

3. Check `cron` for all scheduled programs:

   ```
   $ crontab -l
   ```

   This should show the line you just placed in addition to all the other `cron` entries.

Updating Crontab

Instead of directly editing the crontab entries, you can edit a different file and then replace the crontab entries with the contents of that file. Here are the steps to follow:

1. Put the contents of crontab in a temporary file by issuing this Unix command:

   ```
   $ crontab -l > crontab.txt
   ```

   This creates a text file—crontab.txt—with all the `cron` entries.

2. Open the file crontab.txt using vi or any other editor, and place the line you want to add there. Save this file. Remember this file does not constitute the actual crontab file.

3. Replace the system crontab entries with the contents of the temporary file by issuing the following Unix command:

   ```
   $ crontab crontab.txt
   ```

The crontab file now mirrors the contents of the temporary file.

Both ways of adding a line to crontab—editing directly and editing a work file—do the same thing, but the second option might be less risky. If you make a mistake—even a small typo—while editing the system crontab, it could be a problem. The second approach does not let the crontab entries be replaced if an error is encountered. In addition, you have a backup of the crontab entries as a text file.

Examples of Crontab Schedules

Here are several examples of scheduling times for running a program named rman.sh.

- To schedule the program to run at 10:23 p.m. daily, use the following line:

  ```
  23 22 * * * rman.sh
  ```

Note how the date, month, and weekday entries are *, indicating that they do not matter; this should be run every day.

- To schedule it at 10:23 p.m. every Friday and Sunday, use this:

```
23 22 * * 5,7 rman.sh
```

- To schedule it at 10:23 p.m. on March 10, use this:

```
23 22 10 03 * rman.sh
```

- To schedule it at 10:23 p.m. on the 10th of each month, use this:

```
23 22 10 * * rman.sh
```

- To schedule it at 10 minutes past every hour on Sunday, use this:

```
10 * * * 0 rman.sh
```

- To schedule it every 15 minutes every day, use this:

```
0,15,30,45 * * * * rman.sh
```

How It Works

One of the problems of cron jobs is that they are executed in background, so any output from them does not go to the screen. You must capture the output in some log file. To facilitate that, in the actual task name, you can use a notation like this:

```
<command> > log.log 2>&1
```

This notation uses two special output streams, 1 and 2, for standard output and standard error, respectively. The output of the command that generally goes to the screen is shown as standard output, and any error messages go to standard error. Here the standard output is redirected by the > character to the file log.log. The notation 2>&1 means that the output of standard error (denoted by 2) is being redirected to 1 (standard output), which in turn goes to the file log.log too. So, this way, all the output from the <command > can be captured in the file log.log.

Table 9-2 describes the fields of crontab entries in detail. Remember that fields are delimited from each other by whitespace (space characters, tabs, and the like).

Table 9-2. Crontab Entries

Field Position	Example	Description
1	20	Shows the minute of the time component. You can place multiple values here, such as 10, 20, 30 to execute at the 10th, 20th, and 30th minute. You can also specify a range such as 10-12 to denote the 10th, 11th, and 12th minutes.
2	12	Shows the hour of the time component in 24-hour format. For instance, to set something for 1:23 p.m., you will place 13 in this field and 23 in the minutes field (the first field). Like the minutes, you can place a range here as well. If you place an asterisk on this field, the task is executed every hour, on that minute. For instance, if fields 1 and 2 are 20 and *, the task executes every 20 minutes of every hour.
3	25	Date when this task is run, 25th in this case. An asterisk in this field means every day.
4	12	Month when the task will run. In this example, it will run on December 25. An asterisk in this field means every month on that date, shown in field 3.
4	3	Weekday, starting with 0 for Sunday. So, 3 means it will execute on Wednesday.
5	myrman.sh	The actual task name.

9-3. Developing a Windows Batch File to Run RMAN
Problem

You want to develop a Windows batch file to kick off RMAN to back up the database on a Windows server.

Solution

A batch file in Windows to script RMAN commands is similar in concept to a shell script in Unix, but you need to shift directions. In the Unix script, you used the RMAN commands inline in the script. In Windows, you will use a slightly different approach, as shown here:

1. Create a RMAN command file with all the parameters you want.

2. Call the command file from the RMAN command line.

The batch file needs some utilities outside what are available in Windows:

- A utility to get the date and time in the format you want; here we have used a tool called realdate. We give a source for this utility in the "How It Works" section.

- A utility to send e-mail; here we use a tool called bmail. Again, see "How It Works" for where to find this utility.

Here are the steps for creating a batch file:

1. Check whether realdate is installed. If not, install realdate.

2. Install bmail. Again, see "How It Works" for the source of this utility.

3. Prepare the batch file as shown in the upcoming code. Please note that the lines are preceded by line numbers for easy explanation; they do not actually appear in the code.

4. Schedule the batch file for execution via any scheduler, such as Windows Scheduler or the at command (described in Recipe 9-6).

The following is a Windows batch file to create a full RMAN backup of a database running on Windows. This batch file will accept parameters to back up any database in any server, connecting to any catalog and to any media; after the backup, it will check for errors and e-mail the DBA on completion or send an e-mail to a pager in case of failure.

```
1.  @ECHO OFF
2.  :: Beginning of Script
3.  :: Start of Configurable Section
4.  set ORACLE_HOME=C:\oracle\product\12.1\db_1
5.  set ORACLE_SID=MOBDB10
6.  set TOOLHOME=C:\TOOLS
7.  set BACKUP_MEDIA=DISK
8.  set BACKUP_TYPE=FULL_DB_BKUP
9.  set MAXPIECESIZE=16G
10. set BACKUP_MOUNTPOINT=c:\oracle\flash
11. set DBAEMAIL="dbas@proligence.com"
12. set DBAPAGER="dba.ops@proligence.com"
13. set CATALOG_CONN=%ORACLE_SID%/%ORACLE_SID%@catalog
14. set MS=mail.proligence.com
15. ::
16. :: end of Configurable Section
17. ::
18. set BACKUP_LOC_PREFIX=%BACKUP_MOUNTPOINT%\loc
19. set TMPDIR=C:\temp
20. set NLS_DATE_FORMAT="MM/DD/YY HH24:MI:SS"
21. realdate /d /s="set curdate=" > %TOOLHOME%\tmp_dt.bat
22. realdate /t /s="set curtime=" > %TOOLHOME%\tmp_tm.bat
23. call %TOOLHOME%\tmp_dt.bat
24. call %TOOLHOME%\tmp_tm.bat
25. ::
26. ::
27. set LOG=%TOOLHOME%\%ORACLE_SID%_%BACKUP_TYPE%_%BACKUP_MEDIA%_•
    _%CURDATE%_%CURTIME%.log
28. set TMPLOG=%TOOLHOME%\tmplog.$$
29. ::
30. :: Build the Command File
31. set FORMATSTRING=%BACKUP_LOC_PREFIX%1\%ORACLE_SID%_%%u_%%p.rman
32. set CMDFILE=%TOOLHOME%\%ORACLE_SID%.rman
33. echo run { > %CMDFILE%
34. echo   allocate channel c1 type disk >> %CMDFILE%
35. echo     format '%FORMATSTRING%' >> %CMDFILE%
36. echo     maxpiecesize %MAXPIECESIZE%; >> %CMDFILE%
37. echo   backup >> %CMDFILE%
38. echo     tablespace users; >> %CMDFILE%
39. echo   release channel c1; >> %CMDFILE%
40. echo } >> %CMDFILE%
41. :: End of Command File Generation
42. ::
43. echo Starting the script > %LOG%
44. %ORACLE_HOME%\bin\rman target=/ catalog=%CATALOG_CONN% @%CMDFILE% •
    msglog=%TMPLOG%
45. ::
```

```
46. :: Merge the Logfiles
47. type %TMPLOG% >> %LOG%
48. :: Check for errors
49. ::
50. echo THE OUTPUT WAS %ERRORLEVEL% >> %LOG%
51. findstr /i "error" %LOG%
52. if errorlevel 0 if not errorlevel 1 bmail -s %MS%  -t %DBAPAGER% •
    -f "Database" -m %LOG%
53. @echo on
```

How It Works

The program realdate is freely available at www.huweb.hu/maques/realdate.htm. The program bmail is freely available at http://retired.beyondlogic.org/solutions/cmdlinemail/cmdlinemail.htm. This page also details its usage.

Table 9-3 gives a line-by-line explanation of the solution batch file.

Table 9-3. *Line-by-Line Explanation of the Batch File*

Lines	Description
1	This line instructs the batch program executer to stop displaying the commands in the file; just execute them.
4	We set the Oracle Home.
5	We set the Oracle SID.
6	We set the location of this batch file.
7	We specify the type of the backup, such as disk, tape, and so on. Please note that specifying a type here merely places the type in the name of the log file; it does not impact the type of the backup created by this batch file. The RMAN backup commands in the batch file determine the nature of the backup created.
8	We specify the type of backup, such as full or incremental, so that it becomes part of the name of the log file.
9	The MAXPIECESIZE for the backup is specified here.
10	The variables that hold the location of the backup.
11–12	The addresses where an e-mail will be sent.
13	The catalog connection string. In this script, we have assumed that the rman repository username is the ORACLE_SID and the password is the same as the username.
14	The mail server name. You can ask your e-mail administrator for this. In many small and medium organizations, this may be mail.organization.com.
21	We want to create a log file whose name should have the current date and time. The standard Windows date command does not easily yield a usable form of the date to be used in the log file, as is the case with the time component. Here we have used a special program called realdate. More information about realdate is provided following the table. In this line, we have extracted the current date and issued the command to set a variable curdate to hold the current date. For instance, if this program is executed on February 1, 2007, the command realdate /d /s="set curdate=" returns set curdate=20070201. This line is placed in the file tmp_dt.bat.

(continued)

Table 9-3. (*continued*)

Lines	Description
22	We again use `realdate` to extract the current time. For instance, if the program is executed at 11:15:53 p.m., the command `realdate /t /s="set curtime="` yields `set curtime=231553`. This line places that string in the file tmp_tm.bat.
23–24	We execute the batch files we generated in the previous two lines. These set the variables `curdate` and `curtime`.
27	We set the name of the log file.
28	We create a temporary log file to hold the output of the RMAN commands.
31	We create a variable called `FORMATSTRING` for the name of the backup piece.
32	We create a variable called `CMDFILE` to hold the name of the command file that will be passed to RMAN.
33–40	We put all the RMAN commands to be executed later in the command file.
44	We call the RMAN to execute the command file created dynamically in lines 33–40. The output goes to the log file named in line 28.
47	Now that we have the output of the RMAN output, we place the contents of that RMAN log file to the main log file we have been using.
50	We place the result of the RMAN run, as captured in the variable `ERRORLEVEL`. If the RMAN run was successful, this variable will be 0. The result will be in the log file.
51	If there is any error, the log file will contain that error. This line shows how to use the `findstr` command to find out whether the log file contains the word error in either uppercase or lowercase.
52	If the error was found, the `errorlevel` variable will be nonzero, and we want to e-mail the log file to the address specified in the variable `DBAPAGER`. To send the e-mail, we have used a program called `bmail`, which is described next.

After running the batch file, a log file is produced whose name is in the format `<DbName>_<BackupType>_<What's BeingBackedUp>_BKUP_<Target>_<Date>_<Time>.log`. The log file shows the RMAN command file as well, which confirms the actual command that was run.

9-4. Scheduling a Script in Windows via the GUI

Problem

You want to schedule a batch file or script in Windows to create a backup using the graphical user interface (GUI).

Solution

The Windows operating system has a task-scheduling interface that can be used to schedule tasks such as an RMAN backup. Here are the steps to follow:

1. Click Start ➤ Control Panel ➤ Scheduled Tasks ➤ Add a Scheduled Task. This opens the wizard shown in Figure 9-1.

Figure 9-1. *Adding a scheduled task*

2. Click Next. This takes you to the page shown in Figure 9-2. Click the Browse button, and select the batch file you created earlier in Recipe 9-3.

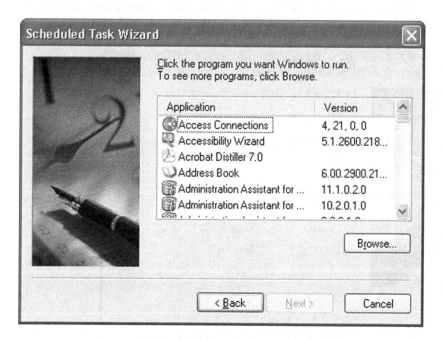

Figure 9-2. *Choosing a program to add to the scheduled tasks*

3. The next page of the wizard, shown in Figure 9-3, allows you to enter the schedule. Choose one of the options: Daily, Weekly, and so on.

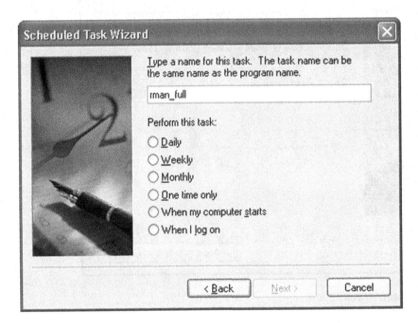

Figure 9-3. *Choosing the batch file and the schedule*

4. The next page allows you to enter the time of execution, as shown in Figure 9-4. On the same page, choose how often the program should be executed, what days the task should run, and so on.

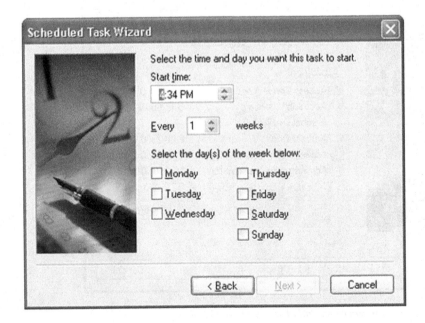

Figure 9-4. *Entering the time of execution*

5. The next page, shown in Figure 9-5, asks you to enter the user ID and password of the user who will run this task. The user ID can be the same as your usual login; otherwise, you can use a special user created just for this. In this example, we have assumed the user oracle will perform the backups and run the task. Enter the password of the user here, as shown in Figure 9-5.

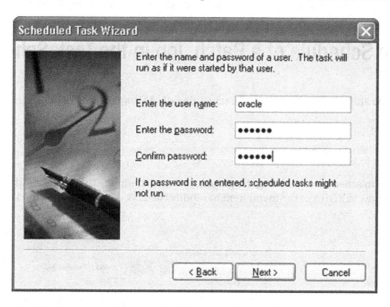

Figure 9-5. *Specifying the user ID and password used to run the scheduled task*

6. When you click the Next button, the task is added to the system, as shown in Figure 9-6.

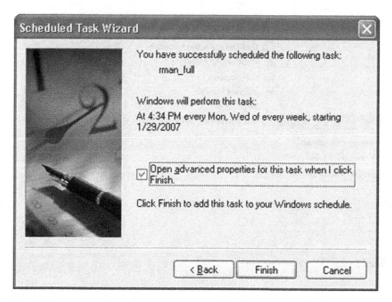

Figure 9-6. *Completion of the task addition*

That's it; the task is now scheduled.

How It Works

The Windows Task Scheduler provides a fairly straightforward way to configure scheduled jobs. The steps are self-explanatory.

Windows also provides for a way to schedule jobs via the command line. To learn how, see Recipe 9-6.

9-5. Changing the Schedule of a Batch Job in the Task Scheduler
Problem

You want to change the schedule and/or other attributes of a scheduled RMAN batch job in Windows using the Task Scheduler.

Solution

In Recipe 9-4, you learned how to schedule a job using the graphical Task Scheduler. That interface also lets you modify jobs. Figure 9-7 shows how to arrive at the menu item to modify the task rman_full from the Windows Start button.

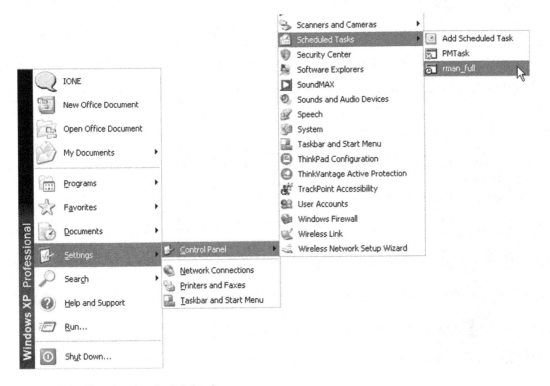

Figure 9-7. *Choosing the scheduled tasks*

From the resulting dialog box, you can change all the attributes of the job, such as the time and date of execution, the user and password being logged in, and so on.

How It Works

When you select the RMAN job in the menu, you'll see the dialog box shown in Figure 9-8.

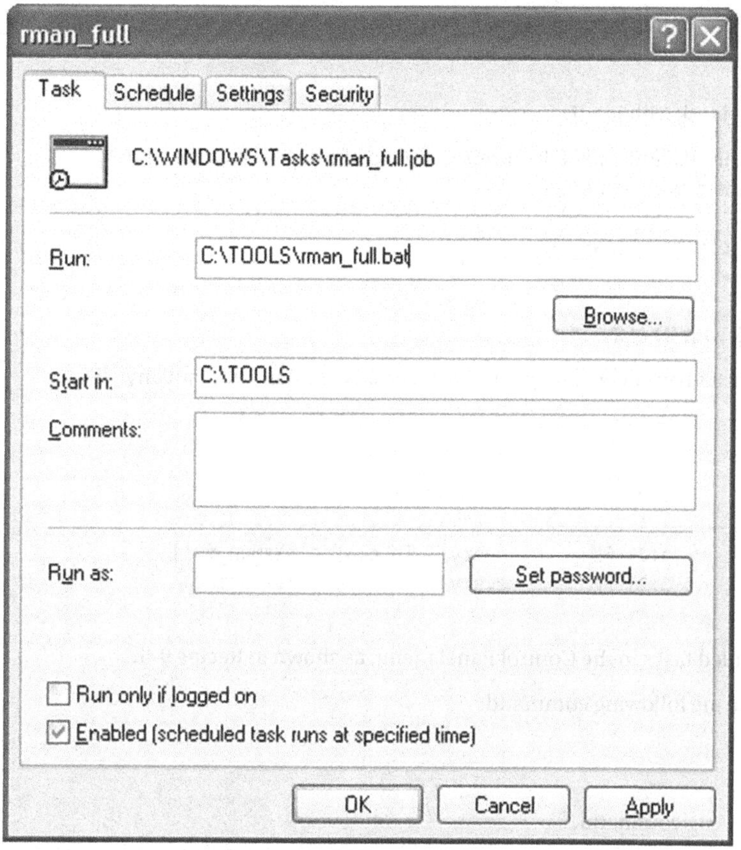

Figure 9-8. *The Task tab*

On the Task tab, you can change the advanced settings, such as the password of the user who runs it and so on. We recommend you take full advantage of the Comments field to describe the purpose of this task and the expected output.

9-6. Scheduling in Windows from the Command Line
Problem

You want to schedule a task in Windows from the command line, without using the GUI.

Solution

The solution is to use a tool called at in Windows. This tool is Windows' equivalent of Unix's cron. You can schedule, display, and delete tasks using this tool. Here are some specific examples showing how to use at to schedule and manage recurring tasks:

- To schedule a batch file called rman_full.bat in the C:\TOOLS directory to be run every Tuesday and Thursday at 1:23 p.m., issue the following command from the command line:

  ```
  C:\TOOLS>at 13:23 every:T,Th c:\tools\rman_full
  Added a new job with job ID = 1
  ```

  The command added a scheduled task with job ID 1.

- If you want the schedule to be every 1st and 2nd of the month, instead of a day of the week, put the dates after the every: parameter, as shown here:

  ```
  C:\TOOLS>at 13:23 every:1,2 c:\tools\rman_inc
  Added a new job with job ID = 2
  ```

- This command added a new task with ID of 2.

- If you want to check how many tasks have been added, just issue the at command without any parameter:

  ```
  C:\TOOLS>at
  Status ID   Day          Time        Command Line
  --------------------------------------------------------------------
          1   Today        1:23 PM     every:T,Th c:\tools\rman_full
          2   Today        1:23 PM     every:1,2 c:\tools\rman_inc
  ```

- You can also examine the scheduled tasks in the Control Panel menu, as shown in Recipe 9-5.

- To delete a task—say, ID 1—issue the following command:

  ```
  C:\TOOLS>at 1 /delete
  ```

- To delete all tasks, issue the following command:

  ```
  C:\TOOLS>at /delete
  ```

- Windows will ask you for a confirmation:

  ```
  This operation will delete all scheduled jobs.
  Do you want to continue this operation? (Y/N) [N]:
  ```

- Enter Y to delete all tasks.

How It Works

For a more complete description of the at command, see Microsoft Knowledge Base article 313565 at http://support.microsoft.com/kb/313565/en-us.

The end results of both the at command and the scheduler are the same, so there is no specific reason to choose one over the other. The choice is primarily whether you prefer using a GUI tool or a command-line tool. Another consideration is how these schedules are set up. If you want to schedule a lot of similar programs, such as backing up several tablespaces through one per script, the at command is far better than the scheduler because you can type them pretty fast.

9-7. Creating Local Stored Scripts
Problem

You want to store often-used scripts in the RMAN catalog and call them whenever needed as local scripts. You are not worried about executing such scripts against any database other than the original target database.

Solution

By default, a script you create can be used against only the target database for which it was created; that is why it's called a local script. A stored script is stored in the catalog, not in the control file of the target database. So, to create a stored script, a catalog connection is necessary. Here are the steps to create a stored script:

1. Connect to the RMAN target database and catalog:

   ```
   $ rman target=/ rcvcat=rmancat/rmancat@idb1
   ```

2. Create the stored script by enclosing it within curly braces. Here is a script named full_disk_db to create a full backup of the database (including the control file) to the disk:

   ```
   RMAN> create script full_disk_db
   2> {
   3>     allocate channel c1 type disk
   4>         format '+DG1/%U.rmb';
   5>     backup
   6>         database
   7>     include current controlfile;
   8>     release channel c1;
   9> }
   starting full resync of recovery catalog
   full resync complete
   created script full_disk_db
   starting full resync of recovery catalog
   full resync complete
   RMAN>
   ```

The script is now created and stored in the catalog database.
Once you've created a stored script, you can execute it in two ways:

- on RMAN prompt

   ```
   RMAN> run { execute script full_disk_db; }
   ```

- from the RMAN command prompt:

```
$ rman target=/ catalog=rmancat/rmancat script full_disk_db

... output truncated ...

connected to target database: IDB1 (DBID=420374953)
connected to recovery catalog database

executing script: full_disk_db

allocated channel: ORA_DISK_1
channel ORA_DISK_1: SID=36 device type=DISK
... output truncated ...
```

How It Works

Stored scripts are stored in the catalog database, not on a file system. After executing the create script command in RMAN, the result came back as follows:

```
created script full_disk_db
```

This output assures you that the script was created successfully. Had there been some issue while creating the script, the output would have been an error message. For instance, imagine that while typing you made a mistake in line 8, as shown here:

```
RMAN> create script full_disk_db
2> {
3>      allocate channel c1 type disk
4>          format '+DG1/%U.rmb';
5>      backup
6>          database
7>      include current controlfile;
8>      release c1;
```

Note the syntax error in line 8, release c1, instead of release channel c1. The moment you press Enter, RMAN immediately comes back with the following error message:

```
RMAN-00571: ===========================================================
RMAN-00569: =============== ERROR MESSAGE STACK FOLLOWS ===============
RMAN-00571: ===========================================================
RMAN-00558: error encountered while parsing input commands
RMAN-01009: syntax error: found "identifier": expecting one of: "channel"
RMAN-01008: the bad identifier was: c1
RMAN-01007: at line 8 column 9 file: standard input
RMAN-00571: ===========================================================
RMAN-00569: =============== ERROR MESSAGE STACK FOLLOWS ===============
RMAN-00571: ===========================================================
RMAN-00558: error encountered while parsing input commands
RMAN-01009: syntax error: found ";": expecting one of: "allocate, alter,
backup, beginline, blockrecover, catalog, change, connect,
```

```
copy, convert, create, crosscheck, configure, duplicate, debug, delete, drop,
exit, endinline, flashback, host, {, library, list,
mount, open, print, quit, recover, register, release, replace, report,
renormalize, reset, restore, resync, rman, run, rpctest, set,
setlimit, sql, switch, spool, startup, shutdown, send, show, test, transport,
upgrade, unregister, validate"
RMAN-01007: at line 8 column 11 file: standard input
```

There are some restrictions on the stored scripts. For example, you can't create the stored scripts within another stored script; they can be created only at the RMAN prompt. If you try to create a script within a script, as shown here, then RMAN throws an error immediately:

```
RMAN> create script parent
2> {
3>    create script child
```

You can't go far:

```
RMAN-00571: ===========================================================
RMAN-00569: =============== ERROR MESSAGE STACK FOLLOWS ===============
RMAN-00571: ===========================================================
RMAN-00558: error encountered while parsing input commands
RMAN-01009: syntax error: found "create": expecting one of: "allocate, alter,
backup, beginline, blockrecover, catalog, change, copy,
convert, crosscheck, configure, duplicate, debug, delete, execute, endinline,
flashback, host, mount, open, plsql, recover,release, replicate, report, restore,
resync, set, setlimit, sql, switch, startup,
shutdown, send, show, transport, validate"
RMAN-01007: at line 3 column 1 file: standard input
```

The run command can't be used within the script.

```
RMAN> create script myscript
2> {
3>    run
```

RMAN immediately throws an error:

```
RMAN-00571: ===========================================================
RMAN-00569: =============== ERROR MESSAGE STACK FOLLOWS ===============
RMAN-00571: ===========================================================
RMAN-00558: error encountered while parsing input commands
RMAN-01009: syntax error: found "run": expecting one of: "allocate, alter,
backup, beginline, blockrecover, catalog, change, copy,convert, crosscheck,
configure, duplicate, debug, delete, execute, endinline,
flashback, host, mount, open, plsql, recover, release,
replicate, report, restore, resync, set, setlimit, sql, switch, startup,
shutdown, send, show, transport, validate"
RMAN-01007: at line 3 column 1 file: standard input
```

The @ and @@ commands, which are the equivalent of run, also can't be put in a script.

9-8. Creating a Global Stored Script

Problem

You want to create a global-stored script that can be called for any target database.

Solution

Stored scripts are stored in the catalog database, and you can call them by name when you want to execute. Here is the RMAN command segment to create a global script called gs_arc_disk_bkup:

```
RMAN> create global script gs_arc_disk_bkup
2> comment 'Global Script to Backup Arc Logs Delete Input'
3> {
4>     allocate channel c1 type disk
5>         format 'C:\oraback\%U.rman';
6>     backup
7>         archivelog
8>         all
9>         delete input;
10>    release channel c1;
11> }
created global script gs_arc_disk_bkup
```

Note that the syntax to create a global script is the same as a local script with one exception: the presence of the clause global before the script keyword.

How It Works

Global scripts are available to more than just the target database to which you were originally connected. After a global script is created, you can connect to any target database and execute the script. So, a natural question is, when is a global script beneficial?

A global script, as the name implies, lets you write once and execute anywhere. So, there is the biggest benefit. You do not need to write scripts for each database, and thus you save on coding and QA costs.

On the other hand, a one-size-fits-all script may not be possible or desirable in all cases. For instance, consider a full backup script. The parameters, such as MAXPIECESIZE and so on, will be different for each database, obviating the usefulness of a single global script.

So, when are these global scripts really useful? Generic, repetitive, non-database-dependent activities are the most suitable for global scripts. Common examples are listing or deleting archived logs, cross-checking backups, and subsequently deleting expired backups.

■ **Note**   The restrictions that apply to local scripts apply to local ones as well. These restrictions are described in the "How It Works" section of Recipe 9-7.

9-9. Updating Stored Scripts

Problem

You want to update a stored script, one that you've stored in a recovery catalog, with new code.

Solution

There is no concept of a line-by-line update to a stored script. You have to replace the entire stored script with a new code. To update a script, issue the `replace script` command followed by new code that you want for the script, as shown here:

```
RMAN> replace script full_disk_db
2> {
3>     allocate channel c1 type disk
4>         format 'c:\backup\rman_%U.rman';
5>     backup
6>         database
7>         include current controlfile;
8>     release channel c1;
9> }
replaced script full_disk_db
```

The script is now replaced by the new code. Remember, you have to replace the entire script.

How It Works

The `replace script` action essentially re-creates the same script. Therefore, the same restrictions applicable to creating a script apply here, too. Check the "How It Works" section of Recipe 9-7 to learn about those restrictions.

The `replace script` command replaces the script in the catalog without leaving behind a copy in some manner. This may not be acceptable to you. You may want to get a copy of the script, and edit that, while the older version of the copy serves as a backup. See Recipe 9-16 on how to accomplish that.

9-10. Commenting on Stored Scripts

Problem

You want to save a comment along with a stored script so you have something to help you remember what that script does when you return to it potentially months later.

Solution

To associate a comment with a script, use the optional `comment` clause in the command to create (or to replace) that script. Enclose your comment within single quotes, as shown here:

```
RMAN> create script full_disk_db
2> comment 'Full Backup as Backupset to Disk'
3> {
4>     allocate channel c1 type disk
```

```
5>        format 'c:\backup\rman_%U.rman';
6>    backup
7>        database
8>        include current controlfile;
9>    release channel c1;
10> }

created script full_disk_db
```

How It Works

Comments help describe the scripts more clearly than just the names you give them. The comments appear when you display or list the scripts, which amounts to a sort of metadata of the scripts.

There is no way to add a comment to an existing script. Instead, you will need to re-create the script using the replace command, as shown here:

```
RMAN> replace script full_disk_db
2> comment 'New Full Backup as Backupset to Disk'
3> {
... and so on ...
```

9-11. Displaying Stored Scripts

Problem

You want to display the code of a script stored in the catalog database.

Solution

The print script command displays the code of the script, as shown here:

```
RMAN> print script full_disk_db;
```

The output, in this case, comes back as follows:

```
printing stored script: full_disk_db
 {allocate channel c1 type disk
format 'c:\backup\rman_%U.rman';
backup
database
include current controlfile;
release channel c1;
}
```

If there are two scripts of the same name—one local and the other global—then the print script command shown earlier displays the local script, not the global one. If you want to display the global script, use the global keyword before the word script, as shown here:

```
RMAN> print global script full_disk_db;
```

How It Works

How the `print` command works should be fairly obvious. It's worth talking a bit, though, about script names having unusual characters. Usually there are no quotes around script names. However, quotes are necessary when the following is true:

- A script name starts with a number.

- A script name contains a reserved word, such as backupset.

- A script name is in mixed case.

Suppose you have a script called 1ClickBackup and you want to display the contents. Use double quotes around the script name:

```
RMAN> print script "1ClickBackup";
printing stored script: 1ClickBackup
 {allocate channel c1 type disk
format 'c:\oracle\flash\loc1\rman_%U.rman';
backup
database include current controlfile;
release channel c1;
}
```

Note if you make a typo in the script name, say, by capitalizing the letter A, as shown here:

```
RMAN> print script "1clickBAckup";
```

then RMAN immediately comes back with an error:

```
RMAN-00571: ===========================================================
RMAN-00569: =============== ERROR MESSAGE STACK FOLLOWS ===============
RMAN-00571: ===========================================================
RMAN-06004: ORACLE error from recovery catalog database: RMAN-20400: stored
script not found
RMAN-06083: error when loading stored script 1clickBAckup
```

The names 1ClickBackup and 1ClickBAckup are not the same; the letter A is capitalized in the latter.

9-12. Listing Stored Scripts
Problem

You want to display a list of stored scripts in the catalog database.

Solution

The `list script names` command lists all the scripts in the database. For example:

```
RMAN> list script names;
```

The output comes back as follows:

```
List of Stored Scripts in Recovery Catalog

    Scripts of Target Database MOBDB10

        Script Name
        Description
        ------------------------------------------------------------------------
        full_disk_db
        Full Backup as Backupset to Disk

    Global Scripts

        Script Name
        Description
        ------------------------------------------------------------------------
        gs_arc_disk_bkup
        Global Script to Backup Arc Logs Delete Input
```

How It Works

The list script names command simply lists the scripts you've saved to your catalog database. The comments of each script, if available, are displayed in the Description column.

The command list script names shows both local and global scripts. If you want to list only global scripts, use the global keyword before the word script:

```
RMAN> list global script names;

List of Stored Scripts in Recovery Catalog

    Global Scripts

        Script Name
        Description
        ------------------------------------------------------------------------
        gs_arc_disk_bkup
        Global Script to Backup Arc Logs Delete Input
```

If you want to find out the global scripts and the local scripts of all the databases using the recovery catalog, you merely use the all qualifier before the script keyword:

```
RMAN> list all script names;
```

9-13. Dropping Stored Scripts

Problem

You want to drop a stored script from the catalog database.

Solution

The RMAN command delete script drops the script from the catalog database. Here is how you drop a script named delete_arc_logs:

```
RMAN> delete script delete_arc_logs;

deleted script: delete_arc_logs
RMAN>
```

How It Works

If you want to drop a script with some special name, such as a number at the beginning of the name or a reserved word, you need to enclose the name in quotes, as shown here:

```
RMAN> delete script "1stDelete";
```

If you have two scripts—one local and one global—in the same name, then the delete script command drops the local one, not the global one. If you want to drop the global script, you must use the keyword global in the command, as shown here:

```
RMAN> delete global script delete_arc_logs;

deleted global script: delete_arc_logs
RMAN>
```

9-14. Executing a Global Script When a Local Script of the Same Name Exists

Problem

You have two scripts of the same name—delete_arc_logs—one local and one global. You want to execute the global script, not the local one.

Solution

To execute the global script, you call that script with the clause global before it, as shown in the following RMAN command:

```
RMAN> run { execute global script delete_arc_logs; }
```

The output is as follows:

```
executing global script: delete_arc_logs
allocated channel: ORA_DISK_1
channel ORA_DISK_1: sid=141 devtype=DISK
List of Archived Log Copies
Key     Thrd Seq    S Low Time          Name
------- ---- ------- - ------------------ ----
116     1    40      A 08/07/12 11:23:15  C:\FLASH\MOBDB10\ARCHIVELOG\2012_08_07\01_
                                          MF_1_40_2V9VWM6T_.ARC
```

... and so on ...

The global script has now executed.

How It Works

When you call a script as follows:

```
RMAN> run { execute script delete_arc_logs; }
```

the local script is executed, if there is a local script. RMAN looks for a local script first and executes that if it is found. Only if no local script exists will RMAN go on to execute the global script. That is the default behavior. You can, however, add the clause global before the word script to make RMAN execute a global script no matter what.

9-15. Converting Stored Scripts to Files
Problem

You want to convert a stored script in the catalog database to an operating system file.

Solution

The print script command shown in Recipe 9-11 has a clause to redirect the output to a file. If you want to store the code in the script delete_arc_logs in the file c:\tools\delete_arc_logs.rman, issue the following command:

```
RMAN> print script delete_arc_logs to file 'c:\tools\delete_arc_logs.rman';
script delete_arc_logs written to file c:\tools\delete_arc_logs.rman
RMAN>
```

This generates a file named delete_arc_logs.rman in the C:\TOOLS directory.

How It Works

Generating files from stored scripts is a good way to protect scripts. You can store the scripts on local file systems as backups against the catalog database. The generated files also are handy while transferring scripts from one database to another. You will learn how to do the reverse—create a script from a file—in Recipe 9-16.

The generated file looks exactly like the code in the script. Here is what the contents of the file look like:

```
{ delete noprompt archivelog all; }
```

However, this file by itself cannot be called from the command line of RMAN directly:

```
RMAN> @delete_arc_logs.rman
RMAN-00571: ===========================================================
RMAN-00569: =============== ERROR MESSAGE STACK FOLLOWS ===============
RMAN-00571: ===========================================================
RMAN-00558: error encountered while parsing input commands
RMAN-01009: syntax error: found ";": expecting one of: "exit"
RMAN-01007: at line 2 column 1 file: standard input
```

So, you need to edit the file to remove the curly braces or put a run keyword before the first curly brace:

```
RMAN> run { delete noprompt archivelog all; }
```

9-16. Creating or Replacing a Stored Script from a File

Problem

You want to create a script from an operating system file generated from a script earlier.

Solution

You can use the create script command with a special from file option. To create a script from the named file, issue the following RMAN command:

```
RMAN> create script delete_arc_logs from file 'c:\tools\delete_arc_logs.rman';

script commands will be loaded from file c:\tools\delete_arc_logs.rman
created script delete_arc_logs

RMAN>
```

This creates the stored script.

How It Works

This is an excellent way to back up and restore the stored scripts outside the database. In Recipe 9-15, you learned how to create a file from a stored script. In this recipe, you learned how to create a stored script from the same file. The approach is also useful when you want to move a stored script from one database to another.

If you want to replace an existing stored script, you issue a modified version of the replace command, as shown here:

```
RMAN> replace script delete_arc_logs from file 'c:\tools\delete_arc_logs.rman';
script commands will be loaded from file c:\tools\delete_arc_logs.rman
replaced script delete_arc_logs
```

This replaces the script delete_arc_logs with the contents of the file.

9-17. Passing Parameters to Stored Scripts

Problem

You want to create a script that can accept parameters during runtime.

Solution

Starting with version 11g Release 1, the RMAN scripts can accept parameters. This applies to both the command file scripts and the stored scripts. To make the stored script delete_archive_log accept a parameter—the log sequence number—you create the script as shown here:

```
RMAN> replace script delete_archive_log { delete noprompt archivelog sequence &1 ; }
```

Note the &1 at the end. This is a placeholder for the parameter. When you execute the command, you may get a message such as the following asking you to enter a value of parameter 1. Enter any number; this does not actually execute the command.

```
Enter value for 1: 1
created script delete_archive_log
```

You can call this script to delete the archived redo log sequence 36, as shown here:

```
RMAN> run {execute script delete_archive_log using 36; }

executing script: delete_archive_log

released channel: ORA_DISK_1
allocated channel: ORA_DISK_1
channel ORA_DISK_1: SID=135 device type=DISK
List of Archived Log Copies for database with db_unique_name IDB1
=================================================================
Key     Thrd Seq     S Low Time
------- ---- ------- - ---------
315     1    36        A 06-AUG-12
        Name: +FRA/idb1/archivelog/2012_08_06/thread_1_seq_36.375.790644523

deleted archived log
archived log file name=+FRA/idb1/archivelog/2012_08_06/thread_1_seq_36.375.790644523 RECID=27
STAMP=790644522
Deleted 1 objects
```

Similarly, to delete archived redo log sequence number 132, you will need to call the same script with the parameter 132.

To execute the script from command line directly, use the script clause of the RMAN command:

```
$ rman target=/ catalog=rmancat/rmancat script del_arc_spec using 37

... output truncated ...
connected to target database: IDB1 (DBID=420374953)
connected to recovery catalog database
```

```
executing script: del_arc_spec

allocated channel: ORA_DISK_1
channel ORA_DISK_1: SID=36 device type=DISK
List of Archived Log Copies for database with db_unique_name IDB1
====================================================================

Key     Thrd Seq     S Low Time
------- ---- ------- - ---------
316     1    37      A 06-AUG-12
              Name: +FRA/idb1/archivelog/2012_08_06/thread_1_seq_37.375.790644523

Do you really want to delete the above objects (enter YES or NO)? yes
deleted archived log
archived log file name=+FRA/idb1/archivelog/2012_08_06/thread_1_seq_37.375.790644523 RECID=28
STAMP=790644522
Deleted 1 objects

Recovery Manager complete.
```

How It Works

The parameterized stored scripts work with positional parameters the same way SQL*Plus does. The parameters are named &1, &2, and so on, relating to their relative positions.

If you need to pass a character value to a parameter, you should use single quotes around the value passed. Here is how you can create a script that expects a character argument:

```
RMAN> replace script delete_archive_log { delete &2 archivelog sequence &1 ; }

Enter value for 2: noprompt

Enter value for 1: 1

replaced script delete_archive_log
```

Now you can call this stored script as follows:

```
RMAN> run {execute script delete_archive_log using 36 'noprompt'; }

executing script: delete_archive_log
... and so on ...
```

If you need to replace the part of a string with the value of the parameter, you can use a period to separate the name from the value passed. For instance, if you want to delete archived redo logs matching a pattern, you can create the script as follows:

```
RMAN> create script del_arc_log_pattern {
2> delete archivelog like '%&1.%'; }
```

```
Enter value for 1: a
```

```
created script del_arc_log_pattern
```

Note how the pattern has been specified as %&1.%. The second % character is separated from the &1 by a period. Now, to delete the archived redo logs with the string 2007_05_11 in them, you can call the script as follows:

```
RMAN> run {execute script del_arc_log_pattern using '2012_08_05'; }
```

```
executing script: del_arc_log_pattern
```

```
released channel: ORA_DISK_1
allocated channel: ORA_DISK_1
channel ORA_DISK_1: SID=134 device type=DISK
List of Archived Log Copies for database with db_unique_name MOBDB11
=====================================================================
Key     Thrd Seq     S Low Time
------- ---- ------- - ---------
75      1    38      A 05-AUG-12
        Name: C:\ORACLE\FLASH\MOBDB11\ARCHIVELOG\2012_08_05\O1_MF_1_38_348WK5OZ_.ARC
76      1    39      A 05-AUG-12
        Name: C:\ORACLE\FLASH\MOBDB11\ARCHIVELOG\2012_08_05\O1_MF_1_39_348WKBQX_.ARC
77      1    40      A 05-AUG-12
        Name: C:\ORACLE\FLASH\MOBDB11\ARCHIVELOG\2012_08_05\O1_MF_1_40_348WKCB8_.ARC
78      1    41      A 05-AUG-12
        Name: C:\ORACLE\FLASH\MOBDB11\ARCHIVELOG\2012_08_05\O1_MF_1_41_348WKJ6C_.ARC
Do you really want to delete the above objects (enter YES or NO)? no
```

Parameterized scripts help significantly in managing the infrastructure with RMAN. You can create just one script and then call it several times with different values of the parameter, which reduces the overall scripting time and potential for errors.

9-18. Creating a Parameterized Command File Script
Problem

You want to create an RMAN command file script that can accept a parameter.

Solution

Starting with Oracle Database 11g Release 1, to create a RMAN command file in Unix (or Windows) that can accept a parameter, you simply create a file with content like this:

```
run { delete noprompt archivelog sequence &1 ; }
```

Note the &1 at the end, which is the positional parameter whose value you will pass later. Name this file delete_arc_logs.rman, and place it in the directory /u01/rmanscripts. Now call the script to delete the archived redo log 36, as shown here:

```
$ rman target=/ @u01/rmanscripts/delete_arc_logs.rman using 36
```

```
... output truncated ...

connected to target database: IDB1 (DBID=420374953)

RMAN> { delete archivelog sequence 36 ; }
2>
using target database control file instead of recovery catalog
allocated channel: ORA_DISK_1
channel ORA_DISK_1: SID=20 device type=DISK
deleted archived log
archived log file name=+FRA/idb1/archivelog/2012_08_06/thread_1_seq_36.376.790643975 RECID=27
STAMP=790643975
Deleted 1 objects

Recovery Manager complete.
```

How It Works

The parameters in the script are positional, which is similar to the parameters in a Unix shell script or a SQL*Plus script. You name the parameters &1, &2, and so on, and pass the values to these parameters in the same order. For instance, here is an example of a script file that accepts two parameters:

```
run { delete &2 archivelog sequence &1 ; }
```

Name the script file delete_arc_logs.rman. Now call the script with the second parameter as noprompt, which is a character string. You can pass the characters by enclosing them in single quotes:

```
C:\tools>rman target=/ @c:\tools\delete_arc_logs.rman using 36 'noprompt'

... output truncated ...

connected to target database: MOBDB11 (DBID=406156306)

RMAN>  { delete noprompt archivelog sequence 36 ; }
2>
using target database control file instead of recovery catalog
allocated channel: ORA_DISK_1
channel ORA_DISK_1: SID=127 device type=DISK
... and so on ...
```

If you need to replace the part of a string with the value of the parameter, you can use a period to separate the string from the value passed. For instance, if you want to delete archived redo logs matching a pattern, you can create the script file with the contents, as shown here:

```
run { delete archivelog like '%&1%' ; }
```

Note how the pattern has been specified as %&1.%. The second % character is separated from the &1 by a period. Name this file del_arc_logs_pattern.rman. Now you can call this script file to delete the archived redo logs matching the pattern %2012_08_08%:

```
C:\tools>rman target=/ @c:\tools\del_arc_logs_pattern.rman using '2012_08_08'
```

On Unix-based systems you have to escape the single quote character by a backslash ("\") since that is interpreted by the Unix shell:

```
$ rman target=/ @delete_arc_logs_pattern.rman using \'2012_08_07\'

... output truncated ...

connected to target database: IDB1 (DBID=420374953)

RMAN> run { delete archivelog like '%2012_08_07%' ; }
2>
using target database control file instead of recovery catalog
allocated channel: ORA_DISK_1
channel ORA_DISK_1: SID=261 device type=DISK
deleted archived log
archived log file name=+FRA/idb1/archivelog/2012_08_07/thread_1_seq_38.374.790678805 RECID=29
STAMP=790678805
deleted archived log
archived log file name=+FRA/idb1/archivelog/2012_08_07/thread_1_seq_39.371.790718425 RECID=30
STAMP=790718426
deleted archived log
archived log file name=+FRA/idb1/archivelog/2012_08_07/thread_1_seq_40.370.790725643 RECID=31
STAMP=790725644
Deleted 3 objects

Recovery Manager complete.
```

Parameterized scripts help significantly in managing the infrastructure with RMAN. You can create just one script and then call it several times with different values of the parameter, making many routine tasks a breeze. This strategy is especially useful in cases where the script remains the same but some output changes to match the date and month, such as when you want to name the backup pieces with the day, month, and year when they were generated. In that case, you can merely call the script with a parameter that accepts the output name. This will reduce the scripting time and the possibility of errors.

CHAPTER 10

Restoring the Control File

Your control file restore method is highly dependent on your backup strategy. The phrase "when you think of backups, think of recovery" applies especially to control files. Depending on your backup methodology, the control file restore can be effortless, or it can be complicated.

If you have enabled a fast recovery area (FRA) or are using a recovery catalog, then you'll find restoring the control file an automated and simple process. Having RMAN do all of the heavy lifting helps ensure that you'll get this critical file restored in a timely and accurate manner.

■ **Note**   We highly recommend that you enable the control file auto backup feature with the
`configure controlfile autobackup on` RMAN command. This will ensure that you have a backup of your control file after every RMAN backup and also after making database structural changes (such as adding a data file).

If you're using neither a FRA nor a recovery catalog, then restoring the control file requires that you perform a few manual steps. Manually performing steps means you must pay extra attention to the details of the task.

Control files aren't usually a source of failure. That's because they're usually multiplexed, which gives you a high degree of protection against failure. However, these are very critical files, and you should know how to restore them if the need arises. This chapter starts with the automated and simple methods for control file restores and then progresses to the more complicated, manual scenarios.

Before you begin, if you have a copy of your current control file, we recommend you make a backup of it before you issue a RMAN `restore controlfile` command. Use the `backup current controlfile` command to back up your control file. In many scenarios, when you restore a control file it will overwrite any existing control files.

■ **Note**   Anytime you restore a control file from a backup (and use it for a recovery), you are required to perform media recovery on your entire database and then open it with the `open resetlogs` command. This is true even if you don't restore any data files (because the control file's SCN is no longer synchronized with the SCNs in the data files and online redo log files). You can determine whether your control file is a backup by querying the CONTROLFILE_TYPE column of the V$DATABASE view. This chapter covers only how to restore your control file and does not show how to restore and recover your entire database. Refer to Chapter 11 for complete recovery scenarios, and refer to Chapter 12 for incomplete recovery situations.

10-1. Restoring Control File Using Fast Recovery Area

Problem

You have enabled a fast recovery area (FRA), and you use it as a repository for your control file backups. You're attempting to start your database and receive this error:

```
ORA-00205: error in identifying control file, check alert log...
```

You inspect the alert.log and determine that you've lost all of your control files and need to restore them.

Solution

When you use the FRA, you can use one of two very different methods to restore the control file depending on whether you enabled the auto backup of the control file. This recipe describes both of these scenarios.

Using FRA and Autobackup Enabled

When you enable the auto backup of your control file and are using a FRA, then restoring your control file is fairly simple. First connect to your target database, then issue a startup nomount command, and then issue the restore controlfile from autobackup command:

```
$ rman target /
RMAN> startup nomount;
RMAN> restore controlfile from autobackup;
```

RMAN restores the control files to the location defined by your control_files initialization parameter. You should see a message indicating that your control files have been successfully copied back from an RMAN backup piece. Here is a partial snippet of the output:

```
channel ORA_DISK_1: AUTOBACKUP
 /u01/fra/O12C/autobackup/2012_07_17/o1_mf_n_788860985_80bw4vbm_.bkp
found in the recovery area
```

■ **Note**   The prior example works only if you have enabled the auto backup of the control file feature and are using a FRA. You can verify whether the auto backup of the control file is enabled via the RMAN show all command. You can verify whether the FRA is enabled by inspecting the db_recovery_file_dest initialization parameter.

You can now alter your database into mount mode and perform any additional restore and recovery commands required for your database.

Using FRA with Auto Backup Disabled

If you don't use the auto backup of the control file feature, then restoring the control file becomes more difficult. If auto backup is disabled, you have to explicitly tell RMAN from which directory and backup piece to restore the control file. Inspect your FRA, look in the backupset directory, and look for the latest directory created in that directory. Use that directory and name to restore the control file. For example:

```
$ rman target /
RMAN> startup nomount;
RMAN> restore controlfile from
'/u01/fra/O12C/backupset/2012_07_17/o1_mf_ncnnf_TAG20120717T0954_80cd0x_.bkp';
```

Here is a partial listing of the output:

```
channel ORA_DISK_1: restoring control file
output file name=/u01/dbfile/o12c/control01.ctl
output file name=/u01/dbfile/o12c/control02.ctl
```

You can now alter your database into mount mode and perform any additional restore and recovery commands required for your database.

How It Works

We highly recommend enabling auto backup of the control file. By default, the auto backup of your control file is not enabled. You can easily enable the auto backup feature via the `configure controlfile autobackup on` command. This ensures that the backup piece is placed in a default location that RMAN can use to automatically restore the target database control file.

Explaining Using FRA and Auto Backup Enabled

When you enable auto backups and use the fast recovery area, no recovery catalog is required (to restore the control file), and you don't have to explicitly provide RMAN with the name and location of backup files or your target database identifier (DBID). This is one of the simplest methods that RMAN provides for restoring a control file. However, this solution works only when you enable auto backups of your control file and use a FRA.

RMAN uses the value of your operating system ORACLE_SID variable to look in the default location for control file backups in the FRA. RMAN deduces the default location of the backup file by combining the values of the db_recovery_file_dest initialization parameter and your operating system ORACLE_SID variable setting. By default RMAN will look in a directory with the following format:

```
/<FRA>/<target database SID>/autobackup/YYYY_MM_DD/<backup piece file>
```

Explaining Using FRA with Auto Backup Disabled

When you don't have the auto backup of your control file enabled, then by default RMAN will place the backup of your control file in a directory path named like this:

```
/<FRA>/<target database SID>/backupset/YYYY_MM_DD/<backup piece file>
```

■ **Note** RMAN will by default back up your control file anytime you back up data file 1, regardless of whether you have the auto backup of your control file feature enabled.

When you restore your control file and when the auto backup feature has not been enabled, then RMAN is unable to determine by itself the default location. You must directly tell RMAN from which backup piece to restore the control file.

▪ **Note** If you are using a FRA and a recovery catalog, then refer to Recipe 10-2 for details about restoring your control file. In that scenario, RMAN will automatically retrieve the backup piece name and location from the recovery catalog.

If you have the RMAN output log from a backup, then you should be able to see which backup piece contains the backup of your control file. For example:

```
Piece Name:
'/u01/fra/O12C/backupset/2012_07_17/o1_mf_ncnnf_TAG20120717T0954_80cd0x_.bkp';
Control File Included: Ckp SCN: 682078
```

In this example, the correct backup piece name is as follows:

```
o1_mf_ncnnf_TAG20120717T0954_80cd0x_.bkp
```

10-2. Restoring Control File Using Recovery Catalog
Problem
You need to restore your control file, and you use a recovery catalog when creating backups.

Solution
Restoring the control file is fairly simple when you use a recovery catalog. All you need to do is ensure that you connect to both your target database and the recovery catalog. Then issue startup nomount, and issue the restore controlfile command.

In this example, the recovery catalog owner and password are both rcat, and also the name of the recovery catalog is rcat. You'll have to change those values to match the username/password@service in your environment.

```
$ rman target /
RMAN> connect catalog rcat/rcat@rcat
RMAN> startup nomount;
RMAN> restore controlfile;
```

RMAN restores the control files to the location defined by your control_files initialization parameter. You should see a message indicating that your control files have been successfully copied back from an RMAN backup piece. Here's a partial listing of RMAN's message stack after a successful control file restore:

```
channel ORA_DISK_1: restore complete, elapsed time: 00:00:03
output file name=/u01/dbfile/o12c/control01.ctl
output file name=/u01/dbfile/o12c/control02.ctl
```

You can now alter your database into mount mode and perform any additional restore and recovery commands required for your database.

How It Works

Using a recovery catalog makes it straightforward to restore the control file. When you issue the `restore controlfile` command, RMAN will retrieve from the recovery catalog the location and name of the file that contains the control file backup and restores the control file appropriately. Because the recovery catalog knows the location of the RMAN backup piece, it doesn't matter whether the backup piece is in a fast recovery area, or in a configured channel location, or if you're using the auto backup of the control file feature.

When you're connected to the recovery catalog, you can view backup information about your control files even while your target database is in nomount mode. To list backups of your control files, use the `list` command as shown here:

```
RMAN> connect target /
RMAN> connect catalog rcat/rcat@rcat
RMAN> startup nomount;
RMAN> list backup of controlfile;
```

Keep in mind the prior command isn't possible if you're not using a recovery catalog. When not using the recovery catalog, the RMAN backup information is stored in the control file. And if you've lost all your control files, you won't be able to place your database in mount mode until you've restored a control file.

If you have registered two databases in the recovery catalog with the same name, then you might receive an error such as this when you attempt to list backups or restore the control file:

```
RMAN-06004: ORACLE error from recovery catalog database:
RMAN-20005: target database name is ambiguous
```

In this situation, you will need to first set your database identifier (DBID) before you can restore your control file. This is because the database name stored in the recovery catalog is not guaranteed to be unique. You can determine the DBID and verify that you have multiple databases with the same name in your recovery catalog by querying the recovery catalog database RC_DATABASE view as shown here:

```
SQL> connect rcat/rcat@rcat
SQL> select db_key, dbid, name from rc_database;
```

See Recipe 10-3 for more details regarding methods to identify your DBID.

10-3. Determining the Database Identifier

Problem

You've experienced media failure with all of your control files. Your backup strategy doesn't take advantage of either a FRA or a recovery catalog. You're trying to restore a control file as follows:

```
$ rman target /
RMAN> startup nomount;
RMAN> restore controlfile from autobackup;
```

However, you receive an error message stating that you must explicitly set the database identifier (DBID):

```
RMAN-06495: must explicitly specify DBID with SET DBID command
```

You don't know the DBID for your database, and you aren't sure how to find the DBID. Without a control file for your database, you can't mount the database and query the DBID value from the V$DATABASE view.

Solution

You can determine the DBID of your target database in one of the following ways:

- You can derive the DBID from an auto backup file.

- You can retrieve the DBID from RMAN output.

- If you've thought ahead, you can write the DBID periodically to a file such as the alert.log.

- You can derive DBID from a file dump.

Deriving the DBID from an Auto Backup File

This solution works only when you're not using a FRA. When the auto backup of the control file is enabled and you're not using a FRA, the format of the file created always includes the format variable %F when naming the file used for the RMAN backup piece. The format of the %F variable is a unique combination of the database identifier, the date, and a sequence, and it follows this format: c-IIIIIIIIII-YYYYMMDD-QQ, which includes the DBID embedded in the IIIIIIIIII string. For example, if the control file backup piece name is c-2601506593-20060918-01, then the DBID substring is 2601506593. Table 10-1 describes the meaning of each section of the %F format variable.

Table 10-1. *Description of %F Format Variable*

String	Meaning
c	Signifies a control file backup
IIIIIIIIII	DBID
YYYYMMDD	Date backup was created. Used by maxdays parameter of the restore controlfile command
QQ	A hex sequence number that is incremented each time a control file auto backup is created for a given day. Used by the maxseq parameter of the restore controlfile command

If you've enabled the auto backup of the control file and haven't specified its location through either the use of a FRA or a configured backup location, then the default location for a control file auto backup on Linux/Unix systems is ORACLE_HOME/dbs, and on Windows platforms it's usually ORACLE_HOME\database. You can inspect the file name and derive the DBID.

▪ **Note** If you are using a FRA, then the control file will not contain the DBID as part of its name. When using a FRA, the control file backup is named using the Oracle Managed File format.

Retrieving the DBID from RMAN Output

Another method for identifying your DBID is to extract it from any RMAN session output that you have previously saved to a log file. The output of an RMAN session will contain the DBID as displayed when you first connect to your target database. For example:

```
RMAN> connect target /
connected to target database: O12C (DBID=3412777350)
```

Writing the DBID to the Alert.log File

Another way of recording the DBID is to write it to the alert.log file on a regular basis using the DBMS_SYSTEM package. For example, you could have this SQL code execute as part of your backup job:

```
COL dbid NEW_VALUE hold_dbid
SELECT dbid FROM v$database;
exec dbms_system.ksdwrt(2,'DBID: '||TO_CHAR(&hold_dbid));
```

After running the previous code, you should see a text message in your target database alert.log file that looks like this:

```
DBID: 3412777350
```

The KSDWRT procedure writes a text message to your database alert.log file. In this case, the hold_dbid SQL variable is populated with the DBID. If you write your target database DBID to the alert.log file on a regular basis, you should be able to identify it easily should the need arise.

■ **Caution** Writing messages to the alert.log file may result in Oracle Support's refusal to use the alert.log file when diagnosing issues.

Dumping Files

If any of the data files, online redo log files, or archived redo log files are physically available, you can use the SQL alter system dump statement to write the DBID to a trace file. Your database does not have to be mounted for this to work. This example shows how to create a data file dump:

```
SQL> connect / as sysdba
SQL> startup nomount;
SQL> alter system dump datafile
     '/u01/dbfile/o12c/system01.dbf' block min 1 block max 10;
```

In the prior line of SQL, you'll have to modify the path and file name to match your environment.
You can also use this syntax to take a dump of an archived redo log file or online redo log file:

```
SQL> alter system dump logfile '<log file name>';
```

The trace file with the DBID will be in your diagnostic trace file destination. If you search for the string "Db ID," you should find something similar to this output:

```
Db ID=3412777350=0xcb6ad986, Db Name='O12C'
```

If you can't find the trace file, use this technique to create and identify it:

```
SQL> oradebug setmypid
SQL> alter system dump datafile
     '/u01/dbfile/o12c/system01.dbf' block min 1 block max 10;
SQL> oradebug tracefile_name
```

You should see the name of the trace file displayed, for example:

```
/u01/app/oracle/diag/rdbms/o12c/o12c/trace/o12c_ora_7126.trc
```

How It Works

If you're using neither a FRA nor a recovery catalog, then you might have to know your DBID before you restore the control file. Every Oracle database has an internal, unique DBID that can be queried from V$DATABASE as follows:

```
SQL> select dbid from v$database;
```

Here is some sample output:

```
    DBID
----------
3412777350
```

RMAN uses the DBID to uniquely identify databases. The DBID helps RMAN identify the correct RMAN backup piece from which to restore the control file. If you don't use a FRA or a recovery catalog, then you should record the DBID in a safe location and have it available in the event you need to restore your control file.

10-4. Restoring Control File with No Fast Recovery Area or Recovery Catalog

Problem

You are using neither a FRA nor a recovery catalog, and you need to restore your control file using RMAN.

Solution

If you're not using a FRA or a recovery catalog, then how you restore the control file is highly dependent on how you configured your backups. We outline four scenarios next.

Using Auto Backup with RMAN Backup Piece in the Default Location

The first example shows how to restore a control file when you've enabled auto backup and have not used the configure command to specify a location for the RMAN backup piece. In this scenario, RMAN will look for the backup in the default location. You need to provide RMAN with the DBID so that it knows from which backup piece the control file should be restored.

■ **Note**   See Recipe 10-3 for details on how to identify your DBID.

Once you know your DBID, you can connect to your target database, issue startup nomount, set the DBID, and issue the restore controlfile command. In this example, the DBID is 3412777350:

```
$ rman target /
RMAN> startup nomount;
RMAN> set dbid 3412777350;
RMAN> restore controlfile from autobackup;
```

RMAN will now display output similar to the following:

```
channel ORA_DISK_1: AUTOBACKUP found: c-3412777350-20120717-07
channel ORA_DISK_1: restoring control file from AUTOBACKUP
c-3412777350-20120717-07
```

When you set the DBID, you are instructing RMAN to search outside the fast recovery area in the default location for a backup file that was formatted with the %F parameter.

■ **Note**   See Table 10-1 for details about the %F format variable.

RMAN will look in the default location for the RMAN backup piece file. The default location varies by operating system. On Linux/Unix, the default location is ORACLE_HOME/dbs. On Windows installations it's usually ORACLE_HOME\database.

RMAN will start with today's date and look for a control file backup with today's date as part of the backup file name. If RMAN doesn't find a backup piece with today's date as part of the file name, it will then look in the default location for a file name with yesterday's date included as part of the name, and so forth.

By default, RMAN will attempt to retrieve from auto backups created within the past seven days only. If you want to modify the default behavior, use the maxdays parameter. This example instructs RMAN to look for a control file backup created in the past 20 days:

```
RMAN> connect target /
RMAN> startup nomount;
RMAN> set dbid 3412777350;
RMAN> restore controlfile from autobackup maxdays 20;
```

You can also instruct RMAN to search for control file backups by sequence number via the maxseq parameter. The sequence number used is defined by the %F format variable and is generated when the control file backup is created. This next example instructs RMAN to look for a control file backup file that has a sequence number of 10 or less:

```
RMAN> connect target /
RMAN> startup nomount;
RMAN> set dbid 3412777350;
RMAN> restore controlfile from autobackup maxseq 10;
```

■ **Note**   The maxdays and maxseq parameters are useful only when your control file backup file names are formatted with the %F format mask. The %F format mask embeds a date and a sequence number in the backup piece name.

Using Auto Backup, with RMAN Backup Piece in a Nondefault Location

If you used the configure controlfile autobackup format command to specify the location of the control file backup to a nondefault location, then you have to tell RMAN where to find the backup file. For example, say you configured your auto backup of the control file like this:

```
RMAN> configure controlfile autobackup format for device type disk
to '/u01/rman/o12c/%F';
```

If you subsequently need to restore a control file, instruct RMAN to look in the directory /u01/rman/012c for a file formatted with %F:

```
$ rman target /
RMAN> startup nomount;
RMAN> set dbid 3412777350;
RMAN> set controlfile autobackup format for device type disk
to '/u01/rman/o12c/%F';
RMAN> restore controlfile from autobackup;
```

RMAN will now display output similar to this:

```
channel ORA_DISK_1: AUTOBACKUP found: /u01/rman/o12c/c-3412777350-20120717-09
channel ORA_DISK_1: restoring control file from
AUTOBACKUP /u01/rman/o12c/c-3412777350-20120717-09
```

This next example is a slight variation of the previous example. Here, instead of using the set command, you directly instruct RMAN to restore from a specific backup piece. In this scenario, you do not need to set the DBID because you're pointing RMAN at a specific backup file.

```
RMAN> connect target /
RMAN> startup nomount;
RMAN> restore controlfile from '/u01/rman/o12c/c-3412777350-20120717-09';
```

You should now see RMAN output similar to this:

```
channel ORA_DISK_1: restoring control file
output file name=/u01/dbfile/o12c/control01.ctl
```

Not Using Auto Backup with RMAN Backup Piece in the Default Location

You can use RMAN without configuring anything. You can start RMAN and back up your database out of the box with a backup database command. In this situation, the system data file would be part of what gets backed up. If you don't configure anything with RMAN, the default behavior is that your control file gets backed up anytime data file 1 is backed up.

The RMAN backup piece will be in a default location that is operating system dependent. On Linux/Unix systems it will be in ORACLE_HOME/dbs; on Windows it's usually ORACLE_HOME\database. The RMAN backup piece name won't be obvious to you; instead it will be something cryptic like 1fh0geg_1_1.

The next example uses the output of the backup database command to determine which backup piece contains the control file. Here you need to identify the correct file and instruct RMAN to restore the control file from the specific backup piece; in this example, the backup file is in the default location on a Linux/Unix box, and the name is 17ngbba3_1_1:

```
$ rman target /
RMAN> startup nomount;
RMAN> restore controlfile from
'/u01/app/oracle/product/12.1.0.1/db_1/dbs/17ngbba3_1_1';
```

Not Using Auto Backup with RMAN Backup Piece in Nondefault Location

You can configure your RMAN backup pieces to be written to a specific location via the `configure channel device` command as follows:

```
RMAN> configure channel device type disk format '/u01/rman/o12c/%d%U.bk';
```

This instructs RMAN to write backups to the `/u01/rman/o12c` directory with the specified file format. When you need to restore from an RMAN backup piece directly, you need to provide RMAN with the directory and backup file name when you issue the restore command. For example:

```
$ rman target /
RMAN> startup nomount;
RMAN> restore controlfile from '/u01/rman/o12c/O12C19ngbbph_1_1.bk';
```

How It Works

If you've enabled the auto backup of your control file feature, RMAN will look for the backup that contains the control file in the default location. If the RMAN backup piece is not in the default location, you can tell RMAN explicitly where to retrieve it from.

When you don't use the FRA or the recovery catalog, then it's more complicated to restore the control file. You need to supply RMAN information such as the DBID or the exact name and location of the backup piece to successfully restore the control file. This can be time-consuming and error prone; therefore, it is recommended that you use a FRA or a recovery catalog when backing up your control file.

10-5. Restoring Control File to Nondefault Location

Problem

You want to restore your control file to a location other than the default location specified by your `control_files` parameter.

Solution

Use the `restore controlfile to` command. The syntax varies slightly depending on whether you're using auto backups or a recovery catalog, or manually configuring the location of the backups.

■ **Note** Your database can be in nomount, in mount, or open when you use the `restore controlfile to` command. If your database is mounted or open, then you must use the `restore controlfile to` command to restore your control file. This is because RMAN will not let you overwrite the current (open) control file. That's a good thing.

Using Auto Backups

This example shows the syntax when restoring to a nondefault location and using an auto backup of the control file:

```
$ rman target /
RMAN> restore controlfile to '/u01/test/control01.ctl' from autobackup;
```

Here is a partial listing of RMAN's output:

```
channel ORA_DISK_1: looking for AUTOBACKUP on day: 20120717
channel ORA_DISK_1: AUTOBACKUP found: c-3412777350-20120717-0b
channel ORA_DISK_1: restoring control file from AUTOBACKUP
c-3412777350-20120717-0b
```

Using a Recovery Catalog

This example shows the syntax when restoring a control file to a nondefault location using a recovery catalog. The recovery catalog knows the location of the last good backup of the control file; therefore, you don't need to use a from autobackup clause.

```
$ rman target /
RMAN> connect catalog rcat/rcat@rcat
RMAN> restore controlfile to '/u01/test/control01.ctl';
```

Using a Manually Configured RMAN Backup Piece

This example shows how to restore to a nondefault location from a backup that was created with a manually configured location for the RMAN backup piece:

```
RMAN> restore controlfile to '/u01/test/control01.ctl'
from '/u01/rman/o12c/O12C19ngbbph_1_1.bk';
```

How It Works

By default, the control files are restored to the location defined by the control_files initialization parameter. If you want the control files restored to a location other than what is defined by the control_files initialization parameter, then use the restore controlfile to command.

▪ **Note**   The restore controlfile to command does not overwrite the current control file. It restores only the control file to the location you specify.

10-6. Restoring Lost Copy of Multiplexed Control File
Problem

You attempt to start your database and receive the following error:

```
ORA-00205: error identifying controlfile, check alert log...
```

You check your target database alert.log file and verify that Oracle can't obtain the status of one of your database control files. You wonder whether you can use a good copy of an existing control file to resolve this issue.

Solution

If you multiplex your control files, you can take a good control file and copy it right over the top of a bad or missing control file. You don't need to issue an RMAN restore controlfile command in this scenario. You have two methods to get your database restarted:

- You can modify your initialization file (spfile or init.ora) so that it references only the good remaining control file(s).

- You can copy a good control file to the location of the bad or missing control file.

Modifying the Initialization File

In the first example, control02.ctl is missing and the database won't start, so we've decided to modify the control_files parameter in the initialization file. This example uses an spfile:

```
SQL> startup nomount;
SQL> alter system
set control_files='/u01/dbfile/o12c/control01.ctl' scope=spfile;
System altered.
SQL> shutdown immediate;
SQL> startup;
```

Copying a Good Control File

In this example, we're copying the good control file (control01.ctl) to the location of the bad control file (control02.ctl). To do this, first shut down your database from either RMAN or SQL*Plus using this:

```
RMAN> shutdown immediate;
```

or this:

```
SQL> shutdown immediate;
```

Even though control02.ctl is bad, we suggest that you first make a copy of it. This may be useful for troubleshooting after the fact. Here we make a copy of the bad control file:

```
$ cp /u01/dbfile/o12c/control02.ctl /u01/dbfile/o12c/control02.ctl.bad
```

Then from the Linux/Unix operating system prompt, copy the good control file to the location of the bad or missing control file:

```
$ cp /u01/dbfile/o12c/control01.ctl /u01/dbfile/o12c/control02.ctl
```

Now from RMAN or SQL*Plus you should be able to start your database normally using the startup command as follows:

```
RMAN> startup;
```

or

```
SQL> startup;
```

How It Works

Before Oracle can start up normally, it must be able to locate and open each of the control files identified by the control_files initialization parameter. The control files are identical copies of each other. If a multiplexed control file becomes damaged, you can either modify the control_files initialization parameter to match the locations of the remaining good control files or copy a good control file to the location of the damaged or missing control file.

If you have one good copy of a control file, you can use that to replace the damaged control files. This minimizes the need to restore your control file from a backup.

■ **Tip** Multiplexing your control files minimizes the chance of failure with these critical files. We highly recommend that you multiplex your control files and try to place each copy on separate devices governed by different controllers.

10-7. Re-creating the Control File

Problem

One of the following situations applies:

- You've experienced a failure and lost all of your control files, and you belatedly realize that you don't have a binary backup of the control file.

- You want to change a database setting that can be modified only by re-creating the control file.

- You are relocating a large number of data files and/or online redo log files, and you find it easier to re-create the control file with the new names and locations (instead of manually renaming the files).

Solution

Use the `alter database backup controlfile` command to create a SQL file that you can use to re-create your control files. Here is the general syntax:

```
alter database backup controlfile to trace [as '<directory/filename>' [reuse]]
[resetlogs|noresetlogs];
```

For example, suppose you want to write a file named recreate.sql written to the /orahome/oracle directory:

```
SQL>alter database backup controlfile to trace
as '/orahome/oracle/recreate.sql' noresetlogs;

Database altered.
```

The prior command creates a file that contains a `create controlfile` SQL statement. Manually edit the newly created file and take out the lines that you don't require (for example, there are a lot of comment lines initially in the file). Here is some sample output for this example:

```
CREATE CONTROLFILE REUSE DATABASE "O12C" NORESETLOGS  NOARCHIVELOG
    MAXLOGFILES 16
    MAXLOGMEMBERS 4
    MAXDATAFILES 1024
```

```
    MAXINSTANCES 1
    MAXLOGHISTORY 876
LOGFILE
  GROUP 1 '/u01/oraredo/o12c/redo01a.rdo'  SIZE 50M BLOCKSIZE 512,
  GROUP 2 '/u01/oraredo/o12c/redo02a.rdo'  SIZE 50M BLOCKSIZE 512
DATAFILE
  '/u01/dbfile/o12c/system01.dbf',
  '/u01/dbfile/o12c/sysaux01.dbf',
  '/u01/dbfile/o12c/undotbs01.dbf',
  '/u01/dbfile/o12c/users01.dbf'
CHARACTER SET AL32UTF8;
--
ALTER DATABASE OPEN;
--
ALTER TABLESPACE TEMP ADD TEMPFILE '/u01/dbfile/o12c/temp01.dbf'
    SIZE 524288000  REUSE AUTOEXTEND OFF;
```

Assuming the prior SQL code is in a file named recreate.sql, here is how to run it:

```
SQL> startup nomount;
SQL> @/orahome/oracle/recreate.sql
```

If successful, you should see this output:

```
Control file created.
Database altered.
Tablespace altered.
```

You should now have control files re-created in every location identified by your control_files initialization parameter.

If you're using a recovery catalog, your backup information is still stored safely in your recovery catalog database. After you re-create the control files, you'll have to connect to the target database and recovery catalog and run a resync catalog command to update the recovery catalog metadata with information about the newly created control file.

```
RMAN> connect target /
RMAN> connect catalog rcat/rcat@rcat
RMAN> resync catalog;
```

You can now back up your target database while connected to the recovery catalog.

How It Works

For critical databases, you should always multiplex your control file and also back it up on a regular basis. This obviates the need to re-create the control file. However, as the Problem section makes clear, sometimes you simply must re-create your control file.

When you re-create the control file, this wipes out any RMAN backup information that was stored in your target database control file. If you need to access historical RMAN backup information (and are not using a recovery catalog), then you will have to do one of the following:

- If using Oracle Database 10g or higher, then use the `catalog` command to repopulate your control file with RMAN backup information (see Recipe 11-18).

- If using Oracle9i Database, then use the `DBMS_BACKUP_RESTORE` package to extract files out of RMAN backup pieces (see Recipe 10-8).

■ **Note** Only the parameters you have set with the RMAN `configure` command are retained after you re-create the control file.

The key to understanding how to re-create a control file is that when you run the `alter database backup controlfile` statement, it in turn creates a file that contains the SQL `create controlfile` statement. You can then modify the file and run it to re-create your controlfiles.

If you don't specify a directory and file name (as shown in the Solution section), then the file is created in your diagnostic trace directory. For example, this next line of code doesn't specify a directory or file name:

```
SQL> alter database backup controlfile to trace;
```

You'll have to find the file in the diagnostic trace directory for your database. You can determine the location via this query:

```
SQL> select value from v$diag_info where name='Diag Trace';
```

Here is some sample output for this example:

```
VALUE
-----------------------------------------
/u01/app/oracle/diag/rdbms/o12c/o12c/trace
```

You might have several trace files in that directory. Usually the most recently created trace file in that directory is the one that contains the SQL `create controlfile` statement.

If you often work with trace files created in the diagnostic trace directory, here's a simple method for easily identifying the name of the trace file that you created:

```
SQL> oradebug setmypid
SQL> alter database backup controlfile to trace;
SQL> oradebug tracefile_name
```

Here is some sample output:

```
/u01/app/oracle/diag/rdbms/o12c/o12c/trace/o12c_ora_4655.trc
```

NAMING A TRACE FILE

If you want to specify a text string to be used as part of the trace filename, then use the tracefile_identifier parameter. This makes finding the trace file generated by your session much easier. For example, if you wanted your trace filename to contain a text string of "MYTRACE," then you would set tracefile_identifier as follows:

```
SQL> alter session set tracefile_identifier='MYTRACE';
```

Every time you modify this parameter, the next trace file that is generated by your session will have the specified value of tracefile_identifier embedded in the trace file name. The format of the trace file name will be as follows:

```
<SID><Oracle process id><tracefile_identifier>.trc
```

10-8. Restoring the Control File Using DBMS_BACKUP_RESTORE

Problem

You're using Oracle Database 9i (or older) with no recovery catalog. You've lost all of your control files. You now want to retrieve a binary copy of the control file from an RMAN backup, but in this version of the database there's no obvious way to instruct RMAN how to restore from a backup piece when you have no control files available (that contain the RMAN backup metadata information). You need to somehow extract the control file from the RMAN backup.

Solution

Use the PL/SQL package DBMS_BACKUP_RESTORE to restore a control file from an RMAN backup. You can access this package whether your database is in nomount or mount mode.

You need to know the name of the backup piece that contains the backup of the control file before you begin. Modify the following anonymous block of PL/SQL to use your backup piece name and control file name:

```
DECLARE
  finished BOOLEAN;
  v_dev_name VARCHAR2(75);
BEGIN
  -- Allocate a channel, when disk then type = null
  -- If tape then type = sbt_tape.
  v_dev_name := dbms_backup_restore.deviceAllocate(type=>null, ident=>'d1');
  --
  dbms_backup_restore.restoreSetDatafile;
  -- Destination and name for restored control file.
  dbms_backup_restore.restoreControlFileTo(cfname=>'/tmp/control01.ctl');
  --
  -- Backup piece location and name.
  dbms_backup_restore.restoreBackupPiece(
    '/u01/rman/c-3412777350-20120722-00', finished);
  --
```

```
if finished then
  dbms_output.put_line('Control file restored.');
else
  dbms_output.put_line('Problem');
end if;
--
dbms_backup_restore.deviceDeallocate('d1');
END;
/
```

If the previous code was stored in a file named rc.sql, then you would execute it as follows:

```
SQL> connect / as sysdba
SQL> startup nomount;
SQL> @rc.sql
```

How It Works

Much of RMAN is internally implemented via the DBMS_BACKUP_RESTORE package. For example, when you issue an RMAN backup or restore command, Oracle calls the DBMS_BACKUP_RESTORE package to initiate the real work. This package is installed when you create a database and run the catproc.sql script and is available in every Oracle database since version 8.0.3.

In very rare situations you may be required to access DBMS_BACKUP_RESTORE package. If you ever need to restore a control file and cannot do it with the normal procedures described throughout this chapter, then you can use DBMS_BACKUP_RESTORE directly. While using this package isn't exactly straightforward, it's not rocket surgery either. You should be able to modify the example in the Solution section of this recipe to meet your requirements.

Keep in mind that if you're using Oracle Database 10g or higher, you can directly restore from a backup piece via the from <backup piece> clause. Also in Oracle Database 10g or higher, you can repopulate a control file with RMAN backup metadata via the catalog command. Additionally, if you're using a recovery catalog, then you can populate a re-created control file with RMAN metadata via the resync catalog command. For all of these reasons, you shouldn't normally have to use the DBMS_BACKUP_RESTORE package.

■ **Tip** One important aspect of DBMS_BACKUP_RESTORE is that this package can be accessed even if your database is in nomount mode. This provides you some flexibility on being able to run RMAN commands even if you can't alter your database into mount mode.

CHAPTER 11

■ ■ ■

Performing Complete Recovery

Be thankful for problems. If they were less difficult, someone else with less ability might have your job.

—James A. Lovell

When an airplane is flying on autopilot through clear skies, you don't worry too much about the pilot's experience level. It's when an engine catches on fire that you want somebody who is prepared and trained to handle the disaster. Or if the pilot isn't trained, hopefully somebody has a comprehensive *Recipes for Disasters* book handy.

That also holds true in the database arena. When the database is up and running smoothly, nobody pays too much attention to the database or the DBA. It's when disaster strikes that companies are thankful they've invested in a DBA who has implemented a solid backup and recovery strategy. It's critical that you have a plan and understand what to do when you see messages like the following:

```
ORA-01157: cannot identify/lock data file 1 - see DBWR trace file
ORA-01110: data file 1: '/u01/dbfile/o12c/system01.dbf'
```

No DBA likes to see that message. However, accidents happen. People do incorrect things. Disks fail. These are all things that can cause failures. A *media failure* occurs when Oracle can't read or write to a required database file. *Media recovery* is the process of restoring files (from backups) and reapplying transactions (from logs) to recover the data files that have experienced media failure. The next several paragraphs will explain the internals of the Oracle restore and recovery process and many terms and definitions used by database administrators.

Background

Most recovery scenarios have two separate phases: restore and recovery. *Restore* is the process of retrieving files from backups. Appropriately named, the RMAN `restore` command is used to retrieve data files, control files, archived redo log files, and server parameter files (spfiles) from backup sets. When RMAN restores a data file, it will reconstruct an exact copy of the data file as it was when it was backed up. RMAN is the only utility that can restore files from RMAN backup pieces.

Recovery is the process of applying transactions from incremental backups (if using) and the redo files (archive and/or online) to the data files. *Complete recovery* means you can recover all transactions that were committed in your database before the failure occurred. You can use either RMAN or SQL*Plus to issue a `recover` command. Aside from a few minor differences, it doesn't matter whether you use RMAN or SQL*Plus to initiate a recovery. Both result in redo being applied to data files to recover transactions. This book focuses on RMAN-initiated restore and recovery examples.

For complete recovery, you do not have to restore and recover all the data files in your database. You have to restore and recover only those data files that are damaged. Depending on the type of failure, that could be all the data files in your database or just one data file. Oracle detects which data files need media recovery by comparing the system change number (SCN) information in the control file and the corresponding SCN information in the data file headers.

Incomplete recovery means that you cannot restore all committed transactions. Incomplete recovery is required when you don't have all the redo required to apply all committed transactions to the data files. You can also initiate incomplete recovery intentionally to restore the database to a previous state to recover data that was accidentally deleted. Incomplete recovery is initiated with the recover database until command. Chapter 12 discusses incomplete recovery. Chapter 13 discusses performing incomplete recovery via various flashback features.

To understand what type of recovery is required, it's helpful to first understand the mechanics of how Oracle handles transactions. Here's a typical transaction:

```
SQL> insert into my_table values(1);
SQL> commit;
Commit complete.
```

When you see Commit complete, Oracle guarantees that a record of that transaction has been safely written to the current online redo log file on disk. That does not mean the modified block has yet been written to the appropriate data file. The transaction information in the online redo log buffer is written very frequently to disk by the log writer background process, whereas changes to the modified blocks in the database buffer are intermittently written to disk by the database writer background process.

Periodically, all changed (dirty) block buffers in memory are written (by database writer) to the data files on disk. This is known as a *checkpoint*. When a checkpoint occurs, the checkpoint process records the current checkpoint SCN in the control files and the corresponding SCN in the data file headers. A checkpoint guarantees that the data files are in a consistent state at a point in time.

The algorithm used by the log writer to write transaction information from the log buffer to the online redo log files is entirely different from the algorithm used by the database writer to write changed blocks from the database buffer to the data files. This is because the log buffer and the database buffer have entirely different goals. The purpose of the log buffer is to temporarily buffer transaction changes and get them quickly written to a safe location on disk (online redo log files), whereas the database buffer tries to keep blocks in memory as long as possible to increase the performance of processes using frequently accessed blocks.

Because the log writer's activities are not synchronized with the database writer's activities, at any point in time you could have committed transactions that exist in the online redo log file but do not yet have the corresponding changed blocks written to the data files. Also, at any given time there might be blocks with uncommitted changes written to the data files. This is the expected behavior. Oracle keeps track of what has been committed (or not) and ensures that you're always presented with a read consistent and committed version of the database. In the event of an unexpected failure, Oracle is able to sort out what was committed or not via information in the redo stream and rollback segments. Figure 11-1 shows a user process initiating data modifications resulting in server processes reading blocks into memory, writing changes to memory, resulting in changed blocks written to data files and change vectors written to redo logs.

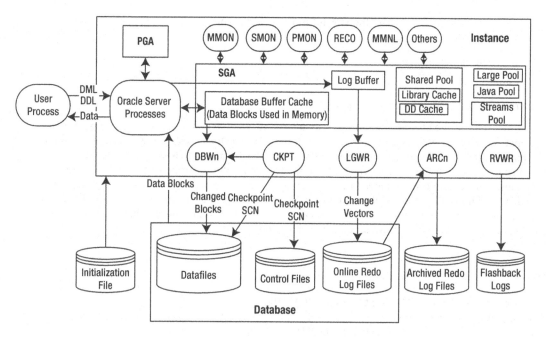

Figure 11-1. *Flow of data changes through an Oracle instance and database*

If You're Still Awake …

An *instance (crash) failure* occurs when the background processes aren't able to shut down normally. When this happens, your data files could be in an inconsistent state—meaning they may not contain all committed changes and may contain uncommitted changes. Instance failures occur when the instance terminates abnormally. A sudden power failure or a shutdown abort are two common causes of instance failure.

Oracle uses *crash recovery* to return the database to a consistent committed state after an instance failure. Crash recovery guarantees that when your database is opened, it will contain only transactions that were committed before the instance failure occurred. Oracle's system monitor will automatically detect whether crash recovery is required.

Crash recovery has two phases: *roll forward* and *roll back*. The system monitor background process will first roll forward and apply to the data files any transactions in the online redo log files that occurred after the most recent checkpoint. Crash recovery uses redo information found in the online redo log files. After rolling forward, Oracle will roll back any of those transactions that were never committed. Oracle uses information stored in the undo segments to roll back (undo) any uncommitted transactions.

■ **Note**   DBAs often use the terms *crash recovery* and *instance recovery* interchangeably. However, Oracle defines crash recovery as either the recovery of a single instance configuration or the crash recovery of all failed instances in an Oracle Real Application Cluster (RAC) configuration, whereas instance recovery is defined to be the recovery of one failed instance by an existing live instance in an RAC configuration.

When you start your database, Oracle uses the SCN information in the control files and data file headers to determine which one of the following will occur:

- Starting up normally

- Performing crash recovery

- Determining that media recovery is required

On startup, Oracle checks the instance thread status to determine whether crash recovery is required. When the database is open for normal operations, the thread status is OPEN. When Oracle is shut down normally (normal, immediate, or transactional), a checkpoint takes place, and the instance thread status is set to CLOSED.

When your instance abnormally terminates (such as from a shutdown abort command), the thread status remains OPEN because Oracle didn't get a chance to update the status to CLOSED. On startup, when Oracle detects that an instance thread was abnormally left open, the system monitor process will automatically perform crash recovery.

The following query demonstrates how a single instance of Oracle would determine whether crash recovery is required. Your database needs to be at least mounted to run this query:

```
SELECT
  a.thread#, b.open_mode, a.status,
  CASE
  WHEN ((b.open_mode='MOUNTED') AND (a.status='OPEN')) THEN
   'Crash Recovery req.'
  WHEN ((b.open_mode='MOUNTED') AND (a.status='CLOSED')) THEN
   'No Crash Rec. req.'
  WHEN ((b.open_mode='READ WRITE') AND (a.status='OPEN')) THEN
   'Inst. already open'
  WHEN ((b.open_mode='READ ONLY') AND (a.status='CLOSED')) THEN
   'Inst. open read only'
  ELSE 'huh?'
  END STATUS
FROM v$thread     a
   ,gv$database b
WHERE a.thread# = b.inst_id;
```

Oracle will start up normally if the SCN information in the control files matches the SCNs in the corresponding data files. If the checkpoint SCN in the data file is less than the corresponding SCN in the control file, Oracle will throw a media recovery error. For example, if you restored a data file from a backup, Oracle would detect that the SCN in the data file is less than the corresponding SCN in the control file. Therefore, a recovery is required to apply changes to the data file to catch it up to the SCN in the control file. Table 11-1 summarizes the checks that Oracle performs to determine whether crash or media recovery is required.

Table 11-1. SCN Oracle Startup Checks

Condition on Startup	Oracle Behavior	DBA Action
CF checkpoint SCN < Data file checkpoint SCN	"Control file too old" error	Restore a newer control file or recover with the using backup controlfile clause.
CF checkpoint SCN > Data file checkpoint SCN	Media recovery required	Most likely a data file has been restored from a backup. Recovery is now required.
CF checkpoint SCN = Data file SCN	Start up normally	None
Database in mount mode, instance thread status = OPEN	Crash recovery required	None. Oracle automatically performs crash recovery.

The following SQL query demonstrates the internal checks that Oracle performs to determine whether media recovery is required:

```
SET LINES 132
COL name FORM a40
COL status FORM A8
COL file# FORM 9999
COL control_file_SCN FORM 999999999999999
COL datafile_SCN FORM 999999999999999
--
SELECT
a.name
,a.status
,a.file#
,a.checkpoint_change# control_file_SCN
,b.checkpoint_change# datafile_SCN
,CASE
WHEN ((a.checkpoint_change# - b.checkpoint_change#) = 0) THEN 'Startup Normal'
WHEN ((b.checkpoint_change#) = 0) THEN 'File Missing?'
WHEN ((a.checkpoint_change# - b.checkpoint_change#) > 0) THEN 'Media Rec. Req.'
WHEN ((a.checkpoint_change# - b.checkpoint_change#) < 0) THEN 'Old Control File'
ELSE 'what the ?'
END datafile_status
FROM v$datafile a       -- control file SCN for datafile
    ,v$datafile_header b -- datafile header SCN
WHERE a.file# = b.file#
ORDER BY a.file#;
```

■ **Tip** The V$DATAFILE_HEADER view uses the physical data file on disk as its source. The V$DATAFILE view uses the control file as its source.

Media recovery requires that you perform manual tasks to get your database back in one piece. This usually involves a combination of restore and recover commands. You will have to issue an RMAN restore command if your data files have experienced media failure. This could be because somebody accidentally deleted files or a disk failed.

When you issue the restore command, RMAN will automatically determine how to extract the data files from any of the following available backups:

- Full database backup
- Incremental level 0 backup
- Image copy backup generated by the backup as copy command

After the files are restored from a backup, you are required to apply redo to them via the recover command. When you issue the recover command, Oracle will examine the SCNs in the affected data files and determine whether any of them need to be recovered. If the SCN in the data file is less than the corresponding SCN in the control file, then media recovery will be required.

Oracle will retrieve the data file SCN and then look for the corresponding SCN in the redo stream to determine where to start the recovery process. If the starting recovery SCN is in the online redo log files, the archived redo log files are not required for recovery.

During a recovery, RMAN will automatically determine how to apply redo. First, RMAN will apply any incremental backups available that are greater than level 0, such as the incremental level 1. Next, any archived redo log files on disk will be applied. If the archived redo log files do not exist on disk, then RMAN will attempt to retrieve them from a backup set.

■ **Note** An RMAN incremental backup contains copies of only those database blocks that have changed from the previous incremental backup. RMAN can more efficiently recover a data file using an incremental backup over applying redo from an archived redo log file.

This chapter guides you through several different common (and not so common) restore and recovery scenarios. Now that you understand the mechanics, you are much better prepared to determine which steps you should take to restore and recover your database.

11-1. Determining How to Restore and Recover
Problem

You just experienced a media failure, and you're not sure what commands you'll need to run to restore and recover your database.

Solution

To be able to perform a complete recovery, all of the following conditions need to be true:

- Your database is in archivelog mode.
- You have a good baseline backup of your database.
- You have any required redo that has been generated since the backup (archived redo log files, online redo log files, or incremental backups that RMAN can use for recovery instead of applying redo).

There are a wide variety of restore and recovery scenarios. How you restore and recover depends directly on your backup strategy and what files have been damaged. Listed next are the general steps to follow when facing a media failure:

1. Determine what files need to be restored.
2. Depending on the damage, set your database mode to nomount, mount, or open.
3. Use the restore command to retrieve files from RMAN backups.
4. Use the recover command for data files requiring recovery.
5. Open your database.

Your particular restore and recovery scenario may not require that all of the previous steps be performed. For example, you may just want to restore your spfile, which doesn't require a recovery step.

The first step in a restore and recovery process is to determine what files have experienced media failure. You can usually determine what files need to be restored from three sources:

- Error messages displayed on your screen, either from RMAN or SQL*Plus

- Alert.log file and corresponding trace files

- Data dictionary views

■ **Note**   See Chapter 20 for details on using the Data Recovery Advisor to determine how to restore and recover your database.

Once you identify which files are damaged or missing, you need to determine what steps to take to restore and recover. Table 11-2 contains general guidelines on what to do when presented with a media failure. You'll have to tailor these guidelines to your type of failure and then find the applicable recipe for specific instructions.

Table 11-2. *Where to Look for Restore and Recovery Instructions*

Files Needing Media Recovery	Action	Chapter/Recipe
Data files with all required redo available	Complete recovery	Chapter 11
Data files without all required redo available	Incomplete recovery	Chapter 12
Control files	Restore control file	Chapter 10
Online redo log files	Combination of clearing and/or re-creating online redo log files and possibly performing incomplete recovery	Chapter 14
Spfile	Restore spfile	Recipe 11-14
Archived redo log files	Restore archived redo log files from another location or from RMAN backup	Recipe 11-15
Control file has no information about RMAN backup piece	Use the catalog command to populate control file with RMAN backup metadata	Recipes 11-18 and 11-19
Need to restore a container root or pluggable database	Restore at root or pluggable database level	Recipe 11-20
Accidentally dropped table or deleted data	Flash back to before drop, SCN, or RMAN restore table to a point in time	Chapter 13

How It Works

When faced with a media failure, you need to have a good understanding of your backup strategy and how that will enable you to restore and recover your database. You should periodically test your backups so that you can confidently recover your database when faced with a media failure (see Recipe 11-21 for details on manually restoring and recovering your database to a different server). When you initially create your backup strategy, you should also design a corresponding restore and recovery strategy. A sound backup strategy should minimize your risk of losing data and minimize the downtime of your database.

If you are missing any redo or incremental backups required for recovery, see Chapter 12 for details on how to perform an incomplete recovery. You can also perform an incomplete recovery using the flashback database feature (assuming you have enabled the flashback feature, described in Chapter 13).

If your database has experienced media failure, you'll see a fairly descriptive message when you attempt to start the database. Usually it's obvious from the error message which files are experiencing problems. For example, this next error message shows that users01.dbf needs media recovery:

```
$ rman target /
RMAN> startup
ORA-01157: cannot identify/lock datafile 4 - see DBWR trace file
ORA-01110: datafile 4: '/u01/dbfile/o12c/users01.dbf'
```

■ **Tip** When Oracle displays errors indicating there has been a media failure, we always recommend you look in the alert.log file for more details. There may be more than one data file that needs to be restored and recovered, and you won't get all of that information from error messages displayed on your screen. Oracle will often just display on your screen the first file that it detects is missing or damaged.

Often there will be a corresponding trace file that contains information that Oracle Support will request when helping diagnose problems. Here's an example of what type of information you'll find in the alert.log file and related trace file when you have a media failure:

```
Errors in file /u01/app/oracle/diag/rdbms/o12c/o12c/trace/o12c_ora_14479.trc
```

■ **Tip** Before you restore the data file from the RMAN backup, verify whether the missing data file physically exists at the OS level. Also confirm that the Oracle software owner has the appropriate read and write privileges on the missing data file and directory.

We also recommend querying the data dictionary for more information. The V$DATAFILE_HEADER view derives its information from the data file headers and reports in the ERROR and RECOVER columns any potential problems. For example, a YES or null value in the RECOVER column indicates there is a problem:

```
SQL> select file#, status, error,recover from v$datafile_header;
```

Here is some sample output:

```
    FILE# STATUS     ERROR                REC
---------- ---------- -------------------- ---
        1 ONLINE                          NO
        2 ONLINE                          NO
        3 ONLINE                          NO
        4 ONLINE     FILE NOT FOUND
```

Also the V$RECOVER_FILE view displays the status of files needing media recovery. The V$RECOVER_FILE reads from the control file and displays information about files needing media recovery:

```
SQL> select file#, online_status, error from v$recover_file;
```

Here is some sample output:

```
  FILE# ONLINE_ ERROR
---------- ------- --------------
      4 ONLINE  FILE NOT FOUND
```

■ **Note** If you restore a control file from a backup, the V$RECOVER_FILE view will not contain accurate information.

11-2. Viewing Backup Files Needed for Restore
Problem

Before you perform a restore and recovery, you would like to first review which backup pieces and archive redo logs will be required for the restore and recovery operation.

Solution

Use the restore ... preview command to report on the backup pieces and archived redo logs required for restore and recovery. For example, if you wanted to view which files would be required to restore and recover the users tablespace, you would do as follows:

```
RMAN> restore tablespace users preview;
```

Here is some sample output:

```
List of Backup Sets
===================
BS Key  Type LV Size       Device Type Elapsed Time Completion Time
------- ---- -- ---------- ----------- ------------ ---------------
42      Full    493.81M    DISK        00:00:53     22-JUL-12
        BP Key: 42   Status: AVAILABLE  Compressed: NO  Tag: TAG20120722T203338
        Piece Name: /u01/app/oracle/product/12.1.0.1/db_1/dbs/1gngolt2_1_1
  File LV Type Ckp SCN    Ckp Time  Name
  ---- -- ---- ---------- --------- ----
  4       Full 836428     22-JUL-12 /u01/dbfile/o12c/users01.dbf

List of Archived Log Copies for database with db_unique_name O12C
=================================================================
Key     Thrd Seq     S Low Time
------- ---- ------- - ---------
60      1    7       A 22-JUL-12
        Name: /u01/app/oracle/product/12.1.0.1/db_1/dbs/arch1_7_788877660.dbf
```

This prior command does not actually restore any files, it just allows you a way to preview which files will be required for a recovery operation.

How It Works

You can run a restore ... preview for any restore command. For example, all of the following are valid:

```
RMAN> restore database preview;
RMAN> restore database from tag TAG20120722T203338 preview;
RMAN> restore datafile 1, 2, 3, 4 preview;
RMAN> restore archivelog all preview;
RMAN> restore archivelog from time 'sysdate - 1' preview;
RMAN> restore archivelog from scn 850000 preview;
RMAN> restore archivelog from sequence 29 preview;
```

When you use the preview command, no data files are actually restored. The restore ... preview command queries the RMAN repository to report which backup pieces and archive redo logs will be needed for the specified restore and recovery operation. It does not check to see whether the RMAN backup files physically exist or verify they are accessible.

You can preview output in the normal verbose mode, or you can have it summarized. This summary mode will reduce the lengthy output. Here are some examples:

```
RMAN> restore tablespace users preview summary;
RMAN> restore database preview summary;
```

If you use a media manager that supports vaulted backups, you can use preview recall to recall media from remote storage. This next example will request that any media needed to restore the database be recalled from remote storage.

```
RMAN> restore database preview recall;
```

11-3. Verifying Integrity of Backup Files
Problem

You need to perform a restore and recovery, but first you want to validate only that the backup pieces are available and structurally sound before restoring data files.

Solution

You can use either the restore ... validate or the validate command to verify the availability and integrity of backup files required by RMAN to perform the restore operation. These commands do not restore any files; rather, they check the soundness of the files that would be used to do a restore.

Using restore ... validate

The validate clause works with any restore command. For example, this validates the backup files required to restore the database:

```
RMAN> restore database validate;
```

If this is successful, you'll see text similar to the following near the bottom of the output:

```
channel ORA_DISK_1: restored backup piece 1
channel ORA_DISK_1: validation complete, elapsed time: 00:00:15
```

By default, RMAN checks only for physical corruption when validating. You can also instruct RMAN to check for logical corruption with the check logical clause:

```
RMAN> restore database validate check logical;
```

■ **Note**   If a backup piece is missing or corrupt, the restore ... validate command will automatically check for the availability of previously taken backups. The behavior of searching sequentially back through backups until a good backup is found is called *restore failover*.

Using Validate

If you need to validate a specific backup set, say, one older than the most recent backup set, then the validate command comes in handy. First, use the list backup command to find the appropriate key.

```
RMAN> list backup summary;
```

Here is some sample output:

```
List of Backups
===============
Key TY LV S Device Type Completion Time #Pieces #Copies Comp Tag
--- -- -- - ----------- --------------- ------- ------- ---- ---
42  B  F  A DISK        22-JUL-12       1       1       NO   TAG20120722T203338
43  B  F  A DISK        23-JUL-12       1       1       NO   TAG20120722T203434
44  B  F  A DISK        24-JUL-12       1       1       NO   TAG20120723T165712
```

In this example, we want to validate an older backup set (42 in this example):

```
RMAN> validate backupset 42;
```

If the validate command works, you should see a message similar to this one at the bottom of the message stack:

```
channel ORA_DISK_1: restored backup piece 1
channel ORA_DISK_1: validation complete, elapsed time: 00:00:16
```

If the validation process discovers a problem, it will display an error message and stop processing.

Another useful feature of the validate command is that you can instruct it to validate all files required for recovery: backup pieces, archive redo log files, data file copies, and control file auto backups. For example:

```
RMAN> validate recovery files;
```

The prior command validates files whether they exist in the FRA or not. It does not validate that flashback logs exist and are available.

To validate all backup pieces in the FRA, use either of the following commands:

```
RMAN> validate recovery area;
RMAN> validate db_recovery_file_dest;
```

How It Works

When you validate backup sets, RMAN actually reads the backup files as if it were doing a restore operation, except that no files are restored or written to disk. This will indicate how much time it takes to read the files during a real restore operation (this could be useful for troubleshooting I/O problems).

The validate clause works with any restore command; here are some examples:

```
RMAN> restore database from tag MON_BCK validate;
RMAN> restore datafile 1 validate;
RMAN> restore archivelog all validate;
RMAN> restore controlfile validate;
RMAN> restore tablespace users validate;
```

■ **Tip**   Periodically run the restore ... validate as part of testing the viability of your backups.

If you have large backup sets, the restore ... validate command can take some time to complete. You can use the header clause to instruct RMAN to check only if the required backup files exist on disk (and not validate its structure). For example:

```
RMAN> restore database validate header;
```

By default the restore ... validate command and the validate command check only for physical corruption. Use the check logical parameter if you want the validation process to also check for logical corruption:

```
RMAN> validate backupset 42 check logical;
```

When RMAN detects logical corruption, it will write relevant error messages to your target database's alert.log file and also reflect this information in the V$DATABASE_BLOCK_CORRUPTION view.

You can see whether a corrupt block is either physically or logically corrupt by querying the CORRUPTION_TYPE column of the V$DATABASE_BLOCK_CORRUPTION view. RMAN can perform block media recovery only on physically corrupt blocks. Blocks tagged with type LOGICAL corruption cannot be recovered by RMAN (through block-level recovery). To recover logically corrupt blocks, restore the data file from a backup and perform media recovery.

■ **Note** Physical corruption is when the block contents don't match the physical format that Oracle expects. By default, RMAN checks for physical corruption when backing up, restoring, or validating data files. Logical corruption is when the block is in the correct format but the contents aren't consistent with logical information Oracle expects to find within the block. Logical corruption would be issues such as corruption in a row piece or an index entry.

Normally when RMAN detects even one corrupt block during validation, it will terminate the operation. You can increase the limit of corrupt blocks that RMAN tolerates via the maxcorrupt clause. You must set the level of corruption allowed per data file. This can be done only within a run{} block. For example, this sets the maximum corruption to 3 for several data files and then runs the validate operation:

```
RMAN> run {set maxcorrupt for datafile 1, 2, 3, 4 to 3;
restore database validate;
}
```

11-4. Testing Media Recovery
Problem

You need to perform a database recovery, but you suspect one of your archived redo log files is bad. You want to test to see whether all of the redo is available and can be applied.

Solution

The recover ... test command instructs Oracle to apply the redo necessary to perform recovery but does not make the changes permanent in the data files. When you recover in test mode, Oracle applies the required redo but rolls back the changes at the end of the process.

This example starts up the database in mount mode, restores the entire database, and then does a test recovery:

```
RMAN> connect target /
RMAN> startup mount;
RMAN> restore database;
RMAN> recover database test;
```

Here is a partial snippet of the output showing a successful test:

```
ORA-10573: Test recovery tested redo from change 862967 to 863288
ORA-10570: Test recovery complete
```

You can test a recovery with most recover commands. Here are some examples:

```
RMAN> recover tablespace users, tools test;
RMAN> recover datafile 1 test;
```

■ **Note** Before performing a test recovery, ensure that the data files being recovered are offline. Oracle will throw an ORA-01124 error for any online data files being recovered in test mode. If you attempt to test recover data files associated with the system tablespace, your database must be in mount mode.

How It Works

The test command allows you to test drive the redo application process without making any permanent changes to the data files. Running this command is particularly useful for diagnosing problems that you're having with the application of redo during the recovery process. For example, you can use the test command with the until clause to test up to a specific trouble point:

```
RMAN> recover database until time 'sysdate - 1/48' test;
RMAN> recover database until scn 2328888 test;
RMAN> recover database until sequence 343 test;
```

■ **Caution**   If you attempt to issue a recover tablespace until ... test, RMAN will attempt to perform a tablespace point-in-time recovery (TSPITR).

If you're missing archived redo log files or online redo log files that are needed for recovery, you'll receive a message similar to this:

```
ORA-06053: unable to perform media recovery because of missing log
```

If you can't locate the missing log, you'll most likely have to perform incomplete recovery. See Chapter 12 for details on how to perform an incomplete recovery.

11-5. Performing Database-Level Recovery

Problem

You've lost all of your data files but still have your online redo log files. You want to perform complete recovery.

Solution

You can perform a complete database-level recovery in this situation with either the current control file or a backup control file.

Use Current Control File

You must first put your database in mount mode to perform a database-wide restore and recovery. This is because the system tablespace data file(s) must be offline when being restored and recovered. Oracle won't allow you to operate your database in open mode with the system data file offline.

In this scenario, we simply start up the database in mount mode, issue the restore and recover commands, and then open the database:

```
$ rman target /
RMAN> startup mount;
RMAN> restore database;
RMAN> recover database;
RMAN> alter database open;
```

If everything went as expected, the last message you should see is this:

```
Statement processed
```

If you're using an older version of the database, the prior message may say "database opened."

At this point you have restored and recovered the database to the point right before the media failure. All committed transactions prior to the point of failure have been recovered.

■ **Note** Your database has to be at least mounted to restore data files using RMAN. This is because RMAN reads information from the control file during the restore and recovery process.

Keep in mind that if you're using a recovery catalog, you should connect to it when performing restore and recover operations, for example:

```
$ rman target / catalog rcat/rcat@rcat
```

You'll have to modify the prior user/pwd@catalog information to match your environment.

Use Backup Control File

This solution uses an auto backup of the control file retrieved from the FRA. If you're using a different strategy to back up your control file, see Chapter 10 for details on restoring your control file.

In this example, we first restore the control file before issuing the restore and recover database commands:

```
$ rman target /
RMAN> startup nomount;
RMAN> restore controlfile from autobackup;
RMAN> alter database mount;
RMAN> restore database;
RMAN> recover database;
RMAN> alter database open resetlogs;
```

If everything went as expected, the last message you should see is this:

```
Statement processed
```

■ **Note** You are required to open your database with the open resetlogs command anytime you use a backup control file during a recovery operation.

How It Works

The restore database command will restore every data file in your database. The exception is when RMAN detects that data files have already been restored; then it will not restore them again. If you want to override that behavior, use the force command (see Recipe 11-11 for details).

When you issue the recover database command, RMAN will automatically apply redo to any data files that need recovery. The recovery process includes applying changes found in the following:

- Incremental backup pieces (applicable only if using incremental backups)

- Archived redo log files (generated since the last backup or last incremental backup that is applied)

- Online redo log files (current and unarchived)

You can open your database after the restore and recovery process is complete. Complete database recovery works only if you have good backups of your database and have access to all redo generated after the backup was taken. You need all the redo required to recover the database data files. If you don't have all the required redo, you'll most likely have to perform an incomplete recovery. See Chapter 12 for details on performing an incomplete recovery.

11-6. Performing Tablespace-Level Recovery
Problem

You're seeing a media error associated with several data files contained in one tablespace. You want to perform complete recovery on all data files associated with that problem tablespace.

Solution

Use the restore tablespace and recover tablespace commands to restore and recover all the data files associated with a tablespace. You can either place the database in mount mode or have the database open (if it's not the system or undo tablespace). In the first scenario, we'll place the database in mount mode for the restore and recovery.

Recover While Database Not Open

This solution works for any tablespace in your database. In this example, we restore the users tablespace:

```
$ rman target /
RMAN> startup mount;
RMAN> restore tablespace users;
RMAN> recover tablespace users;
RMAN> alter database open;
```

If everything was successful, the last message you should see is this:

```
Statement processed
```

Keep in mind that if you're using a recovery catalog, you should connect to it when performing restore and recover operations, for example:

```
$ rman target / catalog rcat/rcat@rcat
```

Recover While Database Is Open

You can take a tablespace offline, restore, and recover it while the database is open. This works for any tablespace except the system and undo tablespaces. Assuming your database is still open, this example takes the users tablespace offline and then restores and recovers before bringing it back online:

```
$ rman target /
RMAN> alter tablespace users offline immediate;
RMAN> restore tablespace users;
RMAN> recover tablespace users;
RMAN> alter tablespace users online;
```

You should see a message similar to this when the tablespace is brought online:

```
Statement processed
```

■ **Tip** New in Oracle Database 12c you can run most SQL statements directly from the RMAN command line without specifying the `sql` command.

If you're using Oracle Database 11g or lower, you'll have to specify the `sql` command to take a tablespace offline and also place the `alter tablespace` command in single quotes:

```
$ rman target /
RMAN> sql 'alter tablespace users offline immediate';
RMAN> restore tablespace users;
RMAN> recover tablespace users;
RMAN> sql 'alter tablespace users online';
```

How It Works

The RMAN `restore tablespace` and `recover tablespace` commands will restore and recover all data files associated with the specified tablespace(s). It's appropriate to perform this type of complete recovery when only data files from a tablespace or set of tablespaces are missing. If your database is open, then all data files in the tablespace(s) being recovered must be offline.

If your database is shut down, yet you want to open it and then perform the restore and recovery of a tablespace, you'll have to use the `alter database datafile` command to take the data files in a tablespace offline (you can't use `alter tablespace` to take a tablespace offline while the database is in mount mode). For example:

```
$ rman target /
RMAN> startup mount;
RMAN> alter database datafile '/u01/dbfile/o12c/users01.dbf' offline;
RMAN> alter database open;
RMAN> restore tablespace users;
RMAN> recover tablespace users;
RMAN> alter tablespace users online;
```

11-7. Performing Data File–Level Recovery

Problem

You have one data file that has experienced media failure. You don't want to restore and recover the entire database or all data files associated with the tablespace. You want to perform complete recovery only on the data file that experienced media failure.

Solution

Use the `restore datafile` and `recover data file` commands to restore and recover one or more data files. The database can be mounted or open to restore data files.

■ **Note** If your database is open, you can't restore and recover data files associated with the system or undo tablespaces. In this scenario, your database must be placed in mount mode.

Recover While Database Not Open

In this scenario we mount the database and then restore and recover a missing data file. You can restore and recover any data file in your database while the database is not open. This example shows restoring the data file 1, which is associated with the system tablespace:

```
$ rman target /
RMAN> startup mount;
RMAN> restore datafile 1;
RMAN> recover datafile 1;
RMAN> alter database open;
```

You can also specify the file name when performing a data file recovery:

```
$ rman target /
RMAN> startup mount;
RMAN> restore datafile '/u01/dbfile/o12c/system01.dbf';
RMAN> recover datafile '/u01/dbfile/o12c/system01.dbf';
RMAN> alter database open;
```

■ **Tip** Use the RMAN `report schema` command to list data file names and file numbers. You can also query the NAME and FILE# columns of V$DATAFILE view to take names and numbers.

Keep in mind that if you're using a recovery catalog, you should connect to it when performing restore and recover operations, for example:

```
$ rman target / catalog rcat/rcat@rcat
```

Recover While Database Is Open

For non-system and non-undo data files, you have the option of keeping the database open while performing the recovery. When your database is open, you're required to take offline any data files you're attempting to restore and recover.

```
$ rman target /
RMAN> alter database datafile 4 offline;
RMAN> restore datafile 4;
RMAN> recover datafile 4;
RMAN> alter database datafile 4 online;
```

If you're using Oracle Database 11g or lower, you'll need to use the sql command combined with alter database commands and quotes:

```
$ rman target /
RMAN> sql 'alter database datafile 4 offline';
RMAN> restore datafile 4;
RMAN> recover datafile 4;
RMAN> sql 'alter database datafile 4 online';
```

Instead of the file number, you can also specify the name of the data file that you want to restore and recover:

```
$ rman target /
RMAN> alter database datafile '/u01/dbfile/o12c/users01.dbf' offline;
RMAN> restore datafile '/u01/dbfile/o12c/users01.dbf';
RMAN> recover datafile '/u01/dbfile/o12c/users01.dbf';
RMAN> alter database datafile '/u01/dbfile/o12c/users01.dbf' online;
```

If you're using Oracle Database 11g or lower, you'll have to do some quoting gymnastics to run the alter database datafile statements:

```
$ rman target /
RMAN> sql "alter database datafile ''/u01/dbfile/o12c/users01.dbf'' offline";
RMAN> restore datafile '/u01/dbfile/o12c/users01.dbf';
RMAN> recover datafile '/u01/dbfile/o12c/users01.dbf';
RMAN> sql "alter database datafile ''/u01/dbfile/o12c/users01.dbf'' online";
```

■ **Note** When using the RMAN sql command, if there are single quote marks within the SQL statement, you are required to use double quotes to enclose the entire SQL statement and then also use two single quote marks where you would ordinarily use a single quote mark.

How It Works

A data file–level restore and recovery works well when you want to specify which data files you want recovered. With data file–level recoveries, you can use either the data file number or the data file name. For non-system and non-undo data files, you have the option of restoring and recovering while the database is open. While the database is open, you have to first take offline any data files being restored and recovered.

It's also possible to restore and recover many data files at the same time. For example:

```
RMAN> alter database datafile 4,5 offline;
RMAN> restore datafile 4,5;
RMAN> recover datafile 4,5;
RMAN> alter database datafile 4,5 online;
```

Also keep in mind that you can run alter database statements directly from SQL*Plus. However, you may find it painful and prone to mistakes to be jumping back and forth between RMAN and SQL*Plus. In Oracle Database 12c and higher, most SQL commands can be run from within RMAN without any special quoting.

11-8. Restoring Data Files to Nondefault Locations

Problem

You've just experienced a serious media failure and won't be able to restore data files to their original locations. In other words, you need to restore data files to a nondefault location.

Solution

Use the set newname and switch commands to restore data files to nondefault locations. Both of these commands must be run from within an RMAN run{} block. In this example, data files 4 and 5 are damaged. The original directory of /u01/dbfile/o12c is not available, so the files are being restored to /u02/dbfile/o12c.

First the database is started in mount mode and then commands are issued to change the location of data files 4 and 5:

```
$ rman target /
RMAN> startup mount;
RMAN> run{
set newname for datafile 4 to '/u02/dbfile/o12c/users01.dbf';
set newname for datafile 5 to '/u02/dbfile/o12c/tools01.dbf';
restore datafile 4, 5;
switch datafile all; # Update control file with new file names.
recover datafile 4, 5;
alter database open;
}
```

This is a partial listing of the output you can expect:

```
starting media recovery
media recovery complete, elapsed time: 00:00:00
Statement processed
```

If the database is open, you can place the data files offline and then set their new names for restore and recovery:

```
RMAN> run{
alter database datafile 4, 5 offline;
set newname for datafile 4 to '/u02/dbfile/o12c/users01.dbf';
set newname for datafile 5 to '/u02/dbfile/o12c/tools01.dbf';
restore datafile 4, 5;
switch datafile all; # Update control file with new file names.
```

```
recover datafile 4, 5;
alter database datafile 4, 5 online;
}
```

If you're running Oracle Database 11g or lower, you'll have to use the sql command to run the alter database datafile command:

```
RMAN> run{
sql 'alter database datafile 4, 5 offline';
set newname for datafile 4 to '/u02/dbfile/o12c/users01.dbf';
set newname for datafile 5 to '/u02/dbfile/o12c/tools01.dbf';
restore datafile 4, 5;
switch datafile all; # Update control file with new file names.
recover datafile 4, 5;
sql 'alter database datafile 4, 5 online';
}
```

How It Works

You can use a combination of the set newname and switch commands to restore and recover a data file to a nondefault location. You must run the set newname command and the switch command from within a run{} block.

The switch command updates the target database control file with the new location of the data file. It's fine to use switch datafile all, which updates all data file locations. The only data file names that will actually change are the ones that you have specified via the set newname command. Alternatively, you can use switch datafile <number> to update the repository with a specific data file number.

■ **Caution**   If you don't run the switch command, RMAN marks the restored data file to be a valid data file copy that can be used for subsequent restore operations.

When restoring files to nondefault locations, you can also use data file names instead of the data file numbers. However, you have to be careful about which name you use and where it comes in the script. This is because the control file doesn't consider the new location to be the current location until you issue the switch command. For example:

```
run{
alter database datafile '/u01/dbfile/o12c/users01.dbf' offline;
set newname for datafile '/u01/dbfile/o12c/users01.dbf'
                    to '/u02/dbfile/o12c/users01.dbf';
restore datafile '/u01/dbfile/o12c/users01.dbf';
switch datafile all; # Update control file with new file names.
recover datafile '/u02/dbfile/o12c/users01.dbf';
alter database datafile '/u02/dbfile/o12c/users01.dbf' online;
}
```

If you're using Oracle Database 11g or lower, you need to use the sql command to run the alter database datafile command and carefully enclose the entire statement in double quotes and use two single quotes to enclose file names:

```
RMAN> run{
sql "alter database datafile ''/u01/dbfile/o12c/users01.dbf'' offline";
set newname for datafile '/u01/dbfile/o12c/users01.dbf'
                    to '/u02/dbfile/o12c/users01.dbf';
restore datafile '/u01/dbfile/o12c/users01.dbf';
switch datafile all; # Update control file with new file names.
recover datafile '/u02/dbfile/o12c/users01.dbf';
sql "alter database datafile ''/u02/dbfile/o12c/users01.dbf'' online";
}
```

At this point, it doesn't hurt to run an RMAN report schema command to ensure that the data files are restored in the correct locations.

11-9. Performing Block-Level Recovery
Problem

When performing daily backups, you notice that RMAN is reporting in your target database alert.log file that there is a corrupt block in a large data file. It could take a significant amount of time to perform the traditional restore and recover of a large data file. You wonder whether there is a method for just recovering the corrupt block and not the entire data file.

■ **Note**   Block-level recovery requires the Oracle Enterprise Edition of the database.

Solution

Use the recover corruption list command to resolve this issue. When RMAN backs up a data file, it will check each used block for physical corruption. You'll be notified of corruption in the output, such as:

```
ORA-19566: exceeded limit of 0 corrupt blocks for file
/u01/dbfile/o12c/tools01.dbf
```

When RMAN detects corrupt blocks, it writes an error to the alert.log file and also populates the V$DATABASE_BLOCK_CORRUPTION view. You can instruct RMAN to recover the blocks listed as corrupt in that view as follows:

```
RMAN> recover corruption list;
```

Here's a partial listing of the expected output:

```
starting media recovery
media recovery complete, elapsed time: 00:00:07
```

■ **Tip**   You can verify the block corruption with the RMAN backup validate or validate command.

How It Works

Block-level corruption is rare and is usually caused by some sort of I/O error. However, if you do have an isolated corrupt block within a large data file, it's nice to have the option of performing a block-level recovery. Block-level recovery is useful when a small number of blocks are corrupt within a data file. Block recovery is not appropriate if the entire data file needs media recovery.

Here are the various locations that Oracle will record block-level corruption:

- RMAN `backup, backup validate,` or `validate` commands automatically populate V$DATABASE_BLOCK_CORRUPTION.

- Trace files.

- Alert.log file.

- Output of `dbverify` utility.

- Output of SQL `analyze ... validate` structure command.

- V$BACKUP_CORRUPTION and V$COPY_CORRUPTION will list corrupt blocks in backup piece files.

Your database can be either mounted or open when performing block-level recovery. You do not have to take the data file being recovered offline. Block-level media recovery allows you to keep your database available and also reduces the mean time to recovery since only the corrupt blocks are offline during the recovery.

Your database must be in archivelog mode for performing block-level recoveries. In Oracle Database 11g or higher, RMAN can restore the block from the flashback logs (if enabled). If the flashback logs are not available, RMAN will attempt to restore the block from a full backup, a level 0 backup, or an image copy backup generated by the `backup as copy` command. After the block has been restored, any required archived redo logs must be available to recover the block. RMAN can't perform block media recovery using incremental level 1 (or higher) backups.

You can instruct RMAN to recover blocks in two ways:

- Use the `corruption list` clause (as shown in the Solution section).

- Specify individual data files and blocks. If you're using Oracle Database 11g or newer, use the `recover data file N block N` command to recover individual blocks within a data file. If you're using Oracle Database 10g or 9i, use the `blockrecover` command to perform block-level recovery. Block-level recovery was not available in Oracle Database 8i.

Here are some examples of using the `recover datafile N block N` command:

```
RMAN> recover datafile 5 block 21 to 25;
RMAN> recover datafile 10 block 24;
RMAN> recover datafile 7 block 22 datafile 8 block 43;
RMAN> recover datafile 5 block 24 from tag=tues_backup;
RMAN> recover datafile 6 block 89 restore until sequence 546;
RMAN> recover datafile 5 block 32 restore until 'sysdate-1';
RMAN> recover datafile 5 block 65 restore until scn 23453;
```

■ **Note**   RMAN cannot perform block-level recovery on block 1 (data file header) of the data file.

CREATING AND FIXING BLOCK CORRUPTION

The purpose of this sidebar is to show you how to corrupt a block so that you can test recovering at the block level. Do not perform this test exercise in a production environment. In a Linux/Unix environment, you can corrupt a specific block in a data file using the dd command. For example, the following dd command populates the 20th block of the tools01.dbf data file with zeros:

```
$ cd /u01/dbfile/o12c
$ dd if=/dev/zero of=tools01.dbf bs=8k conv=notrunc seek=20 count=1
```

You can validate the corruption via the validate command:

```
RMAN> validate tablespace tools;
```

You can now query the V$DATABASE_BLOCK_CORRUPTION view for details:

```
SQL> select * from v$database_block_corruption;
```

FILE#	BLOCK#	BLOCKS	CORRUPTION_CHANGE#	CORRUPTIO	CON_ID
5	20	1	0	ALL ZERO	0

You can now use the RMAN recover command to restore block 20 in data file 5, as shown here:

```
RMAN> recover datafile 5 block 20;
```

You can now verify that the block corruption has been resolved by running a backup or a validate command.

11-10. Restoring Temporary Tablespaces
Problem
RMAN doesn't back up locally managed temporary tablespace tempfiles, and you want to ensure that they're restored as part of your backup strategy.

Solution
Starting with Oracle Database 10g, you don't have to restore or re-create missing locally managed temporary tablespace tempfiles. When you open your database for use, Oracle automatically detects and attempts to re-create locally managed temporary tablespace tempfiles.

When Oracle automatically re-creates a temporary tablespace, it will log a message to your target database alert.log file similar to the following:

```
Re-creating tempfile <your temporary tablespace filename>
```

For example, in our environment the message is as follows:

```
Re-creating tempfile /u01/dbfile/o12c/temp01.dbf
```

How It Works

When you open your database, Oracle will check to see whether any locally managed temporary tablespace tempfiles are missing. If Oracle detects missing temporary tablespace tempfiles, it will automatically re-create them using information from the control files.

■ **Note** Oracle's feature of automatically re-creating temporary tablespace tempfiles applies only to missing locally managed temporary tablespace tempfiles. This feature does not apply to a dictionary-managed temporary tablespace.

If for any reason your temporary tablespace becomes unavailable, you can also re-create it yourself. Since there are never any permanent objects in temporary tablespaces, you can simply re-create them as needed. Here is an example of how to create a locally managed temporary tablespace:

```
CREATE TEMPORARY TABLESPACE temp TEMPFILE
'/u01/dbfile/o12c/temp01.dbf' SIZE 500M REUSE
EXTENT MANAGEMENT LOCAL UNIFORM SIZE 512K;
```

If your temporary tablespace exists but the temporary data files are missing, you can simply add the temporary data file(s) as shown here:

```
ALTER TABLESPACE temp ADD TEMPFILE
'/u01/dbfile/o12c/temp01.dbf' SIZE 500M REUSE;
```

If you have to restore your database to a location that didn't previously exist (say, you had a complete failure and the original mount points are now unavailable), you may need to first take offline and drop the original temporary tablespace tempfile and then add the tempfile to the new directory. For example:

```
SQL> alter database tempfile '/u01/dbfile/o12c/temp01.dbf' offline;
SQL> alter database tempfile '/u01/dbfile/o12c/temp01.dbf' drop;
SQL> alter tablespace temp add tempfile '/u02/dbfile/o12c/temp01.dbf' size 500m;
```

11-11. Forcing RMAN to Restore a File
Problem

As part of a test exercise, you attempt to restore a data file twice and receive this RMAN message:

```
restore not done; all files read only, offline, or already restored
```

In this situation, you want to force RMAN to restore the data file again.

Solution

Use the force command to restore data files and archived redo log files even if they already exist in a location.

■ **Note** When restoring a data file, either your database must be in mount mode or if the database is already open, the data files being restored must be offline.

The following command forces RMAN to restore a file, even if RMAN determines that file doesn't need to be restored:

```
RMAN> restore datafile '/u01/dbfile/o12c/users01.dbf' force;
```

You should see a message similar to this at the bottom of your RMAN messages stack:

```
channel ORA_DISK_1: restore complete, elapsed time: 00:00:03
```

You can now perform recovery on the data files restored and either open the database or if the database is already open, recover and restore the appropriate data files and place them online.

How It Works

By default, RMAN will not restore a data file that is in the correct location and contains the expected information in the data file header. This is known as restore optimization. You rarely will need to use the force feature, but in some circumstances, you may know an aspect about your environment that RMAN is not aware of, and thus need to force a restore. To override RMAN's default behavior, use the force command.

The force command works with any restore command. For example, if you know the particular data file number, you can use the force command this way:

```
RMAN> restore datafile 42 force;
```

Similarly, you can use the force command on a tablespace. Here we use the force command to restore all data files associated with the users tablespace:

```
RMAN> restore tablespace users force;
```

To force RMAN to restore all data files in the database, issue this command:

```
RMAN> restore database force;
```

By default, RMAN won't restore archived redo log files if they already exist on disk. If you want to override this behavior and restore all archive redo logs contained in backup sets, do so as follows:

```
RMAN> restore archivelog all force;
```

11-12. Restoring from an Older Backup
Problem

You want to specifically instruct RMAN to restore from a backup set that is older than the last backup that was taken.

Solution

You can restore an older backup a couple different ways: using a tag name or using the restore ... until command.

Specify a Tag Name

Use the `list backup summary` command to find the tag name of the backup set. Every backup set has a tag name, either the default or one you specified. For example, here's a partial of a `list backup summary` command that shows the tag names output (the date column has been removed so the output fits within the page):

```
List of Backups
===============
Key     TY LV S Device Type #Pieces #Copies Compressed Tag
------- -- -- - ----------- ------- ------- ---------- ---
79      B  F  A DISK        1       1       NO         TAG20120724T210842
80      B  F  A DISK        1       1       NO         TAG20120724T210918
81      B  F  A DISK        1       1       NO         TAG20120729T122948
```

Once you've identified the tag, you can instruct RMAN to use that as follows:

```
$ rman target /
RMAN> startup mount;
RMAN> restore database from tag TAG20120724T210842;
RMAN> recover database;
RMAN> alter database open;
```

If this is successful, you should see the following message:

```
Statement processed
```

Keep in mind you can also use a tag to restore specific tablespaces or data files. Here are some examples:

```
RMAN> restore tablespace users from tag INCUPDATE;
RMAN> restore datafile 2, 3 from tag AUG_FULL;
```

Using restore ... until

You can also tell RMAN to restore data files from a point in the past using the `until` clause of the `restore` command in one of the following ways:

- Until SCN
- Until log sequence
- Until restore point
- Until time

■ **Caution** This recipe uses the `restore ... until` command with the `recover` command to perform complete recovery. If you need to perform an incomplete recovery, you will need to use the `recover ... until` command (not just the `recover` command by itself). See Chapter 12 for details on incomplete recoveries using `restore ... until` in conjunction with the `recover ... until` command.

If you know the SCN in a backup piece that you want to restore from, you can specify the SCN as follows:

```
RMAN> startup mount;
RMAN> restore database until scn 1254174;
RMAN> recover database;
RMAN> alter database open;
```

Or if you know the log sequence number that you want to restore up to, the syntax is as follows:

```
RMAN> startup mount;
RMAN> restore database until sequence 17;
RMAN> recover database;
RMAN> alter database open;
```

If you've created restore points, you can also use the restore point name as follows:

```
RMAN> startup mount;
RMAN> restore database until restore point FRI_RS;
RMAN> recover database;
RMAN> alter database open;
```

You can also specify a point in time from which you want RMAN to restore an older backup. This example instructs RMAN to retrieve the first backup it finds that is more than 1 day old:

```
RMAN> startup mount;
RMAN> restore database until time 'sysdate - 1';
RMAN> recover database;
RMAN> alter database open;
```

Here we're specifically instructing RMAN to restore from a date and time. Since we don't instruct RMAN to recover to a point in time, this example will perform a complete recovery:

```
RMAN> startup mount;
RMAN> restore database until time
"to_date('05-aug-2012 15:45:00', 'dd-mon-rrrr hh24:mi:ss')";
RMAN> recover database;
RMAN> alter database open;
```

How It Works

You can easily instruct RMAN to restore from backups older than the most recent backup set. You can do this by specifying a backup tag name or using the restore ... until command. You may want to do this because you're missing a recent backup file. In this case, the required backup may be one older than the current one.

Keep in mind that starting with Oracle Database 10g, by default RMAN will look in older backups if it can't find a backup piece or if corruption is detected. RMAN will search through backup history until it locates a good backup or until it exhausts all possibilities. This feature is called *restore failover*.

In this example, RMAN cannot find the expected backup piece and automatically searches for a prior backup. Here is the backup operation and its corresponding partial output indicating that RMAN is initiating a restore failover:

```
RMAN> restore database;
...
failover to previous backup
```

11-13. Recovering Through Resetlogs
Problem

You recently performed an incomplete recovery that required you to open your database with the open resetlogs command. Before you could back up your database, you experienced another media failure. Prior to Oracle Database 10g, it was extremely difficult to recover using a backup of a previous incarnation of your database. You now wonder whether you can get your database back in one piece.

Solution

Beginning with Oracle Database 10g, you can restore a backup from a previous incarnation and recover through a previously issued open resetlogs command. You simply need to restore and recover your database as required by the type of failure. In this example, the control files and all data files are restored:

```
$ rman target /
RMAN> startup nomount;
RMAN> restore controlfile from autobackup;
RMAN> alter database mount;
RMAN> restore database;
RMAN> recover database;
RMAN> alter database open resetlogs;
```

When you issue the recover command, you should see redo being applied. RMAN may need to apply redo from the prior incarnation as well as the current incarnation. If this is successful, you should see this:

```
starting media recovery
...
media recovery complete, elapsed time: 00:00:01
```

How It Works

You must open your database with an open resetlogs command in the following scenarios:

- Perform an incomplete recovery

- Recover with a backup control file

- Use a re-created control file and you're missing your current online redo logs

Prior to Oracle Database 10g, you were required to take a backup of your database immediately after you reset the online redo log files. This is because resetting the online redo log files creates a new incarnation of your database and resets your log sequence number back to 1. Prior to Oracle Database 10g, any backups taken before resetting the logs could not be easily used to restore and recover your database.

Starting with Oracle Database 10g, Oracle allows you to restore from a backup from a previous incarnation of your database and issue restore and recovery commands as applicable to the type of failure that has occurred. Oracle keeps track of log files from all incarnations of your database. The V$LOG_HISTORY view is no longer cleared out during a resetlogs operation and contains information for the current incarnation as well as any previous incarnations.

If you're using an FRA (fast recovery area), then Oracle creates the archive redo logs using the Oracle Managed File name format. If you aren't using an FRA, the format mask of the archived redo log files must include the thread (%t), sequence (%s), and resetlogs ID (%r). For example:

```
SQL> show parameter log_archive_format
```

NAME	TYPE	VALUE
log_archive_format	string	%t_%s_%r.dbf

The resetlogs identifier ensures that unique names are used for the archived redo log files across different database incarnations. You can view the incarnation(s) of your database using the list incarnation command:

```
RMAN> list incarnation;
```

■ **Note**   The simplified recovery through resetlogs enhancement works both with RMAN and with user-managed recoveries.

11-14. Restoring the spfile
Problem
You might need to restore the spfile for one of several reasons:

- You accidentally deleted your server parameter file.
- You want to view an old copy of the spfile.
- You can't start your instance with the current spfile.

Solution
First you need to have enabled the auto backup of your control file:

```
RMAN> configure controlfile autobackup on;
```

Also, you need to be using an spfile (not an init.ora file) and have taken a backup since you enabled the auto backup of the controlfile feature.

If you can't start your instance with the current spfile, first rename or move your spfile and then restore the spfile from a backup using one of the techniques described in the following subsections. The approach varies slightly depending on whether you're using a recovery catalog, an FRA, or default locations for backups of the spfile.

Using a Recovery Catalog

If you're using a recovery catalog, then restoring the spfile is fairly straightforward. This example connects to the recovery catalog and then restores the spfile (you'll have to modify the catalog connection string to match the user/pass and recovery catalog for your environment):

```
$ rman target / catalog rcat/rcat@rcat
RMAN> startup nomount;
```

If there is no valid spfile or init.ora file in the default location, then a few errors will be thrown:

```
startup failed: ORA-01078: failure in processing system parameters
LRM-00109: could not open parameter file...
starting Oracle instance without parameter file for retrieval of spfile
```

Now restore the spfile:

```
RMAN> restore spfile;
RMAN> startup force; # startup using restored spfile
```

If you receive an error such as this when running the restore command:

```
RMAN-20001: target database not found in recovery catalog
```

Then first set the DBID (see Recipe 10-3 for details on determining your DBID):

```
RMAN set dbid 3414586809;
```

Not Using a Recovery Catalog, RMAN Auto Backup in Default Location

For this scenario you need to know your database identifier before you can proceed. See Recipe 10-3 for details about determining your DBID.

This recipe assumes that you have configured your auto backups of the spfile to go to the default location. The default location depends on your operating system. For Linux/Unix, the default location is ORACLE_HOME/dbs. On Windows systems, it's usually ORACLE_HOME\database.

```
$ rman target /
RMAN> startup force nomount; # start instance for retrieval of spfile
RMAN> set dbid 3414586809;
RMAN> restore spfile from autobackup;
RMAN> startup force; # startup using restored spfile
```

You should now see your instance start normally:

```
database opened
```

When the auto backup is located in the default location, you can use the parameters maxseq and maxdays to alter the default behavior of RMAN. These parameters also apply to control file restores from the default location. See Recipe 10-4 for examples on how to use maxseq and maxdays.

Not Using a Recovery Catalog, RMAN Auto Backup Not in Default Location

If you're either using an FRA or have the auto backup of your control file configured to a nondefault location, then the spfile will not be backed up to what Oracle calls the default location. In these situations, you have to specifically tell RMAN where to retrieve the backup from.

If you're using an FRA, your spfiles will be backed up in an auto backup directory in the FRA. You'll have to find that directory and backup piece name before you can restore your spfile. You'll also need to know your database identifier before you can proceed. See Recipe 10-3 for determining your DBID. Once you know your DBID, you can restore the spfile as follows:

```
$ rman target /
RMAN> set dbid 3414586809;
RMAN> startup force nomount;  # start instance for retrieval of spfile
RMAN> restore spfile from
'/u01/fra/O12C/autobackup/2012_07_30/o1_mf_s_789989279_81fb00rl_.bkp';
RMAN> startup force; # startup using restored spfile
```

You should now see your instance start normally:

```
database opened
```

How It Works

If you're using an spfile, you can have it automatically backed up for you by enabling the autobackup of the control file. If you're using a recovery catalog, restoring the spfile is simple. The recovery catalog maintains information about what backup piece contains the latest copy of the spfile.

If the auto backups have been configured to create a backup piece in the default location, then you need to set the DBID and issue the restore from autobackup command. When the auto backup is in the default location, you can also use the values maxseq and maxdays to direct RMAN to look at specific ranges of backup files.

If you're not using a recovery catalog and the auto backups are created either in the FRA or in a nondefault location, you will specifically set your DBID and tell RMAN where the backup files are located. This is because when you start your database in nomount mode and it doesn't have access to a parameter file, there is no way for RMAN to know where the FRA is located. If RMAN doesn't know where the FRA is located, then there is no way for it to determine where the auto backups are stored.

Keep in mind it's also possible to use RMAN to create an init.ora parameter file from a backup of an spfile. For example:

```
RMAN> restore spfile to pfile '/tmp/init.ora';
```

You may want to do this because you want to manually inspect and edit the initialization file with a text editor.

11-15. Restoring Archived Redo Log Files

Problem

RMAN will automatically restore any archived redo log files that it needs during a recovery process. You shouldn't normally need to restore archived redo log files. However, you may want to manually restore the archived redo log files if any of the following situations apply:

- You want to restore archived redo log files in anticipation of later performing a recovery; the idea is that if the archived redo log files are already restored, this will speed up the recovery operation.

- You need to restore the archived redo log files to a nondefault location and/or multiple nondefault locations, either because of media failure or because of storage space issues.

- You need to restore specific archived redo log files because you want to inspect them via LogMiner.

Solution

This solution is divided into two sections: restoring to the default location and restoring to a nondefault location.

Restoring to Default Location

The following command will restore all archived redo log files that RMAN has backed up:

```
RMAN> restore archivelog all;
```

If you receive an error such as this:

```
RMAN-06025: no backup of archived log...
```

RMAN can't restore an archive log file that it can't find in a backup piece. Verify which archive redo logs have been backed up via:

```
RMAN> list backup of archivelog all;
```

If you want to restore from a specified sequence, use the from sequence clause. This example restores all archived redo log files from sequence 40:

```
RMAN> restore archivelog from sequence 40;
```

If you want to restore a range of archived redo log files, use the from sequence and until sequence clauses or the sequence between clause, as shown here. These commands restore archived redo log files from sequence 40 through 43 (inclusive) using thread 1.

```
RMAN> restore archivelog from sequence 40 until sequence 43 thread 1;
RMAN> restore archivelog sequence between 40 and 43 thread 1;
```

You can also specify an SCN or a time, for example:

```
RMAN> restore archivelog from scn 900321 until scn 930095;
RMAN> restore archivelog from time 'sysdate - 1';
```

Restoring to Nondefault Location

Use the set archivelog destination clause if you want to restore archived redo log files to a different location than the default. The following example restores to the nondefault location of /u01/archrest. The set archivelog destination command must be run from within the RMAN run{ } block.

```
RMAN> run{
set archivelog destination to '/u01/archrest';
restore archivelog from sequence 40;
}
```

You may have disk space issues and need to spread the restored archived redo logs across multiple locations. You can do so as follows:

```
RMAN> run{
set archivelog destination to '/u01/archrest';
restore archivelog from sequence 1 until sequence 10;
set archivelog destination to '/u02/archrest';
restore archivelog from sequence 11;
}
```

How It Works

To be able to restore archive redo logs, you must have good backups. Usually the archive redo logs are backed up via a command similar to this:

```
RMAN> backup database plus archivelog;
```

or

```
RMAN> backup archivelog all;
```

You can verify which archive redo logs are in which backup sets as shown:

```
RMAN> list backup of archivelog all;
```

If you are uncertain of the sequence numbers to use during a restore of log files, you can query the V$ARCHIVED_LOG view:

```
SQL> select thread#, sequence#, name from v$archived_log;
```

If you've enabled an FRA, then RMAN will by default restore archived redo log files to a subdirectory within the destination defined by the initialization parameter db_recovery_file_dest. Otherwise, RMAN uses the log_archive_dest_N (where 1 is commonly used for N) initialization parameter to determine where to restore the archived redo log files.

If you restore archived redo log files to a nondefault location, RMAN knows the location they were restored to and automatically finds these files when you issue any subsequent recover commands. RMAN will not restore archived redo log files that it determines are already on disk. Even if you specify a nondefault location, RMAN will not restore an archived redo log file to disk if it already exists. In this situation, RMAN will simply return a message stating that the archived redo log file has already been restored. Use the force command to override this behavior:

```
RMAN> restore archivelog all force;
```

If you want to preview what a restore operation would look like without actually restoring any files, then do so as follows:

```
RMAN> restore archivelog all preview;
```

If you want to validate that the backups exist, without restoring them, then do so as shown:

```
RMAN> restore archivelog all validate;
```

■ **Note** When restoring archived redo log files, your database can be either mounted or open.

11-16. Deleting Archived Redo Log Files During Recovery
Problem

You know that you're going to be applying many archived redo log files during a recovery process. You want RMAN to automatically delete the archived redo logs after they're applied.

Solution

Use the recover ... delete archivelog command as shown here:

```
RMAN> recover database delete archivelog;
```

You should see a message like the following in the output after RMAN successfully applies an archived redo log:

```
channel default: deleting archived log(s)
```

How It Works

If you know you're going to restore and apply many archived redo log files, you can use the delete archivelog clause of the recover command. This will cause RMAN to automatically remove any archived redo log files that have been applied and are not needed for recovery any longer. RMAN will not delete any archived redo log files that were already on disk at the time the recover command was issued.

■ **Note** If you restored archived redo log files to the FRA, then RMAN will automatically enable the delete archivelog feature.

You can also instruct RMAN to use a specified amount of space for keeping restored archived redo logs on disk. For example, if you want RMAN to use at most 500MB disk space for restored archived redo log files, you would specify that maximum size, as shown here:

```
RMAN> recover database delete archivelog maxsize 500m;
```

If you don't specify a maximum size, then RMAN deletes archived redo log files after they are applied. If the maximum size is smaller than the backup set containing the archive redo logs, then RMAN issues a warning indicating that the maximum size should be increased.

11-17. Recovering Data Files Not Backed Up

Problem

You recently added a data file to a tablespace and had a failure before the data file was backed up. For example, a backup is taken:

```
RMAN> backup database;
```

Sometime after the backup has finished, a new tablespace is added:

```
CREATE TABLESPACE tools
  DATAFILE '/u01/dbfile/o12c/tools01.dbf'
  SIZE 20m EXTENT MANAGEMENT LOCAL
  UNIFORM SIZE 512k SEGMENT SPACE MANAGEMENT AUTO;
```

Now we have the situation where there currently is no backup of the newly created data file (the tools tablespace in this scenario). Suppose there is a media failure that damages the data file before a fresh backup is taken. You wonder how you're going to restore and recover a data file that was never backed up.

Solution

For this solution to work, you need to have a good baseline backup of your database and any subsequently generated redo up to the point where the data file was created. If you have your current control file, you can restore and recover at the data file, tablespace, or database level. If you're using a backup control file that has no information about the data file, you must restore and recover at the database level.

Using a Current Control File

In this example, we use the current control file and are recovering the tools01.dbf datafile in the newly added tools tablespace.

```
$ rman target /
RMAN> startup mount;
RMAN> restore tablespace tools;
```

You should see a message like the following in the output as RMAN re-creates the data file:

```
creating datafile file number=5 name=/u01/dbfile/o12c/tools01.dbf
```

Now issue the recover command and open the database:

```
RMAN> recover tablespace tools;
RMAN> alter database open;
```

Using a Backup Control File

This scenario is applicable anytime you use a backup control file to restore and recover a data file that has not yet been backed up. First, we restore a control file from a backup taken prior to when the data file was created:

```
$ rman target /
RMAN> startup nomount;
RMAN> restore controlfile from
'/u01/app/oracle/product/12.1.0.1/db_1/dbs/c-3412777350-20120730-05';RMAN> alter database mount;
```

Now you can verify the control file has no record of the tablespace that was added after the backup was taken:

```
RMAN> report schema;
```

When the control file has no record of the data file, RMAN will throw an error if you attempt to recover at the tablespace or data file level. In this situation, you must use the restore database and recover database commands as follows:

```
RMAN> restore database;
RMAN> recover database;
```

Next, you should see quite a bit of RMAN output. Near the end of the output you should see a line similar to this indicating that the data file has been re-created:

```
creating datafile file number=5 name=/u01/dbfile/o12c/tools01.dbf
```

Since you restored using a backup control file, you are required to open the database with the resetlogs command:

```
RMAN> alter database open resetlogs;
```

How It Works

Starting with Oracle Database 10g, there is enough information in the redo stream for RMAN to automatically re-create a data file that was never backed up. It doesn't matter whether the control file has a record of the data file.

Prior to Oracle Database10g, manual intervention from the DBA was required to recover a data file that had not been backed up yet. If Oracle identified that a data file was missing that had not been backed up, the recovery process would halt, and you would have to identify the missing data file and re-create it:

```
SQL> alter database create datafile '/u01/dbfile/o12c/tools01.dbf '
     as '/u01/dbfile/o12c/tools01.dbf' size 10485760 reuse;
```

After re-creating the missing data file, you had to manually restart the recovery session. If you are using an old version of the Oracle database, see MOS note 1060605.6 for details on how to re-create a data file in this scenario.

In Oracle Database 10g and newer, this is no longer the case. RMAN automatically detects that there isn't a backup of a data file being restored and re-creates the data file from information retrieved from the control file and/or redo information as part of the restore and recovery operations.

11-18. Restoring from Uncataloged Backup Pieces

Problem

You had to re-create your control file and you are not using a recovery catalog. Afterward, you attempted to restore data files using RMAN but received the following errors:

```
RMAN-06026: some targets not found - aborting restore
RMAN-06023: no backup or copy of datafile 4 found to restore
```

You want to restore control files, data files, and archived redo logs from RMAN backup pieces, but your control file now contains no information whatsoever about previously taken backups.

Solution

If you're using Oracle Database 10g or higher, use the catalog command to add RMAN metadata directly to your control file about backup pieces. You can do this in several different ways depending on whether you're using an FRA.

Using an FRA

You can have RMAN repopulate the control file with all file information in the FRA. The following command will catalog all backup sets, data file copies, and archived redo log files located in the FRA:

```
RMAN> catalog recovery area;
```

Using a Directory

You can also instruct RMAN to recursively catalog all the backup pieces and image copies located under a directory path. This example instructs RMAN to record metadata in the repository for any backup pieces and image copies located under the /u01/FRA directory:

```
RMAN> catalog start with '/u01/FRA';
```

Using a Backup Piece

For a backup set to be usable, you must catalog all backup pieces in the backup set. In this example, there is only one backup piece in the backup set:

```
RMAN> catalog backuppiece '/u01/rman/o12c/5hnhd8kv_1_1.bk';
```

This writes metadata information about that backup piece into the control file. If this is successful, you should see in the output the following line:

```
cataloged backup piece
```

How It Works

New with Oracle Database 10g, you can now add metadata about backup pieces directly to your control file via the `catalog` command. If you're not using a recovery catalog, this can be particularly useful if you ever have to re-create your control file. This is because when re-creating the control file, all of your RMAN information is wiped out.

You can use the `catalog` command to add the following types of information to your control file:

- Backup pieces
- Archived redo log files
- Control file copies
- Data file copies
- Files in the fast recovery area

■ **Note**   See MOS note 550082.1 for details on how to catalog backup pieces to tape.

You can verify the backup information via the following command:

```
RMAN> list backup;
```

11-19. Restoring Data Files Using DBMS_BACKUP_RESTORE
Problem

You're using an old version of Oracle (9i and lower). You had to re-create your control file, and you are not using a recovery catalog. You want to restore data files from an RMAN backup piece, but your control file now contains no information whatsoever about previously taken backups.

■ **Note**   If you are using Oracle Database 10g or newer, we strongly recommend that you use the `catalog` command and do not use DBMS_BACKUP_RESTORE. See Recipe 11-18 for details on how to add metadata to your control file for uncataloged backup pieces.

Solution

Use the DBMS_BACKUP_RESTORE package to restore files from backup pieces. If you have output logs from your backups, you can visually inspect those and determine the names of the data files within a backup piece. If you don't have any output logs, you'll have to figure out through trial and error which data files are in which backup piece.

In this example, we know from our RMAN backup output logs that three data files are contained within the specified backup piece. You'll need to modify this anonymous block of PL/SQL code to specify the files in your environment:

```
SET SERVEROUTPUT ON
DECLARE
   finished      BOOLEAN;
   v_dev_name    VARCHAR2(10);
   TYPE v_filestable IS TABLE OF varchar2(500) INDEX BY BINARY_INTEGER;
```

```
BEGIN
  -- Allocate channel, when disk then type = null, if tape then type = sbt_tape.
  v_dev_name := dbms_backup_restore.deviceAllocate(type=>null, ident=> 'd1');
  -- Set beginning of restore operation (does not restore anything yet).
  dbms_backup_restore.restoreSetDatafile;
  -- Define datafiles and locations for this backup piece.
  dbms_backup_restore.restoreDatafileTo(dfnumber=>1,
    toname=>'/u01/dbfile/o12c/system01.dbf');
  dbms_backup_restore.restoreDatafileTo(dfnumber=>4,
    toname=>'/u01/dbfile/o12c/users01.dbf');
  dbms_backup_restore.restoreDatafileTo(dfnumber=>5,
    toname=>'/u01/dbfile/o12c/tools01.dbf');
  -- Restore the datafiles in this backup piece.
  dbms_backup_restore.restoreBackupPiece(done => finished,
  handle=>'/u01/app/oracle/product/12.1.0.1/db_1/dbs/38nhakpe_1_1',
          params=>null);
  IF finished THEN
    dbms_output.put_line('Datafiles restored');
  ELSE
    dbms_output.put_line('Problem');
  END IF;
  --
  dbms_backup_restore.deviceDeallocate('d1');
END;
/
```

If you put the prior code into a file named dbr.sql, you would run it as follows:

```
SQL> connect / as sysdba
SQL> startup mount;
SQL> @dbr.sql
```

How It Works

Normally you will never need to know about or use DBMS_BACKUP_RESTORE. You would use it only if you couldn't accomplish a backup and recovery task through the regular RMAN interface. In our example, we're using a pre-10g version of the database and need to restore data files from a backup piece (that the RMAN repository isn't aware of).

Before you can use the DBMS_BACKUP_RESTORE package, you need to know the following:

- Location and names of files in a backup set
- Location and names of backup pieces in the backup set

We recommend that when you create your RMAN backups, you always spool out a log file (see Recipe 17-7 for details). That will ensure that you can determine which data files, control files, and archived redo log files are in which backup pieces. If you don't know what data files are in which backup pieces, you'll have to do some trial-and-error restore operations (guess which data file is in which backup piece).

The basic approach to restore a data file using DBMS_BACKUP_RESTORE is to use an anonymous block of PL/SQL as follows:

1. Allocate a channel with deviceAllocate.
2. Inform Oracle that you're going to restore data files using restoreSetDatafile.

3. Use restoreDatafile to specify data files to be restored.

4. Use restoreBackupPiece to specify the backup piece(s) and perform the actual restore operation.

5. Deallocate the channel with deviceDeallocate.

Interestingly, most of the work that RMAN performs is accomplished through calls to DBMS_BACKUP_RESTORE. Oracle does not readily provide documentation for this package. We suggest that you contact Oracle Support if you need more details on how to use this undocumented package for your particular situation.

■ **Tip**   If you want to view what calls RMAN makes to DBMS_BACKUP_RESTORE, enable PL/SQL debugging as described in Recipe 17-9.

From within SQL*Plus, if you describe DBMS_BACKUP_RESTORE, you'll see that it contains literally hundreds of procedures and functions. You'll need to use only a small subset of those. You can use the DBMS_BACKUP_RESTORE package with any version of Oracle that supports RMAN.

11-20. Restoring a Container Database and/or Its Associated Pluggable Databases

Problem

You've had a failure with a container database (new with Oracle Database 12c) and/or one of its associated pluggable databases and now face one of the following situations:

- All data files have experienced media failure (container root data files as well as all associated pluggable database data files).

- Just the data files associated with the container root database have experienced media failure.

- Only data files associated with a pluggable database have experienced media failure.

Solution

When dealing with container and associated pluggable databases, there are three basic scenarios: all data files need to be recovered, just the data files associated with the root container need to be recovered, or only data files associated with a pluggable database need to be recovered. Solutions to these situations are covered in the following subsections.

Restoring and Recovering All Data Files

To restore all data files associated with a container database (this includes the root container, the seed container, and all of associated pluggable databases), use RMAN to connect to the container database as a user with sysdba or sysbackup privileges and restore and recover all data files associated with the database. Since the data files associated with the root system tablespace are being restored, the database must be started in mount mode (and not open):

```
$ rman target /
RMAN> startup mount;
RMAN> restore database;
RMAN> recover database;
RMAN> alter database open;
```

Keep in mind that when you open a container database, this does not by default open the associated pluggable databases. You can do that from the root container as follows:

```
RMAN> alter pluggable database all open;
```

Restoring and Recovering Root Container Data Files

If just data files associated with the root container have been damaged, you can restore and recover at the root level. In this example, the root container's system data file is being restored, so the database must not be open. The following commands instruct RMAN to restore only the data files associated with the root container database via the keyword root:

```
$ rman target /
RMAN> startup mount;
RMAN> restore database root;
RMAN> recover database root;
RMAN> alter database open;
```

In the prior code, the restore database root command instructs RMAN to restore only data files associated with the root container database. After the container database is opened, you must open any associated pluggable databases. You can do so from the root container as follows:

```
RMAN> alter pluggable database all open;
```

You can check on the status of your pluggable databases via this query:

```
SQL> select name, open_mode from v$pdbs;
```

Restoring and Recovering a Pluggable Database

You have two options for restoring and recovering a pluggable database:

- Connect as the container root user and specify the pluggable database to be restored.
- Connect directly to the pluggable database as a privileged pluggable level user and issue restore and recover commands.

This first example connects to the root container and restores and recovers the data files associated with the salespdb pluggable database. For this to work, the pluggable database must not be open (since the pluggable database's system data file[s] is also being restored and recovered):

```
$ rman target /
RMAN> alter pluggable database salespdb close;
RMAN> restore pluggable database salespdb;
RMAN> recover pluggable database salespdb;
RMAN> alter pluggable database salespdb open;
```

You can also connect directly to a pluggable database and perform restore and recovery operations. When connected directly to the pluggable database, the user has access only to the data files associated with the pluggable database:

```
$ rman target sys/foo@salespdb
RMAN> shutdown immediate;
RMAN> restore database;
RMAN> recover database;
RMAN> alter database open;
```

■ **Note**   When you're connected directly to a pluggable database, you cannot specify the name of the pluggable database as part of the restore and recover commands. In this situation, you'll get an "RMAN-07536: command not allowed when connected to a Pluggable Database" error.

The prior code affects only data files associated with the pluggable database to which you are connected. The pluggable database needs to be closed for this to work. However, the parent container database can be open or mounted. Also, you must have initiated a backup from the pluggable database privileged user. The privileged pluggable database user cannot access backups of data files initiated by the root container database privileged user.

How It Works

Restore and recovery of a container database is very similar to restore and recovery for a non-container database. If you have sysdba or sysbackup access to the root container database, you can perform any type of restore and recovery:

- Restore and recover all data files associated with the database
- Just files associated with the root container
- Initiate restore and recovery operations for any associated pluggable databases

---

■ **Note**   If you need to restore control files and/or archive redo logs, you must do so when connected to the root container database as a sysdba or sysbackup privileged user.

When connected directly to a pluggable database, you can restore and recover only data files associated with the pluggable database. The pluggable database must be shut down while restoring and recovering data file(s) associated with the pluggable database's system tablespace. The parent container database needs to be either open or mounted while restoring a pluggable database's data files. The pluggable database also needs access to RMAN backups that were created while connected as a sysdba or sysbackup privileged user to the pluggable database. In other words, the connection to the pluggable database cannot see backups taken by the root container database privileged user.

When connected to the root container database with sysdba or sysbackup privileges, you can also restore at the tablespace or data file level of granularity. If the tablespace is associated with a pluggable database, include the pluggable database name along with the tablespace name, separated by a colon:

```
$ rman target /
RMAN> alter pluggable database salespdb close;
RMAN> restore tablespace salespdb:sales;
RMAN> recover tablespace salespdb:sales;
RMAN> alter pluggable database salespdb open;
```

If you need to restore and recover a tablespace associated with the seed pluggable database, and the pluggable database name has a special character, such as a $ character, embedded in the name, you'll have to enclose the names in double quotes:

```
$ rman target /
RMAN> restore tablespace "PDB$SEED":"SYSAUX";
```

Since this seed tablespace is static, there should be no need to recover it.

11-21. Restoring and Recovering to a Different Server
Problem

You work in an environment where you need to duplicate a production database to a test server. However, the network security is such that there is no direct network connectivity between the production and test environments. In other words, you won't be able to use the RMAN duplicate database features to automatically re-create a remote database because there is no direct network connection between the production server and test server. You'll have to manually copy your RMAN backups from to a secure server that does have access to production and from there copy the RMAN backups to the test server.

Solution

Follow these high-level steps to re-create a database with an RMAN backup to a different server:

1. Create an RMAN backup on the originating database.

2. Copy RMAN backup from the originating server to the destination server. All steps after this are performed on the destination database server.

3. Ensure that Oracle is installed on destination server (same version as the originating server).

4. Source the required OS variables.

5. Create an init.ora file for the database to be restored.

6. Create any required directories for data files, control files, and online redo logs.

7. Startup the database in NOMOUNT mode.

8. Restore a control file from the RMAN backup.

9. Start up the database in MOUNT mode.

10. Make the control file aware of the location of the RMAN backups.

11. Rename and restore the data files to reflect new directory locations.

12. Recover the database.

13. Set the new location for the online redo logs.

14. Open the database.

15. Add a tempfile.

16. Rename the database (optional).

Each of the prior steps is covered in detail in the next several subsections. Steps 1 and 2 occur on the source database server. All remaining steps are performed on the destination server. For this example, the source database is named o12c, and the destination database will be named DEVDB.

In this example, the originating server and destination server have different mount point names. On the source database, the location of the data files and control files are here:

```
/u01/dbfile/o12c
```

On the destination database, the data files and control files will be renamed and restored to this directory:

```
/ora01/dbfile/DEVDB
```

The destination database online redo logs will be placed in this directory:

```
/ora01/oraredo/DEVDB
```

The destination database archive redo log file location will be set as follows:

```
/ora01/arc/DEVDB
```

Keep in mind these are the directories used on servers in our test environment. You'll have to adjust these directory names to reflect the directory structures on your database servers.

Step 1: Create an RMAN Backup on the Originating Database

When backing up a database, make sure you have the autobackup control file feature turned on. Also include the archive redo logs as part of the backup, like so:

```
RMAN> backup database plus archivelog;
```

You can verify the names and locations of the backup pieces via the list backup command. For example, this is what the backup pieces look like for the source database:

```
1nnht9ot_1_1
1onht9ov_1_1
1pnht9r1_1_1
c-3414586809-20120805-10
```

In the prior output, the file starting with "c-" is the backup piece that contains the control file. You'll have to inspect the output of your list backup command to determine which backup piece contains the control file. You'll need to reference that backup piece in step 8.

Step 2: Copy RMAN Backup to Destination Server

For this step, use a utility such as rsync or scp to copy the backup pieces from one server to another. This example uses the scp command to copy the backup pieces:

```
$ scp 1*  oracle@DEVBOX:/ora01/rman/DEVDB
$ scp c-* oracle@DEVBOX:/ora01/rman/DEVDB
```

In this example, the /ora01/rman/DEVDB directory must be created on the destination server before copying the backup files. Depending on your environment, this step might require copying the RMAN backups twice; once from the production server to a secure server and from the secure server to a test server.

■ **Note** If the RMAN backups are on tape instead of on disk, then the same media manager software must be installed/configured on the destination server. Also, that server must have direct access to the RMAN backups on tape.

Step 3: Ensure that Oracle Is Installed

Make sure you have the same version of Oracle binaries installed on the destination as you do on the originating database.

Step 4: Source the Required OS Variables

You need to establish the operating system variables, such as ORACLE_SID, ORACLE_HOME, and PATH. Initially, we usually set the ORACLE_SID variable to match what it was on the original database. The database name will be changed as part of the last step in this recipe (optional). Here are the settings for ORACLE_SID and ORACLE_HOME on the destination server:

```
$ echo $ORACLE_SID
o12c

$ echo $ORACLE_HOME
/ora01/app/oracle/product/12.1.0.1/db_1
```

Step 5: Create an init.ora File for the Database to be Restored

Copy the init.ora file from the original server to the destination server and modify it so that it matches the destination box in terms of any directory paths. For example, make sure you modify the control_files parameter so that the path names reflect where the control files will be placed on the new server.

For now, the name of the init.ora file is ORACLE_HOME/dbs/inito12c.ora. This file will be renamed when the database is renamed to DEVDB in a later step. For now, the name of the database is o12c; this will be renamed in a later step. Here are the contents of the init.ora file:

```
control_files='/ora01/dbfile/DEVDB/control01.ctl',
               '/ora01/dbfile/DEVDB/control02.ctl'
db_block_size=8192
db_name='o12c'
job_queue_processes=10
memory_max_target=300000000
memory_target=300000000
open_cursors=100
os_authent_prefix=''
processes=100
remote_login_passwordfile='EXCLUSIVE'
resource_limit=true
shared_pool_size=80M
sql92_security=TRUE
undo_management='AUTO'
undo_tablespace='UNDOTBS1'
workarea_size_policy='AUTO'
```

Ensure you change parameters such as control_files to reflect the new path directories on the destination server (/ora01/dbfile/DEVDB in this example).

■ **Note**   If this was an Oracle Database 10*g* example, you would need to set the parameters of: background_dump_dest, user_dump_dest, and core_dump_dest.

Step 6: Create Any Required Directories for Data Files, Control Files, and Dump/Trace Files

For this example, the directories of /ora01/dbfile/DEVDBA and /ora01/oraredo/DEVDBA are created:

```
$ mkdir -p /ora01/dbfile/DEVDBA
$ mkdir -p /ora01/oraredo/DEVDBA
```

Step 7: Start Up the Database in Nomount Mode

You should now be able to start up the database in nomount mode:

```
$ rman target /
RMAN> startup nomount;
```

Step 8: Restore a Control File from the RMAN Backup

Now restore the control file from the backup that was previously copied. For example:

```
RMAN> restore controlfile from '/ora01/rman/DEVDB/c-3414586809-20120805-10';
```

The control file will be restored to all locations specified by the control_files initialization parameter. Here is some sample output:

```
channel ORA_DISK_1: restore complete, elapsed time: 00:00:03
output file name=/ora01/dbfile/DEVDB/control01.ctl
output file name=/ora01/dbfile/DEVDB/control02.ctl
```

Step 9: Start Up the Database in Mount Mode

You should be able to start up your database in mount mode now:

```
RMAN> alter database mount;
```

At this point your control files exist and are opened, but none of the data files or online redo logs exist yet.

Step 10: Make the Control File Aware of the Location of the RMAN Backups

First, use the crosscheck command to let the control file know that none of the backups or archive redo logs are in the same location they were on the original server:

```
RMAN> crosscheck backup; # Crosscheck backups
RMAN> crosscheck copy;   # Crosscheck image copies and archive logs
```

Now use the catalog command to make the control file aware of the location and names of the backup pieces that were copied to the destination server.

■ **Note**   Don't confuse the catalog command with the recovery catalog schema. The catalog command adds RMAN metadata to the control file, whereas the recovery catalog schema is a user created in a separate database (usually) that can be used to store RMAN metadata.

In this example, any RMAN files that are in the /ora01/rman/DEVDB directory will be cataloged in the control file:

```
RMAN> catalog start with '/ora01/rman/DEVDB';
```

Here is some sample output:

```
List of Files Unknown to the Database
=====================================
File Name: /ora01/rman/DEVDB/c-3414586809-20120805-10
File Name: /ora01/rman/DEVDB/1onht9ov_1_1
File Name: /ora01/rman/DEVDB/1pnht9r1_1_1
File Name: /ora01/rman/DEVDB/1nnht9ot_1_1

Do you really want to catalog the above files (enter YES or NO)?
```

Now, type in YES (if everything looks okay). You should be able to use the RMAN list backup command now to view the newly cataloged backup pieces:

```
RMAN> list backup;
```

Step 11: Rename and Restore the Data Files to Reflect New Directory Locations

If your destination server has the exact same directory structure as the original server directories, you can issue the restore command directly:

```
RMAN> restore database;
```

However, when restoring data files to locations that are different from the original directories, you'll have to use the set newname command. Create a file that uses an RMAN run{} block that contains the appropriate set newname and restore commands. We like to use a SQL script that generates SQL to give a starting point. Here is a sample script:

```
set head off feed off verify off echo off pages 0 trimspool on
set lines 132 pagesize 0
spo newname.sql
--
select 'run{' from dual;
--
select
'set newname for datafile ' || file# || ' to ' || '''' || name || '''' || ';'
from v$datafile;
--
select
'restore database;' || chr(10) ||
'switch datafile all;' || chr(10) ||
'}'
from dual;
--
spo off;
```

After you run the script, the newname.sql script that was generated contains the following:

```
run{
set newname for datafile 1 to '/u01/dbfile/o12c/system01.dbf';
set newname for datafile 2 to '/u01/dbfile/o12c/sysaux01.dbf';
set newname for datafile 3 to '/u01/dbfile/o12c/undotbs01.dbf';
set newname for datafile 4 to '/u01/dbfile/o12c/users01.dbf';
restore database;
switch datafile all;
}
```

Now, modify the contents of the newname.sql script to reflect the directories on the destination database server. Here is what the final newname.sql script looks like for this example:

```
run{
set newname for datafile 1 to '/ora01/dbfile/DEVDB/system01.dbf';
set newname for datafile 2 to '/ora01/dbfile/DEVDB/sysaux01.dbf';
set newname for datafile 3 to '/ora01/dbfile/DEVDB/undotbs01.dbf';
set newname for datafile 4 to '/ora01/dbfile/DEVDB/users01.dbf';
restore database;
switch datafile all;
}
```

Now, connect to RMAN and run the prior script to restore the data files to the new locations:

```
$ rman target /
RMAN> @newname.sql
```

Here is a snippet of the output for this example:

```
datafile 1 switched to datafile copy
input datafile copy RECID=5 STAMP=790357985 file name=/ora01/dbfile/DEVDB/system01.dbf
```

All of the data files have been restored to the new database server. You can use the RMAN report schema command to verify that the files have been restored and are in the correct locations:

```
RMAN> report schema;
```

Here is some sample output:

```
RMAN-06139: WARNING: control file is not current for REPORT SCHEMA
Report of database schema for database with db_unique_name O12C
List of Permanent Datafiles
===========================
```

File	Size(MB)	Tablespace	RB segs	Datafile Name
1	500	SYSTEM	***	/ora01/dbfile/DEVDB/system01.dbf
2	500	SYSAUX	***	/ora01/dbfile/DEVDB/sysaux01.dbf
3	800	UNDOTBS1	***	/ora01/dbfile/DEVDB/undotbs01.dbf
4	50	USERS	***	/ora01/dbfile/DEVDB/users01.dbf

```
List of Temporary Files
=======================
```

File	Size(MB)	Tablespace	Maxsize(MB)	Tempfile Name
1	500	TEMP	500	/u01/dbfile/o12c/temp01.dbf

From the prior output, the database name and temporary tablespace data file still don't reflect the destination database (DEVDB). Those will be modified in subsequent steps.

Step 12: Recover the Database

Next, you need to apply any archive redo files that were generated during the backup. These should be included in the backup because the `archivelog all` clause was used to take the backup. Initiate the application of redo via the `recover database` command:

```
RMAN> recover database;
```

RMAN will restore and apply as many archive redo logs as it has in the backup pieces and then may throw an error when it reaches an archive redo log that doesn't exist. For example:

```
RMAN-06054: media recovery requesting unknown archived log for...
```

That error message is fine. The recovery process will restore and recover archive redo logs contained in the backups, which should be sufficient to open the database. The recovery process doesn't know where to stop applying archive redo logs and therefore will continue to attempt to apply until it can't find the next log. Having said that, now is a good time to verify that your data files are online and not in a fuzzy state:

```
select
file#
,status
,fuzzy
,error
,checkpoint_change#,
to_char(checkpoint_time,'dd-mon-rrrr hh24:mi:ss') as checkpoint_time
from v$datafile_header;
```

Step 13: Set the New Location for the Online Redo Logs

If your source and destination servers have the exact same directory structures, you don't need to set a new location for the online redo logs (so you can skip this step).

However, if the directory structures are different, you'll need to update the control file to reflect the new directory for the online redo logs. We sometimes use a SQL script that generates SQL to assist with this step:

```
set head off feed off verify off echo off pages 0 trimspool on
set lines 132 pagesize 0
spo renlog.sql
select
'alter database rename file ' || chr(10)
|| '''' || member || '''' || ' to ' || chr(10) || '''' || member || '''' ||';'
from v$logfile;
spo off;
```

For this example, here is a snippet of the renlog.sql file that was generated:

```
alter database rename file
'/u01/oraredo/o12c/redo01a.rdo' to
'/u01/oraredo/o12c/redo01a.rdo';
...
```

```
alter database rename file
'/u02/oraredo/o12c/redo03b.rdo' to
'/u02/oraredo/o12c/redo03b.rdo';
```

The contents of renlog.sql need to be modified to reflect the directory structure on the destination server. Here is what renlog.sql looks like after being edited for this example:

```
alter database rename file
'/u01/oraredo/o12c/redo01a.rdo' to
'/ora01/oraredo/DEVDB/redo01a.rdo';
...
alter database rename file
'/u02/oraredo/o12c/redo03b.rdo' to
'/ora01/oraredo/DEVDB/redo03b.rdo';
```

Update the control file by running the prior script:

```
SQL> @renlog.sql
```

You can select from V$LOGFILE to verify that the online redo log names are correct:

```
SQL> select member from v$logfile;
```

Here is the output for this example:

```
/ora01/oraredo/DEVDB/redo01a.rdo
/ora01/oraredo/DEVDB/redo02a.rdo
/ora01/oraredo/DEVDB/redo03a.rdo
/ora01/oraredo/DEVDB/redo01b.rdo
/ora01/oraredo/DEVDB/redo02b.rdo
/ora01/oraredo/DEVDB/redo03b.rdo
```

Make sure the directories exist on the new server that will contain the online redo logs. For this example, here's the mkdir command:

```
$ mkdir -p /ora01/oraredo/DEVDB
```

Step 14: Open the Database

You must open the database with the open resetlogs command (because there are no redo logs and they must be re-created at this point):

```
SQL> alter database open resetlogs;
```

If this is successful, you should see this message:

```
Database altered.
```

■ **Note** Keep in mind that all of the passwords from the newly restored copy are as they were in the source database. You may want to change passwords in a replicated database, especially if it was copied from production.

Step 15: Add Tempfile

When you start your database, Oracle will automatically try to add any missing tempfiles to the database. Oracle won't be able to do this if the directory structure on the destination server is different from that of the source server. In this scenario you will have to manually add any missing tempfiles. To do this, first take offline the temporary tablespace tempfile. The file definition from the originating database is taken offline like so:

```
SQL> alter database tempfile '/u01/dbfile/o12c/temp01.dbf' offline;
SQL> alter database tempfile '/u01/dbfile/o12c/temp01.dbf' drop;
```

Next, add a temporary tablespace file to the TEMP tablespace that matches the directory structure of the destination database server:

```
SQL> alter tablespace temp add tempfile '/ora01/dbfile/DEVDB/temp01.dbf'
    size 100m;
```

You can run the report schema command here to verify all files are in the correct locations.

Step 16: Rename the Database

This step is optional. If you need to rename the database to reflect the name for a development or test database, create a trace file that contains the create controlfile statement and use it to rename your database. The basic steps involved are:

1. Generate a trace file that contains the SQL command to re-create the control files:

   ```
   SQL> alter database backup controlfile to trace as '/tmp/cf.sql' resetlogs;
   ```

2. Shut down the database:

   ```
   SQL> shutdown immediate;
   ```

3. Modify the /tmp/cf.sql trace file; be sure to specify SET DATABASE "<NEW DATABASE NAME>" in the top line of the output:

   ```
   CREATE CONTROLFILE REUSE SET DATABASE "DEVDB" RESETLOGS ARCHIVELOG
       MAXLOGFILES 16
       MAXLOGMEMBERS 4
       MAXDATAFILES 1024
       MAXINSTANCES 1
       MAXLOGHISTORY 876
   LOGFILE
     GROUP 1 (
       '/ora01/oraredo/DEVDB/redo01a.rdo',
       '/ora01/oraredo/DEVDB/redo01b.rdo'
     ) SIZE 50M BLOCKSIZE 512,
   ```

```
    GROUP 2 (
      '/ora01/oraredo/DEVDB/redo02a.rdo',
      '/ora01/oraredo/DEVDB/redo02b.rdo'
    ) SIZE 50M BLOCKSIZE 512,
    GROUP 3 (
      '/ora01/oraredo/DEVDB/redo03a.rdo',
      '/ora01/oraredo/DEVDB/redo03b.rdo'
    ) SIZE 50M BLOCKSIZE 512
DATAFILE
   '/ora01/dbfile/DEVDB/system01.dbf',
   '/ora01/dbfile/DEVDB/sysaux01.dbf',
   '/ora01/dbfile/DEVDB/undotbs01.dbf',
   '/ora01/dbfile/DEVDB/users01.dbf'
CHARACTER SET AL32UTF8;
```

If you don't specify SET DATABASE in the top line of the prior script, when you run the script (as shown later in this example), you'll receive an error such as:

```
ORA-01161: database name ... in file header does not match...
```

4. Create an init.ora file that matches the new database name:

```
$ cd $ORACLE_HOME/dbs
$ cp init<old_sid>.ora init<new_sid>.ora
```

For example:

```
$ cp inito12c.ora initDEVDB.ora
```

5. Modify the DB_NAME variable within the new init.ora file (in this example, it's set to DEVDB):

```
db_name='DEVDB'
```

6. Set ORACLE_SID operating system variable to reflect the new SID name (in this example it's set to DEVDB):

```
$ echo $ORACLE_SID
DEVDB
```

7. Start up the instance in nomount mode:

```
SQL> startup nomount;
```

8. Run the trace file to re-create the control file (trace file from step 2):

```
SQL> @/tmp/cf.sql
```

9. Open the database with `open resetlogs`:

    ```
    SQL> alter database open resetlogs;
    ```

    If this is successful, you should have a database that is a copy of the original database. All of the data files, control files, archive redo logs, and online redo logs are in the new locations, and the database has a new name.

10. As a last step, ensure that your temporary tablespace exists:

    ```
    ALTER TABLESPACE TEMP ADD TEMPFILE '/ora01/dbfile/DEVDB/temp01.dbf'
        SIZE 104857600  REUSE AUTOEXTEND OFF;
    ```

■ **Tip**   You can also use the NID utility to change the database name and DBID. For additional information, see MOS note 863800.1 for more details.

How It Works

Manually restoring and recovering a database to a different server is sometimes required. For example, the network security may be such that manually copying an RMAN backup to a remote server is the only way to replicate the database.

The steps covered in the solution section are also an excellent way to test your backup and recovery strategy. If you can completely restore a production backup to a test server, you can be confident that you don't have any missing pieces and that you know how to perform all required tasks. In some environments we schedule an activity like this once every three months. If you understand each step, you'll be better prepared to deal with any type of backup and recovery issue.

The steps covered in the solution section are fairly straightforward. Keep in mind that some of the steps won't be necessary if you have the same directory structures between the two servers. For example, renaming the data files and online redo logs isn't required when the directory structures are the same.

The last step of renaming the database is optional. If you make a copy of a production database, you'll probably want to rename the restored database. This is because you don't ever want to get confused and think you're working with a test database when it is the production database (or vice versa).

■ **Note**   If you don't rename the database, then be careful about connect and resync operations to the same recovery catalog used by the original/source database. This causes confusion in the recovery catalog as to which is the real source database and may jeopardize your ability to recover and restore the real source database.

Performing Incomplete Recovery

One of us once worked in a place where a system administrator saw some *.log files in several directories and decided that since they were just log files, they could be deleted:

```
$ rm *.log
```

The log files that were removed were all of our online redo log files for the database. Oops! Big mistake—we had to perform an incomplete database recovery to get our database back online.

Incomplete database recovery means that you cannot recover all committed transactions. Incomplete means that you do not apply all redo to restore to the point of the last committed transaction that occurred in your database. In other words, you are restoring and recovering to a point in time in the past. For this reason, incomplete database recovery is also called database point-in-time recovery (DBPITR). Usually you perform incomplete database recovery because of one of the following reasons:

- You don't have all the redo required to perform a complete recovery. You're missing either archived redo log files or online redo log files (current or unarchived) that are required for complete recovery. This situation could arise because the required redo files are damaged or missing.

- You purposely want to roll the database back to a point in time. For example, you would do this in the event somebody accidentally truncated a table and you intentionally wanted to roll the database back to just before the truncate table command was issued.

Tip To minimize the chance of failure with your online redo log files, we highly recommend you multiplex them with at least two members in each group and have each member on separate physical devices governed by separate controllers.

Background

Incomplete database recovery consists of two steps: restore and recovery. The restore step will re-create data files, and the recover step will apply redo up to the specified point in time. The restore process can be initiated from RMAN in several ways:

- `restore database until`

- `restore tablespace until`

- `flashback database`

For the majority of incomplete database recovery circumstances, you'll use the `restore database until` command to instruct RMAN to retrieve data files from the RMAN backup files. This type of incomplete database recovery is the main focus of this chapter. The `until` portion of the `restore database` command instructs RMAN to retrieve data files from a point in the past based on one of the following methods:

- Time

- Change (sometimes called system change number [SCN])

- Log sequence number

- Restore point

The RMAN `restore database until` command will retrieve all data files from the most recent backup set or image copy. RMAN will automatically determine from the `until` clause which backup set contains the required data files. If you omit the `until` clause of the `restore database` command, RMAN will retrieve data files from the latest available backup set or image copy. In some situations, that may be the behavior you desire. We recommend you use the `until` clause to ensure that RMAN restores from the correct backup set or image copy. When you issue the `restore database until` command, RMAN will determine how to extract the data files from any of the following:

- Full database backup

- Incremental level 0 backup

- Image copy backup generated by the `backup as copy` command

You cannot perform an incomplete database recovery on a subset of your database's online data files. When performing incomplete database recovery, all of the checkpoint SCNs for all online data files must be synchronized before you can open your database with the `alter database open resetlogs` command. You can view the data file header SCNs and the status of each data file via this SQL query:

```
select
 file#
,status
,fuzzy
,error
,checkpoint_change#,
to_char(checkpoint_time,'dd-mon-rrrr hh24:mi:ss') as checkpoint_time
from v$datafile_header;
```

The FUZZY column of V$DATAFILE_HEADER refers to a data file that contains one or more blocks that have an SCN greater than or equal to the checkpoint SCN in the data file header (meaning there have been writes to the data file since the last checkpoint). During regular database operating conditions, the FUZZY column will normally be YES. However, after you restore a data file, if a data file has a FUZZY value of YES, you cannot open the database normally yet; in this situation more redo needs to be applied before the database can be opened. Table 12-1 summarizes these scenarios.

Table 12-1. Data File State and Corresponding Status of the FUZZY Column

Operation	FUZZY Column Status	DBA Action to Open Database
Normally operating database	YES	N/A
Data file restored from an RMAN offline or cold backup	NO	No redo needs to be applied. However, if CF SCN > DF SCN or CF restored from backup, then open resetlogs must be used.
Data file restored from an RMAN online or hot backup	For an active OLTP database most likely YES; can be NO.	Redo must be applied. After fuzziness cleared, database can be opened. If CF SCN > DF SCN or CF restored from a backup, then open resetlogs must be used.

If you've restored a data file and attempt to open the database before the fuzziness is cleared, you'll receive the following message:

```
ORA-01113: file 1 needs media recovery
```

You can view the SCN to which it must be recovered via the restore database preview command:

```
RMAN> restore database preview;
```

At the bottom of the output you should see the SCN at which to begin recovery and the SCN to which the database must be restored before it can be opened. For example:

```
Media recovery start SCN is 29950
Recovery must be done beyond SCN 29954 to clear datafile fuzziness
```

Figure 12-1 graphically depicts the requirement of restoring data files past the SCN required to clear out fuzziness. As shown in the diagram, you can perform an incomplete recovery for any SCN starting with 29954 up until 29998. Archive log 1 is required to begin the recovery process. Archive redo log 2 is required to recover past the fuzzy SCN. If you apply all of the redo within of archive log 3 and the current online redo log, then a complete recovery is performed.

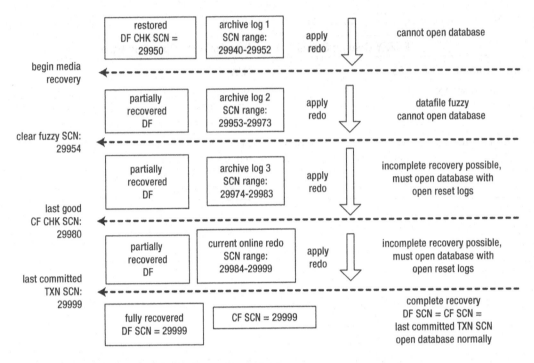

Figure 12-1. *SCN ranges of incomplete and complete recovery*

There are two major exceptions where you can perform incomplete recovery on a subset of your database:

- Tablespace point-in-time recovery (TSPITR)

- Table point-in-time recovery (new in Oracle Database 12c)

Tablespace point-in-time recovery uses the recover tablespace until command. TSPITR is used in rare situations and restores and recovers only the tablespace(s) you specify. This type of recovery is described in Recipe 12-10 and involves many steps to achieve the desired result.

Table point-in-time recovery is a new feature in Oracle Database 12c. This type of recovery uses the RMAN recover table command. This topic is covered in Chapter 13, which deals with various other methods for table-level recovery (like flashback to before drop or flashback to before SCN).

The recovery portion of an incomplete database recovery is usually initiated with the recover database until command. RMAN will automatically recover your database to the point specified with the until clause. Just like the restore command, you can recover until a time, change/SCN, log sequence number, or restore point. When RMAN reaches the specified point, it will automatically terminate the recovery process.

■ **Note**   Regardless of what you specify in the until clause, RMAN will convert that into a corresponding until scn clause and assign the appropriate SCN. This is to avoid any timing issues, particularly those caused by daylight saving time.

During a recovery, RMAN will automatically determine how to apply redo. First, RMAN will apply any incremental backups available. Next, any archived redo log files on disk will be applied. If the archived redo log files do not exist on disk, then RMAN will attempt to retrieve them from a backup set. If you want to apply redo as part of an incomplete database recovery, the following conditions must be true:

- Your database must be in archivelog mode.

- You must have a good backup of all data files.

- You must have all redo required to restore up to the specified point.

When performing an incomplete database recovery with RMAN, you must have your database in mount mode. RMAN needs the database in mount mode to be able to read and write to the control file. Also, while in mount mode the database is not open for general use. Any data files in need of recovery cannot be open for regular user transaction processing while being recovered. Hence the need for the database to be in mount mode.

▪ **Note**   After incomplete database recovery is performed, you are required to open your database with the `alter database open resetlogs` command.

Depending on your scenario, you can use RMAN to perform a variety of incomplete recovery methods. The first recipe in this chapter discusses how to determine what type of incomplete recovery to perform.

12-1. Determining Type of Incomplete Recovery
Problem

You want to perform an incomplete recovery but don't know which method to use.

Solution

Use Table 12-2 to determine which type of incomplete recovery to perform.

Table 12-2. *Deciding Type of Incomplete Recovery to Perform*

Situation	Instructions Location
You know approximately what time you want to stop the recovery process.	Recipe 12-2
You know the particular log file for which you want to stop the recovery process.	Recipe 12-3 or Recipe 12-4
You know the SCN at which you want to end the recovery process.	Recipe 12-6
You want to restore to a defined restore point.	Recipe 12-7
You want to restore one tablespace to a point in time.	Recipe 12-10
You want to restore individual tables to a point in time in the past.	See Chapter 13 for restore table, flashback table to before drop, and flashback table to before SCN.
You want to restore and recover a subset of your database's data files.	Recipe 12-11
You have enabled the flashback database feature and want to flash back your database.	Chapter 13
You have a Data Pump export and want to restore objects to a point in time in the past.	See Oracle Database Utilities guide for details on how to use Data Pump.

How It Works

Time-based restore and recovery is commonly used when you know approximately the date and time to which you want to recover your database. For example, you may know approximately the time you want to stop the recovery process but not a particular SCN.

Log sequence–based and cancel-based recovery work well in situations where you have missing or damaged log files. In such scenarios, you can recover only up to your last good archived redo log file.

SCN-based recovery works well if you can pinpoint the SCN at which you want to stop the recovery process. You can retrieve SCN information from views such as V$LOG and V$LOG_HISTORY. You can also use tools such as LogMiner to retrieve the SCN of a particular SQL statement.

Restore point recoveries work only if you have established restore points. In these situations, you restore and recover up to the SCN associated with the specified restore point.

Tablespace point-in-time recovery is used in situations where you can restore and recover just a few tablespaces. You can use RMAN to automate many of the tasks associated with this type of incomplete recovery.

Table point-in-time recovery may be appropriate if you accidentally dropped a table or erroneously deleted data. See Chapter 13 for all options available with restoring a table back to a time in the past.

Flashing back your database works only if you have enabled the flashback database feature. DBAs often use this feature in environments where the database needs to be rolled back to a baseline (like a test environment), or also in production environments to capture the state of the database right before an application upgrade takes place. This allows you to restore the database back to a point in time in the event the upgrade doesn't go as planned. Chapter 13 covers this topic in detail.

12-2. Performing Time-Based Recovery

Problem

You want to restore your database to a previous date and time.

Solution

You can restore your database to a previous time in one of two ways:

- Specify the time as part of the restore and recover commands.

- Use the set until time command, and then issue unqualified restore and recover commands.

The following example specifies a time when issuing the restore and recover commands:

```
$ rman target /
RMAN> startup mount;
RMAN> restore database until time
    "to_date('28-aug-2012 08:10:00', 'dd-mon-rrrr hh24:mi:ss')";
RMAN> recover database until time
    "to_date('28-aug-2012 08:10:00', 'dd-mon-rrrr hh24:mi:ss')";
RMAN> alter database open resetlogs;
```

If everything went well, you should now see output similar to this:

```
Statement processed
```

■ **Tip**   For time-based incomplete database recovery, we recommend using the TO_DATE function and explicitly specifying the date format. This eliminates any ambiguity about what date format is being used.

You can also specify the time by using the set until time command. This command and the subsequent restore and recover must be executed from within a run{} block:

```
$ rman target /
RMAN> startup mount;
RMAN> run{
set until time "to_date('28-aug-2012 08:25:00', 'dd-mon-rrrr hh24:mi:ss')";
restore database;
recover database;
}
RMAN> alter database open resetlogs;
```

If everything went well, you should now see output similar to this:

```
Statement processed
```

If you're using a recovery catalog you should also connect to it before initiating any restore and recovery commands. For example:

```
$ rman target / catalog rcat/rcat@rcat
```

You'll have to modify the prior line of code to match the username/password and recovery catalog connection string for your environment.

How It Works

To restore and recover your database back to a point in time, you can use either the until time clause of the restore and recover commands or the set until time clause within a run{} block. RMAN will restore and recover the database up to, but not including, the specified time. In other words, RMAN will restore any transactions committed prior to the time specified. RMAN automatically stops the recovery process when it reaches the time you specified.

The default date format that RMAN expects is YYYY-MM-DD:HH24:MI:SS. However, we recommend using the TO_DATE function and specifying a format mask. This eliminates ambiguities with different national date formats and having to set the operating system NLS_DATE_FORMAT variable.

When performing time-based recoveries, sometimes you'll see this error:

```
RMAN-03002: failure of restore command at ...
RMAN-20207: UNTIL TIME or RECOVERY WINDOW is before RESETLOGS time
```

This usually means you're trying to restore from a backup that belongs to a previous incarnation of the database. In other words, the backup that RMAN is trying to use was created prior to the database being opened with the alter database open resetlogs command. See Recipe 12-9 for details on how to restore from a previous incarnation.

12-3. Performing Log Sequence–Based Recovery

Problem

You want to use RMAN to restore up to, but not including, a certain archived redo log file.

Solution

RMAN allows you to apply redo up to (but not including) a specific archived redo log file by specifying its sequence number when restoring and recovering. You can do this in one of two ways:

- Specify until sequence as part of the restore and recover commands.

- Use the set until sequence command.

The following example restores and recovers the target database up to, but not including, log sequence number 5:

```
$ rman target /
RMAN> startup mount;
RMAN> restore database until sequence 5;
RMAN> recover database until sequence 5;
RMAN> alter database open resetlogs;
```

If everything went well, you should now see output similar to this:

```
Statement processed
```

You can also use the set until command from within a run{} block to perform a log sequence-based recovery. The following examples restores and recovers up to but not including log sequence number 5 of thread 1:

```
$ rman target /
RMAN> startup mount;
RMAN> run{
set until sequence 5 thread 1;
restore database;
recover database;
}
RMAN> alter database open resetlogs;
```

If everything went well, you should now see output similar to this:

```
Statement processed
```

How It Works

Usually log sequence-based incomplete database recovery is initiated because you have a missing or damaged archived redo log file. If that's the case, you can recover only up to your last good archived redo log file, because you cannot skip a missing archived redo log file.

How you determine which archived redo log file to restore up to (but not including) will vary by situation. For example, if you are physically missing an archived redo log file and if RMAN can't find it in a backup set, you'll receive the following message when trying to apply the missing file:

```
RMAN-06053: unable to perform media recovery because of missing log
RMAN-06025: no backup of log thread 1 seq 45 lowscn 2149069 found to restore
```

Based on the previous error message, you would restore up to (but not including) log sequence 45.

Another common way to determine which archived redo log file you need to restore up to (but not including) is if files can't be restored from a bad tape. In this situation, you'll work with your system administrator to restore all available archived redo log files and then determine which sequence number to restore up to (but not including) based on what files were restorable.

Each time an online redo log file is generated, it is assigned a sequential log sequence number. When the online redo log file is copied to an archived redo log file, the log sequence number is preserved in the file header. You can view log sequence numbers by querying the SEQUENCE# column of the V$LOG_HISTORY and V$ARCHIVED_LOG views. Both of these views are based on information stored in the control file. You can query sequence number information from V$LOG_HISTORY, as shown here:

```
SELECT
 sequence#
,first_change#
,first_time
FROM v$log_history
ORDER BY first_time;
```

And here's the corresponding query for V$ARCHIVED_LOG:

```
SELECT
 sequence#
,first_change#
,first_time
FROM v$archived_log
ORDER BY first_time;
```

In the prior queries, it's important to order by first_time because that is date based. If you have opened your database with resetlogs in the past, then the sequence number is reset to 1. In that scenario, ordering by something other than first_time (for example sequence number) can sometimes give misleading results.

If you're using a fast recovery area (FRA), the sequence number is automatically embedded in the archive redo log filename. When an archive redo log file is created in the FRA, it uses the Oracle Managed File (OMF) format for the filename. The OMF format for an archived redo log file is O1_MF_<thread number>_<sequence number>_%u.arc.

If you're not using an FRA, then you must specify the file format of the archived redo log file via the log_archive_format initialization parameter. The default format is operating system dependent and usually consists of a combination of %S, %R, and %T. The %S specifies the log sequence number, %R specifies the resetlogs ID, and %T is the thread number.

■ **Note** In Oracle Database 10*g* and higher, when not using an FRA, the log_archive_format initialization parameter must contain the format parameters %S, %R, and %T.

If any of your archived redo log files or online redo log files are physically available, you can also view the sequence number by dumping the file contents to a trace file with the dump logfile command as follows:

```
SQL> alter system dump logfile '<directory/log file>';
```

For example:

```
SQL> oradebug setmypid
SQL> alter system dump logfile
     '/ora01/fra/O12C/archivelog/2012_08_08/o1_mf_1_10_825jth6l_.arc';
SQL> oradebug tracefile_name;
/ora01/app/oracle/diag/rdbms/o12c/o12c/trace/o12c_ora_15002.trc
```

You can search that trace file for the string Seq#, which shows the sequence number for the log file that you dumped. Here's a sample of what you should see in the dump file:

```
descrip:"Thread 0001, Seq# 0000000010, SCN 0x000000102a7c-0x000000102a7f"
```

In this case, the sequence number is 10.

12-4. Performing Cancel-Based Recovery

Problem

You want to perform a cancel-based incomplete database recovery first using RMAN to restore the data files and then using SQL*Plus to recover the data files.

Solution

The following example restores from the latest RMAN backup in preparation for an SQL*Plus cancel-based recovery:

```
$ rman target /
RMAN> startup mount;
RMAN> restore database; # restore database from last backup
```

Once your database is restored, you can start an SQL*Plus session and initiate a cancel-based recovery, as shown here:

```
$ sqlplus / as sysdba
SQL> recover database until cancel;
```

You will now be prompted by SQL*Plus to manually apply each archived redo log file. The following is the prompt that you'll get for each log file:

```
Specify log: {<RET>=suggested | filename | AUTO | CANCEL}
```

Hit the Return/Enter key until you arrive at the archived redo log file where you want to stop the recovery process. When you want to stop the recovery process, type the CANCEL keyword, as shown:

```
CANCEL
```

You should see a message indicating media recovery has been canceled:

```
Media recovery cancelled.
```

You can now open your database with the open resetlogs command:

```
SQL> alter database open resetlogs;
```

How It Works

SQL*Plus cancel-based incomplete database recovery is similar to the RMAN log sequence–based incomplete database recovery described in Recipe 12-3. The only difference is that you're using SQL*Plus to initiate the recovery process and you're manually instructing Oracle at which log to cancel the recovery.

Sometimes it's desirable to use SQL*Plus cancel-based recovery. For example, you may want to view the name and location of each log file before it is applied. Why would you want to view each file name? Sometimes DBAs are paranoid and stressed out in recovery situations, and they feel a little warmer and fuzzier when they can first view the archived redo log file name before applying it.

■ **Note**   With cancel-based recovery, you also have the option of manually entering an archived redo log file or online redo log file name and location.

12-5. Using LogMiner to Find an SCN
Problem

A user accidentally dropped a table. You want to find the SCN associated with that drop statement so that you can restore the database to the SCN just prior to the accidental drop.

■ **Note**   To be able to mine redo for DML statements, you must have database supplemental logging enabled prior to when the archived redo log file was generated. However, LogMiner can search for DDL statements without having supplemental logging enabled.

Solution

Here are the steps for instructing LogMiner to analyze a specific set of archived redo log files for an SCN associated with a SQL statement:

1. Specify a set of archived redo log files for LogMiner to analyze.

2. Start LogMiner, and specify a data dictionary.

3. Perform analysis.

4. Stop the LogMiner session.

First you need to tell LogMiner which online redo log files or archived redo log files you want to analyze. In this scenario, we know the SQL statement that we're looking for is in the archived redo log file with a sequence number of 7.

```
$ sqlplus / as sysdba
SQL> exec dbms_logmnr.add_logfile(-
logfilename=>'/ora01/fra/O12C/archivelog/2012_08_08/o1_mf_1_7_825l7wob_.arc',-
options=>dbms_logmnr.addfile);
```

If you want to mine multiple online redo log files, you can add more using DBMS_LOGMNR.ADD_LOGFILE as follows:

```
SQL> exec dbms_logmnr.add_logfile(-
logfilename=>'/ora01/fra/O12C/archivelog/2012_08_08/o1_mf_1_8_825l7xmh_.arc',-
options=>dbms_logmnr.addfile);
```

You can view which log files will be analyzed by the current LogMiner session by querying the V$LOGMNR_LOGS view:

```
SQL> select log_id, filename from v$logmnr_logs;
```

LogMiner needs access to the data dictionary to translate object IDs into object names. This example starts LogMiner and specifies that we want to use the current data dictionary for metadata information:

```
SQL> exec dbms_logmnr.start_logmnr(-
    options=>dbms_logmnr.dict_from_online_catalog);
```

After you've started LogMiner, you can query the V$LGMNR_CONTENTS view for the SCN of the transaction of interest. This example queries for an SCN associated with a drop of the PAYROLL table:

```
SELECT
 operation
,scn
,sql_redo
FROM v$logmnr_contents
WHERE table_name='PAYROLL';
```

Here is some sample output:

```
OPERATION        SCN SQL_REDO
---------  ---------- ---------------------------------------------------
DDL           1060896 create table payroll(payroll_id number);
DDL           1060905 ALTER TABLE "MV_MAINT"."PAYROLL" RENAME TO
"BIN$xsfqJXV6Pq7gQ4TQTwpu3g==$0" ;

DDL           1060908 drop table payroll AS "BIN$xsfqJXV6Pq7gQ4TQTwpu3g==$0" ;
```

After you've found the SCN of interest, you can end your LogMiner session by calling dbms_logmnr as follows:

```
SQL> exec dbms_logmnr.end_logmnr();
```

How It Works

You can use LogMiner to find SCNs associated with DML and DDL statements. LogMiner requires supplemental logging to be enabled to display information about DML statements. Enable supplemental logging by issuing the following SQL:

```
$ sqlplus / as sysdba
SQL> alter database add supplemental log data;
```

By default, Oracle is not enabled with supplemental logging. LogMiner requires that supplemental logging be enabled prior to the log files' being created so it can extract SCNs associated with DML commands. Once supplemental logging is enabled, you can use LogMiner to analyze and retrieve information such as an SCN associated with a particular DML statement.

You can analyze redo logs based on a time range, schema, SCN range, and so on. See the Oracle Database Utilities Guide for full details on how to use LogMiner. You can download all of Oracle's documentation from the http://otn.oracle.com website.

■ **Tip** Consider using flashback drop, flashback table, flashback query, and/or restore table to restore and recover an erroneously dropped table or deleted data. Chapter 13 describes these techniques in full detail.

12-6. Performing Change/SCN-Based Recovery
Problem

You want to perform an incomplete database recovery to a particular database SCN.

Solution

After establishing the SCN to which you want to restore, use the until scn clause to restore up to, but not including, the SCN specified. The following example restores all transactions that have an SCN that is less than 1399500:

```
$ rman target /
RMAN> startup mount;
RMAN> restore database until scn 1399500;
RMAN> recover database until scn 1399500;
RMAN> alter database open resetlogs;
```

If everything went well, you should now see output similar to this:

```
Statement processed
```

You can also use set until scn within a run{} block to perform SCN-based incomplete database recovery without having to repeat the SCN number for each command:

```
$ rman target /
RMAN> startup mount;
RMAN> run{
set until scn 1399500;
```

```
restore database;
recover database;
}
RMAN> alter database open resetlogs;
```

If everything went well, you should now see output similar to this:

```
Statement processed
```

How It Works

SCN-based incomplete database recovery works in situations where you know the SCN value up to where you want to end the restore and recovery session. RMAN will recover up to, but not including, the specified SCN. RMAN automatically terminates the restore process when it reaches the specified SCN.

To view the current SCN of your database, query the V$DATABASE view:

```
SQL> select current_scn from v$database;
```

You can view historical SCN information for your database in several ways:

- As detailed in Recipe 12-5, you can use LogMiner to determine an SCN associated with a DDL or DML statement.

- You can look in the alert.log file.

- You can look in your trace files.

- You can query the FIRST_CHANGE# column of VLOG, VLOG_HISTORY, and V$ARCHIVED_LOG.

If you have set the initialization parameter log_checkpoints_to_alert to TRUE, then every time a log switch occurs, Oracle will write the SCN of each checkpoint to your target database alert.log file. This feature can be handy when trying to determine historical checkpoint SCN activity. Here's an excerpt from the alert.log file that shows the SCN of a checkpoint for a database that has log_checkpoints_to_alert set to TRUE:

```
Beginning log switch checkpoint up to RBA [0x15.2.10], SCN: 1063491
```

You can also view SCN information by querying data dictionary views. For example, you can query V$ARCHIVED_LOG to display the first SCN and time that it was generated, as shown here:

```
SELECT
 sequence#
,first_change#
,first_time
FROM v$archived_log
ORDER BY first_time;
```

Once you determine the SCN to which you want to recover, you can use the until scn clause of the restore and recover commands to perform incomplete database recovery.

12-7. Recovering to a Restore Point

Problem

You want to restore and recover to a restore point.

Solution

Before you can restore to a restore point, you must have previously created a restore point via the create restore point command. Once you've done this, you can use the until restore point clause of the restore command. For demonstration purposes, we create a restore point to be used in this example:

```
SQL> create restore point MY_RP;
```

You can also view the SCN assigned to your restore point(s):

```
SQL> select name, scn from v$restore_point;
```

This example restores and recovers to the MY_RP restore point:

```
$ rman target /
RMAN> startup mount;
RMAN> restore database until restore point MY_RP;
RMAN> recover database until restore point MY_RP;
RMAN> alter database open resetlogs;
```

If everything went as planned, you should see this message:

```
Statement processed
```

Alternatively, you can use the set until command within a run{} block to specify a target restore point. The restore and recover commands will perform the incomplete database recovery up to the specified restore point:

```
$ rman target /
RMAN> startup mount;
RMAN> run{
set until restore point MY_RP;
restore database;
recover database;
}
RMAN> alter database open resetlogs;
```

If everything worked okay, you should see this message:

```
Statement processed
```

How It Works

A restore point records the SCN of the database at the time the restore point was created. The restore point acts like a synonym for the particular SCN. It allows you to restore and recover to an SCN without having to specify a number. RMAN will restore and recover up to, but not including, the SCN associated with the restore point.

You can view restore point information in the V$RESTORE_POINT view. That view contains information such as NAME, SCN, TIME, and DATABASE_INCARNATION#. Normal restore points are stored in the control file and will eventually age out. Normally there's no need to drop a normal restore point.

If you need to keep a restore point indefinitely, then use a guaranteed restore point:

```
SQL> create restore point MY_G_RP guarantee flashback database;
```

The main difference between a guaranteed restore point and normal restore point is that a guaranteed restore point is not eventually aged out of the control file. A guaranteed restore point will persist until you drop it. If you do need to drop a restore point, you can do so as follows:

```
SQL> drop restore point MY_G_RP;
```

You can view the details of a restore point with this query:

```
SELECT name, scn, time, guarantee_flashback_database
FROM v$restore_point;
```

Guaranteed restore points do require a fast recovery area. However, for incomplete recovery using a guaranteed restore point, you do not have to have flashback database enabled. For a database that does not have flashback database enabled, if you have no guaranteed restore points, your database will indicate that flashback is off:

```
SQL> select flashback_on from v$database;

FLASHBACK_ON
------------------
NO
```

However, after you create a guaranteed restore point (in a database with flashback disabled), the flashback_on column indicates that you can flash back to a restore point only:

```
SQL> select flashback_on from v$database;

FLASHBACK_ON
------------------
RESTORE POINT ONLY
```

12-8. Restoring a Noarchivelog Mode Database

Problem

You used RMAN to back up a database in noarchivelog mode. You now need to restore this database from an RMAN backup.

Solution

When you restore a database in noarchivelog mode, you can choose to use a backup control file or the current control file. You can run the following query to verify the type of control file you used to mount your database:

```
SQL> select open_mode, controlfile_type from v$database;
```

Here is some sample output:

```
OPEN_MODE              CONTROL
-------------------    -------
READ WRITE             CURRENT
```

Using Backup Control File

Our recommended approach is to first restore the control file that was backed up at the same time your noarchivelog mode database was backed up. This way the control file has an SCN that is consistent with the data file SCNs. After you restore the control file, you can then restore the data files and open your database with the open resetlogs command. For example:

```
$ rman target /
RMAN> startup nomount;
RMAN> restore controlfile from autobackup;
RMAN> alter database mount;
RMAN> restore database;
RMAN> alter database open resetlogs;
```

You should see the following message after opening your database with the resetlogs option:

```
Statement processed
```

■ **Note** In this scenario, if you don't restore the control file, then you won't be able to open your database. This is because the control file needs to be in sync with the data files.

Using Current Control File

If you don't restore your control file from the backup, you will have to perform a few extra steps. This example does not restore the control file (uses current control file) and uses SQL*Plus to cancel out of the recovery session:

```
$ rman target /
RMAN> startup mount;
RMAN> restore database;
RMAN> alter database open resetlogs;
```

At this point, you'll get an error message indicating that the resetlogs option is valid only after an incomplete database recovery:

```
ORA-01139: RESETLOGS option only valid after an incomplete database recovery
```

Perform the following steps from SQL*Plus to open your database:

```
SQL> recover database until cancel;
```

You should now be prompted as follows:

```
Specify log: {<RET>=suggested | filename | AUTO | CANCEL}
```

Immediately type in CANCEL. At this point, you should see a message indicating media recovery has been canceled, as shown here:

```
Media recovery cancelled.
```

You can now open your database with the alter database open resetlogs command, as shown here:

```
SQL> alter database open resetlogs;
```

You should see the following message after opening your database with the resetlogs option:

```
Database altered.
```

How It Works

Sometimes in test environments you may not enable archiving. However, it is still possible to use RMAN to back up the database as long as the database is placed in mount mode first.

```
$ rman target /
RMAN> shutdown immediate;
RMAN> startup mount;
RMAN> backup database;
RMAN> alter database open;
```

You can restore a noarchivelog database only to the point at which it was backed up. There is no roll forward of transactions because there are no archived redo log files to apply. This type of restore and recovery is commonly used to reset a test environment database to a baseline point in time.

Since the online redo log files are not included in the RMAN backup, you must issue alter database open resetlogs to create new online redo log files, as well as to synchronize the control files and data files in terms of their checkpoint SCNs.

12-9. Recovering to a Previous Incarnation

Problem

You experience a media failure immediately following an open resetlogs command. For example, you're faced with this scenario:

1. You've recently performed an incomplete recovery and opened your database with the open resetlogs command.

2. Before you can take another backup, you experience a media failure. You determine that you need to restore and recover the database to a point in time prior to the time you opened the database with the open resetlogs command.

3. You initiate a point in time recovery prior to the time the database was opened with the open resetlogs command:

```
RMAN> restore database until time
    "to_date('28-aug-2012 08:22:00','dd-mon-rrrr hh24:mi:ss')";
```

When restoring datafiles, the prior command throws this error:

```
RMAN-03002: failure of restore command at ...
RMAN-20207: UNTIL TIME or RECOVERY WINDOW is before RESETLOGS time
```

In this situation you must restore and recover to a previous incarnation of your database.

Solution

Before starting, ensure that you set the NLS_DATE_FORMAT variable so that you can see the time component in RMAN's output:

```
$ export NLS_DATE_FORMAT="DD-MON-RRRR HH24:MI:SS"
```

This will allow you to see the time component in RMAN's output.

Step 1: Run the List Incarnation Command

You have to restore a control file that knows about the incarnation of the database to which you want to restore. Therefore, you first need to determine which incarnation you will be restoring to. Run the following command to display incarnation information:

```
RMAN> list incarnation;
```

Here is some sample output:

```
DB Key  Inc Key DB Name  DB ID            STATUS  Reset SCN  Reset Time
------- ------- -------- ---------------- --- ---------- ----------
14      14      012C     3415120612       PARENT  1376388    28-aug-2012 08:19
15      15      012C     3415120612       CURRENT 1377144    28-aug-2012 08:35
```

For this example, we want to restore to the time of 8:22 (which would be incarnation 14, which is prior to the current incarnation of 15).

Step 2: Shut Down the Database

```
RMAN> shutdown immediate;
```

Step 3: Start the Database in Nomount Mode

If you're not using a recovery catalog, start up this way:

```
RMAN> startup nomount;
```

If you are using a recovery catalog, use this command:

```
RMAN> startup force nomount;
```

Step 4: Restore the Control File to the Desired Time

This example assumes the use of an FRA and the auto backup of the control file is enabled:

```
RMAN> restore controlfile from autobackup until time
      "to_date('28-aug-2012 08:22:00','dd-mon-rrrr hh24:mi:ss')";
```

If you're not using an FRA and the auto backup of the control file, see Chapter 10 for details on restoring the control file.

Step 5: Mount the Database

```
RMAN> alter database mount;
```

Step 6: Set the Database to the Desired Incarnation

From the output in step 1, for this scenario 14 is the desired incarnation.

```
RMAN> reset database to incarnation 14;
```

Step 7: Restore and Recover the Database

Now restore and recover the database to the same time as you specified when restoring the control file:

```
RMAN> restore database until time
      "to_date('28-aug-2012 08:22:00','dd-mon-rrrr hh24:mi:ss')";
RMAN> recover database until time
      "to_date('28-aug-2012 08:22:00','dd-mon-rrrr hh24:mi:ss')";
RMAN> alter database open resetlogs;
```

When successful, you should see this message:

```
Statement processed
```

■ **Note**   You can restore until a time, SCN, sequence, or restore point.

How It Works

Prior to Oracle Database 10g, it was quite unwieldy (often requiring the assistance of Oracle Support) to restore to previous incarnation of your database. In older versions of Oracle it was mandatory to back up your database immediately after opening it with an open resetlogs operation. Those requirements have been somewhat relaxed, as it is now possible to restore and recover to a prior incarnation.

Anytime you restore your database with a backup control file or perform an incomplete database recovery, you are required to use the `alter database open resetlogs` command to open your database. This resets the online redo log sequence to 1 and creates a new version of your database. Oracle calls this fresh version of your database a new incarnation.

You can view incarnation information by querying the V$DATABASE_INCARNATION view. You can also view database incarnation data from within RMAN by issuing the following:

```
RMAN> list incarnation of database;
```

In rare situations, you may find that you need to restore to a previous incarnation of your database. For example, there may be data that is contained only in a prior incarnation, and the only way to retrieve it is to restore and recover to that previous incarnation of your database. The key here is that when you restore and recover to a prior incarnation, you need to ensure that the control file that you restore is aware of the particular database incarnation that you want to restore.

12-10. Performing Tablespace Point-in-Time Recovery
Problem

A rogue developer thought he was in a test environment and issued commands to delete data from several tables in one tablespace. It turns out he was in the production environment. You want to use tablespace point-in-time recovery (TSPITR) to restore your tablespace to the point in time just before the erroneous DML was issued.

■ **Tip** Before using TSPITR, consider other forms of recovery, such as flashing back a table to before drop or before an SCN, or restoring a single table. See Chapter 13 for full details.

Solution

This recipe shows how to perform fully automated RMAN tablespace point-in-time recovery. Here are the steps:

1. Determine the time to which you want to perform TSPITR.

2. Determine and resolve any dependencies to objects in tablespaces not included in the TSPITR.

3. Determine whether there are objects that will not be recovered.

4. Create a destination on disk to temporarily hold the auxiliary database.

5. Run the `recover tablespace until` command.

6. Back up the restored tablespace and alter it online.

Step 1: Determine the Time to Perform TSPITR

You need to decide what time or SCN to which you want to restore the tablespace. In most scenarios this will be just prior to the point at which the erroneous drop or delete was issued.

Step 2: Determine and Resolve Dependencies

If objects in the tablespaces involved with the TSPITR have constraint relationships to objects not in tablespaces included in the TSPITR, you will not be able to perform a successful TSPITR. Also no SYS-owned objects should reside in a tablespace involved with a TSPITR.

You can use the TRANSPORT_SET_VIOLATIONS view to help you determine whether there are constraint dependencies to objects in tablespaces not included in the TSPITR. Here's a sample query that checks to see whether there are any dependencies to the tools tablespace:

```
$ sqlplus / as sysdba
SQL> execute dbms_tts.transport_set_check('TOOLS', TRUE);
SQL> select * from transport_set_violations;
```

If there are dependencies, consider including dropping or disabling the constraints. Another option would be to include the dependent tablespace in the TSPITR.

■ **Tip**   You cannot perform a TSPITR on the default permanent tablespace for a database.

Step 3: Determine Which Objects Will Not Be Recovered

For objects in tablespaces involved with the TSPITR, you'll lose any transactions that were created after the point to which you restore. If you need to preserve objects created after the time to which you are going to restore, then you'll need to use the Data Pump utility or the export utility to save them (before performing TSPITR). After you have performed TSPITR, you can import these objects.

You can query the TS_PITR_OBJECTS_TO_BE_DROPPED view to help identify objects that need to be preserved. This query identifies objects created after the time to which the TSPITR will be performed:

```
SELECT owner, name, tablespace_name
FROM ts_pitr_objects_to_be_dropped
WHERE tablespace_name ='TOOLS'
AND creation_time > to_date('28-aug-2012 11:06:00','dd-mon-rrrr hh24:mi:ss');
```

Step 4: Create an Auxiliary Destination

First ensure that you have an area on disk that will serve as a temporary container for an auxiliary database. This area will need enough space for a system, undo, and temporary tablespace. We recommend you have at least 1 GB of space in your auxiliary destination.

```
$ mkdir /orahome/oracle/aux
```

Step 5: Run the Recover Command

You can now perform a fully automated TSPITR. You can restore until a time, SCN, or sequence. Notice that your database is open during the TSPITR. In this example, we restore the tools tablespace up to, but not including, the time specified:

```
$ rman target /
RMAN> recover tablespace tools until time
```

```
"to_date('28-aug-2012 11:06:00','dd-mon-rrrr hh24:mi:ss')"
auxiliary destination '/orahome/oracle/aux';
```

In the prior command, ensure you use the recover command (and not restore)! You can recover to an SCN, log sequence number, or time. Also, don't forget to specify the auxiliary destination. RMAN will now perform a fully automated TSPITR recovery of the specified tablespaces.

You should see a large amount of output as RMAN creates an auxiliary database and automatically performs all steps associated with TSPITR. After successful completion, you should see message output similar to the following:

```
Removing automatic instance
Automatic instance removed
```

Step 6: Back Up the Tablespace and Alter It Online

Once the TSPITR completes, you must back up the recovered tablespace and bring it online:

```
RMAN> backup tablespace tools;
RMAN> alter tablespace tools online;
```

If you're using Oracle Database 11g or lower, then you must use the sql command to run most SQL statements from RMAN:

```
RMAN> sql 'alter tablespace tools online';
```

How It Works

RMAN TSPITR allows you to recover one or more tablespaces back to a time that is different from the other tablespaces in your database. Performing TSPITR is useful in the following situations:

- When you have a tablespace or set of them that contains objects owned by only one schema. If there are undesired DML statements that affect several of the schema's objects, you have the option of using TSPITR to restore the schema's objects to a previous point in time.

- There have been erroneous DML statements that affect only a subset of tables isolated to a few tablespaces.

For example, say you have two tablespaces, p_dt and p_idx, and all of the objects in those two tablespaces are owned by prod_own. If there were undesirable DML statements that were issued against tables owned by prod_own, you could use TSPITR to restore and recover to just prior to when the bad SQL was run. In this example, we restore the two tablespaces back to just before SCN 1432:

```
$ mkdir /orahome/oracle/aux
$ rman target /
RMAN> recover tablespace p_dt, p_idx until SCN 1432
      auxiliary destination '/orahome/oracle/aux';
```

You should now see quite a number of RMAN messages displaying the status of each operation. Once it is complete, back up the recovered tablespaces and bring them online:

```
RMAN> backup tablespace p_dt, p_idx;
RMAN> alter tablespace p_dt online;
RMAN> alter tablespace p_idx online;
```

Or when using Oracle Database 11g or lower, use this syntax:

```
RMAN> sql 'alter tablespace p_dt online';
RMAN> sql 'alter tablespace p_idx online';
```

■ **Caution** If you are not using a recovery catalog, you can perform TSPITR only once on a tablespace. You will be allowed to perform another TSPITR only from a backup taken after the first TSPITR was performed. This is because after performing TSPITR, the control file has no record of the previous incarnation of the tablespace you recovered. Therefore, you won't be able to recover this tablespace again from the backup taken before TSPITR was performed. However, when using a recovery catalog, you can "cry mulligan" and perform multiple TSPITRs if you discover that you restored your tablespace(s) to the wrong point. Therefore, we recommend you use a recovery catalog if you foresee the need to perform multiple TSPITRs on a tablespace.

RMAN performs many tedious tasks for you with automated TSPITR. Here are the steps that RMAN performs for you:

1. Creates an auxiliary instance, starts it, and connects to it

2. Takes offline tablespaces that are involved with TSPITR

3. Restores the backup control file that corresponds to the target restore time

4. Restores data files to a destination specified by your AUXILIARY DESTINATION

5. Recovers restored data files in an auxiliary location

6. Opens an auxiliary database with the resetlogs command

7. Exports the auxiliary data dictionary metadata about recovered tablespaces and shuts down the auxiliary database

8. Issues a switch command on the target database to update the control file to point at the recovered auxiliary data files

9. Imports objects associated with recovered tablespaces into the target database

10. Deletes the auxiliary data files

After step 10 is complete, your target database should have the tablespaces recovered to the point listed in the recover command. The rest of the tablespaces in your database should be as they were before you initiated the TSPITR. You need to back up any tablespaces involved in the TSPITR and then alter them online.

Many limitations are involved with TSPITR. Here are some situations where you cannot use TSPITR:

- If the database is not running in archivelog mode or is missing required archive redo logs

- Attempting to recover a tablespace that was renamed to a point in time before it was renamed; you must use the prior name of the tablespace to perform TSPITR

- If there are constraints on objects that refer to objects in other tablespaces, you must perform TSPITR on all tablespaces involved

- Cannot perform TSPITR on the default tablespace for your database

- Cannot perform TSPITR on tablespaces that contain materialized views or partitioned tables unless all of the associated objects are contained within the tablespaces being recovered

- Tablespace cannot contain undo or rollback segments

- Tablespace cannot contain objects owned by SYS such as PL/SQL packages, Java classes, and so on

---

■ **Tip** A wide variety of features are available with TSPITR. This recipe covers only the automated RMAN tablespace point-in-time recovery. For complete details on all features of TSPITR, see the Oracle Backup and Recovery User's Guide.

12-11. Recovering a Subset of Data Files
Problem

You want to perform incomplete recovery on a subset of data files in your database.

Solution

The basic procedure is to determine which datafiles you don't want to restore and recover and then use `alter database datafile ... offline for drop` for the data files to be excluded.

■ **Caution** The data files you offline drop using this procedure will not be available for subsequent restore and recovery operations.

Here are the RMAN commands to perform an incomplete recovery on a subset of data files in your database:

```
$ rman target /
RMAN> startup mount;
```

Use the RMAN `report schema` command to identify which data files you do not want to restore and recover. You can also query V$DATAFILE for the data file details. In this example, the data file 5 is taken offline before the restore and recovery:

```
RMAN> alter database datafile 5 offline for drop;
```

If you're using Oracle Database 11g or lower, you must use the `sql` command to run the prior command:

```
RMAN> sql 'alter database datafile 5 offline for drop';
```

Next restore and recover the database:

```
RMAN> restore database until sequence 5;
RMAN> recover database until sequence 5;
RMAN> alter database open resetlogs;
```

How It Works

This type of recovery is used sometimes if you need to restore and recover only part of your database. For example, if some data is accidentally modified in your production database, you can use this recovery to do the following:

1. Copy production RMAN backup files to a nonproduction database server

2. On the non-production database server, restore and recover just the system, sysaux, undo, and other data files that you're interested in to a point in time just before the data was erroneously modified

3. Export the data out of the database's tablespaces to a point in time

4. Use the exported data to fix data in your production database

---

■ **Note**   Consider using a tablespace point-in-time recovery to restore and recover specific tablespaces to a previous point in time (see Recipe 12-10 for details).

12-12. Performing Incomplete Recovery on a Pluggable Database

Problem

You want to restore a pluggable database to a prior point in time.

Solution

You can restore a pluggable database to a prior SCN, log sequence number, restore point, or timestamp. To do this you must be connected to the root container database with sysdba or sysbackup privileges. You cannot perform this operation while connected as SYS to the pluggable database. The steps for an incomplete recovery of a PDB are as follows:

1. Close the PDB.

2. Specify a point in time in the past using an SCN, log sequence number, restore point, or timestamp.

3. Issue the RESTORE and RECOVER commands.

4. Open the PDB with the OPEN RESETLOGS clause

This example follows the prior steps and performs an incomplete recovery on a pluggable database by specifying an SCN for a prior point in the past:

```
ALTER PLUGGABLE DATABASE salespdb CLOSE;
run {
set until scn 2044500;
restore pluggable database salespdb;
recover pluggable database salespdb;
}
```

Here is a small snippet of the output produced:

```
channel ORA_AUX_DISK_1: starting datafile backup set restore
channel ORA_AUX_DISK_1: specifying datafile(s) to restore from backup set
```

After the PDB has been restored and recovered to the specified point, you must open the PDB with the OPEN RESETLOGS clause

```
ALTER PLUGGABLE DATABASE salespdb OPEN RESETLOGS;
```

If successful, you should see this message:

```
Statement processed
```

The OPEN RESETLOGS in this situation only applies to the PDB. This syntax is required to open the PDB and create a new incarnation of it. It does not reset the online logs for the root container database nor create a new incarnation for the root container database. You can check on the incarnation status of the PDB by querying:

```
select pdb_incarnation#
from v$pdb_incarnation
where status = 'CURRENT'
and con_id = <container_ID>;
```

How It Works

Restoring a pluggable database to a prior point in time is very similar to restoring a non-pluggable database to a previous point in time. The main difference is that you must use the PLUGGABLE clause and specify a specific PDB. You do not have to shut down the parent root container database or any other pluggable databases in the CDB. In other words you can perform an incomplete recovery on an individual pluggable database without impacting the availability of any other databases within the CDB.

When performing a point in time recovery on a PDB, RMAN first restores the PDB data files from the appropriate backup. To perform a PDB point in time recovery, RMAN requires a copy of the root container's undo tablespace as it was for the specified point in time in the past. To accomplish this RMAN creates a temporary auxiliary database which minimally consists of the root container's undo, system, and sysaux tablespaces.

If you're using a FRA, RMAN will create the auxiliary database data files in the FRA in the <FRA>/<SID>/datafile directory. Make sure you have enough space allocated and free in your FRA to accommodate the prior mentioned tablespaces' data files. If you don't have enough space, an ORA-19809: limit exceeded for recovery files error will be thrown.

If you're not using a FRA, RMAN will create the auxiliary database data files in the location specified by the AUXILIARY DESTINATION clause. Again, you need to ensure you have enough disk space in auxiliary destination to allow for the restoration of the auxiliary database.

After RMAN is finished with the PDB point in time recovery, the auxiliary instance is shutdown. Also, when the PDB is opened for use RMAN removes any data files that were restored for the auxiliary database.

12-13. Troubleshooting Incomplete Recovery

Problem

You're attempting to perform an incomplete recovery, and RMAN is returning the following error:

```
ORA-01139: RESETLOGS option only valid after an incomplete database recovery
```

You wonder how to go about determining what is wrong.

Solution

In many situations, problems with incomplete recovery are caused by omitting one of the required steps. Here is the correct sequence of steps for most incomplete recovery scenarios:

1. restore database until <specified point>;

2. recover database until <specified point>;

3. alter database open resetlogs;

The specified point in steps 1 and 2 should be identical. The specified point can be an SCN, a time, a log sequence number, or a restore point.

How It Works

Listed in Table 12-3 are some of the more common incorrect actions performed during an incomplete recovery. If you receive an error listed in the Result column, then ensure you are performing the correct steps for incomplete recovery (detailed in the Solution section of this recipe).

Table 12-3. Incomplete Recovery Incorrect Action and Result

Incorrect Action	Result
Issue `restore database until` and attempt to open database without issuing a corresponding `recover database until` command	ORA-01139: RESETLOGS option only valid after an incomplete database recovery
Restore all data files but perform recovery only on a subset of restored online data files	ORA-01139: RESETLOGS option only valid after an incomplete database recovery
Issue `restore database until`, and then attempt to open database with `alter database open` command	ORA-01113: file 1 needs media recovery
Issue the `alter database open` command after performing incomplete recovery.	ORA-01589: must use RESETLOGS or NORESETLOGS option for database open
The `restore database until <specified point>` command is greater than the `recover database until <specified point>`	RMAN-06556: data file must be restored from backup older than SCN

When performing an incomplete recovery, before you can open the database with a resetlogs option, the checkpoint SCN for all online, read-write datafiles must be identical. You can view the data file checkpoint SCNs via this query:

```
SELECT
 file#
,fuzzy
,status
,checkpoint_change#
,to_char(checkpoint_time,'dd-mon-rrrr hh24:mi:ss')
,error
FROM v$datafile_header;
```

After you open your database with the resetlogs clause, the checkpoint SCN in the control file will be synchronized with the checkpoint SCN in the data file headers.

Performing Flashback Recovery

In Oracle Database 10g Release 1, Oracle introduced a new feature: flashback. Actually, the term is used in three different contexts, making the usage somewhat confusing. There is also a similar-sounding feature—flashback queries—starting with Oracle9i Database, and this doesn't help matters much.

The flashback concepts introduced in Oracle Database 10g are different from the ones introduced in Oracle9i Database. The 10g version of the term—flashback—actually refers to an aid to recoverability. In this chapter, you will learn about the various flavors of flashback and how to use each one. You will also learn how to recover a specific table from the backups without having to recover an entire database.

Introducing Flashback

There are four flavors of flashback:

- Flashing back a database
- Undropping a table
- Flashing back a table
- Recovering a single table from backup

Flashing Back a Database

Many times you might need to roll back the database to a point in time in the past. In earlier releases, this functionality was present but in a very different way. For instance, in Oracle9i Database and prior versions, you would reinstate an older backup and then roll it forward to a point in time in the past. For instance, suppose today is January 21 and the time is 10 a.m. The database backups are taken at 5 a.m. every day. If you wanted to roll the database back to 10 p.m. January 20, you would restore the backup taken at 5 a.m. January 20 and then apply all the archived redo logs to restore it to 10 p.m. But what if you made a mistake in your calculation and the data you wanted to recover was deleted at 9 p.m.? After you recovered the database up to 10 p.m., all your work was in vain. There is no going back to 9 p.m.; you would have to start the process again from the beginning—restore the backup of 5 a.m. and then roll forward all the changes by applying logs up to 9 p.m.

Oracle Database 10g changed all that by introducing a feature called flashback database. You enable flashback on the database. This causes additional logs to be created during the database operation. These logs, called flashback logs, are generated along with the regular archived logs. The flashback logs record changes to the database blocks exclusively for the purpose of rolling back the block changes, so they are different from archived logs. When you flash the database back to a point in the past, these flashback logs are read and applied to the database blocks to undo the changes. The entire database is transported to that point in time.

■ **Note**   The entire database is rolled back during flashback database; you can't perform flashback on individual tables or tablespaces.

Undropping a Table

This has happened to the best of us—you dropped a very important table. What can you do? In versions prior to Oracle Database 10g Release 1, there wasn't any choice other than to restore the backup of the corresponding tablespace to another database, recover the tablespace, export the table, and import the table to the production database. These tasks are time-consuming and risky, and the table is unavailable throughout them.

Starting with Oracle Database 10g, the process is less threatening. When the table is dropped, it's not really erased from the database; rather, it is renamed and placed in a logical container called the recycle bin, similar to the Recycle Bin found in Windows. After you realize the mistake, you can reinstate the dropped table using only one simple command. Who says you can't revive the dead?

Flashing Back a Table

The Oracle9i Database introduced a feature called flashback query. When the data in the database changes, the past images of the changed data are stored in special segments called undo segments. The reason for storing this data is simple—if the changed data is not committed yet, the database must reconstruct the prechange data to present a read-consistent view to the other users selecting the same data item. When the change is committed, the need for the past image is gone, but it's not discarded. The space is reused if necessary. The reason for keeping it around is simple, too.

The read-consistency requirement does not stop after the data changes are committed. For instance, a long-running query needs a read-consistent view when the query started, which could be well in the past. If the query refers to the data that might have been changed and committed in the recent past, after the query has started, the query must get the past image, not the image now, even though it is committed. If the query finds that the past data is no longer available, it throws the dreaded ORA-1555 Snapshot Too Old error.

Anyway, what does the ORA-1555 error have to do with flashback operation? Plenty. Since the past image of the data is available in the undo segment for a while, why should a long-running query be the only one to have fun? Any query can benefit from that past image, too. That thought gave rise to flashback queries in Oracle9i Database where you could query data as of a time in the past. With Oracle Database 10g, that functionality was made richer with flashback version queries, where you can pull the changes made to the row data from the undo segments, as long as they are available in the undo segments, of course. And when you pull the older versions of the table, you can effectively reinstate the entire table to a point in time in the past using these past images. This is known as flashing back the table.

Recovering a Table

Suppose you have dropped a table. Now it is gone from the recycle bin, so you can't get it out from there using the undrop process mentioned earlier in this section. The only option is to get it from the backup. However, database recovery recovers the entire database from backup and will overwrite *all* data as of that point in time in the past. When all you want is to recover a single table from the backup, you can't just surgically extract the table from the backup. Instead, you have to create a temporary instance and recover the tablespace containing the table to the very point just prior to the time the table was dropped. However, you need to restore and recover some other mandatory tablespaces, such as system, sysaux, and one or more undo tablespaces. Once they are restored, you will need to recover that temporary database to the required time, extract the table using Data Pump, and import it into the main database. All this is a lot of work.

Oracle Database 12.1 introduces a new feature to recover a single table, or even a single partition of a table from the backup. A single command accomplishes that objective. The job of recovering a single table is now much easier than before.

In this chapter, you will learn to use all four types of flashback operations.

13-1. Checking the Flashback Status of a Database
Problem

You want to check whether your database is flashback enabled.

Solution

The data dictionary view V$DATABASE contains information about the flashback status of the database. Check the column FLASHBACK_ON on that view to ascertain the flashback status:

```
SQL> select flashback_on from v$database;

FLASHBACK_ON
------------
YES
```

The output shows that the value of the column FLASHBACK_ON is set to YES, which means the database is running in flashback mode. If the database is not in flashback mode, the query would have returned NO.

■ **Note**   Starting with Oracle 12.1, you can run SQL statements from the RMAN prompt, as well as from the SQL*Plus prompt. For simplicity and consistency with older releases, we execute SQL commands from SQL*Plus in this book.

How It Works

If the database is running in flashback mode, it generates additional files known as flashback logs, which record changes to the data blocks. These files are recorded in the fast recovery area, which was described in Chapter 3. In addition, the FLASHBACK_ON column will return a YES indicator so that you know for sure that flashback mode is enabled.

13-2. Enabling Flashback on a Database
Problem

You want to enable a database to flash back to a point in time in the past.

Solution

The database must be running in archivelog mode to enable flashback. The flashback-enabled database generates flashback logs, which are stored only in the fast recovery area (FRA), which used to be called Flash Recovery Area prior to Oracle Database 11g Release 2. So the FRA must be configured prior to enabling the flashback.

These flashback logs are generated in addition to the archived logs. Here are the steps to then follow to enable flashback on the database:

1. Make sure the FRA is defined in the database. To set up the FRA, check out Recipe 3-1. To find out whether the FRA is set, execute the following command via SQL*Plus while logged in as sys or any other sysdba account:

   ```
   SQL> show parameter db_recovery_file_dest
   ```

   If the value of the parameter db_recovery_file_dest is set, then the FRA is defined to that location. Here is a sample output:

   ```
   SQL> show parameter db_recovery_file_dest
   ```

NAME	TYPE	VALUE
db_recovery_file_dest	string	+FRA
db_recovery_file_dest_size	big integer	12G

2. From the output, you'll notice that the parameter db_recovery_file_dest is set to +FRA, which is the location of the fast recovery area. The second parameter, db_recovery_file_dest_size, shows the size of the fast recovery area.

3. Make sure the database is in archivelog mode. You check the mode by issuing the following SQL:

   ```
   SQL> select log_mode from v$database;

   LOG_MODE
   ----------
   ARCHIVELOG
   ```

4. The value of the column LOG_MODE is ARCHIVELOG, which indicates the database is running in archivelog mode.

5. If the result of the query is different, as in the example shown here, then the database is not running in archivelog mode:

   ```
   SQL> select log_mode from v$database;

   LOG_MODE
   ------------
   NOARCHIVELOG
   ```

6. To enable archivelog mode, follow these steps:

   a. Shut down the database by issuing the following SQL statement:

   ```
   SQL> shutdown immediate
   ```

   b. Start the database in mount mode by issuing the following SQL statement:

   ```
   SQL> startup mount
   ```

c.   Enable archivelog mode by issuing the following command:

```
SQL> alter database archivelog;
```

d.   At this point, you can open the database for business, but since your objective is to enable flashback, go to the next step.

7.   Make sure the database is in either mounted or open state by issuing the following SQL statement:

```
SQL> select OPEN_MODE from v$database;

OPEN_MODE
---------
MOUNTED
```

8.   If the database is not even mounted, then mount it:

```
SQL> alter database mount;

Database mounted.
```

The final line confirms that the database is now mounted.

■ **Note**   In some earlier versions of the Oracle Database, you could enable flashback mode only when the database is mounted, not open.

---

9.   Enable flashback for the database by issuing the following SQL statement:

```
SQL> alter database flashback on;

Database altered.
```

The database is now in flashback mode. You can open the database now (if not open already).

How It Works

When the database is in flashback mode, it generates flashback logs as a result of changes to the data. These flashback logs are later used to roll the database to a previous state. However, the flashback logs capture only the changes to the data blocks, which may not be enough for rebuilding a consistent database. In addition to the flashback logs, the rollback process needs archived logs. Therefore, the database must also be in archivelog mode to enable flashback.

The flashback logs are stored in the fast recovery area, which is described in Chapter 3. The fast recovery area is the only place the flashback logs can be stored. Therefore, it's necessary to enable a fast recovery area with the appropriate size to enable flashback in the database. You can learn how to size the fast recovery area in Recipe 3-16. One of the inputs to the calculations is the estimated size of the total flashback logs generated. You will learn how to estimate that value in Recipe 13-8.

13-3. Disabling Flashback on a Database

Problem

You want to disable flashback mode for a database.

Solution

Disable flashback mode by issuing the following SQL statement:

```
SQL> alter database flashback off;
Database altered.
```

Now the database is running in nonflashback mode.

How It Works

When the database is taken out of flashback mode, the flashback logs are not generated anymore. You can check that the database has indeed been taken off flashback mode by issuing the following query:

```
SQL> select flashback_on from v$database;

FLASHBACK_ON
------------
NO
```

The result shows NO, confirming that the database is not running in flashback mode now.

13-4. Flashing Back a Database from RMAN

Problem

You want to flash a database back to a point in time in the past through RMAN.

Solution

When you want to flash the database back to a time in the past, you have a few choices in deciding when to flash back to. You can flash back to the following:

- A specific point in time, specified by date and time
- A specific SCN number
- The last resetlogs operation
- A named restore point

We describe each of these scenarios in the following sections. Each of the solutions, however, has some common tasks before and after the actual flashback.

Common Presteps

The following are the "common presteps" to follow for any type of full database flashback procedure:

1. Check how far back into the past you can flash back to. Refer to Recipe 13-6.

2. Connect to RMAN:

```
rman target=/
```

3. Shut the database down:

```
RMAN> shutdown immediate
```

4. Start the database in mount mode:

```
RMAN> startup mount
```

This completes the preflashback steps.

Common Poststep

After the flashback operation, you will open the database with the clause resetlogs, as shown in the following actions in RMAN:

```
RMAN> alter database open resetlogs;

database opened
```

It's important to open the database in resetlogs mode since the flashback operation performs a point-in-time recovery, which is a form of incomplete recovery. For more information about incomplete recovery, refer to Chapter 12.

Solution 1: Flashing Back to a Specific SCN

In this example, you will see how to flash back a database to a specific SCN, which is the most precise flashback procedure possible. Here are the steps to follow:

1. First, check the SCN of the database now. Connecting as sys or any other DBA account, issue the following SQL statement:

```
SQL> select current_scn
  2  from v$database;

CURRENT_SCN
-----------
    1137633
```

The output shows the current SCN is 1,137,633. You can flash back to an SCN prior to this number only.

2. Execute the "common presteps" 1 through 4.

3. Flash the database back to your desired SCN. For instance, to flash back to SCN 1,050,951, issue the following RMAN command:

```
RMAN> flashback database to scn 1050951;

Starting flashback at 03-AUG-12
using target database control file instead of recovery catalog
allocated channel: ORA_DISK_1
channel ORA_DISK_1: SID=16 device type=DISK

starting media recovery
media recovery complete, elapsed time: 00:00:01

Finished flashback at 03-AUG-12
```

This command flashed the database back to the desired SCN.

4. You can open the database now for regular operations by executing the "common poststep."

5. However, you may not be certain whether you have flashed back to the exact point in time you wanted to be at. To determine whether you have, you can open the database in read-only mode:

```
RMAN> alter database open read only;

Database opened.
```

6. Check the data in the table. For instance, the purpose of the flashback was to undo the changes done to the interest calculation table, so you can check the interest table to see whether the values are 0.

7. If you have not gone far back into the past, you can start the flashback process again to flash back to a different SCN. Start with step 2—shut down the database, start up in mount mode, and then flash back.

```
RMAN> flashback database to scn 2981100;
```

Note that you can use a SCN after the SCN you flashed back to earlier as shown here in this example. Obviously however, you can't flash back to an SCAN more than the current one; that will be akin to flashing back to the future.

8. Once again, open the database in read-only mode, and check the data to make sure you are at a point you want to be. If you are not there, you can redo the steps.

9. Once you are satisfied you have arrived at a point where you want to be, follow step 2 of the "common poststeps" to open the database for regular operation.

Now the database is at the point in time in the past you want to be.

Solution 2: Flashing Back to a Specific Time

You want to flash the database to a specific time, not an SCN. Here are the steps to follow:

1. Follow "common presteps" 1 through 4.

2. Use the following command to flash back to a time just two minutes ago. Since a day has 24 hours, with 60 minutes each, 2 minutes happen to be 2/60/24 of a day:

    ```
    RMAN> flashback database to time 'sysdate-2/60/24';

    Starting flashback at 03-AUG-12
    using channel ORA_DISK_1

    starting media recovery

    archived log for thread 1 with sequence 70 is already on disk as
    file +FRA/cdb1/archivelog/2012_07_22/thread_1_seq_70.279.789267613
    archived log for thread 1 with sequence 71 is already on disk as
    file +FRA/cdb1/archivelog/2012_07_22/thread_1_seq_71.280.789285641
    media recovery complete, elapsed time: 00:00:40
    Finished flashback at 03-AUG-12
    ```

3. If you want to flash back to a specific time, not in reference to a time such as sysdate, you can use the timestamp instead of a formula:

    ```
    RMAN> flashback database to time "to_date('08/03/2012 22:00:00','mm/dd/yyyyhh24:mi:ss')";
    ```

    This flashes the database back to that specific timestamp.

4. As in the first solution, you can open the database in read-only mode at this time to check whether you have traversed far enough into the past.

5. If you haven't, you can start the process once again—shut down immediately, start in mount mode, flash back to a different time, and then open the database in read-only mode.

6. Once you are satisfied you have arrived at the desired point in time, shut the database down and follow the "common poststep" to open the database for regular operation.

The database is now as of August 3rd, 2012 at 10:00:00 p.m.

Solution 3: Flashing Back to a Restore Point

In this solution, you will learn how to flash back the database to a restore point. You can learn about creating restore points in Recipe 13-9 and Recipe 13-10. Here are the steps to follow to flash back to a restore point:

1. Follow "common presteps" 1 through 4.

2. To flash back to a restore point named grp6, issue the following SQL:

    ```
    RMAN> flashback database to restore point grp6;

    Starting flashback at 03-AUG-12
    using channel ORA_DISK_1
    ```

```
starting media recovery

archived log for thread 1 with sequence 70 is already on disk as
file +FRA/cdb1/archivelog/2012_07_22/thread_1_seq_70.279.789267613
media recovery complete, elapsed time: 00:00:01
Finished flashback at 03-AUG-12
```

3. At this time you can open the database in read-only mode and check the data, as described in the first solution of this recipe. If the flashback is not far enough in the past, or too far, you can flash back to another restore point—grp5, for instance. In that case, you repeat the steps: shut down, start, and flash back. To flash back to restore point grp5, you issue the following RMAN command:

```
RMAN> flashback database to restore point grp5;
```

4. Execute the "common poststep" to open the database for normal operation.

The database is now as of the time when the restore point rp5 was created.

Solution 4: Flashing Back to Before the Last resetlogs Operation

You have opened the database with the resetlogs clause, and that was probably a mistake. Now you want to revert the changes to the last resetlogs operation. Here are the steps to accomplish that:

1. Execute the "common presteps" 1 through 4.

2. Use the following command to flash back the database to the last resetlog operation:

```
RMAN> flashback database to before resetlogs;

Starting flashback at 03-AUG-12
allocated channel: ORA_DISK_1
channel ORA_DISK_1: SID=17 device type=DISK

starting media recovery
media recovery complete, elapsed time: 00:00:01

Finished flashback at 03-AUG-12
```

3. The database has now been flashed back to the last restore point. Execute the "common poststep" to open the database for normal operation.

How It Works

When the database is in flashback mode, it generates special log files called flashback logs that can be used to flash back the database to a prior point in time. The flashback logs carry the SCN, allowing you to use the SCN as a measuring point to which to flash back. But SCNs are akin to the internal clock of the database, and they also relate to the wall clock. Therefore, when you issue the commands to flash back to a specific timestamp, Oracle automatically determines the SCN associated with the timestamp and rolls back to that SCN.

Similarly, restore points are merely pointers to specific SCNs, so when you flash back to a specific restore point, the database actually issues a flashback to the SCN associated with that restore point. Finally, the database records the SCN when the database was opened with resetlogs; so, again, your flashback command to the last resetlogs operation is merely the same as issuing the flashback to that SCN. You can check the SCN during the last resetlogs operation by issuing the following query:

```
SQL> select resetlogs_change#
  2    from v$database;

RESETLOGS_CHANGE#
-----------------
1070142
```

Flashback does not work in only one direction; it works both back and forth from a point. Of course, you can't go to a point in time in the future, and you can go only as far back into the past as the flashback logs are available. Figure 13-1 shows how the flashback works in both forward and reverse directions from a point.

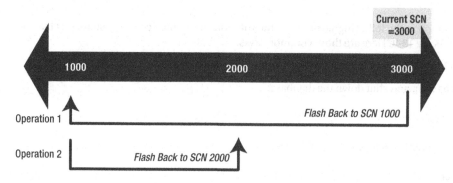

Figure 13-1. *Flashback operations*

Note that Operation 1 flashed the database from the current SCN (3,000) to SCN 1,000. After that was done, before the database opened for read/write access, Operation 2 flashed the database back from SCN 1,000 to SCN 2,000, which is akin to rollforward operations, but we still call it flashback. You can do this operation up to any SCN less than 3,000 any number of times to get to the precise position in time. The lower limit of SCN you can flash back to depends on how much flashback log data is available in the fast recovery area.

■ **Note**   To guarantee the ability to flash back to a point in time, you can create guaranteed restore points, discussed in Recipe 13-10.

13-5. Flashing Back a Database from SQL

Problem

You want to flash the database back to a point in time in the past by using SQL statements, not RMAN.

Solution

Like the RMAN approach, several options are available to you in deciding on a reference point to flash back to. You can flash back to the following:

- A specific point in time, specified by date and time
- A specific SCN
- A named restore point

Common Presteps

We'll describe each option's solution in the following sections. All the solutions have some common steps, just like the RMAN approach described in Recipe 13-4. Here are those common tasks:

1. Check how far back into the past you can flash back to. Refer to Recipe 13-6.

2. Connect as a sysdba user, and shut down the database:

    ```
    SQL> shutdown immediate
    ```

3. Start the database in mount mode:

    ```
    SQL> startup mount
    ```

This completes the preflashback steps.

Common Poststep

After the flashback operation, you will open the database with the clause resetlogs:

```
SQL> alter database open resetlogs;

database opened
```

It's important to open the database in resetlogs mode since the flashback operation performs a point-in-time recovery, which is a form of incomplete recovery. For more information on incomplete recovery, refer to Chapter 12.

Solution 1: Flashing Back to a Time

You have a specific time—such as August 3, 2012, at 10 p.m.—that you want to flash back to. This time must be in the past. Here are the steps to follow:

1. Perform the "common presteps" 1 through 3.

2. Flash the database to your desired timestamp by issuing the following SQL statement:

```
SQL> flashback database to timestamp
  2> to_date('08/03/2012 22:00:00','mm/dd/yyyy hh24:mi:ss');

Flashback complete.
```

The message "Flashback complete" confirms that the database has been flashed back.

3. As described in the RMAN approach, you can open the database now for regular operations by executing the "common poststep."

4. However, you may not be certain that you have flashed back to the exact point in time at which you wanted to be. To determine whether you have, you can open the database in read-only mode:

```
SQL> alter database open read only;

Database opened.
```

5. Check the data in the tables so you can figure out whether you have flashed back enough in the past or you need to go even further. For instance, the purpose of the flashback was to undo the changes to the interest calculation table, so you can check the interest table to see whether the values are 0.

6. If you have not gone far back into the past, you can start the flashback process again to flash back to a different timestamp. Start with step 2, and execute the "common presteps" and flashback:

```
SQL> flashback database to timestamp
  2> to_date('08/03/2012 21:00:00','mm/dd/yyyy hh24:mi:ss');
```

7. Again, open the database in read-only mode, check the data to make sure you are at the point at which you want to be. If you are not there, you can reexecute step 2 through step 6.

8. Once you are satisfied that you have arrived at a point where you want to be, follow the "common poststep" to open the database for regular operation.

The flashback to the timestamp is now complete.

Solution 2: Flashing Back to a Specific SCN

You have a specific SCN to flash back to. This SCN must be less than the current SCN. The steps are the same as for the first solution, except for step 6, in which you substitute the SCN with the timestamp:

1. Find out the current SCN by issuing this query:

    ```
    sql> select current_scn from v$database;

    CURRENT_SCN
    -----------
    1044916
    ```

    From the output, you know that the current SCN is 1,044,916. You can flash back only to a SCN less than this number. These are the steps to flash back to the SCN 1,000,000.

2. Follow the "common presteps" 1 through 3.

3. Issue the following SQL statement to flash back to SCN 1,000,000:

    ```
    SQL> flashback database to scn 1000000;

    Flashback complete.
    ```

4. After the flashback is complete, you can open the database in read-only mode to check the contents.

    ```
    SQL> alter database open read only;

    Database altered.
    ```

5. After the database is opened, you can check the data and determine whether the flashback was done to a time far back enough. If not, you can flash it back once more by repeating the steps: shut down, start up, flash back, and open as read-only.

6. When you want the database to be at a certain point in time, follow the "common poststep" to open the database for normal use.

The database is now flashed back and ready for use.

Solution 3: Restoring to a Restore Point

You can also use the flashback feature to roll a database back to a named restore point. See Recipe 13-9 to learn how to create a restore point. Then use the following steps to revert to such a restore point:

1. Follow the "common presteps."

2. Issue the following SQL statement to flash the database back to, in this example, restore point rp1:

    ```
    SQL> flashback database to restore point rp1;

    Flashback complete.
    ```

3. Similar to the second solution, you can open the database in read-only mode to check whether you have flashed back to a correct place in time:

```
SQL> alter database open read only;

Database altered.
```

4. After the database is opened, you can check the data and determine whether the flashback was done to a time far back enough. If not, you can flash it back once more by repeating the steps: shut down, start up in mount mode, flash back, and open as read-only.

5. When you want the database to be at a certain point in time, follow the "common poststep" to open the database for normal use.

The database is now flashed back and ready for use.

How It Works

The SQL approach works exactly like the RMAN approach described in Recipe 13-4. Refer to the "How It Works" section of that recipe for details.

13-6. Finding Out How Far Back into the Past You Can Flash Back
Problem

You want to flash back the database, and you want to find out how far into the past you can go.

Solution

Query the V$FLASHBACK_DATABASE_LOG view to find out how far into the past you can flash back. For example:

```
SQL> select * from v$flashback_database_log;

OLDEST_FLASHBACK_SCN OLDEST_FL RETENTION_TARGET FLASHBACK_SIZE
-------------------- --------- ---------------- --------------
ESTIMATED_FLASHBACK_SIZE     CON_ID
------------------------ ----------
             2193903 21-JUL-12             1440       367001600
               20570112         0
```

The value of the column OLDEST_FLASHBACK_SCN is 2193903, which indicates you can flash back to the SCN up to that number only, not before that.

The column OLDEST_FLASHBACK_TIME shows the earliest time you can flash back to when you use the timestamp approach shown in Recipe 13-4 and Recipe 13-5. The default display format of a datetime column is just a date, and it does not yield enough information. To see the exact time, you issue the following SQL statement:

```
SQL> select to_char(oldest_flashback_time,'mm/dd/yy hh24:mi:ss')
  2  from v$flashback_database_log;

TO_CHAR(OLDEST_FL)
-----------------
07/21/12 17:39:12
```

The output shows that you can flash back to at most July 21, 2012, at 5:39:12 p.m. when using the timestamp option.

How It Works

You can flash back the database to any point in the past as long as the required flashback logs are available and as long as the required archived logs are available. The archived logs can be either online or on backup, but they must be available.

Information on flashback logs is available on the data dictionary view V$FLASHBACK_DATABASE_LOG.

The dynamic performance view V$FLASHBACK_DATABASE_LOG shows some of the information on flashback operations. Table 13-1 describes the columns of this view.

Table 13-1. *Columns of V$FLASHBACK_DATABASE_LOG*

Column Name	Description
OLDEST_FLASHBACK_SCN	The minimum SCN to which you can flash back the database.
OLDEST_FLASHBACK_TIME	The earliest time to which you can flash back the database.
RETENTION_TARGET	The initialization parameter db_flashback_retention_target determines how long the flashback logs are retained, in minutes. The same parameter is shown in this column. See the note after this table for more information.
FLASHBACK_SIZE	The size of flashback logs as of now.
ESTIMATED_FLASHBACK_SIZE	This column is a bit more interesting and explained in detail after this table.
CON_ID	The container ID, in case of a pluggable database (only in case of Oracle Database 12.1 and above). If you don't use a pluggable database, this column will show the default container ID of 0.

To find the value of the retention target set in the database, you can also issue this SQL:

```
SQL> show parameter db_flashback_retention_target
NAME                              TYPE      VALUE
--------------------------------- --------- ------
db_flashback_retention_target     integer   1440
```

Note that the database initialization parameter db_flashback_retention_target sets the target for the flashback operation. Since this is set to 1440 in the solution example, the database tries to keep the logs for 1,440 minutes. The important word here is "tries," not "guarantees." The actual number of logs kept depends on the size of the fast recovery area, which is determined by another database initialization parameter: db_recovery_file_dest_size. When the flashback logs fill up the fast recovery area, the database removes the oldest logs to make room for the new ones. The age of the oldest logs removed may potentially be less than 1,440 minutes, which is why 1,440 minutes is merely a target, not a guaranteed value of retention.

So, if the database were to retain the flashback logs for the entire 1,440 minutes, what would the combined size of those flashback logs be?

The column ESTIMATED_FLASHBACK_SIZE answers the question. In the example shown here, the value of this column is 20,570,112, or about 20 MB, while the column FLASHBACK_SIZE is 367,001,600, or about 366 MB, much more than the estimated size. This occurred since the fast recovery area has plenty of space and the older flashback logs are still retained in the fast recovery area. Normally, on a small fast recovery area and very active database, this output is reversed—the estimated size is more than the actual size.

13-7. Estimating the Amount of Flashback Logs Generated at Various Times

Problem

You want to find out how much space the flashback logs are expected to consume in the database at various points in time.

Solution

The solution is rather simple. The Oracle database already has a view that shows the estimated database changes and flashback changes in a one-hour period. This view is V$FLASHBACK_DATABASE_STAT. Here is a sample of how to use the view to identify how much flashback and database change data are generated in hour-long intervals:

```
SQL> alter session set nls_date_format = 'mm/dd/yy hh24:mi:ss';

Session altered.

SQL>    select * from v$flashback_database_stat
2       order by begin_time
3       /

BEGIN_TIME         END_TIME           FLASHBACK_DATA    DB_DATA   REDO_DATA
----------------   ----------------   --------------    -------   ---------
ESTIMATED_FLASHBACK_SIZE    CON_ID
------------------------    ---------
08/03/12 23:09:29 08/04/12 00:53:34            8192    1392640           0
                         0           0
... and so on ...
```

The data of interest is the column ESTIMATED_FLASHBACK_SIZE, which shows the expected flashback log generated in the time period shown by the columns BEGIN_TIME and END_TIME. Using this view, you can see an hour-by-hour progress of the flashback data generation. Issue the following query to find out the estimated total size of the flashback logs at the end of each period:

```
SQL> select end_time, estimated_flashback_size
2    from v$flashback_database_stat
3    order by 1
4    /
```

Here is the output:

```
END_TIME           ESTIMATED_FLASHBACK_SIZE
----------------   ---------------------------
08/02/12 19:58:00  73786720
08/02/12 20:53:10 164890123
08/02/12 21:57:37 287563456
... and so on ...
```

Studying the output, you can see the demand for flashback logs went up at 21:57 to 287,563,456, or about 287MB. If you estimate the total size of flashback logs as 190MB, then the older logs will be deleted to make room for the new ones at 21:57. This information helps you when deciding the optimal value of the flashback logs.

How It Works

This view V$FLASHBACK_DATABASE_STAT shows the estimated flashback data within hour-long intervals. Table 13-2 describes the columns of the view.

Table 13-2. *Columns of V$FLASHBACK_DATABASE_STAT*

Column Name	Description
BEGIN_TIME	The beginning of the interval
END_TIME	The end time of the interval
FLASHBACK_DATA	The amount of flashback data generated in bytes in this time interval
DB_DATA	The amount of database change data generated in bytes in this time interval
REDO_DATA	The amount of redo generated in bytes in this time interval
ESTIMATED_FLASHBACK_SIZE	The estimated size of the total flashback logs retained to satisfy the retention target at the end of this time interval, shown in the column END_TIME
CON_ID	The container ID (in case of Oracle Database 12.1 and above)

13-8. Estimating the Space Occupied by Flashback Logs in the Fast Recovery Area

Problem

You want to estimate how much space will be needed for the flashback logs to be retained enough to flash back by a time period specified by the retention target.

Solution

To estimate the total size of all flashback logs required for the retention target, follow these steps:

1. Check the dynamic performance view V$FLASHBACK_DATABASE_LOG:

    ```
    SQL> select * from v$flashback_database_log;

    OLDEST_FLASHBACK_SCN OLDEST_FL RETENTION_TARGET FLASHBACK_SIZE
    -------------------- --------- ---------------- --------------
    ESTIMATED_FLASHBACK_SIZE     CON_ID
    ------------------------ ----------
                 2193903 21-JUL-12             1440      367001600
                21479424              0
    ```

2. Note the value of ESTIMATED_FLASHBACK_SIZE, which is 21,479,424, or about 20MB in this case. This should ideally be your size of the flashback logs.

How It Works

It is not necessary for the database to hold on to the flashback logs. If the space inside the flashback recovery area is under pressure, Oracle automatically deletes the oldest flashback logs to make room for the new ones. Even though the retention target is set, there is no guarantee that Oracle can actually flash back to that point in the past. Since flashback logs are removed only when there is no space, if you size the flashback recovery area large enough, no flashback logs that are required to flash the database back by the retention target need to be deleted. In this recipe, you have identified how many flashback logs would need to be retained to meet the retention target requirement.

13-9. Creating Normal Restore Points

Problem

You want to create normal (or nonguaranteed) restore points that you can later flash back to.

Solution

Execute a statement such as the following, which creates a restore point named rp1:

```
SQL> create restore point rp1;

Restore point created.
```

The restore point is now created. You can flash back to the rp1 restore point later, as explained in Recipe 13-4 and Recipe 13-5.

How It Works

Restore points are named positions in time. While flashing a database back, you can specify a restore point as a destination instead of specifying an SCN or timestamp. However, flashing back to a restore point is possible only if the flashback logs are available for the time associated with the restore point. Because the restore points created by following this recipe are not guaranteed, they are known as unguaranteed or normal restore points. Normal restore points are the default type.

13-10. Creating Guaranteed Restore Points

Problem

You want to create guaranteed restore points to ensure that you can flash back to them as needed. You want to require the database to retain any needed logs to support those points.

Solution

Add the guarantee keyword to your create restore point command. For example:

```
SQL> create restore point rp2 guarantee flashback database;

Restore point created.
```

Restore point rp2 is now created as a guaranteed restore point.

How It Works

For a description of restore points and how they work, refer to the "How It Works" section of Recipe 13-9. As described in that recipe, merely defining a restore point does not mean you can flash back to the associated point in time. Flashback logs are deleted by the database automatically when the space in the fast recovery area is inadequate for an incoming backup. It's entirely possible then for the logs required by a given restore point to be deleted, making that restore point useless.

If you try to flash the database to a point for which no flashback logs are available, you will see the following error message:

```
ORA-38729: Not enough flashback database log data to do FLASHBACK.
```

This message means the database does not have the flashback logs needed to go back to the restore point (or time or SCN) that you've specified. By adding the word guarantee to your create restore point command, you prevent the database from deleting any needed logs for whatever restore point you are creating.

If you have a guaranteed restore point, you can't change the log mode of the database to noarchivelog. Here is the error you will get:

```
SQL> alter database noarchivelog;
alter database noarchivelog
*
ERROR at line 1:
ORA-38781: cannot disable media recovery - have guaranteed restore points
```

This is due to fact that guaranteed restore points allow you to flash the database to that point in time and to accomplish that the Oracle Database must read and access the archived logs.

■ **Caution**   When a guaranteed restore point is defined, the associated flashback logs are never deleted unless the restore point is dropped. This will reduce the available space in the fast recovery area. A filled-up fast recovery area will cause the database instance to abort, with the failure in the recovery writer (RVWR) process. So, create guaranteed restore points only when you need to go back to them after some preestablished event to be completed in the near future, such as doing a test run of the application and then reverting to the starting data sets. After the test is completed, drop the guaranteed restore points.

13-11. Listing Restore Points
Problem

You want to list the various restore points in the database and the information about them.

Solution

Query the view V$RESTORE_POINT. For example:

```
SQL> col time format a32
SQL> col name format a10
```

```
SQL> select name, DATABASE_INCARNATION#, SCN, time
  2  from v$restore_point
  3  order by scn;

NAME        DATABASE_INCARNATION#        SCN TIME
----------  ---------------------  ---------- -------------------------------
RP1                             2     2193924 21-JUL-12 05.39.31.000000000 PM
GRP1                            2     2194050 21-JUL-12 05.44.48.000000000 PM
GRP2                            2     2194061 21-JUL-12 05.44.58.000000000 PM
RP2                             2     2194077 21-JUL-12 05.45.16.000000000 PM
GRP3                            2     2195811 21-JUL-12 06.19.15.000000000 PM
GRP4                            2     2195894 21-JUL-12 06.19.47.000000000 PM
GRP5                            2     2196549 21-JUL-12 06.39.20.000000000 PM
GRP6                            2     2196630 21-JUL-12 06.40.30.000000000 PM
GRP7                            3     2197224 03-AUG-12 11.04.38.000000000 PM
GRP8                            3     2197263 03-AUG-12 11.05.33.000000000 PM
RP9                             3     2197281 03-AUG-12 11.05.50.000000000 PM
GRP11                           4     2199532 04-AUG-12 01.34.37.000000000 AM
... and so on ...
```

The various columns of the view are described in the "How It Works" section.

How It Works

When you create a restore point as guaranteed, the database marks the flashback logs as not to be removed when the fast recovery area runs out of space. The space occupied by these specially marked flashback logs is shown under the column STORAGE_SIZE in the view V$RESTORE_POINT.

Table 13-3 describes the columns of the view V$RESTORE_POINT.

Table 13-3. *Columns of V$RESTORE_POINT*

Column Name	Description
SCN	This is the SCN of the database when the restore point was created.
DATABASE_INCARNATION#	This column displays the incarnation of the database when this restore point was created. If the database was flashed back and then opened with resetlogs, it creates a new incarnation of the database.
GUARANTEE_FLASHBACK_DATABASE	If the restore point is a guaranteed one, this column holds the value YES.
STORAGE_SIZE	This is the storage occupied by the flashback logs of the guaranteed restore points. In case of normal restore points, this value is 0.
TIME	This is the timestamp when the restore point was created.
NAME	This is the name of the restore point.
PRESERVED	This is a new column in Oracle Database 11g. It shows whether the restore point must be explicitly deleted.
RESTORE_POINT_TIME	This shows whether you specified a specific time when the restore point was supposed to be taken. If you didn't specify a time, it's NULL.
CON_ID	The container ID in case of Oracle Database 12.1 and above.

13-12. Dropping Restore Points

Problem

You want to drop a specific restore point.

Solution

To drop a restore point named rp2, whether normal or guaranteed, simply execute the following SQL statement:

```
SQL> drop restore point rp2;

Restore point dropped.
```

To list the restore points defined in the database, use Recipe 13-11.

How It Works

Normal restore points are merely pointers to the SCNs at the time they were defined. They do not consume any space. Guaranteed restore points mark the flashback logs necessary to enable flashback to a specific point in time, and those flashback logs do take up space. When you drop a guaranteed restore point, you will see an immediate increase in the available space in the fast recovery area. To check the available space in the fast recovery area, refer to Recipe 3-4.

13-13. Recovering a Dropped Table

Problem

You accidentally dropped a table that should not have been dropped. You want to reinstate the table without doing a database recovery.

Solution

If you dropped the table just moments ago, it is not actually dropped; it is placed in the recycle bin. Assume that you dropped the table ACCOUNTS and want to revive it. You can resurrect that table from the recycle bin by following these steps:

1. Log on to the database as the table owner.

2. Check whether the table exists in the recycle bin. Issue the SQL*Plus command show recyclebin:

    ```
    SQL> show recyclebin

    SQL> show recyclebin
    ORIGINAL NAME    RECYCLEBIN NAME                   OBJECT TYPE  DROP TIME
    ---------------  -------------------------------   -----------  -------------------
    TEST             BIN$xmtCqONCcZjgQ4CohAoD7Q==$0    TABLE        2012-08-04:01:53:19
    ```

The presence of the table TEST under the column ORIGINAL_NAME indicates that the table is still present in the recycle bin and can be revived. If you see multiple entries with the same ORIGINAL_NAME, it indicates the table was dropped, another table was created with the same name, that table was dropped, too, and so on, for however many duplicate entries you have. Recipe 13-14 shows how to handle a situation in which you have duplicate names in the recycle bin.

3. Revive the table from the recycle bin by issuing the following SQL*Plus command:

```
SQL> flashback table test to before drop;

Flashback complete.
```

The table is now available in the database.

How It Works

In Oracle Database 10g, when you drop a table, the table is not really dropped. Rather, the table is renamed. For instance, in the example in this recipe, when the table TEST was dropped, the table was actually renamed to BIN$xmtCqONCcZjgQ4CohAoD7Q==$0. That name is cryptic enough that it would never be used and thus would never conflict with a real name by any user. Since the table is merely renamed and not dropped, the data in the table is still available. When you issue the flashback command in step 2, Oracle Database starting with 10g merely renames the table to the original name. However, the dropped table does not show up in the data dictionary views USER_TABLES and ALL_TABLES.

```
SQL> select table_name
  2  from user_tables;

no rows selected
```

However, the view TAB shows this renamed table:

```
SQL> select * from tab;

TNAME                           TABTYPE CLUSTERID
------------------------------- ------- ---------
BIN$xmtCqONCcZjgQ4CohAoD7Q==$0 TABLE
```

If you check the USER_SEGMENTS dictionary view, the segments will be there:

```
SQL> col segment_name format a30
SQL> select segment_type, segment_name
  2  from user_segments;
SEGMENT_TYPE     SEGMENT_NAME
---------------------------------------
TABLE     BIN$xmtCqONDcZjgQ4CohAoD7Q==$0
INDEX     BIN$FPl4bnVgTH2ZIr1uc310Hg==$1
INDEX     BIN$c7f1XmKBQjiVXy2j/NcJqA==$1
```

The indexes are those of the table. When the table was dropped, the indexes were not dropped. They were renamed, just like the table.

If you make a mistake in identifying the correct table, Oracle Database returns an ORA-38305 error, as shown in the following example where you are trying to revive a table named ACCOUNTS that does not exist in the recycle bin:

```
SQL> flashback table accounts to before drop;
flashback table accounts to before drop
*
ERROR at line 1:
ORA-38305: object not in RECYCLE BIN
```

The error says it all.

■ **Tip**   If you want to delete a table permanently, without sending it to the recycle bin, then use the purge clause in the drop statement. For example:

```
SQL> drop table test purge;
Table dropped.
```

The table is now completely dropped; similar to the pre-10g behavior, it does not go to the recycle bin.

13-14. Undropping a Table When Another Exists with the Same Name

Problem

You had a table called ACCOUNTS that was dropped, and since then you created another table also called ACCOUNTS. Now you want to reinstate the first table ACCOUNTS from the recycle bin.

Solution

There are two potential solutions:

- Drop the existing table so there will be no conflict for the name of the table undropped.

- Undrop the table but reinstate it to a different name.

Here are the solutions in detail.

Solution 1: Dropping the Existing Table

The easiest approach is, of course, to drop the existing table. The flashed-back table then comes on the database without any problems.

Solution 2: Renaming the Reinstated Table

The alternative approach is safer because you do not need to drop anything. When you flash back a table to undrop it, you can optionally rename it. In this case, when you flash back the table ACCOUNTS, you want to reinstate it as NEW_ACCOUNTS.

```
SQL> flashback table accounts to before drop rename to new_accounts;

Flashback complete.
```

The existing table still remains as ACCOUNTS, but the reinstated table is renamed to NEW_ACCOUNTS.

How It Works

When you flash back a table from the recycle bin, a table with that name must not already exist in the database. Suppose you are trying to revive a table called ACCOUNTS but it already exists. In that case, the flashback statement returns with an error: ORA-38312:

```
SQL> flashback table accounts to before drop;

Flashback complete.

SQL> flashback table accounts to before drop;
flashback table accounts to before drop
*
ERROR at line 1:
ORA-38312: original name is used by an existing object
```

■ **Note** Suppose there are two tables in the recycle bin with the same name—ACCOUNTS, as shown here:

```
ORIGINAL NAME RECYCLEBIN NAME                    OBJECT TYPE  DROP TIME
------------- ---------------------------------- ------------ -------------------
ACCOUNTS      BIN$xmtCqONLcZjgQ4CohAoD7Q==$0 TABLE            2012-08-04:02:09:42
ACCOUNTS      BIN$xmtCqONKcZjgQ4CohAoD7Q==$0 TABLE            2012-08-04:02:09:24
TEST1         BIN$xmtCqONDcZjgQ4CohAoD7Q==$0 TABLE            2012-08-04:02:05:45
```

Now you issue this:

```
SQL> flashback table accounts to before drop;
```

Which table ACCOUNTS will be reinstated?

The table that was dropped last will be reinstated; that is, the table that shows up first will be reinstated. Pay attention to this behavior while reinstating a table from the recycle bin.

13-15. Undropping a Specific Table from Two Dropped Tables with the Same Name

Problem

You had a table called ACCOUNTS, which you dropped. Later you created a table, again called ACCOUNTS, and dropped that, too. Now you want to revive the table ACCOUNTS, the one that was dropped first.

Solution

To reinstate a specific dropped table, follow the steps:

1. First find out the presence of these objects in the recycle bin:

   ```
   ORIGINAL NAME RECYCLEBIN NAME                      OBJECT TYPE  DROP TIME
   ------------- ------------------------------       ------------ -------------------
   ACCOUNTS      BIN$xmtCqONLcZjgQ4CohAoD7Q==$0 TABLE              2012-08-04:02:09:42
   ACCOUNTS      BIN$xmtCqONKcZjgQ4CohAoD7Q==$0 TABLE              2012-08-04:02:09:24
   TEST1         BIN$xmtCqONDcZjgQ4CohAoD7Q==$0 TABLE              2012-08-04:02:05:45
   ```

   Note there are two different tables with the same name—ACCOUNTS.

2. Decide which of the two accounts tables to revive. The column DROP_TIME helps in your decision; it shows when each table was dropped. In your case, you want to recover the one that was dropped earlier. If you issue the statement `flashback table accounts to before drop`, the more recently dropped table will be revived—not what you want in this scenario.

3. To revive the earlier table, the one that was dropped first, issue the `flashback table` command, giving the recycle bin name as the table name:

   ```
   SQL> flashback table "BIN$bQ8QU1bWSD2Rc9uHevUkTw==$0" to before drop;
   Flashback complete.
   ```

   Be sure to put the recycle bin name— BIN$xmtCqONKcZjgQ4CohAoD7Q==$0—in double quotes. The double quotes are necessary because of the presence of special characters in the name.

4. Check the recycle bin. You will see only one table now:

   ```
   SQL> show recyclebin
   ORIGINAL NAME RECYCLEBIN NAME                      OBJECT TYPE  DROP TIME
   ------------- ------------------------------       ------------ -------------------
   ACCOUNTS      BIN$xmtCqONLcZjgQ4CohAoD7Q==$0 TABLE              2012-08-04:02:09:42
   ```

   There is just one table in the recycle bin. You have successfully restored the earlier version of the table.

How It Works

As mentioned in Recipe 13-13, a drop table command in Oracle Database 10g and later does not actually drop a table; it merely renames it to a name with a lot of special characters. An example of such a name is the "BIN$xmtCqONKcZjgQ4CohAoD7Q==$0" name shown in this recipe. While reviving a table in the recycle bin, you can use its original name or the special recycle bin name.

In most cases, you can use the original name. Sometimes, though, you can't use the original name. One such example could be when you drop a table and create another with the same name. When you re-create a table that was dropped before and then drop the re-created one, the table name is same—ACCOUNTS, in this example—but the recycle bin names for each of those two tables are unique. To reinstate a specific dropped table, you should specify the recycle bin name instead of the real name.

13-16. Checking the Contents of the Recycle Bin
Problem

You want to see the objects in the recycle bin.

Solution

You can display the objects in your own recycle bin in two ways:

- Use the SQL*Plus command show recyclebin:

```
SQL> show recyclebin
ORIGINAL NAME RECYCLEBIN NAME                    OBJECT TYPE  DROP TIME
------------- -------------------------------   ----------- -------------------
TEST          BIN$xmtCqONMcZjgQ4CohAoD7Q==$0 TABLE        2012-08-04:02:15:11
TEST1         BIN$xmtCqONDcZjgQ4CohAoD7Q==$0 TABLE        2012-08-04:02:05:45
```

The command SHOW RECYCLEBIN shows some pertinent details for all tables in the recycle bin. However, the command does not show corresponding indexes, triggers, and so on.

- To get information on all objects in the recycle bin, including indexes and triggers, query the view USER_RECYCLEBIN, as shown in the following example:

```
SQL> select * from user_recyclebin;

OBJECT_NAME
--------------------------------------------------------------------------
ORIGINAL_NAME
--------------------------------------------------------------------------
OPERATION TYPE                      TS_NAME
--------- ----------------------- -------------------------------
CREATETIME         DROPTIME            DROPSCN
------------------ ------------------- ----------
PARTITION_NAME
--------------------------------------------------------------------------
CAN CAN    RELATED BASE_OBJECT PURGE_OBJECT      SPACE
--- --- ---------- ----------- ------------ ----------
BIN$xmtCqONDcZjgQ4CohAoD7Q==$0
```

```
TEST1
DROP         TABLE                          SYSAUX
2012-08-04:02:05:30 2012-08-04:02:05:45      2207258

YES YES       90902        90902          90902             8


BIN$xmtCqONMcZjgQ4CohAoD7Q==$0
TEST
DROP         TABLE                          SYSAUX
2012-08-04:02:09:38 2012-08-04:02:15:11      2208461

YES YES       90903        90903          90903             8
```

To check the recycle bin of all users, check the view DBA_RECYCLEBIN:

```
SQL> select * from dba_recyclebin;
```

The columns are the same as user_recyclebin, except the additional column—OWNER—that shows the owner of the dropped object. In Oracle 12.1, a new view CDB_RECYCLEBIN shows the recycle bin for the container database.

How It Works

When a table is dropped in Oracle Database 10g Release 1 and newer, it is not actually dropped. It's merely renamed to a different name, such as BIN$UawCFy69TUyc9DgR50AEMw==$0. A record is placed in the table RECYCLEBIN$ (in the sys schema) for that table. The view USER_RECYCLEBIN is a join between, among other tables, the OBJ$ (the objects in the database) and RECYCLEBIN$ tables in the sys schema.

13-17. Restoring Dependent Objects of an Undropped Table

Problem

You want to recover all the subordinate objects, such as the indexes, constraints, and so on, of a table that has been undropped.

Solution

Here are the steps to restore the dependent objects:

1. First, check the contents of the recycle bin to get an inventory of what is available. This is an important step; do not skip it. The following is the query you want to execute:

```
SQL> col type format a5
SQL> col original_name format a15
SQL> col object_name format a15
SQL> select original_name, object_name, type, can_undrop
  2  from user_recyclebin;

ORIGINAL_NAME   OBJECT_NAME                    TYPE      CAN
--------------  -----------------------------  --------- ---
IN_ACC_01       BIN$xmtCqONUcZjgQ4CohAoD7Q==$0 INDEX     NO
```

```
IN_ACC_02      BIN$xmtCqONVcZjgQ4CohAoD7Q==$0 INDEX    NO
TR_ACC_01      BIN$xmtCqONWcZjgQ4CohAoD7Q==$0 TRIGGER  NO
ACCOUNTS       BIN$xmtCqONXcZjgQ4CohAoD7Q==$0 TABLE    YES
```

The most important column is the column CAN_UNDROP. If this column is YES, then you can undrop an object cleanly without any additional efforts. Objects with CAN_UNDROP = NO can still be reinstated, but you have to change their names to the original names manually.

■ **Tip**   The ORIGINAL_NAME column shows the original names. Once a table is undropped, the recycle bin information is removed, and you will never be able to see the original names of the dependent objects, such as triggers and indexes of that table. So, save the output of this query before you go to the next step.

---

2. Now undrop the table ACCOUNTS by executing the following SQL statement:

    ```
    SQL> flashback table accounts to before drop;

    Flashback complete.
    ```

    The table is now available in the database.

3. Display the constraints of the table:

    ```
    SQL> select constraint_type, constraint_name
      2  from user_constraints
      3  where table_name = 'ACCOUNTS';

    C CONSTRAINT_NAME
    - ------------------------------
    P BIN$ncFOiaduRZeURXatWq8lyA==$0
    C BIN$782qhcPvQbajusPeAEiR3Q==$0
    ```

    The flashback (or the undrop) brought back the primary key and check constraints but not the foreign keys, if there were any. The foreign keys are lost forever.

4. Change the names of the reinstated objects to their original names, if you know what they were. For example, if you know the original name of the constraint BIN$ncFOiaduRZeURXatWq8lyA==$0 was pk_accounts, you can issue the following query to restore the original name:

    ```
    SQL> alter table accounts rename constraint "BIN$ncFOiaduRZeURXatWq8lyA==$0" to
    pk_accounts;

    Table altered.

    SQL> alter table accounts rename constraint "BIN$782qhcPvQbajusPeAEiR3Q==$0" to
    ck_acc_01;

    Table altered.
    ```

    If you don't have the names, use any human-readable name you consider appropriate.

5. Now check the indexes of the newly reinstated table:

```
SQL> select index_name
  2  from user_indexes
  3  where table_name = 'ACCOUNTS';

INDEX_NAME
------------------------------
BIN$9POlL6gfQK6RBoOK4klc3Q==$0
BIN$PookVi5nRpmhmPaVOThGQQ==$0
BIN$fzY77+GmTzqz/3u4dqac9g==$0
```

6. Note the names, and compare them to the names you got in step 1. It's not easy, but you can make a clear connection. Using the output from step 1, rename the indexes:

```
SQL> alter index "BIN$9POlL6gfQK6RBoOK4klc3Q==$0" rename to IN_ACC_01;
Index altered.

SQL> alter index "BIN$PookVi5nRpmhmPaVOThGQQ==$0" rename to SYS_C005457;
Index altered.

SQL> alter index "BIN$fzY77+GmTzqz/3u4dqac9g==$0" rename to in_acc_02;
Index altered.
```

7. Finally, make sure the indexes are in place and have correct names:

```
SQL>    select index_name
  2     from user_indexes
  3     where table_name = 'ACCOUNTS';

INDEX_NAME
--------------------------------------
IN_ACC_01
SYS_C005457
IN_ACC_02
```

8. Check the triggers on the reinstated table:

```
SQL> select trigger_name
  2  from user_triggers;

TRIGGER_NAME
-------------------------------------------------
BIN$dt6tBSIWSn+F5epvjybKmw==$0
```

9. Rename triggers to their original names:

```
SQL> alter trigger "BIN$dt6tBSIWSn+F5epvjybKmw==$0" rename to tr_acc_01;
Trigger altered.
```

10. Check the triggers now to make sure they are named as they were originally:

```
SQL>    select trigger_name
   2    from user_triggers;


TRIGGER_NAME
--------------------------------------
TR_ACC_01
```

This confirms you reinstated all the dependent objects.

How It Works

In Oracle Database 10g Release 1 and newer, when a table is dropped, the table is not actually dropped; it is merely renamed to a system-generated name and marked as being in the recycle bin. Likewise, all the dependent objects of the table—triggers, constraints, indexes—are also not dropped; they are renamed as well and continue to exist on the renamed table. When you flash back the table to before the drop, or undrop the table, these dependent objects are not undropped. But those objects do exist, and you can rename them to their original names. The only exceptions are foreign key constraints, which are lost when a table is dropped.

13-18. Turning Off the Recycle Bin
Problem

You want to turn off the recycle bin behavior; that is, you want behavior like in Oracle9i where a dropped table just gets dropped permanently.

Solution

You can modify the recycle bin behavior so that dropped objects do not go to the recycle bin. Instead, they simply get dropped permanently. The parameter that influences this is recyclebin. You can set this parameter at the session level or the system level.

Set the session parameter to disable the recycle bin at the session level:

```
SQL> alter session set recyclebin = off;

Session altered.
```

After setting recyclebin to off, if you drop a table, the table is completely dropped:

```
SQL> drop table accounts;

Table dropped.
```

Now, if you check the recycle bin:

```
SQL> show recyclebin
```

the command returns no output, indicating that the recycle bin is empty.

You can turn off the recycle bin for the entire database by putting this parameter in the parameter file and restarting the database:

```
recyclebin = off
```

If the recycle bin is turned off at the system level, you can turn it on at the session level, and vice versa.

How It Works

In Oracle Database 10g Release 1 and newer, when the tables are dropped, they are really not dropped. Instead, they are renamed and marked to be in the recycle bin. This is the default behavior. By executing the statement `alter session set recyclebin = off` at the session level, the behavior is changed to the pre-10g one; that is, the table is actually dropped as a result of the `drop` command, not renamed to be placed in the recycle bin.

SHOULD YOU TURN OFF THE RECYCLE BIN?

Even though you can turn off the recycle bin at the system level, in our opinion there is no valid reason to do so. Here are some arguments against recycle bins:

- They take up space, since the dropped objects are not actually dropped.

- They make the free-space calculations erroneous because they are dropped but still counted as occupied space.

- They show up in a user's list of tables, which can be confusing. And the names are confusing.

- In some environments, such as data warehouses, a lot of tables are created and dropped rapidly. Dropping those tables is permanent, and there is never a need to undrop them.

Each of these arguments can be countered, as shown here:

- They take up space, but the space is immediately deallocated and given to the segment that needs it, if there is a space pressure in the tablespace. So, the space is not taken up in a practical sense.

- The free-space calculations exclude the recycle bin objects, so the free space reported is accurate.

- The recycle bin object shows up in TAB but not in the view USER_TABLES. Most scripts are written against USER_TABLES, not against TAB, so this is not a real concern.

The last argument has some merit. Ordinarily, this should not cause any issues, since the recycle bin objects are not counted toward the user's total used space. But if you would rather not see the recycle bin objects, you can turn it off for that session only.

So, as you can see, there is no real reason behind turning off the recycle bin at the system level (or mimicking the 9i behavior). On the other hand, if you disable it, you will lose a valuable feature—a safety net of sorts while dropping tables. So, we strongly recommend against turning off the recycle bin.

13-19. Clearing the Recycle Bin

Problem

You want to remove all dropped objects from the recycle bin.

Solution

You can clean up the recycle bin using the purge statement, which clears the recycle bin of the currently logged-on user. For example:

```
SQL> purge recyclebin;

Recyclebin purged.
```

Each user has a logically individual recycle bin. If you want to clear the recycle bins of all users in the database, you should purge dba_recyclebin, as shown here:

```
SQL> purge dba_recyclebin;

DBA Recyclebin purged.
```

This clears all the data from all the recycle bins.

How It Works

Note from the earlier recipes that when a table is dropped, it's not really dropped. Instead, the table is renamed and marked to be in the recycle bin. The statement purge recyclebin merely drops all the objects that were marked to be in the recycle bin.

CALLING PURGE IN PL/SQL

PURGE is a DDL, not DML, statement. The difference is not significant when you use it in the SQL*Plus command line as shown in the examples, but it is important to understand the difference when writing a PL/SQL routine. You can't call it in PL/SQL code as shown here:

```
SQL> begin
  2      purge recyclebin;
  3  end;
  4  /
    purge recyclebin;
          *
ERROR at line 2:
ORA-06550: line 2, column 10:
PLS-00103: Encountered the symbol "RECYCLEBIN" when expecting one of the
following:
:= . ( @ % ;
The symbol ":=" was substituted for "RECYCLEBIN" to continue.
```

To call purge in a PL/SQL code, you will need to call it as a parameter to execute `immediate`, as shown here:

```
SQL> begin
  2      execute immediate 'purge recyclebin';
  3  end;
  4  /
PL/SQL procedure successfully completed.
```

13-20. Querying the History of a Table Row (Flashback Query)

Problem

You want to find how the values of the columns in a row have changed over a period of time.

Solution

To find all the changes to the row for ACCNO 3760 in table ACCOUNTS, issue the following query:

```
SQL>    select
  2     acc_status,
  3     versions_starttime,
  4     versions_startscn,
  5     versions_endtime,
  6     versions_endscn,
  7     versions_xid,
  8     versions_operation
  9     from accounts
 10     versions between scn minvalue and maxvalue
 11     where accno = 3760
 12     order by 3
 13     /
```

The result comes back as follows:

```
A VERSIONS_STARTTIME     VERSIONS_STARTSCN VERSIONS_ENDTIME      VERSIONS_ENDSCN ➥
VERSIONS_XID     V
- -------------------- ------------------------- ----------- --------------------- -----------
---------------------------------------------
---------------- -
A 12-JUL12 04.38.57 PM            1076867 12-JUL12 04.39.03 PM   1076870
02002F00D8010000 U
I 12-JUL12 04.39.03 PM            1076870 12-JUL12 04.39.12 PM   1076874
08001B00DB010000 U
A 12-JUL12 04.39.12 PM            1076874
07002B0068010000 U
A                12-JUL12 04.38.57 PM    1076867
```

The results show how the values of the column ACC_STATUS were changed at different points in time. Note the column VERSIONS_OPERATION, which shows the DML operation that modified the value of the corresponding row. The values are as follows:

> *I*: Insert
>
> *U*: Update
>
> *D*: Delete

In the example output, you can see that on July 12, 2012, at 4:38:57 p.m. (the value of the column VERSIONS_STARTTIME), someone updated the value of a row by using an Update operation. The SCN at that time was 1076867. The ACC_STATUS column was changed to A at that time. This value was unchanged until July 12, 2012, at 4:39:03 p.m. (the value of column VERSIONS_ENDTIME).

As shown in the second record of the output, on July 12, 2012, at 4:39:03 p.m. and at SCN 1076870, another update operation updated the ACC_STATUS to I. This is how you read the changes to the table row where ACCNO is 3760.

Note the line where VERSIONS_ENDTIME is null. This indicates the current row, which has not been changed yet.

In addition to the SCN, you can also use `timestamp` as a predicate, as shown here:

```
SQL>    select
2       acc_status,
3       versions_starttime,
4       versions_startscn,
5       versions_endtime,
6       versions_endscn,
7       versions_xid,
8       versions_operation
9       from accounts
10      versions between timestamp minvalue and maxvalue
11      where accno = 3762
12      order by 3;
```

In the previous example, you specified the predicate to get all the available records. Note line 10:

```
versions between timestamp minvalue and maxvalue
```

This predicate indicates the minimum and maximum values of the timestamps available. You can specify exact values for these as well. To get the versions on July 12 between noon and 3 p.m., you need to rewrite the query by modifying line 10 to this:

```
versions between timestamp to_date('7/12/2012 12:00:00', 'mm/dd/yyyy hh24:mi:ss')
and to_date('7/12/2012 15:00:00', 'mm/dd/yyyy hh24:mi:ss')
```

Instead of using timestamps, you can use SCNs, such as between 1000 and 2000, to get the versions of the row. In that case, line 10 becomes this:

```
versions between SCN 1000 and 2000
```

If you don't see any data under the pseudocolumns, the reasons could be one of the following:

- The information has aged out of the undo segments.
- The database was recycled after the changes occurred.

How It Works

When a row is updated, the database records the relevant change details in the database blocks, in addition to some other related details, such as the SCN of when the change occurred, the timestamp, the type of operation that resulted in the change, and so on—a sort of "metadata" about the changes, if you will. This metadata is stored in pseudocolumns and can be queried afterward.

Table 13-4 describes the flashback query pseudocolumns. The pseudocolumns that start with VERSIONS, such as VERSIONS_STARTTIME, are not actually part of the table. They are computed and shown to the user at runtime. A good everyday example of such a pseudocolumn is ROWNUM, which denotes the serial number of a row in the returned result set. This column is not stored in the table but is computed and returned to the user when the query is executed. Since these columns are not part of the table's definition, they are called pseudocolumns.

Table 13-4. Flashback Query Pseudocolumns

Pseudo Column Name	Description
VERSIONS_STARTTIME	This is the timestamp when this version of the row became effective. This is the commit time after the row was changed.
VERSIONS_STARTSCN	This is the SCN when this version became effective.
VERSIONS_ENDTIME	This is the timestamp when the version became old, replaced by a new version. This is the time of commit after the row was changed.
VERSIONS_ENDSCN	This is the SCN when the row's version was changed.
VERSIONS_XID	This is the transaction ID that changed the row's version. This can be joined with the XID column of the dictionary view FLASHBACK_TRANSACTION_QUERY to show the transaction that made this change. The view FLASHBACK_TRANSACTION_QUERY also shows other relevant details of the transaction, such as who did it, when, and so on.
VERSIONS_OPERATION	This is the abbreviated activity code—I, U, or D—for Insert, Update, or Delete that resulted in this version of the row.

13-21. Flashing Back a Specific Table

Problem

You want to flash back a specific table, not the entire database, to a point in time in the past.

Solution

The table can be flashed back with a specialized adaptation of flashback queries. Here are the steps on how to do it:

1. Make sure the table has row movement enabled:

```
SQL>    select row_movement
  2     from user_tables
  3     where table_name = 'ACCOUNTS';

ROW_MOVE
--------
ENABLED
```

2. If the output comes back as DISABLED, enable it by issuing this SQL statement:

```
SQL> alter table accounts enable row movement;
```

```
Table altered.
```

This prepares the table for flashback.

3. Check the table to see how far into the past you can flash it back. Use Recipe 13-6 to determine how far back into the past you can go.

4. Flash the table back to a specific timestamp:

```
SQL> flashback table accounts to timestamp to_date ('12-JUL-12 18.23.00', 'dd-MON-YY hh24.mi.ss');
```

```
Flashback complete.
```

You can flash back to a specific SCN as well:

5. Check the data in the table to make sure you have flashed back to the exact point you want. If the flashback was not enough, you can flash the table back once more to a point even further in the past. For instance, the previous step reinstated the table as of 6:23 p.m., which was not enough. In this step, you will flash it back to one more minute in the past—to 6:22 p.m.

```
SQL> flashback table accounts to timestamp to_date ('12-JUL-12 18.22.00',
'dd-MON-YY hh24.mi.ss');
Flashback complete.
```

6. If you have gone too far into the past, you can flash "forward" using the same flashback statement:

```
SQL> flashback table accounts to timestamp to_date ('12-JUL-12 18.24.00',
'dd-MON-YY hh24.mi.ss');
```

```
Flashback complete.
```

As you can see, you can flash the table back and forth until you arrive at the exact point.

The flashback is complete. Since the table was not dropped, all dependent objects, such as triggers and indexes, remain unaffected.

How It Works

Table flashback is entirely different from the database flashback you saw earlier in the chapter. When a table's data changes, the past information is stored in undo segments. Oracle uses this information to present a read-consistent view of the data later. Even if the changes were committed, the undo data is important for the read-consistent image needed by a query that started after the data was changed but before it was committed.

The flashback versions query in Recipe 13-20 uses the information in the undo segments to display past versions of the data at multiple points in time. Flashing back a table uses the same undo data to reconstruct the data at whatever point in the past you specify. If sufficient information is not available in the undo segments, you will get the following error:

```
SQL> flashback table accounts to timestamp to_date ('12-JUL-12 15.23.00', 'dd-MON-YY hh24.mi.ss');
flashback table accounts to timestamp to_date ('12-JUL-12 15.23.00', 'dd-MON-YY hh24.mi.ss')
                 *
ERROR at line 1:
ORA-00604: error occurred at recursive SQL level 1
ORA-12801: error signaled in parallel query server P003
ORA-01555: snapshot too old: rollback segment number 4 with name "_SYSSMU4$" too small
```

This error may not be that intuitive to interpret, but it conveys the message—the undo segment does not have information the flashback operation needs. In that case you can resort to Recipe 13-22 for an alternative mechanism to get the table back from the past.

Contrast this operation with the flashback database operation. In flashback database, the changes at the block level to the entire database are captured in flashback logs, and the flashback operation undoes the block changes. Any database change—the creation of new objects, truncation, and so on—is captured by the logs and can be played back. In a flashback query, the data is reconstructed from the undo segments. Any DDL operations are not reinstated. So if you have added a column at 1:30 p.m. and flash back to 1:25 p.m., the added column is not dropped. By the way, the DDL operation does not restrict your ability to perform a flashback beyond that point.

During the flashback operation, the database might have to move the rows from one block to another. This is allowed only if the table has the property row movement enabled. Therefore, you had to enable that as the first step of the process.

You can flash back a table owned by another user, but to do so you need SELECT, INSERT, DELETE, and ALTER privileges on the table, as well as one of the following:

- FLASHBACK ANY TABLE system privilege
- FLASHBACK privilege on that particular table

Table flashback does not work on the following types of tables:

- Advanced queuing (AQ) tables
- Individual table partitions or subpartitions
- Materialized views
- Nested tables
- Object tables
- Remote tables
- Static data dictionary tables
- System tables
- Tables that are part of a cluster

Some restrictions are relaxed with newer versions of the Oracle Database, so it is possible that some items may not be in this list when you read this book.

There are some important points you should know when you flash back a table. To make our description of those points easier to understand, suppose the following is a time line of events:

```
Time -> ------------------------------------------------------------------
SCN ->          1,000              2,000                  3,000        4,000
Events ->          DDL Occurred      Index Dropped     Table Data
```

The SCNs corresponding to each event are shown on the scale. The current SCN is 4,000. Given this scenario, the following limitations and caveats are true:

- You can't flash back the table to an SCN prior to SCN 1,000 (when a specific type of DDL occurred). These DDL operations are as follows:

  - Adding a constraint to the table.

  - Adding the table to a cluster.

  - Adding, dropping, merging, splitting, coalescing, or truncating a partition or subpartition. Adding a range partition is acceptable.

  - Dropping columns.

  - Modifying columns.

  - Moving the table to a different (or even the same) tablespace.

  - Truncating the table.

- When you flash back the table to a SCN prior to 2,000 (when the index was dropped), the index is not reinstated. Remember, the flashback operation is a data movement operation, not DDL, so dropped objects are not created.

- When you flash back a table, the statistics on the table are not reinstated. When you flash back the table to SCN 1,500, the statistics on the table are as of SCN 4,000.

13-22. Recovering a Specific Table from Backup
Problem

You want to restore a specific table, not the entire database. The table is no longer in the recycle bin, but you do have the RMAN backup.

Solution

Oracle Database 12.1 introduces a new feature that enables you to recover a table or a partition from an RMAN backup. You can restore just the table or partion, without needing to restore the entire, containing tablespace.
Here are the steps to recover a table named ACCOUNTS in the SCOTT schema:

1. Make sure the database is in archivelog mode:

    ```
    SQL> select log_mode from v$database;

    LOG_MODE
    ------------
    ARCHIVELOG
    ```

2. Make sure the database is open in read/write mode:

    ```
    SQL> select open_mode from v$database;

    OPEN_MODE
    ----------
    READ WRITE
    ```

3. Choose where a temporary database can be created for the duration of the RMAN
    operation. Designate a file system or an ASM disk group–the choice is yours. Just be sure
    you choose a destination having enough space to hold SYSTEM, SYSAUX, and Undo
    tablespaces along with the tablespace that holds the table. In this example, we will use the
    disk group DG1.

4. Decide the point in time to restore the table to. You can specify the point in time using
    either of:

    a. The timestamp

    b. The SCN

    In this example, in step 4, we specify recovery up to one minute prior to the current time.
    Since a day has 24 hours, and an hour has 60 minutes, the expression sysdate - 1/60/24
    represents the time just one minute ago.

    Pay careful attention to choosing the time. The table you are recovering must have been
    present in the database at that time. If the table was dropped prior to that time, the
    recovery will fail with "RMAN-05057: Table not found" error.

5. Connect to RMAN:

    ```
    $ rman
    RMAN> connect target '/ as sysdba'
    ```

■ **Caution**   As of the writing of this book, there is bug #14172827 that causes the last step of this process to fail.
To avoid that bug, connect to the target database in RMAN as sysdba or as SYS, i.e., connect target '/ as sysdba',
or as connect target sys/<SysPassword>; do not connect as connect target /.

---

6. Issue the following command from RMAN. Be sure to plug in your chosen point in time:

    ```
    RMAN> recover table SCOTT.ACCOUNTS
    2> until time 'sysdate-1/60/24'
    3> auxiliary destination '+DG1'
    4> ;
    ```

    The command will execute with a long output, which is not reproduced here for the sake
    of brevity. At the end, the table will be reinstated in the database from the backup.

    If you know the SCN, you can use that instead of the timestamp. For example:

    ```
    RMAN> recover table SCOTT.ACCOUNTS
    2> until scn 2012991
    3> auxiliary destination '+DG1'
    4> ;
    ```

■ **Note**   If you have one or more pluggable databases on a container database, the `recover table` command works only when connected to the container database, not to the pluggable ones.

How It Works

From the earlier recipes you learned how to recover a table manually from backup. In summary here are the high-level steps in that operation:

1. Create another database instance.

2. Restore from the backup the tablespace containing that table along with system, sysaux and undo tablespaces in a different location.

3. Open that restored database.

4. Export the table.

5. Import into the main database.

6. Drop this temporary database and delete the instance.

The recover table operation does all this work behind the scenes without you having to worry about the commands and other details. If you examine the very long output after the command, you can see the precise commands used by RMAN.

Let's examine some of the output from the recover command:

1. A temporary instance is created:

```
Creating automatic instance, with SID='ykFp'
 initialization parameters used for automatic instance:
db_name=CDB1
db_unique_name=ykFp_pitr_CDB1
```

RMAN chooses a random string as SID so as not to clash with an existing SID. The unique name of the database ykFp_pitr_CDB1 is also another way to avoid using one of the existing database names.

2. A clone control file is mounted:

```
contents of Memory Script:
{
# set requested point in time
set until  time "sysdate-1/60/24";
# restore the controlfile
restore clone controlfile;
# mount the controlfile
sql clone 'alter database mount clone database';
# archive current online log
sql 'alter system archive log current';
}
```

3. Relevant data files are restored:

```
{
# set requested point in time
set until  time "sysdate-1/60/24";
# set destinations for recovery set and auxiliary set datafiles
set newname for clone datafile  1 to new;
set newname for clone datafile  4 to new;
set newname for clone datafile  12 to new;
set newname for clone datafile  3 to new;
set newname for clone tempfile  1 to new;
# switch all tempfiles
switch clone tempfile all;
# restore the tablespaces in the recovery set and the auxiliary set
restore clone datafile  1, 4, 12, 3;
switch clone datafile all;
}
```

4. The relevant data files are restored to the location specified by the auxiliary parameter in the RMAN recover table command—DG1:

```
channel ORA_AUX_DISK_1: starting datafile backup set restore
channel ORA_AUX_DISK_1: specifying datafile(s) to restore from backup set
channel ORA_AUX_DISK_1: restoring datafile 00001 to +DG1
channel ORA_AUX_DISK_1: restoring datafile 00004 to +DG1
channel ORA_AUX_DISK_1: restoring datafile 00012 to +DG1
channel ORA_AUX_DISK_1: restoring datafile 00003 to +DG1
channel ORA_AUX_DISK_1: reading from backup piece
+FRA/cdb1/backupset/2012_08_04/nnndf0_tag20120804t133222_0.427.790435943
channel ORA_AUX_DISK_1: piece
handle=+FRA/cdb1/backupset/2012_08_04/nnndf0_tag20120804t133222_0.427.790435943
tag=TAG20120804T133222
channel ORA_AUX_DISK_1: restored backup piece 1
channel ORA_AUX_DISK_1: restore complete, elapsed time: 00:00:35
Finished restore at 04-AUG-12
```

5. The clone database is recovered:

```
contents of Memory Script:
{
# set requested point in time
set until  time "sysdate-1/60/24";
# online the datafiles restored or switched
sql clone "alter database datafile  1 online";
sql clone "alter database datafile  4 online";
sql clone "alter database datafile  12 online";
sql clone "alter database datafile  3 online";
# recover and open database read only
recover clone database tablespace  "SYSTEM", "UNDOTBS1", "UNDOTBS2", "SYSAUX";
sql clone 'alter database open read only';
}
```

6. Media recovery starts and completes on these data files:

```
starting media recovery

archived log for thread 1 with sequence 67 is already on disk as file
+FRA/cdb1/archivelog/2012_08_04/thread_1_seq_67.420.790436095
archived log for thread 1 with sequence 68 is already on disk as file
+FRA/cdb1/archivelog/2012_08_04/thread_1_seq_68.425.790436113
archived log for thread 1 with sequence 69 is already on disk as file
+FRA/cdb1/archivelog/2012_08_04/thread_1_seq_69.423.790448453
archived log file name=+FRA/cdb1/archivelog/2012_08_04/thread_1_seq_67.420.790436095
thread=1 sequence=67
archived log file name=+FRA/cdb1/archivelog/2012_08_04/thread_1_seq_68.425.790436113
thread=1 sequence=68
archived log file name=+FRA/cdb1/archivelog/2012_08_04/thread_1_seq_69.423.790448453
thread=1 sequence=69
media recovery complete, elapsed time: 00:00:02
Finished recover at 04-AUG-12

sql statement: alter database open read only
```

7. The table is exported via Data Pump:

```
contents of Memory Script:
{
# create directory for datapump import
sql "create or replace directory TSPITR_DIROBJ_DPDIR as ''
+DG1''";
# create directory for datapump export
sql clone "create or replace directory TSPITR_DIROBJ_DPDIR as ''
+DG1''";
}
executing Memory Script

sql statement: create or replace directory TSPITR_DIROBJ_DPDIR as ''+DG1''

sql statement: create or replace directory TSPITR_DIROBJ_DPDIR as ''+DG1''

Performing export of tables...
    EXPDP> Starting "SYS"."TSPITR_EXP_dscb_CvAe":
    EXPDP> Estimate in progress using BLOCKS method...
    EXPDP> Processing object type TABLE_EXPORT/TABLE/TABLE_DATA
```

8. The table is imported into the main database:

```
Performing import of tables...
    IMPDP> Master table "SYS"."TSPITR_IMP_dscb_zhwf" successfully loaded/unloaded
    IMPDP> Starting "SYS"."TSPITR_IMP_dscb_zhwf":
    IMPDP> Processing object type TABLE_EXPORT/TABLE/TABLE
    IMPDP> Processing object type TABLE_EXPORT/TABLE/TABLE_DATA
    IMPDP> . . imported "SCOTT"."ACCOUNTS"                    5.031 KB
```

9. Finally, the temporary instance is dropped:

```
Removing automatic instance
shutting down automatic instance
Oracle instance shut down
Automatic instance removed
auxiliary instance file +DG1/cdb1/datafile/sysaux.259.790448475 deleted
auxiliary instance file +DG1/cdb1/datafile/undotbs2.257.790448475 deleted
... and so on ...
```

If you encounter an error at any of the steps, it will be clearly visible in the above steps. The most common issues that may come up during this activity are:

- Backup does not have the tablespace that contains the table to be recovered

- The table was not present at the SCN or timestamp given in the recover command

- Not enough storage to restore the auxiliary database

- Not enough memory to create the auxiliary instance

Here are the restrictions on the recover table process:

- SYS owned tables can't be recovered.

- The recover table works by performing a point in time recovery of the tablespace, which is not allowed for SYSTEM and SYSAUX. Therefore, tables in these two tablespaces can't be recovered with this command.

- Tables can't be recovered on a physical standby database.

13-23. Recovering a Partition
Problem

You want to recover a single partition named P1 from a table named ACCOUNTS from the backup.

Solution

Follow the prerequisites explained in Recipe 13-22—e.g., there should be enough space in the auxiliary destination to hold the tablespaces SYSTEM, SYSAUX, and the tablespace where the partition exists. Sufficient memory to run another instance and the backup that contains the partition. After ensuring all those prerequisites are satisfied, follow these steps in RMAN:

1. Connect to RMAN target database:

    ```
    RMAN> connect target "/ as sysdba"
    ```

2. Recover the table's partition with this command:

    ```
    RMAN> recover table  scott.accounts:P1
    2> until scn 1799975
    3> auxiliary destination '+DG1';
    ```

    This creates a table called ACCOUNTS_P1, which is a replica of the partition P1 of the table ACCOUNTS.

3. Create an empty partition on the table. In this case, assume there is a partition called P2.
   So, you will need to split the partition P2.

```
SQL> alter table accounts
  2   split partition p2
  3   at (102)
  4   into
  5   (
  6       partition p1,
  7       partition p2
  8* );

Table altered.
```

This splits the partition P2 into two partitions: P1 and P2. All the data in P2 are still there
and P1 is completely empty.

4. Swap the newly recovered table with this empty partition:

```
SQL> alter table accounts
  2   exchange partition p1
  3   with table accounts_p1
  4   without validation;

Table altered.
```

Now the partition P1 contains the data from the backup.

5. The table ACCOUNTS_P1 is now empty. Drop the table:

```
SQL> drop table accounts_p1;

Table dropped.
```

How It Works

The recovery of a partition follows the same mechanism as the recovery of a table from the backup of the database as
shown in Recipe 13-22. The only difference is that the recovered partitions are created not as partitions, but rather as
independent tables. The syntax of the command used in step 2 of the solution is:

```
recover table <Owner>.<TableName>:<PartitionName>
```

If more than one partition is to be recovered, you can mention them separated by commas:

```
recover table scott.accounts:P1, scott.accounts:P2
```

Each partition is recovered as a separate table with the naming convention as <TableName>_<PartitionName>.
The partition P1 of the table ACCOUNTS will be recovered as ACCOUNTS_P1. If you recover multiple partitions of a
table, each partition is imported into an individual table.

13-24. Recovering a Table into a Different Name

Problem

You want to recover a table, but a table with the same name already exists in the database.

Solution

Suppose you want to recover a table called ACCOUNTS but there is already a table with that same name. Thus, you want to recover the table under a new name: ACCOUNTS_NEW. Ensure the prerequisites explained in Recipe 13-22. As explained in that recipe, use the `recover table` command, but with a little addition: the `remap table` clause.

1. Connect to RMAN:

    ```
    $ rman
    RMAN> connect target "/ as sysdba"
    ```

2. Recover the table but with `remap table` clause that creates a table with a different name—ACCOUNTS_NEW:

    ```
    RMAN> recover table  arup.accounts
    2> until scn 1799975
    3> auxiliary destination '+DG1'
    4> remap table arup.accounts:accounts_new;
    ```

The remap clause at the end causes the table ACCOUNTS to be restored with the name ACCOUNTS_NEW.

How It Works

Recall from Recipe 13-22 that the recover command creates a temporary instance and recovers just the tablespaces that are required for the table. The operation then exports the table and imports it into the main database. The `remap table` clause injects the REMAP_TABLE option in the final import process to import the table into a new name. The `remap table` clause in the recover command does the trick of restoring the table in the new name.

Here is the syntax of the remap table clause:

```
remap table <Owner>.<OldTableName>:<NewTableName>
```

If you want to recover a partition of the table:

```
remap table <Owner>.<OldTableName>:<PartitionName>:<NewTableName>
```

So, had you wanted to recover a partition P1 of table ACCOUNTS to a new table called ACCOUNTS_P1_NEW, you would have used the following clause instead:

```
remap table arup.accounts:p1:accounts_p1_new;
```

When you recover a partition, it always goes to a separate table.

13-25. Recovering a Table into a Different Tablespace

Problem

You want to recover a table, but not to the same tablespace it was in earlier. You don't want the default tablespace, but rather a different tablespace you choose during the recovery operation.

Solution

Follow the prerequisites explained in Recipe 13-22 and recover the table, but with a small change. The recover table statement has a remap tablespace clause that allows substituting tablespace names. Suppose you want to recover a table ACCOUNTS but want it to go to ACCDATA tablespace; not USERS. To do that, follow these steps:

1. Connect to RMAN:

   ```
   $ rman
   RMAN> connect target "/ as sysdba"
   ```

2. Recover the table partition but with remap clause:

   ```
   RMAN> recover table  arup.accounts
   2> until scn 1799975
   3> auxiliary destination '+DG1'
   4> remap tablespace users:accdata;
   ```

The last clause imports the table ACCOUNTS into the database, but instead of the default tablespace, it imports the table into the tablespace ACCDATA.

How It Works

The recipe works the same way as the Recipe 13-22. The remap tablespace clause in recover command does the trick. Here is the syntax of the remap clause:

```
remap tablespace <OldTablespace>:<NewTablespace>
```

The usual preconditions apply to the recover option here, e.g., the tablespace should have sufficient free space, etc. Note from the "How It Works" section of Recipe 13-22 that the recover command creates a new auxiliary instance, recovers just enough tablespaces necessary to recover the table, and exports that table and imports into the main database. The remap tablespace clause alters the IMPDP command to include the remap_tablespace option, which causes the process to import the table to a different tablespace.

13-26. Creating an Export Dump of a Table to be Recovered

Problem

You want to recover a table from backup, but not in the form of a table in a database. Instead, you want to create a Data Pump Export dump file with the table structure and data. What you want is the ability *later* to import the table and data into any database you choose.

Solution

Follow the prerequisites mentioned in Recipe 13-22. Then do the following:

1. Identify the location where the dump file will be created. In this example, we chose '/tmp' files system. You do not need to create a database directory object on this Unix directory.

2. Choose the name of the dump file. In this case we chose the name accounts.dmp.

3. Connect to RMAN:

```
$ rman
RMAN> connect target "/ as sysdba"
```

4. Issue the following command from RMAN prompt:

```
RMAN> recover table scott.accounts
2> until scn 1792736
3> auxiliary destination '+DG1'
4> datapump destination '/tmp' dump file 'accounts.dmp'
5> notableimport;
```

5. Check the existence of the dump file at the location specified - /tmp:

```
$ ls -l /tmp/accounts.dmp
```

Now you can use this file to import into a different database, or the same database later.

How It Works

The mechanics of the process has been described in Recipe 13-22. Like that recipe, this recipe's solution creates a temporary instance, recovers the tablespaces necessary for the table ACCOUNTS, and exports the table. But unlike that other recipe, the solution here does not import the table from that dump file.

Note the additional clause notableimport, which causes the table not to be imported into the database. Instead RMAN leaves the table in the dump file called accounts.dmp in the directory /tmp.

When you use the notableimport clause, you can't use remap tablespace or remap table. When you have the dump file, you can use it to import the table into any tablespace. If needed, you can rename the table as part of issuing the impdp command, so the remap clauses are not relevant and hence not available.

Handling Online Redo Log Failures

One of us worked for a company that had just implemented an expensive database server with redundancy built into every component, or so we thought. We were using RAID disks for all database files and the online redo log groups. We were confident that there was minimal risk of failure with these disks.

Therefore, we decided not to multiplex the online redo log groups. A few days later, an inexpensive battery that maintained the cache for a disk controller failed. This caused corruption in the current online redo log group. As a result, we lost data, experienced costly downtime, and had to perform an incomplete recovery.

How Redo Logs Work

Online redo logs are crucial database files that store a record of transactions that have occurred in your database. Online redo logs serve several purposes:

- Provide a mechanism for recording changes to the database so that in the event of a media failure you have a method of recovering transactions.

- Ensure that in the event of total instance failure, committed transactions can be recovered (crash recovery) even if committed data changes have not yet been written to the data files.

- Allow administrators to inspect historical database transactions through the Oracle LogMiner utility.

You are required to have at least two *online redo log groups* in your database. Each online redo log group must contain at least one *online redo log member*. The member is the physical file that exists on disk. You can create multiple members in each redo log group, which is known as *multiplexing* your online redo log group.

Tip We highly recommend that you multiplex the online redo log groups with at least two members in each group and, if possible, have each member on a separate physical device governed by a separate controller.

The log writer is the background process responsible for writing transaction information from the redo log buffer (in memory) to the online redo log files (on disk). The online redo log group that the log writer is actively writing to is the *current online redo log group*. The log writer writes simultaneously to all members of the current redo log group. The log writer needs to successfully write to at least one member for the database to continue operating. Your database will cease operating if the log writer cannot write successfully to at least one member of the current group.

The log writer writes *redo records* to the online redo log files. A redo record describes how a block of data was changed (and does not normally contain the data block itself), and consists of a group of *change vectors*. Change vectors are generated for modifications to the data segment block, the undo segment block, and the transaction table of the undo segment.

When the current online redo log group fills up, a *log switch* occurs, and the log writer starts writing to the next online redo log group. The log writer writes to the online redo log groups in a round-robin fashion. Since you have a finite number of online redo log groups, eventually the contents of each online redo log group will be overwritten. If you want to save a history of the transaction information, then you must place your database in *archivelog mode*. When your database is in archivelog mode, after every log switch, the archiver background process will copy the contents of the online redo log file to an *archived redo log* file. In the event of a failure, the archived redo log files allow you to recover the complete history of transactions that have occurred since your last database backup.

▓ **Note**   In an Oracle Real Application Cluster (RAC) database, each instance has its own set of online redo logs. This is known as a *thread* of redo. Each RAC instance writes to its own online redo logs and generates its own thread of archive redo log files. Additionally, each instance must be able to read any other instance's online redo logs. This is important because if one instance crashes, then the other surviving instances can initiate instance recovery via reading the crashed instance's online redo logs.

Figure 14-1 displays a typical setup for the online redo log files. This figure shows three online redo log groups, with each group containing two members (physical files). The database is in archivelog mode. In this figure, group 2 has recently filled with transactions, a log switch has occurred, and the log writer is now writing to group 3. The archiver process is copying the contents of group 2 to an archived redo log file. When group 3 fills up, another log switch will occur, and the log writer will begin writing to group 1. At the same time, the archiver will copy the contents of group 3 to archive log sequence 3 (and so forth).

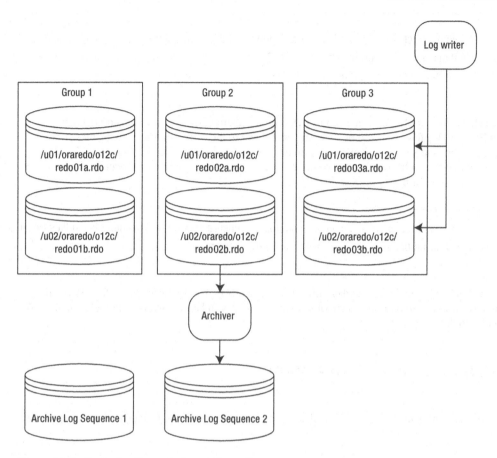

Figure 14-1. *Typical online redo log configuration*

The online redo log files aren't intended to be backed up. These files contain only the most recent redo transaction information generated by the database. When you enable archiving, the archived redo log files are the mechanism for protecting your database transaction history. Therefore, you should back up the archive redo log files.

The contents of the current online redo log files are not archived until a log switch occurs. This means that if you lose all members of the current online redo log file, then you'll most likely lose transactions. Listed next are several mechanisms you can implement to minimize the chance of failure with the online redo log files:

- Multiplex groups to have multiple members.

- If possible, don't allow two members of the same group to share a controller.

- If possible, don't put two members of the same group on the same physical disk.

- Ensure operating system file permissions are set appropriately (restrictive so that only the owner of the Oracle binaries has permissions to write and read).

- Use physical storage devices that are redundant (that is, RAID).

- Appropriately size the log files so that they switch and are archived at regular intervals.

- Consider setting the archive_lag_target initialization parameter to ensure that the online redo logs are switched at regular intervals.

■ **Note**   The only tool provided by Oracle that can protect you and preserve all committed transactions in the event you lose all members of the current online redo log group is Oracle Data Guard implemented in Maximum Protection Mode. Refer to MOS note 239100.1 for more details regarding Oracle Data Guard protection modes.

The online redo log files are never backed up by an RMAN online backup or by a user-managed hot backup. If you did back up the online redo log files, it would be meaningless to restore them. The online redo log files contain the latest redo generated by the database. You would not want to overwrite current files from a backup with old redo information. For a database in archivelog mode, the online redo log files contain the most recently generated transactions that are required to perform a complete recovery.

■ **Tip**   Use the RMAN `backup database plus archivelog` command to ensure your current online redo log files (of all the threads) are switched and archived before and after the backup of the database.

Since RMAN doesn't back up online redo log files, you can't use RMAN to restore these critical files. Given their criticality, we thought it was important to include a chapter on how to deal with failures with online redo log files. We first start by detailing how to decide what to restore.

14-1. Determining a Course of Action
Problem
You've experienced a problem with your online redo log files and need to determine what shape they are in and what action to take.

Solution
Follow these steps when dealing with online redo log file failures:

1. Inspect the alert.log file to determine which online redo log files have experienced a media failure.

2. Query V$LOG and V$LOGFILE to determine the status of the log group and degree of multiplexing.

3. If there is still one functioning member of a multiplexed group, then see Recipe 14-2 for details on how to fix a failed member(s).

4. Depending on the status of the log group, use Table 14-1 to determine what action to take.

Table 14-1. *Determining the Action to Take*

Type of Failure	Status Column of V$LOG	Action	Recipe
One member failed in multiplexed group	N/A	Drop/re-create member.	Recipe 14-2
All members of group	INACTIVE	Clear logfile or drop/re-create log group.	Recipe 14-3
All members of group	ACTIVE	Attempt checkpoint, and if successful, clear logfile. If checkpoint is unsuccessful, perform incomplete recovery.	Recipe 14-4
All members of group	CURRENT	Attempt to clear log, and if unsuccessful, perform incomplete recovery.	Recipe 14-5

Inspect your target database alert.log file to determine which online redo log file member is unavailable. Oracle error messages related to online redo log file failures are ORA-00312 and ORA-00313. Here's an example of errors written to the alert.log file when there are problems with an online redo log file:

```
ORA-00313: open failed for members of log group 2 of thread 1
ORA-00312: online log 2 thread 1: '/u02/oraredo/o12c/redo02b.rdo'
```

Query V$LOG and V$LOGFILE views to determine the status of your log group and the member files in each group:

```
SELECT
 a.group#
,a.thread#
,a.status grp_status
,b.member member
,b.status mem_status
,a.bytes/1024/1024 mbytes
FROM v$log     a,
     v$logfile b
WHERE a.group# = b.group#
ORDER BY a.group#, b.member;
```

Here is some sample output:

```
GROUP#  THREAD# GRP_STATUS MEMBER                          MEM_STA  MBYTES
------  ------- ---------- ------------------------------- -------  --------
     1        1 INACTIVE   /u01/oraredo/o12c/redo01a.rdo            50
     1        1 INACTIVE   /u02/oraredo/o12c/redo01b.rdo            50
     2        1 CURRENT    /u01/oraredo/o12c/redo02a.rdo            50
     2        1 CURRENT    /u02/oraredo/o12c/redo02b.rdo            50
     3        1 INACTIVE   /u01/oraredo/o12c/redo03a.rdo            50
     3        1 INACTIVE   /u02/oraredo/o12c/redo03b.rdo            50
```

If only one member of a multiplexed group has experienced a failure, then proceed to Recipe 14-2. If all members of a redo log group have experienced a failure and your database is open, it will hang (cease to allow transactions to process) as soon as the archiver background process cannot successfully copy the failed online redo log file members.

If your database is closed, Oracle will not allow you to open it if all members of one online redo log group are experiencing a media failure. When you attempt to open your database, you'll see a message similar to this:

```
ORA-00313: open failed for members of log group...
```

Depending on the status reported in V$LOG for the failed group, use Table 14-1 to determine what action to take.

How It Works

Your target database's alert.log file contains the best information for determining what type of failure has occurred. If only one member of a multiplexed group fails, then you will be able to detect this only by inspecting the alert.log file. You can also try to stop and start your database. If all members of a group have experienced media failure, then Oracle will not let you open the database and will display an ORA-00313 error message.

The alert.log file will also tell you where additional error messages have been written to trace files:

```
Additional information: 3
Checker run found 1 new persistent data failures
Errors in file /u01/app/oracle/diag/rdbms/o12c/o12c/trace/o12c_lgwr_10531.trc:
```

When diagnosing online redo log issues, the VLOG, VLOGFILE, and V$LOG_HISTORY views are particularly helpful. You can query these views while the database is mounted or open. Table 14-2 briefly describes each view.

Table 14-2. Useful Views Related to Online Redo Logs

View	Description
V$LOG	Displays the online redo log group information stored in the control file.
V$LOGFILE	Displays online redo log file member information.
V$LOG_HISTORY	History of online redo log information in control file.

The STATUS column of the V$LOG view is particularly useful when working with online redo logs groups. Table 14-3 describes each status and meaning for the V$LOG view.

Table 14-3. Status for Online Redo Log Groups in the V$LOG View

Status	Meaning
CURRENT	The log group that is currently being written to by the log writer.
ACTIVE	The log group is required for crash recovery and may or may not have been archived.
CLEARING	The log group is being cleared out by an alter database clear logfile command.
CLEARING_CURRENT	The current log group is being cleared of a closed thread.
INACTIVE	The log group isn't needed for crash recovery and may or may not have been archived.
UNUSED	The log group has never been written to; it was recently created.

The STATUS column of the V$LOGFILE view also contains useful information. This view contains information about each physical online redo log file member of a log group. Table 14-4 provides descriptions of the status of each log file member.

Table 14-4. *Status for Online Redo Log File Members in the V$LOGFILE View*

Status	Meaning
INVALID	The log file member is inaccessible, or it has been recently created.
DELETED	The log file member is no longer in use.
STALE	The log file member's contents are not complete.
NULL	The log file member is being used by the database.

It's important to differentiate between the STATUS column in V$LOG and the STATUS column in V$LOGFILE. The STATUS column in V$LOG reflects the status of the log group. The STATUS column in V$LOGFILE reports the status of the physical online redo log file member.

14-2. Restoring After Losing One Member of a Multiplexed Group
Problem

You notice this message in your alert.log file:

```
ORA-00312: online log 2 thread 1: '/u02/oraredo/o12c/redo02b.rdo'
```

You are experiencing media failure with one member of a multiplexed online redo log group and need to restore the damaged online redo log file member.

Solution

If your online redo log file members are multiplexed, the log writer will continue to function as long as it can successfully write to one member of the current log group. If the problem is temporary, then as soon as the online redo log file becomes available, the log writer will start to write to the online redo log file as if there were never an issue.

If the media failure is permanent (such as a bad disk), then you'll need to replace the disk and drop and re-create the bad member to its original location. If you don't have the option of replacing the bad disk, then you'll need to drop the bad member and re-create it in an alternate location.

For permanent media failures, follow these instructions for dropping and re-creating one member of an online redo log group:

1. Identify the online redo log file experiencing media failure.

2. Ensure that the online redo log file is not part of the current online log group.

3. Drop the damaged member.

4. Add a new member to the group.

To begin, open your alert.log file and look for an ORA-00312 message that identifies which member of the log group is experiencing media failure. You should see lines similar to these in your alert.log file:

```
ORA-00312: online log 2 thread 1: '/u02/oraredo/o12c/redo02b.rdo'
Errors in file /u01/app/oracle/diag/rdbms/o12c/o12c/trace/o12c_lgwr_10531.trc:
```

This message tells you which log member has failed. The alert.log file output also specifies that a trace file has been generated. You'll find additional information about the bad member in the specified trace file:

```
ORA-00313: open failed for members of log group 2 of thread 1
ORA-00312: online log 2 thread 1: '/u02/oraredo/o12c/redo02b.rdo'
ORA-27037: unable to obtain file status
Linux-x86_64 Error: 2: No such file or directory
ORA-00321: log 2 of thread 1, cannot update log file header
ORA-00312: online log 2 thread 1: '/u02/oraredo/o12c/redo02b.rdo'
```

From the prior output, a member of the online redo log group 2 is having issues. Once you've identified the bad online redo log file, execute the following query to check whether that online redo log file's group has a CURRENT status (in this example, we're interested in group 2):

```
SELECT group#, status, archived, thread#, sequence#
FROM v$log;
```

Here is some sample output indicating that group 2 is not the current log:

GROUP#	STATUS	ARC	THREAD#	SEQUENCE#
1	CURRENT	NO	1	25
3	INACTIVE	NO	1	24
2	INACTIVE	NO	1	23

■ **Note** If you attempt to drop a member of a current log group, Oracle will throw an ORA-01609 error specifying that the log is current and you cannot drop one of its members.

If the failed member is in the current log group, then use the alter system switch logfile command to make the next group the current group. Then drop the failed member as follows:

```
SQL> alter database drop logfile member '/u02/oraredo/o12c/redo02b.rdo';
```

Then re-create the online redo log file member:

```
SQL> alter database add logfile member '/u02/oraredo/o12c/redo02b.rdo'
    to group 2;
```

Keep in mind that the prior commands are examples, and that you'll have to specify the directory and logfile member file and group number for your environment.

If an unused log file already happens to exist in the target location, you can use the reuse parameter to overwrite and reuse that log file. The log file must be the same size as the other log files in the group:

```
SQL> alter database add logfile member '</directory/file_name>' reuse
    to group <group#>;
```

How It Works

Oracle will continue to operate as long as it can write to at least one member of a multiplexed redo log group. An error message will be written to the alert.log file when the log writer is unable to write to a current online redo log file.

You should periodically inspect your alert.log file for Oracle errors. This may be the only way that you'll discover a member of a group has experienced a media failure. We recommend that you run a periodic batch job that searches the alert.log file for any errors and automatically notifies you when it finds potential problems.

Once you've identified the bad member of an online redo log group, then you can drop and re-create the online redo log file. The newly created online redo log file may display an INVALID status in V$LOGFILE until it becomes part of the CURRENT log group. Once the newly created member becomes part of the CURRENT log group, its status should change to NULL. A NULL member status (as described in Table 14-4) indicates that the database is using the online redo log file.

You can drop and add online redo log file members while your database is in either a mounted state or an open state. We recommend that while dropping and re-creating log members, you have your database in a mounted state. This will ensure that the status of the log group doesn't change while dropping and re-creating members. You cannot drop an online redo log file member that is part of the CURRENT group.

■ **Note** When using the `alter database drop logfile member` command, you will not be allowed to drop the last remaining online redo log file member from a redo log group. If you attempt to do this, Oracle will throw an ORA-00361 error stating that you cannot remove the last standing log member. If you need to drop all members of a log group, use the `alter database drop logfile group` command.

SEARCHING THE ALERT LOG FOR ERRORS

Here's a simple Bash shell script that determines the location of the alert.log and then searches the alert.log for an error string. You can use something similar to automatically detect errors in the alert.log.

```
#!/bin/bash
export DBS="ENGDEV STAGE OTEST"
export MAILLIST="larry@support.com"
export BOX=`uname -a | awk '{print$2}'`
#-----------------------------------------------------------
for instance in $DBS
do
# call script to source oracle OS variables
. /etc/oraset $instance
crit_var=$(
sqlplus -s <<EOF
/ as sysdba
SET HEAD OFF TERM OFF FEED OFF VERIFY OFF
COL value FORM A80
select value from v\$diag_info where name='Diag Trace';
EOF)
  if [ -r $crit_var/alert_$instance.log ]
  then
  grep -ic error $crit_var/alert_$instance.log
    if [ $? = 0 ]
```

```
    then
        mailx -s "Error in $instance log file" $MAILLIST <<EOF
Error in $crit_var/alert_$instance.log file on $BOX...
EOF
        fi # $?
    fi # -r
done # for instance
exit 0
```

You can easily modify the above to fit the requirements of your environment. For example, you might need to change the way the Oracle operating system variables are sourced, the databases searched for, the error string, and the e-mail address. This is just a simple example showing the power of using a shell script to automate the search for errors in a file.

14-3. Recovering After Loss of All Members of the INACTIVE Redo Log Group

Problem

You're attempting to open your database and receive this message:

```
ORA-00312: online log 2 thread 1: '/u01/oraredo/o12c/redo02a.rdo'
ORA-00312: online log 2 thread 1: '/u02/oraredo/o12c/redo02b.rdo'
```

The message indicates that all members (two in this example) of an online redo log group in your database have experienced a media failure. You wonder how you're going to get your database open again.

Solution

To recover when you've lost all members of an inactive redo log group, perform the following steps:

1. Verify that all members of a group have been damaged.

2. Verify that the log group status is INACTIVE.

3. Re-create the log group with the clear logfile command.

4. If the re-created log group has not been archived, then immediately back up your database.

If all members of an online redo log group are damaged, you won't be able to open your database. In this situation, Oracle will allow you to only mount your database.

Inspect your alert.log file, and verify that all members of a redo log group are damaged. You should see a message indicating that all members of an online redo log group are damaged and the database cannot open:

```
ORA-00312: online log 2 thread 1: '/u01/oraredo/o12c/redo02a.rdo'
ORA-00313: open failed for members of log group 2 of thread 1
```

Next, ensure that your database is in mount mode:

```
$ sqlplus / as sysdba
SQL> startup mount;
```

Next, run the following query to verify that the damaged log group is INACTIVE and determine whether it has been archived:

```
SELECT group#, status, archived, thread#, sequence#
FROM v$log;
```

Here is some sample output:

```
GROUP# STATUS             ARC    THREAD#   SEQUENCE#
------ ----------------   ---    ---------- ----------
     1 CURRENT            NO            1          25
     3 INACTIVE           NO            1          24
     2 INACTIVE           NO            1          23
```

If the status is INACTIVE, then this log group is no longer needed for crash recovery (as described in Table 14-3). Therefore, you can use the clear logfile command to re-create all members of a log group. The following example re-creates all log members of group 2:

```
SQL> alter database clear logfile group 2;
```

If the log group has not been archived, then you will need to use the clear unarchived logfile command as follows:

```
SQL> alter database clear unarchived logfile group 2;
```

If the cleared log group had not been previously archived, it's critical that you immediately create a backup of your database. See Chapter 7 for details on taking a complete backup of your database.

Keep in mind that in these prior examples the logfile group is number 2. You'll have to modify the group number to match the group number for your scenario.

How It Works

If the online redo log group is inactive and archived, then its contents aren't required for crash or media recovery. Use the clear logfile command to re-create all online redo log file members of a group.

■ **Note**   The clear logfile command will drop and re-create all members of a log group for you. You can issue this command even if you have only two log groups in your database.

If the online redo log group has not been archived, then it may be required for media recovery. In this case, use the clear unarchived logfile command to re-create the logfile group members. Back up your database as soon as possible in this situation.

The unarchived log group may be needed for media recovery if the last database backups were taken before the redo information in the log was created. This means if you attempt to perform media recovery, you won't be able to recover any information in the damaged log file or any transactions that were created after that log.

If the clear logfile command does not succeed because of an I/O error and it's a permanent problem, then you will need to consider dropping the log group and re-creating it in a different location. See the next two subsections for directions on how to drop and re-create a log file group.

Dropping a Log File Group

The alternative to clearing a logfile group (which tells Oracle to re-create the logfile) is to drop and re-create the log file group. You might need to do this if you need to re-create the logfile group in a different location because the original location is damaged or not available.

A log group has to have an inactive status before you can drop it. You can check the status of the log group, as shown here:

```
select group#, status, archived, thread#, sequence#
from v$log;
```

You can drop a log group with the drop logfile group command:

```
SQL> alter database drop logfile group <group #>;
```

If you attempt to drop the current online log group, Oracle will return an ORA-01623 error stating that you cannot drop the current group. Use the alert system switch logfile command to switch the logs and make the next group the current group.

After a log switch, the log group that was previously the current group will retain an active status as long as it contains redo that Oracle requires to perform crash recovery. If you attempt to drop a log group with an active status, Oracle will throw an ORA-01624 error stating that the log group is required for crash recovery. Issue an alter system checkpoint command to make the log group inactive.

Additionally, you cannot issue a drop logfile group command if it leaves you with only one log group left in your database. If you attempt to do this, Oracle will throw an ORA-01567 error and inform you that dropping the log group is not permitted because it would leave you with less than two logs groups for your database (Oracle minimally requires two log groups to function).

Adding a Log File Group

You can add a new log group with the add logfile group command:

```
SQL> alter database add logfile group <group_#>
('/directory/file') SIZE <bytes> K|M|G;
```

You can specify the size of the log file in bytes, kilobytes, megabytes, or gigabytes. The following example adds a log group with two members sized at 50MB:

```
SQL> alter database add logfile group 2
('/u01/oraredo/o12c/redo02a.rdo',
 '/u02/oraredo/o12c/redo02b.rdo') SIZE 50M;
```

If for some reason the log file members already exist on disk, you can use the reuse clause to overwrite them:

```
alter database add logfile group 2
('/u01/oraredo/o12c/redo02a.rdo',
 '/u02/oraredo/o12c/redo02b.rdo') SIZE 50M reuse;
```

MOVING ONLINE REDO LOG FILES

The need may arise to physically move online redo log files. For example, you may want to relocate the online redo logs to a newly installed storage device. Here are the steps for moving online redo log files:

First, shut down the database:

```
SQL> shutdown immediate;
```

Second, from the OS move the online redo logs to the new location.

```
$ mv /u01/oraredo/o12c/redo03a.rdo /u03/oraredo/o12c/redo03a.rdo
$ mv /u02/oraredo/o12c/redo03b.rdo /u04/oraredo/o12c/redo03b.rdo
```

Third, start up the database in mount mode:

```
SQL> startup mount;
```

Fourth, use the alter database rename file clause to rename the online redo logs (this updates the control file):

```
alter database rename file
    '/u01/oraredo/o12c/redo03a.rdo', '/u02/oraredo/o12c/redo03b.rdo'
to '/u03/oraredo/o12c/redo03a.rdo', '/u04/oraredo/o12c/redo03b.rdo';
```

Last, open the database:

```
SQL> alter database open;
```

14-4. Recovering After Loss of All Members of the ACTIVE Redo Log Group

Problem

All the members of an active online redo log group in your database have experienced media failure.

Solution

Perform the following steps when restoring an active online redo log group:

1. Verify the damage to the members.

2. Verify that the status is ACTIVE.

3. Attempt to issue a checkpoint.

4. If the checkpoint is successful, the status should now be INACTIVE, and you can clear the log group.

5. If the log group that was cleared was unarchived, back up your database immediately.

6. If the checkpoint is unsuccessful, then you will have to perform incomplete recovery (see Recipe 14-5 for options).

Inspect your target database alert.log file, and verify the damage. You should see a message in the alert.log file identifying the bad members:

```
ORA-00312: online log 2 thread 1: '/u01/oraredo/o12c/redo02a.rdo'
ORA-00312: online log 2 thread 1: '/u02/oraredo/o12c/redo02b.rdo'
```

Next, verify that the damaged log group has an ACTIVE status as follows:

```
$ sqlplus / as sysdba
SQL> startup mount;
```

Run the following query:

```
select group#, status, archived, thread#, sequence#
from v$log;
```

Here is some sample output:

GROUP#	STATUS	ARC	THREAD#	SEQUENCE#
1	CURRENT	NO	1	92
2	ACTIVE	YES	1	91
3	INACTIVE	YES	1	90

If the status is ACTIVE, then attempt to issue an alter system checkpoint command, as shown here:

```
SQL> alter system checkpoint;
System altered.
```

If the checkpoint completes successfully, then the active log group should be marked as INACTIVE. A successful checkpoint ensures that all modified database buffers have been written to disk, and at that point, only transactions contained in the CURRENT online redo log will be required for crash recovery.

■ **Note**　If the checkpoint is unsuccessful, you will have to perform incomplete recovery. See Recipe 14-5 for a full list of options in this scenario.

If the status is INACTIVE and the log has been archived, you can use the clear logfile command to re-create the log group, as shown here:

```
SQL> alter database clear logfile group <group#>;
```

If the status is inactive and the log group has not been archived, then re-create it with the `clear unarchived logfile` command, as shown here:

```
SQL> alter database clear unarchived logfile group <group#>;
```

If the cleared log group had not been previously archived, it's critical that you immediately create a backup of your database. See Chapter 7 for details on creating a complete backup of your database.

■ **Note**   If you need to drop and re-create the group to an alternate location, see the How It Works section of Recipe 14-3 for an example.

How It Works

An online redo log group with an ACTIVE status is still required for crash recovery. If all members of an active online redo log group experience media failure, then you must attempt to issue a checkpoint. If the checkpoint is successful, then you can clear the log group. If the checkpoint is unsuccessful, then you will have to perform an incomplete recovery.

If the checkpoint is successful and if the log group has not been archived, then the log may be required for media recovery. Back up your database as soon as possible in this situation. The unarchived log group may be needed for media recovery if the last database backups were taken before the redo information in the log was created. This means if you attempt to perform media recovery, you won't be able to recover any information in the damaged log file or any transactions that were created after that log.

14-5. Recovering After Loss of All Members of the CURRENT Redo Log Group

Problem

All of the members of a current online redo log group in your database have experienced media failure.

Solution

Unfortunately, your alternatives are limited when you lose all members of a current online redo log group. Here are some possible options:

- Perform an incomplete recovery up to the last good SCN.
- If flashback is enabled, flash your database back to the last good SCN.
- If you're using Oracle Data Guard, fail over to your physical or logical standby database.
- Contact Oracle Support for suggestions.

In preparation for an incomplete recovery, first determine the last good SCN by querying the FIRST_CHANGE# column from V$LOG. In this scenario, you're missing only the current online redo logs. Therefore, you can perform an incomplete recovery up to, but not including, the FIRST_CHANGE# SCN of the current online redo log.

```
SQL> shutdown immediate;
SQL> startup mount;
```

Now issue this query:

```
SELECT group#, status, archived, thread#, sequence#, first_change#
FROM v$log;
```

Here is some sample output:

```
GROUP# STATUS              ARC  THREAD#   SEQUENCE# FIRST_CHANGE#
------ ------------------- ---  --------  ---------- -------------
     1 INACTIVE            YES       1          86        533781
     2 INACTIVE            YES       1          85        533778
     3 CURRENT             NO        1          87        533784
```

In this case, you can restore and recover up to, but not including, SCN 533784. Here's how you would do that:

```
RMAN> restore database until scn 533784;
RMAN> recover database until scn 533784;
RMAN> alter database open resetlogs;
```

For complete details on incomplete recovery, see Chapter 12. For details on flashing back your database, see Chapter 13.

How It Works

Losing all members of your current online redo log group is arguably the worst thing that can happen to your database. If you experience media failure with all members of the current online redo group, then you most likely will lose any transactions contained in those logs. In this situation, you will have to perform incomplete recovery before you can open your database.

■ **Tip**   If you are desperate to restore transactions lost in damaged current online redo log files, then contact Oracle Support to explore all options.

CHAPTER 15

■ ■ ■

Duplicating Databases and Transporting Data

Oracle DBAs routinely create duplicate databases by using source database backup files or by using *active database duplication*, which lets you duplicate a database without any backups of the source database. Duplicate databases help you test database upgrades and application changes and serve as reporting databases under some circumstances. Duplicating a database comes in handy when you need to test a backup and recovery strategy. You can duplicate a database when you accidentally lose a very large table and must recover it from a backup. Instead of performing a time-consuming database recovery, you can simply create a duplicate database and export the table and then import it into the production database. Starting with Oracle 12c, you can run the RMAN command recover table to restore a table to a point in time in the past by restoring the table from an rMAN backup. However, duplicating a database may be the best solution when dealing with earlier releases.

Besides duplicating databases, RMAN's duplicate database capability also helps you set up *standby databases*, which are not merely one-time copies of the production databases but are continually updated versions of the production database. The primary purpose of a standby database is to serve as the production server during recovery and failover situations. You can't use a duplicate database to perform a standby recovery and failover.

Although you can duplicate databases without using RMAN, there are several advantages to duplicating a database with the help of RMAN:

- You can duplicate a database without even making a backup of the source database by using network-enabled duplication, also called active database duplication.

- You can register a duplicated database in the same recovery catalog as the primary database, since the duplicate database will have its own unique DBID.

- You can exclude certain tablespaces, such as read-only tablespaces.

- You can duplicate the database on the same server or on a remote host.

- You also have the option, if you want, of duplicating a database to a past point in time.

- When you duplicate a database with RMAN, the duplicate command assigns the duplicate database a different DBID (except in cases where you duplicate a database for use as a standby database) so you don't have to change the DBID manually with the DBNEWID utility.

Any database duplication you make with the help of RMAN backups is called *backup-based duplication*. Prior to the Oracle Database 11g release, this was your only means of duplicating a database with RMAN. Backup-based database duplication requires a source database and a backup copy of that source database, either on the source host or on tape. Once you back up the source database, you need to transfer these source database backups to the destination server to create a duplicate database.

You may transfer backups of database files and the archived redo logs in various ways:

- Manually transfer backups from the target host to the host on which you are duplicating the database by using identical directory paths. For example, if the backups are stored in /u01/backup on the source host, move them to the /u01/backup directory on the destination host.

- Manually transfer backups from the target host to the duplicate host using different directory paths (to a different location on the host where you're creating the duplicate database). For example, if the backups are in the /u01/backup directory on the source host, copy them to the /u02/backup directory on the destination host. You must then update the source database control file using the catalog (catalog start with <directory>) command so it's aware of the new location of the backups. You must do this because RMAN checks the backup metadata in the control file for the location of the backup files and archived redo logs. Of course, this means that for the catalog command to work you must have the /u02/backup directory on the source host as well!

- Use a network file system (NFS), and ensure that the source and destination hosts can both access the same NFS mount point.

Starting with the Oracle Database 11g release, RMAN offers an alternative method of duplicating databases, without using any source database backups. This type of database duplication, performed directly over the network, is called active database duplication. In this chapter, we show you how to perform database duplication using both the older backup-based duplication method and the relatively new innovation in database duplication, which performs database duplication over the network without using any backups.

When you're duplicating databases with RMAN, the source and the destination databases can be on the same or different servers. To create a duplicate database, RMAN uses what's called an *auxiliary database instance*. An auxiliary instance is the database associated with the duplicate database. RMAN uses target channels to perform the work involved in active database duplication. For backup-based duplication, auxiliary channels perfom the work of duplication instead.

For active database duplication, RMAN can use image copies or backup sets. The capability to perform active database duplication using backup sets is a new feature introduced in Oracle Database 12c Release 1.

It's important to remember that the most recent point to which you can recover a duplicate database is the last redo log file archived by the source database. This is so because the duplication process doesn't back up and apply the source database online redo log files. Therefore, RMAN will always perform a database point-in-time recovery during database duplication.

You can use RMAN to duplicate a database in any of the following ways:

- Active duplication: duplicate the database files directly over the network

- Backup-based duplication without a target connection: use the recovery catalog and duplicate files from RMAN backup sets and image copies

- Backup-based duplication with a target connection: use RMAN to create duplicate database files from existing RMAN backup sets and image copies

- Backup-based duplication without a target connection or a recovery catalog: RMAN uses backup sets and copies stored in a directory designated by the parameter BACKUP_LOCATION

Also in this chapter, we talk about using RMAN to move data with transportable tablespaces. Oracle's transportable tablespaces feature lets you move large amounts of data much faster than a traditional export and import of data. This is because the transportable tablespace operation requires that you copy just the data files that belong to the tablepspace whose contents you want to transport and merely export and import the metadata relating to the tablespace. The transportable tablespace feature is highly useful when archiving historical data, performing tablespace point-in-time recovery, and exporting and importing large data warehouse table partitions. You can even transport tablespaces across platforms, which means you can use this feature to migrate Oracle databases from one platform to another or move data from data warehouses to data marts running on smaller platforms.

15-1. Renaming Database Files in a Duplicate Database

Problem

You're planning to duplicate a database without OFA or ASM files and learn that there are multiple ways to specify file names for the duplicate database. You want to find out which file-renaming method is best for you.

Solution

There are different file naming strategies you need to follow for naming regular directory structures as against an OMF- or ASM-based data file storage. This solution is devoted to non-OMF and non-ASM file renaming strategies. The next recipe discusses file naming strategies for OMF and ASM files.

There are multiple ways to rename files for a duplicate database when you use non-OMF and non-ASM file storage, as summarized in the following list.

1. Use the set newname command to name the file system data files and tempfiles.

You can employ the set newname command to rename data files before you issue the duplicate database command. You need to include the set newname command inside an RMAN run block, as shown in the following example.

```
run
{
set newname for datafile 1 to '/u01/app/oracle/oradata/system01.dbf';
set newname for datafile 2 to '/u01/app/oracle/oradata/sysaux01.dbf';
set newname for datafile 3 to '/u01/app/oracle/oradata/undotbs01.dbf';
set newname for datafile 4 to '/u01/app/oracle/oradata/users01.dbf';
set newname for datafile 5 to '/u01/app/oracle/oradata/users02.dbf';
set newname for tempfile 1 to '/u01/app/oracle/oradata/temp01.dbf';
duplicate target database to dupdb
...
}
```

The example shown here demonstrates how to rename file names at the individfual data file level, using the set newname command. The following example shows how to execute the set newname command at the *database level*:

```
run
{
set newname for database to '/u01/app/oracle/oradata/%U';
duplicate target database to dupdb
...
}
```

2. Use the configure auxname command to rename data files.

The configure auxname command achieves the same result as the set newname command, with the difference being that once you configure the auxiliary file names, all subseqeuent duplicate database commands can use the renamed file-name settings. With the set newname command, on the other hand, you'll have to specify the command each time you duplicate a database.

If you want to follow this strategy to specify names for your duplicate database data files, you must issue a `configure auxname` command to specify the names for each data file in the database you're duplicating:

```
configure auxname for datafile 1 to '/u01/app/oracle/oradata/system01.dbf';
configure auxname for datafile 2 to '/u01/app/oracle/oradata/sysaux01.dbf';
configure auxname for datafile 3 to '/u01/app/oracle/oradata/undotbs01.dbf';
configure auxname for datafile 4 to '/u01/app/oracle/oradata/users01.dbf';
configure auxname for datafile 5 to '/u01/app/oracle/oradata/users02.dbf';
```

Assuming you have just these five files in the source database, you can then issue the following command to duplicate the database:

```
set newname for tempfile 1 to '/u01/app/oracle/oradata/temp01.dbf';
duplicate target database
to dupdb
logfile
group 1 ('/u01/app/oracle/oradata/duplogs/redo01a.log',
```

You need to execute the `set newname` command to name the tempfile(s), as shown in the preceding example. RMAN then uses the `configure auxname` settings you've configured earlier to rename all the data files.

3. Use the `db_file_name_convert` command to generate file names

You can also use the `db_file_name_convert` command to generate the target file names. You can convert target file names from */oracle* to */dupdb/oracle*, for example. To generate names for log files you can use the analogous command `log_file_name_convert`.

How It Works

When RMAN duplicates a database, it must generate names for all database files, such as the control files, data files, tempfiles, and online redo log files. Oracle recommends the simple strategy of keeping the duplicate database names the same as those for the source database. That is, if you're using ASM disk groups, the disk groups must have the same names in both the source and the duplicate databases. Similarly, if the source database file names contain a path, the duplicate database must have an identical path name. Nothing more in terms of a file naming strategy is required if you choose to adopt this simple strategy. Obviously, you can use this strategy only in cases where the source and destination hosts are different. Even if the two hosts are different, as is the case in most cases, there may be a number of reasons you may want to name the duplicate database's file names differently from those in the source database. In all these cases, you can follow one of the strategies described in the Solution section of this recipe for naming the duplicate database's data files.

15-2. Specifying Alternative Names for OMF or ASM File Systems
Problem

You want to understand the alternatives for renaming files in a duplicate database using OMF- or ASM-based file systems.

Solution

When some or all of the files of a duplicate database use OMF or ASM files, you must set file naming parameters inside the auxiliary instance's initialization parameter file. If you're using an SPFILE for setting the initialization parameters, for example, you must include the following parameters in the SPFILE for the auxiliary instance.

- `db_create_file_dest`: specifies the default location for OMF managed data files

- `db_create_online_log_dest_n`: specifies the default location for OMF-based control files and online redo log files

- `db_recovery_file_dest`: specifies the default location for the fast recovery area

You can't set the `db_file_name_convert` and the `log_file_name_convert` parameters for OMF files. You must also not set the `control_files` parameter if you want the duplicate database's control files in an OMF format.

How It Works

You can include the `db_file_name_convert` command when duplicating a database or specify the parameter in the initialization parameter file for the auxiliary instance. You can use the `db_file_name_convert` parameter to generate file names for both data files and tempfiles.

Unlike the `db_file_name_convert` command, you can't specify the `log_file_name_convert` command in a `duplicate database` clause—you can specify the parameter only in the auxiliary instance's initialization parameter file.

15-3. Creating a Duplicate Database from RMAN Backups
Problem

You want to use RMAN to create a duplicate database from RMAN backups.

Solution

In this sequence of steps to create a duplicate database using RMAN backups, the target database is named *orcl*, and the duplicate database, also known as the *auxiliary database* in RMAN parlance, is named *orcl1*. Here are the steps to duplicate a database to the same server.

1. Back up the target database as follows:

```
RMAN> connect target /
RMAN> backup database plus archivelog;
```

You'll use these backups as the source for the database duplication later. Of course, if you already have made backups of the source database, you can skip this step.

2. Use a dedicated listener configuration for RMAN by making the following additions to your listener.ora file:

```
SID_LIST_LISTENER =
    (SID_LIST =
        (SID_DESC =
            (GLOBAL_DBNAME = orcl1)
            (ORACLE_HOME = /u01/app/oracle/product/12.01.1)
            (SID_NAME =orcl1)
        )
    )
```

3. Once you modify the listener.ora file, restart the listener:

```
$ lsnrctl start
```

4. Add the following information to the tnsnames.ora file, located in the $ORACLE_HOME/network/admin directory:

```
orcl1 =
(DESCRIPTION =
(ADDRESS_LIST =
(ADDRESS = (PROTOCOL = TCP)(HOST = virtual1.vm.alapati.com)(PORT = 1521))
)
(CONNECT_DATA =
(SERVER = DEDICATED)
(SERVICE_NAME = orcl1.vm.alapati.com)
 )
)
```

5. Create the init.ora file for the duplicate database, *orcl1*. During the database duplication process, RMAN will create the control files, the data files, and the redo log files for the duplicate database with the file name structure you provide through the db_file_name_convert and log_file_name_convert initialization parameters. The database duplication process will create a set of control files for the new duplicate database in the location specified by the control_files initialization parameter. Following are the contents of the init.ora file for creating the duplicate database orcl1:

```
db_name = orcl1
db_block_size = 8192
compatible = 12.0.0.0
remote_login_passwordfile = exclusive
control_files = ('/u05/app/oracle/oradata/orcl1/control01.ctl',
'/u05/app/oracle/oradata/orcl1/control02.ctl')
db_file_name_convert = ('/u01/app/oracle/oradata/orcl',
 '/u05/app/oracle/oradata/orcl1')
log_file_name_convert = ('/u01/app/oracle/oradata/orcl',
 '/u05/app/oracle/oradata/orcl1')
```

Only the db_name and the control_files initialization parameters are required. The db_block_size parameter is also required if this parameter is set in the target database. All the other initialization parameters are optional. In this example, the init.ora file for the duplicate database is named *initorcl1.ora*. Save this file in the appropriate location. (On Linux/Unix, the default location is $ORACLE_HOME/dbs, and on Windows it is %ORACLE_HOME%\database.)

6. Start the new auxiliary database (duplicate database) instance. You must start the new instance in nomount mode since you don't have a control file for this new database yet. For example:

```
$ export ORACLE_SID=orcl1
[oracle@virtual1 dbs]$ sqlplus /nolog

SQL*Plus: Release 12.1.0.0.2 Beta on Tue Nov 16 13:28:51 2012

Copyright (c) 1982, 2012, Oracle.  All rights reserved.
```

```
SQL> connect / as sysdba
Connected to an idle instance.

SQL> startup nomount pfile=$ORACLE_HOME/dbs/initorcl1.ora
ORACLE instance started.

Total System Global Area  238034944 bytes
Fixed Size                  2258944 bytes
Variable Size             180357120 bytes
Database Buffers           50331648 bytes
Redo Buffers                5087232 bytes
SQL>
SQL> exit
```

The `startup` command we executed starts the auxiliary instance and mounts the new control file. Once you create a new Oracle instance as shown here, the listener utility will automatically register the new database.

7. Start RMAN, and connect to the target database, after making sure you first set the ORACLE_SID environmental variable to the source database, *orcl*. Note that the target database can be mounted or open.

```
[oracle@virtual1 dbs]$ rman target sys/Ninamma11@orcl auxiliary /

Recovery Manager: Release 12.1.0.0.2 - Beta on Tue Nov 16 14:55:37 2012

Copyright (c) 1982, 2012, Oracle and/or its affiliates.  All rights reserved.

connected to target database: ORCL (DBID=1316762630)
connected to auxiliary database: ORCL1 (not mounted)

RMAN>
```

This has been an example showing how to perform a backup-based duplication with a target connection. We therefore must connect to the source database as the target. We must also connect to the auxiliary instance as auxiliary, but a recovery catalog is purely optional, and we aren't using one here.

■ **Note** If you're duplicating a database to the same host, as is the case in this example, you don't have to use a password file. You can simply choose to use operating system authentication to connect to the auxiliary instance. If you must access a database from a different host, on the other hand, you must use a password file for both the target and auxiliary instances, and they must use the same sysdba password. You must use an Oracle Net service name to connect to the auxiliary instance.

---

8. Issue the `duplicate target database` command to start the database duplication (since the Oracle 11.2 release, the word *target* is optional—that is, you can just issue the following command instead: duplicate database to orcl1).

```
RMAN> duplicate target database to orcl1;

Starting Duplicate Db at 16-NOV-12
using target database control file instead of recovery catalog
allocated channel: ORA_AUX_DISK_1
channel ORA_AUX_DISK_1: SID=21 device type=DISK

contents of Memory Script:
{
   sql clone "create spfile from memory";
}
...
executing Memory Script

connected to auxiliary database (not started)
Oracle instance started

contents of Memory Script:
{
   sql clone "alter system set  db_name =
 ''ORCL'' comment=
 ''Modified by RMAN duplicate'' scope=spfile";
   sql clone "alter system set  db_unique_name =
 ''ORCL1'' comment=
 ''Modified by RMAN duplicate'' scope=spfile";
   shutdown clone immediate;
   startup clone force nomount
   restore clone primary controlfile;
   alter clone database mount;
}
executing Memory Script
executing command: SET until clause
executing command: SET NEWNAME
...
Starting restore at 16-NOV-12
using channel ORA_AUX_DISK_1

channel ORA_AUX_DISK_1: starting datafile backup set restore
...
channel ORA_AUX_DISK_1: restore complete, elapsed time: 00:04:25
Finished restore at 16-NOV-12

datafile 1 switched to datafile copy
input datafile copy RECID=22 STAMP=796835136 file

executing Memory Script
Finished recover at 16-NOV-12
Oracle instance started
...
   Alter clone database open resetlogs;
}
```

```
database opened

Finished Duplicate Db at 16-NOV-12
RMAN>
```

The database duplication is successfully completed. You now have an identical copy of the source database (*orcl*), named *orcl1*.

How It Works

These prerequisites apply to all database duplication jobs:

- You must start the auxiliary instance with the nomount option.

- You can't use a standby database as the target database.

- You'll need the password file for the auxiliary instance only if you're using the RMAN client on a different host than the auxiliary host or if you duplicate from an active database (see Recipe 15-4 and Recipe 15-5).

- The target database can be open or closed.

- Both the source and destination databases must be on the same operating system platform (32-bit and 64-bit versions of a platform are considered identical). However, when duplicating from a 32-bit platform to a 64-bit platform, you must run the *utlrp.sql* script (located in the $ORACLE_HOME/rdbms/admin directory) to convert the code to the new operating system format.

If you're using disk-based backups, you can speed up the database duplication by allocating more channels. If you're using tape backups, however, you can have only as many channels as the number of tape devices you have available.

You may optionally specify the password file option with the duplicate database command when duplicating a database using the backup-based method if you want to make multiple passwords from your target database available on the new duplicate database. Specifying this option will overwrite any existing auxiliary instance password file with the source database password file.

■ **Note** You don't need a password file when you're duplicating a database on the same host as the source database.

The duplicate database command creates the duplicate data files for the new database and recovers them with the help of incremental backups (if you have any) and archived redo logs. It's your job to ensure that the auxiliary channel can access all the necessary data file backups and the archived redo logs necessary to create the duplicate database. You may use a mix of full and incremental backups for this purpose. You can also use the backups of the archived redo log files or the actual archived redo log files during the database duplication process. By default, RMAN will duplicate a database from the most recent available backups of the source database and will recover the duplicate database to the latest SCN contained in the archived redo logs. RMAN can't recover the duplicate database to the latest SCN, since it doesn't use the online redo logs as part of the database duplication. The RMAN client can run on any host as long as it can connect to the source and the auxiliary instances. You must ensure that all the necessary backup files and archived redo log files are accessible by the server session on the duplicate host. The auxiliary channel performs the bulk of the duplication work through the server session it starts on the host where you are duplicating the database. The auxiliary channel restores the backups of the primary database and starts the recovery process as part of the database duplication.

The **duplicate** command will automatically assign the duplicate database a new DBID, and, therefore, you can register both the source and the duplicate databases in the same recovery catalog. The exception is when you create a duplicate database to act as a standby database, because then both the primary database and standby database have the same DB_NAME and DBID. However, the two databases can have a different DB_UNIQUE_NAME to distinguish them when registering in the same recovery catalog. During the database duplication, RMAN does the following:

1. Generates a unique DBID for the new duplicate database.

2. Creates a new control file for the duplicate database.

3. Restores the backups and performs an incomplete recovery using all the backups and archived redo logs. The recovery must be an incomplete recovery since you don't back up the online redo logs (particularly the current online redo logs) on the target database. Therefore, you can't apply the online redo logs to the duplicate database, and thus can recover only to the latest archived redo log.

4. Shuts down and starts up the auxiliary instance.

5. Opens the duplicate database with the resetlogs option, thus clearing the online redo logs.

■ **Caution**   Since you're creating the duplicate database on the same host as the primary database, be extra careful when setting the *_path or *_dest initialization parameter so RMAN doesn't accidentally overwrite the source database files with the duplicate database files.

The Solution section showed you basic backup-based database duplication. Backup-based *database duplication* works the following way regarding the various types of source database files:

- Data files are restored from backups.

- Control files are re-created (to support and implement the targetless duplication feature starting with Oracle Database 11g) but are restored from backups if you specify for standby.

- Tempfiles are re-created in the location set by the db_create_file_dest parameter.

- Online redo log files are re-created.

- Archived redo logs are restored from backups, but only if needed for duplication.

- Server parameter files are restored from backup if you use the spfile clause only.

- Fast recovery area files aren't copied, and flashback log files, password files, and block change tracking files aren't re-created.

As part of the duplication process, RMAN re-creates the control file for the duplicate database using information from the target database. RMAN knows which backups (including incremental backups) and archived redo logs it needs for the duplication by reading backup metadata from the target database's control file. If you don't ensure that all auxiliary channels can access all backups and archived redo logs, the backup will fail.

Once the duplicate database is started, you can comment out or delete the db_file_name_convert and log_file_name_convert parameters from the init.ora file for the duplicate database. You can restart the duplicate database for normal use at this point.

Once you've duplicated the source database, you can register the duplicate database in the same recovery catalog as the primary database, since the two databases will have unique DBIDs.

If you are duplicating a database to the same Oracle home as the primary database, you must use a different DB_UNIQUE_NAME for the duplicate database. You can have an identical DB_NAME for both the original/source database and the duplicate/auxiliary database even if they are hosted on the same server or using the same ORACLE_HOME, as long as they have a different DB_UNIQUE_NAME.

You must also convert the file names (as in the example shown in the Solution section) so they're different from the source database file names. Make sure you don't specify the nofilenamecheck clause while duplicating the database on the same host, because this may cause the duplicate command to overwrite the primary database files.

15-4. Duplicating a Database Without Using RMAN Backups
Problem

You want to duplicate a database from a source database, but realize you don't have any backups of the source database.

Solution

Starting with Oracle Database 11g, you can duplicate a source database entirely without any premade source database backups whatsoever, by using network-based duplication of databases. As we mentioned earlier, this capability is also called active database duplication. The steps are essentially the same as those we showed for the older backup-based database duplication techniques earlier in this chapter, in Recipe 15-2.

Under RMAN's active database duplication strategy, you can use the source database files to duplicate a database directly to the auxiliary instance. In active database duplication, the service name of the auxiliary instance is utilized to copy the source database files and send them to the destination host as either image copies or backup sets. There's absolutely no need for any preexisting backups to duplicate the source database.

In this solution, we describe an example showing how to perform active database duplication by specifying the active database clause of the RMAN duplicate command. In the example, the source and duplicate databases are on the same host, so you do need to use different database file names for the two databases. The source database is named *orcl* and the duplicate database is named *orcl2*. Here's the process:

1. Add the following information to the tnsnames.ora file, located in the $ORACLE_HOME/network/admin directory:

```
ORCL2=
  (DESCRIPTION =
    (ADDRESS = (PROTOCOL = TCP)(HOST = virtual1.vm.alapati.com)(PORT = 1521))
    (CONNECT_DATA =
      (SERVER = DEDICATED)
      (SERVICE_NAME = orcl1.vm.alapati.com)
    )
  )
```

2. We're going to specify the spfile during our database duplication. You need only one parameter, db_name, to denote the name of your new duplicate database. You don't need to set the initialization parameters such as db_file_name_convert and log_file_name_convert, because you're going to set these parameters directly in the duplicate database command itself. So, the contents of the SPFILE for the auxiliary instance will look like this:

```
db_name = orcl2
```

3. In this example, the init.ora file for the duplicate database is named *initorcl2.ora*. Save this file in the appropriate location. (On Linux/Unix, the default location is $ORACLE_HOME/dbs, and on Windows, it's %ORACLE_HOME%\database.)

4. Create a password file for connecting remotely to the auxiliary instance with the sysdba privilege. This is because when you perform active database duplication, the target database instance must connect directly to the auxiliary database instance. Note that the password file connection requires the same sysdba password as that of the source database. Create the password file manually with the orapwd utility, as shown here, with just a single password to start the auxiliary instance:

```
[oracle@virtual1 dbs]$ export ORACLE_SID=orcl2
[oracle@virtual1 dbs]$ orapwd password=Ninamma11 file=orapworcl2
```

5. Start the auxiliary database (duplicate database) instance. You must start the new instance in the nomount mode since you don't have a control file for this new database yet.

```
$ export ORACLE_SID=orcl2
$ sqlplus /nolog

SQL> connect / as sysdba
Connected to an idle instance

SQL> startup nomount
Oracle Instance started.
Total System Global Area    113246208 bytes
Fixed Size                     218004 bytes
Variable Size                58722860 bytes
Database Buffers             50331648 bytes
Redo Buffers                  2973696 bytes
SQL> exit
```

The startup nomount command will start the auxiliary instance in the nomount mode. If you're using a Windows server, you create a new instance by using the oradim utility.

6. Start up RMAN, and connect to the target database after making sure you first set the ORACLE_SID environmental variable to the source database, which is named *orcl* in our case. The target database can be mounted or open.

```
RMAN> connect target sys/Ninamma11@orcl
connected to target database: ORCL (DBID=1316762630)
RMAN>
```

■ **Note** If you're duplicating a database to the same host, as is the case in this example, you don't have to use a password file. You can simply choose to use operating system authentication to connect to the auxiliary instance. If you're performing active database duplication, on the other hand, you must use a password file for both the target and auxiliary instances, and they must use the same sysdba password. You must use an Oracle Net service name to connect to the auxiliary instance.

7. Connect to the duplicate database using the keyword auxiliary through an SQL*Net connection:

```
RMAN> connect auxiliary orcl1
auxiliary database Password:
connected to auxiliary database: ORCL1 (not mounted)
RMAN>
```

8. Issue the duplicate target database command to start the database duplication process. For example:

```
RMAN> duplicate target database
   2> to orcl1
   3> from active database;

Starting Duplicate Db at 27-NOV-12
using target database control file instead of recovery catalog
allocated channel: ORA_AUX_DISK_1
channel ORA_AUX_DISK_1: SID=22 device type=DISK

contents of Memory Script:
{
   sql clone "alter system set  db_name =
 ...
   alter clone database mount;
}
executing Memory Script

sql statement: alter system set  db_name =  ''ORCL''  comment= ''Modified by RMAN
duplicate'' scope=spfile
Oracle instance shut down
Oracle instance started

Starting restore at 27-NOV-12
Finished restore at 27-NOV-12
...
executing command: SET NEWNAME
...
datafile 1 switched to datafile copy
...
contents of Memory Script:
{
   set until scn  2514656;
   recover
   clone database
    delete archivelog
   ;
}
sql statement: alter system set  db_name =  ''ORCL1''  comment= ''Reset to original value
by RMAN'' scope=spfile
```

```
sql statement: CREATE CONTROLFILE REUSE SET DATABASE "ORCL1" RESETLOGS ARCHIVELOG
   ...
contents of Memory Script:
{
   set newname for tempfile  1 to
 "/u05/app/oracle/oradata/orcl1/temp01.dbf";
   switch clone tempfile all;
   switch clone datafile all;
}
executing Memory Script
datafile 2 switched to datafile copy
input datafile copy RECID=7 STAMP=797777727 file
name=/u05/app/oracle/oradata/orcl1/example01.dbf
...
sql statement: alter tablespace  USERS online

Finished Duplicate Db at 27-NOV-12

RMAN>
```

How It Works

Make sure you follow these guidelines for network-enabled database duplication:

- Both the source and destination databases must be known to Oracle Net.

- The source database can be mounted or open.

- If the source database is mounted, you must have shut it down cleanly prior to starting it up in mount mode.

- If the source database is open, it must be running in archivelog mode.

- You can continue to use the source database normally while the database duplication is going on, but be aware that there's an overhead cost of CPU and network bandwidth consumption for sending the data.

You start the active database duplication process by using the from active database clause of the RMAN duplicate command. The inter-instance network connection is used to copy the source database files to the specified destination on the auxiliary instance. Since we didn't specify backup sets explicitly in the duplicate database command, RMAN copies the source data files over to the destiantion server as RMAN image copies. At the end of the data file copying process, RMAN uses a "memory script" to complete the recovery before opening the new duplicate database. RMAN decides the end time for the duplication based on when it completes the copying of the online data files.

You must use a password file during active database duplication, unlike in the case of backup-based duplication, where a password file isn't necessary. The password file makes it possible to connect to the auxiliary instance with the same SYSDBA password as the source database. You must use the same SYSDBA password for both the source and the auxiliary database. Alternatively, you can specify the password file option within the duplicate database command. When you do this, RMAN copies the source database password file to the destination server.

If you were to perform the active database duplication on a different host with the same directory structure, your database duplication command must include the `nofilenamecheck` clause, as shown here:

```
RMAN> duplicate database
    to newdb
    from active database
    nofilenamecheck;
```

Note that you still have to specify the `nofilenamecheck` clause, just as in the case of a backup-based duplication, since you're going to use identical directory structures and file names for both the source and destination databases. You also could use the optional `password file` option as part of the `duplicate database` command, if you want RMAN to copy the entire source database password file to the duplicate database. We chose to create the password file manually in this recipe.

Active *database duplication* works as follows regarding the various types of source database files:

- Data files are copied from the source database.

- Control files are re-created but will be copied from the source database if you specify the `for standby` clause.

- Tempfiles are re-created in the location set by the `db_create_file_dest` parameter.

- Online redo log files are re-created.

- Archived redo logs are copied from the source database, but only if needed for duplication.

- Server parameter files are copied from the source database if you use the `spfile` clause only.

- Password files are always copied for standby databases, but for a duplicate database, they're copied only if you specify the `password file` option in the `duplicate database` command.

Fast recovery area files aren't copied, and flashback log files, password files, and block change tracking (BCT) files aren't re-created. If block change tracking is enabled in the original/source database, then the BCT file is actually created at the auxiliary/duplicate database.

In this example, we don't specify any auxiliary channels. RMAN will use only image copies and not backup sets during this active database duplication, when you don't allocate any auxiliary channels. This example uses RMAN image copies to transfer all source database files over to the auxiliary database. Using image copies is also called push-based method for active database duplication and this method uses quite a bit of resources on the source database. When you perform active duplication and specify backup sets, the auxiliary instance gets the database files from the source database, a method also known as the pull-based method. This method uses fewer resources on the source database. Using backup sets instead of image copies for active database duplication also means you can take advantage of features such as the encryption and compression of the source database backup sets. In addition, you can parallelize the creation of backup sets, so this could be a much faster method for transporting large databases.

As mentioned earlier, the example in the Solution section used image copies. To let RMAN use backup sets instead, you must specify a net service name for the target database and also ensure that the number of auxiliary channels that you allocate is at least as large as the number of target channels allocated. Finally, you must add one of the following clauses to the `duplicate ... from active database` command:

- `using backupset`

- `using compressed backup set`

- `section size`

If you'd rather create a standby database instead of a duplicate database, all you have to do is replace the to auxdb part of the duplicate database command with the for standby clause, as shown here:

```
RMAN> duplicate target database
      for standby
      from active database;
```

It's easy to duplicate a non-ASM file-based database to an ASM file system-based database. Here we'll show you a simple example to demonstrate how to do this. First create an ASM disk group, named +DISK1. Following is the database duplication command to create an ASM file system-based duplicate database. This duplicate database command will create a database whose data files, control files, and online redo logs are all in the ASM disk group +*DISK1*.

RMAN> duplicate target database

```
to newdb
from active database
spfile
parameter_value_convert
'/u01/app/oracle/oradata/sourcedb/','+DISK1'
set db_create_file_dest = +DISK1;
```

You can speed up active database duplication by increasing the parallelism setting of disk channels on the source database. Doing so will lead to parallel copying of the source database files over the network.

■ **Tip** Make sure you don't use the nofilenamecheck clause with the duplicate command when duplicating a database on the same host as the source database, as is the case in this recipe. The nofilenamecheck clause keeps RMAN from checking whether the source and target file names are identical. Use it only when duplicating a database to a different host.

If you get an error such as PLS-561, it means the duplicate database doesn't have the same value for the nls_lang parameter as the source database. In this case, you must set the correct nls_lang environment variable to get past the error. Use the following query to find out the value of the nls_lang parameter in the source database:

```
SQL> select parameter, value from nls_database_parameters
      where parameter in
      ('NLS_LANGUAGE','NLS_TERRITORY','NLS_CHARACTERSET'
      ,'NLS_NCHAR_CHARACTERSET');
```

To change the value of the nls_lang variable, use the export or setenv command (in Linux/Unix) to set the value for the variable you get from the previous query.To avoid problems because of inadequate memory, you may use a higher memory for the duplicate database when you're duplicating it.

15-5. Specifying Options for Network-based Active Database Duplication

Problem

You want to specify various options such as encryption and compression during active database duplication.

Solution

In this recipe, we'll show you how to specify three key options—*encryption, compression,* and *parallelization*—during active database duplication.

Specifying Encryption

Simply add the set encryption command before the duplicate command, to perform active database duplication using encrypted backup sets. Here's an example:

```
RMAN> set encryption algorithm 'AES128';
RMAN> connect target sysbackup@prod;
RMAN> connect auxiliary sysbackup@dup_db
RMAN> duplicate target database to dup_db
      from active database
      password file;
```

Specifying Compression

You can compress backup sets that you create to transfer the source database files to the destination database. You can compress backup sets that you're using for active database duplication, by specifying the using compressed backupset clause of the duplicate command. Here's an example:

```
RMAN> duplicate target database to dup_db
      from active database
      password file
      using compressed backupset;
```

Specifying Parallelization

You can speed up active database duplication by parallelizing the duplication propcess. You do this by taking advantage of RMAN's *multisection backups* feature. Specify the section size option of the duplicate command to create multisection backups, which can be used in the duplication process. Here's an example:

```
RMAN> duplicate target database to dup_db
      from active database
      password file
      section size 400M;
```

This duplicate command creates and uses multisection backup sets, which are limited to 400 MB each in size.

How It Works

The ability to encrypt backup sets during active database duplication provides additional security when transmitting the contents of the data files over a network. You can specify encryption during active database duplication, but only if you're using push-based duplication, which uses RMAN backup sets and not image copies. Since backup sets can be used in database duplication only starting with Oracle Database 12.1 release, you can specify encryption only if your database is atleast 12.1 or newer releases.

Using compressed backup sets will provide better performance during the duplication of a database, because you'll be dealing with smaller backup sets. RMAN supports the compression of the backupsets used for active database duplication starting with Oracle Database 12c Release 1.

If you're dealing with very large source database data files, using multisection backups during active database duplication provides faster performance during the backup. RMAN will back up the large data files in parallel and create multiple backup pieces with separate RMAN channels dedicated to creating each backup piece. As with the encryption and compression features, the ability to create multisection backups is also a new feature introduced in the 12.1 release.

15-6. Duplicating a Database with Several Directories

Problem

You want to duplicate a source database with data spread out over several directories.

Solution

If the source database files are spread over multiple directories, you must use the set newname parameter instead of the db_file_name_convert parameter to rename the files in the duplicate database.

The following example shows how to create a duplicate database when the target database uses several directories:

```
RMAN> run
{
set newname for datafile 1 to '/u01/app/oracle/testdata/system01.dbf';
set newname for datafile 2 to '/u01/app/oracle/testdata/sysaux01.dbf';
set newname for datafile 3 to '/u01/app/oracle/testdata/data01.dbf';
set newname for datafile 4 to '/u01/app/oracle/testdata/index01.dbf';
set newname for datafile 5 to '/u01/app/oracle/testdata/undotbs01.dbf';
duplicate target database to newdb
logfile
    group 1 ('/u01/app/oracle/testdata/logs/redo01a.log',
      ('/u01/app/oracle/testdata/logs/redo01b.log') size 10m reuse,
    group 2 ('/u01/app/oracle/testdata/logs/redo02a.log',
      ('/u01/app/oracle/testdata/logs/redo02b.log') size 10m reuse;
}
```

The run block shown here duplicates the target database and supplies file names for both data files and online redo log files for the duplicate database.

How It Works

You must use a `run` block when duplicating database with the `set newname for datafile` clause, since that's a requirement for using the `set newname` clause. Before you run the `duplicate database` command, copy the source database initialization file from the source database host to the host where you're creating the duplicate database. Specify a path name in this initialization parameter file for all parameters that end with _dest. However, you mustn't set any values for the db_file_name_convert and log_file_name_convert parameters, because the `run` command specifies file names for both the data files and the online redo log files.

15-7. Duplicating a Database to a Past Point in Time
Problem

You want to create a duplicate database to a past point in time.

Solution

To create an auxiliary database to a past point in time, you use essentially the same steps as shown in Recipe 15-2. The only difference comes at the end, during the execution of the `duplicate` command. You must specify the `until` time clause to create an auxiliary database to a past period in time. Here's an example that shows how to duplicate the database to a past point in time using the `until time` clause:

```
RMAN> connect target sys/<sys_password>@targdb
RMAN> connect auxiliary sys/<sys_password.@dupdb
RMAN> duplicate target database
      to dupdb
      spfile
      nofilenamecheck
      until time 'sysdate-1';
```

The `duplicate ... until time` command shown here will create a duplicate database that'll be in the same state as the source database was 24 hours ago.

How It Works

Use the `until time` clause when you want to specify a database duplication but don't want the duplicate database to be quite as up-to-date as the source database. You can provide the archived redo logs in the form of an already backed-up RMAN backup set or in their original form from the archived redo log destination.

You can also perform incomplete database duplication to a past point in time by placing the `set until time` clause before the `duplicate database` command, as shown in the following example:

```
run
 {
  allocate channel C1 device type disk;
  allocate auxiliary channel C2 device type disk;
  set until time "to_date('Nov 16 2012 12:00:00',
  'Mon DD YYYY HH24:MI:SS')";
  duplicate target database to aux;
 }
```

The set until time clause will ensure that the duplicate target database won't be up-to-date but rather be current only to the November 16, 2012, point in time that you specified in the duplicate database command.

▪ **Note**   The until or to restore point clause, which allows you to perform an incomplete recovery when duplicating a database, is usable only in backup-based duplication. You can't use these incomplete duplication techniques when using *active database duplication*, which doesn't use any preexisting backups.

Note that in addition to specifying a point in time (until time), you can also specify an SCN or a log sequence number for an incomplete database duplication job. Or you may specify the to restore point clause, which results in an incomplete database duplication with the SCN corresponding to the restore point as the inclusive limit point for the database duplication.

15-8. Skipping Tablespaces During Database Duplication
Problem

You want to skip certain tablespaces when duplicating a database.

Solution

Specify the skip tablespace clause to omit specific tablespaces when duplicating a database. In the following example, the skip tablespace clause leads to the omission of the *users* and *tools* tablespaces from the duplicate database named aux:

```
run
  {
    allocate channel C1 device type disk;
    allocate auxiliary channel C2 device type disk;
    duplicate database to aux
    skip tablespace users, tools;
  }
```

The result of this command will be a duplicate database that's exactly the same as the source database, but without the two tablespaces: *users* and *tools*.

How It Works

As soon as RMAN opens the new auxiliary database, it'll start dropping all tablespaces that are part of the skip tablespace command. The tablespace drop is done using the option including contents cascade constraints. RMAN drops the tablespaces in a reverse sorted list of tablespace names. You'll get errors if you try to exclude tablespaces that contain indexes used for enforcing unique or primary keys.

You don't have to specify the temporary tablespaces as part of the excluded tablespaces since RMAN doesn't back up the temporary tablespace. Since leaving out LOBs may cause a database duplication to fail, it's a good idea not to exclude tablespace containing LOBs. You can't exclude the default permanent tablespace (such as the *users* tablespace in most Oracle databases). If you do, RMAN will receive an error because it'll try to drop the default permanent tablespace from the new duplicate database. One way around this is to change the default permanent tablespace to a different tablespace.

15-9. Duplicating a Database with a Specific Backup Tag

Problem

You want to specify a particular backup tag during the duplication of a database.

Solution

You can "force" RMAN to use a specific backup during a database duplication process by simply making other backups unavailable. Here are the steps to follow:

1. Use the `list backup of database` command to find out the primary key of the backup set you plan to use in the duplication process:

    ```
    RMAN> list backup of database;
    ```

2. Make all the backup sets except the one you choose unavailable to RMAN during the database duplication process by using the following command for each of the backups you want to make inaccessible to RMAN:

    ```
    RMAN> change backupset <primary key> unavailable;
    ```

3. Follow the steps in Recipe 15-2 or Recipe 15-3 to duplicate the source database.

4. Once the database duplication is finished, make all the backups available to RMAN again by issuing the following command for each of the backup sets you had made unavailable prior to the database duplication:

    ```
    RMAN> change backupset <primary key> available;
    ```

All the backup sets are once again "available" for use by RMAN.

How It Works

The ability to specify a particular tag to back up a database is handy when you're moving a production database to a test platform. You may have multiple backups of the production database available to RMAN, and you may not necessarily want the latest backup to serve as the basis of database duplication. In such cases, you can choose a specific version of the production database by picking a specific backup denoted by a backup tag and make just that backup available to RMAN for duplicating the database.

15-10. Resynchronizing a Duplicate Database

Problem

You want to synchronize a duplicate database with its parent database.

Solution

Once you create a duplicate database from a source database, you can periodically "update" or synchronize the duplicate database by simply rerunning the `duplicate` command over again, in essence re-creating the duplicate database (reduplicating the target database). In the following example, we first perform a one-time setup of the new data file names by using the `configure auxname` clause, as shown here:

```
RMAN> connect target /
RMAN> connect catalog rman/rman@catdb
RMAN> connect auxiliary sys/Nicholas11@dupdb
RMAN> run {
configure auxname for datafile 1 to '/u01/app/oracle/oradata1/system01.dbf';
configure auxname for datafile 2 to '/u01/app/oracle /oradata2/sysaux01.dbf';
configure auxname for datafile 3 to '/u01/app/oracle /oradata3/undotbs01.dbf';
configure auxname for datafile 4 to '/u01/app/oracle /oradata4/drsys01';
configure auxname for datafile 5 to '/u01/app/oracle /oradata5/example01.dbf';
configure auxname for datafile 6 to '/u01/app/oracle /oradata6/indx01.dbf';
configure auxname for datafile 7 to '/u01/app/oracle /oradata7/users01.dbf';
}
```

Synchronize the duplicate database with the source database by periodically executing the `duplicate target database` command to re-create the duplicate database. For example:

```
RMAN> connect target /
RMAN> connect catalog rman/rman@catdb
RMAN> connect auxiliary sys/Ninamma11@dupdb

RMAN> duplicate target database to dupdb
logfile
group 1 ('/u01/app/oracle/duplogs/redo01a.log',
'/u02/app/oracle/duplogs/redo01b.log') size 200k reuse,
group 2 ('/u01/app/oracle/duplogs/redo02a.log',
'/u02/app/oracle /duplogs/redo02b.log') size 200k reuse;
```

You can schedule this script for running on a daily or a weekly basis, thus creating a new and up-to-date duplicate database on a continuous basis.

How It Works

To synchronize a duplicate database with the parent database, you must in essence re-create the duplicate database by transferring the latest copies of the source database files to the duplicate database.

To set up a database for periodic synchronization, you must first use the `configure` command to set persistent new names for the data files. Once you set the persistent data file names, the file names will be recorded in the control file, and RMAN will use the same file names each time you synchronize the duplicate database by using the `duplicate` command.

Remember that you have to employ the `configure auxname` clause only once—the first time you duplicate the database. RMAN will reuse the same file names anytime you execute the `duplicate` command.

15-11. Duplicating Pluggable Databases and Container Databases

Problem

You want to duplicate a pluggable database or a container database.

Solution

In this Solution, we explain first how to duplicate a container database. Then we show how to duplicate a pluggable database.

Duplicating a Container Database

To duplicate a whole container database, you follow the same initial steps as you do for a regular database, as shown in Recipe 15-3. Make sure that when you connect to the target and the auxiliary databases that you connect to *root*. Also ensure that the credentials are the same in both the source and the auxiliary database.

Back up the data files for the container database with the following command:

```
RMAN> backup copy of database;
```

If there are no image copies, you may experience the following error:

```
RMAN-06585: no copy of datafile 1 found
```

Duplicating a Pluggable Database

Follow these steps to duplicate a pluggable database.

1. First, complete steps 1-6 shown in Recipe 15-3.

You can transfer just the backup files for a pluggable database (in this case *pdb3*), by using the backup command with the pluggable option. For example:

```
RMAN> backup copy of pluggable database pdb3;
```

If there are no image copies, you may experience the following error:

```
RMAN-06585: no copy of datafile 1 found
```

2. Duplicate a pluggable database, called *pdb1* in this example, with the following command:

```
RMAN> duplicate database to cdb1 pluggable database pdb1;
```

This command duplicates the pluggable database *pdb1* to the container database *cdb1*.

3. You can duplicate all the databases in a container database, with the exception of the pluggable database *pdb3*, by executing the following command:

```
RMAN> duplicate database to cdb1 skip pluggable database pdb3;
```

The `skip pluggable` database option lets you duplicate all pluggable databases in a container database, except the pluggable databases that you specify in the command. You can specify multiple pluggable databases by using a comma-delimited list, as we explain in the How It Works section of this recipe.

How It Works

As you learned in the Solution section, you use the same `duplicate` command to duplicate pluggable databases as you do for a normal database. You must log in to the root as a user with the SYSDBA or the SYSBACKUP role.

You can duplicate one or more pluggable databases with the same `duplicate` command. During the duplication of a pluggable database, RMAN duplicates the root (CDB$ROOT) and the seed database (PDB$SEED) of the container database, of which the pluggable database is a part. You can duplicate multiple pluggable databases by using the `duplicate` command in the following way:

```
RMAN> duplicate database to cdb1 pluggable database pdb1, pdb2, pdb;
```

You might experience the following error message when duplicating a pluggable database:

```
RMAN-06136: ORACLE error from auxiliary database: ORA-65093: container database not set up properly
```

To avoid this error, make sure to set the following parameter in the auxiliary database.

```
_enable_pluggable_database=true
```

You can duplicate specific tablespaces within a pluggable databhase as well. First, complete the requirements for database duplication as explained in steps 1–6 in Recipe 15-3. Once you do this, execute the `duplicate` command with the `tablespace` option.:

The `duplicate` command shown in this first example duplicates the *example* tablespace from the pluggable database *pdb1*:

```
RMAN> duplicate database to cdb1 tablespace pdb1:example;
```

This next example shows how to duplicate both a pluggable database (pdb1) and a tablespace (named *example*) from a different pluggable database (*pdb2*) at the same time:

```
RMAN> duplicate database to cdb1 pluggable database pdb1 tablespace pdb2:example;
```

15-12. Transporting Tablespaces on the Same Operating System Platform
Problem

You want to transport tablespaces using RMAN backups instead of performing the transportable tablespaces operation on the "live" production database.

■ **Tip** You can also transport tablespaces using the "live" data files from a database instead of using RMAN backups of those data files. However, the live tablespace transport requires the tablespaces to be open read-only during the transport. Using RMAN backups thus enhances database availability, especially when transporting huge tablespaces.

Solution

You create a transportable tablespace set by executing the RMAN command transport tablespace. The following example shows how to transport tablespaces between identical operating system platforms by utilizing RMAN backups. Here are the steps you must follow to transport tablespaces from one database to another.

1. Connect to the recovery catalog and to the target database.

    ```
    RMAN> connect catalog rman@catdb

    recovery catalog database Password:
    connected to recovery catalog database

    RMAN> connect target sysbackup

    target database Password:
    connected to target database: ORCL (DBID=1316762630)
    ```

2. Generate the transportable tablespace set by issuing the transport tablespace command. During a regular (non-RMAN) tablespace transport, you use an operating system utility, such as the scp command, to copy the database files that belong to the tablespaces in the transportable tablespace set. Here, however, since we're using RMAN to transport the tablespaces, we use the RMAN backups for this purpose.

    ```
    RMAN> transport tablespace test2
    2> tablespace destination '/u01/app/oracle/oradata/transportdest'
    3> auxiliary destination '/u01/app/oracle/oradata/auxdest';

    Creating automatic instance, with SID='nFya'

    initialization parameters used for automatic instance:
    db_name=ORCL
    db_unique_name=nFya_pitr_ORCL
    compatible=12.0.0.0.0
    ...
    starting up automatic instance ORCL

    Oracle instance started
    Running TRANSPORT_SET_CHECK on recovery set tablespaces
    TRANSPORT_SET_CHECK completed successfully

    contents of Memory Script:
    {
    # set requested point in time
    set until  scn 2413098;
    # restore the controlfile
    restore clone controlfile;
    # mount the controlfile
    sql clone 'alter database mount clone database';
    # archive current online log
    sql 'alter system archive log current';
    ```

```
# resync catalog
resync catalog;
}
executing Memory Script

executing command: SET until clause

Starting restore at 23-NOV-12
Finished restore at 23-NOV-12
sql statement: alter database mount clone database
sql statement: alter system archive log current
starting full resync of recovery catalog
full resync complete
Starting restore at 23-NOV-12
contents of Memory Script:
contents of Memory Script:
{
# make read only the tablespace that will be exported
sql clone 'alter tablespace  TEST2 read only';
# create directory for datapump export
sql clone "create or replace directory STREAMS_DIROBJ_DPDIR as ''
/u01/app/oracle/oradata/transportdest''";
}
Performing export of metadata...
    EXPDP> Starting "SYSBACKUP"."TSPITR_EXP_nFya_xCjA":
    EXPDP> Datafiles required for transportable tablespace TEST2:
    EXPDP>    /u01/app/oracle/oradata/transportdest/test02_01.dbf
    EXPDP> Job "SYSBACKUP"."TSPITR_EXP_nFya_xCjA" successfully completed at Tue Nov 23
15:29:14 2012 elapsed 0 00:02:22
Export completed
/*
    The following command may be used to import the tablespaces.
    Substitute values for <logon> and <directory>.
    impdp <logon> directory=<directory> dumpfile= 'dmpfile.dmp' transport_datafiles=
/u01/app/oracle/oradata/transportdest/test02_01.dbf
-----------------------------------------------------------------
-- Start of sample PL/SQL script for importing the tablespaces
-----------------------------------------------------------------
-- End of sample PL/SQL script
-----------------------------------------------------------------
Removing automatic instance
shutting down automatic instance
Oracle instance shut down
Automatic instance removed
RMAN>
```

3. The transport tablespace command generates a Data Pump export file with the
    necessary metadata to transport the tablespace named *test2*. It also copies the data files for
    the tablespace you're going to transport.

4. Import the tablespace set into the target database by running the Data Pump import
    script generated by the `transport tablespace` command. You can perform the import by
    using the Data Pump Import utility from the command line, but it's a whole lot simpler to
    use the import script prepared for you by RMAN during the creation of the transportable
    tablespace set, with the default name *impscrpt.sql*.

```
SQL> @impscrpt.sql
Directory created.
Directory created.
PL/SQL procedure successfully completed.
Directory dropped.
Directory dropped.
SQL>
```

5. Use the DBA_TABLESPACES view to check that the tablespace test2 has been imported to
    the target database.

How It Works

In this recipe, we showed you how to transport tablespaces to the same operating system platform using RMAN
backups. The next recipe, Recipe 15-13, shows how to do this on different platforms.

This recipe shows how you can create transportable tablespace sets from RMAN backups. You must have a prior
backup of all the data files that belong to the transportable tablespace set and the archived redo logs, so RMAN can
use them to recover to the target point in time.

You can also transport tablespaces from a "live" database using an alternative transport tablespace technique
explained in the Oracle documentation (specifically, the Administrator's Guide). However, the big disadvantage in
using that method is that the transportable tablespaces must be put into read-only mode, thus affecting database
availability. It not only may be time-consuming to put the tablespaces into read-only mode, but users can't write
to those tablespaces during the tablespace transport. You don't have any of these limitations when you use RMAN
backups as the basis of your transportable tablespace operation.

You may use this capability of RMAN for creating transportable tablespace sets for reporting purposes.
Transportable tablespace sets are also highly useful during the instantiation of Oracle Streams. The one big
requirement for using RMAN backups to create transportable tablespaces is that your RMAN backups must be
recoverable to the SCN at which you want the transportable tablespaces to be.

RMAN first creates an auxiliary database instance through which it creates the transportable tablespace sets.
RMAN does quite a few things to prepare the transportable table set. Here's a summary of the actions set off when you
execute the `transport tablespace` command:

1. RMAN checks to make sure that the tablespaces you want to transport are self-contained.
    To be considered self-contained, the tablespace set you want to transport mustn't contain
    references pointing outside those tablespaces, such as an index on a table that doesn't
    belong to one of the tablespaces you're transporting. RMAN automatically executes
    the `transport_set_check` procedure of the DBMS_TTS package at the beginning of the
    tablespace transport process, to verify whether the tablespaces are self-contained, as
    shown here:

```
Running TRANSPORT_SET_CHECK on recovery set tablespaces
TRANSPORT_SET_CHECK completed successfully
```

2. RMAN starts an auxiliary instance in nomount mode first. You don't have to specify a parameter file for this auxiliary instance, since RMAN automatically creates the file. The name of the auxiliary instance is also made up by RMAN, as shown here:

```
Creating automatic instance, with SID='nFya'
```

3. RMAN restores a backup of the target database control file and uses it to mount the auxiliary database.

4. Using the switch operation, RMAN restores all data files from the target database for the auxiliary instance. These files are restored to the location specified by the auxiliary destination clause in the transport tablespace command.

5. RMAN also stores the files pertaining to the tablespaces in the transportable tablespace set in the location you specify with the tablespace destination parameter in the transport tablespace command.

6. Once the data files from the target database are all restored to the auxiliary database location, RMAN performs a point-in-time recovery of the auxiliary instance. In our example, since we didn't specify a target time, a complete database recovery is performed. Note that all applicable archived redo logs are also automatically restored and applied by RMAN during the recovery process. Once the recovery is finished, an open resetlogs operation is performed on the auxiliary database by RMAN.

7. RMAN invokes the Data Pump Export utility (in the transportable tablespace mode) to create the export dump file containing the tablespaces in the transportable tablespace set. By default, the export dump file is placed in the location you specify with the tablespace destination clause of the transport tablespace command.

8. RMAN also simultaneously generates a Data Pump import script you can use to plug in the transported tablespaces into the target database. The default script name is *impscrpt.sql*, and this script is located in the directory specified by the tablespace destination clause of the transport tablespace command.

9. RMAN shuts down the auxiliary instance and automatically deletes all the files created and used during the transport tablespace process. The only files that remain are the transportable set files, the Data Pump export log, and the sample Data Pump import script.

In the example shown in the solution, the RMAN-created *impscrpt.sql* script was used to import the tablespaces into the target database. The script utilizes a PL/SQL script to import the tablespaces.

Alternatively, you can use the following Data Pump import command to import the tablespaces. For example:

```
$ impdp sys/sammyy1
directory=exp_data_dir
dumpfile= 'dmpfile.dmp'
transport_datafiles= /u05/app/oracle/transportdest/test2_01.dbf
```

■ **Note**   You can also use non-RMAN backups to create transportable tablespace sets, as long as you record the data file copies and archived redo logs in the RMAN repository using the catalog command.

You can also use the `transport tablespace` command to perform a tablespace transport to a past point in time. Simply add the `until scn` clause to the `transport tablespace` command, as shown here:

```
RMAN> transport tablespace test1,test2
2> tablespace destination '/u05/app/oracle/transportdest'
3> auxiliary destination '/u05/app/oracle/auxdest'
4> until SCN 259386;
```

The preceding command will recover the transportable tablespaces only up to the specified SCN. Instead of the SCN, you can also specify a target point in time or a restore point as well.

15-13. Performing a Cross-Platform Tablespace Transport by Converting Files on the Source Host

Problem

You want to transport a set of tablespaces from a database running on a certain platform to a database running on a different operating system. You're using RMAN image copies for the tablespace transport and you need to convert files on the destination host for the transport of the tablespaces.

Solution

In this solution, we show you how to transport a set of two tablespaces—*users* and *example*—from a source database named *orcl* running on a Linux host to a destination database named *orcl2* running on a Sun Solaris host. Here are the steps to follow for transporting the tablespaces.

1. Find the correct name for the destination operating system by querying the V$TRANSPORTABLE_PLATFORM view in the source database.

```
. SQL>  select platform_id,platform_name,endian_format
2       from v$transportable_platform
3*      where upper(platform_name) like 'SOLARIS%';
```

PLATFORM_ID	PLATFORM_NAME	ENDIAN_FORMAT
1	Solaris[tm] OE (32-bit)	Big
2	Solaris[tm] OE (64-bit)	Big
17	Solaris Operating System (x86)	Little
20	Solaris Operating System (x86-64)	Little

```
SQL>
```

From the query's output, you get the full name of the destination platform, which is "Solaris Operating System (x86-64)."

2. The next step is to place the two tablespaces you want to transport—*users* and *example*—into read-only mode.

```
SQL> alter tablespace users read only;

Tablespace altered.

SQL> alter tablespace example read only;

Tablespace altered.

SQL>
```

3. Create a directory to store the converted data files. You'll specify this directory with the format command in the next step when you convert the data files.

```
$ mkdir /tmp/transport_Solaris
```

4. Connect to the source database as the target from RMAN and run the convert tablespace command to convert the data files that belong to the two tablespaces (*users* and *example*) into the endian format of the destination host.

```
RMAN> convert tablespace users,example
2> to platform 'Solaris[tm] OE (64-bit)'
3> format '/tmp/transport_Solaris/%U';

Starting conversion at source at 25-NOV-12
using target database control file instead of recovery catalog
allocated channel: ORA_DISK_1
channel ORA_DISK_1: SID=54 device type=DISK
channel ORA_DISK_1: starting datafile conversion
input datafile file number=00002 name=/u01/app/oracle/oradata/orcl/example01.dbf
converted datafile=/tmp/transport_Solaris/data_D-ORCL_I-1316762630_TS-EXAMPLE_FNO-2_9dnokrhi
channel ORA_DISK_1: datafile conversion complete, elapsed time: 00:00:46
channel ORA_DISK_1: starting datafile conversion
input datafile file number=00006 name=/u01/app/oracle/oradata/orcl/users01.dbf
converted datafile=/tmp/transport_Solaris/data_D-ORCL_I-1316762630_TS-USERS_FNO-6_9enokrj1
channel ORA_DISK_1: datafile conversion complete, elapsed time: 00:00:03
Finished conversion at source at 25-NOV-12

RMAN>
```

You now have the set of converted data files in the */tmp/transport_Solaris* directory. The data will be in the correct endian format for the Solaris (64-bit) platform.

5. On the source database, use Data Pump to create the dump file for the two tablespaces: *users* and *example*.

6. Using an OS utility, move the converted data files and the export dump file to a directory on the destination server.

7. Use Data Pump import to plug the new tablespaces into the destination database.

8. Place the transported tablespaces into the read/write mode.

How It Works

RMAN's convert command lets you perform a cross-platform transport of tablespaces or databases with image copies. You must execute the convert command during a tablespace transport, when the source and destination platforms are different and the endian formats are different as well. If the endian formats are the same, you can perform a simple copy of the files between the two systems, without having to execute the convert command.

In the solution example we have different endian formats on the source and destination hosts, so we had to convert the tablespaces. In this recipe, we showed how to perform the conversion on the source server. The next recipe shows how to convert files on the destination server.

In this recipe we performed the tablespace conversion with the convert tablespace command. You can use the convert tablespace command only on the source host and not on the destination host, where you must use the convert datafile command, as the next recipe shows. It's reassuring to know that the convert command doesn't actually alter or convert any of the existing data files on the source host—it merely generates output files in the correct format for use on the destination server.

In the convert tablespace command shown in the Solution, we used the format option to name the output files. Alternatively, you may choose to specify the db_file_name_convert argument and name the output files that way. You can specify either the format or the db_file_name_convert arguments with the convert tablesapce command to tell RMAN how to name the output files. If you specify both options, the db_file_name_convert clause takes precedence over the format clause. Any file not named per the db_file_nme_convert clause is named based on the file naming pattern you specify with the format clause.

15-14. Performing a Cross-Platform Tablespace Transport by Converting Files on the Destination Host

Problem

You want to transport a set of tablespaces from a database from a certain platform to a database running on a different operating system. You're using RMAN image copies for the transport and you need to convert files on the destination host for the transport of the tablespaces.

Solution

Often you can't convert data on the source host when you're performing a cross-platform tablespace transport. This solution shows how to convert the data files belonging to a set of tablespaces you want to transport from one platform to another. Following are the steps to perform the cross-platform tablespace transport by converting files on the destination host.

1. Find the correct name for the source operating system by querying the V$TRANSPORTABLE_PLATFORM view in the source database.

```
SQL>  select platform_id,platform_name,endian_format
  2     from v$transportable_platform
  3*  where upper(platform_name) like '%LINUX%';

PLATFORM_ID    PLATFORM_NAME                    ENDIAN_FORMAT
-----------    ----------------------------     ---------------
         10    Linux IA (32-bit)                Little
         11    Linux IA (64-bit)                Little
          9    IBM zSeries Based Linux          Big
         13    Linux x86 64-bit                 Little
         18    IBM Power Based Linux            Big
SQL>
```

In this case, the source host's complete platform name is *Linux x86 64-bit.*

2. Place the tablespaces you want to transport to the destination database into the read-only mode at the source database.

```
SQL> alter tablespace users read only;

Tablespace altered.

SQL> alter tablespace example read only;

Tablespace altered.

SQL>
```

3. Using Data Pump, create an export dump file to capture the metadata for the two tablespaces (users, example) that you want to transport to the destination database.

4. Using OS utilities, move the export dump file and the data files belonging to the two tablespaces to the destination server. Once you copy all the files over, the data files are stored on the destination server as follows in our case:

```
/tmp/transport_Linux/users/users01.dbf
/tmp/transport_Linux/example/example01.dbf
```

5. Connect to RMAN with the destination database as the target:

```
$ rman
RMAN> connect target sysbackup@orcl2 as sysbackup
```

6. Convert the data files you copied from the source database into the endian format of the destination server.

```
RMAN> convert datafile
        '/tmp/transport_Linux/users/users01.dbf',
        'tmp/transport_Linux/example/example01.dbf'
        db_file_name_convert
        'tmp/transport_Linux/users','/u01/app/oracle/oradata/users',
        'tmp/transport_Linux/example','/u01/app/oracle/oradata/example'
        from platform 'Linux x86 64-bit';
```

We specified the db_file_name_convert parameter to assign the file names for the converted data files. We could have alternatively specified the from_platform clause instead. You'll now have a set of converted data files in the /u01/app/oracle/oradata directory on the destination server, with the files from the two transport tablespaces named as follows:

```
/u01/app/oracle/oradata/users/users01.dbf
/u01/app/oracle/oradata/example/example01.dbf
```

7. Use the Data Pump utility to plug in the metadata for the two tablespaces into the destination database.

8. Place the new tablespaces into the read/write mode on the destination server.

How It Works

RMAN lets you transport tablespaces from a database that runs on a certain operating system platform to another database running on a different platform. Although you can convert a database on the source host, at times you may choose to convert the data files on the destination host, for reasons such as avoiding a performance overhead on the source during the conversion. In addition, if you want to distribute tablespaces from the source database to multiple databases running on different operating systems, converting the data files on the destination host is the best bet.

The V$TRANSPORTABLE_PLATFORM view shows the internal names used by the database for various operating system platforms. You must specify the exact name of the operating system in the convert command.

As with the case (explained in the previous recipe) where you perform a conversion on the source host, RMAN doesn't actually alter any of the source database data files. In this example, we used the convert datafile command instead of the convert tablespace command for converting the tablespaces we want to transport across platforms. The reason for this is that you can't use the convert datafile command on the source host, but can use it on the destination host.

■ **Note** You can't generate output file names by specifying the db_file_name_convert parameter with the convert command when both source and destination database files are in the OMF format.

15-15. Transporting a Database by Converting Files on the Source Database Platform
Problem

You want to transport an entire database from one operating system platform to another by converting the data files on the source database host.

Solution

You can copy an entire database from one OS platform to another with the help of RMAN's convert command (convert database). Here are the steps to follow.

1. Ensure that both the source and the destination OS platforms share the same endian format. That is, the two hosts can have a different OS platform, but the endian format must be the same, whether it's little-endian or big-endian. You can do this by executing the following command and comparing the endian format of the two OS platforms.

```
SQL> select platform_id,platform_name,endian_format
     from v$transportable_platform;
```

2. Shut down the source database if it's running, and restart it in read-only mode.

```
SQL> alter database open read only;
```

3. Make sure the server output is on in SQL*Plus.

```
SQL> set serveroutput on
```

4. Execute the dbms_tdb.check_db function to make sure that there are no conditions such as incompatible endian formats between the source and the destination platforms.

```
SQL> declare
  2  db_ready boolean;
  3  begin
  4  db_ready := dbms_tdb.check_db('Microsoft Windows IA (64-bit)');
  5  end;
  6  /

PL/SQL procedure successfully completed.

SQL>
```

In this example, we execute the check_db function on a 64-bit Linux platform to transport the database to a 64-bit Windows platform. The check_db function didn't return any warnings or the value FALSE, so we can continue on and transport the database to the other platform.

5. Execute the dbms_tdb.check_external function to ensure there aren't any external tables, directories or BFILEs that would prevent RMAN from automatically transporting the files.

```
SQL> declare
  2  external boolean;
  3  begin
  4  external := dbms_tdb.check_external;
  5  end;
  6  /

PL/SQL procedure successfully completed.

SQL>
```

In our case, there are no errors at this point, so we can move on. If there are any external tables or directories, you need to copy the files yourself and create the necessary database directories.

6. Make sure that the source DB is in the read-only mode, before using RMAN to connect to the source database as the target and issuing the convert database command shown here. Before you run the convert database command, ensure that you create a directory to hold the converted data files. In our example, we created the directory */u02/app/oracle/convertdb* for this purpose.

```
RMAN> connect target /

connected to target database: ORCL (DBID=1316762630)

RMAN> convert database
2> new database 'newdb'
3> transport script '/u02/app/oracle/convertdb/transportscript.sql'
4> to platform 'Microsoft Windows IA (64-bit)'
5> DB_FILE_NAME_CONVERT '/u01/app/oracle/oradata/orcl','/u02/app/oracle/convertdb';

Starting conversion at source at 25-NOV-12
using target database control file instead of recovery catalog
allocated channel: ORA_DISK_1
channel ORA_DISK_1: SID=29 device type=DISK

External table SYS.OPATCH_EXT_TAB found in the database
External table SH.SALES_TRANSACTIONS_EXT found in the database

Directory SYS.STREAMS_DIROBJ_DPDIR found in the database
Directory SYS.SUBDIR found in the database
Directory SYS.SS_OE_XMLDIR found in the database
Directory SYS.MEDIA_DIR found in the database
Directory SYS.LOG_FILE_DIR found in the database
Directory SYS.DATA_FILE_DIR found in the database
Directory SYS.XMLDIR found in the database
Directory SYS.ORACLE_OCM_CONFIG_DIR2 found in the database
Directory SYS.ORACLE_OCM_CONFIG_DIR found in the database
Directory SYS.DATA_PUMP_DIR found in the database
Directory SYS.SCHEDULER$_LOG_DIR found in the database
Directory SYS.OPATCH_SCRIPT_DIR found in the database
Directory SYS.OPATCH_LOG_DIR found in the database

BFILE PM.PRINT_MEDIA found in the database

User SYS with SYSDBA and SYSOPER privilege found in password file
channel ORA_DISK_1: starting datafile conversion
input datafile file number=00001 name=/u01/app/oracle/oradata/orcl/system01.dbf
converted datafile=/u02/app/oracle/convertdb/system01.dbf
channel ORA_DISK_1: datafile conversion complete, elapsed time: 00:03:16
...
channel ORA_DISK_1: starting datafile conversion
input datafile file number=00006 name=/u01/app/oracle/oradata/orcl/users01.dbf
converted datafile=/u02/app/oracle/convertdb/users01.dbf
channel ORA_DISK_1: datafile conversion complete, elapsed time: 00:00:01
...
Edit init.ora file /u01/app/oracle/product/12.1.0/db_1/dbs/init_00nolft7_1_0.ora. This
PFILE will be used to create the database on the target platform
Run SQL script /u02/app/oracle/convertdb/transportscript.sql on the target platform to
create database
```

```
To recompile all PL/SQL modules, run utlirp.sql and utlrp.sql on the target platform
To change the internal database identifier, use DBNEWID Utility
Finished conversion at source at 25-NOV-12

RMAN>
```

7.   Once the convert database command completes its execution, open the source database read/write.

```
SQL> alter database open read write;
```

8.   The conversion process creates files in the directory you specified with the transport script and the db_file_name_convert parameters. Copy these files, including the *transportscript.sql* file, to a location on the destination server.

9.   Edit the *transportscript.sql* file so the file reflects the correct data file locations on the destination server.

10.   The *transportscript.sql* file contains a pfile for the database you'll be transporting to the destination server. In our case, the name of the pfile is listed toward the end of the *transportscript.sql* file as follows:

```
PFILE='/u01/app/oracle/product/12.1.0/db_1/dbs/init_00nolft7_1_0.ora'
```

The pfile in the *transportscript.sql* file has several initialization parameters, grouped under the following sections:

```
# Please change the values of the following parameters:
# Please review the values of the following parameters:
# The values of the following parameters are from source database:
```

Obviously, you must review the parameters carefully and change any parameters that you must, including the names of the control files as well as the value of the db_name initialization parameter for the new database. You must also, at this point, if necessary, change any of the converted data files as well as any memory settings for the new database.

11.   Go to the destination server and connect to the destination database as shown here.

```
SQL> connect / as sysbackup
```

12.   Create the new database on the destination server by executing the script *transport.sql* that the convert database command has created for you.

```
SQL> @transportscript
```

Once the script *transport.sql* completes executing, your new duplicate database is ready for you.

How It Works

A major requirement for performing a cross-platform database transport is that the source and destination operating systems must have the same endian format. That is, both endian formats must be either little-endian or big-endian. You can't transport an entire database using RMAN image copies (or backup sets) if the endian formats of the source and destination servers don't match.

Even when the endian formats match, you can't simply copy certain files, such as files containing undo segments, directly from the source to the destination server—you must perform an RMAN conversion of these files to ensure that the source files are compatible with the destination operating system.

The `convert database` command processes all the data files in the source database and copies the files to the location you specify with the `db_file_name_convert` parameter. In our example, we specified the following:

```
DB_FILE_NAME_CONVERT '/u01/app/oracle/oradata/orcl','/u02/app/oracle/convertdb'
```

By default the `convert database` command processes all files, including those to which it doesn't need to make any changes. You may optionally specify the `skip unnecessary datafiles` option with the `convert database` command to instruct RMAN to process only those files to which it needs to make changes. In this case, you must manually copy the rest of the data files to the destination server. You must first open the source database in the read-only mode before copying the files over to the destination server.

In cases where the source and destination servers have different endian formats, you can't use the `convert database` command to transport a database. You can still, however, get the job done by first creating a skeleton database on the destination database and transporting all the required tablespaces from the source database to the destination database. This is so because, as demonstrated earlier in Recipes 15-13 and 15-14, you can perform a cross-platform tablespace transport even when the two platforms don't share an endian format.

The `convert database` command converts all data files on the source host as part of the database transport. Executing the `dbms_tdb.check_db` function ensures that the following conditions aren't present before you attempt the conversion of the source database's data files with the `convert database` command:

- Incompatible endian formats between the source/destination servers
- Incorrect compatibility settings
- Active or in-doubt transactions

You can specify the following parameters when you execute the `check_db` function:

- `target_patform_name`: this is an optional parameter that denotes the full name of the destination platform as shown in the output of the V$DB_TRANSPORTABLE_PLATFORM view. If you omit this, RMAN assumes that the two operating system platforms are compatible for the purposes of the database transport.

- `skip_option`: you can specify which parts of the database to skip during the transport checks before starting the transport of the data files. If you leave this parameter out, the database checks all data files in the database.

15-16. Transporting Tablespaces to a Different Platform Using RMAN Backup Sets

Problem

You want to transport a set of tablespaces to a different operating system using RMAN backup sets.

Solution

You can use RMAN backup sets for a cross platform transport of tablespaces. In the following example, we'll show you how to do this when you're transporting tablespaces from a non-Linux to a Linux platform. Follow these steps to perform the transport of the tablespaces.

1. Connect to the source database through RMAN.

    ```
    $ RMAN
    RMAN> connect target sysbackup@orcl as sysbackup;
    ```

2. Make the tablespace you want to transport read-only. In this case, the tablespace we want
    to transport is named *demo*, so we set it to a read-only status.

    ```
    RMAN> alter tablespace demo read only;
    Statement processed
    RMAN>
    ```

3. Select a method for naming the output files of the backup commmand. We chose to specify
    the format clause of the RMAN backup command for this purpose. You can specify the
    clause to new instead, to denote that you want RMAN to make sure that the restored
    "foreign" data files use new OMF-format file names in the destination database. In our
    backup command in step 6, we use the format clause in the following manner:

    ```
    format '/u02/app/oracle/oradata/transport_%u'
    ```

4. Find out the exact name of the destination platform with the following query:

    ```
    RMAN> select platform_id, platform_name,endian_format
          from v$transportable_platform
          where upper(platform_name) like '%LINUX%';
    ```

The full name of the destination platform in our case is *Linux x86 64-bit*.' This is what we'll specify in our RMAN
backup command in step 6.

5. Connect to RMAN with the source database as the target.

    ```
    RMAN> connect target /
    connected to target database: ORCL (DBID=1316762630)
    RMAN>
    ```

6. Back up the source database tablespaces by specifying the to platform clause in the
    RMAN backup command. You must also specify the datapump clause, so the export dump
    file for the tablespace metadata is created as a separate backup piece.

    ```
    RMAN> backup to platform 'Linux x86 64-bit'
    2> format '/u02/app/oracle/oradata/transport_%u'
    3> datapump format '/u02/app/oracle/oradata/export/trans_ts_%U'
    4> tablespace demo;

    Starting backup at 27-NOV-12
    using target database control file instead of recovery catalog
    allocated channel: ORA_DISK_1
    channel ORA_DISK_1: SID=20 device type=DISK
    Running TRANSPORT_SET_CHECK on specified tablespaces
    TRANSPORT_SET_CHECK completed successfully
    ```

```
Performing export of metadata for specified tablespaces...
    EXPDP> Starting "SYSBACKUP"."TRANSPORT_EXP_ORCL_omwi":
    EXPDP> Processing object type TRANSPORTABLE_EXPORT/PLUGTS_BLK
    EXPDP> Processing object type TRANSPORTABLE_EXPORT/STATISTICS/MARKER
    EXPDP> Processing object type TRANSPORTABLE_EXPORT/POST_INSTANCE/PLUGTS_BLK
    EXPDP> Master table "SYSBACKUP"."TRANSPORT_EXP_ORCL_omwi" successfully loaded/unloaded
    EXPDP> ***********************************************************************
    EXPDP> Dump file set for SYSBACKUP.TRANSPORT_EXP_ORCL_omwi is:
    EXPDP>    /u01/app/oracle/product/12.1.0/db_1/dbs/backup_tts_ORCL_87665.dmp
    EXPDP> ***********************************************************************
    EXPDP> Datafiles required for transportable tablespace DEMO:
    EXPDP>    /u01/app/oracle/oradata/orcl/demo01.dbf
    EXPDP> Job "SYSBACKUP"."TRANSPORT_EXP_ORCL_omwi" successfully completed at Sat Nov 27
17:29:48 2012 elapsed 0 00:01:34
Export completed

channel ORA_DISK_1: starting full datafile backup set
channel ORA_DISK_1: specifying datafile(s) in backup set
input datafile file number=00010 name=/u01/app/oracle/oradata/orcl/demo01.dbf
channel ORA_DISK_1: starting piece 1 at 27-NOV-12
channel ORA_DISK_1: finished piece 1 at 27-NOV-12
piece handle=/u02/app/oracle/oradata/transport_aknoqnt8 tag=TAG20121027T172711 comment=NONE
channel ORA_DISK_1: backup set complete, elapsed time: 00:00:03
channel ORA_DISK_1: starting full datafile backup set
input Data Pump dump file=/u01/app/oracle/product/12.1.0/db_1/dbs/backup_tts_ORCL_87665.dmp
channel ORA_DISK_1: starting piece 1 at 27-NOV-12
channel ORA_DISK_1: finished piece 1 at 27-NOV-12
piece handle=/u02/app/oracle/oradata/export/trans_ts_alnoqntd_1_1 tag=TAG20121027T172711
comment=NONE
channel ORA_DISK_1: backup set complete, elapsed time: 00:00:01
Finished backup at 27-NOV-12

RMAN>
```

In this example, we chose to use the to platform clause, so any necessary conversion of the endian format of the destination database data files is performed on the source database. If you want the conversion of the endian formats to take place on the destination server, you must specify the for transport clause instead with your backup command (backup for transport ...). Note that the format clause specifies the format of the backup piece.

The backup to platform command produces both a Data Pump dump file set with the metadata for the tablespace *demo*, as well as an RMAN backup set that contains the backup of the tablespace *demo*, which we want to export to the destination database.

7. Use OS utilities to move the backup sets you've made in the previous step to the destination database host.

8. Connect to RMAN with the destination database as the target.

```
$ RMAN
$ connect target sysbackup@orcl1 as sysbackup;
```

9. Finally, restore the backup sets that you transported from the source database (orcl) into the destination database (orcl1).

```
RMAN> restore foreign tablespace demo
   2> format '/u01/app/oracle/oradata/orcl1'
   3> from backupset '/u02/app/oracle/oradata/transport_aknoqnt8'
   4> dump file from backupset    '/u02/app/oracle/oradata/export/trans_ts_alnoqntd_1_1';

Starting restore at 27-NOV-12
using channel ORA_DISK_1

channel ORA_DISK_1: starting datafile backup set restore
channel ORA_DISK_1: specifying datafile(s) to restore from backup set
channel ORA_DISK_1: restoring all files in foreign tablespace DEMO
channel ORA_DISK_1: reading from backup piece /u02/app/oracle/oradata/transport_aknoqnt8
channel ORA_DISK_1: restoring foreign file 10 to /u01/app/oracle/oradata/orcl1
channel ORA_DISK_1: foreign piece handle=/u02/app/oracle/oradata/transport_aknoqnt8
channel ORA_DISK_1: restored backup piece 1
channel ORA_DISK_1: restore complete, elapsed time: 00:00:01
channel ORA_DISK_1: starting datafile backup set restore
channel ORA_DISK_1: specifying datafile(s) to restore from backup set
channel ORA_DISK_1: restoring Data Pump dump file to
/u01/app/oracle/product/12.1.0/db_1/dbs/backup_tts_ORCL1_91741.dmp
channel ORA_DISK_1: reading from backup piece /u02/app/oracle/oradata/export/trans_ts_alnoqntd_1_1
channel ORA_DISK_1: foreign piece handle=/u02/app/oracle/oradata/export/trans_ts_alnoqntd_1_1
channel ORA_DISK_1: restored backup piece 1
channel ORA_DISK_1: restore complete, elapsed time: 00:00:01

Performing import of metadata...
   IMPDP> Master table "SYSBACKUP"."TSPITR_IMP_ORCL1_ntuf" successfully loaded/unloaded
   IMPDP> Starting "SYSBACKUP"."TSPITR_IMP_ORCL1_ntuf":
   IMPDP> Processing object type TRANSPORTABLE_EXPORT/PLUGTS_BLK
   IMPDP> Processing object type TRANSPORTABLE_EXPORT/POST_INSTANCE/PLUGTS_BLK
   IMPDP> Job "SYSBACKUP"."TSPITR_IMP_ORCL1_ntuf" successfully completed at
Sat Nov 27 17:42:42 2012 elapsed 0 00:00:24
Import completed

Finished restore at 27-NOV-12

RMAN>
```

How It Works

When you're transporting tablespaces using RMAN backup sets, the terms *foreign data file* and *foreign tablespace* refer, respectively, to the source database data files and tablespaces that you're transporting and plugging into the destination database. A *datapump destination* is the location on the target database's host server where you're storing the Data Pump–related files, including the Data Pump export dump file and the log files.

The source and destination databases can be running on different platforms that use different endian formats. If the endian formats on the two platforms are different, you must first convert the data. How this conversion is performed depends on the clause you specify with the backup command. The backup command during a cross-platform transport can contain either the for transport or the to platform clause. If you specify the for transport clause, you can transport the backup set to any destination database and the endian format conversion will be done on the destination server. If you specify the to platform clause, RMAN performs the endian format conversion on the source database itself. In the example we showed in the Solution section, we chose to specify the to platform clause.

In the backup to platform command shown in the Solution section, the format clause specifies the location and names for the restored files. If you omit this clause, you must set the db_file_create_dest initialization parameter in the target database. RMAN will then restore all data files using OMF file names, to the location you specify with this parameter.

A *foreign tablespace* is defined as the set of *foreign data files* that together form a tablespace in the source database. The foreign data files that are part of a foreign tablespace don't belong to the target database, but are being transported into it from the source database. The clause backupset in the restore foreign tablespace command refers to the backup set you've made earlier in the source database, and it contains the data that RMAN will restore. You can specify only some of the tablespaces or data files during a cross-platform transport. The option to new (restore foreign database to new) specifies that the new foreign data files in the destination database must use new OMF-format file names. We used the option format and chose not to specify the option to new in our example.

When transporting tablespaces from one platform to another, you can specify either the for transport or the to platform clause. During the tablespace transport, RMAN needs to export the tablespace metadata, in order to plug the source tablespaces into the destination database. When the endian format is different on the source and destination hosts, the endian format needs to be converted. If you specify the for transport clause, the endian format conversion is performed on the destination database. By specifying the to platform clause, you ensure that the conversion is performed on the source database.

15-17. Transporting a Database to a Different Platform Using RMAN Backup Sets
Problem

You want to transport a database to a different operating system using RMAN backup sets.

Solution

Follow these steps to transport a database to a database running on a different OS platform. You must be working with an Oracle 12c release database to use backup sets for this purpose.

1. Execute the SYS.DBMS_TDB_CHECK_DB procedure.

    ```
    SQL>    declare
      2       db_ready boolean;
      3  begin
      4       db_ready :=
      5       dbms_tdb.check_db('Microsoft Windows IA (32-bit)',dbms_tdb.skip_readonly);
      6* end;
    SQL> /

    PL/SQL procedure successfully completed.
    SQL>
    ```

2. Make the database read-only:

    ```
    SQL> alter database open read only;

    Database altered.

    SQL>
    ```

3. Back up the source database by specifying the to platform clause of the backup command.

```
RMAN> backup to platform
   2> = 'Microsoft Windows IA (64-bit)'
   3> format '/u01/app/oracle/oradata/backups/special/transport_db%U'
   4> database;

Starting backup at 11-NOV-12
using target database control file instead of recovery catalog
allocated channel: ORA_DISK_1
channel ORA_DISK_1: SID=29 device type=DISK
channel ORA_DISK_1: starting full datafile backup set
channel ORA_DISK_1: specifying datafile(s) in backup set
input datafile file number=00001 name=/u01/app/oracle/oradata/orcl/system01.dbf
input datafile file number=00003 name=/u01/app/oracle/oradata/orcl/sysaux01.dbf
input datafile file number=00005 name=/u01/app/oracle/oradata/orcl/cattbs_01.dbf
input datafile file number=00002 name=/u01/app/oracle/oradata/orcl/example01.dbf
input datafile file number=00007 name=/u01/app/oracle/oradata/orcl/virt_catalog_01.dbf
input datafile file number=00004 name=/u01/app/oracle/oradata/orcl/undotbs01.dbf
input datafile file number=00006 name=/u01/app/oracle/oradata/orcl/users01.dbf
channel ORA_DISK_1: starting piece 1 at 11-NOV-12
channel ORA_DISK_1: finished piece 1 at 11-NOV-12
piece handle=/u01/app/oracle/oradata/backups/special/transport_db87nng24s_1_1
tag=TAG20121011T130116 comment=NONE
channel ORA_DISK_1: backup set complete, elapsed time: 00:03:46
Finished backup at 11-NOV-12

RMAN>
```

4. At this point, you can disconnect from the source database.

5. Move the backup sets produced by step 3 to the destination host using OS commands such as scp.

6. Go the destination server and start up RMAN, and connect to the destination database as the target:

```
$ rman
RMAN> connect target sys@orcl
```

7. In this example, *orcl* is the name of the destination database where you want to transport the database.

8. Restore the backup sets from the source database by executing the following restore command:

```
RMAN> restore foreign database to new from backupset
'/u01/app/oracle/backup/db_transport_01';
```

The example shown here will restore the cross-platform backup contained in the backup set *db_transport_01*, which is saved in the directory */u01/app/oracle/backup*.

How It Works

The two important requirements for creating an RMAN backup set for performing a cross-platform transport of an entire database are, first, your database must be running at a `compatible` parameter value of 12.0 or greater, and second, you must open the source database in the read-only mode.

When you restore the cross-platform backup sets created in the source database to the destination database, notice that you must specify the `foreign database` clause with your `restore` command. The option `to new` (`restore foreign database to new`) specifies that the new foreign data files in the destination database must use new OMF-format file names.

CHAPTER 16

■ ■ ■

Tuning RMAN

For most backup and recovery scenarios, you'll find that RMAN's out-of-the-box performance is acceptable. RMAN is a reliable and efficient tool for backing up, restoring, and recovering your database. However, sometimes (especially with large databases) you will be required to tune and increase the performance of RMAN jobs. These are the most common reasons you'll encounter for needing to tune RMAN:

- Your backups are taking too long.

- The performance of the overall system is unacceptable during backups.

- Restore and recovery operations take too long.

Before you start the tuning process, you must first clearly identify what you want to accomplish and how to measure success. If you can't measure performance, then it is difficult to manage it. Without specific criteria, you won't know when you have successfully improved the job being tuned.

For example, your business may require that the production database not be down for more than six hours. As part of your backup and recovery strategy, you have regularly been testing how long a complete restore and recovery of your database will take. If you discover that the test environment restore times have been steadily increasing and are now taking close to six hours, you should start the tuning process.

In the situation we've just described, you would have a specific requirement that the restore and recovery operation must take less than six hours. You also have been testing and gathering metrics and can show a historical trend toward unacceptable performance. Having specific goals and a way to measure performance are the first steps toward being able to tune successfully (RMAN or otherwise).

Here are the general steps that we recommend when trying to improve backup and recovery performance:

1. Identify measurable business performance requirements.

2. Collect data and measure performance.

3. Identify bottlenecks.

4. Make adjustments that will alleviate the worst bottleneck.

5. Repeat steps 1–4 until your performance goals are achieved.

You'll have to work with your business to figure out what the specific and measurable performance goals are for your backup and recovery processes. This chapter will assist you with steps 2, 3, and 4 in the tuning process.

Before going any farther, we feel compelled to point out the obvious, which is that isolated tuning of single components of your system will not necessarily lead to a holistic optimized result. Your backup and recovery performance will be impacted by the architecture of your entire system. This includes components such as the following:

- CPU

- Memory

- Operating system

- Disk technology and configuration

- Network

- Database architecture

- Tape technology and configuration

- Application design

- Design of data model and its physical implementation

- Robustness of SQL statements

■ **Note** We realize that oftentimes performance tuning and troubleshooting are inherently intertwined. The topics specific to troubleshooting have been placed in Chapter 17. Keep in mind you may need to refer to recipes in this chapter (tuning) and in Chapter 17 (troubleshooting) to resolve a particular performance issue.

In reality, you rarely have control over all aspects of your system. However, you should be aware of the system as a whole and do everything you can to work with the appropriate personnel to identify and address performance issues that aren't directly related to RMAN or Oracle. You'll also find yourself in the position of trying to convince other people (managers, application developers, and so on) that Oracle and RMAN are not the cause of the system performance issues. If you're not holistically aware of your system, you won't consider all relevant variables related to performance issues.

Having said that, the primary focus of this chapter is on tuning RMAN backup and recovery operations. Take a few minutes to analyze Figure 16-1. This diagram shows the primary architectural components involved when taking an RMAN backup (if restoring, then reverse the "blocks" data flow arrows).

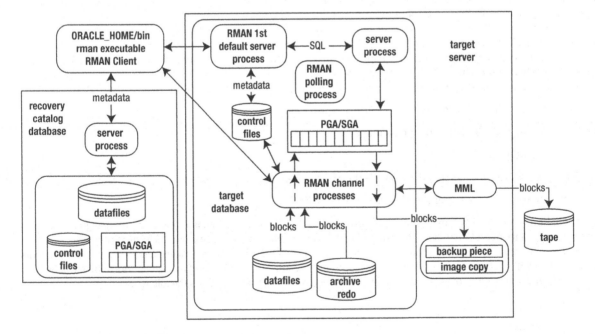

Figure 16-1. RMAN backup flow of information and data

When you start an RMAN backup job, two target database server processes are initially created: the first default server process and a polling process. The polling process can be ignored. The first default server process is responsible for querying the target database control file (for RMAN metadata) and running any SQL statements issued from within RMAN. If you're using a recovery catalog, an additional process is started on the recovery catalog server. This process handles the communication between the RMAN client and recovery catalog (RMAN metadata).

Additionally, another server process is started for each channel that is allocated. These channel processes are responsible for reading blocks from data files on disk, placing these blocks into a memory area, and then writing these blocks to the backup pieces (either on disk or on tape).

Having said that, when you experience RMAN backup performance problems, we recommend you start by investigating these architectural components:

- RMAN reading metadata from the target database control file

- RMAN reading metadata from the recovery catalog (if using)

- SQL statements issued from RMAN client

- Reading data file blocks from disk into memory

- Writing blocks from memory to the backup location (either disk or tape)

Basically anywhere in Figure 16-1 where there is a data flow related to "metadata," "blocks," or "SQL" is where you'll most likely experience RMAN performance issues. This is where you should initially focus your tuning efforts. Most of the recipes in this chapter are in some way related to the prior bullets.

When first tuning RMAN, you should identify the extent of performance problems (see Recipes 16-1 through 16-3). Next determine whether the bottleneck is related to querying the RMAN repository metadata (Recipes 16-4 and 16-5). If the bottleneck is not related to querying the repository, you must figure out whether the issue is caused by reading the data files or writing to the backups (Recipes 16-6 through 16-9). The remaining recipes in this chapter deal with increasing RMAN performance, such as implementing parallelism, using incremental features, and so on.

■ **Tip**   See My Oracle Support (MOS) note 247611.1 for known RMAN performance issues. This note lists issues, fixes, and workarounds for several performance problems.

16-1. Identifying RMAN Processes
Problem

An RMAN backup job is running too long. You would like to identify the database sessions and operating system processes associated with any RMAN jobs.

Solution

The following query will provide you a wealth of information regarding RMAN processes currently connected to your target database:

```
COL username    FORM a10
COL kill_string FORM A12
COL os_id       FORM A6
COL client_info FORM A24
COL action      FORM A21
```

```
--
SELECT
 a.username
,a.sid || ',' || a.serial# AS kill_string
, b.spid AS OS_ID
,(CASE WHEN a.client_info IS NULL AND a.action IS NOT NULL THEN 'First Default'
       WHEN a.client_info IS NULL AND a.action IS NULL     THEN 'Polling'
  ELSE a.client_info
  END) client_info
,a.action
FROM v$session a
    ,v$process b
WHERE a.program like '%rman%'
AND  a.paddr = b.addr;
```

Before running the prior query, start a separate terminal session and connect to your target database without issuing any backup commands:

```
$ rman target /
```

After connecting to RMAN, execute the query; here is some sample output:

```
USERNAME    KILL_STRING  OS_ID  CLIENT_INFO               ACTION
----------  -----------  -----  ------------------------  --------------------
SYSBACKUP   46,119       22470  First Default             0000001 FINISHED70
SYSBACKUP   47,125       22471  Polling
```

Now from your RMAN connection issue a backup command:

```
RMAN> backup datafile 4;
```

Run the SQL query again and notice the additional line in the output:

```
USERNAME    KILL_STRING  OS_ID  CLIENT_INFO               ACTION
----------  -----------  -----  ------------------------  --------------------
SYSBACKUP   46,119       22470  First Default             0000013 FINISHED129
SYSBACKUP   47,127       24164  Polling
SYSBACKUP   51,175       24165  rman channel=ORA_DISK_1   0000034 FINISHED129
```

From the prior output, there are four crucial pieces of information that lay the foundation for RMAN tuning. *First*, when you connect to RMAN, two processes are allocated: the first default process and the polling process. For tuning purposes, ignore the polling process. However, the first default is critical; this process is responsible for communication between the RMAN client and target database control file and any SQL statements issued (from the client).

Second, is one default disk channel is allocated when you issue a command requiring I/O, such as backup, restore, and so on. You will see a process for every channel that you allocate.

Third, the KILL_STRING provides you the information required to terminate a connection to the database via the alter system kill session SQL statement.

Fourth, the OS_ID provides the operating system identifier. This can be used in conjunction with Linux/Unix OS commands to monitor a process via operating system utilities such as ps and top. The OS_ID also can be used with the Linux/Unix kill command to terminate a session (from the OS command prompt).

How It Works

The query in the Solution section of this recipe is almost always where you will initiate the tuning process. The query identifies the first default process. When you troubleshoot performance issues, this process is often targeted for enabling RMAN debug tracing (see Recipe 17-9) and/or SQL tracing (see Recipe 16-5). Tracing helps isolate whether performance issues are with the RMAN client querying the RMAN repository (see Recipe 16-4) or SQL issues, or whether the bottleneck is with channel I/O processes (see Recipe 16-6).

If you ever need to terminate a RMAN process from SQL, you must first identify the SID (session identifier) and SERIAL number. For example, say you want to terminate a channel process that appears to be hung that has a SID of 51 and a SERIAL number of 175:

```
SQL> alter system kill session '51,175';
```

With the operating system identifier you can use ps and top to monitor resource consumption. For example, the following ps command shows how long a process has been running:

```
$ ps -ef | grep 24165
```

The output indicates that the process started today at 14:17:

```
oracle   24165 22465  0 14:17 ?        00:00:01 oracleo12c...
```

This slightly more complicated ps command shows the percentage of CPU resources the process is consuming:

```
$ ps -e -o pcpu,pid,user,tty,args | grep -i 24165
```

Here is some sample output indicating the process is using 1.2 percent of the CPU:

```
1.2 24165 oracle   ?        oracleo12c...
```

If you have access to a utility such as top, you can monitor all aspects of the process, such as the time running, percentage of CPU and memory usage, and so on:

```
$ top -p 24165
```

Here is a snippet of the top output:

```
 PID USER      PR  NI  VIRT  RES  SHR S %CPU %MEM    TIME+  COMMAND
24165 oracle    20   0  622m  63m  38m S  9.0  3.2  0:16.92 oracle_24165_o1
```

We should mention that there are a couple of other ways of identifying RMAN processes. One method is to inspect RMAN's output messages to your terminal to identify your SID. If you're sending output to a log file, look for the SID in that file. When you start an RMAN job (and subsequently allocate one or more channels), you should see output similar to this on your screen. In this example, the SID is 51:

```
allocated channel: ORA_DISK_1
channel ORA_DISK_1: SID=51 device type=DISK
```

You can also use set command id to label a process. This will help you identify a specific channel process if you have many RMAN jobs running at the same time. This example sets the command ID to my_session:

```
RMAN> set command id to 'my_session';
RMAN> backup database;
```

Your session identifier will show up as extra information in the CLIENT_INFO column of V$SESSION. For example, if we execute the query from the Solution section, here is some sample output:

```
USERNAME    KILL_STRING  OS_ID  CLIENT_INFO               ACTION
----------  -----------  -----  ------------------------  --------------------
SYSBACKUP   46,119       22470  id=my_session             0000039 FINISHED66
SYSBACKUP   47,127       24164  Polling
SYSBACKUP   51,175       24165  id=my_session,rman chann  0000117 STARTED16
                                el=ORA_DISK_1
```

16-2. Monitoring RMAN Job Progress

Problem

You have a long-running RMAN job, and you wonder how much longer it will take to complete.

Solution

To monitor the progress of an RMAN backup or restore command, query V$SESSION_LONGOPS via SQL*Plus:

```
COL sid FORM 99999
COL serial# FORM 99999
COL opname FORM A35
COL sofar FORM 999999999
COL pct_complete FORM 99.99 HEAD "% Comp."
--
SELECT sid, serial#, sofar, totalwork, opname,
round(sofar/totalwork*100,2) AS pct_complete
FROM    v$session_longops
WHERE   opname LIKE 'RMAN%'
AND     opname NOT LIKE '%aggregate%'
AND     totalwork != 0
AND     sofar <> totalwork;
```

If you have an RMAN backup running, you should see output similar to this:

```
  SID SERIAL#     SOFAR  TOTALWORK OPNAME                                % Comp.
------ -------  --------- ---------- ----------------------------------- -------
  352   47427    388472    5517824 RMAN: incremental datafile backup       7.04
  331   28937   1946552    5636096 RMAN: incremental datafile backup      34.54
  181   49581    370166    5636096 RMAN: incremental datafile backup       6.57
```

For RMAN operations, the columns SOFAR and TOTALWORK are usually measured in database blocks. If you're running a restore operation, the output will look something like this:

```
  SID SERIAL#     SOFAR  TOTALWORK OPNAME                                % Comp.
------ -------  --------- ---------- ----------------------------------- -------
   12      13     56234     238080 RMAN: full datafile restore            23.62
```

Oracle also provides a view, V$RECOVERY_PROGRESS, that reports on just the recovery operations (either RMAN or user-managed). This view is a subview of the V$SESSION_LONGOPS view. To report on the progress of a recover command, you can run a SQL query as shown here:

```
COL type FORM A20
COL item FORM A20
--
SELECT type, item, units, sofar, total
FROM v$recovery_progress;
```

If you are running an RMAN recovery operation, you should see output similar to this:

TYPE	ITEM	UNITS	SOFAR	TOTAL
Media Recovery	Log Files	Files	39	39
Media Recovery	Average Apply Rate	KB/sec	2928	2928
Media Recovery	Redo Applied	Megabytes	40	40
Media Recovery	Last Applied Redo	SCN+Time	0	0

How It Works

The V$SESSION_LONGOPS view contains information about long-running jobs (SQL statements, RMAN operations, and so on) in your database. You can use this view to monitor the progress of RMAN backup, restore, and recovery operations.

Often it's useful to join V$SESSION_LONGOPS to both V$SESSION and V$PROCESS. This query allows you to see the RMAN channel session ID and the OS process ID:

```
SELECT s.client_info,
       sl.opname,
       sl.message,
       sl.sid, sl.serial#, p.spid,
       sl.sofar, sl.totalwork,
       round(sl.sofar/sl.totalwork*100,2) "% Complete"
FROM   v$session_longops sl, v$session s, v$process p
WHERE  p.addr = s.paddr
AND    sl.sid=s.sid
AND    sl.serial#=s.serial#
AND    opname LIKE 'RMAN%'
AND    opname NOT LIKE '%aggregate%'
AND    totalwork != 0
AND    sofar <> totalwork;
```

For RMAN jobs, the view V$SESSION_LONGOPS contains two types of rows:

- Aggregate

- Detailed

Aggregate rows capture the progress of the backup or restore operation as each job step completes. A job step is the creation or restore operation of a backup set or image copy. Aggregate rows are updated only after the completion of each job step in the backup or restore operation.

Detailed rows show the progress of individual job steps. Typically several data files are associated with one job step. Detailed rows are updated after every buffer I/O associated with the restore or recover operation.

If your backup or restore command is interacting with several backup sets, you may want to report at an aggregate level. To report at the aggregate level, run a query similar to the one shown next:

```
select sid, serial#, sofar, totalwork,opname,
round(sofar/totalwork*100,2) "% Complete"
from    v$session_longops
where   opname LIKE 'RMAN%aggregate%'
and     totalwork != 0
and     sofar <> totalwork;
```

You can also use V$SESSION_LONGOPS to estimate when a job will complete for an RMAN backup or restore operation, because the total amount of work, the time the job began, and the amount of work left are known values. Here is such a query:

```
SET LINES 200
COL opname FORM A35
COL pct_complete FORM 99.99 HEAD "% Comp."
COL start_time FORM A15 HEAD "Start|Time"
COL hours_running FORM 9999.99 HEAD "Hours|Running"
COL minutes_left FORM 999999 HEAD "Minutes|Left"
COL est_comp_time FORM A15 HEAD "Est. Comp.|Time"
--
SELECT sid, serial#, opname,
ROUND(sofar/totalwork*100,2) AS pct_complete,
TO_CHAR(start_time,'dd-mon-yy hh24:mi') start_time,
(sysdate-start_time)*24 hours_running,
((sysdate-start_time)*24*60)/(sofar/totalwork)-(sysdate-start_time)
  *24*60 minutes_left,
TO_CHAR((sysdate-start_time)/(sofar/totalwork)+start_time,'dd-mon-yy hh24:mi')
  est_comp_time
FROM   v$session_longops
WHERE  opname LIKE 'RMAN%'
AND    opname NOT LIKE '%aggregate%'
AND    totalwork != 0
AND    sofar <> totalwork;
```

The prior query is very useful if you have a long-running backup or restore job and people keep asking, "When will it be done?" This seems to occur especially during stressful restore scenarios where all eyes are on the DBA recovering the database.

16-3. Measuring Backup Performance
Problem

You want to determine whether backups are taking longer (than prior backups) and see if the size of RMAN backups is increasing.

Solution

Use information in V$RMAN_BACKUP_JOB_DETAILS for statistics on backups. The following query displays useful information regarding the length of time a backup has run and the size of recent backups:

```
SET PAGESIZE 50
COL time_taken_display FORM A10 HEAD "Time|Taken|HH:MM:SS"
COL rman_end_time      FORM A17
COL i_size_gig         FORM 999.99 HEAD "Input|Gig"
COL o_size_gig         FORM 999.99 HEAD "Output|Gig"
COL compression_ratio  FORM 99.99 HEAD "Comp.|Ratio"
COL status             FORM A12
COL input_type         FORM A14
--
SELECT
 time_taken_display
,TO_CHAR(end_time,'dd-mon-rrrr hh24:mi') AS rman_end_time
,input_bytes/1024/1024/1024 i_size_gig
,output_bytes/1024/1024/1024 o_size_gig
,compression_ratio
,status
,input_type
FROM v$rman_backup_job_details
ORDER BY end_time;
```

Here is a snippet of the output:

```
Time
Taken                       Input  Output  Comp.
HH:MM:SS  RMAN_END_TIME       Gig     Gig  Ratio STATUS       INPUT_TYPE
--------- ----------------- ------- ------- ------ ------------ --------------
03:06:51  09-aug-2012 18:52  130.12   25.58   5.09 COMPLETED    DB INCR
03:05:27  10-aug-2012 18:50  130.06   25.48   5.10 COMPLETED    DB INCR
03:06:31  11-aug-2012 18:52  129.90   25.43   5.11 COMPLETED    DB INCR
00:00:43  12-aug-2012 09:48     .05     .05   1.00 COMPLETED    CONTROLFILE
```

This output gives you a good indication of RMAN performance. It shows how long the backups are running, when they finish, input size (in gigabytes) of blocks read, output size of the backup, and so on.

■ **Tip**   Keep in mind that V$RMAN_BACKUP_JOB_DETAILS has many other useful columns that you may want to report on such as START_TIME, INPUT_BYTES_PER_SEC_DISPLAY and OUTPUT_BYTES_PER_SEC_DISPLAY. If you are trouble-shooting I/O issues, you may especially want to report on those columns.

How It Works

Measuring the duration of your backups provides a starting point from which you can begin tuning your RMAN backups. The V$RMAN_BACKUP_JOB_DETAILS view contains a plethora of information about backup durations and I/O rates.

■ **Note** If you're using a recovery catalog, you can query RC_RMAN_BACKUP_JOB_DETAILS for the same information as found in V$RMAN_BACKUP_JOB_DETAILS. The view RC_RMAN_BACKUP_JOB_DETAILS may contain a longer history than what's available in V$RMAN_BACKUP_JOB_DETAILS.

The rows in V$RMAN_BACKUP_JOB_DETAILS are aggregated for all backup jobs that have run during a connection to RMAN. That means the first timestamp recorded is for the first backup operation that the session performs, and the last timestamp recorded is when the last backup command finishes (for the connected session).

Be careful about interpreting the contents of the view. The view records statistics, such as the aggregated duration and number of bytes, but it does not report on what actual backup or restore commands were executed during a session.

You are limited only by your imagination as to what you can report on with RMAN backups. For example, suppose you wanted to report the average amount of time for an RMAN backup, rank the backups by time taken, and also report on the average of the prior three backups. Here is a query that uses analytic (window) functions to display the desired information:

```
SELECT
 ROUND((end_time - start_time)*24*60,2) AS minutes
,end_time
,RANK() OVER (ORDER BY end_time - start_time DESC) rank_row
,ROUND(
    AVG((end_time - start_time)*24*60) OVER ()
    ,2) average_all
,ROUND(
    AVG((end_time - start_time)*24*60)
      OVER (ORDER BY rownum
            ROWS BETWEEN 3 PRECEDING AND 1 PRECEDING)
 ,2) average_prev_3
FROM v$rman_backup_job_details
ORDER BY end_time;
```

Here is some sample output:

MINUTES	END_TIME	RANK_ROW	AVERAGE_ALL	AVERAGE_PREV_3
49.25	27-JUL-12	15	54.05	
57.68	28-JUL-12	8	54.05	49.25
52.40	29-JUL-12	11	54.05	53.47
52.05	30-JUL-12	13	54.05	53.11
47.52	31-JUL-12	17	54.05	54.04
49.20	01-AUG-12	16	54.05	50.66
67.00	02-AUG-12	2	54.05	49.59
52.17	03-AUG-12	12	54.05	54.57
56.52	04-AUG-12	10	54.05	56.12
64.23	05-AUG-12	5	54.05	58.56
51.20	06-AUG-12	14	54.05	57.64
64.77	07-AUG-12	4	54.05	57.32
60.67	08-AUG-12	6	54.05	60.07
64.98	09-AUG-12	3	54.05	58.88
67.72	10-AUG-12	1	54.05	63.47
57.78	11-AUG-12	7	54.05	64.46
57.50	12-AUG-12	9	54.05	63.49

The prior output indicates that the RMAN backups took a little longer on August 10 (number 1 rank), but nothing really out of the ordinary.

Refer to Table 16-1 for the view that you should inspect if you need to analyze backup performance information on a more granular basis than what's available in V$RMAN_BACKUP_JOB_DETAILS. The view names in Table 16-1 are somewhat descriptive of each view's content. For example, if you want to analyze what is happening at the backup set level, then V$BACKUP_SET or V$BACKUP_SET_DETAILS will provide information at that level. The recovery catalog (RC) views are available only in your recovery catalog database. The RC views can be more valuable to you in that they are capable of providing a longer history of information than the V$ views.

Table 16-1. *Description of Detailed Performance Views*

View Name	Recovery Catalog View
V$RMAN_BACKUP_SUBJOB_DETAILS	RC_RMAN_BACKUP_SUBJOB_DETAILS
V$BACKUP_SET	RC_BACKUP_SET
V$BACKUP_SET_DETAILS	RC_BACKUP_SET_DETAILS
V$BACKUP_SET_SUMMARY	RC_BACKUP_SET_SUMMARY
V$BACKUP_PIECE	RC_BACKUP_PIECE
V$BACKUP_PIECE_DETAILS	RC_BACKUP_PIECE_DETAILS
V$BACKUP_DATAFILE	RC_BACKUP_DATAFILE
V$BACKUP_DATAFILE_DETAILS	RC_BACKUP_DATAFILE_DETAILS
V$BACKUP_DATAFILE_SUMMARY	RC_BACKUP_DATAFILE_SUMMARY
V$BACKUP_FILES	RC_BACKUP_FILES
V$BACKUP_COPY_DETAILS	RC_BACKUP_COPY_DETAILS
V$BACKUP_COPY_SUMMARY	RC_BACKUP_COPY_SUMMARY
V$BACKUP_REDOLOG	RC_BACKUP_REDOLOG
V$BACKUP_ARCHIVELOG_DETAILS	RC_BACKUP_ARCHIVELOG_DETAILS
V$BACKUP_ARCHIVELOG_SUMMARY	RC_BACKUP_ARCHIVELOG_SUMMARY
V$BACKUP_CONTROLFILE_DETAILS	RC_BACKUP_CONTROLFILE_DETAILS
V$BACKUP_CONTROLFILE_SUMMARY	RC_BACKUP_CONTROLFILE_SUMMARY
V$BACKUP_SPFILE	RC_BACKUP_SPFILE
V$BACKUP_SPFILE_DETAILS	RC_BACKUP_SPFILE_DETAILS
V$BACKUP_SPFILE_SUMMARY	RC_BACKUP_SPFILE_SUMMARY

QUERYING FROM RC_BACKUP_FILES

If you get an ORA-20021 error when querying RC_BACKUP_FILES, you'll need to call the DBMS_RCVMAN. SETDATABASE procedure to resolve this problem. Follow the steps outlined in this sidebar to do this. These steps are also documented in My Oracle Support's note 363125.1.

1. First connect to SQL*Plus in your recovery catalog database as the recovery catalog owner:

```
SQL> connect rcat/rcat@rcat
SQL> select count(*) from rc_backup_files;
*
ERROR at line 1:
ORA-20021: database not set
```

2. To fix this issue, call the DBMS_RCVMAN package. The fourth parameter to the SETDATABASE procedure needs to be your target database ID:

```
SQL> call dbms_rcvman.setdatabase(null, null, null, 378401810, null);
SQL> select count(*) from rc_backup_files;

  COUNT(*)
---------------
       205
```

16-4. Determining Whether Repository Queries Are a Bottleneck
Problem
Your RMAN backups are taking a long time. You want to determine whether the problem is related to querying the RMAN metadata repository.

Solution
Find the difference between when RMAN started and when RMAN began its first backup command. To do this, first set the NLS_DATE_FORMAT variable to include a time dimension. This will enable RMAN to report timings down to the second. Here's a shell script that sets NLS_DATE_FORMAT and then runs several RMAN commands:

```
export NLS_DATE_FORMAT='dd-mon-rrrr hh24:mi:ss'
rman log=rman_output.log <<EOF
connect target /
connect catalog rcat/rcat@rcat
set echo on;
backup incremental level=0 database plus archivelog;
spool log off;
EOF
exit 0
```

Now inspect the output log file. There will be a timestamp at the very top showing when the connection to RMAN was initiated. Here is some sample output:

```
Recovery Manager: Release 12.1.0.0.2 ... on Sun Aug 12 14:27:37 2012
```

Now search the log file and identify the time that the backup command starts:

```
Starting backup at 12-aug-2012 14:27:41
```

That shows in this example that RMAN spent only a few seconds from the time it connected and queried the repository to the time it started the backup command. In this environment, there are no performance issues with querying the RMAN repository metadata. If the time between the connection and the start of the backup job had been several minutes, then you would have a performance problem with querying RMAN metadata.

How It Works

When you first connect to RMAN and run commands, the RMAN client needs to communicate with the target database and the recovery catalog (if using). For example, before an RMAN backup command can execute, the repository needs to be queried to determine which files need to be backed up and where the backups should be written to.

If you have a performance problem with querying the RMAN metadata, you'll have to dig a little deeper into the internals of RMAN to determine the exact problem. It could be either a problem with communication between the RMAN client and the target database, or a problem with querying the recovery catalog (if using).

When you start RMAN, two processes are started on the target database (see Figure 16-1). One is the first default process; the other is a polling process. The default process is the one responsible for querying the target database control file and running any SQL statements issued from within RMAN. If you're using a recovery catalog, then a server process is started on the recovery catalog server. This process is responsible for handling communication between the RMAN client and the recovery catalog.

There are two basic techniques for gathering in-depth details on the communication between the RMAN client and the target database first default process and/or the recovery catalog:

- Enable RMAN debug tracing
- Enable SQL tracing

RMAN debug tracing provides information on internal RMAN operations. When working with Oracle Support, support personnel oftentimes will request that you enable RMAN debug tracing. This topic is covered in detail in Recipe 17-9.

You can also enable tracing of any SQL that RMAN is running. This is useful to determine whether a particular SQL query is the cause of performance issues. See Recipe 16-5 for further details on enabling SQL tracing.

If you eliminate the querying of the RMAN metadata as a problem, then you need to focus efforts on where the backup operation is spending its time. For example, is the performance issue with reading data files or with writing to the backup pieces (see Recipe 16-6 for further details on isolating read or write performance issues).

16-5. Enabling SQL Tracing for an RMAN Session
Problem

You suspect you have performance problems related to RMAN processes that query the RMAN repository. You want to determine which SQL statements RMAN is executing and how long the queries are running.

> ■ **Note** Keep in mind that SQL tracing is entirely different from RMAN debug tracing. SQL tracing captures SQL state-
> ments (and associated statistics) executed by a session. RMAN debug tracing captures information regarding RMAN
> internal processing. See Recipe 17-9 for details on enabling RMAN debug tracing.

Solution

Enable SQL tracing for the process of interest. There are two processes where you would want to capture the SQL:

- First default process connected from the RMAN client to the target database
- Process connected to the RMAN recovery catalog

The prior two connections are most likely where you will have issues with long-running SQL statements related to RMAN. Enabling SQL tracing for these sessions is described in the following two subsections.

First Default Process

Here we enable SQL tracing on the first default process by connecting to the target database and issuing the following statements:

```
$ rman target /
RMAN> alter session set events '10046 trace name context forever, level 12';
RMAN> select 'RMAN SQL TRACE FILE' from dual;
RMAN> backup datafile 4;
RMAN> exit;
```

If you're running Oracle Database 11g or below, then the prior code needs to use the sql command:

```
RMAN> sql "alter session set events ''10046 trace name context forever,
    level 12''";
RMAN> sql "select ''RMAN SQL TRACE FILE'' from dual";
RMAN> backup datafile 4;
RMAN> exit;
```

The line in the prior code bits where we select a text string from dual is there simply to help find the correct trace file.

You should now have a trace file in your trace diagnostic directory. See the subsection "Analyzing Trace File Information" in the Solution section of this recipe for details on extracting information from the trace file.

Recovery Catalog Process

A simple approach to enabling SQL tracing on the recovery catalog process is to create an after-logon trigger (in the recovery catalog database) that automatically starts tracing for the recovery catalog user when it connects. This next bit of code shows how to do that:

```
create or replace trigger trace_rcat
after logon on database
declare
  trace_string varchar2(100);
```

```
begin
if user='RCAT' then
  dbms_monitor.session_trace_enable(null, null, true, true);
  SELECT 'RMAN SQL TRACE FILE' INTO trace_string FROM dual;
end if;
end;
/
```

The prior bit of code assumes the recovery catalog user is named RCAT. You'll have to modify that to match the recovery catalog user name in your environment. Ensure that your recovery catalog user has alter session privileges:

```
SQL> grant alter session to rcat;
```

Now when a connection to the recovery catalog is made via the RCAT user, a trace file is created that contains the SQL statements and statistics for that session. See the subsection "Analyzing Trace File Information" in this recipe for details on processing the trace file.

Ensure you drop the trigger after you're done gathering SQL tracing information:

```
SQL> drop trigger trace_rcat;
```

Analyzing Trace File Information

To view the trace file, first determine its location:

```
SQL> select value from v$diag_info where name = 'Diag Trace';

VALUE
--------------------------------------------
/ora01/app/oracle/diag/rdbms/rcat/rcat/trace
```

Now navigate to the trace file directory:

```
$ cd /ora01/app/oracle/diag/rdbms/rcat/rcat/trace
```

> ■ **Note** If you're using a version prior to Oracle Database 11g, you can determine the trace file directory by inspecting the user_dump_dest initialization parameter.

Next search for the string RMAN SQL TRACE FILE in the trace files (this string was embedded into the trace file via SQL from the prior two subsection examples):

```
grep "RMAN SQL TRACE FILE" *.trc
rcat_ora_23006.trc ...
```

In this example, the name of the trace file is rcat_ora_23006.trc. Now run the TKPROF (trace kernel profiler) utility to transform information in the trace file into a human readable form:

```
$ tkprof rcat_ora_23006.trc myout.txt
```

You should now have a file named myout.txt that contains the SQL statements and associated statistics (executed by the session being traced). When running TKPROF, consider sorting the SQL by elapsed time for fetches or by executions. For example:

```
$ tkprof rcat_ora_23006.trc myout.txt sort=fchela
$ tkprof rcat_ora_23006.trc myout.txt sort=exeela
```

This will help you identify the problem SQL in that the most problematic statements (either by elapsed time for fetches or executions) will be sorted to the top of the output file.

How It Works

There are several techniques for enabling SQL tracing for a session. In the Solution section we showed how to enable tracing via setting the 10046 event (for the client) and also using dbms_monitor (for the recovery catalog). Keep in mind there are many other techniques for enabling SQL Tracing (oradebug, alter session set sql_trace=true, dbms_session, and so on). For example, say you wanted to enable SQL tracing for the first default process using the oradebug utility, then first identify the operating system ID of the first default process (see Recipe 16-1 for details). Next enable oradebug for that process:

```
SQL> oradebug setospid 22470
SQL> oradebug unlimit
SQL> oradebug event 10046 trace name con'ext forever, level 12
```

Now display the name of the file with SQL tracing information:

```
SQL> oradebug tracefile_name
```

Normally you wouldn't need to enable SQL tracing for RMAN sessions. If you are having performance problems with RMAN processes that are querying the RMAN repository, then the technique described in the Solution section provides you a method for identifying poorly performing SQL statements (executed by the client or in the recovery catalog).

Once you have a trace file, you can run the TKPROF utility to produce a file that contains the SQL statements and associated statistics. Refer to the Oracle Database Performance Tuning guide for full details on using TKPROF and SQL tracing.

■ **Tip** If you suspect Oracle Net is the bottleneck, see MOS note 1230493.1 for details on enabling SQL*Net tracing on RMAN processes.

If you're working with Oracle Support on an issue, they may ask you to turn on debugging and tracing at the same time. Here is an Oracle Database 12c example of that:

```
rman msgno log=rman_debug01.log trace rman_debug01.trc << EOF
set echo on
connect target /
alter session set max_dump_file_size=UNLIMITED;
alter session set tracefile_identifier='rmanbackup_10046_trace_file';
alter session set events '10046 trace name context forever, level 12';
debug all;
backup database;
debug off;
EOF
```

The prior code generates a log file, a tracing log file, and a trace file with the string "rmanbackup_10046_trace_file" included in the file name (the trace file is created in your diagnostic trace directory). If you're using Oracle Database 11g or lower, you'll need to use the `sql` command to issue SQL statements from within RMAN:

```
rman msgno log=rman_debug01.log trace rman_debug01.trc << EOF
set echo on
connect target /
sql "alter session set max_dump_file_size=UNLIMITED";
sql "alter session set tracefile_identifier=''rmanbackup_10046_trace_file''";
sql "alter session set events ''10046 trace name context forever, level 12''";
debug all;
backup database;
debug off;
EOF
```

16-6. Determining Whether Bottleneck Is Read or Write

Problem

You've eliminated the querying of the RMAN metadata as a performance issue. You now want to determine whether backup performance is related to reading the data files or writing to backup pieces.

Solution

Issue a backup `validate` command to provide the time required to read data files. Compare the time that command takes to execute to the time it takes to perform a regular backup. The difference will give you the time RMAN is spending on writing.

For example, you can instruct RMAN to read the data files only via the `validate` clause of the backup command. This tells RMAN to read the data files as if it were going to back them up, but doesn't actually write anything to the backup storage device. Ensure that you set the NLS_DATE_FORMAT operating system variable before running any commands, as this will provide timings down to the second:

```
$ export NLS_DATE_FORMAT='dd-mon-rrrr hh24:mi:ss'
```

Now connect to RMAN and issue a backup command with the `validate` clause:

```
$ rman target /
RMAN> backup validate database;
...
Starting backup at 12-aug-2012 15:26:27
...
<there will be a lot of output here>
...
Finished backup at 12-aug-2012 15:28:11
```

The difference between the start and finish time tells you how much time RMAN is spending reading files. Compare that time to how long a regular backup takes (both reading and writing files):

```
RMAN> backup database;
```

If the time reading is a short amount compared to how long your backups are taking, this tells you that reading is not an issue. If the time spent reading files is much greater than the time it takes to back up the database, then you need to look at what RMAN is doing while reading files.

How It Works

When you issue a backup command, RMAN will start at least one channel session that is responsible for reading the files to be backed up, writing blocks to memory, and then writing blocks from memory to the backup piece files. When diagnosing performance issues, it's useful to determine whether the problem is with reading the data files or with writing to the backup set. As shown in the Solution section of this recipe, the backup validate command can assist with this task.

If the problem is with the reads, then focus on issues related to reading data files. For example:

- If you're using the BIGFILE feature, consider using multisection backups to enable the reading of a BIGFILE in parallel.

- If you're using incremental backups, consider enabling block change tracking so that the number of blocks read is reduced.

- Consider allocating multiple channels if your data files are spread across many different disks or ASM disk groups.

- If your OS supports direct I/O, consider enabling this feature (see MOS note 555601.1 for further details).

Keep in mind that if you're using compression, no compression takes place during the reading of the files. The blocks are compressed after the read takes place and before the write to the backup piece.

In the Solution section, we presented a simple technique for determining whether the issue was with reading or writing files. If you want to further isolate the I/O issue to a particular data file or mount point, then consider turning on RMAN debug io as shown here:

```
rman msgno log=rman_debug01.log trace rman_debug01.trc << EOF
set echo on
connect target /
debug io;
backup database;
debug off;
EOF
```

The debug output will show the elapsed time and I/O rate when RMAN reads the blocks of the individual data files from the disk to the memory, as well as the elapsed time and I/O rate when writing the blocks from the memory to the RMAN backup pieces. This will help narrow down the investigation to the specific/selected data file(s) having read issue, and identify the problematic disk or mount points.

16-7. Identifying I/O Bottlenecks
Problem

You want to determine I/O bottlenecks in your RMAN backup and recovery jobs.

Solution

Query V$BACKUP_ASYNC_IO and V$BACKUP_SYNC_IO to determine I/O bottlenecks. Ideally, the EFFECTIVE_BYTES_PER_SECOND column should return a rate that is close to the capacity of the backup device. The following query returns statistics for asynchronous I/O for backup and restore operations that have occurred within the past seven days:

```
SELECT sid, serial, filename, type, elapsed_time,
       effective_bytes_per_second
FROM v$backup_async_io
WHERE close_time > sysdate - 7;
```

If you have identified your SID and SERIAL number (see Recipe 16-1), you can specifically query for records associated with your current session:

```
SELECT filename, sid, serial, close_time, long_waits/io_count as ratio
FROM    v$backup_async_io
WHERE   type != 'AGGREGATE'
AND     SID = &SID
AND     SERIAL = &SERIAL
ORDER BY ratio desc;
```

If you are using tape drives, query the EFFECTIVE_BYTES_PER_SECOND column of V$BACKUP_SYNC_IO. If the effective rate is less than the tape device's maximum throughput, this may indicate that your tape device is not streaming (continuously writing).

For tape devices, you can also identify bottlenecks by using the backup validate command. You can compare the time it takes for a regular backup job to tape versus just a backup validate command. A backup validate command performs the same reads as a regular backup but does not write to tape. If the time to perform a backup validate is significantly less than a regular backup job to tape, then writing to tape is most likely the bottleneck.

How It Works

Most operating systems now support asynchronous I/O. When backing up to disk, asynchronous I/O is advantageous because a server process can perform more than one I/O operation at a time. Contrast that with synchronous I/O, where the server process has to wait for each I/O operation to complete before starting the next I/O operation.

The initialization parameter disk_asynch_io controls Oracle's asynchronous behavior. If your operating system supports asynchronous I/O, then Oracle recommends that you leave this parameter set to its default value of TRUE. Oracle will take advantage of asynchronous I/O if it's available. If asynchronous I/O is not available with your operating system, you can tune I/O performance by setting the dbwr_io_slaves initialization parameter to a nonzero value.

■ **Note**   Enabling multiple I/O slaves will increase the number of processes that your database uses. You will need to adjust the processes initialization parameter accordingly.

You can use two views to monitor asynchronous and synchronous I/O. As its name implies, V$BACKUP_ASYNC_IO contains information for asynchronous backup or restore operations. Likewise, V$BACKUP_SYNC_IO contains information for synchronous operations. For each backup or restore operation, you will see a row in the view for the following events:

- Each data file read or written

- Each backup piece read or written

- An aggregate record for overall performance of files read or written during an operation

The TYPE column of V$BACKUP_ASYNC_IO and V$BACKUP_SYNC_IO can have the following values: INPUT for files read, OUTPUT for files written, and AGGREGATE for aggregated rows.

The EFFECTIVE_BYTES_PER_SECOND column specifies the read/write rate for the backup or restore operation. For aggregated rows, the EFFECTIVE_BYTES_PER_SECOND should be close to the maximum throughput of the backup device. If the value of EFFECTIVE_BYTES_PER_SECOND is significantly less than the backup device's maximum I/O rate, then you probably have a system performance issue with something other than your database (such as a busy CPU).

■ **Note** The V$BACKUP_ASYNC_IO and V$BACKUP_SYNC_IO views have information only since the last time your instance was started.

RMAN will record information about asynchronous backup operations to V$BACKUP_ASYNC_IO. If your operating system or backup device (such as a tape drive) doesn't support asynchronous I/O, you can use V$BACKUP_SYNC_IO for diagnosing I/O bottlenecks.

■ **Note** Refer to Oracle's operating system–specific documentation to determine whether your operating system supports asynchronous I/O.

16-8. Improving Tape I/O Performance
Problem

You have identified your tape drive as an I/O performance bottleneck (see Recipe 16-7). You want to improve RMAN's I/O performance with your tape device.

Solution

We have two recommendations for improving RMAN's I/O performance with tape devices:

- Use an incremental backup strategy with block change tracking.
- Adjust multiplexing of backup sets.

The RMAN incremental block change tracking backup strategy is detailed in Recipe 7-11. For information about multiplexing backup sets, refer to Recipe 16-9.

How It Works

Improving tape I/O can be difficult because many of the variables are not dependent on RMAN. Some factors are dependent on the tape device and Media Management Layer (MML) software. Here are some variables to consider when tuning tape I/O:

- MML software configuration
- Network configuration
- Level of tape compression
- Tape streaming
- Tape block size

Variables that you can control from RMAN are your incremental backup strategy and the level of multiplexing. If your tape device is not streaming (continuously writing), then consider using an incremental backup strategy. Incremental backups usually have fewer writes than full backups and therefore should lessen the bottleneck writing to tape.

The block change tracking feature enables RMAN to quickly identify which blocks have changed since the last incremental backup. This feature can significantly improve the performance of incremental backups.

Also, consider altering the default multiplexing behavior of RMAN. Setting filesperset high and maxopenfiles low may increase the efficiency of writing to your tape device. You can also use the diskratio parameter to instruct RMAN to balance the load if data files are distributed across several different disks. See Recipe 16-9 for details on how to adjust the multiplexing of backup sets.

16-9. Maximizing Throughput to Backup Device

Problem

You suspect that your backup device is a bottleneck for backup operations. You want to adjust the throughput to the backup device.

Solution

You can tune the throughput to backup devices by adjusting RMAN's level of multiplexing. RMAN multiplexing is controlled by three parameters:

- filesperset
- maxopenfiles
- diskratio

Using filesperset

Use the fileperset clause of the backup command to limit the number of data files in each backup set. For example, if you wanted to limit the number of files being written to a backup set to only two files, you would use filesperset, as shown here:

```
RMAN> backup database filesperset 2;
```

Using maxopenfiles

Use the maxopenfiles clause of the configure channel command or the allocate channel command to limit the number of files that can be simultaneously open for reads during a backup. If you want to limit the number of files being read by a channel to two files, use maxopenfiles as follows:

```
RMAN> configure channel 1 device type disk maxopenfiles 2;
```

To reset the channel maxopenfiles to the default setting, use the clear parameter as shown here:

```
RMAN> configure channel 1 device type disk clear;
```

Using diskratio

The diskratio parameter of the backup command instructs RMAN to read data files from a specified number of disks. For example, if you wanted RMAN to include data files located on at least four different disks into one backup set, then use diskratio as follows:

```
RMAN> backup database diskratio 4;
```

If you specify filesperset and not diskratio, then diskratio will default to the value of filesperset. The diskratio parameter works only on operating systems that can provide RMAN with information such as disk contention and node affinity.

How It Works

Multiplexing backup sets is RMAN's ability to read multiple data files simultaneously and write them to the same physical backup piece file. The level of multiplexing is defined by the number of files read simultaneously.

As of Oracle Database 10g, RMAN will automatically tune the level of multiplexing of your backup sets. RMAN will automatically divide the files being read during a backup across the available channels. Therefore, under most scenarios you will not be required to tune throughput. If you're working with tape devices, you may need to adjust the parameters described in this recipe to ensure that writes to tape are continuously streaming. Setting filesperset high and maxopenfiles low may increase the efficiency of writing to your tape device.

You can alter the default levels of multiplexing by using the filesperset and maxopenfiles parameters. The value of filesperset specifies the maximum number of files in each backup set. The default value of filesperset is 64.

The default value of maxopenfiles is 8. This places a limit on the number of files that RMAN can read in parallel. For example, if you set maxopenfiles for a channel to 2, then only two data files would be read and then written to the backup piece at a time (for that channel).

■ **Note** See MOS note 1072545.1 for details on adjusting database initialization parameters to maximize memory buffer throughput.

16-10. Tuning Media Recovery
Problem

You want to manually adjust the degree of parallelism that Oracle uses for media recovery to match the number of CPUs on your database server.

Solution

Starting with Oracle Database 10g, when you issue a recover command from either within RMAN or within SQL*Plus, Oracle's default behavior is to automatically perform media recovery operations in parallel. However, if you want to override this default behavior, you can use the recover parallel or recover noparallel command. This next line of code instructs Oracle to spawn four parallel processes to apply redo:

```
RMAN> recover database parallel 4;
```

If you don't want Oracle to recover in parallel, then specify the noparallel clause as shown here:

```
RMAN> recover database noparallel;
```

How It Works

Ordinarily you don't need to adjust the degree of parallelism for media recovery. This is because Oracle automatically parallelizes media recovery for you. Oracle determines the number of parallel processes to spawn for media recovery from the initialization parameter cpu_count. This parameter is set by default to the number of CPUs on your database server.

For example, if your server has two CPUS, then by default cpu_count will be set to 2 when you create your database. For this server, Oracle will spawn two processes to apply redo anytime you issue a recover command (from either RMAN or SQL*Plus).

Oracle's documentation states that systems with efficient asynchronous I/O see little benefit from parallel media recovery. You should test whether adjusting the degree of parallelism improves performance before you attempt this in a production environment.

■ **Note**   The initialization parameter recovery_parallelism has no effect on media recovery.
The recovery_parallelism parameter affects only crash recovery.

16-11. Slowing RMAN Down
Problem

Users are complaining about poor application performance. You've noticed that the performance degradation occurs while the RMAN backups are running. You want to reduce RMAN's I/O rate so that it spreads out its impact on the system over a period of time.

■ **Tip**   Consider using compressed backups to slow down RMAN. This will result in more CPU usage, but fewer writes spread out over a longer period of time. If you have plenty of CPU power, this is a simple but effective way to slow RMAN down. If you take this approach, remember that your restore time will be greater because RMAN must uncompress the backups as part of the restore operation.

Solution

Use one of the following to control RMAN's I/O rate:

- The backup duration ... minimize load command
- The rate clause of the allocate channel or configure channel command

Using backup duration ... minimize load

Use the backup duration ... minimize load command to evenly distribute RMAN I/O over a period of time. This example shows how to spread the I/O of an RMAN backup over a 45-minute period:

```
RMAN> backup duration 00:45 minimize load database;
```

RMAN will report the time taken for the backup operation in the output, as shown in this snippet:

```
channel ORA_DISK_1: throttle time: 0:44:43
```

Using rate

You can also use the rate clause of the allocate channel command or the configure channel command to control RMAN's I/O rate. This example configures channel 1 to have a maximum read rate of 5MB per second:

```
RMAN> configure channel 1 device type disk rate=5M;
```

The rate can be set using M, K, or G (for megabytes, kilobytes, and gigabytes). If you need to clear the channel rate setting, use this command:

```
RMAN> configure channel 1 device type disk clear;
```

■ **Tip** See My Oracle Support note 369573.1 for details on minimizing the impact of an RMAN backup on an OLTP database.

How It Works

RMAN is engineered to perform backup and recovery tasks as fast as possible. When you initiate a backup, the backup's execution will increase the I/O on the server as the blocks are read from data files and written to backup pieces. Sometimes you may want to slow down RMAN so that it doesn't impact application performance while the backup is running. You can slow down RMAN with the duration clause or by specifying a rate.

The duration clause specifies the amount of time you want an RMAN backup to take. When you use the minimize load clause, this instructs RMAN to spread out the I/O load over the duration of the specified time. When minimizing the load, RMAN will monitor and adjust the I/O rate so that the resources are consumed evenly across the duration of the backup. The format for the time value of the duration clause is HH:MM (HH is hours and MM is minutes). You must specify the hour and colon components of the time even if the hour component is zero.

If a backup does not complete within the specified duration period, then RMAN will abort the backup. If you are running backup commands from within a run{} block, then RMAN will not execute subsequent commands. You can use the partial clause to instruct RMAN to continue running subsequent commands within a run{} block (even if the backup doesn't finish in the specified time).

In this example, the partial clause instructs RMAN to execute all subsequent commands in the run{} block even if the first command doesn't finish within the specified time:

```
RMAN> run {
backup duration 1:00 partial minimize load database;
backup archivelog all;
backup current controlfile;
}
```

Whether or not you use the partial clause, RMAN will still consider any backup sets that were created successfully (before the time limit was exceeded) to be usable for restore operations. If you want to force RMAN to include only one data file per backup set, you can use the filesperset parameter as shown here:

```
RMAN> backup duration 01:00 minimize load database filesperset 1;
```

When you set the filesperset parameter to 1, it forces RMAN to create each backup set with only one data file within it. Any backup sets that complete before the duration time is exceeded will be marked as successful.

■ **Note** Oracle does not recommend using `backup duration ... minimize load` when using tape devices. When using minimize load, RMAN could reduce its I/O to a rate that is too low to keep the tape device streaming.

You can also instruct to minimize the time that RMAN takes to perform a backup. This example instructs RMAN to try to complete the backup in two minutes or less:

```
RMAN> backup duration 0:02 minimize time database;
```

Minimizing time is default behavior, and this instructs RMAN to back up as quickly as possible within the specified time. When you use the minimize time clause, RMAN will prioritize the files to be backed up, giving the most recently backed-up data file the lowest priority.

16-12. Improving Performance Through Parallelism
Problem

You want to improve RMAN performance by utilizing multiple I/O channels. You want backup and/or restore operations to run as fast as possible.

Solution

Use the `parallel` clause of the `configure` command to instruct RMAN to allocate multiple channels for backup and restore operations. The approach slightly varies depending on whether you're using a FRA.

Using a FRA

The following command instructs RMAN to open multiple channels when performing backup operations:

```
RMAN> configure device type disk parallelism 2;
RMAN> backup database;
```

If you're using a FRA, RMAN will automatically allocate the specified number of channels, which are then used to read files and write in parallel to your FRA.

You can also implement parallelism by using the `allocate` command. This command must be run within a run{} block (there's no need to specify the degree of parallelism because it's derived from the number of allocated channels):

```
RMAN> run{
allocate channel d1 device type disk;
allocate channel d2 device type disk;
backup database;
}
```

Not Using a FRA

You may have an environment where you have multiple backup locations on disk and you want to perform RMAN operations in parallel. In this situation you can manually configure channels to write backups to separate locations. For example, say you have two separate mount points where you want to write the backups. You can configure that as follows:

```
RMAN> configure device type disk parallelism 2;
RMAN> configure channel 1 device type disk format '/u01/rman/o12c/rman1_%U.bk';
RMAN> configure channel 2 device type disk format '/u02/rman/o12c/rman2_%U.bk';
RMAN> backup database;
```

When the backup command is executed, RMAN will spread the backup pieces across the two configured channels. If you set the degree of parallelism to 1, then RMAN will back up using only the first channel device defined (even if you have configured two or more channels).

Keep in mind that the disk location specified in this example may not match your environment. You will have to change the directory paths to match backup locations that exist on your sever. If the directories don't exist, you'll receive this error:

```
ORA-19504: failed to create file...
ORA-27040: file create error, unable to create file
```

■ **Note** The %U in the configuration statement instructs RMAN to create unique backup piece names.

Another method for enabling parallelism is to format the allocate channel command. This command must be run within a run{} block and there's no need to specify a degree of parallelism (it's derived from the number of allocated channels):

```
RMAN> run{
allocate channel d1 device type disk format '/u01/rman/o12c/rman1_%U.bk';
allocate channel d2 device type disk format '/u02/rman/o12c/rman2_%U.bk';
backup database;
}
```

Another technique for enabling parallelism is to format the backup command with multiple locations. Here you do have to specify the degree of parallelism:

```
RMAN> configure device type disk parallelism 2;
RMAN> backup database format '/u01/rman/o12c/rman1_%U.bk',
    '/u02/rman/o12c/rman1_%U.bk';
```

It's mostly a personal preference as to which technique you use to enable parallelism.

■ **Note** If you enable parallelism, are not using a FRA, and don't configure explicitly the location of the backup pieces, then RMAN will write in parallel backup pieces to the default location (usually ORACLE_HOME/dbs).

How It Works

An easy way to improve performance is to allocate multiple channels for backup and restore operations. The following factors will influence whether parallelism improves the performance of these operations:

- Files being backed up are spread across multiple storage devices. This could be multiple disks, RAID storage, or ASM disk groups. In this situation RMAN read performance may improve.

- Backup location is spread across multiple storage devices. This could be multiple tapes, disks, RAID storage, or ASM disk groups. In this situation RMAN write performance may improve.

- Server has multiple CPUs. This can especially help with compressed backups in which the CPU load is higher.

The default degree of parallelism for a backup is 1 (and can be up to 255). If you change the degree of parallelism, RMAN will start the number of server sessions to match the degree of parallelism that you specify. For example, if you specify a degree of parallelism of 2, then RMAN will start two channels for the backup or restore operation.

A good rule of thumb is to have the degree of parallelism match the number of physical devices. For example, if you have data files distributed over two physical drives, then a parallelism degree of 2 would be appropriate. If you have only one physical drive, then setting the degree of parallelism to a higher value generally may not help improve performance (as there is overhead associated with starting multiple channels). When using tape devices, the guideline is to make the number of channels allocated equal to the number of tape devices divided by the number of duplexed copies.

To view the degree of parallelism for the default device type, use the show device type command as shown here:

```
RMAN> show device type;
```

Here is some sample output:

```
CONFIGURE DEVICE TYPE DISK PARALLELISM 2 BACKUP TYPE TO BACKUPSET;
```

You can view the channel configuration information as shown here:

```
RMAN> show channel;
```

Here is the corresponding output:

```
CONFIGURE CHANNEL 1 DEVICE TYPE DISK FORMAT '/u01/rman/o12c/rman1_%U.bk';
CONFIGURE CHANNEL 2 DEVICE TYPE DISK FORMAT '/u02/rman/o12c/rman1_%U.bk';
```

You can clear the device type and channel settings with these commands:

```
RMAN> configure device type disk clear;
RMAN> configure channel 1 device type disk clear;
RMAN> configure channel 2 device type disk clear;
```

■ **Note** If you're using a FRA and manually configuring channels, then you may end up with some backup pieces in your FRA and some backup pieces located in the directories specified during manual channel configuration. For example, if you manually configure two channels and specify a degree of parallelism of 4 (and are using a FRA), then RMAN will write backup pieces to the two manually configured disk locations as well as creating two backup pieces in the FRA.

16-13. Speeding Up Compressed Backup Sets

Problem

You've enabled compression for your backups and they're running slow. You want to improve the performance of compressed backups.

Solution

There are two techniques for improving the performance of compressed backups:

- Use the Oracle Advanced Compression option
- Enable parallelism

If you're using Oracle Database 11g or higher, consider using the Advanced Compression option:

```
RMAN> configure compression algorithm 'MEDIUM';
```

The prior command instructs RMAN to use the medium compression algorithm (of the Oracle Advanced Compression option). From our experience, this compression algorithm runs about twice as fast as basic (default) compression.

■ **Note** Oracle Advanced Compression requires the Enterprise Edition of Oracle and is an extra-cost option (as of the writing of this book).

Another method for potentially speeding up compression is to allocate multiple channels:

```
RMAN> configure device type disk parallelism 2;
```

The idea is that compression is CPU intensive and if your server has multiple CPUs, you can spread the CPU load.

How It Works

Starting with Oracle Database 11g release 2, four levels of compression are available with RMAN:

- BASIC
- LOW
- MEDIUM
- HIGH

The BASIC compression is the default compression and doesn't require an extra license. The other levels (LOW, MEDIUM, and HIGH) are part of the Oracle Advanced Compression option. You can verify the compression being used via:

```
RMAN> show compression algorithm;
```

To view descriptions of available compression, run this query:

```
select algorithm_name, algorithm_description, is_default
from v$rman_compression_algorithm;
```

Here is some sample output:

```
ALGORITHM_ ALGORITHM_DESCRIPTION                              IS_
---------- -------------------------------------------------- ---
BZIP2      good compression ratio                             NO
BASIC      good compression ratio                             YES
LOW        maximum possible compression speed                 NO
ZLIB       balance between speed and compression ratio        NO
MEDIUM     balance between speed and compression ratio        NO
HIGH       maximum possible compression ratio                 NO
```

Specifying BZIP2 and ZLIB level compression is deprecated as of Oracle Database 11g release 2.

16-14. Improving Performance Using Incremental Features
Problem

You wonder whether you can improve performance by using one or more of RMAN's incremental backup features.

Solution

RMAN provides three main incremental backup features:

- Incremental backups
- Change tracking
- Incremental update

Table 16-2 describes how each feature can improve performance with backup and restore operations. You'll have to test these features in your environment to see whether they give you the desired performance boost.

Table 16-2. Matrix of Incremental Features Available to Increase RMAN Performance

	Incremental Backups	Change Tracking	Incremental Update
Backup	Reduces disk space and time writing to the backup device. Good choice when most of your blocks aren't updated often. See Recipe 7-10 for details.	Significantly improves performance when using incremental backups. See Recipe 7-11 for details.	Backup time becomes proportional to amount of redo generated. See Recipe 7-27 for details.
Restore	Dependent on number of incremental backups taken since level 0 backup.	N/A	Significantly decreases time to restore database.

How It Works

Incremental backups are a good choice for databases in which a small percentage of blocks are updated from one backup to the next. Incremental backups would be less ideal for databases in which most of the blocks are updated between backups.

You can significantly improve the performance of incremental backups by using change tracking. Change tracking can slightly decrease the performance of your database activities (because Oracle has to keep track of which blocks are changing). However, if the performance of backups is paramount, then you should consider implementing this feature.

If you want to minimize the mean time to recovery, you should consider using the RMAN incremental update feature. Incremental updates use image copies as a basis for the backup.

Restoring a data file from an image copy is much more efficient than restoring from a backup set. This is because an image copy is an identical copy of the data file and RMAN can simply copy the image to the location from where it was backed up.

■ **Tip**   If you use Oracle Data Guard, consider a strategy where you use RMAN to take backups of the physical standby database. This will give the same protection as backing up your primary database but will offload the impact of RMAN backups from the primary database server to the standby database server.

16-15. Setting the Large Pool Size

Problem

You either are using a tape device or have disabled native asynchronous I/O. In these scenarios setting the large pool size may help performance.

Solution

Oracle recommends using this formula for setting the large pool size:

```
number_of_allocated_channels * (16 MB + (4 * size_of_tape_buffer))
```

Use the `alter system` command to set a value for the `large_pool_size` parameter, for example:

```
SQL> alter system set large_pool_size = 64M scope=both;
```

You can verify its value via:

```
SQL> show parameter large_pool_size;
```

How It Works

You should rarely have to enable the use of the large pool. If you are backing up to disk and have native asynchronous IO turned off, you may want to set a value for the large pool. You can tell whether asynchronous I/O is off if `disk_asynch_io` is set to `false` and `dbwr_io_slaves` is greater than zero.

If you are backing up to tape and have enabled multiple I/O slaves, you may want to set a value for the large pool. You can tell whether you're using multiple I/O slaves if the value of `backup_tape_io_slaves` is set to `true`.

When I/O slaves are enabled, RMAN will use memory in the large pool if it is allocated; otherwise it will allocate memory in the shared pool. If you're using I/O slaves, we recommend that you enable a large pool to avoid contention in the shared pool. If you're not using I/O slaves, then RMAN will not use the large pool.

Troubleshooting RMAN

Not many things are more vexing to a DBA than experiencing problems when backing up and recovering a mission-critical database. The good news is that RMAN is a tried-and-true backup and recovery tool. RMAN has been available since version 8.0. Many companies routinely use RMAN as their backup and recovery (B&R) solution. As a result, vast sources of RMAN information are available (web sites, white papers, presentations, blogs, forums, user groups, and so on). This means you can usually find somebody who has already encountered the problem you're facing.

For example, if you visit Oracle's RMAN technical forum web site, you'll see that there have been thousands of postings for problems that DBAs have encountered. We can't cover all these potential RMAN issues and corresponding solutions in a book. However, we can cover helpful RMAN troubleshooting techniques and some of the more common types of problems you'll encounter. We begin by helping you determine where to look for answers when facing an RMAN issue.

■ **Note** We realize that oftentimes troubleshooting and performance tuning are inherently intertwined. The topics specific to performance tuning have been placed in Chapter 16. Keep in mind you may need to refer to recipes in Chapters 16 and 17 to resolve a particular issue.

17-1. Determining Where to Start
Problem

You just issued an RMAN command, and it returned a long error stack message. You wonder where to start to resolve the issue.

Solution

When dealing with RMAN issues, here are the general steps we recommend you follow to resolve problems:

1. Start at the bottom of the error stack and work your way back up until you spot the most relevant error message(s).

2. If you suspect the problem is a syntax error, use the checksyntax option as described in Recipe 4-15, or look in Oracle's RMAN Reference Guide for syntax descriptions.

3. Look for relevant error messages in these files: the alert log, trace files, and sbtio.log (if using an MML).

4. Follow a recipe in this book that helps resolve the issue.

5. Use your favorite search engine to search the Web for information from other DBAs who have encountered similar situations.

6. Ask other DBAs for help.

7. Search Oracle's RMAN backup and recovery documentation at `http://otn.oracle.com`.

8. Search Oracle's My Oracle Support (MOS) web site at `http://support.oracle.com`.

9. Search for an answer or post a question on Oracle's RMAN forum at `http://forums.oracle.com`.

10. Open a service request (SR) with Oracle Support.

11. Enable more output logging and debugging (see Recipes 17-7, 17-8, and 17-9).

■ **Note** Before you can use the MOS web site to open an SR, you must first purchase a valid Oracle support license.

How It Works

With RMAN troubleshooting, usually you start with the error message displayed on your terminal or recorded in a log file. This section discusses a typical RMAN error stack. To begin with, you'll almost always see the following text as the first part of the output when there's an RMAN error:

```
RMAN-00571: ===========================================================
RMAN-00569: =============== ERROR MESSAGE STACK FOLLOWS ===============
RMAN-00571: ===========================================================
```

RMAN error messages can sometimes be frustrating to interpret. Even for something as simple as an incorrectly typed RMAN command, you'll be presented with a lengthy output describing the error. For example, you might receive the following message stack:

```
RMAN-01009: syntax error: found "identifier": expecting one of: "advise,
allocate, alter, analyze, associate statistics, audit, backup, begin, @, call,
catalog, change, comment, commit, configure, connect, convert, copy, create,
create catalog, create global, create script, create virtual, crosscheck, declare
...
```

When presented with an RMAN error message stack, follow the steps outlined in the Solution section of this recipe. You'll have to vary the steps depending on your scenario. For example, if you have a priority-one (P1) production problem, you may want to open an SR with Oracle Support as your first step. For most other situations, you'll use a subset of the solution steps and resolve the problem on your own.

17-2. Resolving Connection Permission Issues

Problem

You're trying to log in to RMAN from the command prompt, and you receive the following message:

```
$ rman target /

RMAN-00554: initialization of internal recovery manager package failed
RMAN-04005: error from target database:
ORA-01031: insufficient privileges
```

Solution

If you're attempting to use operating system authentication (not supplying a username and password) when starting RMAN, you need to ensure your OS user account is part of a privileged DBA OS group. If you're not using OS authentication, you need to make sure you have correctly enabled a password file.

Using OS Authentication

In Linux/Unix, the privileged OS group is usually named dba. This is the group you specified when installing the Oracle software. To verify that your OS account belongs to the proper group, use the Linux/Unix id command:

```
$ id
uid=500(oracle) gid=500(oinstall) groups=500(oinstall),501(dba)
```

In a Windows environment use this process to verify that your OS user is part of the Oracle DBA group:

1. Go to Control Panel, and then go to Administrative Tools.

2. Click Computer Management.

3. Click Local Users and Groups, then click Groups.

4. You should see a group named ora_dba; double-click it.

5. Make sure your OS user is a member of the Oracle DBA group.

Using a Password File

If you're not using OS authentication, then you must supply a username and password combination that is recorded in the password file that has appropriate privileges:

```
$ rman target <username>/<password>
```

If you don't supply a correct username and password, you'll get an ORA-01031 "insufficient privileges" error. Ensure that you use a correct username and password when using a password file.

■ **Tip** Recipe 2-1 has complete details on how to use OS authentication and also how to implement a password file.

How It Works

Most RMAN tasks require that you connect to the target database with a user who has the sysdba database privilege. You can connect to your target database with sysdba privileges in one of two ways:

- Use an OS-authenticated account.
- Use a password file that contains the username and password information of schemas granted the sysdba privilege.

■ **Tip** A new sys level privilege is available in Oracle Database 12c named sysbackup. You can grant this privilege to database users to allow them to specifically perform RMAN backup and recovery tasks. This allows you to grant a user the privileges required to back up, restore, and recover the database without having to grant them all of the privileges associated with sysdba.

A useful way to troubleshoot the root cause of an ORA-01031 error is to attempt to log in to SQL*Plus with the same authentication information as when trying to connect through RMAN. This will help verify either that you are using an OS-authenticated account or that the username and password are correct.

If OS authentication is working, then you should be able to log in to SQL*Plus as follows:

```
$ sqlplus / as sysdba
```

If you're using a password file, you can verify that the username and password are correct (and that the user has sysdba privileges) by logging in as shown here:

```
$ sqlplus <username>/<password> as sysdba
```

If you receive an ORA-01031 error from attempting to log in to SQL*Plus, then either you aren't using an OS-authenticated account or your username and password combination does not match what is stored in the password file (for users attempting to connect as sysdba).

If you are using an OS-authenticated account, it doesn't matter what you specify for the username and password. You can specify any text strings for the username and password, and Oracle will allow you to connect. This is because Oracle performs OS authentication first. If that OS authentication succeeds, the username and password combination is not validated.

Another issue that you might encounter when first connecting to and using RMAN is this:

```
RMAN-00554: initialization of internal recovery manager package failed
RMAN-04005: error from target database:
ORA-06553: PLS-213: package STANDARD not accessible
RMAN-04015: error setting target database character set to US7ASCII
```

If you receive the prior messages, ensure your data dictionary has been properly created (via catalog.sql and catproc.sql).

Another error commonly encountered when first accessing RMAN is as follows:

```
$ rman target /
rman: can't open target
```

If you encounter the prior error, ensure that the directory ORACLE_HOME/bin in your PATH variable comes before any X11 software related directories. You can verify that you're using Oracle's rman executable via the which command:

```
$ which rman
```

```
/u01/app/oracle/product/12.1.0.1/db_1/bin/rman
```

If the which command displays this:

```
/usr/X11R6/bin/rman
```

Then you need to set your PATH variable as previously indicated.

17-3. Handling Disk Space Issues
Problem

You're attempting to create a backup, and you receive an error similar to the following:

```
RMAN-03009: failure of backup command on ORA_DISK_1 channel ...
ORA-19502: write error on file ...
ORA-27072: File I/O error
```

Solution

The error described in the Problem section is usually caused by a lack of disk space. Verify from the operating system that the location you're backing up to is indeed full. In a Linux/Unix environment, you can use the df command to verify this. In a Windows environment, you can right-click the backup directory and view its properties.

If your backup location is full, you can do one of the following to correct the problem:

- Change the backup location to an area that has more space.

- Add disk space to the backup location.

- If using a fast recovery area (FRA), either move the FRA or increase its size.

- Change the RMAN retention policy to fewer days or fewer backups and delete obsolete backup files and/or archive redo log files that are no longer required.

Changing your backup location and deleting obsolete backup files are trivial tasks to perform, and you'll need to see your system administrator about adding space to your backup location. The other two options, though, require a bit more explanation.

Moving and/or Resizing the FRA

The following SQL statement uses the alter system command to move the FRA:

```
SQL> alter system set db_recovery_file_dest='/oraback02/FRA' scope=both;
```

If disk space is available, you can increase the size of the FRA to an appropriate value. This example changes the FRA size to 100GB:

```
SQL> alter system set db_recovery_file_dest_size=100g scope=both;
```

■ **Note** If you're not using an spfile, make sure you update the new initialization settings in your init.ora file.

You can verify what the new FRA settings are with this query:

```
SQL> select * from v$recovery_file_dest;
```

■ **Tip** See Chapter 3 for complete details on how to manage your FRA.

Changing Retention Policy and Deleting Old Backups

This section shows how to change a retention policy and use the delete obsolete command to free up space consumed by obsolete backups. First use the report obsolete command to view backups that are candidates to be deleted:

```
RMAN> report obsolete;
```

This command will show the retention policy and which backups and archived redo log files are obsolete. Here is a snippet of the output:

```
RMAN retention policy will be applied to the command
RMAN retention policy is set to redundancy 6
...
no obsolete backups found
```

In this example, no obsolete backups were reported. We'll use the configure command to change the retention policy from a redundancy policy of six down to two:

```
RMAN> configure retention policy to redundancy 2;
```

Now the report obsolete command shows that there are several obsolete files:

```
Type                 Key    Completion Time    Filename/Handle
-------------------- ------ ------------------ --------------------
Backup Set           7      30-JUL-12
  Backup Piece       7      30-JUL-12
/u01/app/oracle/product/12.1.0.1/db_1/dbs/c-3412777350-20120730-00
...
```

Now we can use the delete obsolete command to have RMAN remove the backups from the backup media and also update the repository:

```
RMAN> delete obsolete;
```

How It Works

If you're encountering disk space issues, the error message will vary depending on whether you're using a FRA and which operating system you're using. You can resolve disk space issues in a number of ways. If you're in an emergency situation, the quickest way to resolve the issue may be to change the location of the backup directory. If you're looking for a long-term solution, you'll probably want to consider adding more disk space to the backup location and/or changing your RMAN retention policy.

If you're using a FRA, then you can dynamically issue an `alter system` command to change the location and size of the backup directory. If you're not using a FRA, you can use the `configure` command to change the location of the backups (see Recipe 5-16 for an example of how to do this).

If there are old archived redo log files, consider backing them up and then deleting them from disk. You can use commands such as `report obsolete` to show which RMAN backup files and archived redo log files are no longer required as per the retention policy. If there are obsolete files, then you can use the `delete obsolete` command to have RMAN remove them from the backup media.

■ **Tip** Consider using compressed backups to decrease the amount of disk space consumed. RMAN's basic default compression algorithm produces a significant reduction in the size of the backups.

17-4. Dealing with the RMAN-06059 Error
Problem

You've just switched from user-managed backups to using RMAN backups and are attempting to run the following command:

```
RMAN> backup database plus archivelog;
```

Your backup process doesn't get very far when RMAN throws this error:

```
RMAN-03002: failure of backup plus archivelog command at...
RMAN-06059: expected archived log not found, loss of archived log
compromises recoverability
```

Your boss happens to be in your office when you are attempting to back up the database and lets you know that "compromised recoverability" will translate into "compromised job security."

Solution

The problem is that the control file has information regarding archive redo logs that are no longer on disk (or have been manually moved). You must update RMAN's repository to reflect that archived redo log files have been either physically deleted or moved to another location on disk. Use the `crosscheck` command to inform RMAN that archived redo log files have been physically removed from disk, as shown here:

```
RMAN> crosscheck archivelog all;
```

Now run your backup command again; this time it should succeed:

```
RMAN> backup database plus archivelog;
```

If the issue is that your archived redo logs are still on disk, but RMAN is unaware of the location (because either the archive redo logs were created before you started using RMAN or for some reason you've moved the files), then use the catalog command to update the RMAN repository with the new location of the files:

```
RMAN> catalog start with '/oradump01/oldarchive';
```

The start with clause of the catalog command instructs RMAN to look in the specified directory and update its repository with any archive redo log files, backup pieces, or image copies located within that directory (and its subdirectories).

How It Works

When you switch from user-managed backups to RMAN backups, you will most likely have many historical archived redo log files that have been generated and removed from disk by your user-managed backup scripts. The control file will still retain information regarding these old files. In situations where you have used operating system commands to remove or move archived redo log files, you must inform RMAN that files have been deleted or moved. The crosscheck command instructs RMAN to check to see if the files physically exist in the last known location. If the files have been moved, then use the catalog command to update the RMAN repository.

You can tell RMAN to back up data files and archived redo log files with the backup database plus archivelog command, or you can just back up archived redo log files via the backup archivelog all command. Both of these commands instruct RMAN to back up any archived redo log files that have an AVAILABLE status in the V$ARCHIVED_LOG view. You can query the STATUS column of V$ARCHIVED_LOG as follows:

```
select thread#, sequence#,
decode(status,'A','available','D','deleted','U','unavailable','X','expired')
from v$archived_log;
```

If RMAN can't find on disk an archived redo log file that has an AVAILABLE status, then it will throw the RMAN-06059 error and abort the backup. If you are not using RMAN to delete archived redo log files from disk, then the archived redo log file status remains AVAILABLE, even though the file isn't in the expected location.

When running the crosscheck archivelog all command, RMAN will change the status of an archived redo log file to EXPIRED if it cannot locate the file. RMAN will not attempt to back up an archived redo log file with an EXPIRED status.

The catalog command is handy because you can use it to update the RMAN repository with information about relocated archived redo log files, RMAN backup pieces, and image copies. Use the catalog start with command to tell RMAN which directory to look in for your relocated files. Alternatively, you can tell RMAN to catalog just one archived redo log file, as shown here:

```
RMAN> catalog archivelog '/oldarchvies/arch1_3144_234562.arc';
```

Now you can query from V$ARCHIVED_LOG, and it will reflect the new location of the archived redo log file.

■ **Tip** We strongly recommend that you always use RMAN to delete archived redo log files and backup pieces from the backup media. If you use an OS command to delete these files, then RMAN is unaware that the files have been removed from the backup media. This causes issues when you run subsequent backup, restore, and recover commands.

17-5. Terminating RMAN Processes

Problem

You have an RMAN job that appears to be hung. You want to terminate the job.

Solution

You can terminate an RMAN job by using one of the following techniques:

- Press Ctrl+C from the RMAN client. This approach, of course, works only if performed from the terminal session responsible for the process you want to stop.

- Manually kill the OS process.

- Terminate the server session corresponding to an RMAN channel using an `alter system kill` SQL statement.

Pressing Ctrl+C from the RMAN interface is the easiest way to terminate a job (when it works). If that isn't successful or if you did not initiate the job interactively, then you'll have to try one of the following solutions.

Terminating a Unix Process

In a Linux/Unix environment, you can identify an RMAN operating system process number using the Unix `ps` command as follows:

```
$ ps -ef | grep -v grep | grep -i rman
```

The process number is displayed in the second column of the output:

```
oracle   5000  1853  0 17:30 pts/0    00:00:01 rman target /
```

In this example, the process to terminate is 5000. You can then use the Linux/Unix `kill` command, as shown here:

```
$ kill -9 5000
```

Terminating a Windows Process

On a Windows server, you can use the Task Manager utility to identify background processes. You can start Task Manager in one of the following ways:

- Ctrl+Alt+Delete.

- Ctrl+Shift+Esc.

- Right-click an empty space in the taskbar, and choose Task Manager.

From the Task Manager, click Applications, and select the RMAN process you want to terminate. Click End Task to terminate the process.

Using SQL to Terminate an RMAN Channel

Use the `alter system kill session` SQL statement to terminate a hung RMAN job. To do this, you need to first identify the serial ID and serial number:

```
SELECT
 a.username
,a.sid
,a.serial#
,b.spid AS OS_ID
,a.client_info
FROM v$session a
     ,v$process b
WHERE a.program like '%rman%'
AND   a.paddr = b.addr;
```

Here's some sample output:

```
USERNAME        SID   SERIAL# OS_ID      CLIENT_INFO
----------  -------- ---------- ---------- -------------------------
SYSBACKUP        28      4605 5215
SYSBACKUP       114       275 5877
SYSBACKUP       112      2733 5880      rman channel=ORA_DISK_1
```

Now use the `alter system kill session` SQL statement and provide the SID and SERIAL# for the process you want to terminate:

```
SQL> alter system kill session '112,2733';
```

If multiple RMAN jobs are running, you'll have to identify the serial ID number of the particular job you are interested in terminating. When you start RMAN, two sessions are initiated, the default first process and the polling process. Also an additional process is started for each channel that is allocated.

How It Works

On rare occasions, you might encounter the need to terminate a hung RMAN job. For example, when backing up to tape, RMAN jobs might sometimes hang because of problems with the media manager. In these situations, you'll have to manually kill the appropriate RMAN job with one of the techniques shown in this recipe.

We recommend that before terminating an RMAN job you first query the V$SESSION_LONGOPS view to see whether the job is making any progress:

```
SELECT sid, serial#, sofar, totalwork, opname,
round(sofar/totalwork*100,2) AS pct_complete
FROM   v$session_longops
WHERE  opname LIKE 'RMAN%'
AND    opname NOT LIKE '%aggregate%'
AND    totalwork != 0
AND    sofar <> totalwork;
```

■ **Tip**   You can find full details on how to monitor RMAN jobs in Recipes 16-1, 16-2, and 16-3.

17-6. Diagnosing NLS Character Set Issues

Problem

You're trying to connect to RMAN, and you get an NLS error similar to the following:

```
ORA-12705: Cannot access NLS data files or invalid environment specified
```

Solution

There are usually two reasons for NLS character set problems:

- There's a mismatch between the NLS character set of the client and that of the database server.

- You have an NLS-related operating system variable that has been set incorrectly.

To determine whether there is an NLS character set mismatch, compare your target database character set to your client character set. To display your target database character set, issue the following SQL statement:

```
SQL> select value from v$nls_parameters where parameter = 'NLS_CHARACTERSET';

VALUE
----------------------
WE8ISO8859P1
```

Compare that to the operating system NLS_LANG setting on your client. In Linux/Unix, use the echo command to display the relevant NLS parameters:

```
$ echo $NLS_LANG
```

In Windows, search the Registry Editor for the value of NLS_LANG as shown here: Start ➤ un ➤ regedit ➤ Edit ➤ Find ➤ NLS_LANG.

If you find that there is an NLS_LANG mismatch, then you can override the OS variable manually. For example, in a Linux/Unix C shell environment, use the setenv OS command:

```
$ setenv NLS_LANG american_america.we8iso8859p1
```

In a Linux/Unix Korn or Bash shell environment, use the OS export command as follows:

```
$ export NLS_LANG=american_america.we8iso8859p1
```

In a Windows environment, use the set command, as shown here:

```
c:\> set NLS_LANG=american_america.we8iso8859p1
```

If you set NLS_LANG to a value that RMAN doesn't recognize, then you may receive an error like this:

```
RMAN-00554: initialization of internal recovery manager package failed
RMAN-04005: error from target database:
ORA-12705: Cannot access NLS data files or invalid environment specified
```

If you receive an error like that, ensure that your NLS_LANG operating system parameter is set to a valid value.

■ **Tip**   To view valid NLS values, query the V$NLS_VALID_VALUES view.

How It Works

When faced with potential NLS character set issues, first verify the settings on both your target server and your client. The value of NLS_LANG should match between the client OS and the target database server. To troubleshoot this, you can manually override the client setting and force it to match your target database NLS_LANG setting.

When troubleshooting NLS issues, it can sometimes be difficult to pin down where the NLS values are being set. This is because you can have variables set at the database, instance, session, and client OS. Table 17-1 describes useful NLS views that can help verify at what level the NLS parameters have been set.

Table 17-1. *Useful NLS Troubleshooting Views*

NLS View Name	Description
V$NLS_VALID_VALUES	Lists all valid values for NLS settings.
NLS_SESSION_PARAMETERS	Contains NLS values for the current session. These can be modified via an alter session command.
V$NLS_PARAMETERS	Contains current values of NLS parameters.
NLS_INSTANCE_PARAMETERS	Contains NLS values set at the instance level. These values are set through the initialization file or an alter system command.
NLS_DATABASE_PARAMETERS	Contains NLS values defined when your database was created. These can be overridden by the instance, client OS, or client session.

17-7. Logging RMAN Output

Problem

You're trying to debug a difficult issue and want to capture the output of an RMAN session.

Solution

You can enable RMAN logging in two ways:

- From the OS prompt
- From the RMAN command line

From the OS Prompt

From the OS prompt you can use the log parameter to instruct RMAN to send any output to an OS file (instead of to your screen):

```
$ rman target / log=rman_output.log
```

■ **Note**   The keyword msglog has been deprecated in favor of the keyword log.

From the RMAN Command Line

You can also spool the output to a log file from the RMAN command line, as shown here:

```
RMAN> spool log to rman_output.log
RMAN> set echo on
RMAN> backup database;
```

To turn off logging, use the `log off` parameter, as shown here:

```
RMAN> spool log off;
```

You should now have captured in your log file all the output associated with the `backup database` command.

■ **Tip** We recommend that when you capture the output to a log file that you also use the `set echo on` command. This will ensure that the RMAN command is displayed before actually running it.

USING THE UNIX SCRIPT COMMAND

If you're in a Linux/Unix environment, you can use the `script` command to record everything printed to your screen. For example, if you wanted to capture all output from an RMAN session in a file named rman.log, then use the Linux/Unix `script` command as shown here:

```
$ script rman.log
Script started, file is rman.log
$ rman target /
RMAN> backup database;
```

You should see several RMAN output messages at this time:

```
RMAN> exit
```

Now press Ctrl+D (or type `exit`) to end the script session. After you press Ctrl+D (or type `exit`), you should see this message:

```
$ Script done, file is rman.log
```

You should now see all the output from your `backup database` command in the rman.log file.

How It Works

You can use the RMAN command-line `log` option or the `spool` command to capture output in a log file. When you are troubleshooting RMAN, it's often helpful to capture all the output in a log file so that it can be analyzed later. If you request assistance from Oracle Support, often they will ask you to capture the complete RMAN session output and send it to them.

If the log file that you specify already exists, then by default RMAN will overwrite the file. If you want RMAN to append to an existing file, use the append parameter. Here's how to append to a file from the OS command line:

```
$ rman target / log=rman_output.log append
```

Here's how you would append to a file from the RMAN prompt:

```
RMAN> spool log to rman_output.log append
```

You cannot use the spool command from within a run{} block. You must set spooling outside the run{} block, as shown here:

```
RMAN> spool log to rman_output.log
RMAN> set echo on
RMAN> run{allocate channel d1 type disk;
backup database;
release channel d1;
}
```

■ **Note** When spooling to a log file, RMAN will not display on your screen the output. You'll have to inspect the log file to determine whether the commands ran successfully. You can also view the RMAN command history via the V$RMAN_OUTPUT view (see Recipe 17-8 for details).

17-8. Viewing RMAN Command History
Problem

You didn't log your output to an OS file, and you now wonder whether there is a way to view the RMAN command stack output.

Solution

Use V$RMAN_OUTPUT to view the text messages that RMAN produces when performing tasks. Run this query to view the historical RMAN command messages:

```
select
 sid
,recid
,output
from v$rman_output
order by recid;
```

Here's a small sample of the output:

```
  SID   RECID OUTPUT
------ ------- ----------------------------------------------------------------
    99     108 using channel ORA_DISK_1
    99     109 channel ORA_DISK_1: starting full datafile backup set
    99     110 channel ORA_DISK_1: specifying datafile(s) in backup set
```

You can also join V$RMAN_OUTPUT to V$RMAN_STATUS to get additional information. This useful query shows the type of command RMAN is running, its current status, and its associated output messages:

```
select
 a.sid
,a.recid
,b.operation
,b.status
,a.output
from v$rman_output a
    ,v$rman_status b
where a.rman_status_recid = b.recid
and   a.rman_status_stamp = b.stamp
order by a.recid;
```

How It Works

The V$RMAN_OUTPUT view contains messages recently reported by RMAN. It is an in-memory view that can hold up to a maximum of 32,768 rows. Information in this view is cleared out when you stop and restart your database. The OUTPUT column of V$RMAN_OUTPUT contains the messages that RMAN logs to your terminal when running commands.

Another handy use of this view is to query the output in the event that you are using a log file. If you are writing RMAN output to a log file, then RMAN will not display messages to your terminal. In this situation, you can query V$RMAN_OUTPUT to check on the status of currently running RMAN operations:

```
select
 a.sid
,a.recid
,b.operation
,b.status
,a.output
from v$rman_output a
    ,v$rman_status b
where a.rman_status_recid = b.recid
and   a.rman_status_stamp = b.stamp
and   b.status = 'RUNNING'
order by a.recid;
```

17-9. Enabling RMAN's Debug Output
Problem

You're working with Oracle Support and they have requested that you enable RMAN debugging and send them the output.

Solution

You can turn on debugging in several different ways:

- From the OS prompt or RMAN command line
- When allocating a channel
- When configuring a channel

From the OS Prompt or RMAN Command Line

This first example enables all debugging and places the debug messages in a separate file from the regular RMAN output:

```
$ rman target / debug=all trace=rman.trc log=rman.log
```

The prior command will enable verbose debugging and send the debug output to a file named rman.trc. The regular logging of RMAN commands and output will be placed in the rman.log. We recommend that you put the debug messages in a separate file (as shown in the prior line of code). This is particularly helpful when working with Oracle Support and they request a file that contains just the debug information.

You can also turn on debugging around particular RMAN commands. For example:

```
$ rman target /
RMAN> spool log to rman.log
RMAN> spool trace to rman.trc
RMAN> run{
debug on;
backup datafile 4;
debug off;
}
RMAN> spool trace off;
RMAN> spool log off;
```

Again as a best practice, in the prior output debug messages are directed to a separate file from the regular RMAN output.

When Allocating a Channel

This example uses debug with the trace parameter. Tracing at level 1 gives you the least amount of information, and tracing at level 5 gives you the most verbose output. Run the allocate command from within the run{} block, as shown here:

```
RMAN> run{
allocate channel d1 type disk debug=5 trace=5;
backup datafile 4;
release channel d1;
}
```

You should now have a trace file located in the directory specified for your diagnostic trace files. You can display the directory of the trace files via this query:

```
SQL> select value from v$diag_info where name='Diag Trace';
```

If you're using an older version of Oracle, you can locate the trace file directory by displaying the value of the user_dump_dest initialization variable:

```
SQL> show parameter user_dump_dest
```

When Configuring a Channel

This example configures a channel to debug and trace at level 5:

```
RMAN> configure channel device type disk debug=5 trace=5;
RMAN> backup datafile 4;
```

You should now have a trace file located in the directory specified for your diagnostic trace files. To clear the channel debug settings, use the clear parameter as shown here:

```
RMAN> configure channel device type disk clear;
```

How It Works

The debug command produces a detailed report of internal operations executed by RMAN. You'll notice that the performance of RMAN will suffer when debugging is enabled. Therefore, we don't recommend running commands in debug mode on a production database. You should turn on debugging only in test environments or at the recommendation of Oracle Support.

Debugging Basics

The debug on command is equivalent to debug all. Both of those commands turn on all available types of debugging. You also have the option of enabling debugging just for certain types of operations. Listed next are specific areas for which you can turn on debugging:

- io
- sql
- plsql
- rcvman
- rpc

For example, if you wanted to debug just I/O-related operations when backing up your users' tablespace, you would enable I/O debugging as shown here:

```
$ rman target /
RMAN> spool log to rman.log
RMAN> spool trace to rman.trc
RMAN> set echo on
RMAN> debug io
RMAN> backup datafile 4;
RMAN> debug off
RMAN> spool trace off;
RMAN> spool log off;
```

Your output file (rman.trc in this example) should indicate that IO debugging has been enabled:

```
RMAN-03036: Debugging set to level=9, types=IO
```

The default level for debugging is 9. Valid ranges of debug levels are from 1 to 15, with level 1 the least verbose and level 15 generating the most output. Usually the default debugging level of 9 is sufficient. You can alter the default level of debugging by using the level parameter. For example, this sets the debug level of PL/SQL operations to the maximum level of 15:

```
RMAN> debug plsql level=15
```

You should now see an informative message like this indicating debugging is on:

```
RMAN-03036: Debugging set to level=15, types=PLSQL
```

Advanced Debugging and Troubleshooting

When you work with Oracle Support, they may request that you simultaneously enable debugging, logging, and tracing and then upload the subsequently generated output files for analysis. For example, you might be asked to run a shell script such as the following:

```
#!/bin/bash
export NLS_DATE_FORMAT="DD-MON-RRRR HH24:MI:SS"
export dateNOW=$(date +%Y%m%d%H%M%S)
rman msgno log=${ORACLE_SID}_${dateNOW}_rmanout.log \
  trace=${ORACLE_SID}_${dateNOW}_rmanout.trc << EOF
set echo on
connect target /
show all;
report schema;
host "sqlplus '/ as sysdba' @precmd.sql";
host "mv precmd.lst ${ORACLE_SID}_${dateNOW}_precmd.lst";
run {
 sql "alter session set max_dump_file_size=UNLIMITED";
 sql "alter session set tracefile_identifier=''rmanbackup_10046_trace_file''";
 sql "alter session set events ''10046 trace name context forever, level 12''";
 debug all;
 <<<INSERT_RMAN_COMMAND_HERE_THAT_YOU_WANT_TO_MONITOR>>>
 debug off;
}
host "sqlplus '/ as sysdba' @postcmd.sql";
host "mv postcmd.lst ${ORACLE_SID}_${dateNOW}_postcmd.lst";
EOF
```

Do the following before running the previous prior script:

1. Modify the prior shell script and place within it the RMAN commands that you want to monitor.

2. Copy the precmd.sql and postcmd.sql script to the directory from which you're running the prior shell script (the SQL scripts are provided below, and can be downloaded from www.apress.com).

After running the script, you may be asked to upload the following files:

- ${ORACLE_SID}_${dateNOW}_rmanout.log

- ${ORACLE_SID}_${dateNOW}_rmanout.trc

- ${ORACLE_SID}_${dateNOW}_precmd.lst

- ${ORACLE_SID}_${dateNOW}_postcmd.lst

- Trace file generated by RMAN backup with event 10046

- Latest alert.log

Listed next is the precmd.sql script. Inspect this script carefully before running this to ensure the table names used in the script do not match any existing table names in your environment:

```
spool precmd;
set line 2000
set echo on;
alter session set nls_date_format = 'DD-MON-YYYY HH:MI:SS';
drop table pre_cmd_wait_time;
drop table cmd_start_time;
drop table pre_backup_sync_io;
drop table pre_backup_async_io;
drop table pre_cmd_ksfq_events;
create table pre_cmd_wait_time
as select sum (time_waited_micro/1000000) time_waited_secs
from v$system_event where event like '%sbt%';
create table pre_backup_async_io
as select * from v$backup_async_io;
create table pre_backup_sync_io
as select * from v$backup_sync_io;
create table cmd_start_time
as select sysdate start_time from dual;
create table pre_cmd_ksfq_events
as select * from v$system_event
where event in ('i/o slave wait', 'io done');
exit;
```

Here is the postcmd.sql script:

```
spool postcmd;
set echo on;
-- Look for STATISTICS SECTION below for relevant statistics that will help
-- analyse RMAN backup performance problems
set line 2000
alter session set nls_date_format = 'DD-MON-YYYY HH:MI:SS';
drop table cmd_end_time;
create table cmd_end_time as select sysdate end_time from dual;
drop table post_cmd_wait_time;
drop table backup_async_io;
drop table backup_sync_io;
create table backup_async_io
as (select * from v$backup_async_io
```

```
where (sid, serial) not in (select sid, serial from pre_backup_async_io));
--
create table backup_sync_io
as (select * from v$backup_sync_io
where (sid, serial) not in (select sid, serial from pre_backup_sync_io));
--
create table post_cmd_wait_time
as select sum (time_waited_micro/1000000) time_waited_secs from v$system_event
where event like '%sbt%';
--
variable sbttime_in_secs number;
begin
  select post.time_waited_secs  - nvl(pre.time_waited_secs, 0)
  into :sbttime_in_secs from pre_cmd_wait_time pre, post_cmd_wait_time post;
end;
/
variable cmdtime_in_secs number;
begin
  select (end_time - start_time)*24*60*60 into :cmdtime_in_secs
  from cmd_start_time, cmd_end_time;
end;
/
variable total_input_bytes number;
begin
  select sum(bytes) into :total_input_bytes
  from (select sum(bytes) bytes
        from backup_async_io where type='INPUT'
        union
        select sum(bytes) bytes
        from backup_sync_io where type='INPUT');
end;
/
variable total_output_bytes number;
begin
  select sum(bytes)
  into :total_output_bytes
  from (select sum(bytes) bytes
        from backup_async_io where type='OUTPUT'
        union
        select sum(bytes) bytes
        from backup_sync_io where type='OUTPUT');
end;
/
variable non_sbttime_in_secs number;
begin
  :non_sbttime_in_secs := :cmdtime_in_secs - :sbttime_in_secs;
end;
/
-- STATISTICS SECTION
-- Relevant statistics that are useful to identify
-- RMAN performance problems are displayed below.
-- SBTTIME_IN_SECS is amount of time that was spent in SBT library
```

```
print sbttime_in_secs;
--  CMDTIME_IN_SECS is total command execution time
print cmdtime_in_secs;
-- NON_SBTTIME_IN_SECS is time spent in non-SBT code
print non_sbttime_in_secs;
-- TOTAL INPUT BYTES read
print total_input_bytes;
-- TOTAL OUTPUT BYTES written
print total_output_bytes;
-- Effective output bytes per second
select :total_output_bytes/:cmdtime_in_secs effective_output_bytes_per_sec
  from dual;
-- Effective input bytes per second
select :total_input_bytes/:cmdtime_in_secs effective_input_bytes_per_sec
  from dual;
-- Input file that is bottleneck for the backup operation
select long_waits, io_count, filename input_bottleneck_filename
from backup_async_io
where type='INPUT'
and long_waits/io_count = (select max(long_waits/io_count)
                             from backup_async_io where type='INPUT' );
-- Critical I/O event information
select
  pre.event, (post.total_waits-pre.total_waits) total_waits,
 (post.total_timeouts-pre.total_timeouts) total_timeouts,
 (post.time_waited-pre.time_waited) time_waited,
 (post.time_waited_micro - pre.time_waited_micro) time_waited_micro,
 (post.time_waited_micro-pre.time_waited_micro)/
 (post.total_waits-pre.total_waits) average_wait_micro
from pre_cmd_ksfq_events pre, v$system_event post
where pre.event=post.event;
-- IO_SLAVES parameter settings for the instance
show parameter io_slaves;
set line 2000
-- Contents of V$BACKUP_ASYNC_IO generated for the RMAN command executed
select * from backup_async_io;
-- Contents of V$BACKUP_SYNC_IO generated for the RMAN command executed
select * from backup_sync_io;
-- Pre and Post command statistics for important KSFQ events
select * from v$system_event where event in ('i/o slave wait', 'io done');
exit;
```

Again, this level of debugging and tracing often is required only when requested by Oracle Support. The output is helpful in diagnosing difficult performance and troubleshooting issues.

17-10. Enabling Granular Time Reporting
Problem

You're troubleshooting an issue, and you notice that the output from the list command specifies the date but without an hours:minutes:time component. You want to capture the exact second when your RMAN operations started and finished.

Solution

Use the operating system NLS_DATE_FORMAT variable to specify a date format that includes a time component. In a Unix C shell environment, use the setenv OS command as shown here:

```
$ setenv NLS_DATE_FORMAT 'dd-mon-yyyy hh24:mi:ss'
```

In a Linux/Unix Korn or Bash shell environment, use the OS export command as follows:

```
$ export NLS_DATE_FORMAT='dd-mon-yyyy hh24:mi:ss'
```

In a Windows environment, use the set command as shown here:

```
c:\> set NLS_DATE_FORMAT=dd-mon-yyyy hh24:mi:ss
```

How It Works

We recommend that you always set your NLS_DATE_FORMAT variable so that you see the hour, minute, and second components of the date when issuing RMAN commands. If you spool a log file when issuing backup, restore, and recovery commands, this will ensure that a timestamp component is displayed. This can be useful when trying to troubleshoot RMAN issues. If you're working with Oracle Support on an RMAN problem, they will almost always ask you to set this parameter to enable the viewing of the time component (down to the second).

You can verify the value of NLS_DATE_FORMAT from your OS environment with the echo command. In Linux/Unix, use echo as follows:

```
$ echo $NLS_DATE_FORMAT
```

Here is a Windows example of displaying NLS_DATE_FORMAT using the echo command:

```
C:\> echo %NLS_DATE_FORMAT%
```

■ **Caution**   If you accidentally set NLS_DATE_FORMAT to an invalid Oracle date format, RMAN may complain and not let you start a session "RMAN-03999: Oracle error occurred while converting a date." Refer to Oracle's SQL Reference Guide for valid Oracle date formats. The SQL Reference Guide is available for download at Oracle's http://otn.oracle.com web site.

To unset an OS variable, simply make it blank. For example, to unset NLS_DATE_FORMAT in a Unix C shell environment, use the unsetenv OS command:

```
$ unsetenv NLS_DATE_FORMAT
```

In a Linux/Unix Korn or Bash shell environment, use the OS export command as follows:

```
$ export NLS_DATE_FORMAT=
```

In a Windows environment, use the set command as shown here:

```
c:\> set NLS_DATE_FORMAT=
```

17-11. Working with Oracle Support
Problem

You ran into an RMAN problem, and you want to get help from Oracle Support.

Solution

Go to My Oracle Support's web site (http://support.oracle.com) and open a service request (SR). When working with Oracle Support, you'll get a faster and better response by providing the following documentation when you open a request for service:

- Test case that illustrates step-by-step details to reproduce the problem

- Complete RMAN script or command(s) that were run

- Complete RMAN output log

- Database alert.log file

- Remote Diagnostic Agent (RDA) output (optional)

How It Works

If you've purchased a support license from Oracle, then you should open an SR when you run into an RMAN problem that you can't solve. You'll need your customer support identifier (CSI) number when you open a service request.

From our experience, documenting steps to reproduce the problem at hand is perhaps the most useful task when requesting help from Oracle Support. We know that not all problems are easily reproducible. However, if at all possible, document clearly the conditions and steps that produce the problem and send those to Oracle Support when you first request help.

Usually we open an SR as soon as we suspect that we have run into an issue that won't be easily resolved. This way we get a support person working on our issue in parallel with our own efforts. Then if we can't solve the problem, we already have Oracle in the loop and working on a solution.

■ **Tip** It doesn't hurt to open an SR early in your problem resolution process. In many cases, you may solve the problem before Oracle Support gets a chance to look at it. However, for the cases that you don't solve quickly, the sooner you get Oracle Support involved, the greater chance you'll have to escalate your SR and get a more experienced support analyst working on your request.

17-12. Resolving RMAN Compatibility Issues
Problem

Your RMAN executable is version 8.1.6, and you're trying to connect to a version 10.2 database. You are receiving this error message:

```
database not compatible with this version of RMAN
```

You wonder which versions of the RMAN executable are compatible with which versions of your target database.

Solution

Table 17-2 lists Oracle's RMAN compatibility matrix. The easiest way to use this matrix is to find the version of your database in the "Target/Auxiliary DB" column and then use that row for determining the compatibility required for other RMAN components in your environment.

Table 17-2. RMAN Compatibility Matrix

Target/Auxiliary DB	RMAN Executable	Catalog DB	Catalog Schema
8.1.7.4	8.1.7.4	>=8.1.7	8.1.7.4 or >=9.0.14
9.0.1	9.0.1	>=8.1.7	>= RMAN executable
9.2.0	>= 9.0.1.3 and <= target database	>=8.1.7	>= RMAN executable
10.1.0	>= 9.0.1.3 and <= target database	>=9.0.1	>= RMAN executable
10.2.0	>= 9.0.1.3 and <= target database	>=9.0.1	>= RMAN executable
11.1.0	>= 9.0.1.3 and <= target database	10.2.0.3	>= RMAN executable
11.2.0	>= 9.0.1.3 and <= target database	10.2.0.3	>= RMAN executable
12.1.0	TBD	TDB	TBD

■ **Tip**   You can also find the RMAN compatibility matrix information in MOS note 73431.1.

How It Works

Ideally, you'd like all your environments to be at the same Oracle version. In reality, that rarely is the case. Therefore, in most environments, you will have to deal with some RMAN compatibility issues. Here are the general rules of thumb when dealing with RMAN compatibility problems:

- Whenever possible, the version of the rman executable should be the same as your target/auxiliary database version.
- The version of the catalog schema must be at the same version or newer than the rman executable.
- The version of the catalog database is backward compatible with earlier versions of the target database.

If you're not sure which version of the catalog schema you are using, connect via SQL*Plus to the recovery catalog as the catalog owner and run this query:

```
SQL> select * from rcver;
```

17-13. Dealing with an ORA-19511 Error
Problem

You're receiving an ORA-19511 error message from your media management layer (MML).

Solution

Inspect the contents of the sbtio.log file. It should have more detailed information about the root cause of the problem. The sbtio.log file is usually located in a directory within the automatic diagnostic repository or in the $ORACLE_HOME/rdbms/log directory.

How It Works

When your MML returns the ORA-19511 error, this usually indicates one of the following:

- The MML software has not been configured or installed correctly.

- An OS variable related to the MML has not been set correctly.

In this situation, Oracle is only passing back the error from the MML. If the text of message ORA-19511 does not provide enough information to resolve the problem, you should contact the third-party MML vendor and engage their assistance to resolve the problem.

When you receive an ORA-19511 error message, it will typically be accompanied by other media management layer or OS error messages. Table 17-3 lists the error messages and their meanings.

Table 17-3. *Media Management Layer Error Messages*

Message Number	Description
sbtopen 7000	Backup file not found
sbtopen 7001	File exists
sbtopen 7002	Bad mode specified
sbtopen 7003	Invalid block size specified
sbtopen 7004	No tape device found
sbtopen 7005	Device found, but busy
sbtopen 7006	Tape volume not found
sbtopen 7007	Tape volume in use
sbtopen 7008	I/O error
sbtopen 7009	Can't connect with media manager
sbtopen 7010	Permission denied
sbtopen 7011	OS error
sbtopen 7012	Invalid argument to sbtopen
sbtclose 7020	Invalid file handle or file not open
sbtclose 7021	Invalid flags to sbtclose
sbtclose 7022	I/O error
sbtclose 7023	OS error
sbtclose 7024	Invalid argument to sbtclose
sbtclose 7025	Can't connect with media manager

(continued)

Table 17-3. (*continued*)

Message Number	Description
sbtwrite 7040	Invalid file handle or file not open
sbtwrite 7041	End of volume reached
sbtwrite 7042	I/O error
sbtwrite 7043	OS error
sbtwrite 7044	Invalid argument to sbtwrite
sbtread 7060	Invalid file handle or file not open
sbtread 7061	EOF encountered
sbtread 7062	End of volume reached
sbtread 7063	I/O error
sbtread 7064	OS error
sbtread 7065	Invalid argument to sbtread
sbtremove 7080	Backup file not found
sbtremove 7081	Backup file in use
sbtremove 7082	I/O error
sbtremove 7083	Can't connect with media manager
sbtremove 7084	Permission denied
sbtremove 7085	OS error
sbtremove 7086	Invalid argument to sbtremove
sbtinfo 7090	Backup file not found
sbtinfo 7091	I/O error
sbtinfo 7092	Can't connect with Media Manager
sbtinfo 7093	Permission denied
sbtinfo 7094	OS error
sbtinfo 7095	Invalid argument to sbtinfo
sbtinit 7110	Invalid argument to sbtinit
sbtinit 7111	OS error

17-14. Dealing with an ORA-27211 Error
Problem

When attempting to allocate a channel for tape I/O, you receive an ORA-27211 error.

Solution

The ORA-27211 error usually indicates that the media management library is not loading properly (specifically the libobk.so file). When you receive this error, usually a corresponding trace file is generated. Look for a trace file in a directory within the automatic diagnostic repository. The trace file should have additional information about MML errors or OS errors.

The libobk.so is usually located in the directory /lib. If it's not there, then create a link to your third-party media manager vendor library, as shown in the example here:

```
# ln -s /usr/local/oracle/backup/lib/libobk.so /lib/libobk.so
# ls -l /lib/libobk.so
lrwxrwxrwx  1 root root 38 Sep 18 06:24 /lib/libobk.so ->
/usr/local/oracle/backup/lib/libobk.so
```

Another solution is to explicitly set the OS environment variable SBT_LIBRARY when allocating the SBT_TAPE channel, and point it to the third-party media manager vendor library, as shown in the example here:

```
run {
 allocate channel t1 device type sbt_tape
  parms 'SBT_LIBRARY=/usr/local/oracle/backup/lib/libobk.so';
 backup current controlfile;
}
```

How It Works

The ORA-27211 error is usually thrown when you have not correctly installed your MML. Consult your vendor's MML documentation, and ensure that you have correctly integrated the software with Oracle. You can manually simulate this error by setting the SBT_LIBRARY to a nonexistent file (libobkx.so):

```
RMAN> run {
allocate channel t1 device type sbt_tape
parms 'SBT_LIBRARY=/usr/local/oracle/backup/lib/libobkx.so';
backup current controlfile;
}
```

```
using target database control file instead of recovery catalog
RMAN-00571: ===========================================================
RMAN-00569: =============== ERROR MESSAGE STACK FOLLOWS ===============
RMAN-00571: ===========================================================
RMAN-03009: failure of allocate command on t1 channel at 09/18/2012 06:35:10
ORA-19554: error allocating device, device type: SBT_TAPE, device name:
ORA-27211: Failed to load Media Management Library
```

This may help you diagnose the problem (which is usually related to a missing libobk.so file).

17-15. Dealing with an ORA-04031 Error
Problem

You're using I/O slaves and are getting an ORA-04031 error written to your alert.log file.

Solution

Set up a large pool memory area on your database. If you are using Oracle Database 10g or newer, then consider using automatic shared memory management (ASMM) to have Oracle automatically allocate memory to the large pool.

If you're not comfortable with using ASMM, then you can manually set the initialization parameter large_pool_size. If you want to manually set the large pool size, here is Oracle's recommended formula for sizing it:

```
large_pool_size = num_of_allocated_channels * (16 MB + (4 * size_of_tape_buffer ))
```

How It Works

If you have enabled the use of I/O slaves, we recommend that you set up a large pool memory area. When using I/O slaves for synchronous I/O, RMAN will use memory in the large pool if it is available. If a large pool memory is not available, RMAN will allocate memory from the shared pool. If RMAN cannot allocate enough memory, it will acquire memory from the PGA and write an ORA-04031 message to your alert.log file.

Using I/O slaves can improve performance when performing I/O to synchronous devices such as tape drives. You enable tape I/O slaves by setting the backup_tape_io_slaves parameter to TRUE. This causes an I/O server processes (slaves) to be assigned to each tape channel being used.

■ **Tip** See MOS note 73354.1 for details on how the use of I/O slaves can affect RMAN's use of memory buffers for backup and recovery operations.

If you are working with an OS that doesn't support asynchronous I/O, then you can enable disk I/O slaves via the dbwr_io_slaves parameter. If you set this parameter to a nonzero value, RMAN will use four server processes to perform backup and recovery operations.

■ **Tip** You can display the component name and associated memory area (shared, large, Java, or streams pool) of structures using the SGA by querying the V$SGASTAT view. For example:

```
SQL> select pool, name, bytes from v$sgastat;
```

17-16. Managing Files in an ASM Environment
Problem

You're using Oracle's automatic storage management (ASM) to manage your disks. You want to view the data files and RMAN backup pieces that are stored on ASM disk groups.

Solution

Use the ASMCMD utility to manage RMAN files and database files when using ASM-managed disks. Ensure that your ORACLE_SID and ORACLE_HOME environment variables are set properly for your ASM instance. Type asmcmd -p from the operating system to invoke the utility:

```
C:\> asmcmd -p
```

You should now see the ASMCMD prompt:

```
ASMCMD [+]>
```

The -p option will set your prompt to display the current working directory as part of the prompt. For example, the ASMCMD prompt changes as we use the cd command to change the current directory:

```
ASMCMD [+] > cd +data/prmy/datafile
ASMCMD [+data/prmy/datafile] >
```

If you are familiar with Unix commands, it should be easy for you to manage your ASM environment using ASMCMD commands. For example, the ls command will list the files in an ASM directory. Table 17-4 lists the disk management commands available with ASMCMD.

Table 17-4. *ASMCMD Disk Management Commands*

Command	Description
cd	Changes the current directory to the specified directory
cp	Enables copying of files between disk groups, and between disk groups and the operating system
lsof	Lists open files
du	Displays the total disk space occupied by ASM files in the specified ASM directory and all its subdirectories, recursively
exit	Exits ASMCMD
find	Lists the paths of all occurrences of the specified name (with wildcards) under the specified directory
help	Displays the syntax and description of ASMCMD commands
ls	Lists the contents of an ASM directory, the attributes of the specified file, or the names and attributes of all disk groups
lsct	Lists information about current ASM clients
mkalias	Creates an alias for a system-generated file name
mkdir	Creates ASM directories
pwd	Displays the path of the current ASM directory
rm	Deletes the specified ASM files or directories
rmalias	Deletes the specified alias, retaining the file to which the alias points
repair	Repairs range of physical blocks on the ASM disk (Oracle Database 11g only)

Table 17-5 lists the group management commands available with ASMCMD.

Table 17-5. ASMCMD Group Management Commands

Command	Description
chdg	Changes a disk group
chkdg	Check and/or repair a disk group
dropdg	Drops a disk group
iostat	Displays I/O statistics
isattr	Lists attributes of disk group
lsdg	Lists all disk groups and their attributes
lsdsk	Lists the ASM disks (new starting with Oracle Database 11g)
lsod	Lists open devices
md_backup	Creates a metadata backup script of mounted disk groups (new starting with Oracle Database 11g)
md_restore	Restores a disk group backup (new starting with Oracle Database 11g)
mkdg	Makes a disk group
mount	Mounts a disk group
offline	Takes offline a disk or disk group
online	Places online a disk or disk group
rebal	Rebalances a disk group
remap	Remaps a data in a range of blocks
setattr	Sets attributes for a disk group
umount	Unmounts a disk group

How It Works

You can view and manage ASM disk groups and ASM files via one of the following tools:

- Enterprise Manager
- SQL*Plus
- ASMCMD

The focus of this recipe is on using the ASMCMD utility. See Chapter 19 for details on using RMAN with Enterprise Manager. If you're familiar with SQL*Plus, the following query is useful for viewing files within your ASM environment:

```
SELECT concat('+'||gname, sys_connect_by_path(aname, '/')) full_alias_path FROM
(SELECT g.name gname, a.parent_index pindex, a.name aname,
a.reference_index rindex FROM v$asm_alias a, v$asm_diskgroup g
WHERE a.group_number = g.group_number)
START WITH (mod(pindex, power(2, 24))) = 0
CONNECT BY PRIOR rindex = pindex;
```

The ASMCMD utility will also allow you to view and display information about your ASM environment. Before running the asmcmd, ensure that you set the ORACLE_SID variable of the ASM instance as follows:

```
C:\> set ORACLE_SID=+ASM
```

If the ORACLE_SID variable is not properly set to the correct ASM instance, then you will get the following error message:

```
asmcmd: command disallowed by current instance type
```

Also ensure that ORACLE_HOME is set properly. If it isn't, then Oracle will display an error such as this:

```
asmcmd: the environment variable ORACLE_HOME is not set.
```

Once you set your environment variables, you should be able to invoke the ASMCMD utility and use its Linux/Unix-like commands to manage your ASM environment. If you want to view more information about ASM commands, use the help option:

```
ASMCMD> help
ASMCMD> help md_backup
```

■ **Note** The asmcmd is not available by default in Oracle Database 10g Release 1, but you can copy the two required files from the Oracle Database 10g Release 2 installation, namely, asmcmdcore and asmcmd for Linux/Unix or asmcmd. bat for Windows. You can find these files in the ORACLE_HOME/bin directory.

17-17. Automatically Determining Whether Backups Are Working
Problem
You want an automated method of determining whether RMAN backups are running successfully.

Solution
Use a combination of SQL, shell scripting, and a scheduler such as cron to automatically detect when the RMAN backups have not completed successfully. The following shell script queries the data dictionary to determine whether backups have run within a specified number of days:

```
#!/bin/bash
#
if [ $# -ne 2 ]; then
  echo "Usage: $0 SID threshold"
  exit 1
fi
# source oracle OS variables
. /var/opt/oracle/oraset $1
crit_var=$(sqlplus -s <<EOF
/ as sysdba
```

```
SET HEAD OFF FEEDBACK OFF
SELECT COUNT(*) FROM
(SELECT (sysdate - MAX(end_time)) delta
 FROM v\$rman_backup_job_details) a
WHERE a.delta > $2;
EOF)
#
if [ $crit_var -ne 0 ]; then
  echo "rman backups not running on $1" | mailx -s "rman problem" dbasupport@gmail.com
else
  echo "rman backups ran ok"
fi
#
exit 0
```

You'll have to adjust this code to work in your environment. The code uses a script named oraset to establish the Oracle operating system variables, such as ORACLE_HOME, ORACLE_SID, and PATH. You'll have to replace the invocation of that script with whatever method you use to instantiate these operating system variables. Also you'll need to replace the e-mail address with one of your own.

Assuming the script is placed in a file named rman_chk.bsh, you can determine whether the backups have run for the DWREP database within the past day by running the script as follows:

```
$ rman_chk.bsh DWREP 1
```

If no RMAN jobs have run at all within the past day, an e-mail will be sent indicating that there may be an issue.

You can automate the script in a Linux/Unix environment by placing an entry in cron. The following entry runs the RMAN check job on a daily basis:

```
25 6 * * * /u01/oracle/bin/rman_chk.bsh DWREP 1>/u01/oracle/bin/log/rman_chk.log 2>&1
```

■ **Tip** Many Oracle data dictionary views contain a $ character as part of the view name. When referencing a V$ view within a shell script, you must escape the $ character and tell the shell to not treat it as a shell variable. This is done with a \ character.

How It Works

It's extremely important to have some automated method for detecting whether the RMAN backups are running successfully. You can modify the shell script presented in the Solution section to meet the needs of your environment. The script in the solution section is a very simple yet effective way of determining whether RMAN is running. The script won't detect every issue, but it will let you know if RMAN hasn't run a successful job within the specified period.

Along those lines, here's another simple script that will let you know if there's a data file that hasn't been backed up within the specified time period:

```
#!/bin/bash
#
if [ $# -ne 2 ]; then
  echo "Usage: $0 SID threshold"
  exit 1
fi
```

```
# source oracle OS variables
. /var/opt/oracle/oraset $1
crit_var2=$(sqlplus -s <<EOF
/ as sysdba
SET HEAD OFF FEEDBACK OFF
SELECT COUNT(*)
FROM
(
SELECT name
FROM v\$datafile
MINUS
SELECT DISTINCT
 f.name
FROM v\$backup_datafile d
    ,v\$datafile        f
WHERE d.file#      = f.file#
AND   d.completion_time > sysdate - $2);
EOF)
#
if [ $crit_var2 -ne 0 ]; then
  echo "datafile not backed up on $1" | mailx -s "backup problem" dbasupport@gmail.com
else
  echo "datafiles are backed up..."
fi
#
exit 0
```

The foregoing script will check the data dictionary. If there's a data file that has not been backed up within the specified period of time, a notification e-mail is sent out. Assuming the script is placed in a file named rman_chk2.bsh, you can check as follows to see whether there are any data files in the DWREP database that have not been backed up in the past day:

```
$ rman_chk2.bsh DWREP 1
```

The script provides a count of every data file name in the database minus every data file name in the database that has not been backed up within the specified period. Normally that count should be zero. The V$BACKUP_DATAFILE view is based on information in the control file, and is populated when RMAN backs up each data file. If you've never run RMAN backups, then the view will be empty, which is why you can't just check V$BACKUP_DATAFILE by itself. You need to also know the total number of data files in your database, regardless of whether they've been backed up.

CHAPTER 18

■ ■ ■

Using Oracle Secure Backup as a Media Management Layer

RMAN comes preconfigured to work with a single disk channel. To back up and restore from a tape device, you need to configure a media management layer (MML), which works with the actual storage devices. When you instruct RMAN to work with a tape device, RMAN sends the media management layer the necessary information so the MML can send instructions to the actual storage media. In other words, RMAN doesn't deal directly with tape devices. You can use Oracle's own freely available Oracle Secure Backup (OSB) as your media management layer, or you can choose to go with a third-party MML. The OSB is an excellent product that can make both database and operating system file backups. In this chapter, we'll provide recipes for using Oracle Secure Backup as your MML. Your first step in using OSB as an MML is to install OSB and configure RMAN to work with OSB. Before you can use OSB as your MML for your database (and file-system) backups, you must first configure RMAN to make backups to OSB. You use the sbt_library parameter in the allocate channel or configure channel command to specify the path name to the media management library when you're configuring channels for RMAN to use with OSB. You use values for the parms parameter inside a command such as configure channel to send instructions to the media manager.

   Once you install and configure the OSB media manager library to work with RMAN and your databases, test to confirm that RMAN can successfully be backed up to the media manager. Make a test backup and restore it before you start using the media manager with RMAN. After you make the test backups, issue the list backup command, which shows you whether the backup really went to the media manager. The easiest way to perform a backup to OSB is by configuring automatic sbt channels and setting the default device type to sbt.

A Quick Introduction

OSB acts as a media management layer for RMAN by providing a built-in media management software library that RMAN uses to make tape backups. This software library is also called an *sbt interface*. Although it's a free product, note that OSB provides advantages you can't get from other MMLs, such as the ability to directly make RMAN-encrypted backups to tape. You can use OSB with Oracle9*i* Database, Oracle Database 10g, Oracle Database 11g, and Oracle Database 12c.

Advantages of Using OSB

OSB costs much less than other third-party products in terms of license costs. Competing third-party MML products need you to license each client, such as the host, the application, the storage device, the media server, and the administrative server, separately. OSB licensing is based strictly on the number of physical tape drives you use, and you can use an unlimited number of clients without licensing costs.

Other advantages of using OSB include:

- It offers automatic integration with Oracle products, such as Real Application Clusters (RAC), Automatic Storage Management (ASM), and Data Guard.

- The OSB encryption module is within the Oracle database and encrypts the data before it's recorded on media. In addition, the data on tape is stored in encrypted form, providing you a secure backup of your data.

- OSB can back up both database files and the operating system files.

- OSB can duplex backups so each backup goes to a different tape device.

- OSB provides the ability to perform multilevel incremental backups.

- Because of OSB's tight integration with RMAN, it helps optimize storage access, resulting in a 15 to 30 percent performance improvement over other third-party products, according to Oracle.

Introducing the OSB Architecture

The OSB architecture depends primarily on three components, called *domains*:

- *Administrative server*: Each OSB domain contains one administrative server, which manages the entire backup and recovery information that's stored in a special OSB catalog. On a Linux server, for example, the catalog is stored in the /usr/local/oracle/backup directory by default.

- *Media server*: This is the OSB component that manages the actual media devices, such as the physical tape drives, virtual tape libraries, and physical tape libraries. OSB supports a variety of tape backup devices made by third-party vendors, such as NetApp and EMC.

- *Client*: Client applications are mostly the Oracle databases you want to back up and recover with OSB. OSB also supports backup appliances, such as network-attached storage (NAS), as clients.

The obtool command-line program is the main OSB command-line interface. You can use obtool to back up and recover file systems and to configure and manage OSB. You can use obtool on any host that's part of the administrative domain. Please refer to the *Oracle Secure Backup Reference* for details about obtool.

Understanding How OSB and RMAN Work Together

The process of RMAN backup and recovery operations with OSB is straightforward, as summarized in the following steps:

1. When you initiate a backup or restore command through RMAN (using the command line or Enterprise Manager) and allocate a tape channel, generically known as a *system backup to tape* (sbt) channel for it, a server session starts on the target database.

2. The server session on the target database makes a request to the OSB to execute the backup job or restore job.

3. OSB creates the backup or restore job and assigns it a unique identifier.

4. OSB reserves the tape drive to perform the backup job and starts the tape-loading process in motion. If no tape drives are available, OSB queues the job request.

5. OSB creates the backup or restores the backup pieces, depending on the backup or restore request.

Managing Backup and Recovery with RMAN and OSB

You can run RMAN backup and recovery commands in three ways using OSB:

- You can use the normal RMAN client. Note the following:

  - You must install OSB on the target host where the target database is running.

  - The client can be run from any Oracle Home, even if it's not a member of the OSB administrative domain.

  - The database host must be part of the administrative domain.

- You can use the Oracle Enterprise Manager (OEM) Database Control. Database Control must be running on the administrative server of OSB. You can use the OEM Grid Control. Grid Control is the way to go if you want to perform tape backups of several databases through a centralized control interface. Grid Control can run on any host in the administrative domain.

RMAN Client, OEM Database Control, or OEM Grid Control provides you with an interface for performing database backup and recovery functions when working with RMAN and OSB. If you want to work with file-system backups, you can do so by using the following tools:

- You can use the OSB web interface, called the web tool, for OSB-related tasks.

- You can use the obtool utility, which you invoke by typing obtool at the command line.

■ **Note**   You can determine the version of obtool on your server by executing the command obtool --version/-V.

We assume you've already installed OSB before trying to use the OSB-related recipes in this chapter. We also assume that you've configured the OSB environment and set up your tape devices and virtual tape libraries. The following OSB-related recipes focus strictly on how to configure and use an OSB tape device as part of an RMAN backup and recovery strategy.

18-1. Installing Oracle Secure Backup on Linux
Problem

You want to install Oracle Secure Backup on a Linux server.

Solution

Following are the summary steps to follow to install OSB on a Linux server.

1. Create a directory with enough space to hold the installation file:

   mkdir /tmp/osbdownload

2. Download the OSB installation software from one of the following web locations:

   http://www.oracle.com//technetwork/products/secure-backup/overview/index.html
   or: http://www.oracle.com/technetwork/products/secure-backup/downloads/index.html

3. Create the Oracle Security Backup home, by logging into the server as the root user and executing the following command:

```
$ mkdir -p /usr/local/oracle/backup
```

4. Move to the OSB home and load the OSB software by executing the Oracle-provided *setup* script. For example:

```
$ cd /usr/local/oracle/backup

[root@virtual1 backup]# /tmp/osbdownload/OB/setup

Welcome to Oracle's setup program for Oracle Secure Backup.  This
program loads Oracle Secure Backup software from the CD-ROM to a
filesystem directory of your choosing.

This CD-ROM contains Oracle Secure Backup version 10.4.0.2.0_LINUX64.

Please wait a moment while I learn about this host... done.


 - - - - - - - - - - - - - - - - - - - - - - - - - - - - - - - - - - -
    1. linux86_64
       administrative server, media server, client

 - - - - - - - - - - - - - - - - - - - - - - - - - - - - - - - - - - -
Loading Oracle Secure Backup installation tools... done.
Loading linux86_64 administrative server, media server, client... done.

 - - - - - - - - - - - - - - - - - - - - - - - - - - - - - - - - - - -
Oracle Secure Backup has installed a new obparameters file.
Your previous version has been saved as install/obparameters.savedbysetup.
Any changes you have made to the previous version must be
made to the new obparameters file.
```

5. The setup script offers you two choices: *yes* and *no*. Enter *yes* to run the *installob* script, to install Oracle Secure Backup on the local host.

```
Would you like to continue Oracle Secure Backup installation with
'installob' now?  (The Oracle Secure Backup Installation Guide
contains complete information about installob.)

Please answer 'yes' or 'no' [yes]: yes

 - - - - - - - - - - - - - - - - - - - - - - - - - - - - - - - - - - -

Welcome to installob, Oracle Secure Backup's installation program.

For most questions, a default answer appears enclosed in square brackets.
Press Enter to select this answer.

Please wait a few seconds while I learn about this machine... done.
```

Alternatively, you can run the installob script by executing the following command from the OSB home directory:

```
$ /install/installob
```

6. Confirm the settings in the *obparameters* file, which is automatically created by the installer. If you've already edited this file and set customized obparameters to yes, the *installob* script will use those parameters. Enter *yes* or press the *Enter* key to confirm that you don't want to customize the obparaemters file.

```
Have you already reviewed and customized install/obparameters for your
Oracle Secure Backup installation [yes]? yes
```

- -

7. Specify the host role by choosing option a, b, or c for administrative server, media server, or client, respectively. The following example chooses (a), for administrative server:

```
Oracle Secure Backup is not yet installed on this machine.

Oracle Secure Backup's Web server has been loaded, but is not yet configured.

Choose from one of the following options. The option you choose defines
the software components to be installed.

Configuration of this host is required after installation completes.

You can install the software on this host in one of the following ways:
    (a) administrative server, media server and client

    (b) media server and client

    (c) client

If you are not sure which option to choose, please refer to the Oracle
Secure Backup Installation Guide. (a,b or c) [a]?

Beginning the installation.  This will take just a minute and will produce
several lines of informational output.

Installing Oracle Secure Backup on virtual1 (Linux version 2.6.32-300.10.1.el5uek)
```

8. Enter the password for the Oracle Secure Backup keystore:

```
Please enter the key store password:
Re-type password for verification:
```

9. Enter a password for the Oracle Secure Backup administrative server:

```
You must now enter a password for the Oracle Secure Backup 'admin' user.
Oracle suggests you choose a password of at least 8 characters in length,
containing a mixture of alphabetic and numeric characters.
```

```
Please enter the admin password:
Re-type password for verification:
```

10. Enter an e-mail address where you want Oracle Secure Backup to send notifications:

```
You should now enter an email address for the Oracle Secure Backup 'admin'
user.  Oracle Secure Backup uses this email address to send job summary
reports and to notify the user when a job requires input.  If you leave this
blank, you can set it later using the obtool's 'chuser' command.

Please enter the admin email address: salapati@casham.com
```

11. At this point the installation and configuration process begins:

```
generating links for admin installation with Web server
    updating /etc/ld.so.conf
    checking Oracle Secure Backup's configuration file (/etc/obconfig)
    setting Oracle Secure Backup directory to /usr/local/oracle/backup in /etc/obconfig
    setting local database directory to /usr/etc/ob in /etc/obconfig
    setting temp directory to /usr/tmp in /etc/obconfig
    setting administrative directory to /usr/local/oracle/backup/admin in /etc/obconfig
    protecting the Oracle Secure Backup directory
    creating /etc/rc.d/init.d/observiced
    activating observiced via chkconfig
    initializing the administrative domain

***************************** N O T E *****************************
On Linux systems Oracle recommends that you answer no to the next two
questions. The preferred mode of operation on Linux systems is to use
the /dev/sg devices for attach points as described in the 'ReadMe'
and in the 'Installation and Configuration Guide.'

Is virtual1 connected to any tape libraries that you'd like to use with
Oracle Secure Backup [no]?

Is virtual1 connected to any tape drives that you'd like to use with
Oracle Secure Backup [no]?

Installation summary:

    Installation  Host            OS       Driver      OS Move    Reboot
          Mode    Name            Name     Installed?  Required?  Required?

      admin       virtual1        Linux    no          no         no

Oracle Secure Backup is now ready for your use.

[root@virtual1 backup]#
```

As the message indicates, Oracle Secure backup is installed and ready for your use.

How It Works

In our example installation shown in the Solution section, we chose to install all three components of Oracle Secure backup—the administrative server, the media server, and the client—on the same Linux host. That's the reason we chose option (a) in Step 7. By choosing option (a), you're telling the installer to install the software for the administrative server, media server, and client on this host. This is okay on a test server. In real production environments dealing with a large number of databases and huge storage arrays, you'll most likely choose a separate server for each OSB component.

Here's what the three key OSB components stand for:

- Administrative server: the host server that contains a copy of the OSB software as well as the OSB catalog.

- Media server: the host server that contains storage devices, such as tape libraries, connected to it.

- Client: the host server whose locally accessed data OSB will back up.

The administrative server in our example here also plays the additional role of a media server. The host on which we installed the adminsitrative server and the media server won't be recognized automatically as a media server, however. Here's how you can verify the roles a host can play:

```
ob> lshost
virtual1.vm.casham.com admin,client              (via OB)   in service
ob>
```

For our single host to be recognized as a media server, we must execute the chhost command and explictly grant the host the media server role. Here's an example that shows how to do this:

```
ob> lshost
virtual1.vm.casham.com admin,client              (via OB)   in service
ob> chhost --addrole mediaserver virtual1.vm.casham.com
ob> lshost
virtual1.vm.casham.com admin,mediaserver,client  (via OB)   in service
ob>
```

18-2. Verifying the MML Installation
Problem

You want to verify that your media manager layer (MML) has been installed correctly.

■ **Note** This recipe is valid for any Oracle environment that ships with the sbttest utility. The sbttest utility works with any media management layer (Oracle Secure Backup, Veritas NetBackup, EMC NetWorker Module for Oracle, IBM Tivoli, HP OmniBack, and so forth).

Solution

On some Unix platforms there is an `sbttest` utility that can be used to verify that your MML has been installed and configured correctly. From the Unix command line, run the `sbttest` utility. To run this utility, you must specify a dummy file for the utility to interact with. In this example, the file name is mml.tst:

```
$ sbttest mml.tst
```

If the test is successful, you should see lights blinking on your tape device and output on the screen similar to the following:

```
The sbt function pointers are loaded from libobk.so library.
-- sbtinit succeeded
-- sbtinit (2nd time) succeeded
sbtinit: Media manager supports SBT API version 2.0
sbtinit: vendor description string=NMO v4.2.0.0
```

If your MML has not been installed correctly, the utility will report errors such as the following:

```
libobk.so could not be loaded. Check that it is installed.
```

If you receive the previous message, ensure that the libnwora file is in the correct directory and is correctly linked to the libobk file (this will vary by MML vendor).

How It Works

The `sbttest` utility is designed to test whether you can use your MML to back up and restore files to and from tape. This utility will test functionality, such as the following:

- Is MML installed correctly?

- Can you write files to tape through the RMAN SBT API?

- Can you read files from tape via the RMAN SBT API?

This utility is located in your $ORACLE_HOME/bin directory. If you don't find it there, check with Oracle Support for the availability of `sbttest` for your operating system.

The `sbttest` utility requires that you list a file name for it to use as part of the test. This file does not have to exist before you run the test. If you want to view all options available with the `sbttest` utility, then don't specify any parameters on the command line, as shown here:

```
$ sbttest
```

You should now see a long listing of the parameters available with the `sbttest` utility. Table 18-1 describes these parameters.

Table 18-1. Description of sbttest Parameters

Parameter Name	Purpose
backup_file_name	The only required parameter. If this file doesn't exist, the sbttest utility will create it for use during the test and then delete it upon completion.
dbname	The database name that sbt uses to identify the backup file (the default is sbtdb).
trace	The trace file name where the MML software writes diagnostic messages.
remove_before	When specified, the backup file will be deleted before it is opened. This is useful when a previous run of sbttest didn't complete successfully and didn't delete the backup file.
noremove_after	Instructs sbttest to not remove the backup file after successful completion.
read_only	When specified a backup file must already exist. Instructs sbttest to validate the backup file contents.
no_regular_backup_restore	Instructs sbttest to skip the nonproxy backup and restore.
no_proxy_backup	Instructs sbttest to skip proxy copy backup.
no_proxy_restore	Instructs sbttest to skip proxy copy restore.
file_type	File type can be 1, 2, or 3.
copy_number	Specifies the copy_number parameter to sbtpcbackup.
media_pool	Specifies the media_pool parameter to sbtpcbackup.
os_res_size	Determines the size of the operating system reserved block (in bytes).
pl_res_size	Determines the size of the platform reserved block (in bytes).
block_size	Determines the size of blocks written to the backup file (default is 16,384 bytes).
block_count	Specifies number of blocks written to backup file (default is 100).
proxy_file	Specifies the operating system file name, backup file name, operating system reserved size, block size, and block count for the proxy file.
libname	Determines the sbt library to test. The default library is libobk.so. You can specify oracle.disksbt for Oracle's disk sbt library.

Listed next is an example showing how to specify parameters when running the sbttest utility. This example shows how to limit the number of blocks written to tape to 10:

```
$ sbttest mml.tst -block_count 10
```

The next example shows how to store the diagnostic messages in a file named mml.trc:

```
$ sbttest mml.tst -trace /orahome/mml.trc
```

You can also test the backup of an existing data file. This example instructs the sbttest utility to use an existing data file with the name of data_ts06.dbf in the BRDSTN database:

```
$ sbttest data_ts06.dbf -dbname BRDSTN
```

■ **Note** There's no sbttest utility for the Windows environment. However, you can request that Oracle Support provide you with the *loadsbt.exe* utility for Windows. The loadsbt.exe utility isn't as robust as sbttest, but it does provide you with a way to troubleshoot your media management layer in a Windows environment.

18-3. Working with obtool
Problem

You want to work with the OSB's utility *obtool,* to perform various backup-related tasks pertaining to the use of OSB with RMAN.

Solution

The obtool utility is the main command line interface to Oracle Secure Backup. You invoke the obtool utility by typing in "obtool" at the operating system prompt:

```
$ obtool
```

The very first time you invoke obtool, the utility prompts you to provide a username and password, as shown here:

```
[root@virtual1 backup]$ obtool
Oracle Secure Backup 10.4.0.2.0
login: admin
Password:
ob>
```

On subsequent logins, you can log in without providing any credentials:

```
[root@virtual1 backup]$ obtool
ob>
```

The prompt *ob>* shows that the obtool session has started and that you can start issuing obtool commands.
To exit from an obtool session, type the exit or quit command. Here's an example that shows how to end a session with the exit command:

```
ob> exit
```

When you finish an obtool session by typing in *exit* or *quit,* the login token of the user preserves the user's credentials, so you won't need to enter the user credentials the next time you start obtool.
You can completely log out of obtool by issuing the *logout* command. Unlike the *exit* or *quit* command, the *logout* command destroys the user's login token, so the user is forced to enter the credentials during a subsequent obtool session.
You can start obtool as a specific user by adding the *–u* option to the obtool command, as shown here:

```
[root@virtual1 backup]$ obtool -u admin
Password:
ob>
```

You can view all available help topics by entering the following command:

```
ob> help topics
You can view a list of commands on a particular topic, by entering help followed by the name of the
command:ob> help class
Class definition commands:
chclass change the attributes of a user class
lsclass list the names and attributes of one or more user classes
mkclass define a user class
renclass assign a new name to a user class
rmclass remove a user class from the administrative domain
ob>
```

In this example, the *help* command displays available obtool *class* commands.

To find out the correct syntax for a specific command, enter *help* followed by the name of the command:

```
ob> help lssection
Usage: lssection [ --long | --short ] [ --noheader/-H ] [ --incomplete/-i ]
[ --oid/-o oid-list ]...
[ { { --vid/-v vid-list } | { --void/-V oid-list } }
[ --file/-f filenumber-list ]...]
```

You can get the glossary of terms for a specific topic by entering *help* with the topic name and the keyword *glossary*, as shown here:

```
ob> help snapshot glossary
<filesystem-name> the logical or physical name of a file system that is
logically connected to a host
<hostname> a name of a host assigned by the user via mkhost or renhost
<numberformat> the format in which to display large numbers, one of:
friendly displays large values in "KB", "MB", ...
precise shows precise values (with commas)
plain like precise, but eschews commas
(unspecified) uses "numberformat" variable or, if
unset, "friendly"ob>
```

How It Works

Oracle recommends the following tools for accessing OSB.

- Use OEM for managing OSB.

- Use OSB Web Tool to manage file-system backups.

- Use the obtool utility or OSB Web Tool to access the OSB configuration file. (Do not access the configuration file directly through a text editor.)

The obtool command-line client includes the complete functionality of OSB. Behind the scenes, both OEM and the Oracle Secure Backup Web Tool invoke obtool to perform their tasks. Oracle recommends that you access configuration data through the obtool utility, or through the Oracle Secure backup web tool, which is based on the obtool utility.

During installation, OSB automatically creates the *admin* user. When you first invoke the obtool utility after installing OSB, you must use the password that you chose for the *admin* user during the installation.

The obtool utility is quite powerful, with a vast array of commands organized under various command categories. For example, the command category backup includes the following commands:

- backup: creates a file-system backup request (not a database backup)

- lsbackup: lists each file-system backup request you created with the backup command

- rmbackup: removes backup requests queued in obtool

18-4. Using obtool in Noninteractive Mode

Problem

You want to use obtool in a noninteractive mode. For example, you want to write a script that will run unattended.

Solution

You can avoid the obtool command prompt and issue OSB-related commands directly on the operating system command line by using the following syntax:

```
obtool [ cl-option ]... command-name [ option ]... [ argument ]...
```

For example, here's how you issue the *lshost* command on the command line:

```
% obtool lshost
Output of command: lshost
brhost2 client (via OB) in service
brhost3 mediaserver,client (via OB) in service
br_filer client (via NDMP) in service
stadv07 admin,mediaserver,client (via OB) in service
%
```

Once an interactive command completes executing, obtool exits and you're back to the operating system prompt.

You can enter multiple obtool commands interactively at the command line, by separating the commands with a semicolon:

```
$ obtool lshost ; lsdev
```

On some types of operating system shell sessions, you may have to enclose the semicolon with quotes, as shown here:

```
$ obtool lshost ';' lsdev
```

Often you'll need to execute multiple obtool commands in sequence. Instead of entering each command separately, you can use a text file containing all the obtool commands you want to execute. You can then run the commands sequentially by redirecting the obtool input to the script, as shown here:

```
ob> < /my_dir/my_script.txt
```

The obtool utility will run all the commands in the *my_script.txt* file and will return the *ob>* prompt.

How It Works

The Solution section shows how you can avoid the obtool interactive mode altogether by directly entering commands at the operating system command line. When entering a set of commands, you can choose to specify them directly on the command line, or in the case of a large number of obtool commands, use a script file to pass the commands to obtool, which will then sequentially execute the set of commands contained in the file.

18-5. Configuring an OSB Virtual Device

Problem

You want to configure a virtual test device to test Oracle Secure Backup in a non-production environment.

Solution

Perform the following steps on the server that has the media server role in an OSB environment. In our example, the same host serves as the administrative server and the media server, but you could choose a different host for the media server role.

1. Log in as the user oracle:

    ```
    $ su - oracle
    ```

2. Create a directory to host the various virtual storage components and the virtual storage devices:

    ```
    $ mkdir/osb_vdevices
    ```

3. Log in to obtool as the admin user:

    ```
    $ obtool -u admin
    Password:
    ```

4. Execute the mkdev command to configure the virtual tape library:

    ```
    ob> mkdev -t library -v -S20 -I2 -o -B yes -a virtual1.vm.mydomain.com:/osb_vdevices/
    vlib1 vlib1
    ```

5. You can confirm that the mkdev command worked, by executing either the lsdev or the lsdev -long commands, as shown here:

    ```
    ob> lsdev
    library            vlib1            in service
    ob>

    ob> lsdev --long
    vlib1:
        Device type:        library (virtual)
        Model:              [none]
        Serial number:      [none]
        In service:         yes
        Debug mode:         no
    ```

```
                Barcode reader:          yes
                Barcodes required:       no
                Auto clean:              no
                Clean interval:          (not set)
                Clean using emptiest:    no
                Ejection type:           auto
                Min writable volumes:    0
                UUID:                    39b28964-0ce4-1030-93c1-000c292f9d8f
                Attachment 1:
                    Host:                virtual1.vm.casham.com
                    Raw device:          /osb_vdevices/vlib1
        ob>
```

6. Execute the mkdev command again, this time to configure the virtual tape devices:

```
ob> mkdev -t tape -v -o -l vlib1 -d1 -a virtual1.vm.casham.com:/osb_vdevices/vdrive1  vdrive1
ob>
```

You can see that although you've created the virtual tape device, there are no volumes in the tape device, as shown by the lsvol command here:

```
ob> lsvol --long --library vlib1
Inventory of library vlib1:
    in    mte:          vacant
    in    1:            vacant
    in    2:            vacant
    in    3:            vacant
    in    4:            vacant
    in    5:            vacant
    in    6:            vacant
    in    7:            vacant
    in    8:            vacant
    in    9:            vacant
    in    10:           vacant
    in    11:           vacant
    in    12:           vacant
    in    13:           vacant
    in    14:           vacant
    in    15:           vacant
    in    16:           vacant
    in    17:           vacant
    in    18:           vacant
    in    19:           vacant
    in    20:           vacant
    in    iee1:         vacant
    in    iee2:         vacant
ob>
```

7. Manually insert a volume into the tape library by executing the insertvol command.

```
ob> insertvol -L vlib1 unlabeled 1-20
```

8. Execute the lsvol command to confirm that you've successfully inserted the volume in the tape library vlib1:

```
ob> lsvol -l -L vlib1
Inventory of library vlib1:
    in    mte:           vacant
    in    1:             unlabeled, barcode 67538cc80ce51039e51000c292f9d8f, oid 100
    in    2:             unlabeled, barcode 6767c9ea0ce51039e51000c292f9d8f, oid 101
    in    3:             unlabeled, barcode 67758a940ce51039e51000c292f9d8f, oid 102
    in    4:             unlabeled, barcode 6783d4be0ce51039e51000c292f9d8f, oid 103
    in    5:             unlabeled, barcode 6792854a0ce51039e51000c292f9d8f, oid 104
    in    6:             unlabeled, barcode 67a06c140ce51039e51000c292f9d8f, oid 105
    in    7:             unlabeled, barcode 67af1c460ce51039e51000c292f9d8f, oid 106
    in    8:             unlabeled, barcode 67bdaf7c0ce51039e51000c292f9d8f, oid 107
    in    9:             unlabeled, barcode 67ceaa660ce51039e51000c292f9d8f, oid 108
    in    10:            unlabeled, barcode 67dc0d280ce51039e51000c292f9d8f, oid 109
    in    11:            unlabeled, barcode 67e97ff80ce51039e51000c292f9d8f, oid 110
    in    12:            unlabeled, barcode 67f7bfa00ce51039e51000c292f9d8f, oid 111
    in    13:            unlabeled, barcode 680539d20ce51039e51000c292f9d8f, oid 112
    in    14:            unlabeled, barcode 681310020ce51039e51000c292f9d8f, oid 113
    in    15:            unlabeled, barcode 6821d5ec0ce51039e51000c292f9d8f, oid 114
    in    16:            unlabeled, barcode 682f970e0ce51039e51000c292f9d8f, oid 115
    in    17:            unlabeled, barcode 683ddecc0ce51039e51000c292f9d8f, oid 116
    in    18:            unlabeled, barcode 684b804a0ce51039e51000c292f9d8f, oid 117
    in    19:            unlabeled, barcode 6859849c0ce51039e51000c292f9d8f, oid 118
    in    20:            unlabeled, barcode 68682cc20ce51039e51000c292f9d8f, oid 119
    in    iee1:          vacant
    in    iee2:          vacant
    in    dte:           vacant
ob>
```

How It Works

Creating virtual devices to test OSB before moving it to a production setup is often a very useful idea—just don't do this as part of a production backup strategy! In the first mkdev command that we executed to create the virtual media library, we executed the command with the following options:

```
mkdev -t library -v -S20 -I2 -o -B yes -a virtual1.vm.mydomain.com:/osb_vdevices/vlib1 vlib1
```

In this command, here's what the various options stand for:

- -t library: specifies the device as a tape library

- -v: specifies the verbose option for printing the output of this command

- -S: tells OSB how many slots it should create for this virtual tape library

- -o: tells OSB that this virtual tape library is available immediately for use

- -a: this option constructs the path to the OSB's tape library attachments and is also called the attachment specification

- vlib1: name of the tape library

In the second mkdev command we executed to create the virtual tape devices, we executed the command with the following options:

```
mkdev -t tape -v -o -l vlib1 -d1 -a virtual1.vm.casham.com:/osb_vdevices/vdrive1  vdrive1
```

And here's what the various options stand for:

- -t tape: specifes that we're creating a tape device

- -v: specifies the verbose option for the output of this command

- -o: lets OSB know that this tape device is available for use immediately

- -l vlib1: denotes the tape library (vlib1) that's assigned to the tape device we're creating

- -d1: The Data Transfer Element tag assigned to the tape device. In this case, we're asking OSB to configure a single tape.

- -a: constructs the path to the tape device attachment

- vdrive1: name of the tape device

You can issue the ls command from the virutal directory osb_vdevices that you've created earlier. The ls command shows a virtual directory named vdrive1 and a virtual library named vlib1. If you then issue the cd vlib1 command, you can view the contents of the virtual library, as shown in the following example.

```
[oracle@virtual1 osb_vdevices]$ ls
vdrive1   vlib1
[oracle@virtual1 osb_vdevices]$ cd vdrive1
[oracle@virtual1 vdrive1]$ ls
[oracle@virtual1 vdrive1]$ cd ../vlib1
[oracle@virtual1 vlib1]$ ls
67538cc80ce51039e51000c292f9d8f   67e97ff80ce51039e51000c292f9d8f
6767c9ea0ce51039e51000c292f9d8f   67f7bfa00ce51039e51000c292f9d8f
67758a940ce51039e51000c292f9d8f   680539d20ce51039e51000c292f9d8f
6783d4be0ce51039e51000c292f9d8f   681310020ce51039e51000c292f9d8f
6792854a0ce51039e51000c292f9d8f   6821d5ec0ce51039e51000c292f9d8f
67a06c140ce51039e51000c292f9d8f   682f970e0ce51039e51000c292f9d8f
67af1c460ce51039e51000c292f9d8f   683ddecc0ce51039e51000c292f9d8f
67bdaf7c0ce51039e51000c292f9d8f   684b804a0ce51039e51000c292f9d8f
67ceaa660ce51039e51000c292f9d8f   6859849c0ce51039e51000c292f9d8f
67dc0d280ce51039e51000c292f9d8f   68682cc20ce51039e51000c292f9d8f
[oracle@virtual1 vlib1]$
```

18-6. Configuring RMAN to Work with Oracle Secure Backup

Problem

You want to configure RMAN so you can make tape backups through Oracle Secure Backup.

Solution

Once you've configured the tape library and the tape drives (if you're testing with virtual tape libraries and tape drives, please see Recipe 18-5), you must grant RMAN necessary permissions for it to be able to work with the OSB devices you've configured. In the following example, we show you how to create a preauthorized Oracle Secure Backup user for performing RMAN backup and recovery tasks.

1. Invoke the obtool utility as the admin user:

    ```
    [oracle@virtual1 ~]$ obtool --user admin --password Ninamma11
    ob>
    ```

2. Check the current OSB authorized users by issuing the lsuser command:

    ```
    ob> lsuser
    admin           admin
    ob>
    ```

    The lsuser command shows that we just have the admin user that was created during the OSB installation.

3. Create an OSB preauthorized user named oracle:

    ```
    ob> mkuser -c oracle -p oracle -U oracle -G dba -N no -h *:*:*+rman+cmdline oracle
    ```

4. Confirm the creation of the user *oracle* with the following lsuser command:

    ```
    ob> lsuser
    admin           admin
    oracle          oracle
    ob>
    ```

The lsuser command shows that the OSB user *oracle* was successfully created.

How It Works

In the mkuser command, here's what the various flags stand for:

- -c: specifies that the user you're creating beliogns to the predefined Orcle OSB account class.

- -p: denotes the Oracle OSB account class

- _U: specifes the OS accout name for the OSB user

- -G: specifes the OS group name for the OSB user

- -N: tells OSB that this user isn't authorized to log into an NDMP server.

- Oracle: this is the name of the OSB account and is different than the user *oracle* that owns typical Oracle database software installations.

18-7. Configuring RMAN Access to the Oracle Secure Backup sbt Library
Problem

You want to configure RMAN access to Oracle Secure Backup via Oracle Enterprise Manager Database Control.

Solution

The easiest way to make RMAN backups through the OSB interface is to use the Oracle Enterprise Manager Grid Control or Database Control. In this recipe, we show you how to use OEM Database Control to manage RMAN tape backups through OSB.

You must follow these steps to configure RMAN access to Oracle Secure Backup through OEM Database Control:

1. Log in to Database Control as a user with `sysdba` privileges.

2. Click the Availability tab on the Home page of Database Control.

3. In the Oracle Secure Backup section, click Oracle Secure Backup Device and Media.

4. On the Add Administrative Server page that appears, perform the following two steps to register the administer server with Database Control:

    a. In the Oracle Secure Backup Home directory, enter the full Oracle Secure Backup Home directory. This is the same directory in which you originally installed OSB. By default, this is the /usr/local/oracle/backup directory on Unix/Linux and the C:\Program Files\Oracle\Backup directory on Windows.

    b. Enter an OSB administrator name and password in the Username and Password boxes, respectively.

5. On the Host Credentials Page that appears next, enter the credentials (needs root privileges on Unix/Linux) for the administrative user on the administrative server.

6. The *hostname* page appears next, which you can use to load tapes.

Once you've registered the administrative server by following these steps, you're ready to work with OSB through the OEM Database Control or through manual commands.

How It Works

When you install OSB on a Linux/Unix platform, the installer automatically copies the sbt library to the subdirectory named lib, under the OSB home, which is the /usr/local/oracle/backup directory on Unix/Linux systems and the C:\Program Files\Oracle\Backup directory on Windows. You can use the parameter `sbt_library` to specify a location to replace the default sbt library location. When you allocate an sbt channel, RMAN will automatically load the OSB sbt library. Here's an example showing how to configure a default media management library using the `sbt_library` parameter:

```
configure default device type to sbt;
configure channel device type sbt parms="sbt_library=?/lib/med_li1.so";
backup database;
```

The `backup database` command backs up the database using the media management library you configured in the previous command. The following example shows how to set a value for the `sbt_library` parameter by using the keyword parms:

```
run
{
  allocate channel device type sbt
  parms="sbt_library=?/lib/med_lib1.so";
  backup database;
}
```

The previous run block backs up the database using the media management library specified by the sbt_library parameter.

18-8. Managing Authorized OSB Accounts

Problem

You want to create and manage an operating system user account to perform backup and recovery tasks with OSB.

Solution

You can create the special OSB user and perform the necessary preauthorization during the OSB installation. In this Solution, we'll show you how to handle user management after tse installation is complete by using obtool, the OSB command-line interface. Execute the obtool command mkuser to create the OSB user, as shown in the following example:

```
ob> mkuser --class oracle --preauth prod1:+rman obuser
```

The previous command creates the account named obuser. Note the following about the mkuser command that creates the new OSB user:

- obuser is the name of the new OSB user.

- class denotes that the new user obuser is assigned to the oracle class.

- The preauth option +rman preauthorizes sbt backups through RMAN. The prod1 here stands for the host of the operating system user who has been granted preauthorized access to OSB.

You've now successfully configured an RMAN preauthorization, wherein you authorized an operating system user to make RMAN tape backups using OSB.

In addition to the mkuser command, obtool provides several other commands that help you manage OSB accounts. The following examples show how to employ the most useful of these commands.

Listing Users

Use the lsuser command to list the names and attributes of one or more users. The simple lsuser command provides the names of the users:

```
ob> lsuser
```

Use the lsuser command with the --long option to get a user's attributes, as shown here:

```
ob> lsuser --long salapati
```

Changing User Attributes

Use the chuser command to change an OSB user's attributes, as shown in the following example:

```
ob> chuser --password sammyy1 --email samalapati@casham.com
```

Renaming Users

The renuser command lets you rename an OSB user, as shown here:

```
ob> renuser salapati sam_alapati
```

The renuser command shown here renames user salapati to sam_alapati.

Removing Users

You can remove an OSB user with the rmuser command, as shown here:

```
ob> rmuser -nq salapati
```

The rmuser command in this example removes the OSB user salapati from the administrative domain after displaying a confirmation message. The nq option is optional and specifies that there is no need for a prompt.

How It Works

You must "preauthorize" an OS user to access OSB and perform backup and recovery actions. Your OSB interaction will be successful only if you've first authenticated the operating system user who starts the Oracle server session as an Oracle Secure Backup user. The server session can use only the OSB user account that you create to perform backup and recovery jobs.

You can also use the browser-based Oracle Secure Backup web tool to configure RMAN preauthorization. The OSB web tool helps you configure an administrative domain, browse the backup catalog, and back up and restore the file system. Once you configure a preauthorized OSB user account, the easiest way to make a connection between this OSB account and RMAN is to simply use Database Control for that purpose.

18-9. Creating OSB Media Families for RMAN Backups
Problem

You want to create separate groups of tape volumes for different types of RMAN backup sets.

Solution

You can create named groups of tape volumes called *media families* that share common characteristics. You can create separate media families for the data files and the archived redo logs, and you can assign them different expiration and recycling policies, for example.

You can create a media family using the Enterprise Manager, the Oracle Secure Backup web tool, or the mkmf command in obtool. In this recipe, we show you how to create a media family using the mkmf command.

You can create two types of media families: time-managed and content-managed. We provide an example showing how to create a time-managed media family first. Here's the example:

```
ob> mkmf --vidunique --writewindow 14days --retain 28days family_time
```

You can use the `mkmf` command with numerous options. In the simple example here, the options are as follows:

- `vidunique` creates a unique volume ID for the new media family.

- `writewindow` specifies a time window for the *write window*, which is the time during which you can update the volume set by adding backup images to it. OSB can use the volume family for backups until the write window remains open. In the example here, the write window is set to 14, which means all volumes in this media family will be available for update for 14 days.

- `retain` specifies the amount of time for which the volumes in the media family are retained before being possibly overwritten. In the example, the retention parameter is set to 28 days. However, each volume in the backup expires only after 42 days after the first time OSB makes a backup to the volume, since OSB adds the write window duration (14 days) to volume retention time (28 days) to arrive at the volume expiration time (42 days).

- The last item in the command, `family_time`, is the name of the media family. The next example shows how to create a content-managed media family, again by executing the `mkmf` command:

```
[oracle@virtual1 ~]$ obtool --user admin --password Ninamma11

ob>  mkmf --vidunique --writewindow forever family_content_1
ob>
```

By giving the value `forever` for the `writewindow` parameter, you're specifying that OSB can update all volumes in this media family indefinitely. The name of the media family is `family_content_1`.

How It Works

Create media families to separate your OSB tape volumes into meaningful groups. For example, if you want to retain a set of tape volumes for six months, you can do so by using a time-based media family and specifying 180 days as the value for the `retain` parameter.

The key thing to understand is that all volumes that are members of a media family share the same retention and other characteristics. Note that this applies to all volumes, no matter when they were created.

The default volume expiration policy for a media family is the content-managed policy. A volume that's a member of such a family expires when the status of all the backup pieces stored on that volume is set to be deleted. Media volumes that belong to time-managed policy-based media families, on the other hand, will expire only when the expiration time is reached, as explained in the Solution section of this recipe.

18-10. Creating an OSB Database Backup Storage Selector
Problem

You want to create a database backup storage selector for OSB.

Solution

You can configure a database backup storage selector by using the web tool or the `mkssel` command in `obtool`, or by using the Enterprise Manager. In this recipe, we show you how to create a database backup storage selector using the `mkssel` command in `obtool`.

Execute the `mkssel` command to create database backup storage selectors for OSB. Make sure you have the right to modify the administrative domain's configuration. The `mkssel` command has several options you can use. Here's a simple example showing how to create a backup storage selector named `stor_sel1`:

```
ob> mkssel --dbid 2233353479 --host prod1 --content full --family med_fam1 stor_sel1
```

The storage selector `stor_sel1` applies to the database with a specific DBID on the prod1 host. If you want this storage selector set to all databases, specify an asterisk (*) instead of the DBID. The content option specifies that full rather than incremental backups can be made with this storage selector. The media family `med_fam1` will be used for backups under this storage selector.

You can use other commands from the `obtool` utility to manage database backup storage selectors, as shown in the following sections.

Changing a Database Storage Selector

Once you create a backup storage selector, you can modify it with help from the `chssel` command, shown here:

```
ob> chssel --dbid 5123449812 --host prod1 --content full --family f1 ssel_new
```

The previous command replaces the current media family with the new media family `ssel_new`.

Renaming a Database Storage Selector

You can use the `renssel` command to rename a backup storage selector, as shown in the following example:

```
ob> renssel ssel_old ssel_new
```

The command shown here renames the `ssel_old` storage selector to `ssel_new`.

Removing a Database Storage Selector

Use the `rmssel` command to remove a database backup storage selector, as shown in this example:

```
ob> rmssel ssel_old
```

This command deletes the database backup storage selector `ssel_old`.

How It Works

OSB uses the database backup storage selectors to represent the backup attributes of an Oracle database. The backup storage attributes that are required are as follows:

- Database name or ID
- Host name
- Name of the media family to use for the backups

Optionally, you can specify settings of backup storage selectors indicating the backup contents (full/incremental) and the copy number of duplexed backups.

18-11. Configuring OSB Parameters in RMAN

Problem

You want to configure Oracle Secure Backup (OSB) media management parameters in RMAN.

Solution

You can specify the following OSB parameters in a backup or restore job in RMAN:

- `ob_media_family [_n]`: specifies the media family to use for a job
- `ob_device [_n]`: specifies the tape drive to be used for the job
- `ob_resource_wait_time`: specifies the length of time for which a job should wait for a necessary resource to become available

You can specify media management parameters in RMAN in two ways. You can use environment variables via the `configure` or `allocate` channel command. Or you can use the `send` command. We'll illustrate both methods in this solution.

Using the Configure or Allocate Channel Command

Use the `parms` parameter to send instructions to the media manager from RMAN. In the following example, we use the `configure` channel command to specify values for the `ob_device` and `ob_media_family` parameters:

```
RMAN> configure channel device type sbt
      parms='env=(ob_device=drive3,
      ob_media_family=med_fam1)';
```

The previous command specifies the `ob_device` parameter to direct the backup to the tape drive drive3 and the `ob_media_family` parameter to specify the media family med_fam1 for the backup.

You can also use the `allocate` channel command to specify media management parameters, as shown in the following example:

```
RMAN> run
      {
      allocate channel ch1 device type sbt
      parms 'env=(ob_device=drive3, ob_media_family=med_fam1)';

      }
```

This `allocate` channel command uses the env parameter of the `parms` option to specify the media family med_fam1 for the backup.

Using the Send Command

The RMAN send command lets you send a vendor-specific string to a channel that's supported by a media manager. The following example shows how to issue the send command to specify a tape drive by sending the value for the ob_device parameter to Oracle Secure backup:

```
RMAN> run
        {
        allocate channel ch1 device type sbt;
        send 'ob_device drive3';
        send 'ob_media_family med_fam1';
        backup database;
        }
```

The send command specifies the tape drive device3 as the value for the ob_device parameter for channel ch1, which communicates with the media manager.

How It Works

When you issue the send command, if you don't specify a channel for a backup or restore job, RMAN uses all allocated channels for the job. The send command will accept only those commands that are supported by the specific media manager you are using. The database has nothing to do with the interpretation of the strings that you enter as input to the send command strings—that's left entirely to the MML.

18-12. Making Oracle Database Backups Using Oracle Secure Backup

Problem

You want to perform a backup using Oracle Secure Backup and RMAN.

Solution

You use the same backup commands as you would when you back up to disk, but you specify a tape channel when using Oracle Secure Backup. Here's an example that shows how to back up a database using OSB-managed tape devices. We use bold text in the output of the backup command, to show details about the tape devices used in the backup.

```
[oracle@virtual1 ~]$ rman

Recovery Manager: Release 12.1.0.0.2 - Beta on Fri Nov 9 11:21:58 2012

Copyright (c) 1982, 2012, Oracle and/or its affiliates.  All rights reserved.

RMAN> connect target /
```

```
connected to target database: ORCL (DBID=1316762630)

RMAN> CONFIGURE DEFAULT DEVICE TYPE TO sbt;

new RMAN configuration parameters:
CONFIGURE DEFAULT DEVICE TYPE TO 'SBT_TAPE';
new RMAN configuration parameters are successfully stored

RMAN> backup database;

Starting backup at 09-NOV-12
allocated channel: ORA_SBT_TAPE_1
channel ORA_SBT_TAPE_1: SID=74 device type=SBT_TAPE
channel ORA_SBT_TAPE_1: Oracle Secure Backup
channel ORA_SBT_TAPE_1: starting full datafile backup set
channel ORA_SBT_TAPE_1: specifying datafile(s) in backup set
input datafile file number=00001 name=/u01/app/oracle/oradata/orcl/system01.dbf
input datafile file number=00003 name=/u01/app/oracle/oradata/orcl/sysaux01.dbf
input datafile file number=00005 name=/u01/app/oracle/oradata/orcl/cattbs_01.dbf
input datafile file number=00002 name=/u01/app/oracle/oradata/orcl/example01.dbf
input datafile file number=00007 name=/u01/app/oracle/oradata/orcl/virt_catalog_01.dbf
input datafile file number=00004 name=/u01/app/oracle/oradata/orcl/undotbs01.dbf
input datafile file number=00006 name=/u01/app/oracle/oradata/orcl/users01.dbf
input datafile file number=00010 name=/u01/app/oracle/oradata/orcl/demo01.dbf
input datafile file number=00008 name=/u01/app/oracle/oradata/orcl/test01_01.dbf
input datafile file number=00009 name=/u01/app/oracle/oradata/orcl/test02_01.dbf
channel ORA_SBT_TAPE_1: starting piece 1 at 09-NOV-12
channel ORA_SBT_TAPE_1: finished piece 1 at 09-NOV-12
piece handle=amnpsbar_1_1 tag=TAG20121109T112411 comment=API Version 2.0,MMS Version 10.4.0.2
channel ORA_SBT_TAPE_1: backup set complete, elapsed time: 00:04:36
Finished backup at 09-NOV-12

Starting Control File Autobackup at 09-NOV-12
piece handle=c-1316762630-20121109-00 comment=API Version 2.0,MMS Version 10.4.0.2
Finished Control File Autobackup at 09-NOV-12

RMAN>
```

How It Works

You can configure either a content-based or a time-based backup expiration policy for backups made to tape. If you delete any backup made through the sbt interface by using RMAN's delete command, OSB updates its catalog automatically to account for the deleted backup pieces. However, when you delete a backup piece from tape using an OSB command (rmpiece) or when you overwrite a backup piece on tape, RMAN's repository won't be automatically updated. Always make it a policy to use RMAN's crosscheck command to avoid discrepancies between the actual backups on tape and RMAN's repository backup metadata.

Once you make the backup with OSB and RMAN, check the backup status by issuing the list backup command in RMAN (we use bold text in the output of the backup command, to show details about the tape devices used in the backup):

```
RMAN> list backup;

using target database control file instead of recovery catalog

List of Backup Sets
===================

BS Key  Type LV Size       Device Type Elapsed Time Completion Time
------- ---- -- ---------- ----------- ------------ ----------------
221     Full   1.23G       SBT_TAPE    00:04:28     09-NOV-12
        BP Key: 232   Status: AVAILABLE  Compressed: NO  Tag: TAG20121109T112411
        Handle: amnpsbar_1_1   Media: RMAN-DEFAULT-000001
  List of Datafiles in backup set 221
  File LV Type Ckp SCN    Ckp Time  Name
  ---- -- ---- ---------- --------- ----
  1       Full 2558079    09-NOV-12 /u01/app/oracle/oradata/orcl/system01.dbf
  2       Full 2443713    25-OCT-12 /u01/app/oracle/oradata/orcl/example01.dbf
  3       Full 2558079    09-NOV-12 /u01/app/oracle/oradata/orcl/sysaux01.dbf
  4       Full 2558079    09-NOV-12 /u01/app/oracle/oradata/orcl/undotbs01.dbf
  5       Full 2558079    09-NOV-12 /u01/app/oracle/oradata/orcl/cattbs_01.dbf
  6       Full 2443701    25-OCT-12 /u01/app/oracle/oradata/orcl/users01.dbf
  7       Full 2558079    09-NOV-12 /u01/app/oracle/oradata/orcl/virt_catalog_01.dbf
  8       Full 2558079    09-NOV-12 /u01/app/oracle/oradata/orcl/test01_01.dbf
  9       Full 2558079    09-NOV-12 /u01/app/oracle/oradata/orcl/test02_01.dbf
  10      Full 2530714    27-OCT-12 /u01/app/oracle/oradata/orcl/demo01.dbf

222     Full   9.75M      SBT_TAPE    00:00:28     09-NOV-12
        BP Key: 233   Status: AVAILABLE  Compressed: NO  Tag: TAG20121109T112847
        Handle: c-1316762630-20121109-00   Media: RMAN-DEFAULT-000001
  Control File Included: Ckp SCN: 2558193       Ckp time: 09-NOV-12

RMAN>
```

To test OSB's integration with RMAN, let's now delete the backups you've made with OSB. The output of the delete backup command shows that RMAN is using OSB as it's supposed to.

```
RMAN> delete backup;
allocated channel: ORA_SBT_TAPE_1
channel ORA_SBT_TAPE_1: SID=38 device type=SBT_TAPE
channel ORA_SBT_TAPE_1: Oracle Secure Backup
allocated channel: ORA_DISK_1
channel ORA_DISK_1: SID=37 device type=DISK
...

List of Backup Pieces
BP Key  BS Key  Pc# Cp# Status      Device Type Piece Name
------- ------- --- --- ----------- ----------- ----------
232     221     1   1   AVAILABLE   SBT_TAPE    amnpsbar_1_1
233     222     1   1   AVAILABLE   SBT_TAPE    c-1316762630-20121109-00

Do you really want to delete the above objects (enter YES or NO)?
```

```
Do you really want to delete the above objects (enter YES or NO)? yes
deleted backup piece
backup piece handle=amnpsbar_1_1 RECID=232 STAMP=798895453
deleted backup piece
backup piece handle=c-1316762630-20121109-00 RECID=233 STAMP=798895730
Deleted 2 objects

RMAN>
```

This recipe showed you how to make database backups with RMAN and OSB. You can also use the obtool backup command set to create an OSB-based operating system file backup. For example, the backup --go command starts a scheduled backup.

18-13. Restoring Using Oracle Secure Backup
Problem
You want to restore and recover a data file with Oracle Secure Backup and RMAN.

Solution
Once you configure the OSB sbt interface, restoring data files requires using the same RMAN commands as you would for disk-based restore operations. Here's an example showing how to restore a data file from tape and recover it using the recover command. You are missing a data file or it's corrupted, so when you start the database, you're getting error message ORA-01157 saying that a file can't be identified. Follow these steps to perform a media recovery:

1. Start the database in the mount mode.

2. Run the following query to see exactly which data files are missing and need to be restored:

    ```
    SQL> select * from v$recover_file;
    ```

3. The restore preview command shows you what RMAN backups you need for restoring a missing data file, as shown in the following example:

    ```
    RMAN> restore preview datafile 1;
    ```

4. Next, restore the data file using the restore command, and then perform a media recovery of the restored data file by using the recover command, as shown here:

    ```
    RMAN> run
          {
           allocate channel device type sbt
           parms 'env=(ob_media_family=test_mf)';
           restore datafile 1;
           recover datafile 1;
          }
    ```

    The run block shown here will restore data file 1 from tape and recover it.

5. Open the database:

    ```
    SQL> alter database open;
    ```

The recovery is successful because the database opens without any errors.

How It Works

You can perform all RMAN restore and recover commands with OSB-based tape backups. You can also use the obtool utility's restore command set to restore operating system files from an OSB backup of operating system files. The lsrestore command lets you see the restore jobs that have been submitted.

18-14. Accessing RMAN Backup Data in Oracle Secure Backup

Problem

You want to access and manage information about RMAN backups made with the OSB sbt interface.

Solution

You can use various commands in obtool to view important information about backup and restore jobs made through the OSB interface. For example, the lsjob command lists the information about backup and restore jobs for a database. Here's a typical lsjob command:

```
ob> lsjob --all

Job ID Sched time Contents State
--------------- ----------- ------------------------------ --------------
oracle/1 none database orcl (dbid=1091504057) completed successfully at 2012/08/11.11:29
oracle/1.1 none datafile backup completed successfully at 2012/08/11.11:29
oracle/2 none database orcl (dbid=1091504057) completed successfully at 2012/08/11.11:56
oracle/2.1 none datafile backup completed successfully at 2012/08/11.11:56
oracle/3 none database orcl (dbid=1091504057) completed successfully at 2012/08/11.11:57
oracle/3.1 none restore piece '06grqejs_1_1' completed successfully at 2012/08/11.11:57
ob>
```

The lsjob command shows the backup job IDs, the contents (data file backup, restore piece, and so on), and their *states*, which tell you whether they completed successfully. The lsbackup command shows what OSB backups currently exist:

```
ob> lsbackup --long

        Dataset:            prod1.ds
        Media family:       (null)
        Backup level:       full
        Priority:            2
        Privileged op:       yes
        Eligible to run:    2012/06/21.21:50:00
        Job expires:        2012/06/24.12:00:00
        Restriction:         any device
```

Use the catxcr command (again, in obtool) to obtain job transcripts, which provide detailed information such as the media family and volume information for an RMAN job. Here's a typical catxcr command:

```
ob> catxcr --noninput  --follow  --level warning  sbt/1.2
```

The example shown here disables any input requests and displays all warning and error messages for the job sbt/1.2. The `follow` option specifies that the job be monitored continually and new lines be shown as they appear. Instead of using the `catxcr` command, you can use the web tool to obtain job transcripts that contain information about RMAN jobs.

How It Works

OSB's catalog of backup metadata is maintained separately from RMAN'S recovery catalog and is directly managed by OSB. OSB's administrative server stores the backup catalog.

You can view all active OSB-related jobs by issuing the following command:

```
ob> lsj –aljrRLC
```

Issue the following command to view all jobs generated today:

```
ob> lsj -A –today
```

You can view all jobs in a date range by issuing the following command:

```
ob> lsj -AljrRLC -f 2012/11/20.02:00:00 -t 2012/11/21.00:00:00
```

Instead of using the `obtool` commands shown in the Solution section of this recipe, you can also use the OSB web tool to view OSB's backup catalog metadata.

Of course, you can also use all RMAN commands, such as the `list backup` command, to view both disk-based and tape-based backups, including those made through the OSB interface.

■ ■ ■

Performing Backup and Recovery with Enterprise Manager

This chapter shows you the basics of using Enterprise Manager (EM) for backup and recovery. EM provides you with an interface to RMAN through several screens. You can access most of RMAN's many features via these screens. The main goal of this chapter is to show you how to successfully perform fundamental backup and recovery tasks via EM. You should find the layout of Enterprise Manager fairly intuitive and easy to navigate to the desired feature. One nice aspect of EM is that the screens visually show you the various RMAN features and possible configurations. The screenshots in this chapter are based on Enterprise Manager Cloud Control 12c.

■ **Note** It is beyond the scope of this book to show you how to implement and use all the features available through EM. Oracle has a whole set of books on how to implement and use EM. You can download EM documentation from Oracle's OTN website at `http://otn.oracle.com`.

19-1. Creating a Backup

Problem

You want to use Enterprise Manager to back up your database.

Solution

Ensure you have the following in place before you begin:

- Enterprise Manager installed and running
- Target database created and running in archivelog mode
- A credentialed OS user created (usually the `oracle` operating system account)

If all of the previous items are available, then you are ready to begin with step 1.

Step 1: Log In and Navigate to Availability

Log in to Enterprise Manager, and click the Availability tab, then pick Backup and Recovery, and then choose Schedule Backup. At this point you may be prompted for a privileged user. Normally this is the sys user or a similar user that has sysdba privileges or sysbackup (new in Oracle Database 12c) privileges. Enter the proper username and password for your target database. At this point you should see a screen similar to Figure 19-1.

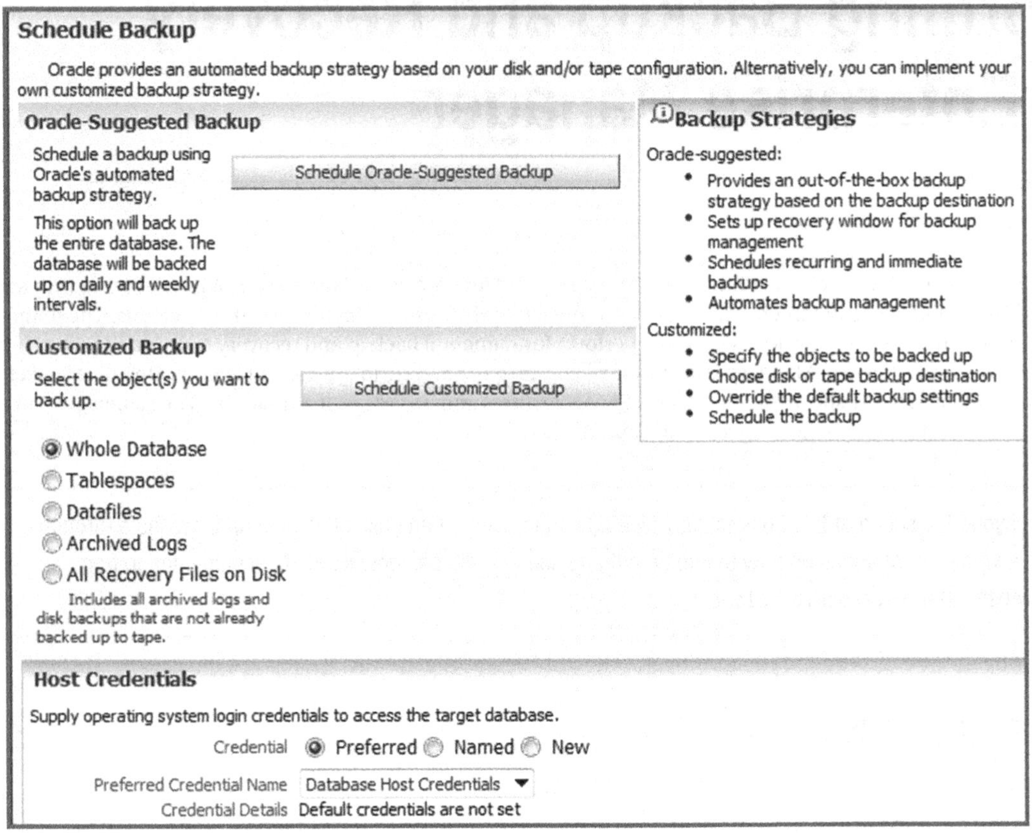

Schedule Backup

Oracle provides an automated backup strategy based on your disk and/or tape configuration. Alternatively, you can implement your own customized backup strategy.

Oracle-Suggested Backup

Schedule a backup using Oracle's automated backup strategy.

This option will back up the entire database. The database will be backed up on daily and weekly intervals.

[Schedule Oracle-Suggested Backup]

Customized Backup

Select the object(s) you want to back up.

[Schedule Customized Backup]

◉ Whole Database
◯ Tablespaces
◯ Datafiles
◯ Archived Logs
◯ All Recovery Files on Disk
Includes all archived logs and disk backups that are not already backed up to tape.

ⓘ **Backup Strategies**

Oracle-suggested:
• Provides an out-of-the-box backup strategy based on the backup destination
• Sets up recovery window for backup management
• Schedules recurring and immediate backups
• Automates backup management

Customized:
• Specify the objects to be backed up
• Choose disk or tape backup destination
• Override the default backup settings
• Schedule the backup

Host Credentials

Supply operating system login credentials to access the target database.

Credential ◉ Preferred ◯ Named ◯ New
Preferred Credential Name Database Host Credentials ▼
Credential Details Default credentials are not set

Figure 19-1. Schedule backups

At this point you also need to enter Host Credentials. This is usually an operating system user and password that has privileges on the target database. In Linux/Unix environments this is usually the oracle OS account (the account used to install the Oracle binaries). If you don't enter a valid credentialed user, an error message will be displayed and you won't be allowed to perform any backup and recovery tasks. After you have set up a credentialed user, you should be able to click on either the Schedule Oracle-Suggested Backup or the Schedule Customized Backup link. In this example we click on Schedule Customized Backup.

Step 2: Schedule a Customized Backup

You should now see a screen similar to Figure 19-2. We use default settings for this example and then click on the Next button.

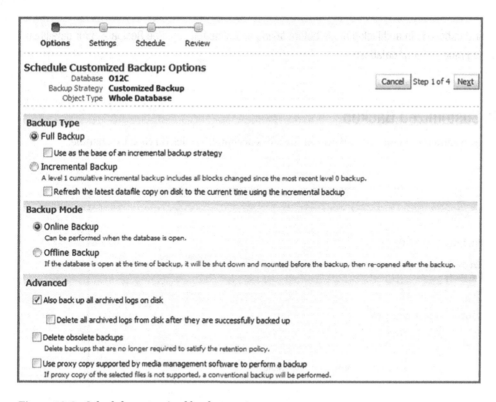

Figure 19-2. *Schedule customized backup options*

Step 3: Choose Backup Options

You should now see a screen similar to Figure 19-3. From here you set the destination to be disk or tape (tape requires that an MML be installed). You can also review the default settings. If everything looks okay, click on Next.

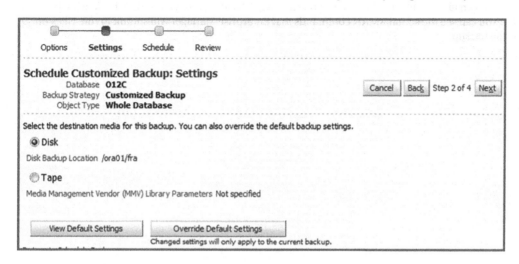

Figure 19-3. *Schedule customized backup settings*

■ **Note** Ensure that your database is in archivelog mode before taking an online backup. See Recipe 2-3 for details on how to toggle the archivelog mode of your database.

Step 4: Schedule Customized Backup

You should now see a screen similar to Figure 19-4. If everything looks acceptable, click on Next to schedule the backup.

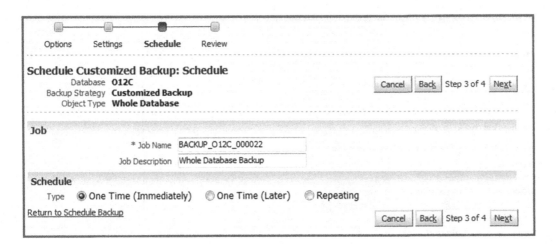

Figure 19-4. *Schedule customized backup*

Step 5: Review and Submit the Backup Job

You should now see a screen like Figure 19-5. From here you can review the details of your RMAN backup job before you submit it to run. You can see the actual RMAN commands that Enterprise Manager will submit to run. Click on Submit Job to start the backup.

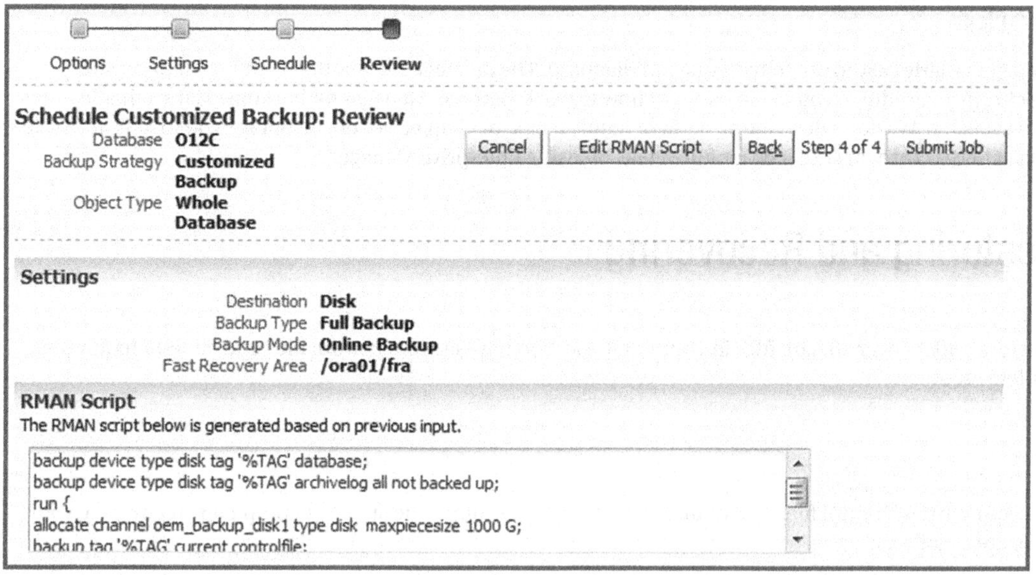

Figure 19-5. Review and submit backup job details

Step 6: Review Status of Backup Job

To review the status of backup jobs, from the main Enterprise Manager screen, choose the Availability tab, then pick Backup and Recovery, then choose Backup Reports. From here you should see your backup job in the Results section. Figure 19-6 shows the results screen for this example. From here you can click on the Backup Name and view the results of your backup job.

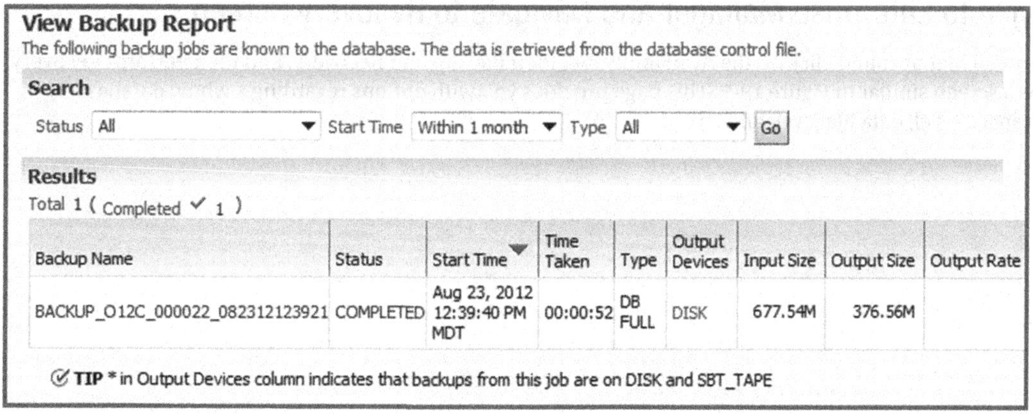

Figure 19-6. Review the results

How It Works

Enterprise Manager is fairly easy to use to back up your database. The default configuration is sufficient to get you started. This recipe just introduces you to the basics of how to use Enterprise Manager for backups. Many other features and options are available. We don't describe all of them in this recipe or chapter. We do encourage you to look at Oracle's documentation at http://otn.oracle.com for full details on using Enterprise Manager.

19-2. Restoring and Recovering

Problem

You want to restore and recover all data files in your database. You have current control files and all redo required to perform complete recovery.

Solution

Assuming that your current control files and online redo log files are intact, the steps for completely recovering your whole database are as follows:

1. Shut down your database.

2. Start up the database in mount mode.

3. Issue the restore and recovery commands.

4. Open your database for general access.

Enterprise Manager will automatically perform all of the prior steps for you. You will be presented with a series of screens from which you will provide instructions to Enterprise Manager regarding what type of restore and recovery you need it to perform.

Step 1: Log In to Enterprise Manager and Navigate to Recovery Screen

Log in to Enterprise Manager and click on the Availability tab, then Backup and Recovery, and then Perform Recovery. You should see a screen similar to Figure 19-7. This page provides you with options regarding a whole database recovery, tablespace level, data file level, and so on.

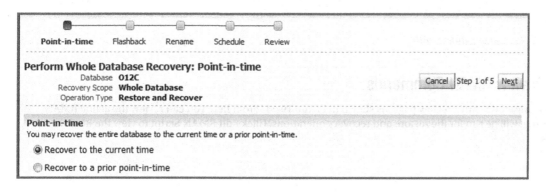

Perform Recovery

Oracle Advised Recovery

Oracle did not detect any failures.   [Advise and Recover]

User Directed Recovery

Recovery Scope Whole Database ▼   [Recover]

Operation Type ◉ Recover to the current time or a previous point-in-time
       Datafiles will be restored from the latest usable backup as required.
       ○ Restore all datafiles
         Specify Time, SCN or log sequence. The backup taken at or prior to
         that time will be used. No recovery will be performed in this operation.
       ○ Recover from previously restored datafiles

▷ **Decrypt Backups**

Host Credentials

Supply operating system login credentials to access the target database.

               Credential ◉ Preferred ○ Named ○ New
Preferred Credential Name [Database Host Credentials ▼]

Attribute	Value
UserName	oracle
Password	******
More Details	

Credential Details

ⓘ Overview

• Recover database failures as advised by Oracle
• Restore and/or recover the entire database or selected objects
• Restore files to a new location
• Recover tablespaces to a point-in-time based on a timestamp, system change number (SCN), or log sequence number
• Recover datafile data blocks that are marked as corrupted, or based on datafile block IDs or tablespace block addresses
• Flashback database or tables to a specific system change number (SCN) or timestamp

Figure 19-7. *Initiating a recovery*

For this example we'll perform a whole database restore and recover to the current time. This process is initiated by clicking on the Recover link.

Figure 19-7 also provides you with a graphical interface into the Data Recovery Advisor. If Oracle automatically detects an issue with the database, you will be allowed to click on the Advise and Recover link. See Chapter 20 for details on manually running the Data Recovery Advisory.

Step 2: Recover to Current Time

You should now see a screen similar to Figure 19-8. We accept the default value of recovering to the current time and click on Next.

Point-in-time ── Flashback ── Rename ── Schedule ── Review

Perform Whole Database Recovery: Point-in-time
        Database **O12C**
Recovery Scope **Whole Database**
Operation Type **Restore and Recover**

[Cancel] Step 1 of 5 [Next]

Point-in-time
You may recover the entire database to the current time or a prior point-in-time.
◉ Recover to the current time
○ Recover to a prior point-in-time

Figure 19-8. *Perform whole database recovery*

Step 3: Determine Where to Restore Data Files

You should now see a screen similar to Figure 19-9. In this example, we're restoring the data files to the default location. Click the Next button.

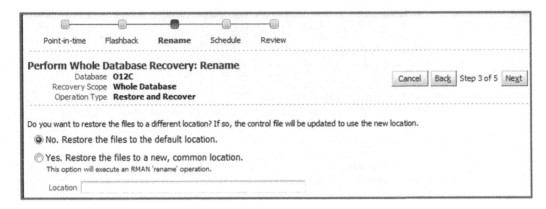

Figure 19-9. *Restoring data files to the default location*

Step 4: Schedule Job Details

As shown in Figure 19-10, you now are presented with a screen that details the job name and description. If everything looks good, click on Next.

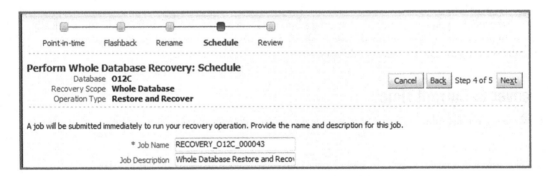

Figure 19-10. *Review schedule details*

Step 5: Review RMAN Commands

You now are presented with a review page, as shown in Figure 19-11. From here you can review the actual RMAN commands that will be run for the restore and recovery operations. Click Edit RMAN Script to view the RMAN commands.

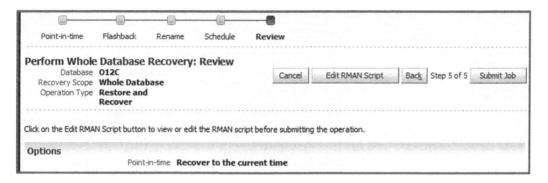

Figure 19-11. *Review RMAN script*

We recommend that you review the RMAN commands to verify that it is going to do what you want it to do. Here are the actual RMAN commands that will be run in this recipe:

```
run {
restore database;
recover database;
}
```

Click on Submit Job to initiate the restore and recover operation. RMAN will shut down your database and place it in mount mode before it runs the prior commands.

Step 6: View the Job Status

The next screen (Figure 19-12) indicates the job was submitted successfully. Click on View Job to view the job details.

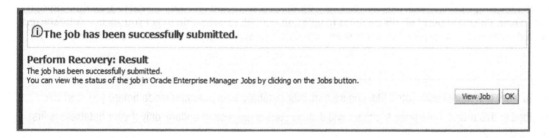

Figure 19-12. *View submitted job status*

Step 7: Review the Status of Restore and Recovery

If everything goes well, you should see a screen similar to Figure 19-13. From this screen you can click on the status of each step of the job to view the result.

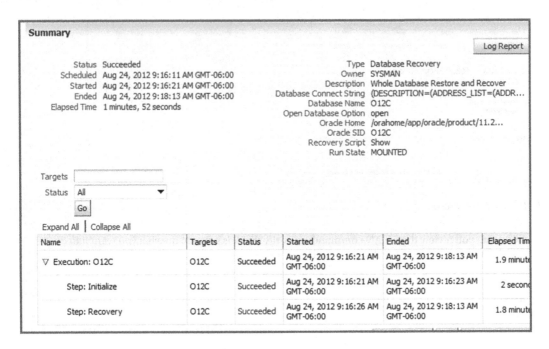

Figure 19-13. *Viewing the status of the job operation*

How It Works

In this example, we restored and recovered the entire database. We used the current control file and had all redo required to recover the data files up to the last transaction that was committed in the database. You can use Enterprise Manager to perform almost every restore and recovery scenario. The actual screens used in a restore and recovery operation will vary by quite a bit depending on the type of failure and your backup strategy.

It is beyond the scope of this book to describe every different restore and recovery scenario available through Enterprise Manager. The main point of this recipe is to give you enough information to get you successfully started with restore and recovery. Enterprise Manager is pretty good at displaying what options are available and how to use them.

■ **Note** If you want to restore your control file, ensure that your database is in nomount mode before you start the process described in this recipe. Enterprise Manager will display control file restore options only if your database is first placed in nomount mode.

19-3. Performing Routine RMAN Maintenance Tasks

Problem

You want to perform routine RMAN maintenance tasks, such as cross-checking or deleting obsolete backups.

Solution

From the main EM screen, click on Availability, then Backup and Recovery, and then Manage Current Backups. At this point you may be asked for SYS login credentials; if so, enter the username and password of a user with sysdba privileges. You should see a screen similar to Figure 19-14. From this screen, you can perform RMAN maintenance tasks.

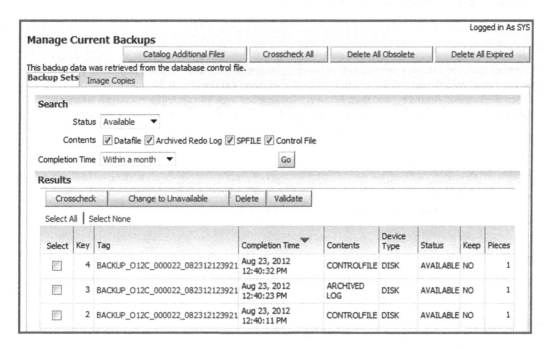

Figure 19-14. Managing current backups

How It Works

The Manage Current Backups screen shown in Figure 19-14 allows you to perform tasks such as:

- Cross-checking files
- Deleting obsolete and expired files
- Changing the status of backups
- Validating backup sets
- Cataloging files

The options on the Manage Current Backups screen are fairly self-explanatory. You can switch back and forth between managing image copies and backup sets by clicking either the Backup Sets tab or the Image Copies tab. You can also view backups by a date range. For example, you can use the Completion Time drop-down list to work with just a subset of your backup files.

The Manage Current Backups screen retrieves the data that it displays about backups from the control file or from the recovery catalog (if you are using one). Therefore, you will see information for all RMAN backups whether or not a given backup was initiated from Enterprise Manager.

19-4. Configuring a Recovery Catalog
Problem

You want to configure a recovery catalog using Enterprise Manager.

Solution

First you need to create another database to contain the recovery catalog (see Chapter 6 for details). Once your recovery catalog database has been created, you can use EM to configure a recovery catalog. From the main EM screen click on Availability, then Backup and Recovery, and then Recovery Catalog Settings. You should see a screen similar to Figure 19-15. Click on the Use Recovery Catalog Button and then Add Recovery Catalog to set up a catalog.

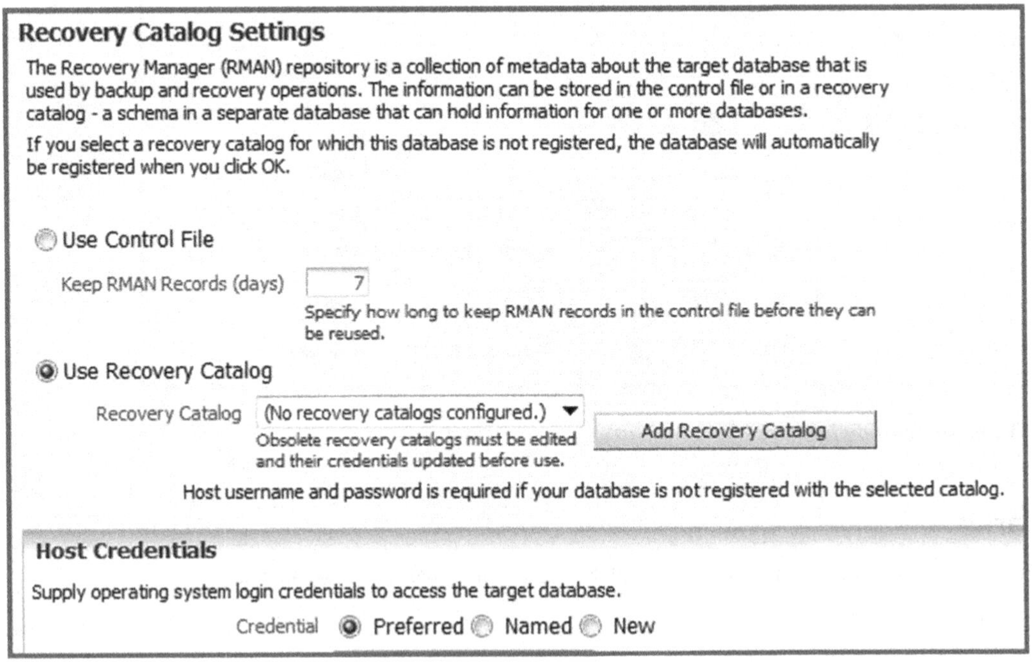

Figure 19-15. *Recovery catalog settings*

You should now see a screen similar to Figure 19-16. Fill in the details for your environment and click on Next.

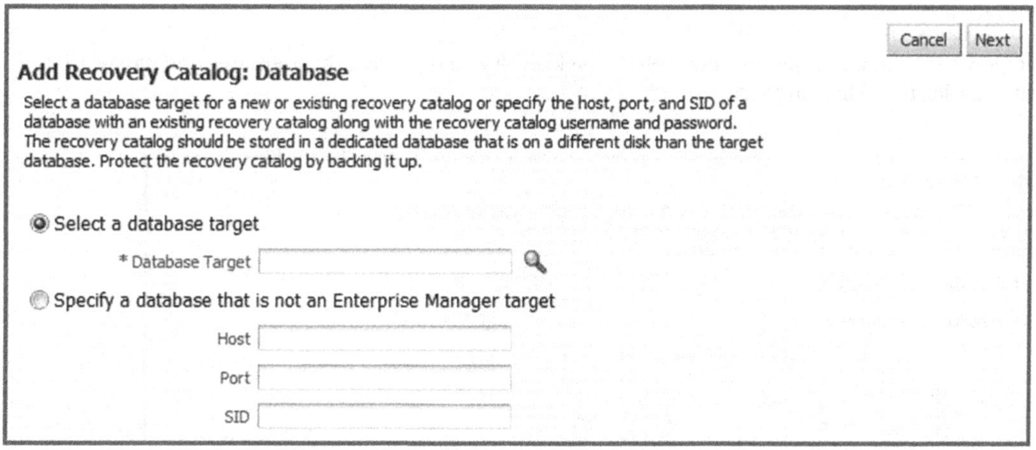

Figure 19-16. *Adding a recovery catalog*

As shown in Figure 19-17, you should now see a screen asking for host and database credentials. Fill in the information for your environment and click on Next.

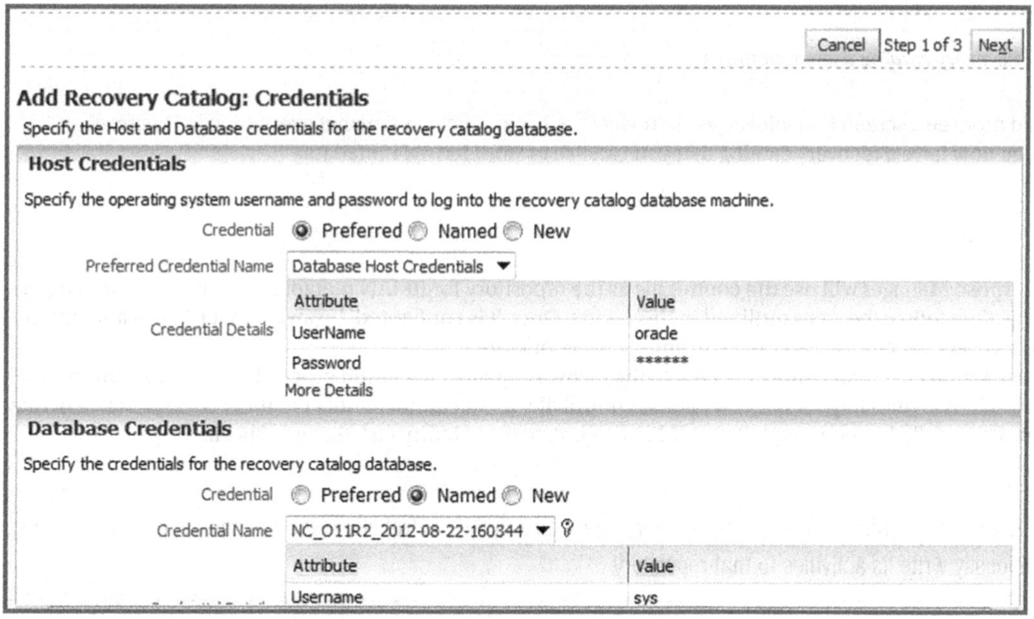

Figure 19-17. *Add host and database credentials*

■ **Tip** See Recipe 6-1 for details on configuring a recovery catalog schema.

You should now see a screen similar to Figure 19-18. Click on New and provide the username and password of the recovery catalog user, then click on Next.

Add Recovery Catalog: User
Specify an existing recovery catalog user that will be used to connect to the recovery catalog database during backup and recovery operations. The recovery catalog user will be granted the necessary roles and privileges, if needed, to create and access the recovery catalog.

Recovery Catalog User Credentials
Specify the recovery catalog user credentials.

Credential	⦿ Preferred ⦿ Named ◉ New
* Username	rcat
* Password	••••••
* Confirm Password	••••••
Role	NORMAL ▼
	☑ Save As NC_O11R2_2012-08-24-132433
	☐ Set As Preferred Credentials
	Test

Cancel   Back   Step 2 of 3   Next

Figure 19-18. *Recovery catalog user credentials*

You should now see a screen that allows you to review the setup. Click on Finish if everything looks correct. If successful, you now have a recovery catalog that you can use to store RMAN metadata.

How It Works

By default, Enterprise Manager will use the control file as the repository for RMAN metadata. If you want EM to use a recovery catalog, then follow the steps outlined in this recipe. Once it is configured, be aware that EM will attempt to connect to the recovery catalog for every backup and recovery operation.

If Enterprise Manager cannot connect RMAN to the recovery catalog, it will still proceed with the operation, and RMAN will record its activities in your target database control file. If EM cannot connect to the recovery catalog, it may report an operation as failed, even though it was able to complete the primary task that you specified.

■ **Note** RMAN always records its backup and recovery operations in the control file. If you are using a recovery catalog, RMAN will additionally write its activities to that repository.

19-5. Configuring the Recovery Settings

Problem

You want to use Enterprise Manager to configure various recovery features, such as the fast recovery area.

Solution

From the main EM screen click on Availability, then Backup and Recovery, and then Recovery Settings. You should see a screen similar to what is shown in Figure 19-19 (you may have to scroll down a bit to see this portion of the screen). From this screen, you can specify a location and size for your target database fast recovery area.

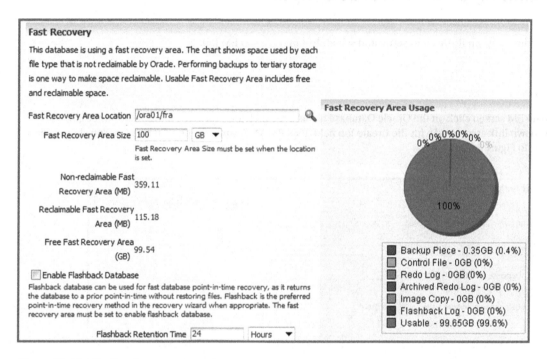

Figure 19-19. *Configuring recovery settings*

How It Works

The recovery settings screen actually allows you configure a wide variety of recovery features, such as:

- Fast recovery area
- Mean time to recovery
- Archive log destination and format
- Supplemental logging
- Flashback database

This provides you with a visual way to manage these various features. Most of the options here are fairly intuitive and don't require any extra explanation. The main point here is to make you aware that you can manage these features all from one screen.

■ **Tip** See Chapter 3 for complete details on fast recovery area internals. See Chapter 13 for instructions on how to perform flashback recovery.

19-6. Running Custom RMAN Scripts
Problem
You want to write a custom RMAN and script and schedule it to run as an EM job.

Solution
From the main EM screen click on the Oracle Database tab and the pick Job Activity. On the far bottom right, click on the drop-down link associated with the Create Job field. Pick RMAN Script and then click on Go. You should see a screen similar to Figure 19-20.

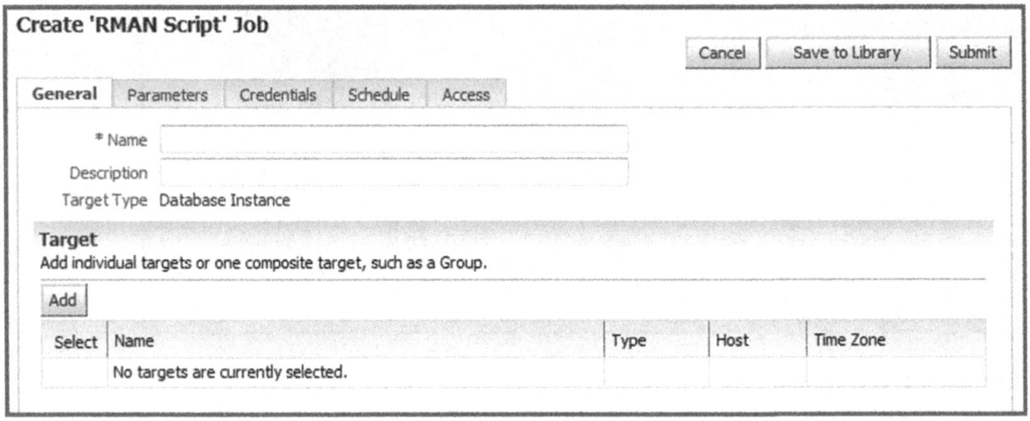

Create 'RMAN Script' Job

| | | | | Cancel | Save to Library | Submit |

General | Parameters | Credentials | Schedule | Access

* Name

Description

Target Type Database Instance

Target
Add individual targets or one composite target, such as a Group.

Add

Select	Name	Type	Host	Time Zone
	No targets are currently selected.			

Figure 19-20. *Create RMAN script*

Fill in a name and description for your job. You will also need to specify your target database information. To do this, click the Add button to select your database as the target of this job.

Now click on the Parameters tab. You should see a screen like Figure 19-21. Here is where you enter your special RMAN script.

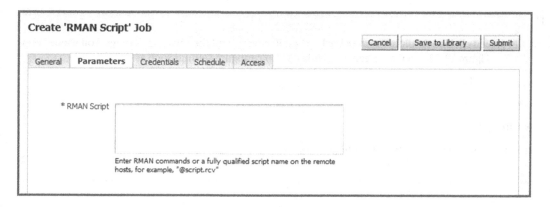

Figure 19-21. *Create special RMAN script*

After you've entered the RMAN script, click on the Credentials tab and make sure you fill in the host and database credentials for your environment. You can now click on Submit to have the job run immediately. If you want the job to run a specific time, then enter those details in the Schedule section.

How It Works

It's fairly easy to schedule custom RMAN scripts through Enterprise Manager. You need to navigate to the appropriate screens, create the custom RMAN job, and then schedule the job to be run.

You can view job information from the Job Activity screen or you can also query the Enterprise Manager repository directly. To view job information from SQL*Plus, connect as the repository owner (usually named sysman), and query the MGMT_JOB table:

```
SQL> connect sysman/<your password>
SQL> select job_name, job_description from mgmt_job;
```

Here is some sample output:

```
JOB_NAME                          JOB_DESCRIPTION
------------------------------    ----------------------------------------------------
RECOVERY_012C_000043              Whole Database Restore and Recover
BACKUP_012C_000022                Whole Database Backup
RMAN SCRIPT                       RMAN script
```

19-7. Configuring Backup Settings
Problem

You want to configure backup settings, such as degree of parallelism, backup location, default backup type, and MML settings.

Solution

From the main EM screen click on Availability, then Backup and Recovery, and then Backup Settings. You should now see a screen similar to Figure 19-22. On this screen, it is fairly easy to configure settings such as:

- Degree of backup and restore parallelism

- Backup location

- Backup type

- Tape and media management layer configuration

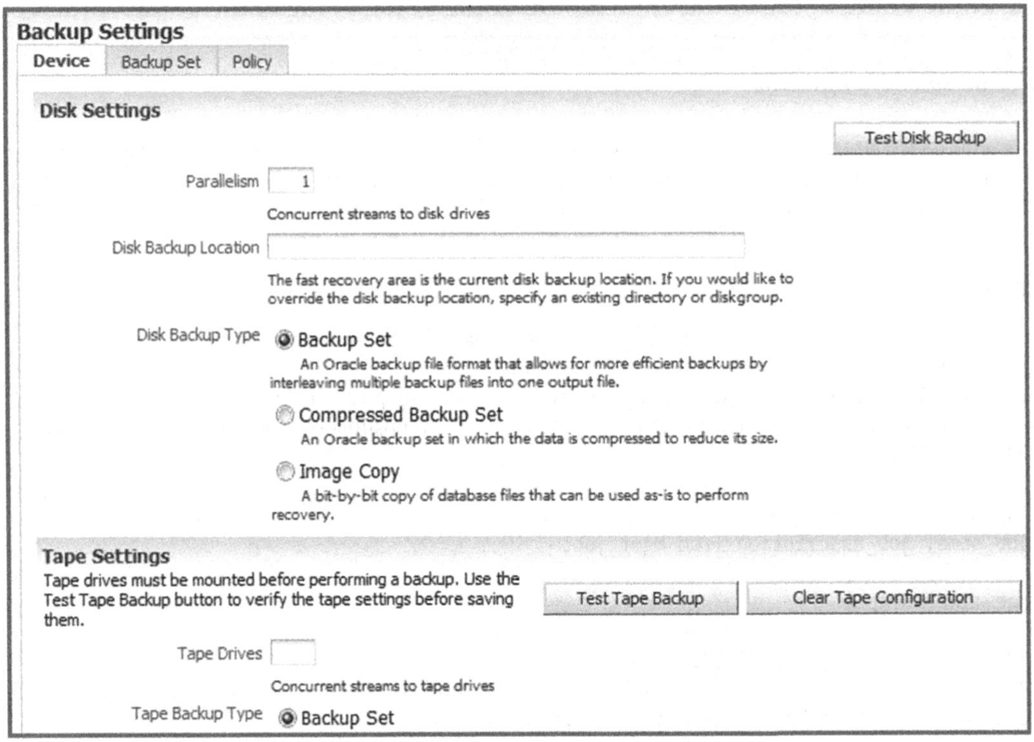

Figure 19-22. *Viewing the backup settings*

How It Works

From the screen displayed in Figure 19-22, you can perform tasks such as enabling multiple degrees of parallelism for RMAN channels, setting the backup location on disk, specifying the default backup type (backup set, compressed, or image copy), and specifying the MML settings.

You can query backup setting details from the EM repository owner's (usually the sysman schema) MGMT_BACKUP_CONFIGURATION table, as shown here:

```
SQL> connect sysman/<your password>
SQL> select use_disk, disk_location, disk_parallelism from mgmt_backup_configuration;
```

Here is some sample output:

```
USE_ DISK_LOCATION          DISK_PARALLELISM
---- -------------------- ----------------
YES  /ora02/O12R2/rman                   3
```

19-8. Configuring Backup Policies
Problem

You want to configure your RMAN auto-backup control file and retention policies.

Solution

From the main EM screen navigate to Availability, then Backup and Recovery, and then Backup Settings. Now click on the Policy tab. You should now see a screen similar to Figure 19-23. On this screen, you can configure RMAN policies, such as the following:

- Backing up the control file and server initialization file automatically

- Not backing up files that haven't changed since the previous backup

- Enabling block change tracking

- Excluding tablespaces from backups

- Establishing retention policies

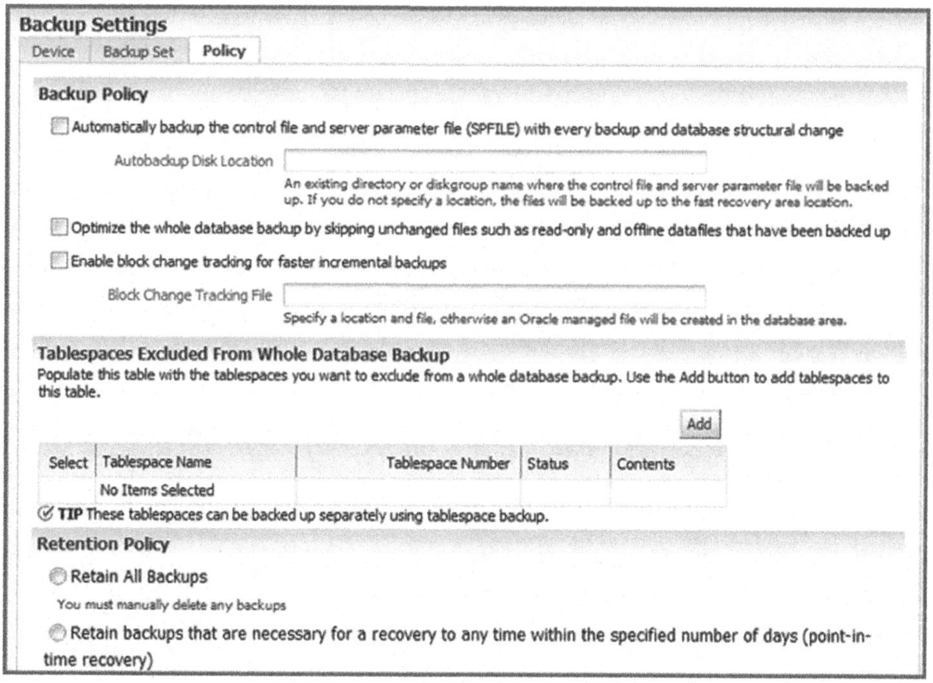

Figure 19-23. *Setting up backup policies*

How It Works

Enterprise Manager allows you to perform RMAN tasks such as enabling the automatic backup of your control file, backup optimization, and retention polices. The Backup Policy screen provides an easy point-and-click interface for configuring your RMAN backup policies. This screen provides you a summary of the various features and possible configurations.

CHAPTER 20

■ ■ ■

Using the Data Recovery Advisor

If your database experiences a failure and the subsequent stress causes you to have a heart attack, hopefully you'll have time to call for an emergency medical technician (EMT) or paramedic to assist you with your heart problems. If your heart goes into ventricular fibrillation, the EMT or the paramedic has the option of using an automatic defibrillator machine to shock you back to normal.

Interestingly, an EMT doesn't have the same options that a paramedic has when operating a defibrillator. The EMT is limited to pushing the power button followed by the analyze button. The defibrillator then generates a message from the machine recommending whether to press the shock button. If the machine recommends a shock, then the EMT is free to give you a good zap.

The paramedic typically has more training and experience than an EMT. The paramedic has the option of running the defibrillator in manual mode, which means she can instruct the machine when to perform certain actions. The difference between an EMT and a paramedic in this situation is who is calling the shots. For an EMT, the defibrillator machine instructs him what to do; the machine is in charge. For a paramedic, it's the other way around. The paramedic can instruct the machine when to perform certain actions.

Assuming either the EMT or the paramedic saves you (if they don't, stop here), you can now return to trying to resolve the issue with your database. The Data Recovery Advisor tool was added to RMAN in Oracle Database 11*g*. This tool automatically detects problems with your database that may require you to perform restore and recovery operations. The Data Recovery Advisor will list failures, give you advice on how to resolve issues, and allow you to push the button that instructs RMAN to run the commands required to fix the problem.

When you use the Data Recovery Advisor, it helps to have a combination of EMT (junior DBA) and paramedic (senior DBA) skills. At an entry level, you should be trained in backup and recovery concepts and know how to use RMAN to restore and recover your database.

On a higher level, you also want to be able to determine whether the advice you're getting from the tool will correctly resolve the failure. You want the option of manually overriding anything the tool recommends. You might choose to override the tool because of training, prior experience with a particular type of failure, or knowledge about your environment.

The Data Recovery Advisor tool can assist with diagnosing media failures, making recommendations, and providing the RMAN commands to resolve the problem. You can use the Data Recovery Advisor from either the RMAN command line or Enterprise Manager. This chapter focuses on running the Data Recovery Advisor from the RMAN command line. There are four RMAN commands associated with the Data Recovery Advisor:

- `list failure`
- `advise failure`
- `repair failure`
- `change failure`

The first several recipes in this chapter discuss listing, advising, and repairing failures. The last recipe in this chapter describes how to change the status of a failure.

20-1. Listing Failures

Problem

You suspect you have a media failure in your database. You want to use the Data Recovery Advisor to list media failures.

Solution

Use the list failure command as shown here:

```
RMAN> list failure;
```

Here is some sample output:

```
List of Database Failures
==========================
```

Failure ID	Priority	Status	Time Detected	Summary
62	HIGH	OPEN	15-JUL-12	One or more non-system data files are missing

The prior output indicates that the database has at least one data file that is missing. At this point you should next run the advise failure command, which is covered in Recipe 20-2.

How It Works

When using the Data Recovery Advisor, list failure is the first command you should run. This will alert you to any problems with database files such as control files, data files, and online redo logs.

The Data Recovery Advisor stores its information outside the database in the Automatic Diagnostic Repository (ADR). This allows you to run the list failure command even when your database is started in nomount mode and is also not dependent on the availability of the recovery catalog (if using one). You can determine the location of the base directory for the ADR by viewing the diagnostic_dest initialization parameter:

```
SQL> show parameter diagnostic_dest
```

Here is some sample output:

NAME	TYPE	VALUE
diagnostic_dest	string	/u01/app/oracle

You can view the names and values of directories in the ADR with this query:

```
SQL> select name, value from v$diag_info;
```

If you suspect there is a problem with your database and the Data Recovery Advisor is not reporting a failure, you can proactively initiate a database health check by running the following RMAN command:

```
RMAN> validate database;
```

If a failure is detected, it will be recorded in the ADR. Once a failure is recorded in the ADR, then you can use the `advise failure` and `repair failure` commands to resolve the issue.

Failures with a `critical` status usually make your database unavailable and are typically diagnosed when attempting to start the database. For example, a missing control file would be considered a `critical` failure. A high failure is an issue that makes your database partially unavailable, such as a damaged or missing non-system data file.

If you want to see more detail about a given failure, then use the `list failure ... detail` command. In this example, we are listing more details on a failure with an ID of 62:

```
RMAN> list failure 62 detail;
```

Here is some sample output:

```
Database Role: PRIMARY

List of Database Failures
=========================

Failure ID Priority Status    Time Detected Summary
---------- -------- --------- ------------- -------
62         HIGH     OPEN      15-JUL-12     One or more non-system
                                            data files are missing
  Impact: See impact for individual child failures
  List of child failures for parent failure ID 62
  Failure ID Priority Status    Time Detected Summary
  ---------- -------- --------- ------------- -------
  445        HIGH     OPEN      15-JUL-12     Data file 4:
'/u01/dbfile/o12c/users01.dbf' is missing
    Impact: Some objects in tablespace USERS might be unavailable
```

If you want to see all failures that have been resolved and closed, then use the `closed` clause:

```
RMAN> list failure closed;
```

Table 20-1 describes the types of failures that can be reported from the `list failure` command.

Table 20-1. *Data Recovery Advisor List Failure Options*

Failure Type	Description
all	Lists all failures
critical	Lists only critical failures with an open status
high	Lists only high-priority failures with an open status
low	Lists only low-priority failures with an open status
closed	Lists failures with a closed status
exclude failure	Excludes failures by a specified failure number
detail	Provides verbose description of the failure

20-2. Getting Advice

Problem

You've experienced a media failure. You want to get advice from the Data Recovery Advisor about how to restore and recover your database.

Solution

First use the `list failure` command to display all failures (see Recipe 20-1 for details). If you have only one failure associated with your database, then you can run the `advise failure` command without any parameters:

```
RMAN> advise failure;
```

The output will vary quite a bit depending on the failure. Here's a partial snippet of the output for a media failure that has occurred with a data file in the users tablespace:

```
Mandatory Manual Actions
========================
no manual actions available

Optional Manual Actions
=======================
1. If file /u01/dbfile/o12c/users01.dbf was unintentionally renamed or moved, restore it

Automated Repair Options
========================
Option Repair Description
------ ------------------
1      Restore and recover data file 4
  Strategy: The repair includes complete media recovery with no data loss
  Repair script: /u01/app/oracle/diag/rdbms/o12c/o12c/hm/reco_1129363368.hm
```

How It Works

The `advise failure` command gives advice about how to recover from potential problems detected by the Data Recovery Advisor. If you have multiple failures with your database, then you can directly specify the failure ID to get advice on a given failure. You obtain the failure ID by viewing the output of the `list failure` command. This example gets advice on the failure ID of 62:

```
RMAN> advise failure 62;
```

If you have a combination of `critical`, `high`, and `low` failures, you must use the `advise failure` command to obtain advice about `critical` failures before you can get advice about lower-priority failures. You can get specific advice about the priority of failure by specifying one of the following keywords: `all`, `critical`, `high`, or `low`. This example displays advice about just the critical errors:

```
RMAN> advise failure critical;
```

Depending on your situation, the advise failure output will contain one or both of the following sections:

- Manual Checklist

- Automated Repair Options

The Manual Checklist section gives you advice for manually resolving the issue. For example, you may not have the required backups to restore a file, so the advice might be to find a copy of the file and restore it manually.

The Automated Repair Options section provides you with RMAN commands that you can use to resolve the problem. Table 20-2 describes the columns contained in the Automated Repair Options output.

Table 20-2. *Descriptions of Automated Repair Options*

Column	Description
Option	An identifying number for a repair operation
Strategy	A complete recovery strategy (no data loss) or an incomplete recovery (data loss) strategy
Repair Description	A brief description of the proposed repair operation
Repair Script	A script that contains the proposed commands to resolve the problem

The Automated Repair Options section will list the location and name of a repair script that contains RMAN commands to resolve the problem. At this point, you may want to open another terminal session and inspect the contents of the repair script (with a text editor such as vi or Notepad). Here is some sample content for this example:

```
# restore and recover datafile
restore ( datafile 4 );
recover datafile 4;
sql 'alter database datafile 4 online';
```

By analyzing the script you can gain a greater understanding of the failure and how RMAN intends to resolve the problem. If you want RMAN to automatically repair the failure, then run the repair failure command as described in Recipe 20-3.

20-3. Repairing Failures

Problem

You've experienced a media failure. You want to use the Data Recovery Advisor to perform a restore and recovery.

Solution

We recommend that you always run the following RMAN commands in this order (without exiting RMAN between each command):

1. list failure

2. advise failure

3. repair failure

By running list failure and advise failure, you will gain an understanding as to what the problem is and how to fix it. You can use the repair failure command to run the repair script generated by the Data Recovery Advisor:

```
RMAN> repair failure;
```

Here is a partial listing of the output for this example:

```
Strategy: The repair includes complete media recovery with no data loss
Repair script: /u01/app/oracle/diag/rdbms/o12c/o12c/hm/reco_1800500206.hm

contents of repair script:
   # restore and recover datafile
   restore ( datafile 4 );
   recover datafile 4;
   sql 'alter database datafile 4 online';
```

You will be prompted to specify whether you want to run the repair script:

```
Do you really want to execute the above repair (enter YES or NO)?
```

If you're satisfied with the repair script commands, then enter YES and hit Enter. The output will vary based on the type of restore and recovery that is performed. Here's a partial snippet of the output of restoring and recovering just one data file:

```
channel ORA_DISK_1: piece handle=/u01/app/oracle/product/12.1.0.1/db_1/dbs/05ng5lcb_1_1
tag=TAG20120715T152811
channel ORA_DISK_1: restored backup piece 1
Finished restore at 15-JUL-12
Starting recover at 15-JUL-12
using channel ORA_DISK_1
starting media recovery
media recovery complete, elapsed time: 00:00:01
Finished recover at 15-JUL-12
sql statement: alter database datafile 4 online
repair failure complete
```

The prior output indicates RMAN successfully repaired the failure. You can validate that the failure has been fixed by running list failure:

```
RMAN> list failure;
no failures found that match specification
```

How It Works

We recommend that you run the repair failure command only after you have run the list failure and advise failure commands. Repairing the problem should be the last step performed. You should use the Data Recovery Advisor to repair failures only after you thoroughly understand what the failure is and what commands will be run to repair the failure.

If you want to inspect what the repair failure command will do without actually running the commands, then use the preview clause:

```
RMAN> repair failure preview;
```

The preview clause instructs RMAN to display only the commands that it recommends be run to resolve the failure. If you want to spool the output of a preview command to a file, then use the spool log command:

```
RMAN> spool log to rmanout.txt;
RMAN> repair failure preview;
RMAN> spool log off;
```

If you don't want to be prompted during a repair session, then use the noprompt clause:

```
RMAN> repair failure noprompt;
```

■ **Caution**   Use the noprompt clause with caution. We recommend you use this only when you're sure you know exactly what the repair failure command will execute.

Oracle has added several views related to the Data Recovery Advisor tool. You can query these views for more details regarding failures. Table 20-3 lists the Data Recovery Advisor related views and their descriptions.

Table 20-3. *Data Recovery Advisor Related Views*

Data Recovery Advisor View	Description
V$IR_FAILURE	Displays information regarding failure
V$IR_FAILURE_SET	Provides information on advice associated with the failure
V$IR_MANUAL_CHECKLIST	Provides details on how to resolve the problem
V$IR_REPAIR	Provides information regarding the repair script

20-4. Changing Failure Status
Problem

You have a failure that is listed with a high priority. However, you know that the failure isn't that critical for your particular database. You want to use the Data Recovery Advisor to change the priority of a failure from high to low.

Solution

Use the change failure command to alter the priority of a failure. In this example, we have a missing data file that belongs to a noncritical tablespace. First, obtain the failure priority via the list failure command:

```
RMAN> list failure;
```

Here is some sample output:

```
Database Role: PRIMARY
List of Database Failures
=========================
Failure ID Priority Status    Time Detected Summary
---------- -------- --------- ------------- -------
62         HIGH     OPEN      15-JUL-12     One or more non-system
                                            data files are missing
```

Second, change the priority from high to low with the change failure command:

```
RMAN> change failure 62 priority low;
```

You will be prompted to confirm that you really do want to change the priority:

```
Do you really want to change the above failures (enter YES or NO)?
```

If you do want to change the priority, then type YES, and hit the Enter key. If you run the list failure command again, you'll see that the priority has now been changed to low:

```
RMAN> list failure low;
```

Here is some sample output:

```
Failure ID Priority Status    Time Detected Summary
---------- -------- --------- ------------- -------
62         LOW      OPEN      15-JUL-12     One or more non-system
                                            data files are missing
```

How It Works

For most problems, you should never have to change the priority or status of a failure. However, sometimes you may want to change the status or priority of a failure. In those cases, you can use the change failure command. For example, you may have a data file missing that is in a tablespace that you know is not being used. In that case, you can change the priority to low.

The priority of a failure can be one of the following: critical, high, or low. The status of failure can be open or closed.

If you fix a problem manually without using the repair failure command, the Data Recovery Advisor will detect that the problem has been resolved when the next list failure command is issued. At that time, the Data Recovery Advisor will change the status of any fixed failures to closed.

If you want to manually change the status of a failure from open to closed, then you can use the closed clause as shown here:

```
RMAN> change failure 62 closed;
```

Table 20-4 lists all the options of the change failure command.

Table 20-4. *Options of Change Failure*

Option	Description
all	Changes all failures with an open status
critical	Changes all failures with a critical status
high	Changes all failures with a high status
low	Changes all failures with a low status
failure number	Changes a specific failure
exclude failure <failure number>	Excludes a failure from the operation
closed	Changes the status to closed
priority high	Changes the priority to high
priority low	Changes the priority to low

CHAPTER 21

■ ■ ■

Using RMAN on Windows

Microsoft Windows has always been a favorite platform for many people and organizations—for personal and business applications including Oracle Database. A sizable number of production databases, estimated at about 25 percent by Oracle Corporation, run on Windows. Needless to say, where there is a production Oracle Database, there is a need to protect it, and there is a place for RMAN. That's the purpose of this chapter: to help you put the power of RMAN to the most effective use on the Windows platform.

We will start with a general discussion on Oracle on Windows. Since we have covered some of the Windows-related issues regarding RMAN in other chapters, you may already be familiar with them. In this chapter, instead of repeating the content applicable for the Windows environment, we will point out the relevant recipes in other chapters and mention only the differences or important points to consider.

21-1. Understanding Oracle Database Architecture on Windows
Problem

You want to understand the Oracle Database architecture on the Windows platform, especially how it differs from the architecture on Unix-based systems.

Solution

To begin understanding how to use Oracle on Windows, it's helpful to review the Oracle architecture in general. Most people look at Oracle on Unix as the general case, and we do the same in this book. One of the key differences between Oracle on Unix and Oracle on Windows is that Oracle on Windows is organized into threads rather than processes.

The Oracle Database Instance

An Oracle instance under Windows is a collection of threads such as the system monitor (SMON), the process monitor (PMON), the database writer (DBWn), and so on, and a bunch of memory areas, such as a system global area (SGA) and a program global area (PGA). The SGA is further broken into the database buffer cache, shared pool, and log buffer memory areas. Figure 21-1 shows the memory structures and threads for the Oracle Database instance on Windows.

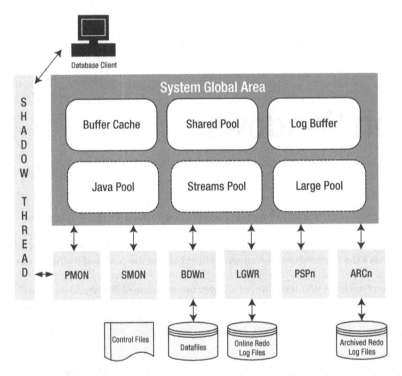

Figure 21-1. *Oracle Database instance architecture on Windows*

The *buffer cache* is a memory area to hold the blocks of the table data retrieved from the database data files. When the user requests a piece of data from a table, the Oracle database gets it from the disk and places it in the buffer cache. The data is then served from the buffer cache to the user. If another user requests the same data, the database gets it from the buffer cache instead of from the disk again.

When the user sessions make changes to the database, the pre-change and post-change images of the data are written to a memory area called the *log buffer*. When the user commits, the contents of the log buffer are written to the disk to special files called *online redo log files*. If the instance crashes, all the memory areas disappear. By examining the online redo log files, the database can find out which operations have been successful and which ones need to be discarded. The log buffer contents are flushed to the online redo log files by a process known as the *log writer* (LGWR). The flushing occurs when any one of the following happens:

- The log buffer is one-third full.

- It has been three seconds since the last flush.

- The log buffer is 1MB full.

- A session commits.

- The checkpoint occurs.

When a user changes the data, the change occurs in the buffer cache only, not on the disk. This way, the slowest operation—the physical I/O to the disk—does not become the bottleneck as the database changes. The changed blocks in the buffer cache—known as dirty blocks—are written to the data files by a process known as the data buffer writer (DBWn). There can be more than one DBWn process; hence, they are named DBW0, DBW1, and so on. On Windows, however, there is no need to define multiple DBWn processes, because the I/O is asynchronous anyway and one database writer is enough. The event of flushing data from the cache to the data files is called checkpointing.

The third most important memory area is called *shared pool*, which houses several types of memory areas, such as the library cache and the row cache. The *library cache* is a shared memory area that holds the parsed object definition as well as SQL queries. The *row cache* is an area that holds information on data dictionary objects.

In addition, the instance may also have some optional memory areas, such as *large pool*, *Java pool*, and *streams pool* (Oracle Database 10g Release 2 and newer). These areas appear in Figure 21-1 in dotted boxes.

Now let's turn to the threads. In addition to the threads described already—DBWn and LGWR—there are several other threads to know and understand. PMON monitors all other processes. SMON performs process cleanups, among other things. If the database is in archivelog mode, the online redo log files are written to a special type of file called *archived redo log files* before they are overwritten. The thread that writes the online redo log files to the archived redo log files is called the *archiver* (ARCn). There can be more than one archiver process; hence, they are named ARC0, ARC1, and so on.

■ **Note**   The Oracle instance is built around processes in Unix and Linux, and around threads in Windows. All the threads are under the same Windows process called ORACLE.EXE, the main Oracle Database executable. You will learn later in this recipe the significance of Oracle on Windows being designed the way that it is. See the section "Why Threads on Windows?" under How It Works.

When a client connects to the database, it connects to a shadow thread, which in turn connects to the database instance, or more specifically the PMON thread. The client process communicates to the shadow thread only, and the shadow thread does all the work. This is why the Oracle architecture is sometimes called a *two-task* architecture.

How It Works

Unlike Unix, where the Oracle instance starts as a number of processes, on Windows the Oracle database starts as a service. A *service* allows the database instance to start without a user being logged in. A service is conceptually similar to, though not quite the same as, a Unix daemon.

So, an Oracle instance consists of two parts: the Windows service and the instance itself. The service has to start first before you can connect to it and start the instance. Contrast this with Unix, where you make a connection first to start the instance. When you install the Oracle database software, this service is automatically created. To check for the service, select Start ➤ Programs ➤ Administrative Tools ➤ Services. This opens the main services screen. Figure 21-2 shows part of this screen.

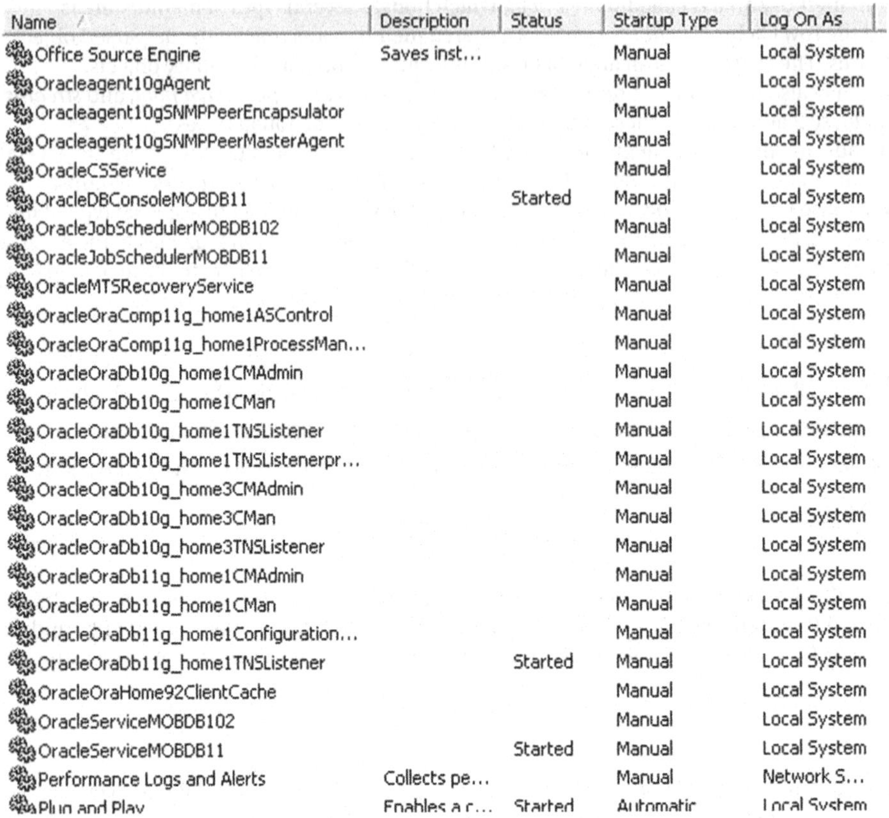

Name	Description	Status	Startup Type	Log On As
Office Source Engine	Saves inst...		Manual	Local System
Oracleagent10gAgent			Manual	Local System
Oracleagent10gSNMPPeerEncapsulator			Manual	Local System
Oracleagent10gSNMPPeerMasterAgent			Manual	Local System
OracleCSService			Manual	Local System
OracleDBConsoleMOBDB11		Started	Manual	Local System
OracleJobSchedulerMOBDB102			Manual	Local System
OracleJobSchedulerMOBDB11			Manual	Local System
OracleMTSRecoveryService			Manual	Local System
OracleOraComp11g_home1ASControl			Manual	Local System
OracleOraComp11g_home1ProcessMan...			Manual	Local System
OracleOraDb10g_home1CMAdmin			Manual	Local System
OracleOraDb10g_home1CMan			Manual	Local System
OracleOraDb10g_home1TNSListener			Manual	Local System
OracleOraDb10g_home1TNSListenerpr...			Manual	Local System
OracleOraDb10g_home3CMAdmin			Manual	Local System
OracleOraDb10g_home3CMan			Manual	Local System
OracleOraDb10g_home3TNSListener			Manual	Local System
OracleOraDb11g_home1CMAdmin			Manual	Local System
OracleOraDb11g_home1CMan			Manual	Local System
OracleOraDb11g_home1Configuration...			Manual	Local System
OracleOraDb11g_home1TNSListener		Started	Manual	Local System
OracleOraHome92ClientCache			Manual	Local System
OracleServiceMOBDB102			Manual	Local System
OracleServiceMOBDB11		Started	Manual	Local System
Performance Logs and Alerts	Collects pe...		Manual	Network S...
Plug and Play	Enables a c...	Started	Automatic	Local System

Figure 21-2. The Windows services screen

This screen shows the name of the various services on the left side. Note the service names related to Oracle; they all start with the word *Oracle*. In particular, note the service OracleServiceMOBDB11, which is the service for the database instance named MOBDB11. When you install Oracle, this service is created, and the start-up property is set to Automatic; that is, the service starts automatically when Windows starts. This functionally is similar to the placement of files in the /etc/init.d directory in Unix. You may decide to change it so you have to start it manually. To change the start-up option to Manual, right-click the service name, and choose Properties. In the dialog box that appears, choose Manual from the Startup Type drop-down list, and click the button Apply.

Another way to check the service name command is to use the SC command. Here is how you can check the database service:

```
C:\>sc query OracleServiceMOBDB11
```

This returns with the following output, which shows the status of the service:

```
SERVICE_NAME: OracleServiceMOBDB11
        TYPE               : 10  WIN32_OWN_PROCESS
        STATE              : 4  RUNNING
                                (STOPPABLE,PAUSABLE,ACCEPTS_SHUTDOWN)
        WIN32_EXIT_CODE    : 0  (0x0)
```

```
SERVICE_EXIT_CODE        : 0  (0x0)
CHECKPOINT               : 0x0
WAIT_HINT                : 0x0
```

If the service is set to Manual, then you must start it. To start it, you can right-click the name of the service and click Start. Alternatively, you can execute the following command from the command prompt:

```
C:> net start OracleServiceMOBDB11
```

This command starts the service OracleServiceMOBDB11. Typically it also starts up the instance.

Another command used on Windows is oradim. This command is used for a variety of things—from creating an Oracle service to starting/stopping and even removing the services. Here is how you can start the Oracle service using this tool:

```
C:\> oradim -startup -sid MOBDB11 -starttype srvc,inst
```

You can also use the oradim command to stop the service. To see a complete list of oradim commands and options, type oradim at the command line without any arguments; this gives you the syntax, as shown here:

```
C:\> oradim
ORADIM: <command> [options].  Refer to manual.
Enter one of the following commands:
Create an instance by specifying the following options:
    -NEW -SID sid | -ASMSID sid | -MGMTDBSID sid | -IOSSID sid | -APXSID sid|
 -SRVC srvc | -ASMSRVC srvc | -MGMTDBSRVC srvc | -IOSSRVC srvc |
 -APXSRVC srvc  [-SYSPWD pass] [-STARTMODE auto|manual]
[-SRVCSTART system|demand] [-PFILE file | -SPFILE] [-MAXUSERS maxusers]
[-SHUTMODE normal|immediate|abort] [-TIMEOUT secs] [-RUNAS osusr/ospass]
Edit an instance by specifying the following options:
    -EDIT -SID sid | -ASMSID sid | -MGMTDBSID sid | -IOSSID sid | -APXSID sid
[-SYSPWD pass]  [-STARTMODE auto|manual] [-SRVCSTART system|demand]
[-PFILE file | -SPFILE] [-SHUTMODE normal|immediate|abort]
[-SHUTTYPE srvc|inst] [-MAXUSERS maxusers] [-RUNAS osusr/ospass]
Delete instances by specifying the following options:
    -DELETE -SID sid | -ASMSID sid | -MGMTDBSID sid | -IOSSID sid |
 -APXSID sid| -SRVC srvc | -ASMSRVC srvc | -MGMTDBSRVC srvc |
 -IOSSRVC srvc | -APXSRVC srvc
Start up services and instance by specifying the following options:
    -STARTUP -SID sid | -ASMSID sid | -MGMTDBSID sid | -IOSSID sid
 | -APXSID sid [-SYSPWD pass] [-STARTTYPE srvc|inst|srvc,inst]
[-PFILE filename | -SPFILE]
Shut down service and instance by specifying the following options:
    -SHUTDOWN -SID sid | -ASMSID sid | -MGMTDBSID sid | -IOSSID sid |
 -APXSID sid [-SYSPWD pass] [-SHUTTYPE srvc|inst|srvc,inst]
[-SHUTMODE normal|immediate|abort]
Manipulate ACLs by specifying the following options:
    -ACL -setperm|-addperm|-removeperm  dbfiles|diag|registry
 -USER username  -OBJTYPE file|dir|registry  -OBJPATH object-path
 -RECURSE true|false [-HOST hostname]
 Query for help by specifying the following parameters: -? | -h | -help
```

If you use ASM, you can use oradim to manage ASM instances, too.

Threads, Not Processes

An Oracle instance under Unix is a collection of several processes, such as PMON, SMON, LGWR, and so on, running on the server and several areas of memory. In Unix, these are operating system processes, and you can find them by entering the following command at the Unix command line:

```
$ ps -aef | grep ora_
  oracle 11221    1  0  May  7  ?         31:04  ora_lck0_PRODB1
  oracle 10723    1  0  May  7  ?        221:11  ora_lmon_PRODB1
  oracle 11306    1  0  May  7  ?          3:43  ora_asmb_PRODB1
  oracle 10775    1  0  May  7  ?          8:50  ora_dbw1_PRODB1
  oracle 10785    1  0  May  7  ?        332:07  ora_lgwr_PRODB1
  oracle 11312    1  0  May  7  ?          0:43  ora_rbal_PRODB1
... and so on ...
```

In the output, the first column shows the owner of the process, that is, `oracle`. The second column shows the Unix process ID (the numbers 11221, 10723, and so on) for those processes. Being processes, they can be killed and monitored independently.

Why Threads on Windows?

On the Windows platform, however, the Oracle server processes are not shown as Windows processes but as *threads* inside a single Oracle process. Threads are separate execution paths inside a process.

Why is it important for Oracle on Windows to run instance background processes as threads rather than as regular Windows processes? Here are the reasons:

- On Windows, programs can run either as processes or as threads. When run as processes, they can potentially affect the Windows kernel code and crash Windows. You might have seen, probably more than once, the dreaded Blue Screen of Death, which occurs when some application performs an illegal operation. That is an example of an illegal operation performed by an application process that compromised the Windows kernel stability, and hence the kernel just had to crash. Threads, however, are different; they don't attach to the kernel, and nothing happening in a thread will affect kernel stability.

- When a process needs to call another process, significant time is wasted in context switching between different processes. This context switching is less expensive between multiple threads of the same process.

- When the Oracle instance creates a new server process to serve a client, it's easier and faster to create a thread than a Windows process.

- Solving the problem of allocating memory for an Oracle SGA in a threaded architecture does not require shared memory, while in the processes model it does. This important difference helps Windows manage its overall memory in a much better way compared to the processes model, where each process has to have its own shared memory segment that is just not efficient.

- Therefore, the Oracle Database architecture on Windows is based on threads and not processes.

21-2. Monitoring Threads on Windows

Problem

You want to identify and monitor the threads related to an Oracle instance in Windows.

Solution

You can use a number of tools that show threads. There is one that comes with the Windows Resource Kit, but this is not part of the Windows distribution; you have to buy it from Microsoft as a separate product. In addition to the threads viewer, the Windows Resource Kit has other cool tools, too, such as `tail.exe`, which is similar in functionality to the `tail` command in Unix. You can also find tools to view threads from third parties on the Internet.

We searched the Internet and downloaded a tool called Process Viewer for Windows from www.teamcti.com/pview/prcview.htm. Using Process Viewer, you can see the Windows processes, as shown in Figure 21-3. This is pretty similar to what you would expect to see in the Task Manager that comes with Windows. Note the process called ORACLE.EXE. This is the single Oracle process, and all the server processes inside an Oracle instance run within this process as threads.

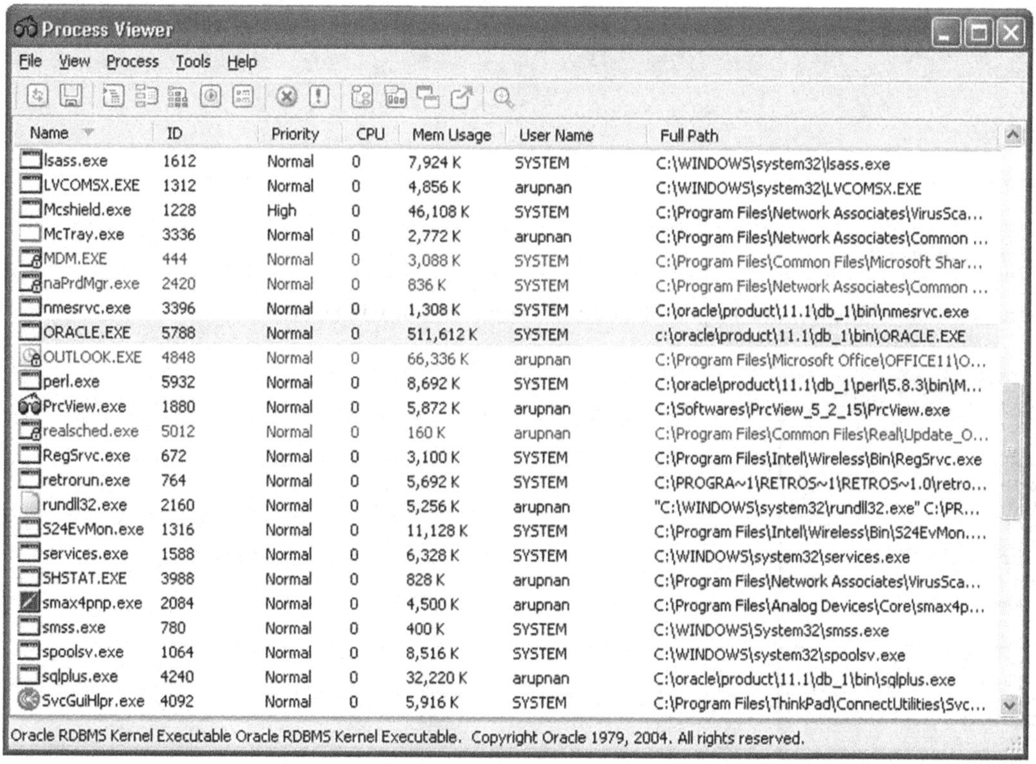

Name	ID	Priority	CPU	Mem Usage	User Name	Full Path
lsass.exe	1612	Normal	0	7,924 K	SYSTEM	C:\WINDOWS\system32\lsass.exe
LVCOMSX.EXE	1312	Normal	0	4,856 K	arupnan	C:\WINDOWS\system32\LVCOMSX.EXE
Mcshield.exe	1228	High	0	46,108 K	SYSTEM	C:\Program Files\Network Associates\VirusSca...
McTray.exe	3336	Normal	0	2,772 K	arupnan	C:\Program Files\Network Associates\Common ...
MDM.EXE	444	Normal	0	3,088 K	SYSTEM	C:\Program Files\Common Files\Microsoft Shar...
naPrdMgr.exe	2420	Normal	0	836 K	SYSTEM	C:\Program Files\Network Associates\Common ...
nmesrvc.exe	3396	Normal	0	1,308 K	SYSTEM	C:\oracle\product\11.1\db_1\bin\nmesrvc.exe
ORACLE.EXE	5788	Normal	0	511,612 K	SYSTEM	c:\oracle\product\11.1\db_1\bin\ORACLE.EXE
OUTLOOK.EXE	4848	Normal	0	66,336 K	arupnan	C:\Program Files\Microsoft Office\OFFICE11\O...
perl.exe	5932	Normal	0	8,692 K	SYSTEM	C:\oracle\product\11.1\db_1\perl\5.8.3\bin\M...
PrcView.exe	1880	Normal	0	5,872 K	arupnan	C:\Softwares\PrcView_5_2_15\PrcView.exe
realsched.exe	5012	Normal	0	160 K	arupnan	C:\Program Files\Common Files\Real\Update_O...
RegSrvc.exe	672	Normal	0	3,100 K	SYSTEM	C:\Program Files\Intel\Wireless\Bin\RegSrvc.exe
retrorun.exe	764	Normal	0	5,692 K	SYSTEM	C:\PROGRA~1\RETROS~1\RETROS~1.0\retro...
rundll32.exe	2160	Normal	0	5,256 K	arupnan	"C:\WINDOWS\system32\rundll32.exe" C:\PR...
S24EvMon.exe	1316	Normal	0	11,128 K	SYSTEM	C:\Program Files\Intel\Wireless\Bin\S24EvMon....
services.exe	1588	Normal	0	6,328 K	SYSTEM	C:\WINDOWS\system32\services.exe
SHSTAT.EXE	3988	Normal	0	828 K	arupnan	C:\Program Files\Network Associates\VirusSca...
smax4pnp.exe	2084	Normal	0	4,500 K	arupnan	C:\Program Files\Analog Devices\Core\smax4p...
smss.exe	780	Normal	0	400 K	SYSTEM	C:\WINDOWS\System32\smss.exe
spoolsv.exe	1064	Normal	0	8,516 K	SYSTEM	C:\WINDOWS\system32\spoolsv.exe
sqlplus.exe	4240	Normal	0	32,220 K	arupnan	C:\oracle\product\11.1\db_1\bin\sqlplus.exe
SvcGuiHlpr.exe	4092	Normal	0	5,916 K	SYSTEM	C:\Program Files\ThinkPad\ConnectUtilities\Svc...

Oracle RDBMS Kernel Executable Oracle RDBMS Kernel Executable. Copyright Oracle 1979, 2004. All rights reserved.

Figure 21-3. Process Viewer for Windows main screen

To find out the threads, right-click the process ORACLE.EXE to open the menu shown in Figure 21-4.

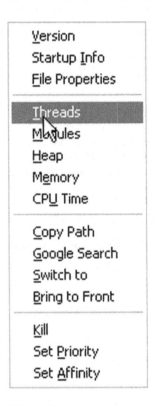

Figure 21-4. *Process submenu*

From this menu, choose Threads, which opens the threads viewer, as shown in Figure 21-5.

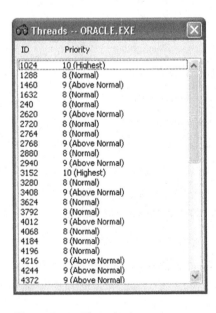

Figure 21-5. *Threads viewer*

This viewer shows the various threads under the Windows process ORACLE.EXE. You can find these threads in the view V$PROCESS as Oracle instance processes. The following is one example, taken from the threads viewer, of the thread 5852. If you look in V$PROCESS for a process whose ID is 5852, you will identify the instance process that is associated with this Windows thread.

```
SQL> select * from v$process
  2  where spid = 5852;

ADDR           PID SPID                         USERNAME         SERIAL#
-------- ---------- ------------------------ ---------------- ---------------------------
----------
TERMINAL
----------------
PROGRAM
-----------------------------------------------------------------------------------------
TRACEID
-----------------------------------------------------------------------------------------
--------------------------------
B LATCHWAI LATCHSPI PGA_USED_MEM PGA_ALLOC_MEM PGA_FREEABLE_MEM PGA_MAX_MEM
- -------- -------- ------------ ------------- ---------------- ------------------------------
--------------------------------
5AA754CC         2 5852                         SYSTEM                     1
STARUPNANT60
ORACLE.EXE (PMON)
1                      708318        859134                 0        859134
```

This SPID column, which shows the operating system process ID, actually shows the thread ID on Windows, not the process ID. The only process related to Oracle is ORACLE.EXE, and its process ID is 5788.

21-3. Identifying Oracle Home and SID on Windows

Problem

You want to set up Oracle SID and Oracle Home environment variables in Windows.

Solution

In Unix-based systems, you are familiar with the environmental variables that define the Oracle SID and Oracle Home, where the Oracle binaries are stored. If you want to change the Oracle SID or Home, all you have to do is export the variables. For example:

```
$ export ORACLE_SID=PROBE2
$ export ORACLE_HOME=/opt/oracle/products/10.2/db_1
```

On Windows, however, this technique will not necessarily work. So, let's see how the Oracle Home and other details are set on Windows.

On Windows, the information is kept in a place called the *registry*, which is sort of the brain of the Windows operating system. To check the Oracle Home and the location of the installation, check the registry. Select Start ➤ Run. In the text box, type **regedit** (**reg.exe** in later versions of Windows), and press the Enter key. This action opens the Registry Editor. Open HKEY_LOCAL_MACHINE/SOFTWARE/ORACLE. Figure 21-6 shows part of the screen.

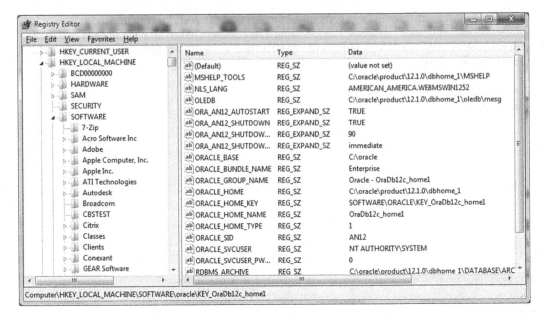

Figure 21-6. *Registry Editor for Oracle Home*

The right pane shows the information about Oracle Home and other details. Note the key named `inst_loc`. The data value of that key in our case is C:\Program Files\Oracle\Inventory, which is the location of the Oracle software inventory.

When the Oracle software is installed, the installer creates the directory C:\Program Files\Oracle\Inventory. This is where the inventory of the Oracle software is stored. In this directory you will find a file called oui.loc, which stores the location of the Oracle Universal Installer. Here is some example output of the file:

```
InstLoc=C:/Program Files/Oracle/oui
InstVer=2.2.0.12.0
```

The first line indicates that the installation location is C:/Program Files/Oracle/oui, which indicates the location of the installer files. This directory has a subdirectory called HomeSelector. In that subdirectory you will see a file called ohsel.exe. That file is used to choose a different Oracle Home. So, unlike in Unix, where you export the variable ORACLE_HOME to change the Oracle Home, you will need to execute this program and choose the Oracle Home.

21-4. Setting Oracle Groups on Windows
Problem

You want to add a user to a privileged group in Windows that allows the users in that group to connect to the database as SYSDBA without entering the password.

Solution

In Unix, the users belonging to the operating system group called dba have the sysdba privilege. In the Windows environment, this group is usually called ORA_DBA. When the Oracle Database software is installed, the group is automatically created, and the user doing the installation is placed in that group. To add a user to the group, follow these steps:

1. To locate the group, you have to use the Local Groups and User Administration screen. To go there, select Start ➤ Program ➤ Administrative Tools ➤ Computer Management. This opens a screen similar to the one shown in Figure 21-7.

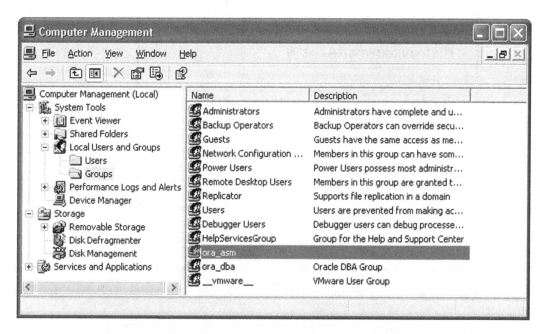

Figure 21-7. *The DBA group on Windows*

2. In the left pane, you will see several items. Click the + sign next to the Local Users and Groups item, and then click Groups. On the right side you will see all the groups defined on this computer, as shown in Figure 21-7. The last group is ORA_DBA.

3. Once in that screen, double-click the group ORA_DBA to open the properties of the group, as shown in Figure 21-8. From the output, note that only two users are part of the ORA_DBA group. Suppose you want to put a local user called arup in this group, too. To do that, click the Add button, which opens the dialog box shown in Figure 21-9.

Figure 21-8. *Viewing the properties of the group ORA_DBA*

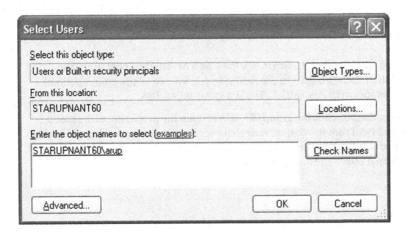

Figure 21-9. *Adding a local user to the ORA_DBA group*

4. In this dialog box, click the Locations button, and choose the name of this machine instead of the network name. In this example, the machine name is STARUPNANT60.

5. Type **arup** in the Enter the Object Names to Select box, and click the Check Names button, which will validate the presence of the user. If the user actually exists, the name will be highlighted by an underline under its name in the box, as shown in Figure 21-9. Click the OK button.

6. Now, make sure the user is indeed part of the ORA_DBA group by checking the group properties again. The dialog box should look something like Figure 21-10.

Figure 21-10. *Checking for user arup in the group ORA_DBA*

You can also use the following command to see the users in the ORA_DBA group:

```
c:\>net localgroup ora_dba
Alias name     ora_dba
Comment        Oracle DBA Group

Members

-------------------------------------------------------------------------------------------
----------
arup
CORP\arupnan
NT AUTHORITY\SYSTEM
The command completed successfully.
```

From now on, the user arup can log in to Oracle as sysdba without entering a password, as shown here:

```
C:\> sqlplus / as sysdba
```

Ideally, you would want to create separate Windows user IDs for each of the DBAs and place each in the ORA_DBA group.

How It Works

When you install Oracle in Windows, it creates a group called ORA_DBA that is special. The Oracle software running on that Windows server identifies the group as privileged. Any user that is part of ORA_DBA can log in to the database with SYSDBA role by entering sqlplus / as sysdba, i.e., no password. However, for this to work, the value of the parameter SQLNET.AUTHENTICATION_SERVICES should also be set to (NTS) in the file sqlnet.ora file, as described in Recipe 21-10.

21-5. Setting Path for Oracle Binaries on Windows
Problem

You want to set path of the Oracle binaries on the Windows server so that the users can execute the executables, such as SQL*Plus, anywhere on the command.

Solution

In Unix, the Oracle binaries are located in the directory ORACLE_HOME/bin, and this directory is placed in the PATH variable of the user oracle. If you change the Oracle Home, all you have to do is put the new directory in the PATH variable, as shown here:

```
$ export PATH=$PATH:$ORACLE_HOME/bin
```

On Windows, paths are usually global and apply to all users, not just locally in a session. To check for the PATH set for a Windows environment, follow these steps:

1. Go to the Desktop, right-click My Computer, and choose Properties. This opens the System Properties dialog box, as shown in Figure 21-11.

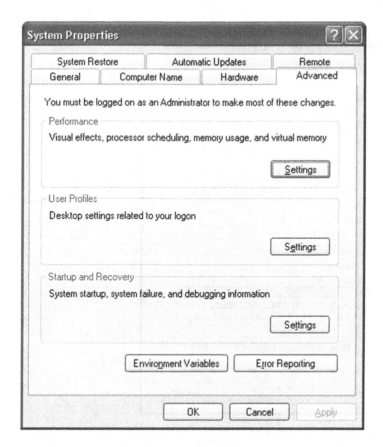

Figure 21-11. *Windows system properties*

2. Now select the Advanced tab.

3. Click the Environment Variables button, which opens the Environment Variables dialog box, as shown in Figure 21-12.

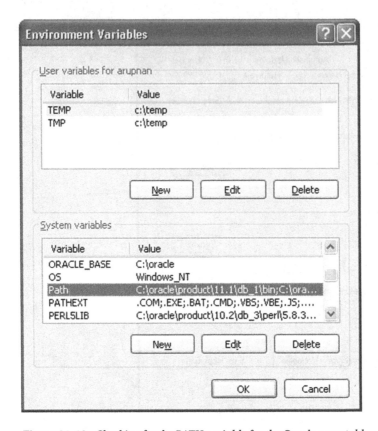

Figure 21-12. *Checking for the PATH variable for the Oracle executable*

4. The lower part of the screen shows the system variables. Scroll down the list until you see the Path variable, as shown in Figure 21-12.

■ **Note** You may want to click the Edit button to see the complete path. If you want to change the path, you can do so in this dialog box.

21-6. Managing Oracle via Management Console

Problem

You want to use the Management Console. However, it is not installed by default.

Solution

Windows provides a tool called the Management Console that allows you to control certain administrative functions through a GUI. It is handy for performing repetitive commands fairly easily and quickly. In the console, you as the user can create and add stand-alone console add-ins, also known as *snap-ins*. Oracle takes advantage of the tool and provides a snap-in for managing Oracle Databases. However, it is not installed by default. While installing Oracle Database software, choose a custom installation rather than an express one, and explicitly choose the Management Console for Oracle.

After the database is installed, you can configure this Management Console plug-in. Follow these steps to configure the Management Console for Oracle:

1. Click Start ➤ Run, enter **mmc** in the Run window, and press Enter.

2. This action opens the Management Console, similar to the window shown in Figure 21-13. Select File ➤ Add/Remove Snap-In.

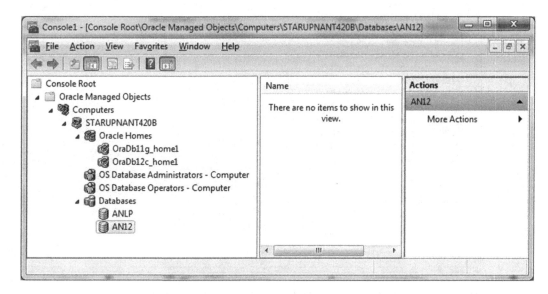

Figure 21-13. *Management Console window*

3. This opens the Add/Remove Snap-In dialog box, as shown in Figure 21-14. In this dialog box, click the Add button near the bottom-left corner. Please note that in this figure you can already see the Oracle Management Console in the dialog box, which shows up as Oracle Managed Objects. This is because we have already added it.

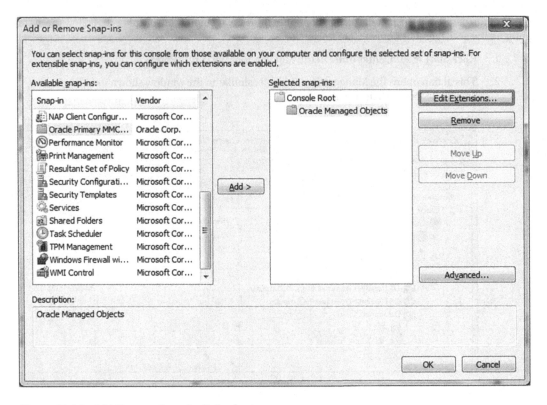

Figure 21-14. *Add/Remove Snap-In dialog box*

4. Clicking the Add button opens the Add Standalone Snap-In dialog box, as shown in Figure 21-15. Scroll down, and select Oracle Primary MMC Snap-In. Then click Add.

Figure 21-15. Adding the Oracle Management Console snap-in

5. From the File menu, choose Save As, and when prompted, enter **Oracle Management Console** as the name of the console.

6. From this point on, you can access this MMC directly from the menu. Choose Start ➤ Programs ➤ Administrative Tools ➤ Oracle Management Console. Choosing the menu item opens the Oracle Management Console, as shown earlier in Figure 21-13. From this console, you can perform several management tasks as a DBA. The first action will be to connect to the database. Right-click the database name, which in this example is AN12. This action opens the pop-up menu shown in Figure 21-16.

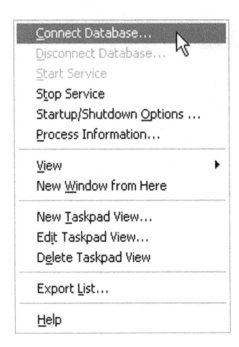

Figure 21-16. *Pop-up menu for database*

7. Click Connect Database, and it will connect to the database as the sysdba user. From this menu you can perform several administrative tasks, such as stopping the Oracle service. The most useful, in our opinion, is perhaps the item called Process Information. Clicking Process Information will open a dialog box with information on the threads related to Oracle, as shown in Figure 21-17.

Name	Type	User	Thread ID	CPU	%
PMON	Backgrou...	SYS	6772	0:00:00	0%
VKTM	Backgrou...	SYS	5724	0:00:00	0%
GEN0	Backgrou...	SYS	7316	0:00:00	0%
DIAG	Backgrou...	SYS	8996	0:00:00	0%
DBRM	Backgrou...	SYS	8968	0:00:01	0%
VKRM	Backgrou...	SYS	8876	0:00:00	0%
PSP0	Backgrou...	SYS	5336	0:00:00	0%

Process Information for AN12

This list displays information about Oracle threads.

Kill Thread   OK   Help

Figure 21-17. *Oracle threads information*

How It Works

The dialog box shown in Figure 21-17 shows the threads of the Oracle-related programs and processes. Note how all the programs and background processes are listed. Thread 6772 is the PMON process, while 8968 is the DB Resource Manager. In this dialog box you can monitor the processes running inside the Oracle instance and how much CPU each is consuming.

21-7. Killing Oracle Processes in Windows
Problem

You want to kill a specific Oracle server process in Windows.

Solution

In Unix, it's rather simple to kill a process by issuing the `kill` command. On Windows, this becomes a little complicated. You can kill the processes by opening the Task Manager, right-clicking the process to be killed, and choosing End Process. However, remember that the process is the entire Oracle instance; you don't want to kill that. You want to kill only a specific thread. So, you can't use the Task Manager's End Process approach.

Oracle provides a utility to kill Oracle threads, called `orakill`. Type `orakill` on the command line to see how to use this tool:

```
C:\>orakill

Usage:  orakill sid thread
where sid     = the Oracle instance to target
       thread = the thread id of the thread to kill

  The thread id should be retrieved from the spid column of a query such as:

      select spid, osuser, s.program from
      v$process p, v$session s where p.addr=s.paddr
```

The usage is pretty straightforward. To kill thread 6776 in SID MOBDB11, you issue the following command:

```
C:\>orakill MOBDB11 6776

Kill of thread id 6776 in instance MOBDB11 successfully signaled.
```

How It Works

Recall from the previous recipes in this chapter that unlike in the case of Unix, the Oracle instance in Windows does not have operating system processes. Instead it has threads. So you have to kill the thread of the Oracle process that you want to kill. In the V$PROCESS view, the column SPID shows the thread# under Windows platform (it shows process ID under Unix platforms). To get the thread# of the session in question, you have to use this query:

```
select spid as thread#
from v$process p, v$session s
where s.sid = <sessionID>
and p.addr = s.paddr;
```

Once you have the thread#, you can kill with the command as shown.

Another way to kill the thread is from the Oracle Management Console, as explained in Recipe 21-6. Choose Process Information from the pop-up menu shown in Figure 21-16, highlight the thread 6776, and click the Kill Thread button in the lower-left corner.

21-8. Choosing Oracle Homes
Problem

You want to choose a specific Oracle Home from multiple Oracle Homes defined in a Windows server.

Solution

Unlike Unix, where you can choose a specific Oracle Home by exporting the ORACLE_HOME environment variable, you have to follow a slightly different approach for accomplishing the same in Windows. If you have more than one Oracle Home in Windows, you have to choose a menu item to choose one over the other. Here are the steps:

1. Choose Start ➤ Program ➤ Oracle – OraDb12c_home1 ➤ Oracle Installation Products ➤ Universal Installer. It brings up a window similar to the one shown in Figure 21-18.

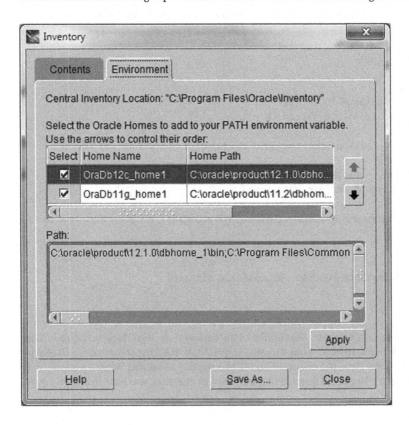

Figure 21-18. *Selecting Oracle Home*

2. Click on the tab labeled Environment. In that pane, you will see the Oracle Homes defined in the machine. Unselect the Oracle Homes you don't want and select the one you want.

How It Works

In Figure 21-18, the dialog box shows all the Oracle Homes in that server. The order in which they are displayed determines the order in which the commands will be searched. For instance, in this example the Oracle Home named OraDb12c_home1 will be the first to be searched. That means when you give a command called sqlplus.exe, it will be searched in the bin directory of that Oracle Home first and then in the other home, called OraDb11g_home1.

If you want to change the order in which the Oracle Homes are searched for executables, click on the Up or Down arrows toward the right hand of the window to move the Oracle Homes.

21-9. Copying Open Files in Windows
Problem

You want to copy a file already opened by Windows.

Solution

If you want to copy an "open" file, such as a data file already opened by the Oracle Database, you should use the ocopy utility instead of the regular copy or xcopy utilities. Here is the basic syntax of ocopy:

```
C:\> ocopy <SourceFile> <DestinationFile>
```

How It Works

On Windows, the file copy utilities are copy and xcopy, both similar to the cp utility in Unix. Although you can use copy or xcopy for many occasions, you can't use them to copy files that are held open by a process. The copy created in that case is considered to be "fuzzy" by the operating system, and may not be completely readable. For instance, while performing hot backups, when you place tablespaces into backup mode, Oracle Database is aware of the fuzzy nature of the files, but not the Windows operating system. Windows sees that the files are still used by Oracle and hence it marks the copies created by the copy and xcopy commands as useless.You may not use copy or xcopy to copy those files to a backup destination.

To avoid this issue, Oracle provides a utility called ocopy available in ORACLE_HOME\bin folder. You can use ocopy to copy any file, not just Oracle data files, but it's especially useful when making hot backups. The utility can be used for copying raw devices as well. Here is an example of copying a raw device:

```
C:\>ocopy \\.\lun1 c:\lun1.dbf
C:\LUN1.DBF
```

In addition to copying files for hot backup, you can also use ocopy for other open file copies, such as copying the Oracle Cluster Ready Services voting and quorum disks.

21-10. Connecting as sysdba Using OS Authentication
Problem
You want to connect as SYSDBA from certain users in Windows without needing to enter a password for SYS.

Solution
To enable operating system authentication for sysdba—that is, to let a Windows user connect to the database as sysdba without entering a password—follow these steps:

1. Make sure the Windows user is part of the group ORA_DBA. You can see the exact steps to accomplish this in the section "Oracle Groups" in Recipe 21-5.

2. Place the following line in the file SQLNET.ORA in the directory network\admin in the Oracle Home directory. The line may already exist in the file SQLNET.ORA.

    ```
    SQLNET.AUTHENTICATION_SERVICES = (NTS)
    ```

3. Now the user can connect to the database as sysdba merely by executing the following:

    ```
    C:\> sqlplus / as sysdba
    ```

There is no need to enter the password.

How It Works
The user connects to the SYSDBA role without a password due to two settings you have completed in this recipe:

*   The user belongs to the ORA_DBA group, which lets the Oracle Database treat this as a special user that is allowed to connect to the SYSDBA role without needing a password.

*   The setting SQLNET.AUTHENTICATION_SERVICES = (NTS) instructs the Oracle database to accept the authentication from Windows and not from the database. So a password is no longer needed.

Both these conditions must be true to allow the user to connect to SYSDBA role without a password. If you leave one out, it will not work. For instance, if you don't set the parameter in the SQLNET.ORA file and try to connect, you will get the following result:

```
C:\>sqlplus / as sysdba

SQL*Plus: Release 12.1.0.0.2 Beta on Tue Oct 16 13:08:31 2012

Copyright (c) 1982, 2012, Oracle.  All rights reserved.

    ERROR: ORA-01031: insufficient privileges
```

The error says it all.

21-11. Simulating a Failure

If you want to simulate a failure in the Windows environment and use RMAN to recover the database or data file, all the details are available in Recipe 2-6.

21-12. Creating a Fast Recovery Area

If you want to create a fast recovery area, refer to Recipe 3-1. In the Windows environment, merely replace the Unix directory name with a Windows folder. For instance, to define the fast recovery area on the folder c:\flash, issue the following SQL statement:

```
alter system set db_recovery_file_dest = 'c:\flash';
```

All other details are the same as described in Recipe 3-1.

21-13. Placing Data Files, Control Files, and Online and Archived Redo Log Files in the FRA

To place the data files, control files, online redo log files, and archived redo log files in the fast recovery area, follow the steps shown in Recipe 3-8 and Recipe 3-9.

21-14. Switching Back from Image Copies

In Recipe 3-13, you can learn how to reinstate the image copy of the data file in the fast recovery area to cut down the time significantly during recovery. In Recipe 3-14, you can learn how to switch back to the main data file location from the fast recovery area. The steps are all the same in the Windows environment, except you remove the files by using the del command instead of rm. For example:

```
C:\> del c:\oradata\flash\sys01.dbf
```

21-15. Using the Fast Recovery Area

The tasks of creating and using the fast recovery area for various tasks—such as enabling the flashback for the database, storing database backups, and creating other supporting files, such as control files and online/archived redo log files—have been described in Chapter 3 in various recipes. These recipes also apply to Windows platforms. In Real Application Clusters (RACs) on Windows, there is another way to define the location of the FRA. Recall from the recipes in Chapter 3 that the location must be visible to all nodes of the RAC, and it can't be a raw device. On Windows, however, it can be a raw partition, which is the Windows equivalent of the raw device in Unix. Of course, you can use a clustered file system, such as ACFS or ASM, and Oracle recommends using ASM up to Oracle Database 11.2 and ACFS now.

Raw files are typically named as a drive letter. For instance, you can specify the drive letter Z for a physical or logical partition. To use the raw files in the fast recovery area, issue the following statement:

```
SQL> alter system set db_recovery_file_dest = '\\.\Z:';
```

Note the backslashes before the drive letter; these are necessary when specifying a raw partition.

21-16. Developing a Windows Batch File

You may need to develop a Windows batch file to automate various tasks including RMAN backup. In Recipe 9-3 you can learn how to develop a complete batch file that accepts parameters as database names, input types, and so on, so that it can be used in many databases with little or no modification. This batch file also checks for errors and sends out notification in both success and failure cases.

21-17. Scheduling Windows Jobs

After developing a batch file on Windows, you will nevertheless want to schedule it through some mechanism so that it can be run automatically. In Recipe 9-4, you can learn how to schedule a batch file or an executable through a command-line utility called at.

Schedules are not cast in stone; they need to be changed to reflect business conditions. If you prefer a GUI version, Recipe 9-5 shows how to change a schedule through a GUI tool. To learn how to change a schedule through the command line, see Recipe 9-6.

21-18. Transporting Tablespaces to/from Windows

When you want to transport a tablespace from one database to the other across multiple platforms, Oracle Database starting with version 10*g* makes it easier. If both the source and target databases are on the same platform, then it's as simple as copying the data files to the target server. Even if they are not on the same platform, you can still copy the data files if the byte order (or *endianness*) of the platforms is the same. For instance, both Linux x86 and Windows are little endian, so transporting a tablespace merely requires copying the files between them. You can learn all about that activity in Recipe 15-12.

If the operating systems are not of the same endianness—that is, you are transporting between Windows and an operating system that is big endian (such as HPUX)—you will need to convert the data files before plugging them into the target system. Recipe 15-12 shows you how to perform the conversion through RMAN. To convert the data files on the target system, instead of the source system, refer to Recipe 15-14.

21-19. Transporting an Entire Database to/from Windows

Sometimes you want to transport an entire database, not just a few tablespaces, to or from Windows. Oracle Database 10*g* Release 2 provides this functionality. As when you transport tablespaces, if the platforms of both the source and target databases are the same, the task is reduced to merely copying the files. Even if they are not the same platform, if the byte order (the endianness) of the platforms is the same, you can merely copy the data files to the target environments as well. For instance, to transport to or from a Windows environment where the source or target platform is little endian, you merely copy the files. Recipe 15-13 shows you how to perform that operation.

If you want to transport a database from Windows to another platform that is a big-endian platform or you want to transport a database from a platform like that to Windows, you will need to use RMAN to convert the datafiles. You will find the relevant details in Recipe 15-13.

RMAN in an Oracle Data Guard Environment

You can use RMAN to simplify the administration of your Oracle Data Guard setup. You can employ all the standard RMAN backup and recovery strategies in a Data Guard environment. RMAN lets you perform backups on the primary database and enables quick recovery from the loss of data files, control files, or even the entire database.

It's important to understand that RMAN commands work similarly across both the primary and the standby database. You can back up a tablespace, for example, on a primary database and restore and recover that tablespace in a standby database and vice versa. The recovery catalog keeps track of which database files and which backup files belong to which database, by associating all database and backup files with a db_unique_name.

RMAN treats disk backups and tape backups differently when it comes to accessibility. It considers disk backups accessible only to the database with which the backup is associated. The recovery catalog considers tape backups created on one database as accessible to all databases. You can copy a backup from a standby server to a primary server and vice versa and catalog the backup in the server where you moved the backup. Once you connect as target to the database on the destination server and catalog the backup, that backup file will be associated with the target database.

Since only a physical standby is a block-by-block copy of the primary database, you can't use a logical database to back up your primary database.

22-1. Synchronizing a Physical Standby Database
Problem

You want to synchronize a physical standby database with the primary database.

Solution

You can use RMAN incremental backups to synchronize a physical standby database with its primary database. Here are the steps to follow:

1. Stop the application of redo on the standby database:

    ```
    SQL> alter database recover managed standby database cancel;
    ```

2. If the standby database has lagged far behind the primary database, find the current SCN of the standby database by executing the following query (on the standby database):

    ```
    SQL> select current_scn from v$database;
    ```

3. Create an incremental backup of the primary database from the current SCN, as shown here:

```
RMAN> backup incremental from scn 123456 database
          format '/tmp/ForCatchup_%U' tag 'ForCatchp';
```

4. The RMAN backup command shown in step 3 will create data file backups and a control file backup. Move all the backup pieces that you've created on the primary database server to the standby database server:

```
$ scp /tmp/Forcatchup_* standby:/tmp
```

5. On the standby database, execute the following command to catalog the backup pieces you moved from the primary server to the standby server:

```
RMAN> catalog start with '/tmp/ForCatchp';
```

6. Check that the file names at the standby database site are registered, by executing the following command:

```
RMAN> report schema;
```

7. Apply the incremental backups to the standby database by executing the following set of commands:

```
RMAN> connect target /
RMAN> startup force nomount;
RMAN> restore standby controlfile from tag 'FORSTANDBY';
RMAN> alter database mount;
RMAN> recover database noredo;
```

8. Start the apply of redo on the physical standby:

```
SQL> alter database recover managed standby database disconnect from session;
```

How It Works

You can sometimes use RMAN incremental backups to synchronize a standby with the primary database. First create a backup on the primary database using the RMAN backup incremental from SCN command. The backup starts at the current SCN of the standby, so you can then roll the standby database forward in time by applying this incremental backup from the primary database.

You can use this strategy of applying RMAN incemental backup in the following situations:

- The physical standby lags far behind the primary database.

- The physical database has a large number of nologging changes.

- Several data files in the physical standby have nologging changes.

Although a recovery catalog isn't absolutely essential to follow the incremental backup strategy described here, Oracle recommends you use the recovery catalog so you don't have to correct the file names in the restored control file.

In the example shown in this recipe, we used the current SCN of the standby database as the starting point of the primary database backup. However, if you're dealing with a standby with a large number of nologging changes, you must use the first_nologged_scn from the V$DATAFILE view, as shown here:

```
SQL> select min(first_nologged_scn_) from v$datafile where first_nologged_scn > 0;

MIN(FIRST_NONLOGGED_SCN)
------------------------
223948
```

If you are using a recovery catalog, RMAN will automatically set the path names for all data files in the standby control file. If not, you must execute the RMAN set newname command to set the data file names. You must be connected to the recovery catalog during the execution of the restore standby controlfile command, for that command to work. The alternative is to execute the restore standby controlfile from '<control_file backup filename>' command.

22-2. Configuring Archive Log Deletion Policies on the Primary and Standby Databases

Problem

You want to correctly configure the deletion policy for archived redo logs on a standby database.

Solution

You can specify automatic archived redo log deletion or you can manually delete the logs yourself. We explain both strategies here.

Configuring Automatic Deletion of Archived Logs

Execute an RMAN configure command to enable automatic deletion of those archived logs on the primary database that have been applied to a standby destination or destinations. Here's an example:

```
RMAN> configure archivelog deletion policy to applied on standby;
```

You must issue this command at the primary database and after connecting to each of the other standby databases and the recovery catalog.

Manually Deleting Archived Redo Logs

You can delete archived redo logs that you've already backed up, with the delete archivelog command. The following command, for example, will delete all the archived logs generated prior to 3 days ago and have at least 2 copies on tape.

```
RMAN> delete archivelog all backed up 2 times to sbt
        completed before 'sysdate -3';
```

How It Works

On the primary database, the first command shown in the solution will enable the automatic deletion of archived logs that have already been applied to remote standby destinations. This configuration also requires that you set at least one remote destination to mandatory.

When you apply the same command to each of the other standby databases where you're taking backups, the archived logs on the standby database that have been applied to all other remote standby destinations are automatically deleted. You must connect to each of the other standby databases and to the recovery catalog when issuing the command.

When you switch over to the secondary, or when a failover occurs, database roles will change and, therefore, you must re-execute the appropriate `configure` commands on the new primary and the new standby databases.

If you haven't set up the automatic deletion of archived logs at any standby database, you can execute the `delete archivelog` command shown under "Manually Deleting Archived Redo Logs" to explicitly delete archive logs that you've backed up to tape one or more times. The `backed up` clause ensures that you don't delete any archived logs that you haven't already backed up first.

You can also remove expired archived logs with the `delete` command, as shown here:

```
RMAN> delete expired archivelog like '/archivelog/SF%';
```

In this case, we specify the `like` option to select appropriate archived logs for deletion.

If you've configured the fast recovery area, any archived logs that aren't required to satisfy your retention period, or those you've already backed up to tape, will automatically be deleted when the FRA needs space for accommodating new files. In this case, you need to execute the `delete` command manually only if you want to immediately free up some space in the FRA.

22-3. Instantiating a Standby Database with RMAN

Problem

You want to instantiate a standby database with RMAN.

Solution

Follow these steps to instantiate a standby database with RMAN. Before you start to create the standby database, ensure that the correct Oracle database binaries are installed on the target server.

1. Create a standby database initialization parameter file. In this example we restore the SPFILE:

    ```
    RMAN> restore spfile;
    ```

2. Start the standby instance in the *nomount* mode, using the SPFILE.

3. Configure Oracle Net to connect to the standby database host.

4. Connect to the primary database as the target and to the recovery catalog as well, and back up the control file by issuing the following command.

    ```
    RMAN> backup current controlfile for standby;
    ```

5. Connect to the primary database, the recovery catalog, and the standby database instance as follows:

    ```
    $ rman target <primary_db> catalog <catalog_db> auxiliary <standby_db>
    ```

6. Create the standby database with the `duplicate database` command as shown here.

    ```
    RMAN> duplicate target database for standby
            nofilenamecheck dorecover;
    ```

How It Works

The `duplicate` command shown in the Solution section will use the control file and data file backups and the archived logs from the primary database to instantiate a standby database.

The command restores the backup sets from the primary database and recovers the database by applying both incremental backups as well as backups of the archived logs. The new standby database will be created with the current time and SCN by default, as in our solution example. However, you can recover the new standby database to a certain time or SCN by specifying the `until` clause with the `duplicate` command.

You can use the procedure described here not only to create a new standby database, but also to reinstantiate a primary database as a standby database following a failover operation. You can also employ this procedure to recover a standby database after a media failure.

22-4. Resynchronizing After Structural Changes on the Primary Database

Problem

You want to make sure that the standby database is made aware of all the structural changes you make on the primary database.

Solution

You must ensure that the recovery catalog is resynchronized frequently, especially following structural changes to the primary database, to make the standby database aware of these changes. You can resynchronize the recovery catalog by issuing the following `resync` ommand:

```
RMAN> resync catalog;
```

Make sure that you connect to the primary database as the target database and to the recovery catalog before issuing the `resync catalog` command.

How It Works

The resyncing of the recovery catalog following structural changes on the primary database ensures that the standby database becomes aware of the changes. The solution shows how you can resync by manually running the `resync catalog` command. You can also perform an *implicit resync* of the recovery catalog by daily backing up of the control and SPFILE auto backups to tape. Use the following command to back up the primary database control file and SPFILE auto backups to tape:

1. Connect to the primary database as the target database and to the recovery catalog:

    ```
    RMAN> connect target /
    RMAN> connect catalog rman/rman@catdb
    ```

2. Issue the following backup command:

    ```
    RMAN> backup device type sbt backupset all;
    ```

Oracle recommends that you back up the control file from the primary database to tape at least on a weekly basis. Of course, your recovery window determines the frequency of the control file backup. The more frequently you run this backup, the less redo the database needs to apply to a backed up control file during a recovery. The older the controls file, therefore, the longer it takes to get the backup control file up to date.

22-5. Implementing Oracle's Recommended Backup Strategy

Problem

You want to understand the backup strategy that Oracle recommends in a Data Guard setup.

Solution

We summarize the backup strategy recommended by Oracle for protecting your Data Guard setup with RMAN backups.

Primary Database Backup Procedures

Use the following procedures to back up the primary database:

1. Connect to the primary database as the target database and to the recovery catalog:

    ```
    RMAN> connect target /
    RMAN> connect catalog rman/rman@catdb
    ```

2. Back up the primary database control file including the SPFILE auto backup to tape, with the following RMAN command:

    ```
    RMAN> backup device type sbt backupset all;
    ```

Any older backups from a different backup strategy will be stored on tape after the backup command shown here finishes executing.

Standby Database Backup Procedures

The recommended strategy for a standby database is to perform a daily and a weekly backup. The standby backups depend heavily on Oracle's well-known *incrementally updated backup strategy*, wherein a data file image copy is rolled forward with the help of incremental backups, thus minimizing the overhead and time involved in making daily full-image copies of the database.

Daily Backup Procedure

Following are the steps involved in performing the daily backup of the standby database, using Oracle's suggested backup strategy:

1. Connect to the standby database as the target database and to the recovery catalog:

    ```
    RMAN> connect target /
    RMAN> connect catalog rman/rman@catdb
    ```

2. Execute the following recover command to roll forward the level 0 copy (full-image copy) of the database by applying the level 1 incremental backup taken the day before:

    ```
    RMAN>  recover copy of database with tag 'prod';
    ```

3. Create a new level 1 incremental backup:

```
RMAN> backup device type disk
            incremental level 1
            for recover of copy with tag 'prod' database;
```

4. Back up the archive logs daily:

```
RMAN> backup archivelog all not backed up to sbt;
```

5. Issue the following command to back up everything to tape:

```
RMAN> backup backupset all;
```

Weekly Backup Procedure

The weekly backup procedure for a standby database is simple: you back up all recovery area files on disk to tape, as shown here:

```
RMAN> backup recovery files;
```

This weekly backup command backs up available image copies, incremental backups and archivelog backups on disk to tape.

How It Works

Your recovery window determines the frequency of the primary database control file backups. Naturally, making a backup control file more frequently means you can recover faster than when you're using an older backup control file. Oracle recommends that you make a tape backup of the primary database at least weekly.

RMAN can use incremental backups for media recovery. You thus get the benefits of up-to-date data file image copies without the time and overhead involved in making fresh daily image copies of those data files. In addition, the recovery time is drastically reduced, since image copies are updates with just the actual block changes and you'll need a lot fewer redo logs (at most a day's worth) to recover the database to the current time.

Let's review the individual commands you need to execute as part of the daily backup strategy for a standby database:

- `recover copy of database with tag 'prod'`: This command instructs RMAN to roll forward the level 0 copy of the database by applying to it the level 1 incremental backup from the day before. The incremental backup has the same tag as the image copy, *prod,* and is generated by the backup command in Step 2. Following is how the recovery of the image copy takes place:

  - When you first execute this command, of course, there's no incremental level 1 backup, hence there's not going to be any recovery and rolling forward of the image copy with tag *prod.*

  - On the second day, when the `recover copy` command runs, nothing happens, as you have only a level 0 incremental backup. Step 2 will create the level 1 incremental backup tagged *prod.*

  - On the third and subsequent days, RMAN will roll forward the backup using the level 1 incremental backup (with tag prod) that it created the previous day. RMAN merges the incremental backup of the previous day with the data file copy.

- `backup device type disk ... with tag 'prod' database`: This command creates a new level 1 incremental backup tagged *prod*. The very first time this script runs (day 1), it creates a level 0 incremental backup (a full database backup), since there's none prior to this. On all following days, this command generates a new level 1 incremental backup thatwill be available for step 1 on the next day.

- `backup archivelog all not backed up to sbt`: This command backs up all archive logs not previously backed up to tape.

- `backup backupset all`: The very first time this script runs, it copies any previously existing backups to tape. On subsequent runs, the command will back up all archived log and incremental backups in the recovery area to tape.

RMAN can use the up-to-date full database copy and the current incremental backups to recover the database to any point within the past day. It can use the archived redo logs and the online redo logs to recover the database to any point in time during the current day.

22-6. Recovering from the Loss of Data Files
Problem

You want to recover from the loss of data files in a standby environment.

Solution

Use the following steps to recover a standby database data file:

1. Start RMAN and connect to the standby database as well as to the recovery catalog:

   ```
   RMAN> connect target /
   RMAN> connect catalog rman/rman@catdb
   ```

2. Connect to the standby database through SQL*Plus and stop the managed recovery process (MRP):

   ```
   RMAN> alter database recover managed standby database cancel;
   ```

3. Establish the current SCN of the standby database:

   ```
   SQL> select max(next_change#)+1 until_scn
        from v$log_history
        where resetlogs change#=(select resetlogs change# from v$database);

   UNTIL_SCN
   ----------------
   967786
   ```

4. Restore the data files using the RMAN restore command:

   ```
   RMAN> restore datafile 6;
   ```

5. Issue the recover command and specify that RMAN recover the data file until the current SCN of the database, which you've already established in step 3:

    ```
    RMAN> recover database until scn 967786;
    ```

6. Restart the managed recovery process (MRP) to start redo apply again:

    ```
    SQL> alter database recover managed standby database disconnect;
    ```

How It Works

You must ensure that the archived logs are available on disk to satisfy the MRP requirements of the standby database. When recovering data files belonging to a standby database, RMAN automatically restores any archived logs that aren't on disk and applies them during the recovery process that follows the restoration of a data file.

On the primary database, you can also restore and recover at the tablespace level. Simply replace *datafile* with *tablespace* in the restore and recovery commands, as shown here, which restores and recovers the tablespace *users*:

```
RMAN> restore tablespace users;
RMAN> recover tablespace users;
```

As you might have noticed, recovering a data file or a tablespace of the primary database in an Oracle Data Guard environment really doesn't differ from the procedures in a non–Oracle Data Guard setup.

22-7. Recovering Data Files on the Primary Database

Problem

You want to recover from the loss of data files on the primary database.

Solution

You can recover from the loss of data files on a primary database in two ways: by using the backups or by taking recourse to the standby database data files. We show both methods in this section.

Recovering Using Backups

Let's say you want to recover data files 6 and 7. Here are the steps to follow:

1. Connect to the primary database and the recovery catalog.

2. Restore the data files.

    ```
    RMAN> restore datafile 6,7;
    ```

3. Recover the data files.

    ```
    RMAN> recover datafile 6,7;
    ```

In the case of a tablespace recovery, you use the same procedure, but use the `restore tablespace` and the `recover tablespace` commands instead.

Recovering Using Standby Database Files

You can use the network-based backup strategy to recover the data files on the primary database. Follow these steps to recover the primary database by using the data files on the standby database:

1. Connect to the standby database:

    ```
    RMAN> connect target sys@standby
    ```

2. Connect to the primary database as auxiliary database:

    ```
    RMAN> connect auxiliary sys@primary
    ```

3. Use a network-based method to back up the necessary data files on the standby host to a location on the primary host:

    ```
    RMAN> backup as copy datafile 6 format '/u01/app/oracle/backup/dbf6copy.dbf';
    ```

4. Exit from RMAN:

    ```
    RMAN> exit;
    ```

5. Connect to the primary database as the target and to the recovery catalog as well:

    ```
    $ rman
    RMAN> connect target sys@primary
    RMAN> connect catalog rman@catdb
    ```

6. Before recovering the data files on the primary database, make sure to catalog the data file copy you've made in step 3, so RMAN is aware of this backup:

    ```
    RMAN> catalog datafilecopy '/u01/app/oracle/backup/dbf6copy.dbf';
    ```

    Switch the data file copy to make the copy the current data file in the primary database:

    ```
    RMAN> run {
              set newname for datafile 6 to '/u01/app/oracle/backup/dbf6copy.dbf';
              switch datafile 6;
              recover datafile 6;
              alter database datafile 6 online;
          }
    ```

How It Works

The examples shown in the Solution section assume that you're restoring the backup files from a tape backup to the same system on which you've created the backups. If you want to restore to a different system, you must first configure appropriate RMAN backup channels before you can issue the restore and recover commands.

22-8. Recovering the Control File(s) of a Standby Database
Problem

You've lost one or more control files on the standby database in your Oracle Data Guard environment.

Solution

There are several alternatives when it comes to recovering from the loss of control files of a standby database, as explained in the following examples.

Loss of a Single Control File

If you've lost even a single copy of a multiplexed control file, the standby database will shut itself down. Here are the steps to get the standby database going again:

1. Find the location of the control files using the following command:

    SQL> show parameter control_files;

2. Copy one of the surviving control files over to the location of the lost control file as specified in the SPFILE (or the init.ora file).

3. Startup the standby database instance in the mount state:

    SQL> startup mount;

4. Restart the managed recovery process:

    SQL> alter database recover managed standby database disconnect from session;

Loss of All Control Files

If you lose all standby control files, the first option is to restore the backup control file from RMAN backups. Here are the steps:

1. Connect to the standby database as the target database as well as to the recovery catalog.

2. Restore the backup control file from the backups with the following command:

    SQL> restore standby controlfile;

3. You must also manually catalog all archived logs generated since the last archived log backup.

If you've lost all of the control files of the standby database and you don't happen to have a backup control file for the standby database, of course, you can't restore the standby control file. You must create a brand-new standby control file from the primary database using the following steps:

1. Create a new standby control file from the primary database.

2. Copy the new control file to all the multiplexed control file locations on the standby host as specified in the initialization parameter file (SPFILE or the init.ora file).

3. Mount the standby database:

   ```
   SQL> startup mount;
   ```

4. Restart the managed recovery process:

   ```
   SQL> alter database recover managed standby database disconnect from session;
   ```

How It Works

In the Solution section, we show how to copy a good control file to replace a lost or damaged standby database control file. Alternatively, you can edit the initialization parameter `control_files` to remove the reference to the lost or damaged control file, and restart the standby database.

22-9. Recovering File(s) for a Primary Database
Problem

You've lost one or more primary database control files and would like to recover from the loss.

Solution

The way you handle the loss of control files of the primary database is similar to how you do so in the case of a single database running in a non–Oracle Data Guard environment. We divide the solution into the case where you lose only a single control file and a case where you lose all the primary database control files.

Recovering from the Loss of a Single Control File

If you've lost just a single copy of the control file (or it's corrupted and the database can't access it), simply place a good copy of one of the surviving control files over the inaccessible or missing control file and restart the primary instance. You do not need to perform a restore or a recovery in this case.

Recovering from the Loss of All Control Files

If you lose all of the control files of the primary database, you have three basic options. The choice depends on the downtime you're willing to accept.

Failover to a Standby Database

Since the primary database can't use flashback because all of its control files are gone, you must restore and recover. Failing over to a standby database incurs the least downtime of all three methods we discuss here. You can flash back to the failover SCN if the primary database is intact, this being the SCN at which an old standby database became the new primary database. Once you flash back, the standby will catch up automatically with the redo from the new primary database.

■ **Note**   If the old primary database isn't intact, you need to re-create it from a backup of the new primary database and bring it back as a new standby database.

Create a New Control File

You can execute the following SQL statement on the standby database to generate a trace file that will help you re-create the control file on the primary database:

```
SQL> alter database backup controlfile to trace noresetlogs;
```

Once you generate the trace file, edit the SQL script contained in the trace file and run it on the primary database, after starting the database in the nomount state, as shown here:

```
SQL> startup nomount
SQL> @create_ctl.sql
```

Recovering with a Backup Control File

Finally, you can use a backup control file from the primary database and recover the database, as shown here:

```
RMAN> connect target sys@primary
RMAN> restore controlfile;
RMAN> alter database mount;
RMAN> recover database;
RMAN> alter database open resetlogs;
```

How It Works

Recovering with a backup control file takes the most time of all the options we've reviewed here, but it's the only option if a failover or the re-creation of the control file from standby proves impossible. The resetlogs (alter database open resetlogs) option creates a new redo branch (new incarnation). When the archived redo log from this new redo branch reaches the standby database, it registers the new redo branch and stops the managed recovery process (MRP). When you restart MRP at the standby database later on, the database follows the new redo branch.

22-10. Configuring RMAN on a Primary Database
Problem

You want to configure RMAN optimally on the primary database in an Oracle Data Guard environment.

Solution

Oracle recommends several specific configurations for RMAN for the primary database. The following steps show how to configure RMAN for the primary database:

1. Connect to the primary database, as well as to the recovery catalog.

2. Configure the backup retention policy for the primary database:

    ```
    RMAN>configure retention policy to recovery window of 14 days.
    ```

    In this example, we chose 14 days as an example—you can set to the exact number of days dictated by your retention requirements.

3. Configure an archive log deletion policy. There are two basic archive log retention-related configuration settings you can choose. The first deletes all archive logs after they're shipped to all destinations, as shown here:

    ```
    RMAN> configure archivelog deletion policy to shipped to all standby;
    ```

    Alternatively the following archive log-related configuration directive ensures that logs are deleted only after they're applied on all standby destinations:

    ```
    RMAN> configure archivelog deletion policy to applied on all standby;
    ```

4. You must also configure the connect identifiers for the primary database and all standby databases in your Data Guard configuration:

    ```
    RMAN> configure db_unique_name boston connect identifier 'boston_conn_str';
    ```

    Once you're done, issue the `list db_unique_name` command to verify that connect identifiers for all the standby databases have been configured.

How It Works

The configuration of the primary database described here assumes that you're taking backups only on the standby database. Oracle also requires you to use a recovery catalog so you can restore backups taken on one database server on a different database server.

Oracle recommends that you

- Configure a fast recovery area local to each database

- Use a server parameter file (SPFILE)

- Enable Flashback Database on both the primary and the standby databases

22-11. Configuring RMAN in a Standby Database

Problem

You want to configure RMAN in a standby database.

Solution

You can use the following steps to optimally configure RMAN in a standby database. We're assuming that the standby database is one for which you take backups.

1. Log in to RMAN and connect to the standby database, as well as to the recovery catalog:

    ```
    $ rman target sys@standby catalog rman@catdb
    ```

2. Configure the automatic backup of the SPFILE and the control file:

    ```
    RMAN> configure controlfile autobackup on;
    ```

3. Configure backup optimization:

    ```
    RMAN configure backup optimization on;
    ```

4. Configure a tape channel for the backups:

    ```
    RMAN> configure channel device type sbt parms 'channel parameters';
    ```

5. Configure the deletion of the archived logs after backing up n times (n=2, for example):

    ```
    RMAN> configure archivelog deletion policy backed up 2 times to device type sbt;
    ```

How It Works

As mentioned in the Solution section, we're assuming that you're using the standby database for backups. If you aren't performing backups on the standby database, you can configure the deletion of archived logs once they're applied at the standby database. Thus, Step 5 in the Solution section becomes:

```
RMAN> configure archvielog deletion policy to applied on all standby;
```

22-12. Registering Databases in a Data Guard Environment
Problem

You want to register both the primary and the standby database in an Oracle Data Guard environment with RMAN.

Solution

To register a primary database, execute the `register database` command, as shown here:

```
$ rman target sys@primary catalog sys@catdb
RMAN> register database;
```

The `register database` command registers the primary database with RMAN. You don't need to explicitly register the standby database with RMAN. RMAN will automatically register the standby database in the catalog when you connect to the standby database.

How It Works

As you learned in the Solution section, there's no need to run the `register database` command to register a standby database. Even if you don't connect to a standby database, RMAN will automatically register a standby database when you execute the `configure db_unique_name` command to configure the connect identifier for a standby database.

To *unregister* a primary database, you must execute the `unregister database` command:

```
RMAN> connect target sys@primary;
RMAN> unregister database;
```

To unregister a standby database, use the `unregister db_unqiue_name` command, as shown in the following paragraphs.

Let's say your primary database has two standby databases, stdby1 and stdby2, associated with it. You'd like to unregister stdby2 but, since its backups are still used by other databases in your organization, you want to retain the backup metadata for this database. In the following example, we set the DBID of the standby database stdby2 and subsequently unregister it:

```
RMAN> connect catalog rman@catdb
recovery catalog database password: password
connected to recovery catalog database
RMAN> SET DBID 1234567899
executing command: SET DBID
database name is "PROD" and DBID is 1234567899
RMAN> unregister db_unique_name stdby2;
Database db_unique_name is "stdby2", db_name is "PROD" and DBID is 1234567899
Want to unregister the database with target db_unique_name (enter YES or NO)? YES
Database with db_unique_name stdby2 unregistered from the recovery catalog
RMAN>
```

22-13. Maintaining RMAN Backups in a Data Guard Environment
Problem

You want to maintain your RMAN backups in a Data Guard environment.

Solution

It's very important to understand how RMAN determines which backup files are associated with which database, in an Oracle Data Guard that by definition consists of multiple databases. Two things determine which files RMAN can access during a backup and recovery operation. The first of these is the set of values you specify for the db_unique_name parameter for each of the databases in the Data Guard environment. The second factor is the role played by file sharing attributes.

According to the file sharing attributes policy, the following are true:

- RMAN can access only those files on disk that are explicitly associated with a specified database.

- RMAN can access any files on tape for all databases.

How It Works

In the recovery catalog, a backup file unassociated with any database shows the value NULL in the SITE_KEY column in the row describing that database. RMAN associates backup files with the value of NULL for the SITE_KEY column with the target database.

You can execute RMAN commands such as backup and restore on any backup accessible in a Data Guard environment. Let's say you have a primary database named PROD and a standby database named stdby1 living on two different hosts. Let's say data file 1 is backed up to disk as well as to tape on the standby host. If you connect to RMAN with the PROD database as the target, you can access the tape backup of data file 1 but not the disk backup of data file 1 made on the standby database server stdby1. However, you can restore the tape backup of data file 1 made on the stdby1 database on the primary database.

22-14. Reinstating a Physical Standby Using RMAN Backups

Problem

You want to reinstate the primary database with the help of RMAN backups, following a Data Guard failover.

Solution

The following applies to all database versions 10.2.0.2 and higher. You must first ensure that you have backups for all data files. You must also have the standby control file backups, taken at the failed primary database with the alter database create standby controlfile command following a database backup. Here are the steps to follow to reinstate the primary database after a failover:

1. Get the standby_become_primary_scn from the new primary database, following the Data Guard failover:

   ```
   SQL> select to_char(STANDBY_BECAME_PRIMARY_SCN) from v$database;
   ```

2. Delete all archive logs created at or after the failover operation on the failed primary database. Issue the following command to delete the divergent archived logs from the fast recovery area:

   ```
   RMAN> delete archivelog from scn standby_become_primary_scn;
   ```

3. Restore the original failed primary database from backups:

   ```
   RMAN> restore database;
   ```

4. Using the physical standby control file, start up the standby database:

   ```
   SQL> startup mount
   ```

   If you must restore the standby database's control file backup, make sure that the initialization file you use points to the standby control file. If you don't have a standby control file from the failed primary database, you must do the following:

   a. Clean up the fast recovery area.

   b. Create a new standby control file from the new primary database.

   c. Using the new standby control file, restart the new standby database.

   d. Rename all the data and log files.

5.   Send a new archive log from the primary database to the new standby database:

```
SQL> alter system set log_archive_dest_state_n = enable;
SQL> alter system archive log current;
```

6.   Verify that the standby database has received the new archive log:

```
SQL> select dest_id, dest_name,status, type, error, destination
            from v$archive_dest_status
            where dest_id = <standby_dest#>;
```

7.   Restart the managed recovery process (MRP):

```
SQL> recover managed standby database using current logfile through all
        switchover disconnect;
```

8.   Once the standby database is in sync with the primary database, verify that the new standby database data files and control files are in sync. To do this, you must first stop the managed recovery process:

```
SQL> recover managed standby database cancel;
```

9.   Perform the validation check after opening the physical standby database read-only:

10. If you don't see any rows returned, that means the list of data files in the data dictionary matches the data files listed in the control file:

```
SQL> alter database open;
SQL> select file#, CRSCNBAS from file$
        MINUS
        select file#, creation_change# from v$datafile;
```

11. Restart managed recovery after your validation check is successful:

```
SQL> recover managed standby database using current logfile through all
        switchover disconnect;
```

How It Works

Oracle recommends that you actually use Flashback Database to reinstate the original primary database after a Data Guard failover to a physical standby database, because it gets the job done much faster than any other method. However, you sometimes may not have access to Flashback Database, either because you didn't enable it or because the flashback data isn't accessible for some other reason. In such cases, you can reinstate the original primary database using RMAN backups, as shown in the Solution section.

Since a backup control file may not always reflect the same list of data files as that recorded in the data dictionary, it's a good practice to create a standby control file after each backup.

In the Solution section, we showed how to remove any archive logs created at or after the failover operation. If the primary database was isolated from the standby for any length of time, the archive logs on the standby could be inconsistent with those on the current primary database. To avoid problems from applying these divergent archive logs, you must delete them from both your backups, as well as from the fast recovery area.

RMAN and RAC

RAC (Real Application Cluster) technology is pretty common for serious databases that have stringent availability requirements. Today many databases are on RAC. In this chapter you will learn about some of the nuances of RMAN specifically on RAC.

23-1. Specifying a Location for the Snapshot Controlfile

Problem

You want to set the location of the snapshot controlfile in the RMAN job on a RAC database.

Solution

The snapshot controlfile must be in location accessible from all nodes of a RAC database. The location could be as simple as a NFS mountpoint; or an ASM diskgroup. We will show both approaches.

Here's what to do:

1. Decide a common location, e.g. an NFS mountpoint called /commonfs or an ASM diskgroup called BACKUP.

2. Configure the snapshot controlfile to that location:

   ```
   RMAN>  configure snapshot controlfile name to '+PRODBDATA1/snapcf_PRODB.ctl';

   old RMAN configuration parameters:
   CONFIGURE SNAPSHOT CONTROLFILE NAME TO '+DATA';
   new RMAN configuration parameters:
   CONFIGURE SNAPSHOT CONTROLFILE NAME TO '+PRODBDATA1/snapcf_PRODB.ctl';
   new RMAN configuration parameters are successfully stored
   ```

3. Make sure the snapshot controlfile is indeed there:

   ```
   RMAN> show snapshot controlfile name;

   RMAN configuration parameters for database with db_unique_name PRODB are:
   CONFIGURE SNAPSHOT CONTROLFILE NAME TO '+PRODBDATA1/snapcf_PRODB.ctl';
   ```

If you wanted to locate the snapshot controlfile in /commonfs, you would have given:

```
RMAN> configure snapshot controlfile name to '/commonfs/snapcf_PRODB.ctl';
```

The technique is the same. The difference lies in whether you begin the target name with a + or with a /, indicating an ASM group or a mount point respectively.

How It Works

When an RMAN job executes, it has to read the information from the controlfile repeatedly. But the controlfile is a constantly updated file - a moving target. Therefore RMAN takes a snapshot of the controlfile before starting the job. This "copy" of the controlfile is known as snapshot controlfile. It is used only for RMAN; nothing else. After the backup job is complete, RMAN updates the actual controlfile from the snapshot controlfile. Therefore the controlfile is locked only twice - one during the creation of snapshot controlfile and later during the update from the snapshot to the real controlfile.

Since the snapshot controlfile is pretty critical in the backup operation, it's important that (a) it's on a highly performant disk and (b) the RMAN sessions can access it. If you let the RMAN process run on all the nodes of the cluster, then this file must be visible to all the nodes. The default location of the file is on Oracle Home. You can confirm that by using the following command:

```
RMAN> show snapshot controlfile name;

RMAN configuration parameters for database with db_unique_name PRODB are:
CONFIGURE SNAPSHOT CONTROLFILE NAME TO '/ndsint/oradb/db2/dbs/snapcf_PRODB1.f'; # default
```

The default location, as you can see above, is $ORACLE_HOME/dbs directory and the name is snapcf_<InstanceName>.f. Normally, Oracle Home is a local file system; so other RAC nodes can't access it. You should change it to a new location that is common to all the nodes.

23-2. Parallelizing a Backup Across All Nodes in a Cluster (11.2 and Higher)

Problem

In your Oracle 11.2 RAC database you have more than one node, and you want to leverage the full power of all the nodes during the backup rather than taxing only one node.

Solution

RMAN is an operating system program that is invoked from the command line. Operating systems are specific to a server (or a node), and hence the program can run on only one node. The RMAN command creates the channels to be used for backup, and all the channels are created on the same node where the RMAN command is invoked—making it heavily used while underutilizing the rest of the nodes. Your objective is to spread the channels across all the nodes of the cluster regardless of the node on which the RMAN command was invoked.

The solution changes beginning in Oracle Database 11.2. That version introduces the Single Client Access Name (SCAN) feature. In this recipe, we will explain the approach with the SCAN concept. The next recipe shows the pre-11.2 method.

1. Create a service called RMAN (it can be of any name) that can be on all the instances of the cluster:

```
proltestdb01.oradb:/home/oradb # srvctl add service -d prodb -s RMAN -r "PRODB1,PRODB2"
-P BASIC -e SESSION -m BASIC -j LONG -B NONE
```

2. Start that service:

```
proltestdb01.oradb:/home/oradb # srvctl start service -d prodb -s RMAN
```

3. Confirm that the service is running on all the instances of the cluster:

```
proltestdb01.oradb:/home/oradb # srvctl status service -d prodb -s RMAN
Service RMAN is running on instance(s) PRODB1,PRODB2
```

4. If the service is already created, confirm that it has the necessary properties:

```
proltestdb01.oradb:/home/oradb # srvctl config service -d prodb -s RMAN
Service name: RMAN
Service is enabled
Server pool: prodb_RMAN
Cardinality: 2
Disconnect: false
Service role: PRIMARY
Management policy: AUTOMATIC
DTP transaction: false
AQ HA notifications: false
Failover type: SESSION
Failover method: BASIC
TAF failover retries: 0
TAF failover delay: 0
Connection Load Balancing Goal: LONG
Runtime Load Balancing Goal: NONE
TAF policy specification: BASIC
Edition:
Preferred instances: PRODB1,PRODB2
Available instances:
```

The output shows "Preferred instances: PRODB1,PRODB2", which is what I needed to see.

5. Define a TNS alias that uses the SCAN names and the RMAN service to connect to the database. In all the nodes of the database, put this entry in the TNSNAMES.ORA file:

```
RMAN=
    (DESCRIPTION=
        (ADDRESS = (PROTOCOL =TCP)(HOST = prodb01-scan.proligence.com)(PORT=1521))
        (CONNECT_DATA =
            (SERVER=DEDICATED)
            (SERVICE_NAME=RMAN)
        )
    )
```

6. Test to make sure this TNS entry is valid:

```
prolin101.oradb: # tnsping RMAN

TNS Ping Utility for IBM/AIX RISC System/6000: Version 11.2.0.3.0 - Production on
31-AUG-2012 20:37:12

Copyright (c) 1997, 2011, Oracle.  All rights reserved.

Used parameter files:

Used TNSNAMES adapter to resolve the alias
Attempting to contact (DESCRIPTION= (ADDRESS = (PROTOCOL =TCP)(HOST = prodb01-scan)
(PORT=1521)) (CONNECT_DATA = (SERVER=DEDICATED) (SERVICE_NAME=RMAN)))
OK (200 msec)
```

7. Create an RMAN user in the database:

```
SQL> grant dba to rman identified by secretsauze;

Grant succeeded.
```

8. Connect a session to this TNS entry to make sure the service name, etc. are valid:

```
prolin101.oradb # sqlplus rman/secretsauze@RMAN

SQL*Plus: Release 11.2.0.3.0 Production on Fri Aug 31 20:40:41 2012

Copyright (c) 1982, 2011, Oracle.  All rights reserved.

Connected to:
Oracle Database 11g Enterprise Edition Release 11.2.0.3.0 - 64bit Production
With the Partitioning, Real Application Clusters, Automatic Storage Management, OLAP,
Data Mining and Real Application Testing options
```

9. Now that this setup is complete, create channels in the following manner to use this
    service name:

```
RMAN> connect rman/secretsauze@rman
2> run {
3>      allocate channel c1 type disk format '+BACKUP/%u.rmb';
4>      allocate channel c2 type disk format '+BACKUP/%u.rmb';
5>      allocate channel c3 type disk format '+BACKUP/%u.rmb';
6>      allocate channel c4 type disk format '+BACKUP/%u.rmb';
7>      allocate channel c5 type disk format '+BACKUP/%u.rmb';
8>      allocate channel c6 type disk format '+BACKUP/%u.rmb';
9>      ... backup commands come here ...
10> }
```

It will produce the following output:

```
connected to target database: PRODB (DBID=3290063591)

using target database control file instead of recovery catalog
allocated channel: c1
channel c1: SID=2 instance=PRODB2 device type=DISK

allocated channel: c2
channel c2: SID=966 instance=PRODB2 device type=DISK

allocated channel: c3
channel c3: SID=194 instance=PRODB1 device type=DISK

allocated channel: c4
channel c4: SID=147 instance=PRODB1 device type=DISK

allocated channel: c5
channel c5: SID=1397 instance=PRODB2 device type=DISK

allocated channel: c6
channel c6: SID=1445 instance=PRODB2 device type=DISK
```

The output has been truncated for the sake of brevity. The output shows that the channels created—c1 through c6—are spread over the instances PRODB1 and PRODB2.

10. While this is running, connect to SYS on a different session and find out the sessions created for RMAN:

```
select inst_id, sid, username, service_name
from gv$session
where program like '%rman%'
/

    INST_ID      SID USERNAME SERVICE_NAME
    ------ ---------- -------- ------------
         1      100 SYS      RMAN
         1      147 SYS      RMAN
         1      194 SYS      RMAN
         2        2 SYS      RMAN
         2      966 SYS      RMAN
         2     1299 SYS      RMAN
         2     1397 SYS      RMAN
         2     1445 SYS      RMAN
```

Note the sessions are all spread out on both the instances.

11. Wait until the RMAN job completes.

How It Works

You know that RMAN channels are nothing but database sessions that facilitate data movement. Unlike regular user sessions, they extract data blocks and write to a target device—either disk or tape—but they are sessions nonetheless. The trick is to spread these sessions across all the instances of the RAC cluster instead of concentrating them on only the node where the RMAN command was given. This is where the connection to the SCAN listener comes in.

To begin, do not connect via the usual sort of command that depends upon operating system authentication:

```
connect target /
Instead, connect using a TNS alias as shown below:connect target rman/secretsauze@rman
```

Use of a TNS alias causes RMAN to connect using Oracle Net. Your session is then connected to the SCAN listener using the service name—in this case, RMAN. You have defined the service on all the instances of the RAC cluster. Therefore, any sessions connected to the SCAN service will be automatically spread over all the instances.

In addition, note one specific property of the service from the srvctl config service command given in the solution:

```
Runtime Load Balancing Goal: NONE
```

This property ensures that the sessions will be distributed over the instances in a round-robin manner. They will be distributed in equal numbers rather than possibly being concentrated onto nodes based on load. This even distribution is desirable, because you won't know in advance how the nodes will be loaded over the whole period of the RMAN backup. A relatively less loaded node might become highly loaded in the next few hours due to application demands. If you create more RMAN sessions on that node because it is less loaded, the node might end up becoming highly overloaded, and it might even crash or cause other performance issues.

23-3. Parallelizing a Backup Across All Nodes in a Cluster (Below 11.2)

Problem

In your pre-11.2 RAC database you have more than one node. You want to leverage the full power of all the nodes during a backup rather than taxing only one node.

Solution

The solution is similar to that in Recipe 23-2, but unlike that recipe, this solution is for all RAC databases; it is not restricted to Oracle 11.2 and above. Note that for databases 11.2 and above, you should choose Recipe 23-2.

1. Put the following two TNS entries into the TNSNAMES.ORA file:

```
RMAN1=
    (DESCRIPTION=
      (LOAD_BALANCE=NO)
      (ADDRESS_LIST=
          (ADDRESS = (PROTOCOL =TCP)(HOST = prolin1-oravip)(PORT=1521))
          (ADDRESS = (PROTOCOL =TCP)(HOST = prolin2-oravip)(PORT=1521))
      )
      (CONNECT_DATA =
```

```
                    (SERVER=DEDICATED)
                    (SERVICE_NAME=RMAN1)
            )
        )

RMAN2=
      (DESCRIPTION=
        (ADDRESS_LIST=
        (LOAD_BALANCE=NO)
        (FAILOVER=ON)
            (ADDRESS = (PROTOCOL =TCP)(HOST = prolin2-oravip)(PORT=1521))
            (ADDRESS = (PROTOCOL =TCP)(HOST = prolin1-oravip)(PORT=1521))
        )
        (CONNECT_DATA =
            (SERVER=DEDICATED)
            (SERVICE_NAME=RMAN2)
        )
      )
```

2. Create two service names:

```
# srvctl add service -d PRODB -s RMAN2 -r "PRODB2" -a "PRODB1" -P BASIC -e SESSION -m
BASIC -j LONG -B NONE
# srvctl add service -d PRODB -s RMAN1 -r "PRODB1" -a "PRODB2" -P BASIC -e SESSION -m
BASIC -j LONG -B NONE
```

3. Start the services:

```
# srvctl start service -d PRODB -s RMAN1
# srvctl start service -d PRODB -s RMAN2
```

4. Make sure the services are correctly defined:

```
# srvctl config service -d PRODB -s RMAN1
Service name: RMAN1
Service is enabled
Server pool: PRODB_RMAN1
Cardinality: 1
Disconnect: false
Service role: PRIMARY
Management policy: AUTOMATIC
DTP transaction: false
AQ HA notifications: false
Failover type: SESSION
Failover method: BASIC
TAF failover retries: 0
TAF failover delay: 0
Connection Load Balancing Goal: LONG
Runtime Load Balancing Goal: NONE
TAF policy specification: BASIC
Edition:
```

```
Preferred instances: PRODB1
Available instances: PRODB2
```

Repeat the command for service RMAN2.

5. Connect to make sure the TNS entries are correct:

```
# sqlplus rman/secretsauze@rman1

SQL*Plus: Release 11.2.0.3.0 Production on Sun Sep 2 03:44:25 2012

Copyright (c) 1982, 2011, Oracle.  All rights reserved.

Connected to:
Oracle Database 11g Enterprise Edition Release 11.2.0.3.0 - 64bit Production
With the Partitioning, Real Application Clusters, Automatic Storage Management, OLAP,
Data Mining and Real Application Testing options
```

Repeat for the other service—RMAN2.

6. Run the RMAN commands as shown:

```
connect target /
run {
        allocate channel c1 type disk connect rman/secretsauze@rman1 format '+BACKUP/%u.rmb';
        allocate channel c2 type disk connect rman/secretsauze@rman2 format '+BACKUP/%u.rmb';
        host "sleep 120";
        backup tablespace rmantest;
}
```

The output comes back as:

```
using target database control file instead of recovery catalog
allocated channel: c1
channel c1: SID=678 instance=PRODB1 device type=DISK

allocated channel: c2
channel c2: SID=724 instance=PRODB2 device type=DISK
... output truncated ...
```

7. Check the sessions when RMAN is running:

```
select inst_id, sid
from gv$session
where program like '%rman%'
/

INST_ID    SID
-------  -------
      1      678
      2      724
```

The output here shows that the channels are created on both the instances, not on just one of them. This is what you want to see.

How It Works

Prior to 11.2 and the introduction of SCAN, the way to get multiple channels, with each going to a different instance, is to define them separately. For example:

```
allocate channel c1 type disk connect rman/secretsauze@rman1 ...
allocate channel c2 type disk connect rman/secretsauze@rman2 ...
```

Notice the connect commands each specify a TNS alias name. Their doing so causes RMAN to start the channels using the TNS aliases called RMAN1 and RMAN2. The aliases RMAN1 and RMAN2 have been defined on node 1 and node 2, respectively, of the RAC cluster. Therefore, channel c1 connects automatically to node 1, and channel c2 to node 2, even if the RMAN command is given on node 1.

In addition, note the two specific properties of the service RMAN1 from the srvctl config service command given in the solution. These two properties are:

```
Preferred instances: PRODB1
Available instances: PRODB2
```

These mean that the service runs on only instance PRODB (node 1). But if that node is down, the service will automatically fail over to instance PRODB2 (node 2). So, the RMAN job will be successful even if instance 1 is down.

23-4. Restoring on Multiple Nodes
Problem

You are restoring the database from the backup and you want to ensure that all the nodes of the RAC cluster are used in the restore process and not just the node where you kicked off the restore job.

Solution

The trick is to use a little-known syntax in restore command for specifying the channel name.

1. Follow steps 1 through 5 in Recipe 23-2.

2. Decide which files to restore in which nodes. For instance, you may decide to restore files 1, 3, and 5 through node 1, and files 2, 4, and 6 through node 2.

3. Then issue the following restore command from within RMAN:

```
connect target /
run {
        allocate channel c1 type disk connect rman/secretsauze@rman1;
        allocate channel c2 type disk connect rman/secretsauze@rman2;
        restore
                (datafile 1,3,5 channel c1)
                (datafile 2,4,6 channel c2);
}
```

Choose the data files contained within one backup set to be restored through one channel. In this example I am assuming that the data files 1, 3, and 5 are in one backup set and 2, 4, and 6 are in the other. If you decide to restore the entire database, use:

```
connect target /
run {
        allocate channel c1 type disk connect rman/secretsauze@rman1;
        allocate channel c2 type disk connect rman/secretsauze@rman2;
        restore database;
}
```

How It Works

RMAN channels are nothing but sessions. When you allocate a channel, by default it creates the sessions in the instance running on that node.

Normally you allocate a channel as follows:

```
allocate channel c2 type disk;
```

But you can choose instead to specify the connect clause in the allocate channel command:

```
allocate channel c2 type disk connect rman/secretsauze@rman2;
```

When you take this approach, sessions will be connected as specified in the connect string—rman2, in this case. Since rman2 points to the service name RMAN2, and since that service runs on node 2, the session will be created on instance 2. The RMAN command can be executed in node 1, but channel c2 will still be created in node 2.

The (datafile <Datafile#> channel <ChannelName>) syntax in restore command forces the restores through the named channel, and consequently through the node on which the channel is created. That is how the solution example directs different files to be restored by different nodes.

23-5. Backing Up a RAC Database to Tape
Problem

You have an RAC database with multiple instances. While backing up this database to tape, you want the tape channels to be open and running on all the nodes of the cluster.

Solution

Follow steps 1 through 5 of Recipe 23-3. After that, there are two options for accomplishing your objective. In both the options, we have assumed a NetBackup environment for tape backup.

Option 1: Runtime Channel Creation

Allocate channels in the following manner.

```
run {
    allocate channel c1 type sbt PARMS='ENV=(NB_ORA_CLIENT=RMAN1)' connect='rman/secretsauze@rman1';
    allocate channel c2 type sbt PARMS='ENV=(NB_ORA_CLIENT=RMAN2)' connect='rman/secretsauze@rman2';
    backup database;
}
```

Option 2: Pre-configuration of Channels

Configure the channels before starting the actual backup:

```
RMAN> configure channel 1 device type 'sbt' connect 'rman/secretsauze@rman1' PARMS
    "ENV=(NB_ORA_CLIENT=RMAN1)";
RMAN> configure channel 2 device type 'sbt' connect 'rman/secretsauze@rman2' PARMS
    "ENV=(NB_ORA_CLIENT=RMAN2)";
```

Then back up normally from the RMAN prompt.

```
run {
    backup database;
}
```

How It Works

As mentioned in the previous recipes, RMAN connects to the database via a session and uses that session to extract data blocks. The session makes up a channel. By specifying the connect clause in the channel command, you can connect to a specific node. The NB_ORA_CLIENT environmental parameter of the NetBackup command also allows you to specify a TNS alias that points to a specific node. This new channel creation syntax in NetBackup allows you to create channels on different nodes as your needs dictate.

CHAPTER 24

■ ■ ■

RMAN and ASM

In this chapter you will learn about using RMAN in an environment where Automatic Storage Management (ASM) is used as source storage, target storage, or both. The broad principles are the same as for any other use of RMAN. However, there are some ASM-specific aspects to be aware of.

24-1. Defining ASM Diskgroups as Backup Destinations
Problem

You want to use an ASM disk group as a backup destination.

Solution

RMAN does not differentiate between ASM and file systems, so the overall approach remains the same. The only difference is that ASM disk groups are designated by a "+" before the name instead of "/" as in the case of file systems. Here is an example of using the disk group DG1 as the backup location.

1. Set the environment to point to the ASM instance:

    ```
    [oragrid@prolabtst11 ~]$ . oraenv
    ORACLE_SID = [oragrid] ? +ASM
    The Oracle base has been set to /u01/app/oragrid
    ```

2. Check that the ORACLE_SID is indeed set to +ASM:

    ```
    [oragrid@prolabtst11 ~]$ echo $ORACLE_SID
    +ASM
    ```

3. Log into the ASM instance using ASMCMD:

    ```
    [oragrid@prolabtst11 ~]$ asmcmd -p
    ASMCMD [+] >
    ```

4. Find out the available space in the disk group to ensure your backup will fit in.

    ```
    ASMCMD [+] > lsdg
    State    Type    Rebal  Sector  Block      AU  Total_MB  Free_MB  Req_mir_free_MB
    Usable_file_MB  Offline_disks  Voting_files  Name
    ```

MOUNTED	NORMAL	N		512	4096	1048576	204796	189697		51199
69249			0		N	DATA/				
MOUNTED	NORMAL	N		512	4096	1048576	102398	86072		0
43036			0		N	DG1/				
MOUNTED	EXTERN	N		512	4096	1048576	102398	84198		0
84198			0		N	FRA/				

From the above output checking under the column "Free_MB" you can see that DG1 has 86072 MB, which is more than enough for the backup.

5. If you want to separate the backup files from the rest, you should create a separate directory called, say, rman:

```
ASMCMD [+] > cd dg1
ASMCMD [+dg1] > mkdir rman
```

6. Set the environment to the database instance now:

```
[oragrid@prolabtst11 ~]$ . oraenv
ORACLE_SID = [oragrid] ? IDB1
The Oracle base has been set to /u01/app/oragrid
```

7. Connect to RMAN:

```
[oragrid@prolabtst11 ~]$ rman target=/

Recovery Manager: Release 12.1.0.0.2 - Beta on Sat Aug 18 10:51:25 2012

Copyright (c) 1982, 2012, Oracle and/or its affiliates.  All rights reserved.

connected to target database: IDB1 (DBID=420374953)
```

8. Take a backup in the directory:

```
RMAN> run {
2> allocate channel c1 type disk format '+DG1/RMAN/%U.rmb';
3> allocate channel c2 type disk format '+DG1/RMAN/%U.rmb';
4>   backup datafile 1;
5> }

allocated channel: c1
channel c1: SID=15 device type=DISK

allocated channel: c2
channel c2: SID=267 device type=DISK

Starting backup at 18-AUG-12
channel c1: starting full datafile backup set
channel c1: specifying datafile(s) in backup set
input datafile file number=00001 name=+DATA/idb1/datafile/system.282.790482827
channel c1: starting piece 1 at 18-AUG-12
channel c2: starting full datafile backup set
```

```
channel c2: specifying datafile(s) in backup set
including current control file in backup set
channel c2: starting piece 1 at 18-AUG-12
channel c2: finished piece 1 at 18-AUG-12
piece handle=+DG1/rman/Omniuq8u_1_1.rmb tag=TAG20120818T105733 comment=NONE
channel c2: backup set complete, elapsed time: 00:00:01
channel c2: starting full datafile backup set
channel c2: specifying datafile(s) in backup set
including current SPFILE in backup set
channel c2: starting piece 1 at 18-AUG-12
channel c2: finished piece 1 at 18-AUG-12
piece handle=+DG1/rman/Onniuq9O_1_1.rmb tag=TAG20120818T105733 comment=NONE
channel c2: backup set complete, elapsed time: 00:00:01
channel c1: finished piece 1 at 18-AUG-12
piece handle=+DG1/rman/Olniuq8u_1_1.rmb tag=TAG20120818T105733 comment=NONE
channel c1: backup set complete, elapsed time: 00:00:17
Finished backup at 18-AUG-12
released channel: c1
released channel: c2
```

9. Check for the existence of this backup in the ASM disk group:

```
ASMCMD [+dg1/rman] > ls
Olniuq8u_1_1.rmb
Omniuq8u_1_1.rmb
Onniuq9O_1_1.rmb
```

You can see that these backup piece files have been created by the RMAN command.

How It Works

While RMAN is operationally similar whether it is backing up to a file system or to a disk group, you have to be aware of a very important property of the ASM volume manager. The following example shows how to get the list of files in that directory.

```
ASMCMD [+dg1/rman] > ls
Olniuq8u_1_1.rmb
Omniuq8u_1_1.rmb
Onniuq9O_1_1.rmb
```

The files may appear to be there. But they are actually aliases, not real files. To find out the actual files, use the "-ls" modifier to the ls command. For example:

```
ASMCMD [+dg1/rman] > ls -ls
Type       Redund  Striped  Time           Sys  Block_Size  Blocks    Bytes      Space       Name
BACKUPSET  MIRROR  COARSE   AUG 18 10:00:00 N         8192    87974  720683008  1445986304
Olniuq8u_1_1.rmb => +DG1/IDB1/BACKUPSET/2012_08_18/nnndf0_TAG20120818T105733_0.256.791636255
BACKUPSET  MIRROR  COARSE   AUG 18 10:00:00 N        16384      630   10321920    20971520
Omniuq8u_1_1.rmb => +DG1/IDB1/BACKUPSET/2012_08_18/ncnnf0_TAG20120818T105733_0.258.791636255
BACKUPSET  MIRROR  COARSE   AUG 18 10:00:00 N        16384        6      98304     2097152
Onniuq9O_1_1.rmb => +DG1/IDB1/BACKUPSET/2012_08_18/nnsnf0_TAG20120818T105733_0.278.791636257
```

Note the actual files are located in +DG1/IDB1/BACKUPSET/<DateOfBackup> directory, not in the +DG1/RMAN directory as you intended. What is the consequence of this? Fortunately, not much, at least not to users of that disk group. The backup still shows up under the rman directory. Notice the value for "Piece Name" in the output to the following list backup command:

```
RMAN> list backup of datafile 1;

List of Backup Sets
===================

BS Key  Type LV Size        Device Type Elapsed Time Completion Time
------- ---- -- ---------- ----------- ------------ ---------------
16      Full    687.29M    DISK          00:00:10    18-AUG-12
        BP Key: 16   Status: AVAILABLE  Compressed: NO  Tag: TAG20120818T105733
        Piece Name: +DG1/rman/0lniuq8u_1_1.rmb
  List of Datafiles in backup set 16
  File LV Type Ckp SCN    Ckp Time  Name
  ---- -- ---- ---------- --------- ----
  1       Full 2500061    18-AUG-12 +DATA/idb1/datafile/system.282.790482827
```

Note from the output that the backup piece is still shown as:

```
+DG1/rman/0lniuq8u_1_1.rmb
```

In other words, you see the alias in the rman directory, not the actual file name of:

```
+DG1/IDB1/BACKUPSET/2012_08_18/nnndf0_TAG20120818T105733_0.256.791636255
```

So, why does RMAN not keep the actual files in the rman directory? The reason is due to a property of ASM, which manages and organizes files under a scheme called Oracle Managed Files (OMF). ASM reads the metadata of a file and places the file under an appropriate directory by default. For instance, it placed the backup pieces under the directory called BACKUPSETS, in turn under the directory IDB1, which is the name of the database. Furthermore, ASM also put the files under a directory named after the date on which the backup was executed. This keeps the files organized in a tidy manner. Note that you did not create the directories IDB1, BACKUPSET, and 2012_08_18; ASM did that for you.

What will happen if you delete the alias? Let's see:

```
ASMCMD [+dg1/rman] > rm 0lniuq8u_1_1.rmb
ASMCMD [+dg1/rman] > cd  +DG1/IDB1/BACKUPSET/2012_08_18
ASMCMD [+DG1/IDB1/BACKUPSET/2012_08_18] > ls -ls
Type       Redund  Striped  Time          Sys  Block_Size  Blocks      Bytes      Space  Name
BACKUPSET  MIRROR  COARSE   AUG 18 10:00:00  Y       16384     630   10321920   20971520  ncnnf0_TA
G20120818T105733_0.258.791636255
BACKUPSET  MIRROR  COARSE   AUG 18 10:00:00  Y       16384       6      98304    2097152  nnsnf0_TA
G20120818T105733_0.278.791636257
```

Note that the actual file was deleted as well, automatically. Similarly, if you remove all the files, the directories created by ASM will also disappear. For example:

```
ASMCMD [+dg1/rman] > rm *
You may delete multiple files and/or directories.
Are you sure? (y/n) y
```

```
ASMCMD [+dg1/rman] > ls
ASMCMD [+dg1/rman] > cd +DG1/IDB1
ASMCMD [+DG1/IDB1] > ls
TEMPFILE/
```

There is no directory called BACKUPSETS anymore. Since ASM created that directory for you, ASM will delete it when it is no longer needed.

Now that you know that the actual files created will be different from the names you gave and they will be under directories different from what you gave, should you bother creating directories under the ASM disk group? In our opinion, you should. It will be easier to locate and administer backup pieces in that location rather than directly on the DG1 disk group. If you have multiple databases being backed up to the same disk group, putting them under different directories will make organization a breeze. Remember, RMAN repository—whether controlfile or catalog—knows about the aliases alone, not the real file. So, you might find it useful to organize backups under appropriately named directories, leaving ASM to create the necessary system directories and files as needed.

24-2. Specifying ASM Diskgroups as Archivelog Locations

Problem

You want to define the archived logs to go to an ASM disk group instead of to a file system.

Solution

Suppose you want archived logs to go into a disk group called +DG. Use the following steps:

1. Set the log_archive_dest_1 parameter in the database:

    ```
    SQL> alter system set log_archive_dest_1 = 'LOCATION=+DG1';

    System altered.
    ```

2. Enable that destination, if not enabled already:

    ```
    SQL> alter system set log_archive_dest_state_1 = enable;

    System altered.
    ```

3. Confirm that the archived log location is set:

    ```
    SQL> archive log list;
    Database log mode              Archive Mode
    Automatic archival             Enabled
    Archive destination            +DG1
    Oldest online log sequence     92
    Next log sequence to archive   94
    Current log sequence           94
    ```

    The output "Archive destination +DG1" confirms that the location was set properly.

4. Now that the archived log destination is set, you want to back up the archived log to an
    ASM storage location, more specifically to a disk group RMANBAK. Here's how:

```
RMAN> backup archivelog sequence 94 format '+RMANBAK/%U.rmb';

Starting backup at 18-AUG-12
using channel ORA_DISK_1
channel ORA_DISK_1: starting archived log backup set
channel ORA_DISK_1: specifying archived log(s) in backup set
input archived log thread=1 sequence=94 RECID=85 STAMP=791648751
channel ORA_DISK_1: starting piece 1 at 18-AUG-12
channel ORA_DISK_1: finished piece 1 at 18-AUG-12
piece handle=+RMANBAK/0vniv6pv_1_1.rmb tag=TAG20120818T143126 comment=NONE
channel ORA_DISK_1: backup set complete, elapsed time: 00:00:01
Finished backup at 18-AUG-12
```

You have now completed the placement of archived logs on an ASM disk group.

How It Works

When you point archived logs into a specific directory in ASM, the archived logs are not actually created there.
This is due to the property of Oracle Managed Files (OMF) in ASM volume manager (described in Recipe 24-1).
You can confirm that by checking for the actual files and aliases inside the disk group DG1:

```
ASMCMD> cd +dg1
ASMCMD> ls -l
Type  Redund  Striped  Time         Sys  Name
                                     Y    ASM/
                                     Y    IDB1/
                                     N    rman/
                                     N    rmanbackup/
```

Note that the archivelog file created earlier is nowhere to be seen in the directory +DG1. Where did it go? To find
out, check the Oracle Managed File structure. The OMF file is created inside IDB1 (the name of the database).

```
ASMCMD> cd IDB1
ASMCMD> ls -ls
Type  Redund  Striped  Time         Sys  Block_Size  Blocks  Bytes  Space  Name
                                     Y                                      ARCHIVELOG/
                                     Y                                      BACKUPSET/
                                     Y                                      TEMPFILE/
ASMCMD> cd ARCHIVELOG
ASMCMD> ls
2012_08_18/
ASMCMD> ls -ls
Type  Redund  Striped  Time         Sys  Block_Size  Blocks  Bytes  Space  Name
                                     Y                                      2012_08_18/
```

```
ASMCMD> cd 2012_08_18
ASMCMD> ls -ls
Type         Redund  Striped  Time            Sys  Block_Size  Blocks    Bytes      Space     Name
ARCHIVELOG   MIRROR  COARSE   AUG 18 14:00:00  Y          512   13260  6789120   14680064   thread_1_
seq_94.279.791648751
```

The archived log is in the structure <DB Unique Name>/ARCHIVELOG/YYYY_MM_DD. Note that there is no alias. The file just got created there.

What about the location of the backup of the archived logs? Suppose you specify DG1 as the backup location for the archived logs:

```
RMAN> backup archivelog sequence 94 format '+RMANBAK/%U.rmb';

Starting backup at 18-AUG-12
using channel ORA_DISK_1
channel ORA_DISK_1: starting archived log backup set
channel ORA_DISK_1: specifying archived log(s) in backup set
input archived log thread=1 sequence=94 RECID=85 STAMP=791648751
channel ORA_DISK_1: starting piece 1 at 18-AUG-12
channel ORA_DISK_1: finished piece 1 at 18-AUG-12
piece handle=+RMANBAK/0vniv6pv_1_1.rmb tag=TAG20120818T143126 comment=NONE
channel ORA_DISK_1: backup set complete, elapsed time: 00:00:01
Finished backup at 18-AUG-12
```

If you check in ASM for the RMAN backup piece created, you'll get results as follows:

```
ASMCMD> cd +RMANBAK
ASMCMD> ls -ls
Type        Redund  Striped  Time            Sys  Block_Size  Blocks    Bytes      Space     Name
BACKUPSET   MIRROR  COARSE   AUG 18 14:00:00  N          512   13263  6790656   14680064
0vniv6pv_1_1.rmb => +RMANBAK/IDB1/BACKUPSET/2012_08_18/annnf0_TAG20120818T143126_0.280.791649087
                                             Y                                              ASM/
                                             Y                                              IDB1/
                                             N                                              rman/
                                             N                                              rmanbackup/
```

As you can see in the output, the backup piece "0vniv6pv_1_1.rmb " was created as an alias. The actual file was "annnf0_TAG20120818T143126_0.280.791649087" under directory structure "IDB1/BACKUPSET/2012_08_18," following the established OMF structure. If you check in that directory for the presence of the actual file, you will find it:

```
ASMCMD> cd +RMANBAK/IDB1/BACKUPSET/2012_08_18
ASMCMD> ls -ls
Type        Redund  Striped  Time            Sys  Block_Size  Blocks      Bytes        Space     Name
BACKUPSET   MIRROR  COARSE   AUG 18 14:00:00  Y          512   13263    6790656     14680064   annnf0_
TAG20120818T143126_0.280.791649087
BACKUPSET   MIRROR  COARSE   AUG 18 13:00:00  Y        16384     632   10354688     20971520   ncsnf0_
TAG20120818T130056_0.258.791643673
BACKUPSET   MIRROR  COARSE   AUG 18 13:00:00  Y         8192   87974  720683008   1445986304   nnndf0_
TAG20120818T130056_0.278.791643657
```

It's very important to keep this property in mind. The files of known types—data files, archived logs, backup sets, etc.—are stored in appropriate locations in an ASM disk group, regardless of the location given in RMAN.

24-3. Copying Files to or from ASM
Problem

You want to copy a file to or from an ASM disk group using RMAN.

Solution

You have three options for copying files into or out of an ASM disk group:

- Through ASMCMD
- Through DBMS file transfer utility
- Through RMAN

Although the only option relevant to this section is the last one—through RMAN—we will explain the others as well to show the differences among them.

ASMCMD Approach

Oracle Database 10.2 introduced ASMCMD, a command line tool to manage files and directories under ASM disk groups. Using that tool is one of the ways to copy files. Here is an example:

1. Set the environment to point to the ASM instance:

```
[oragrid@prolabtst11 ~]$ . oraenv
ORACLE_SID = [oragrid] ? +ASM
The Oracle base has been set to /u01/app/oragrid
```

2. Check that the ORACLE_SID is indeed set to +ASM:

```
[oragrid@prolabtst11 ~]$ echo $ORACLE_SID
+ASM
```

3. Log into the ASM instance using ASMCMD:

```
[oragrid@prolabtst11 ~]$ asmcmd -p
ASMCMD [+] >
```

4. Inside the ASMCMD prompt, use the cp command to copy the source file to the destination file, along with the proper directory:

```
ASMCMD [+DG1/rman] > cp 0oniv1g8_1_1.rmb +dg1/rmanbackup/0oniv1g8_1_1.rmb
copying +DG1/rman/0oniv1g8_1_1.rmb -> +dg1/rmanbackup/0oniv1g8_1_1.rmb
ASMCMD>
```

5. Note that the file "0oniv1g8_1_1.rmb" is not actually placed in the RMANBACKUP directory; only the alias is put there. You can confirm that by:

```
ASMCMD [+DG1/rman] > cd ../rmanbackup
ASMCMD [+DG1/rmanbackup] > ls -l
```

```
Type        Redund  Striped  Time            Sys  Name
BACKUPSET   MIRROR  COARSE   AUG 18 13:00:00  N   0oniv1g8_1_1.rmb => +DG1/ASM/
BACKUPSET/0oniv1g8_1_1.rmb.256.791643731
```

The file was an alias to +DG1/ASM/BACKUPSET/0oniv1g8_1_1.rmb.256.791643731, as an OMF file is supposed to be.

6. If you want to copy a file to a file system from ASM, you can do that, too:

```
ASMCMD> cp 0pniv1go_1_1.rmb /tmp/a.dbf
copying +dg1/rman/0pniv1go_1_1.rmb -> /tmp/a.dbf
```

DBMS File Copy Approach

If the ASMCMD command line tool is not available, or you are on a version prior to Oracle Database 10.2, you can use a package dbms_file_transfer to copy files. Here is an example:

1. First, create the directory object on each of the source and destination ASM disk groups:

```
SQL> create directory rman as '+DG1/RMAN';

Directory created.

SQL> create directory rmanbackup as '+DG1/RMANBACKUP';

Directory created.
```

2. Now use the following PL/SQL block to copy the file to a new name:

```
1  begin
2    dbms_file_transfer.copy_file (
3            SOURCE_DIRECTORY_OBJECT       => 'RMAN',
4            SOURCE_FILE_NAME              => '0oniv1g8_1_1.rmb',
5            DESTINATION_DIRECTORY_OBJECT  => 'RMANBACKUP',
6            DESTINATION_FILE_NAME         => '0oniv1g8_1_1.new.rmb'
7    );
8  end;
```

DBMS file transfer utility allows you to copy files between the operating system and ASM in versions prior to Oracle Database 10.2.

■ **Caution**   Using either of these approaches—ASMCMD and DBMS file transfer—merely allows you to copy the files to new destinations. The target files are not placed in the data dictionary and therefore are not recognized by RMAN, unless you explicitly catalog them in RMAN.

RMAN Approach

The RMAN approach is the easiest when converting files to and from the ASM disk groups. Follow these steps:

1. Connect to RMAN.

2. Issue the convert command to convert the data file users.283.790482893 on ASM to a file system:

```
RMAN> convert datafile '+DATA/idb1/datafile/users.283.790482893' format '/u01/oradata/%u';

Starting conversion at target at 18-AUG-12
using channel ORA_DISK_1
channel ORA_DISK_1: starting datafile conversion
input file name=+DATA/idb1/datafile/users.283.790482893
converted datafile=/u01/oradata/Orniv31f
channel ORA_DISK_1: datafile conversion complete, elapsed time: 00:00:01
Finished conversion at target at 18-AUG-12
```

3. Catalog the new file just created. Since you used %u as the file name, RMAN will generate a unique name not so easily recognizable. Instead of trying to type the exact name, you can ask RMAN to read all the files:

```
RMAN> catalog start with '/u01/oradata';

searching for all files that match the pattern /u01/oradata

List of Files Unknown to the Database
=====================================
File Name: /u01/oradata/Orniv31f
```

4. RMAN will ask you to confirm. Enter YES:

```
Do you really want to catalog the above files (enter YES or NO)? yes
cataloging files...
cataloging done

List of Cataloged Files
=======================
File Name: /u01/oradata/Orniv31f
```

5. At this time the database does not know about the file you just moved. You can let the database know about it by using the switch command. But first you have to offline the file:

```
RMAN> alter database datafile 6 offline;

Statement processed
```

6. Switch the file to copy:

```
RMAN> switch datafile 6 to copy;

datafile 6 switched to datafile copy "/u01/oradata/Orniv31f"
```

7. Recover the file:

```
RMAN> recover datafile 6;

Starting recover at 18-AUG-12
using channel ORA_DISK_1

starting media recovery
media recovery complete, elapsed time: 00:00:00

Finished recover at 18-AUG-12
```

8. Make it online:

```
RMAN> alter database datafile 6 online;

Statement processed
```

9. Confirm that the copied file, not the older file, is part of the database now:

```
RMAN> report schema;

Report of database schema for database with db_unique_name IDB1

List of Permanent Datafiles
===========================
File Size(MB) Tablespace           RB segs Datafile Name
---- -------- -------------------- ------- ------------------------
1    810      SYSTEM               ***     +DATA/idb1/datafile/system.282.790482827
2    340      EXAMPLE              ***     +DATA/idb1/datafile/example.290.790482945
3    970      SYSAUX               ***     +DATA/idb1/datafile/sysaux.281.790482773
4    125      UNDOTBS1             ***     +DATA/idb1/datafile/undotbs1.284.790482893
6    31       USERS                ***     /u01/oradata/0rniv31f

List of Temporary Files
=======================
File Size(MB) Tablespace           Maxsize(MB) Tempfile Name
---- -------- -------------------- ----------- --------------------
1    106      TEMP                 32767       +DATA/idb1/tempfile/temp.289.790482937
```

File 6 is shown as the new location.

How It Works

RMAN's convert command works in much the same way as the backup as copy command, but with an important difference. Convert merely copies the file; it does not record the existence of the file in the RMAN repository, as you saw in the solution section. Therefore, you had to catalog the copied file to ensure its proper recording. The catalog command looks at the header of the file and from there it knows the type of file: data file, archived log, etc. The catalog command does not need to be told what type of file it is.

Contrast the use of RMAN with the DBMS file transfer and ASMCMD commands. DBMS file transfer is the most versatile. It can be used to copy files not only within the server but from remote servers as well. However, both ASMCMD and this approach are merely for copying; there is no database interaction. The convert command in RMAN interacts with the database data file and copies the file block by block. In the process of doing so, it validates the structural integrity of the file and flags an error if something is amiss. ASMCMD and DBMS file transfer utilities do not have that ability. This is a very good reason to use RMAN when you copy database-related files to and from ASM, even though the other two ways may sound more flexible and seem simpler.

■ ■ ■

RMAN in Exadata

RMAN is the preferred option to back up a database on Exadata. In this chapter you will learn a few nuances of RMAN when used in the Exadata environment. When we wrote this book, Exadata was still on Oracle Database 11g Release 2; so none of the Oracle Database 12c specific features described elsewhere in this book applied to Exadata.

The Lay of the Land

Let's start with a general explanation of Exadata. Boiled down to its most rudimentary concepts, Exadata is just a special-purpose RAC cluster with database servers, storage, and network switches, all within a single enclosure called a "rack." An Exadata rack comes in two models, X3-2 and X3-8, and in four sizes: full rack, half rack, quarter rack and eighth rack. Figure 25-1 shows a schematic representation of the organization of an Exadata X3-2 full rack.

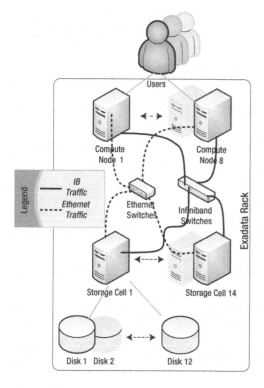

Figure 25-1. *Components of an Exadata full rack*

An Exadata rack holds two kinds of servers. Since the rack has to run one or more Oracle databases, it needs to have Oracle software installed and running on database servers. The storage in Exadata resides on the other type of servers: Storage Cell Servers (or called just "Cells"). The Oracle database software runs on the Compute Nodes (or just "Nodes"), which are blade servers running either Oracle Enterprise Linux or Solaris x86.

There are eight Nodes in a full rack of an X3-2 system. Both the Grid Infrastructure and the RDBMS software run on the Nodes. The software is the regular Oracle Database 11.2 software with the Real Application Cluster option—the same as you can download from oracle.com yourself (along with the newer patch sets from the My Oracle Support site).

There is no special RDBMS or Grid Infrastructure software for Exadata. This makes the RAC cluster running on the Nodes the same as a regular non-Exadata configuration running on a Linux system. So, all of the concepts and recipes you learned in this book, especially in Chapter 23 on RMAN and RAC, apply to Exadata as well.

The disks used for the database are attached to the Cell, which is also a blade server running Oracle Enterprise Linux. The option of Solaris operating system does not exist for this server. The Cells run a special software called Exadata Storage Server (ESS), which enables the exclusive features of the Exadata storage. These features include Smart Scans, Storage Indexes, and Cell Offloading. There are 14 Cells in a full rack of Exadata (in both X3-2 and X3-8 models).

Along with the disks, the Cells also hold 384 GB worth of flash memory cards each—making for a total of about 5.25 TB of pure flash memory. All this flash memory can be added as database disks to the Cells, or used for the Smart Flash Cache—a secondary buffer area between the hard disks and the Nodes. When the Nodes request blocks from the Cells for the first time, the blocks are retrieved from the disk and placed in the Smart Flash Cache. Subsequent requests for blocks are fulfilled from the Smart Flash Cache rather than from the disk—reducing the I/O significantly in the process.

Once again, note that the disks used for database are attached to the Cells, not to the Nodes. Each Cell has 12 disks of either 600 GB (high-performance) or 3 TB (high-capacity) SAS (Serial Attached SCSI)–type drives. The raw disks are divided into several smaller partitions before being used, as shown in Figure 25-2.

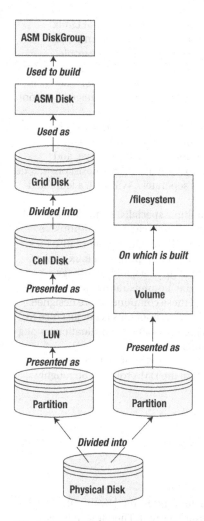

Figure 25-2. *Disk organization in an Exadata Storage Cell*

In Figure 25-2, the first two disks are split into two different partitions; each partition is presented to the cell server as a LUN. One of the LUNs is used to build the root file system on the cell server where the operating system is installed. The Exadata Storage Server (ESS) software is also installed on the file system. Since the file system has to be on a mirrored volume for high redundancy, two such partitions are used from two different disks.

The other LUN (on the other partition of the disk) is presented to the Cell as a celldisk, The celldisk is divided into griddisks, which are then presented to the ASM instance running on the Nodes to be used in ASM diskgroups. So, the ASM disks are actually griddisks on Cells. Once the ASM diskgroup is created and online, the database is built on top of that.

The disks from the cells are presented to the nodes through an Infiniband (IB) network housed inside the Exadata rack. There are three IB switches inside a full rack for redundancy. IB offers very high throughput and very low latency—perfect for Nodes accessing the disks on the Cells. The rack also has regular Ethernet switches—both 10 Gbps and 1 Gbps. These are used to connect to the servers from the outside. The users connect to the Nodes using the normal Ethernet network. They can also use Infiniband to connect to the nodes, which may be beneficial for high-throughput applications, such as reporting or ETL.

Since the servers run Oracle Enterprise Linux (or Solaris in some cases on the nodes), all the normal Linux commands are used for administration of the servers. For instance, the disks are partitioned by the normal `fdisk` command. The database and Grid Infrastructure software are managed by their respective tools—for example, SQL*Plus (for database and ASM), SRVCTL (for cluster resources), and ASMCMD (for managing ASM from command line). These tools are the same as what is found in the non-Exadata system; there is nothing special about Exadata in these tools. The only difference is the tool to manage the Exadata Storage Server. The ESS storage is managed by a tool called CellCLI (Cell Command Line Interface).

Perhaps the last important question you have is about the administration. In a traditional database system, specialist teams manage the individual components in a database infrastructure. For example, DBAs manage the database and ASM, system administrators manage the servers, storage administrators manage the storage, and network admins manage the network components, such as switches and routers. But Exadata has all these constituent components inside a single rack and carefully configured to work well together, not separately. Will such a federated management structure work?

While it is possible to divide the responsibility of managing Exadata across multiple specialist teams just like with a normal database system, we recommend against that. The servers inside Exadata are not really general-purpose servers; they serve a specific purpose of providing database services. Similarly, the Cells run Linux just because they have to run some type of operating system, which happens to be Linux. They are not general-purpose Linux servers.

Many activities performed by system administrators on a "normal" server—creating users, adding storage, mounting file systems, etc.—are not relevant to the servers in Exadata. This makes the "administration" of the servers extremely simple and does not warrant a full-time specialist. On the other hand, all these components are designed to work together and a thorough knowledge and coordinated administration of all the components is not just nice to have, but a *must-have*. One specific example of such necessity is patching, which requires careful coordination among all the different specialized areas. Division of labor may actually prove to be detrimental.

Therefore, a single role that manages the Exadata rack may be better than the federated approach. A person in such a role is known as a Database Machine Administrator (DMA). The skill sets of the DMA role can be roughly broken up as shown below:

- Oracle 11gR2 RAC Database, ASM, and Clusterware administration: 60%

- Exadata Storage Cell administration: 20%

- Linux Administration: 15%

- Others (network, Infiniband, etc.): 5%

This is only a rough division of the skills required, not a breakup of the actual tasks performed by the DMA. On average, about 95% of the activities of a DMA are on the Oracle Database software portion. Therefore, it is very easy for a DBA to transition to the DMA role. The DBA-to-DMA role change is the most common career path, although other specialists, such as Linux administrators, have also made successful transitions.

The foregoing is a very rudimentary explanation of the structure of Exadata. While we sincerely hope that it helps your understanding of the various components, it by no means is expected to be a complete treatise on Exadata. For a thorough understanding of Exadata along with the commands to manage it, please refer to the article series "Exadata Command Reference" on Oracle Technology Network at `www.oracle.com/technetwork/articles/oem/exadata-commands-intro-402431.html`.

Since the Nodes run the regular Oracle Database and Grid Infrastructure software, you will need to enter the RMAN command on a command prompt on those servers (Nodes), not the Cells.

25-1. Configuring RMAN on Exadata
Problem

You want to back up a database on Exadata using RMAN.

Solution

Configuring RMAN is no different in Exadata from in a normal Oracle 11.2 RAC database. The most important determining factor is the location of the backup. You have many choices:

- Inside the same Exadata rack

  - in the Fast Recovery Area

  - on a regular ASM diskgroup (non-FRA)

- Outside the Exadata rack

  - on an ASM diskgroup as FRA

  - on an NFS mount point

  - directly from database to tape

  - from backup on disk to the tape

Your first task is to decide which option to choose. That choice will lead to different recipes in this chapter. In the How It Works section you will find some guidelines to base your decision on.

How It Works

Each Node has four possible interfaces over which backups can be sent to the backup destination.

- directly to an ASM diskgroup inside the rack

- the InfiniBand interface (there are two of these)

- the 10 Gbps Ethernet interface (there are two of these)

- the 1 Gbps Ethernet interface (there is only one)

Of course, the fastest path is to back up directly within the Exadata rack itself, but it may not be desirable for reason of being the single point of failure. For external backups, the Infiniband interface is the most efficient one with the highest throughput and lowest latency, but it also requires a compatible device as a backup location, such as a tape drive or a disk pool with IB interface. If you don't have access to such a device, you can choose the 10 Gbps Ethernet interface to back up to a device with a similar interface.

Most datacenters today are equipped with 10 Gbps network – making this option a fairly easy one. If all else fails, you can use the 1Gbps interface; but the low throughput and high latency makes it the least effective backup interface. The presence of only one such port also makes this option the least highly available.

On the FRA Inside the Exadata Rack

Your easiest option is to back up to the fast recovery area (FRA) inside the Exadata rack. Why is it the easiest? Because the storage space is already available inside the frame and the on-site engineer from Oracle has probably already configured it that way.

Advantages of using the FRA inside the rack approach include:

- The FRA is managed by Oracle, so space is automatically freed up when new files come in and obsolete files are removed automatically.

- You can back up the entire FRA—essentially backing up your backups—to an off-the-rack tape device using a single comment.

- When Exadata is configured, a diskgroup called RECO is usually created by default. This diskgroup is created on the partitions closer to the center of the disk, which are slower in performance. The high-performance peripheral parts of the disk are used for database storage.

- Since the backup does not have to go over a transport medium, such as a network, this option offers the fastest backup approach.

- Finally, this is probably how it was configured by the Oracle on-site engineer. That means there is nothing else to be done except starting up the RMAN command prompt.

There are always trade-offs. Disadvantages include:

- The backups are inside the same rack. If the rack suffers a failure, both database and backups are lost.

- The overall space inside the Exadata rack is usually limited, especially for high-performance disk configurations. If you create an FRA from those disks, you are going to deplete the space even further for database use.

- The special storage software is highly attractive for databases; not so much for backups. For instance, Hybrid Columnar Compression available on Exadata storage is relevant only for databases, not for backups. So using the storage for backups is a waste of their potential.

- As of the writing of this book, Exadata doesn't support mixing different types of disk inside a rack. If you have a high-performance disk configuration, you also have to use that configuration for RMAN backups, which do not usually require a high-performance disk. wwSuch a configuration is therefore a waste of valuable resources.

- Since database and backup are on the same physical disk, there is a possibility of contention.

- Backup to tape needs RMAN media management layer (MML), which is generally an extra-cost option, unless you use Oracle Secure Backup.

- If you have many Exadata racks, you can't use the storage from all of them as a pool. You can back up the database on one Exadata rack into the same rack, not another. If you want to use the storage from the other racks, you have to cluster them together, which is complex and also affects the databases running on the rack.

On an ASM Group Inside the Rack

Still within the rack, you have the option of backing up to an ASM diskgroup rather than to the FRA. Some organizations do not allow FRAs to be created. Others have a strong preference against them. For whatever reason, if you choose not to create an FRA, you do have the option to back up internally to the rack using an ASM diskgroup as your target destination.

As you might surmise, the pros and cons of backing up to an internal ASM group are largely the same as for backing up to an internal FRA. The approach is generally easy to use and performs well, but your backups are still subject to failure of the rack.

On an ASM Group Outside the Rack

The single most obvious issue with the previous two approaches is the issue of single point of failure. If the Exadata Rack fails, so does the backup. So, the equally obvious solution is to move the backup outside the rack. You could create an ASM diskgroup on an external storage and use that as a backup location.

This option offers some very attractive advantages:

- You don't need to use the expensive and limited storage inside Exadata rack, leaving all that storage space to database and related files.

- Backup is outside of the Exadata rack, so a rack failure will not destroy both the database and backup. This eliminates the single-point-of-failure problem.

- You can leverage some other type of storage, for example, ZFS storage appliance, for backups, which are much cheaper than the Exadata storage. You can also use an Exadata Storage Expansion Pack with high-capacity disk configuration.

- In this approach, you don't have to lose the advantages of a fast recovery area. If you designate the ASM diskgroup as an FRA, Oracle manages the contents automatically.

- Since database storage does not share the backup storage, there is no contention for disks inside the Exadata storage when the RMAN backup is running.

- You can use a single device to back up many Exadata racks. For instance, you can have a single ZFS appliance to serve as a backup location for all databases on multiple Exadata racks.

Like the other side of a coin, this option has its own share of disadvantages:

- Since Exadata doesn't have a fiber channel port, traditional SANs can't be presented as backup locations. This limitation leaves NAS as the only viable alternative and NAS may not be as great for ASM as a regular SAN.

- The backup is taken to an ASM diskgroup. To move it to tape, you need to use MML in RMAN—an extra-cost option, unless you use Oracle Secure Backup.

On an NFS Mountpoint Outside of Exadata Rack

ASM is not the only option for database backups. You can also use a regular file system on any storage location outside Exadata rack and mount it on all nodes of Exadata as NFS (Network File Share). This allows all the nodes of Exadata to see this file system and use it as a backup location. You may choose between specialized devices such as ZFS Appliance from Oracle, Celera from EMC, or just about any generic storage such as a small NAS device.

Here are the advantages of this option:

- The backup is outside the Exadata rack, so backup is protected separately from the database. If the Exadata rack fails, the backup is still available for restoration elsewhere.

- Since the backup does not share the physical disks used by the database, there is no contention for disks inside Exadata when the RMAN backup runs.

- Since the backup pieces are created as regular files on a file system, they can be backed up to tape using any backup software without the need for MML. This could translate to huge cost savings.

- If the external storage device allows Infiniband connectivity, the backup throughput is high and the latency is low compared to Ethernet channels. This makes backups faster and more effective.

This is not without its limitations:

- NFS is usually slower compared to the in-rack storage, so backup may be longer compared to the in-rack option described earlier.

- To be 100% effective the device has to have a NAS server. Otherwise you can mount it on one node locally and then NFS mount the local file system across all nodes of Exadata. This approach works, but if the node where the file system is local fails, the entire NFS file system becomes unavailable. So you have to have a NAS server to be a really feasible solution. The NAS server costs money.

Directly from Database to Tape

On the previous approaches we talked about backing up to a disk-based location. While they work, disks are not considered true backups; tapes are. Tapes can be sent off-site, making the backup physically different from the database location. If there is a data center collapse, the backups are not affected. So you may need to back up to the tape anyway. To that end, you may decide to forgo the disk-based backup altogether and back up to the tape directly. There are some strong incentives for this approach:

- Since there is disk-based backup, no disk is needed at all, so you save space inside the Exadata rack allowing you to dedicate all available storage for the database. Furthermore, there is no need to have external disk storage.

- Most organizations put backups on the tape eventually anyway; this option just accomplishes that ultimate objective faster and with fewer resources—i.e., disks.

- There is an emergence of VTLs (Virtual Tape Libraries) that appear as tape drives to servers but have disks instead of tapes. They are usually orders of magnitude faster than tapes making the backup process faster. VTLs also allow optimization activities, such as deduplication, to make efficient use of storage.

But like everything else, the approach of backing up directly to tape is not without limitations, some of which are pretty serious. Here they are:

- You need to have media management layer for RMAN to back up to tape directly. MML is usually an extra-cost option, unless you use Oracle Secure Backup.

- You can't use RMAN image merging of incremental backups if the backup location is tape. This could be a serious limitation since incremental merge significantly reduces the need to have full backups.

- Writing to tape is usually slow compared to disk. This extends the time for backup and may lead to performance issues in regular database processing.

- Tape backups usually work in prearranged schedules to ensure that the proper tapes are mounted in the drives. This makes the backup options somewhat limited. For instance, the backup must start at the prearranged time and must complete by a set time. Otherwise the backups will be on many tapes, making restores difficult.

Moving a Backup from Disk to Tape

Now that you know the options of backing up to the disk and going to the tape directly, you can combine the two options to have a two-phase solution: backing up to the disk, and then moving the backup to the tape. This approach has a number of very attractive benefits:

- This option represents the best of both worlds: the benefits of disk (regardless of the storage inside or outside of Exadata) and tape.

- Since the first backup of the database is to the disk, it allows you to merge the RMAN incremental backup to the image copy on disk. This feature reduces the need to take full backups often.

- Allows you to take advantage of the VTLs (Virtual Tape Libraries), explained above.

- When recovery is needed, and the on-disk backup is not available, the restore can be done from tape to the database directly. There is no need to restore to disk first and then to the database.

- The dual staged backup approach—(a) DB to Disk and (b) Disk to Tape—makes it possible to decouple the stages. Stage (a) can be done anytime that is good for the database, while stage (b) can be made to fit the schedule of the tape facility.

- You can use the space inside the Exadata rack, which is simpler when backing up to disk. The risk of putting the backup inside the Exadata rack is mitigated by the eventual presence of the backup on tape.

The option has some drawbacks.

- It needs space—on both the disk and the tape.

- If you used ASM as a location for the disk-based backup, you need to use Media Management layer (MML) to move the backup to the tape. You can avoid the use of ASM by putting the disk location on an NFS mount point but it has the same issues described earlier under the option of NFS.

25-2. Backing Up Inside the Exadata Rack

Problem

You want to back up the database on Exadata inside the same rack.

Solution

To back up the database to a space inside the same Exadata rack, you first have to decide on the location of the backup. You have two choices:

- In the fast recovery area (FRA) location

- On a specially created ASM diskgroup

Option A: Backing Up to an FRA Location

To back up in the FRA location, follow these steps:

1. Log on to any of the Compute nodes as the Grid Infrastructure owner user. It is generally named "grid" or "oragrid." It could be "oracle" as well in your environment.

2. Log in to the ASM instance as SYSASM:

```
$ sqlplus / as sysasm

SQL*Plus: Release 11.2.0.2.0 Production on Fri Sep 7 22:54:21 2012

Copyright (c) 1982, 2010, Oracle. All rights reserved.

Connected to:
Oracle Database 11g Enterprise Edition Release 11.2.0.2.0 - 64bit Production
With the Real Application Clusters and Automatic Storage Management options
```

3. Make sure the RECO diskgroup is mounted. Note: The diskgroup may not be named exactly as "RECO." Ask the Database Machine Administrator for the specific diskgroup name:

```
SQL> select state
  2  from v$asm_diskgroup
  3  where name = 'RECO';

STATE
-------
MOUNTED
```

4. If it is not mounted, mount it:

```
SQL> alter diskgroup reco mount;
```

5. Find out the space needed for the fast recovery area (Recipe 3-16). Suppose it comes out to be 5.5 TB.

6. Make sure the RECO diskgroup has enough space in the ASMCMD interface:

```
$ asmcmd
ASMCMD> lsdg
State    Type   Rebal Sector Block       AU Total_MB  Free_MB Req_mir_free_MB Usable_file_
MB
Offline_disks Voting_files Name
MOUNTED NORMAL N       512 4096 4194304  4175360  4172528          379578         1896475
             0            N DBFS_DG/
MOUNTED NORMAL N       512 4096 4194304 67436544 62908780         6130594        28389093
             0            N DATA/
MOUNTED HIGH   N       512 4096 4194304 23514624 21332640         4275386         5685751
             0            Y RECO/
```

From the output, it's clear that the RECO diskgroup has 5,685,751 MB. Assume it is more than enough for the FRA.

7. Log on to the Compute Node as the Oracle Database Software owner, which may be named "oradb." (Note that in some installations the owner for both the Database Software and Grid Infrastructure may be the same.)

8. Log on to the database as SYSDBA:

```
$ sqlplus / as sysdba
```

9. Set the fast recovery area parameters—location and size:

```
SQL> alter system set db_recovery_file_dest_size = 5520G;

System altered.

SQL> alter system set db_recovery_file_dest = '+RECO';

System altered.
```

10. On the Compute Node, add a special service called RMAN that is available on all eight nodes of the Exadata rack:

```
$ srvctl add service -d PROPRD -s RMAN -r
"PROPRD1,PROPRD2,PROPRD3,PROPRD4,PROPRD5,PROPRD6,PROPRD7,PROPRD8"
```

Note   The exact database name, instance names, and the nodes will need to be used in the above command. In this example we have shown a database called PROPRD that runs on all eight nodes, so there are eight instances.

---

11. Start the newly created service:

```
$ srvctl start service -d PROPRD -s RMAN
```

12. While still on the Compute Node, under $ORACLE_HOME of Oracle Database, go to the directory network/admin:

```
$ cd $ORACLE_HOME/network/admin
```

13. Open the file tnsnames.ora and place the following entry there:

```
RMAN =
  (DESCRIPTION =
    (ADDRESS = (PROTOCOL = TCP)(HOST = pprd-scan)(PORT = 1521))
    (CONNECT_DATA =
      (SERVER = DEDICATED)
      (SERVICE_NAME = RMAN)
    )
  )
```

In this example we have used pprd-scan as the SCAN name and the port 1521 as the listener port. Substitute with the specific values from your database.

14. Log on to the database as SYSDBA. Create a user called RMAN with SYSDBA role:

```
SQL> grant sysdba to rman identified by secretpass1;

Grant succeeded.
```

15. Copy the file orapwPROPRD1 in $ORACLE_HOME/dbs to all the other Compute nodes to make sure that RMAN can connect to all the nodes using the password file:

```
[oradb@dwhpdb01 dbs]$ scp orapwPROPRD1 oradb@dwhpdb02:`pwd`/orapwPROPRD2
orapwPROPRD1                              100% 1536     1.5KB/s    00:00
[oradb@dwhpdb01 dbs]$ scp orapwPROPRD1 oradb@dwhpdb03:`pwd`/orapwPROPRD3
orapwPROPRD1                              100% 1536     1.5KB/s    00:00
[oradb@dwhpdb01 dbs]$ scp orapwPROPRD1 oradb@dwhpdb04:`pwd`/orapwPROPRD4
orapwPROPRD1                              100% 1536     1.5KB/s    00:00
[oradb@dwhpdb01 dbs]$ scp orapwPROPRD1 oradb@dwhpdb05:`pwd`/orapwPROPRD5
orapwPROPRD1                              100% 1536     1.5KB/s    00:00
[oradb@dwhpdb01 dbs]$ scp orapwPROPRD1 oradb@dwhpdb06:`pwd`/orapwPROPRD6
orapwPROPRD1                              100% 1536     1.5KB/s    00:00
[oradb@dwhpdb01 dbs]$ scp orapwPROPRD1 oradb@dwhpdb07:`pwd`/orapwPROPRD7
orapwPROPRD1                              100% 1536     1.5KB/s    00:00
[oradb@dwhpdb01 dbs]$ scp orapwPROPRD1 oradb@dwhpdb08:`pwd`/orapwPROPRD8
orapwPROPRD1                              100% 1536     1.5KB/s    00:00
```

16. Start RMAN and connect to the target using the new service name and the RMAN user created earlier:

```
RMAN> connect target rman/secretpass1@rman

connected to target database: PROPRD (DBID=1716317401)
```

17. Allocate multiple channels as shown below and start the backup:

```
RMAN> run {
2> allocate channel c1 type disk;
3> allocate channel c2 type disk;
4> allocate channel c3 type disk;
5> allocate channel c4 type disk;
6> allocate channel c5 type disk;
7> allocate channel c6 type disk;
8> allocate channel c7 type disk;
9> allocate channel c8 type disk;
10> backup database;
11> }
```

The above command produces the following output:

```
connected to target database: PROPRD (DBID=1716317401)

using target database control file instead of recovery catalog
allocated channel: c1
channel c1: SID=2316 instance=PROPRD1 device type=DISK

allocated channel: c2
channel c2: SID=2832 instance=PROPRD1 device type=DISK

allocated channel: c3
channel c3: SID=2316 instance=PROPRD6 device type=DISK

allocated channel: c4
channel c4: SID=2832 instance=PROPRD6 device type=DISK

allocated channel: c5
channel c5: SID=2574 instance=PROPRD2 device type=DISK

allocated channel: c6
channel c6: SID=2832 instance=PROPRD4 device type=DISK
... output truncated ...
```

18. Note the channel definitions. The channels are all connected to different instances. That's exactly what we wanted. Now the backups will be spread across all the Compute nodes.

Option B: Backing Up to a Specialty ASM Disk Group

This solution assumes that you don't want to use a fast recovery area for some reason, ostensibly because it's not allowed at your site, or you choose not to use it. The steps are identical to the previous option, except on two groups of steps.

Steps 1 through 9 need to change. Instead of a diskgroup called RECO, you have identified a different diskgroup for backup. Replace the name RECO with this new diskgroup. Assume that diskgroup is named ORABACK. Since you will not be using FRA, do not execute step 9.

Step 17 will need to change. Since you don't use FRA you have to mention the ASM diskgroup explicitly:

```
RMAN> run {
2> allocate channel c1 type disk format '+ORABACK/%u.rmb';
3> allocate channel c2 type disk format '+ORABACK/%u.rmb';
4> allocate channel c3 type disk format '+ORABACK/%u.rmb';
5> allocate channel c4 type disk format '+ORABACK/%u.rmb';
6> allocate channel c5 type disk format '+ORABACK/%u.rmb';
7> allocate channel c6 type disk format '+ORABACK/%u.rmb';
8> allocate channel c7 type disk format '+ORABACK/%u.rmb';
9> allocate channel c8 type disk format '+ORABACK/%u.rmb';
10> backup database;
11> }
```

Now the backups will be created in the diskgroup +ORABACK.

How It Works

The RECO diskgroup is a special diskgroup that is usually created during the initial installation and configuration of Exadata—a task normally undertaken by the Oracle Advanced Customer Service staff, but occasionally by the customer or a third party as well. The diskgroup is created by using the griddisks closer to the center of the disk, which are usually slower compared to the griddisks created by areas near the periphery of the disk.

When you use a fast recovery area, RMAN automatically puts the backup files there. Therefore, you don't have to mention the location explicitly. When you use a diskgroup not defined as an FRA, you have to use that in the format clause of the allocate channel command.

25-3. Backing Up Outside the Exadata Rack

Problem

You want to back up the database on Exadata to a location outside the Exadata rack.

Solution

Three solutions are possible. The first two involve treating an external disk as an FRA. Your choice comes down to whether that external disk is in the form of an ASM diskgroup, or in the form of an NFS mount point. Your third option is to back up to an NFS mount point that you do not configure as an external FRA.

Option A: Using an External ASM Disk Group as an FRA

This solution is very similar to that in Recipe 24-2. The only difference is that the storage comes from the outside. Here are the general steps:

1. Identify the location of external storage. This could be a general-purpose network attached storage device connected via some network transport mechanism, such as Infiniband (preferred due to its high throughput and low latency), or 10 Gbps Ethernet, which is more versatile. This location is visible to the Compute Nodes.

2. Make sure the network is configured for jumbo frames.

3. Logging in as the Grid Infrastructure owner on the Node, and create the diskgroup.

4. Referring to Recipe 24-2, issue the following commands shown in step 9 for creating the fast recovery area.

5. Referring to Recipe 24-3, follow the rest of the steps from step 10 and beyond.

Option B: Using an External NFS Mount Point as an FRA

This is exactly the same as the previous option, except that the location is not an ASM diskgroup but a mount point. Referring to Recipe 24-2, replace steps 1 through 8 as follows:

1. Mount a file system on a NAS location. Let's assume it is called /oraback. Confirm its presence by issuing the following command:

```
# df -h
Filesystem            Size  Used Avail Use% Mounted on
/dev/mapper/VGExaDb-LVDbSys1
                      30G   19G  9.8G  66% /
```

```
/dev/sda1                   124M   34M   85M   29% /boot
/dev/mapper/VGExaDb-LVDbOra1
                            99G   69G   25G   74% /u01
tmpfs                       81G  224M   81G    1% /dev/shm
x.y.z.38:/dwbackup1
                            25T   22T  2.8T   89% /dwbackup1
```

The IP address has been masked to protect the innocent.

2. Make this file system owned by oradb (or the user who owns the Oracle software):

```
# chown oradb:dba /dwbackup1
```

3. In step 9, use this syntax instead:

```
SQL> alter system set db_recovery_file_dest_size = 5520G;

System altered.

SQL> alter system set db_recovery_file_dest = '/dwbackup1';

System altered.
```

4. Follow steps 10 and beyond.

Option C: Using an External NFS Mount Point, but Not as an FRA

This solution is exactly the same as the previous option, except that there is no FRA. So do not execute step 9. Since there is no FRA, you have to let RMAN know the location where the backup should be placed, as shown below:

```
RMAN> run {
2> allocate channel c1 type disk format '/dwbackup1/%u.rmb';
3> allocate channel c2 type disk format '/dwbackup1/%u.rmb';
4> allocate channel c3 type disk format '/dwbackup1/%u.rmb';
5> allocate channel c4 type disk format '/dwbackup1/%u.rmb';
6> allocate channel c5 type disk format '/dwbackup1/%u.rmb';
7> allocate channel c6 type disk format '/dwbackup1/%u.rmb';
8> allocate channel c7 type disk format '/dwbackup1/%u.rmb';
9> allocate channel c8 type disk format '/dwbackup1/%u.rmb';
10> backup database;
11> }
```

25-4. Setting RMAN Buffer Size
Problem

The default size and number of input and output buffers are usually adequate for regular Oracle databases, but they may be inadequate for Exadata due to the higher performance numbers. You need to set up the correct buffer parameters or at least confirm that their values are set.

Solution

First decide whether you are backing to an ASM diskgroup, to a tape, or to a file system. The solution depends on the location used.

1. If you are using an ASM diskgroup as the backup location, do nothing.

2. If you are backing up to a tape drive (or a virtual tape library) and using a media management library (MML), do nothing.

3. If you are using a file system as the backup location, set the following initialization parameters in the database and restart the instance:

```
_backup_file_bufcnt=64
_backup_file_bufsz=4194304
_backup_disk_bufcnt=64
_backup_disk_bufsz=4194304
```

4. In the backup command, use filesperset value of 1.

5. Take the backup as usual.

■ **Note**   Starting with Oracle 11.2.0.2, RMAN automatically sets the correct values, so you do not need to set them explicitly. However, we still recommend setting them explicitly, as the potential benefits outweigh the risks.

How It Works

When an RMAN channel starts backing up, it pulls up a chunk of data from the input data file. This chunk of data is known as an Input Buffer. RMAN pulls up multiple input buffers and processes them in parallel. As you know, a regular backup set–based RMAN backup does not back up never-used blocks or, in case of incremental backup, the blocks that have been backed up earlier and do not need to be in the backup piece. Due to these reasons the output buffer may be smaller than the input buffer, and often is dramatically smaller.

The parameter ending with _bufsz specifies the size of the buffer, and _bufcnt specifies the number of buffers. The higher the number of the buffers, the more the memory consumption. Conversely, the smaller the number, the less the memory consumption but the RMAN channel session will need to open the input file more often. By setting the value to 64, each RMAN channel opens 64 input buffers and 64 output buffers at the same time. The buffer size is set to 4194304, which is 4 MB. Therefore, each RMAN channel consumes about 4 MB X (64 + 64) = 512 MB.

Each RMAN channel by default doesn't just operate on one data file. It opens up several files—which defaults to eight. However, opening many files at the same time is not good for performance either. The reason multiple files are opened is simple: it's possible that the files are busy and the RMAN open command will fail, prompting retry later. By opening several files, RMAN can strike a balance between the negative impact of too many files and the positive impact of not waiting for a busy file. In this tuning recipe you have specified 64 as the buffer count. RMAN will open 64 buffers from each file. With eight files, RMAN will open a large number of buffers, consequently leading to a huge memory consumption. To avoid this possibility, you need to set the files per set parameter to 1, so only one file will be opened by RMAN, not eight.

The default configuration depends on the backup type (image or backupset) and whether the target is ASM or not. Let's see with some examples. You can check the actual buffer count and buffer size used in a previously executed backup by this query:

```
SQL> select set_count, sid, type, substr(filename,1,30) filename,
  2         buffer_size, buffer_count bc, elapsed_time et, bytes
  3  from v$backup_async_io a
  4  where set_stamp = 793415558;
```

Following is the output of a query showing how RMAN executed a regular backup set backup going to an ASM diskgroup. The output shows the results from a default configuration:

SET_COUNT	SID	TYPE	FILENAME	BUFFER_SIZE	BC	ET	BYTES
11	2316	AGGREGATE		0	0	3700	4.0291E+10
11	2316	INPUT	+DWPDATA/proprd/datafile/unica	4194304	21	3700	5075099648
11	2316	INPUT	+DWPDATA/proprd/datafile/cmart	4194304	21	2100	3989839872
11	2316	INPUT	+DWPDATA/proprd/datafile/crmdw	4194304	21	1200	
... output truncated for brevity ...							
11	2316	INPUT	+DWPDATA/proprd/datafile/crmbk	4194304	21	200	58712064
11	2316	OUTPUT	+DWPRECO/proprd/backupset/2012	4194304	64	3500	801103872

Note the buffer details for input (reading of the data files) and output (writing to the backuppieces). The buffer size is 4 MB and the buffer count is 21 for input. For output, the buffer count is 64. Since this backup goes to ASM, the defaults are used.

When the same query is issued after an image copy backup going to an NFS mounted file, here is the output:

SET_COUNT	SID	TYPE	FILENAME	BUFFER_SIZE	BC	ET	BYTES
30497	5164	AGGREGATE		0	0	503451	6.0922E+10
30497	5164	INPUT	+DWNDATA/dwhdr/datafile/crmdw_	4194304	4	503451	6.0922E+10
30497	5164	OUTPUT	/dwbackup1/incr2/data_D-DWHDR_	4194304	16	503551	6.0922E+10

However, after the parameters explained in the recipe are put in place:

SET_COUNT	SID	TYPE	FILENAME	BUFFER_SIZE	BC	ET	BYTES
30497	3345	AGGREGATE		0	0	298500	6.0922E+10
30497	3345	INPUT	+DWNDATA/dwhdr/datafile/crmdw_	4194304	64	298500	6.0922E+10
30497	3345	OUTPUT	/dwbackup1/incr2/data_D-DWHDR_	4194304	64	298600	6.0922E+10

Note the buffer counts are set to 64 (as per the parameter). It also reduced the elapsed time from 503551 to 298600 seconds.

25-5. Detecting Skipped Blocks
Problem

You want to find out how much of the performance enhancement in RMAN (faster time and lesser CPU resources due to less I/O) is due to the workings of the ESS software running on the Cell.

Solution

The Exadata Storage Server (ESS) software can skip blocks at the Cell level directly while taking an incremental backup. To find out how many blocks were skipped, issue the following query while connected as a user with access to the dynamic performance views, typically SYS:

```
col blocks_skipped_in_cell head 'Cell Skip'
col cell_rman_eff head 'RMAN Eff%' format 999.99
select file#, blocks, blocks_read, datafile_blocks, blocks_skipped_in_cell, 100*
blocks_skipped_in_cell/blocks_read cell_rman_eff
from v$backup_datafile
/
```

Here is the output:

```
     FILE#     BLOCKS BLOCKS_READ DATAFILE_BLOCKS  Cell Skip RMAN Eff%
---------- ---------- ----------- ---------------- ---------- ---------
       547       2033       92801           102400          0       .00
       618       1529       77441            89600          0       .00
       622       1397       72321            76800          0       .00
       303       1697       77441            89600          0       .00
       595       1865       87681            89600          0       .00
       616       1265       62081            76800          0       .00
       301       1697       77441            89600          0       .00
       369       1517       77441            89600          0       .00
       496       1421       72321            76800          0       .00
       731       2640       94721           102400          0       .00
       803       2385       82433            89600          0       .00
... output truncated ...
```

From the output you can see that RMAN didn't skip any blocks at the Cell level. You might ask if it means the Exadata software was not effective enough. Actually the blocks read by the RMAN channel (shown under BLOCKS_READ) are less than total blocks of the data file (DATAFILE_BLOCKS). So RMAN did perform some type of filtering. However, that filtering did not occur at the Cell level. To understand the reason for these results, see the How It Works section below.

How It Works

Before explaining the cause of the behavior shown in the Solution, let us explain some relevant columns of the view V$BACKUP_DATAFILE. Take a look at Table 25-1.

Table 25-1. *Explanation of Some Relevant Columns of V$BACKUP_DATAFILE*

Column Name	Description
FILE#	The file ID as shown in v$datafile
COMPLETION_TIME	The timestamp when the backup was completed
DATAFILE_BLOCKS	The total blocks of the data file—both used and unused
BLOCKS_READ	The number of blocks read by RMAN to determine whether it satisfies the incremental backup condition. This number may be less than the total blocks of the data file since the blocks never used, if any, will be skipped by RMAN.
BLOCKS	The actual number of blocks actually backed up. This number may be less than the blocks read because: (a) RMAN will skip once-used but unused-now (as opposed to never used) blocks and (b) the presence of block change tracking information may allow RMAN to skip reading blocks to determine their change status.
USED_CHANGE_TRACKING	Whether the RMAN backup job could take advantage of a block change tracking file to determine the changed blocks.

To see the effect of the Cell filtering in RMAN jobs, turn off the block change tracking on the database before taking incremental backup. Here's how:

```
SQL> alter database disable block change tracking;

Database altered.
```

Now take an RMAN incremental backup of a specific data file only. For example:

```
RMAN> backup incremental level 1 datafile 547;

Starting backup at 08-SEP-12
using target database control file instead of recovery catalog
allocated channel: ORA_DISK_1
channel ORA_DISK_1: SID=5399 instance=PROPRD1 device type=DISK
channel ORA_DISK_1: starting incremental level 1 datafile backup set
channel ORA_DISK_1: specifying datafile(s) in backup set
input datafile file number=00547 name=+DWPDATA/proprd/datafile/crmdw_gen_y11_indx_1.dbf
channel ORA_DISK_1: starting piece 1 at 08-SEP-12
channel ORA_DISK_1: finished piece 1 at 08-SEP-12
piece handle=+DWPRECO/proprd/backupset/2012_09_08/nnndn1_tag20120908t213011_0.887.793488611
tag=TAG20120908T213011 comment=NONE
channel ORA_DISK_1: backup set complete, elapsed time: 00:00:01
Finished backup at 08-SEP-12
```

Now, issue the same SQL used in the Solution for identifying the filtering at the Cell level, but instead of checking for all files, check for the specific data file that you backed up:

```
SQL> select completion_time, blocks, blocks_read, datafile_blocks, blocks_skipped_in_cell,
  2> 100* blocks_skipped_in_cell/blocks_read cell_rman_eff, used_change_tracking
  3> from v$backup_datafile
  4> where file# = 547;
```

COMPLETIO	BLOCKS	BLOCKS_READ	DATAFILE_BLOCKS	Cell Skip	RMAN Eff%	USE
03-JAN-12	2033	92801	102400	0	.00	YES
08-SEP-12	1	1	102400	102399	#######	NO
08-SEP-12	1	1	102400	102399	#######	NO

Ignore the formatting of the RMAN Eff% column. It's clear that the value is so large that it overruns the formatting. You can see that the backup taken on January 3, 2012, used a block change tracking (BCT) file, since USED_CHANGE_TRACKING column shows YES. Since a BCT file was used to filter out unchanged blocks, there was nothing left for the Cell to filter, so the Cell Skip column shows 0—i.e., the Cell didn't filter anything. This led to an RMAN efficiency of 0%.

However, the backup taken on the next occasion—September 8, 2012—did not make use of a BCT file, as shown by the NO value under the USED_CHANGE_TRACKING column. Since RMAN couldn't use a BCT file to filter unchanged blocks, it would have had to scan all the blocks of the data file—i.e., all 102,400 blocks. On a non-Exadata database, RMAN would have read that many blocks and the column BLOCKS_READ would have shown that value. Here is a similar activity and output from a non-Exadata database for a data file of that many blocks:

```
SQL> select completion_time, blocks, blocks_read, datafile_blocks
  2> used_change_tracking
  3> from v$backup_datafile
  4> where file# = 5;
```

COMPLETIO	BLOCKS	BLOCKS_READ	DATAFILE_BLOCKS	USE
08-SEP-12	12141	64321	102400	YES
... [block change tracking was dropped here] ...				
08-SEP-12	1	102400	102400	NO

Note the output carefully. When the BCT file was used (i.e., the USED_CHANGE_TRACKING column showed YES), RMAN read only 64,321 blocks from the 102,400 blocks of the file. However, when the BCT file was dropped, RMAN read all 102,400 blocks of the file and backed up only one block (as shown under the column BLOCKS in the output above). Without BCT, RMAN doesn't have any way of knowing which blocks have changed unless it visits the block to make that determination. In Exadata, the presence of metadata of a block at the Cells enables RMAN to skip unchanged blocks even if BCT is not used. Notice the value of the column BLOCKS_READ in Exadata when the BCT file is not used—it's 1, i.e., only one block was read. The column Cell Skip shows 102399, which indicates that 102,399 blocks were eliminated as not changed at the cell level, leaving just one block to be read.

The ability of an Exadata Cell server to reduce the amount of I/O during RMAN jobs is a very powerful property of Exadata. Reducing the amount of I/O, especially when block change tracking is not used, significantly improves the performance of an RMAN job.

25-6. Tuning RMAN Write Performance on Exadata
Problem

An RMAN backup going to internal disks inside the Exadata frame seems to be sluggish and you want to determine the reason. Alternatively, you want to make sure that the RMAN backup is properly configured for best performance.

Solution

Remember that Exadata is merely an Oracle Database 11g Release 2 RAC database with up to eight nodes. So, all the performance tuning techniques you learned in Chapter 16 apply to Exadata as well. In this recipe you will learn about a few specifics relating to Exadata.

The storage for the database in Exadata comes from inside the rack. If you choose the RECO diskgroup as the fast recovery area location, that also comes from the disks inside the Exadata and therefore there is a possibility of disk contention. If you do see performance deteriorating for the RMAN output to the RECO diskgroup, you should check the total I/O requests against that diskgroup. To that end, do the following:

1. Log in as root to any one of the eight cell servers (not the Compute Node).

2. Enter into CellCLI environment:

   ```
   # cellcli
   ```

3. Issue the following command in CellCLI:

   ```
   CellCLI> list metriccurrent attributes metricObjectName, metricValue where name =
   'GD_IO_RQ_W_LG' and metricObjectName like 'DWPRECO.*';
   ```

   Here is the output:

```
DWPRECO_CD_00_dwhpcel01          3,933 IO requests
DWPRECO_CD_01_dwhpcel01          4,107 IO requests
DWPRECO_CD_02_dwhpcel01          4,106 IO requests
DWPRECO_CD_03_dwhpcel01          4,186 IO requests
DWPRECO_CD_04_dwhpcel01          3,947 IO requests
DWPRECO_CD_05_dwhpcel01          4,093 IO requests
DWPRECO_CD_06_dwhpcel01          3,765 IO requests
DWPRECO_CD_07_dwhpcel01          3,919 IO requests
DWPRECO_CD_08_dwhpcel01          4,067 IO requests
DWPRECO_CD_09_dwhpcel01          4,037 IO requests
DWPRECO_CD_10_dwhpcel01          4,007 IO requests
DWPRECO_CD_11_dwhpcel01          4,051 IO requests
```

The output shows that all the griddisks making up the RECO diskgroup on cell 01 have seen about the same number of I/O requests. Had you seen a significant difference, you would have been concerned about a potential issue on any griddisk showing a variance from the general trend.

Suppose you notice that the I/O requests coming to griddisk DWPRECO_CD_00_dwhpcel01 is very high compared to the other griddisks. That by itself should not necessarily be a concern. You should examine whether the upward swing in the I/O requests was consistent or just a blip. To know that, you should look at the history of this specific metric on this griddisk by using the following CellCLI command (we have used a filter on the collection time to limit the output to only the recent past):

```
CellCLI> list metrichistory attributes collectiontime, metricvalue where  name = 'GD_IO_RQ_W_LG' and
metricObjectName = 'DWPRECO_CD_00_dwhpcel01' and collectionTime > '2012-09-08T00:00:00-04:00';
```

Here is the output:

```
2012-09-08T10:54:58-04:00          3,933 IO requests
2012-09-08T10:55:58-04:00          3,933 IO requests
2012-09-08T10:56:58-04:00          3,933 IO requests
2012-09-08T10:57:58-04:00          3,933 IO requests
2012-09-08T10:58:58-04:00          3,933 IO requests
2012-09-08T10:59:58-04:00          3,933 IO requests
2012-09-08T11:00:58-04:00          3,933 IO requests
2012-09-08T11:01:58-04:00          3,933 IO requests
2012-09-08T11:02:58-04:00          9,933 IO requests
2012-09-08T11:03:58-04:00          3,933 IO requests
2012-09-08T11:04:58-04:00          3,933 IO requests
2012-09-08T11:05:58-04:00          3,933 IO requests
2012-09-08T11:06:58-04:00          3,933 IO requests
2012-09-08T11:07:58-04:00          3,933 IO requests
2012-09-08T11:08:58-04:00          3,933 IO requests
2012-09-08T11:09:59-04:00          3,933 IO requests
2012-09-08T11:10:59-04:00          3,933 IO requests
2012-09-08T11:11:59-04:00          3,933 IO requests
2012-09-08T11:12:59-04:00          3,933 IO requests
2012-09-08T11:13:59-04:00          3,933 IO requests
2012-09-08T11:14:59-04:00          3,933 IO requests
... output truncated ...
```

As you can see from the output, almost all the I/O requests are the same over a period of time, except at 11:02:58 on September 8, 2012. At this point, the number of I/O requests jumped up to 9,933—almost three times the normal period. So, you can conclude that the increased number of I/O requests to this griddisk was not really sustained; it was just a spike at a specific point that came back to normal immediately afterward.

Had you seen something different, i.e., the number of I/O requests fluctuating over a period of time, you would have plotted a graph of the values. This graph would have helped you identify patterns in the I/O requests.

How It Works

CellCLI is the tool to get various metrics and administer the Cells in Exadata. The commands follow this general structure:

```
<verb> <object> <filtering condition>
```

The command we used earlier to get the I/O requests was:

```
CellCLI> list metriccurrent attributes metricObjectName, metricValue where name = 'GD_IO_RQ_W_LG'
and metricObjectName like 'DWPRECO.*';
```

Let's dissect the command:

> list: Asks the CellCLI command to list something. It's similar to SELECT in SQL.

> metriccurrent: It's the object of our interest. This is what we want to list. This is equivalent to a column we are selecting.

attributes `metricObjectName, metricValue`: We don't want to list every attribute of the object metriccurrent; but only two.

`where name = 'GD_IO_RQ_W_LG'`: This specifies that we want to filter the output and show only where the name of the metric (one of the attributes of metriccurrent) is GD_IO_RQ_W_LG, which is the number of large I/O written to the griddisks.

`metricObjectName like 'DWPRECO.*'`: There are several griddisks. We are interested in the griddisks used in the DWPRECO diskgroup, so we used this filtering condition. Unlike SQL, in CellCLI the wildcard character is not "%." CellCLI follows regular expression syntax, and the wildcard character is an asterisk ("*").

In the next activity we checked the history of the metric by issuing the command list metrichistory. We followed the same type of command structure: Verb:Object:Filter. However, we introduced a new type of filter:

```
collectionTime > '2012-09-08T00:00:00-04:00'
```

This is a timestamp filter. In CellCLI you specify the timestamp as YYYY-MM-DDThh24:mi:ss-<GMT Offset>. The GMT Offset specifies many hours behind the local time is with respect to Greenwich mean time. In this case, it's four hours behind.

 **For the Complete Technology & Database Professional**

IOUG represents the **voice of Oracle technology and database professionals** - empowering you to be **more productive in your business** and career by **delivering education,** sharing **best practices** and providing technology direction and **networking opportunities.**

Context, Not Just Content

IOUG is dedicated to helping our members become an #IOUGenius by staying on the cutting-edge of Oracle technologies and industry issues through practical content, user-focused education, and invaluable networking and leadership opportunities:

- *SELECT Journal* is our quarterly publication that provides in-depth, peer-reviewed articles on industry news and best practices in Oracle technology

- Our #IOUGenius blog highlights a featured weekly topic and provides **content driven by Oracle professionals and the IOUG community**

- Special Interest Groups provide you the chance to collaborate with peers on the specific issues that matter to you and even take on leadership roles outside of your organization

- COLLABORATE is our once-a-year opportunity to connect with the members of not one, but three, Oracle users groups (IOUG, OAUG and Quest) as well as with the top names and faces in the Oracle community.

Who we are...

... more than 20,000 database professionals, developers, application and infrastructure architects, business intelligence specialists and IT managers

... a **community of users** that share experiences and knowledge on issues and technologies that matter to you and your organization

Interested? Join IOUG's community of Oracle technology and database professionals at www.ioug.org/Join.

Independent Oracle Users Group | phone: (312) 245-1579 | email: membership@ioug.org
330 N. Wabash Ave., Suite 2000, Chicago, IL 60611

Index

■ S

Printed in the United States
by Baker & Taylor Publisher Services